JN113530

2025 代ゼミ
代々木ゼミナール編

大学入学共通テスト

実戦問題集

英語

リスニング
音声配信

[リーディング・リスニング]

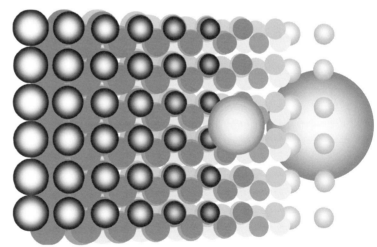

代々木ライブラリー

は じ め に

　この問題集は，大学入学共通テスト（以下，「共通テスト」と略）対策用として，これまでに実施された共通テスト本試験，追試験，2022年に公表された令和7年度共通テスト試作問題などを分析し，これらの出題傾向に基づいて作成したものです。作成には，これまで多くの共通テスト系模試やテキストなどを作成してきた代々木ゼミナール教材研究センターのスタッフが当たり，良問を精選して編集しました。

　共通テストは，「高等学校の段階における基礎的な学習の達成の程度を判定し，大学教育を受けるために必要な能力について把握する」ことを目的に実施されています。出題に当たっては，高等学校において「主体的・対話的で深い学び」を通して育成することとされている「深い理解を伴った知識の質を問う問題や，知識・技術を活用し思考力，判断力，表現力等を発揮して解くことが求められる問題を重視する。その際，言語能力，情報活用能力，問題発見・解決能力等を，教科等横断的に育成することとされていることについても留意する」と公表されています（大学入試センター「大学入学共通テスト問題作成方針」による）。

　また，「知識・技術や思考力・判断力・表現力等を適切に評価できるよう，出題科目の特性に応じた学習の過程を重視し，問題の構成や場面設定等を工夫する。例えば，社会や日常の中から課題を発見し解決方法を構想する場面，資料やデータ等を基に考察する場面などを問題作成に効果的に取り入れる」とされています。

　過去のセンター試験・共通テストの傾向に加えて，思考力・判断力・表現力を重視した出題，社会生活や日常生活に関する問題発見型の出題，さらに複数の資料やデータを関連づける出題が今後も増加すると予想されます。そのような問題に適切に対処するには，同傾向の問題に幅広く触れ，時間配分をも意識して，実践的な演習を積むことが不可欠です。

　本問題集の徹底的な学習，攻略によって，皆さんが見事志望校に合格されることを心より願っています。

代々木ゼミナール教材研究センター

特色と利用法

1. 共通テスト対策の決定版

① 代々木ゼミナール教材研究センターのスタッフが良問を厳選

これまで実施された代々木ゼミナールの共通テスト向け模擬試験やテスト，テキストなどから，本番で出題が予想され，実戦力養成に役立つ良問を厳選して収録しています。また一部の科目では新課程入試に対応するよう新規作成問題を収録しています。

② 詳しい解答・解説付き

2. 共通テストと同一形式

出題形式，難易度，時間，体裁など，本番に準じたものになっています（一部，模試実施時の形式のものがあります）。実戦練習を積み重ねることによって，マークミスなどの不注意な誤りを防ぎ，持てる力を 100％発揮するためのコツが習得できます。

3. 詳しい解答・解説により実力アップ

各回ともにポイントを踏まえた詳しい解説がついています。弱点分野の補強，知識・考え方の整理・確認など，本番突破のための実戦的な学力を養成できます。

4. 効果的な利用法

本書を最も効果的に活用するために，以下の3点を必ず励行してください。

① 制限時間を厳守し，本番に臨むつもりで真剣に取り組むこと
② 自己採点をして，学力のチェックを行うこと
③ 解答・解説をじっくり読んで，弱点補強，知識や考え方の整理に努めること

5. 共通テスト本試験問題・試作問題と解答・解説を収録

2024 年 1 月に実施された「共通テスト本試験」，ならびに 2022 年 11 月に公表された「令和 7 年度共通テスト試作問題」の問題と解答・解説を収録しています。これらも参考にして，出題傾向と対策のマスターに役立ててください。

※「リーディング」問題構成について

2022 年に大学入試センターにて実施された「2025 年度大学入学共通テスト試作問題モニター調査」では，大問数が第 8 問構成へと変更されています。ただしこの問題構成はモニター調査で必要な情報を収集するために構成したもので，本番に向けて問題構成は今後も引き続き検討をするとの付記があります。

この問題集では新しい第 8 問構成の問題（第 5 回）とこれまで通りの第 6 問構成の問題（第 1 ～ 4 回）の両パターンの問題を収録しています。

CONTENTS

大学 入学 共通テスト "出題傾向と対策"

[リーディング]

1．出題傾向

■ 2024 本試験（試験時間：80 分　配点：100 点満点）

第1問　（情報検索）

A は「国際交流イベント」についてのチラシを読んで、2つの設問に答える問題。昨年に比べて分量が増えているが、該当箇所の特定はそれほど困難ではない。B は「3つの観光ツアー」についての情報を題材とし、3つの設問に答える問題。いずれの設問も3つのツアーの内容を横断的に読んで解答する必要があった。A・B ともに英文は平易で、解答に迷う設問も少なく解きやすい。

第2問　（情報検索・情報整理）

A は「戦略ゲームクラブ」のチラシ、B は「海外旅行保険」についてのレビューが題材であった。A・B ともに設問数は5問で、形式的には昨年から大きな変化はない。本文中の意見として正しいものを問う設問のほか、本文に直接的には書かれていない内容を問う問題もあり、慎重に読み解く必要がある。

第3問　（ブログや（雑誌）記事の概要把握）

A は「フォトラリーイベント」についてのブログを読んで、2つの問題に答える問題。昨年と同様に、イラストを選択する問題が出題されている。B は「バーチャル校外学習」についての学校新聞が題材で、設問数は3問。例年通り、時系列順に並べ替える問題が出題されている。A・B ともに英文は読みやすいが、ブログに対してのコメントを考える、あるいは筆者が帰路に見たものを推測するといった、本文の内容に基づいて推測する思考力が求められる。

第4問　（2つの視点から書かれた英文・図表の読み取り）

「よい教室の空間デザイン」について書かれた記事と、アンケート結果が題材。これに加え、両方の資料をまとめたディスカッション用の資料が設けられている。設問数は5問。記事自体は理解しやすいが、複数箇所に基づいて答える問いが含まれ、情報を丁寧に整理する能力が求められる。

第5問　（物語文の概要把握）
英文を読んで発表資料の空所を埋める問題で、設問数は5問。今年は3人の男女の高校卒業後についての物語であった。英文の内容は比較的平易であるが、昨年は1人の人物を中心に物語が進行していたのに対し、今年は3人の人物に関する情報が文章各所に点在しており、内容の整理がやや難しい。

第6問　（文章の要旨・論理展開の把握）
A・Bともに説明文を題材にした長文読解問題である。Aは「時間の知覚」についての英文を読み、発表用メモの空所を埋める問題。設問数は4問。解答に関係するキーワードが太字で表記されていることもあり、解答根拠となる箇所を見つけやすい設問もある。Bは「トウガラシ」についての英文を読み、プレゼンテーション用スライドの空所を埋める問題。設問数は5問。細かい指標の説明を踏まえなければ誤りの選択肢を選んでしまうような、やや難しい問いも含まれている。

なお、2022年に大学入試センターにて実施された「2025年度大学入学共通テスト試作問題モニター調査」では、大問が6問構成から8問構成へと変更されている。追加された2つの大問は次の通りである。
　　第A問：1つのテーマについて複数の意見や資料を読み、見解をまとめる問題。（設問数　5）
　　第B問：生徒が書いたエッセイを教師のコメントを踏まえて改善する問題。（設問数　4）
ただし、この問題構成はモニター調査を通じて必要な情報を収集するために構成したものであり、本番に向けて引き続き検討をするとの付記がある。

2．対　策＜学習法＞
　大学入学共通テストの英語［リーディング］は、読解力の測定に特化した問題である。本文と選択肢の語数を合わせた総語数は6000語を超え、膨大な分量の英文を試験時間内に読み切り、処理する力が求められる。
　英文は説明文・物語文だけでなく、ブログや広告、インターネットのウェブサイトなどの実用的な英文も読解問題の題材になる。そのため、英語の文章を幅広くたくさん読む「多読」の経験を積むことが重要となる。英文読解に苦手意識のある人は、いきなり「速く」読むことに意識を向けるのではなく、まずは平易な文章を一文一文正確に読む「精読」のトレーニングに重点的に取り組んでほしい。ある程度読めるようになってきたら平易な文章を時間内に読んで理解する練習を行い、徐々に内容の難しい英文に取り組んでいくと良いだろう。大学入学共通テストのリーディングの問題は、本文と選択肢の内容を照合するだけでなく、複数の意見を整理する力や、英文の構成や趣旨（最も言いたいこと）を把握する力などが求められる。そのため、一文一文の理解に支障がなくなった段階で、パラグラフや文章全体の趣旨は何かを考えて読むように意識しよう。

［リスニング］

1．出題傾向

■ 2024 本試験（試験時間：60 分　解答時間：30 分　配点：100 点満点）

第 1 問　（短い発話の聞き取り：2 回読み）
A は短い発話の内容に合う英文を選ぶ問題が 4 問、B は短い発話の内容に合うイラストを選ぶ問題が 3 問出題される。英語の音声が聞き取れるだけでなく、発話の内容を理解して正答するには文法・語法の知識も要する。

第 2 問　（短い対話の聞き取り：2 回読み）
短い対話と問いを聞き、答えとして適切なイラストを選ぶ問題が 4 問出題される。第 1 問 B のイラスト問題では問われている内容が比較的ストレートに表現されていたのに対し、第 2 問では間接的に表現されている設問も含まれる。

第 3 問　（短い対話の聞き取り：1 回読み）
短い対話を聞き、問題冊子に書かれた問いの答えとして適切なものを選ぶ問題が 6 問出題される。対話の概要や要点を把握する問題のほか、複数の要素から選択肢を総合的に判断する問題も含まれる。また、イギリス英語話者による読み上げも含まれる。

第 4 問　（モノローグ・説明の聞き取り・複数の情報の比較：1 回読み）
A では、モノローグを聞いて設問に答える問題が 2 問出題される。今年は、問 1 は「遊園地での出来事」についてのイラストを時系列順に並べる形式、問 2 は「夏季講座のスケジュール」の表を完成させる問題であった。音声は 1 回しか流れないので、聞き漏らしがないようメモを取りながら聞くことが重要である。
B は「文化祭の出し物」について 4 人の話者の説明を聞き、問題冊子に記載された条件に最も合う選択肢を選ぶ問題の 1 問のみ。非ネイティブの話者による読み上げも含まれる。音声が流れる前に、与えられた 3 つの条件をしっかりと把握しておくことが重要である。問題冊子に記載された表の空所を埋めながらそれぞれの話者の説明を聞くと、情報を整理しやすい。

第5問　（講義の聞き取り：1回読み）
「ガラス」についての講義を聞いて、4つの設問に答える問題。設問内容としては、講義の概要をまとめたワークシートの空欄を埋める問題、講義の内容と一致する英文を選ぶ問題、グラフおよび講義全体の内容と一致する英文を選ぶ問題がある。音声が流れる前に問題冊子に記載された状況と設問に目を通す時間が約1分間与えられ、［講義のリスニング→6つの小問に解答→講義の続きのリスニング→1つの小問に解答］という流れで解答する。ワークシートを活用して、講義を聞きながらメモを取ることが重要である。

なお2022年に実施された試作問題では、第5問とほぼ同形式の問題が第C問として出題された。［講義のリスニング→5つの小問に解答→2人のメンバーによる短い発言と、講義後の短いディスカッションを聞いて、2つの小問に解答］という流れなっており、講義後のリスニング内容や設問形式に変更が見られる。

第6問　（対話・意見の聞き取り：1回読み）
Aでは「旅行中の移動方法」についての2人の対話を聞いて、それぞれの話者に関する問いに答える問題。1人の意見を問う問題と、会話終了時までに2人で合意したことを問う問題の2問が出題された。Bは「運動を始めること」についての4人の話者による会話の聞き取りで、話者の立場を問う問題が1問と、1人の話者の発言内容に関する図表を選ぶ問題が1問出題された。A・Bともに、意見の要旨を大まかに把握し、話者がそれぞれどのような立場を取っているかを考えることが重要である。

2．対　策＜学習法＞
　大学入学共通テスト［リスニング］は6問構成で、音声は第1問と第2問は2回、第3問以降は1回のみ流される。問題の全体的な特徴としては、細かい情報を聞き取るだけでなく、発言の要旨を理解したり、複数の意見を比較・整理して正誤を判断したりする力も求められることが挙げられる。また、問題冊子に記載されたノートにメモを取りながら解く問題や、ワークシートの空欄に入る語句を選ぶ問題など、音声を聞きながら英語「で」作業することが求められる問題も出題されている。
　このような問題に対処する前提として、聴解力の向上が必須である。リスニングの対策は試験直前に集中的に取り組むのではなく、日頃から少しずつ英文を聞く訓練をすることが肝要である。まずは短い会話文から始めて、スピードに慣れてきたら長めのモノローグを聞くようにすると良いだろう。また、放送内容のスクリプトを音読することも有効である。まずはスクリプトを見ずに音声を聞き、音声を真似て発音する。その後、スクリプトを見て聞き取れなかったところを確認しながら、自然なスピードの音声と一緒に音読を行う。自ら声に出して読むことで、その単語が聞き取れるようになる。さらに英語のリズムが身につくため、聞いた英語が理解しやすくなる。聴解力の向上を目指したこのような学習を積み重ね、本書などで演習を積み多様な問題形式にも慣れていくことが、大学入学共通テスト［リスニング］で得点することに結びつくだろう。

リスニング問題音声配信について

本書に掲載のリスニング問題の音声は，音声専用サイトにて配信しております。
サイトへは下記アドレスよりアクセスしてくだい。ユーザー名とパスワードの入力が必要です。

https://www.yozemi.ac.jp/yozemi/download/book2025shirohoneigo

■ユーザー名：lib7ET8p
■パスワード：8696Xs5K
■利用期間
　2024 年 7 月 10 日〜 2027 年 6 月 30 日 (期限内でも配信は予告なく終了する場合がございます)

推奨 OS・ブラウザ (2024 年 6 月現在)

▶パソコン
Microsoft Edge ※ ／ Google Chrome ※ ／ Mozilla Firefox ※ ／ Apple Safari ※
※最新版
▶スマートフォン・タブレット
Android 4.4 以上／ iOS 9 以上

ご利用にあたって

※音声専用サイトの音声のご利用は、『2025 大学入学共通テスト実戦問題集英語』をご利用いた
　だいているお客様に限らせていただきます。それ以外の方の、本サイトの音声のご利用はご遠
　慮くださいますようお願いいたします。
※音声は無料ですが、音声を聴くこと、ダウンロードには、別途通信料がかかる場合があります（お
　客様のご負担になります）。
※ファイルは MP3 形式です。音声はダウンロードすることも可能です。ダウンロードした音声
　の再生には MP3 を再生できる機器をご使用ください。また、ご使用の機器や音声再生ソフト、
　インターネット環境などに関するご質問につきましては、当社では対応いたしかねます。各製
　品のメーカーまでお尋ねください。
※本サイトの音声データは著作権法等で保護されています。音声データのご利用は、私的利用の
　場合に限られます。
※本データの全部もしくは一部を複製、または加工し、第三者に譲渡・販売することは法律で禁
　止されています。
※本サービスで提供されているコンテンツは、予告なしに変更・追加・中止されることがあります。
※お客様のネット環境および端末により、ご利用いただけない場合がございます。ご理解、ご了
　承いただきますようお願いいたします。

リーディング────第1回

時間　80分　　　　　100点　満点

1 ── 解答にあたっては，実際に試験を受けるつもりで，時間を厳守し真剣に取りくむこと。

2 ── 巻末にマークシートをつけてあるので，切り離しのうえ練習用として利用すること。

3 ── 解答終了後には，自己採点により学力チェックを行い，別冊の解答・解説をじっくり読んで，弱点補強，知識や考え方の整理などに努めること。

※「リーディング」問題構成について

　2022 年に大学入試センターにて実施された「2025 年度大学入学共通テスト試作問題モニター調査」では，大問数が第 8 問構成へと変更されています。ただしこの問題構成はモニター調査で必要な情報を収集するために構成したもので，本番に向けて問題構成は今後も引き続き検討をするとの付記があります。

　この問題集では新しい第 8 問構成の問題（第 5 回）とこれまで通りの第 6 問構成の問題（第 1 ～ 4 回）の両パターンの問題を収録しています。

英　語（リーディング）

各大問の英文や図表を読み，解答番号 $\boxed{1}$ ～ $\boxed{47}$ にあてはまるものとして最も適当な選択肢を選びなさい。

第1問 （配点　10）

A　Your classmate Irene has sent a text message to the group chat of an upcoming musical.

Hello, members!

Thank you for joining us in the production of our musical for the upcoming school festival in fall. About the casting, we have decided to hold auditions for the following popular roles.　Please check the date, time, and location, and leave a message in this chat if you would like to apply. You may also send me a private message.

　Anne, April 26, 12:20 p.m. in room C302
　Eliza, April 28, 12:20 p.m. in room C310
　Olag, May 1, 4:00 p.m. in the audio-visual room in Building A
　Christopher, May 1, 3:50 p.m. at the gym in Building D

We would like to see singing and dancing for Anne and Eliza, simple acting for Olag, and simple acting and physical ability for Christopher.　For the role of Olag, we would like someone with a charming and cheerful personality.　If you have any special skills, please write them in your application message.
We look forward to receiving lots of applications!

問1　According to the schedule, you cannot attend the auditions for both 　1　 .

① Anne and Eliza

② Anne and Olag

③ Christopher and Olag

④ Eliza and Olag

問2　If you really want to win the role of Olag, you should 　2　 .

① put on a funny act to make the judges laugh

② send a personal message that you've taken singing lessons for six years

③ show the judges how elegantly you can dance

④ tell people in this group chat that you are tall and can do a backflip

B You are planning to see the major summer festivals in Tohoku, including Nebuta in Aomori. You are looking at the website of a travel agency.

Tohoku Great Summer Festivals Tour from Tokyo
Aomori Nebuta Festival + Akita Kanto Festival
2 nights & 3 days for just 49,800 yen!!

Enjoy the two major summer festivals in Tohoku. Aomori Nebuta Festival, Akita Kanto Festival and beautiful Tohoku sightseeing spots are all packed into three days! Experience the energy of each festival! The tour will also take you to Lake Tazawa, home to the statue of Princess Tatsuko, and many other attractive sightseeing spots in Tohoku.

Day	Schedule	Meals included in the price

1	6:00 Depart from Tokyo terminal
	16:30 Arrive at Aomori bus terminal
	    Enjoy the night at the Aomori Nebuta Festival
	    ～Stay at a hotel near Aomori Station～
		breakfast: ×
		lunch: ○ (Bento box in the bus)
		dinner: ×

2	7:30 Depart from Aomori Station
	8:30 Arrive at Hirosaki Castle
	    Enjoy sightseeing in Hirosaki city
	13:00 Depart for Akita City
	16:40 Arrive at Akita bus terminal
	    Enjoy the night at the Akita Kanto Festival
	    ～Stay at a hotel in Akita City～
		breakfast: ○
		lunch: ○ (in Hirosaki City)
		dinner: ×

3	8:30 Depart for Lake Tazawa Enjoy the beautiful lake 13:00 Depart for Tokyo 22:50 Arrive at Tokyo terminal	breakfast: ○ lunch: ○ (at Lake Tazawa) dinner: × (There'll be a 50-min break at the Gunma SA)

✧ All seats on the bus are reserved. There is no need to line up early at the bus stop, as seats are not determined on a first-come, first-served basis. You will always have the same seat during the tour. We do not accept any seat requests from passengers.

✧ The tour guide will accompany you on the tour of Hirosaki Castle and Lake Tazawa, but not on the night festivals on Day 1 and Day 2.

✧ Day 1 and Day 2, you will be free to explore the city upon arrival. For this reason, dinner is not included in the price for both days. We do not serve any alcohol with meals.

✧ Dinner for Day 3 is not included in the price, but we will have a stop at Gunma Service Area on the way back. Toilet facilities are also available near the rear seats of the bus.

問1　If you leave Tokyo on August 5, you will be ⬚3⬚ at noon of August 7.

① arriving at Tokyo Terminal

② enjoying the Kanto Festival

③ having lunch in Hirosaki City

④ walking around a beautiful lake

問2　Which of the following is included in the price? ⬚4⬚

① A beer at the souvenir shop in Lake Tazawa

② The bento box on the bus to Aomori

③ The breakfast for Day 1 and Day 2

④ Yakisoba noodles eaten at a stall during the Nebuta Festival

問3　Which of the following is appropriate based on what you learn from the website? ⬚5⬚

① If you get injured during the Akita Kanto Festival, you can ask the tour guide to help you.

② If you want to get a good seat on the bus, you should get in line early.

③ There will be plenty of time to pick up souvenirs if you don't have dinner at the Gunma SA on the way back.

④ You will have a breakfast break on the way to Aomori.

第2問 （配点 20）

A You are attending an educational programme held at the Institute for Research on Learning in the UK. You are reading the information about the programme and the Institute's facilities.

Institute for Research on Learning
Monday - Friday: 9 am – 9 pm

Entrance Pass: When visiting the institute, please print out the entrance pass attached to the welcome email in A4 size and in colour and bring it to the institute.

Study Counselling

We support you in your quest to become a globally competent person. Develop your likes, strengths, interests and concerns, and maximise your ability to be active in the world. Counselling is offered, from 10 am to 8 pm in the Interview Area to the right of the ground floor entrance, to find out what topics interest you and work on exercises to give shape to your ideas.

Learning Records

You are required to write a *Learning Record* for every visit to the Institute, so that you can record what you learnt that day. The form can be found in the Study Areas on the second and third floors. Staff with expertise in many fields are available for 20 to 60 minutes a day to conduct lessons designed for you so take advantage of this when filling in the form.

Facility Information

You are required to show your entrance pass when visiting the institute. Wi-Fi access is available on all floors. The password that you need will be given to you when you arrive at the institute. The Computer Areas are located on the first floor on the left and on the second floor and are available all day.

Comments from Past Students

- This programme is so awesome. It gives you an idea as to how your studying contributes to society, regardless of your school grades.
- Taking lessons is easier in the morning or during the day, and lessons are crowded in the evening. The racks for learning record forms on the second floor are crowded, so you should get them on the third floor.
- There is a library of about 20,000 books so research work is never a problem. You can't bring in food, but bottled drinks are allowed.
- The building has calm background music and lots of plants, so just being there is relaxing. It is a headache to have to get an entrance pass every time you use the photocopier, though.
- The photocopier located next to the Interview Area is free to use, so you can photocopy the pages you need in any book. Some books can be borrowed, others cannot.

問1　6 are two things you can do at the institute.

A：bring your own food and eat it in the library

B：get an entry pass on the ground floor

C：receive counselling in the Study Area

D：research on your area of interest

E：use a photocopier to copy parts of books

① A and B

② B and C

③ C and D

④ C and E

⑤ D and E

問2　You are now in the Computer Area on the first floor and want to get a learning record form.　You can 7 to get one.

① go down one floor

② go up two floors

③ go up three floors

④ stay on the same floor

問3　8 is right next to where the photocopier is located.

① One of the Computer Areas

② One of the Study Areas

③ The Interview Area

④ The Wi-Fi base station

問4　If you want a 50-minute lesson and want to avoid the crowds, you could ⒐ .

① start your lesson no later than 3:00 pm

② start your lesson no later than 7:10 pm

③ take your lesson 25 minutes in the morning and 25 minutes in the evening

④ take your lesson 30 minutes during the day and 20 minutes in the evening

問5　One **fact** stated by a previous student is that ⒑ .

① the entrance pass can be printed out in colour in the Computer Area

② the institute has a collection of less than 30,000 books

③ the institute's calm music helps heal students' headaches from long studying hours

④ the learning record forms are easier to get on the third floor

B You are the editor of your school's English language newspaper. Bill, an exchange student from the U.S., has written an article for the newspaper.

The history of school lunches in Japan dates back to the Meiji era, but it was not until after World War II that it made the most progress. In the late 1940s, *koppepan*, or hot dog buns, and skimmed milk powder became a major part of the school lunch menu. The Japanese diet changed dramatically when bread, made from wheat imported from the United States, began to be eaten throughout the country.

As Japanese society became more affluent in the 1960s, fried bread, raisin bread and soft noodles, or soupless udon noodles topped with curry or meat sauce, were added to the school lunch menu. Around that time, skimmed milk powder, which wasn't popular among children, was replaced by milk. These newly added food items helped to enrich the variety of school lunches.

Eventually, in the 1980s, rice became the staple food of school lunches as it was served more than bread, and since then the school lunch menu has become even more diverse.

In a survey conducted in 2020, people in their 20s to 50s were asked, "What is your favorite food on the school lunch menu that you ate as a child?" The following are the top four food items mentioned by the four generations, extracted from their answers to that question.

▶50s—1. fried bread   2. curry rice   3. soft noodles   4. deep-fried whale
▶40s—1. curry rice   2. fried bread   3. soft noodles   4. frozen mandarin oranges
▶30s—1. curry rice   2. fried bread   3. soft noodles   4. seaweed rice
▶20s—1. fried bread   2. curry rice   3. fried chicken 4. seaweed rice

In the latter part of the 1980s, commercial whaling was prohibited and deep-fried whale disappeared from school lunches, but before then it had been among children's favorite lunch menu items. Similarly, soft noodles were quite popular among people in their 30s through 50s. They stopped being served at school lunches sometime in the 1990s, so the youngest generation didn't know how they tasted.

問1　According to Bill's article, which of the following food items are NOT currently on the Japanese school lunch menu? ☐ 11 ☐

① Curry rice, fried bread, soft noodles, and seaweed rice

② Deep-fried whale, frozen mandarin oranges, and milk

③ Fried bread, soft noodles, and skimmed milk powder

④ *Koppepan*, fried bread, and raisin bread

⑤ Skimmed milk powder, deep-fried whale, and soft noodles

⑥ Soft noodles, fried bread, and seaweed rice

問2　According to Bill, which of the following events was a part of the most significant change in the history of Japanese school lunches? ☐ 12 ☐

① A variety of bread and noodles were added to the school lunch menu.

② *Koppepan* appeared on the school lunch menu.

③ Rice became a staple food of the school lunch.

④ Skimmed milk powder was replaced by milk.

問3　Which of the following statements about the difference between the generations is correct? ☐ 13 ☐

① Curry rice is the most popular food at school among people in their 30s or older.

② People in their 20s didn't eat soft noodles at school.

③ People in their 30s and 40s ate seaweed rice lunches.

④ People in their 30s were the last generation that ate whale meat at school.

問4 Which of the following statements is true about Bill's article about Japanese school lunches? 14

① As Japan became affluent, school lunches became more varied.

② Bread and rice are both equally important food items for school lunches.

③ Eating whale meat should not be banned for any cultural reasons.

④ Soft noodles should be revived because they were so popular and tasty.

問5 Which is the most suitable title for the article? 15

① Do the Japanese Love Their School Lunches?

② How Has School Lunch Evolved in Japan?

③ What Is the Japanese School Lunch Like?

④ Why Has Bread Become So Popular in Japan?

第3問 (配点 15)

A You are interested in the sewage system. You are reading a blog post by a university student in the UK studying engineering.

Michael Wilson

I am interested in sewage. I know I have a strange hobby, but I think it's an interesting one. I recently attended an event called the Sewage Disposal Works Exhibition held in London with a friend of mine.

We first visited the booth of a company that manufactures manholes. I once slipped on a manhole while riding my bicycle. We were impressed to see that manholes nowadays are non-slip and have various designs including local ones.

Next, we listened to a presentation on attempts to repair sewer lines efficiently with digital technology. I thought this technology would be more useful if combined with AI and robotics in the future. Though I found the presentation interesting, the way the presenter spoke was somewhat monotonous and my friend did not seem to be interested.

Finally, we experienced a virtual reality system where we could see a sewage construction site. Wearing special goggles, we felt like we were actually there at the site.

After lunch, we stopped at a gift shop to buy some unique biscuits in the shape of sewage pipes. We were planning to buy five for each of us and give them as souvenirs to our friends. However, they were so popular that we could buy only one per person, much to our disappointment.

Various other new technologies were also introduced at the exhibition, which reminded us that sewage is an important infrastructure that is also related to problems such as heavy rains caused by global warming. We enjoyed the exhibition very much.

問 1　According to Michael's blog, you know that both he and his friend 16 .

① felt the construction site seen through the goggles was very real

② found the presentation on digital technology boring

③ thought manholes nowadays to be monotonous

④ were able to buy as many biscuits as they had planned

問 2　Michael and his friend thought that 17 .

① the digital technology was of little use in sewage repairs

② the manholes still need to improve because they are slippery

③ the presenter made the presentation well

④ the sewage system had to do with environmental problems

B You are planning to visit the UK this summer and have found an interesting article introducing day trip destinations from London in a travel magazine.

Best Day Trips from London

by Daniel Johnson

London is known around the world as a metropolis full of tourist attractions. However, there are many other attractive cities around this gigantic one. I recommend you visit the following tourist places: Oxford, Bath, and Liverpool.

Oxford: This city is home to 40 old and historic universities. A particularly famous tourist attraction is "Christ Church College," founded in 1546. Its dining hall, "the Great Hall," was used as a filming location for the Harry Potter movies. Oxford is also home to "The Bodleian Library," which boasts a collection of more than 7 million volumes. "St. Mary's Church," located in the centre of the Oxford colleges, is famous for its beautiful stained-glass windows. The church's observation deck overlooks this beautiful city.

Bath: The whole city of Bath is listed as a World Heritage site for its historical and architectural values. The biggest tourist attraction is "The Roman Baths." This ancient public bath was built by the Romans about 2,000 years ago. Also worth visiting is "Bath Abbey," a Gothic church. You will see beautiful arches and stained glass inside the church. "The Royal Crescent," today used as a luxury hotel, was built between 1767 and 1774. The entire building was originally made up of 30 houses laid out in a curve.

Liverpool: This city in northwest England is known as the birthplace of the Beatles. Even today, their fans come from all over the world. "The Beatles Story" is a museum dedicated to the Beatles, where visitors can see photographs and rare items of the most important rock band in history. Tourists can also visit the café "Penny Lane," which appears in the lyrics of the Beatles' songs, and the nightclub "The Cavern Club," where the four young musicians played live in the 1960s. The club first opened in 1957.

These three cities can be reached by train from London. For example, about an hour train ride will take you to Oxford, and it will take about an hour and twenty minutes to get to Bath. Liverpool can be reached by train in a little over two hours. Yet, there is another means of transport called "Coach." This long-distance bus service connects prominent cities such as these throughout the UK. It takes more than two hours to get to Oxford by coach, but the fare is much lower.

問1　Put the following sightseeing spots (①～④) in the order they were built.

① Christ Church College

② The Roman Baths

③ The Royal Crescent

④ The Cavern Club

問2　Which building has a fine view of the whole city? 　22

① Bath Abbey

② Christ Church College

③ St. Mary's Church

④ The Royal Crescent

問3　Which of the following statements is true about transport from London?
23

① It takes an hour and a half to get to Oxford from London by train.

② Travelling by coach is more expensive than using the train.

③ You can get to Liverpool in one hour and a half by train.

④ You can get to Oxford, Bath or Liverpool by taking a coach.

第4問　(配点　16)

You are a new student at Garvard University in the US. You are reading the blogs of two students, Luis and Gerald, and you are reading them to find useful information.

Having trouble starting your first year at Garvard University?
Posted by Luis at 3:00 a.m. on September 1st, 2024

Are you excited about starting your very first university year? There are lots of new things you can do, whether joining a new club, applying for an internship, but most importantly going to the gym and gaining muscle. University years are the best time in life to do so. But before taking your first step to the gym, you may wonder what to buy to start your long journey into bodybuilding or fitness successfully. Not to worry as there is a store that has all the products you need. The store is called Gymgear. Although they do not sell online and there are no shipping options, their wide selection of products attracts many students of gym goers from beginner to advanced every day. Here are some items worth checking out especially for beginners.

Recommended items at Gymgear	Protein Powder (1kg) $80	EAA (0.5kg) $55
Wrist wraps $55	Weight belt $110	Knee wraps $60

https://gymgear.web

I would like to mention that the gym equipment items above are not mandatory but if you want to gain muscle efficiently and avoid injury, I highly recommend you buy them. You won't regret it!

Welcome to Garvard University!

Posted by Gerald at 1:00 a.m. on September 13th, 2024

To the new freshman eagerly waiting to start his/her university life at Garvard University, I would like to say, welcome! There are many different activities you can do in the university, but my top choice is going to the gym.

You're going to be here for four years, so why not gain muscle as much as possible before graduating and entering the workforce? I heard that once you start working, it is difficult to gain muscle as you have to wake up everyday early in a punctual manner and work under stress daily. The great thing about university life is that you're in a stress-free environment and you have the freedom to plan your daily life. The downside is that you're always on a budget. My struggle when I first started working out was that I bought whatever I needed at one shop. A year or two later, I found there were multiple options that were cheaper. I wish I had compared the prices before purchasing.

I found a site called savemoneyforgymtools.com, which was very useful for comparing the prices of different e-shops. Let's look at the site's table and compare the prices of the popular products from the 3 sites.

Item	Monster Gear.com	Bomb Muscle.com	All Hard.com
Protein Powder (1kg)	$70	$60	$45
EAA(0.5kg)	$55	$60	$65
Wrist Wraps	$45	$50	$55
Weight Belt	$120	$135	$125
Knee Wraps	$48	$50	$45

https:// savemoneyforgymtools.com

Monster Gear and Bomb Muscle has an optional annual membership, with discounts and free shipping. Monster Gear's membership fee is $80 per year with a 20-dollar discount for every item price. Bomb Muscle's membership fee is $100 per year with a 10-dollar discount for every item price. You cannot cancel the membership during the year. Without joining the membership, the shipping cost for both sites are $30 per item. As for All Hard.com, they do not offer membership and the shipping cost is $20 per item.

問1　Luis recommends buying from Gymgear because ┃ 24 ┃.

① it has a wide variety of items for gym goers of all levels

② it offers discounts for university students

③ it will help with the store's reputation

④ the items are necessary for gym exercise

問2　Gerald believes it's better to buy ┃ 25 ┃.

① all your items from one shop

② items from stores with membership discounts

③ items online as it saves time

④ the cheapest items from several options

問3　Both Luis and Gerald think that ┃ 26 ┃.

① buying gym items is important, especially if you are a beginner

② it is best to start training before graduating from university

③ it is important to choose the cheapest option when buying gym items

④ purchasing gym equipment is important for gaining muscle in the least
amount of time

問4　You are planning to buy a weight belt but since it is heavy, you would like for it to be shipped to your house. Without joining any membership, the cheapest option with shipping cost included is buying from ☐ 27 ☐ .

①　All Hard.com
②　Bomb Muscle.com
③　Gymgear
④　Monster Gear.com

問5　Without joining any membership, the cheapest option to buy only a single order of 1kg protein powder is buying from ☐ 28 ☐ . With the membership fees and free shipping taken into consideration, the cheapest option to buy 1kg of protein powder once every 2 months for a year is buying from ☐ 29 ☐ .

①　All Hard.com
②　Bomb Muscle.com
③　Gymgear
④　Monster Gear.com

Your group is preparing a poster presentation of "The Man Who Spread Potatoes" using information from the magazine article below.

Antoine-Augustin Parmentier was born in 1737 in a small town called Montdidier in northern France. He was a pharmacist by profession, but also an agronomist and nutritionist. He is credited with several accomplishments, the most prominent of which is the promotion of the potato in France and Europe.

Below is the story of how he became a potato advocate and how he promoted the potato. While serving as a pharmacist in the French army during the Seven Years' War (1756-1763), he was taken prisoner by the Prussian army. While in prison in Prussia (now Germany), he was forced to eat potatoes, which were known only as pig feed to the French. Potatoes were brought to Europe from South America by the Spanish around the 16th century; by 1640 they had been introduced to the rest of Europe, but outside of Ireland they were generally used only as livestock feed. King Frederick II of Prussia (1712-1786), who had noticed that the potato could grow even in cold, barren lands, required farmers to cultivate it under strict penalties.

In France, on the other hand, potatoes were thought to cause disease, and in 1748 the cultivation of potatoes was even banned. After returning to Paris in 1763, Parmentier conducted nutritional research on the potato; following famines in 1769 and 1770, a contest was held in 1771 with a prize for a food that would be useful in the event of a famine. Parmentier proposed the use of potatoes and won the prize in 1773. Also, thanks to his efforts, the medical faculty of the University of Paris approved the potato for human consumption in 1772. However, resistance to potatoes still continued, and he experienced hardships, including being forbidden to use the test farm at the hospital where he worked as a pharmacist and being prevented from taking the post he had hoped for at the hospital, but still, he never gave up.

Parmentier's way of promoting the potato was unique. First, he did so by inviting celebrities to dinner parties, serving potato dishes, and presenting bouquets of potatoes to the king and queen. The most interesting way was to have soldiers guard the potato fields during the day to make people believe that they were growing a valuable crop, and then have them pulled out at night to let people steal them. The year 1785 was a bad harvest year, but the potatoes helped northern France escape famine. This was the beginning of the spread of the potato in France.

Today, Parmentier's name remains among us in two forms. One is that many potato dishes are named in honor of him, such as Hachis parmentier, a French home-style dish of minced beef and potatoes. Another is that the Paris metro has a station called Parmentier to commemorate his achievements. On the platform of this station stands a statue of him handing out potatoes to farmers.

From the end of the 17th century to the 19th century, not only Europe but the entire globe was in a period of unusually low temperatures. The potato, which could be grown even in barren and cold areas, saved many people from starvation. It can be said that Parmentier's success in eliminating people's prejudice against the potato was a great achievement.

Your presentation notes:

The Man Who Spread Potatoes

■ Sequence of Key Events

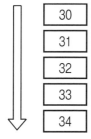

| 30 |
| 31 |
| 32 |
| 33 |
| 34 |

■ Potatoes in Europe before Parmentier
· They were brought from South America by the Spanish around the 16th century.
· ▢ 35

■ Parmentier and potatoes
· ▢ 36
· ▢ 37

⇒ He succeeded in getting rid of Europeans' bias toward potatoes.

■ Parmentier's personality
Parmentier's personality can be described as : ▢ 38 .

問1　Members of your group listed important events related to Parmentier's life. Put the events into the boxes | 30 | ~ | 34 | in the order that they happened.

   ① Cultivation of potatoes was prohibited in France.

   ② Parmentier was given a prize for his proposal.

   ③ Parmentier was made to eat potatoes as a prisoner.

   ④ Parmentier returned from Prussia to France.

   ⑤ The University of Paris declared potatoes to be good for human consumption.

問2　Choose the best item for | 35 | .

   ① Potatoes were generally not used for human consumption.

   ② Potatoes became popular soon after they were introduced.

   ③ Potatoes were prohibited from being grown by the King of Prussia.

   ④ Potatoes were regarded as pig feed by the Irish people.

問3　Choose the best items for | 36 | · | 37 | . (The order does not matter.)

   ① He gave the French king and queen the flowers of potatoes.

   ② He gave the name Parmentier to the dishes he created.

   ③ He had citizens steal the potatoes to spread them.

   ④ He invited ordinary people to dinner parties to serve potatoes.

   ⑤ He threatened people to grow potatoes under strict penalties.

問4　Choose the best item for | 38 | .

   ① ambitious and strict

   ② cheerful and friendly

   ③ conservative and gentle

   ④ ingenious and strong-willed

第6問 （配点 24）

A Your study group is learning about how "decisions are made." You have found an article you want to share. Complete the summary notes for your next meeting.

Brain Makes Decisions Before You Even Know It

Your brain makes up its mind up to ten seconds before you realize it, according to researchers. By looking at brain activity while making a decision, the researchers could predict what choice people would make before they themselves were even aware of having made a decision. The work calls into question the 'consciousness' of our decisions and may even challenge ideas about how 'free' we are to make a choice at a particular point in time.

"We think our decisions are conscious, but these data show that consciousness is just the tip of the iceberg," says John-Dylan Haynes, a neuroscientist at the Max Planck Institute in Germany, who led the study. "The results are quite dramatic," says Frank Tong, a neuroscientist at Vanderbilt University. Ten seconds is "a lifetime" in terms of brain activity, he adds.

Haynes and his colleagues imaged the brains of 14 volunteers while they performed a decision-making task. The volunteers were asked to press one of two buttons when they felt the urge to. Each button was operated by a different hand. At the same time, a stream of letters was presented on a screen at half-second intervals, and the volunteers had to remember which letter was showing when they decided to press their button.

When the researchers analyzed the data, the earliest signal the team could pick up started seven seconds before the volunteers reported having made their decision. Because there is a delay of a few seconds in the imaging, this means that the brain activity could have begun as much as ten seconds before the conscious decision. The signal came from a region called the frontopolar cortex, at the front of the brain, immediately behind the forehead. This area may well be the brain region where decisions are initiated, says Haynes, who reports the results online in Nature Neuroscience.

The next step is to speed up the data analysis to allow the team to predict people's choices as their brains are making them. The results build on some well-known work on free will done in the 1980s by the late neurophysiologist Benjamin

---

Libet, then at the University of California, San Francisco. Libet used a similar experimental set-up to Haynes, but with just one button and measuring electrical activity in his subjects' brains. He found that the regions responsible for movement reacted a few hundred milliseconds before a conscious decision was made.

But Libet's study has been criticized in the intervening decades for its method of measuring time, and because the brain response might merely have been a general preparation for movement, rather than activity relating to a specific decision. Haynes and his team improved the method by asking people to choose between two alternatives — left and right. Because moving the left and right hands generates distinct brain signals, the researchers could show that activity genuinely reflected one of the two decisions.

But the experiment could limit how 'free' people's choices really are, says Chris Frith, who studies consciousness at University College London. Although subjects are free to choose when and which button to press, the experimental set-up restricts them to only these actions and nothing more, he says. "The subjects hand over their freedom to the experimenter when they agree to enter the scanner," he says. What might this mean, then, for the unclear concept of free will? If choices really are being made several seconds ahead of awareness, "there's not much space for free will to operate", Haynes says.

But results aren't enough to convince Frith that free will is an illusion. "We already know our decisions can be unconsciously controlled," he says. The brain activity could be part of this control, as opposed to the decision process, he adds.

Part of the problem is defining what we mean by 'free will'. But results such as these might help us settle on a definition. It is likely that "neuroscience will alter what we mean by free will", says Tong.

Your summary notes:

Brain Makes Decisions Before You Even Know It

Vocabulary

consciousness: things you are aware of

frontopolar cortex: | 39 |

The Main Points

- Research is needed to find out whether the will is truly free when people make decisions.
- A scientist says that in decision-making, consciousness is only a small factor.
- For the brain, ten seconds is as long as a human life, according to a neuroscientist.
- A series of experiments has shown that | 40 | .
- People may make decisions out of unconscious habits before they make conscious decisions.

Interesting Details

- In his experiment, Haynes had volunteers press buttons on their left and right hands in order to | 41 | .
- Tong thinks neuroscience will change the definition of ' | 42 | '.

問1　Choose the best option for | 39 | .

① immediately behind the brain

② the front of the forehead

③ the most forward part of the brain

④ the signal from the cortex

問2　Choose the best option for ☐ 40 ☐ .

① human hand responses are based on the signals delivered from the brain

② unlike your conscious mind, your brain makes decisions in hundreds of milliseconds

③ when there is awareness of a decision to do something, the brain evaluates many options before choosing one

④ your brain has already made the decision before you are even aware that you have made any decision

問3　Choose the best option for ☐ 41 ☐ .

① confirm that brain responses are linked to specific conscious decision-making

② demonstrate that the speed of the brain response differs by the hand being used

③ ensure that there is consciousness and subconsciousness in the human mind

④ show that hand movements can be separated from the workings of consciousness

問4　Choose the best options for ☐ 42 ☐ .

① brain activity

② creativity

③ free will

④ illusion

⑤ sense of self

B You are in a student group preparing a poster for a scientific presentation with the theme "What we should do to improve our health." You have been using the following passage to create the poster.

Essential Amino Acids

Protein is the essential building block of the human body. It is found throughout the bones, muscles, eyes, nails and even hair. Protein can be broken down into smaller substances called amino acids. Amino acids make up about 20% of the body and there are 20 types in total. Eleven of them are called non-essential amino acids and the rest are called essential amino acids (EAA). While our bodies can produce non-essential amino acids, this is not the case for EAA. The only way to obtain EAA is by eating food that contains them. Animal protein such as meat and soy products such as tofu and edamame are major sources of EAA. When food containing protein is consumed, the protein is broken down into amino acids.

Out of the essential amino acids, three of them are called leucine, isoleucine, and valine. They are characterized by a molecular structure in the form of branches and are called branched-chain amino acids (BCAA). BCAAs are popular among athletes as they have common functions in our bodies, which are muscle growth and recovery. When examined closely, however, there are certain differences in how they affect our body. For example, leucine has the ability to support making proteins within our bodies. Leucine consumption has been shown to improve liver function and balance blood sugar. It may also promote weight loss as leucine supplements have shown to increase leptin, a hormone that controls hunger cravings. Isoleucine has the same function as leucine in strengthening muscles, improving liver function and blood sugar control. Isoleucine, however, differs from leucine in that it helps build hemoglobin in the red blood cells, making it an important amino acid for blood loss recovery. Hemoglobin is a protein molecule that combines with oxygen and carries it throughout the body. Valine supports liver function and controls the amount of nitrogen in the blood. It is also said to contribute to skin firmness, as it is one of the main compositions of elastin, which is a type of protein that strengthens the bonds of collagen in the skin. Lack of elastin may result in sagging skin.

Other EAAs excluding BCAAs also contribute greatly to the human body as well. Histidine is unique in that it is the only essential amino acid that can be generated by the body. However, it can only be done in adults and not in children. A study showed that taking histidine supplements can reduce body fat. Another research showed that the body uses histidine to create urocanic acid in the skin, a substance that absorbs UV rays from the sunlight, thus protecting the skin from damage. Threonine is known to prevent fat build-up in the liver. In addition, threonine contributes to stomach health as it is said to play a major role in producing a sticky liquid that protects the stomach. Phenylalanine is known to facilitate recovery from skin disorders, and it is the material for making dopamine, which contributes to physical and mental health. Because phenylalanine has the effect of raising blood pressure, it should not be taken in too large amounts. Methionine is unique in that it is the only EAA containing sulfur. Therefore, the human body requires methionine to create molecules that require sulfur. One example is a protein called keratin, the main component of hair. A study shows lack of methionine to cause hair loss. Tryptophan is an amino acid originally discovered from milk. The human body uses tryptophan to produce a substance called serotonin in the brain, which help us maintain mental health. When at night, the body makes melatonin from serotonin, which helps correct the body's sleep/wake cycle. Lysine, like tryptophan, is found in milk and contains about 2-10% of the body's protein. Some research suggests that lysine consumption helps the human body absorb more calcium. Also, both methionine and lysine are helpful material for burning fat as the body uses them to create carnitine, a substance that helps the body turn fat into energy.

The knowledge of each of the essential amino acids presented above is useful for faster recovery from the disorders caused by insufficient amino acids. When it comes to muscle building and maintenance, taking concentrated BCAAs is common knowledge in the fitness industry. However, research has shown that EAAs allow the body to absorb BCAAs more efficiently, so taking EAAs all in one is gradually becoming the mainstream. Whether you are an athlete or not, learning about amino acids is highly beneficial to your physical and mental health.

Your presentation poster draft:

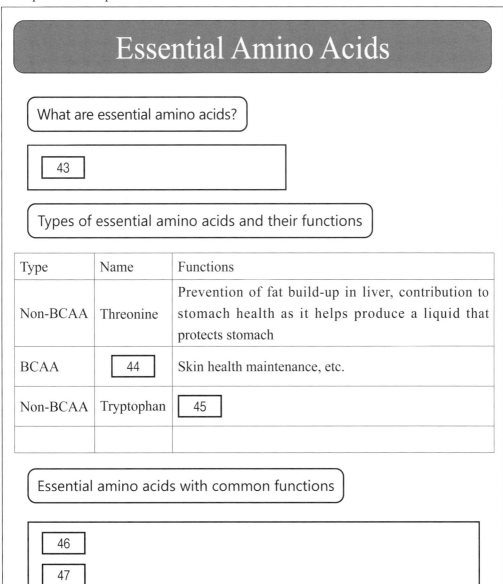

Essential Amino Acids

What are essential amino acids?

| 43 |

Types of essential amino acids and their functions

Type	Name	Functions
Non-BCAA	Threonine	Prevention of fat build-up in liver, contribution to stomach health as it helps produce a liquid that protects stomach
BCAA	44	Skin health maintenance, etc.
Non-BCAA	Tryptophan	45

Essential amino acids with common functions

| 46 |
| 47 |

問1　Under the first poster heading, your group wants to introduce the essential amino acids as explained in the passage. Which of the following is the most appropriate?　43

①　They are certain types of protein that can only be obtained from soy products, each type contributing to health improvement in their own way.

②　They are molecules that are made from 20 different types of protein and essential for muscle gaining and recovery.

③　They are smaller substances of protein that the human body cannot create on its own and must obtain from outside sources.

④　They are the 11 different types of protein molecules which the human body can make on its own.

問2　Choose the best options for　44　·　45　.

44

①　Isoleucine

②　Histidine

③　Phenylalanine

④　Valine

45

①　Absorption of melatonin to create serotonin, which contributes to mental health and correct sleep/wake cycle

②　Contribution in creating serotonin for good mental health and to carry melatonin throughout the body to correct sleep/wake cycle

③　Contribution in creating serotonin for good mental health, which is then changed to melatonin for correcting sleep/wake cycle

④　Removal of serotonin and melatonin for good mental health and correct sleep/wake cycle

問3　You are making statements about some essential amino acids which share common properties. According to the article, which two of the following are appropriate? (The order does not matter.)　46 ・ 47

　① Both histidine and phenylalanine are proven to facilitate urocanic acid production.

　② Both isoleucine and leucine help regulate blood sugar level.

　③ Both lysine and methionine help the body store energy.

　④ Taking isoleucine and leucine supports producing red blood cells.

　⑤ Taking keratin and methionine may prevent hair loss.

　⑥ When it comes to depression, taking phenylalanine and tryptophan is beneficial.

リーディング──第2回

時間　80分　　　　　100点　満点

1 ══ 解答にあたっては，実際に試験を受けるつもりで，時間を厳守し真剣に取りくむこと。

2 ══ 巻末にマークシートをつけてあるので，切り離しのうえ練習用として利用すること。

3 ══ 解答終了後には，自己採点により学力チェックを行い，別冊の解答・解説をじっくり読んで，弱点補強，知識や考え方の整理などに努めること。

　※「リーディング」問題構成について

　2022 年に大学入試センターにて実施された「2025 年度大学入学共通テスト試作問題モニター調査」では，大問数が第 8 問構成へと変更されています。ただしこの問題構成はモニター調査で必要な情報を収集するために構成したもので，本番に向けて問題構成は今後も引き続き検討をするとの付記があります。

　この問題集では新しい第 8 問構成の問題（第 5 回）とこれまで通りの第 6 問構成の問題（第 1 ～ 4 回）の両パターンの問題を収録しています。

英　語（リーディング）

各大問の英文や図表を読み，解答番号 1 ～ 49 にあてはまるものとして最も適当な選択肢を選びなさい。

第1問 （配点 10）

A You are going on a school field trip in August. The following printout will be passed out to students regarding the destination.

Name _____

Field Trip Report

AQUARIUM OF THE BLUE

Discover the wonders of many kinds of marine life!

‣ Hours: 8:00 AM – 8:00 PM

‣ Adult: $42.00　Child (3-11): $21.00

‣ Dolphin feeding experience

‣ No outside food or drinks allowed

AMIGO WILDLIFE PARK

Experience creatures from all over the world

‣ Hours: 10:00 AM – 5:00 PM

‣ Adult (13-61): $21.95　Child: $17.95

‣ Observe the life of Asian elephants

‣ Wear comfortable clothes

‣ Smoking and alcohol are prohibited

What You Should Do

Carefully compare the two options listed above. Choose one location for your field trip report assignment. (Circle the place you have decided to go and submit this printout to your teacher.)

問1　What does the printout tell you to do about the field trip? ☐ 1

　　① Ask the teacher to carefully choose which place to visit.

　　② Fill out the printout and submit it to the teacher.

　　③ Find out about the location of the field trip for next summer.

　　④ Write a report focusing on your most favorite animal you saw.

問2　Which of the following applies to both places? ☐ 2

　　① No food or drinks are allowed in the facility.

　　② Their hours of operation are the same.

　　③ Ticket prices are different for adults and seniors.

　　④ You will meet a wide variety of creatures.

B You are a high school student interested in exploring the wonders of the universe during the summer break. You find a website advertising a fun summer camp about the stars and the universe, hosted by an observatory and research institute.

Eric's Space Workshop (ESW) has been offering immersive space exploration camps for senior high school students since 2001. Immerse yourself in a two-week adventure under the beautiful stars!

Dates: August 3-17, 2024
Location: Mount Saurus observatory in Hannibal Park
Cost: 1,000 dollars, including food and accommodation (additional fees for optional activities such as building robots and telescopes)

Courses Offered
◆ **ASTROGEOLOGY**: Besides observing the starry sky, you'll analyze authentic meteorites under a unique microscope, create a poster with other students highlighting the findings of the analysis and classification of these pieces, research meteorites that have previously landed on Earth, write a document and prepare a presentation for August 17th.

◆ **SOCIAL STUDIES**: In addition to watching the stars, you will observe the Space Station as it orbits the Earth. You will also find out how high above the ground the station is, how long it takes to travel around the Earth, and the role of the Space Station with assigned study partners. Then, prepare a report before the presentation on the final day.

◆ **LITERATURE**: You'll investigate the stories associated with the constellations, their connection to national events, and discover cultural differences. No need to feel burdened as you will be assigned to a study group. You will compile a report on your findings through the presentation on the final day of the program.

▲ **2024 Summer Application: JUNE 27 - JULY 28**
Step 1: Complete the online application form to register.
Step 2: ESW will contact you about scheduling an online interview.
Step 3: On the day of the interview, you'll be asked to describe the course you want to attend and what you expect from it.
Step 4: ESW will notify you when your course registration is complete.

問1   All ESW courses have 3 .

① group studying

② hands-on experiments

③ observation with a telescope

④ presentation of a certificate

問2   During the end of all ESW courses, participants will 4 .

① attend the graduation ceremony

② complete their course registration

③ grade each other's presentations

④ write a report on their studies

問3   What will you do after you submit the online application? 5

① You will contact the staff member for an online interview.

② You will describe space from what you already know about.

③ You will explain what you seek in the workshop.

④ You will upload your student ID card.

第2問　（配点　20）

A　You wanted to buy portable dumbbells for exercising when travelling. You were searching on a UK website and found this advertisement.

Fitness Mozart presents the new Mozart Dumbbells

Mozart Dumbbells are easily adjustable dumbbells with designs by world-class mechanical engineers to achieve the perfect at-home weightlifting experience.

Special Features

Mozart Dumbbells have weight-adjusting systems inside that allow you to switch weights in three ways:
1. Manually, turn the dial on the handle to add or remove weight.
2. Enter the desired weight into the Mozart Dumbbell app and the dumbbells will respond accordingly.
3. Select the Auto-Adjustment Mode in the Mozart Dumbbell app and the AI will automatically select the weight according to your performance.

The app also records your training results. It tracks your performance such as how many times you lifted the dumbbells, what weight you lifted, how long your performance was, and more! You can even instantly share them with the app community. This allows you to be part of a global community that encourages and supports each other's fitness progress. You can also select fitness programs designed by world-famous fitness instructors and join online fitness classes.

The Mozart Dumbbells will innovate the fitness industry and fitness experience.

Advantages

Better Balance: Mozart Dumbbells are precisely made so that both ends are of equal weight to decrease the risk of injuries during usage.

Increased Mobility: The weight of dumbbells can easily be removed for easier storage.

Promotes Exercise: The app offers unique exercises based on the user's body. It is as if the user is playing a weightlifting video game.

Information Security: Your app records can be public, private, or only shared with selected members of your choice.

Customer's Comments
- I like how you can adjust the dumbbells' weight physically and also digitally!
- I lost 10 kgs just by following the fitness program in the app, because it was so much fun!
- These dumbbells are great, but I needed a couple of days to get used to the app.
- I had no problem using these dumbbells! I had trouble using other adjustable dumbbells as their dials break easily.
- Sharing your performance with the app community is motivating! But since it was just released recently, there are only a few members.

問1　According to the maker's statement, which best describes the new dumbbells?

[6]

① affordable dumbbells

② colourful dumbbells

③ ingenious dumbbells

④ old-fashioned dumbbells

⑤ waterproof dumbbells

問2　Which benefit offered by the dumbbells is most likely to appeal to you?

[7]

① Getting motivated to exercise more

② Making the dumbbells more mobile

③ Recording your performance and keeping the information private

④ Reducing the risk of injuries

問3　One opinion stated by a customer is that ☐8☐ .

① it is difficult to add or remove the weights of the dumbbells

② it is fun to share your performance data with other app members

③ the dumbbells are more durable than others

④ you can lose weight so fast only by using the dumbbells and without using the apps

問4　One customer's comment mentions the fitness program. Which benefit is this comment based on? ☐9☐

① Better Balance

② Increased Mobility

③ Information Security

④ Promotes Exercise

問5　According to one customer's opinion, ☐10☐ is recommended.

① allowing time to get familiar with the app

② charging the dumbbells' battery to the max before using

③ comparing the dumbbells' dials with others

④ downloading the app before using the dumbbells

B You are a member of the student council. The members have been discussing a student project that motivates students to study more. To get ideas, you are reading a report about a school challenge. It was written by an exchange student who studied at another school in Japan.

Glued to the screen

Last year, we conducted a survey about how students in our school use their time. The result showed that they spend too many hours on smartphones and playing games. That is why we started this Studying App Tournament so that students would use those hours spent on studying, instead of playing games on their smartphones. Students took part in quizzes from January 17th to February 17th. Students would win prizes based on the total amount of points they earned from these quizzes. First place would win 2,000 yen, second place would win 1,000 yen, and third place would win 500 yen. A total of 30 students out of the whole school participated: more than two-thirds of them were second-year students; 7 were first-year students; and the rest were third-year students. How come so few third-years participated? The following feedback may help answer that question.

Feedback from participants

AB: I spent most of the time on the bus using the studying app, and it helped me understand the classes better. Also, you can add notes on the app, which is useful during class. I felt like I didn't need to review the classes when I got back home because I had already done it on my bus ride!

AJ: I heard some of my second-year friends didn't even know about this Studying App Tournament. The tournament had already ended by the time they found out about it. Even if they had known about this, they wouldn't have felt like taking part because 2,000 yen was way less than what they earn in their part-time jobs.

NI: Most of the time I used the app on my small smartphone. I used it a little bit on my home computer, too. Besides, I'm better at studying audio material, though the app does not have any.

RT: I got the highest score ever on the math test! The Studying App Tournament really helped me to study more! There are 4 choices for each question, and you choose the correct one. Simple as that!

VA: The studying app itself was easy to use. However, it's not surprising that third-year students didn't participate in the Studying App Tournament, because they were so busy and focused on preparing for the university entrance exam.

問1　The aim of the Studying App Tournament was to ☐11☐ .

   ① create an online community so students could help each other outside of school hours

   ② give students the opportunity to create their own app

   ③ help encourage students to study more

   ④ motivate students to learn about self-learning apps

問2　One **fact** about the Studying App Tournament is that ☐12☐ .

   ① fewer than 50% of the participants were second-year students

   ② it was held for about four weeks during the winter

   ③ students had to use smartphones to participate

   ④ the majority of participants were male

問3　From the feedback, | 13 | were activities reported by participants you could do in the studying app.

A : answering questions related to class

B : connecting with other students

C : listening to audio files

D : making notes on the app

① A and B

② A and C

③ A and D

④ B and C

⑤ B and D

⑥ C and D

問4　One of the participants' opinions about the studying app tournament is that
| 14 | .

① the audio materials in the app were useful

② the prize money helped motivate students

③ the studying app was especially effective for improving history scores

④ there was no problem in terms of operating the app

問5　The author's question is answered by | 15 | .

① AB

② AJ

③ NI

④ RT

⑤ VA

第3問 (配点 15)

A You are reading a post by a blogger named Greg. There he explains how to pack bags efficiently when shopping.

The Best Way to Organize Shopping Bags

Hi, I'm Greg. Have you ever worked in a supermarket or convenience store? I've been working at a convenience store for half a year, and learned how to place goods in bags well and quickly.

Putting things in bags is just like building a house. The first thing to do is to put tall and hard items in the corners of the bag. Isn't this the same as putting up the poles of a house? Next, you need to place the heavy items on the bottom of the bag as if you were making a floor with them. Then you should put flat items on the sides like the walls of a house. So far, the basic structure has been completed.

Now, you will notice that there is a wide, open space in the middle. There, you should stack items in order from the heaviest to the lightest. If you are buying potato chips or small snacks, you should place them on top.

Finally, place long, thin, soft items such as newspapers, green onions, or candy bars in a way that you fill in the gaps. This will be the final touch.

Is everything good? If you remember the directions I gave you here, you can organize your shopping bags without damaging fragile items. The items in your bag won't fall out when you are carrying them around.

問1 If you take Greg's advice, how should you organize your bag? ☐16☐

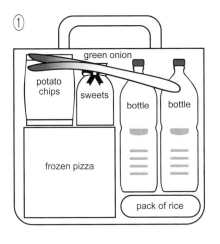

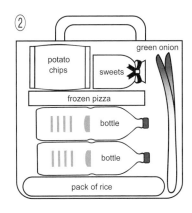

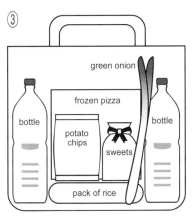

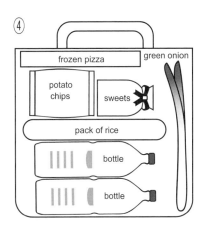

問2 According to Greg, the best way to put things in your bag is ☐17☐.

① filling the gaps with hard and small items

② making a wide, open space in the corner

③ placing items so frozen foods go to the bottom

④ putting in items as if you were building a house

—55—

B You are planning to visit Northern Europe this summer and have found an interesting article on the capital city of Denmark in a travel magazine.

What Makes Copenhagen So Special?

Copenhagen is known as the most bicycle-friendly city in the world. In Copenhagen, bicycles account for about 50% of all transportation to and from school and work. Why do so many people in the Danish capital use bicycles?

The answer is that the Copenhagen government has been promoting a bicycle-focused lifestyle. In 1995, Copenhagen introduced CitiBike, a free bike-share system to create a new, environmentally friendly mode of transport for its citizens and tourists. It was funded by advertising and managed by a city-supported fund. Users can unlock their bicycles from a docking station by inserting refundable coins.

Furthermore, Copenhagen's bicycle system includes a system called "Green Wave" which manages the timing of traffic lights during commuting hours so that cyclists can proceed at the intersections they pass more easily. Before the system was first established on the main bicycle routes in 2007, traffic lights were coordinated in favor of cars. Later, cyclists have to stop for a red light less frequently than before. This system makes their commute to work much more easier.

In 2010, the City of Copenhagen launched a website to receive requests from cyclists. It began accepting a variety of requests, including information about road damage and the establishment of dedicated waiting zones for cyclists at intersections. According to the Copenhagen city government, they received 7,944 requests for repairing road damage and repaired 6,396 of them in 2013.

Copenhagen aims to be the first CO_2-neutral capital by 2025, the leader in green technology and innovation in Europe. It is building 45 routes (746 km in total) of "bicycle superhighway" between the city and the countryside. The construction is expected to end by the year 2045. As general bicycle use is

---

currently increasing in large cities, the government expects the 'bicycle superhighway' to increase the number of cyclists in rural areas. When the superhighway is complete, it is expected to reduce CO_2 emissions by 1,500 tons per year.

問1　Put the following events (①～④) into the order in which they happened or will happen.　18 → 19 → 20 → 21

①　Building a superhighway for bicycles between the city and the countryside

②　Introducing the "Green Wave" system

③　Launching a free public bicycle-sharing system

④　Launching a website to accept requests from cyclists

問2　How does the "Green Wave" system work?　22

①　Cyclists can bring their own bicycles into trains or buses.

②　Cyclists can pass through intersections with less frequent red traffic lights.

③　Cyclists can request when the traffic lights turn green on a website in advance.

④　Cyclists do not have to stop pedaling at red traffic lights during commute hours.

問3　Which of the following is true about the "bicycle superhighway"? 23

① It is aimed to increase cyclists outside of cities.

② It is being built and will be completed in 2025.

③ It is planned to be built only in the countryside for the time being.

④ It will be free from the risk of surface damage compared to other roads.

第4問 （配点 16）

You are studying the benefits gained from keeping pets. You are going to refer to the two articles below to discuss what you learned in the next class.

How a pet benefits you: Why not keep one?
Karim Woodson
Veterinary Surgeon, at Moth Municipal Animal Clinic

Why do people keep pets? Many of you may answer, "No reason. I just want a loving companion." But without realizing it, pets benefit you more than you think. Let me explain this from several points of view. Firstly, keeping pets can lower the levels of stress hormones and reduce symptoms of anxiety. A study published in the International Journal of Workplace Health Management reported that keeping a dog in the office lowered the levels of perceived stress among employees.

Interacting with pets can also boost mood and increase feelings of happiness. Therefore, pet owners often have higher self-esteem and are happier than non-pet owners. In fact, one study found that spending just 15 minutes with a dog can increase levels of oxytocin, a hormone associated with social bonding and pleasure in the brain.

Spending time with pets requires owners to perform more daily routines than non-pet owners. They may play with them, feed them, clean the floor or their cages and walk them, which will force the owners to become more physically active. Dogs, in particular, can benefit their owners in this respect. Dog owners are more likely to meet daily physical activity guidelines than non-dog owners. In addition, a report found that dog walking is associated with healthier body weight and fewer doctor visits.

Lastly, pets can provide their owners with companionship and reduce feelings of social isolation. This is because having a pet can reduce levels of loneliness and ownership promotes social interaction with people you may meet while taking care of your pet, such as vets and other owners.

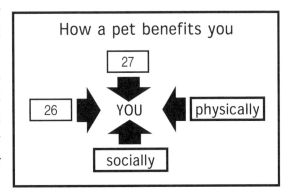

How a pet benefits you

27

26 → YOU ← physically

socially

Effects keeping pets can have on you: Not just good ones

Seth Atwood

Animal Therapy Teacher, at Bkeren Animal College

I teach students who want to be animal therapists and am a dog owner myself. Over the past few years, I have studied the effects of pet ownership on owners' communication skills. Several studies have explored these effects.

Firstly, owning a pet can increase the chances to interact with other pet owners, leading to the development of new friendships. A study published in the International Journal of Workplace Health Management found that pet owners reported higher levels of social support from colleagues than non-pet owners. Positive effects on communication skills can result from increased interaction with others. Additionally, pets communicate non-verbally, so owners of pets become accustomed to understanding their pets' feelings and intentions through body language and vocalizations. This, in turn, can improve owners' ability to interpret and use non-verbal communication when interacting with people.

However, the benefits of living with pets can have negative effects. Although pets can increase social interaction with other pet owners, the same cannot be said for interactions with non-pet owners. Limiting the types of people you interact with can lead to social isolation and reduced communication skills, especially if owners' dependency on pets is excessive. Owners may become less sympathetic towards values and tastes that differ from their own.

If you wish to ensure that your life with your pets is enjoyable and beneficial, you should be aware of the potential negative effects while maintaining a balance between interactions with pets and with other humans.

問1　Woodson says that ⬚24⬚ .

① dog owners are healthy because they usually get up early

② keeping a dog can lead to a pleasant atmosphere in a workplace and active
lifestyle

③ keeping pets does far more good than harm to owners

④ people prefer specific kinds of pets without realizing it

問2　According to a study, keeping a dog in the office lowered stress levels of
⬚25⬚ .

① the dog itself

② the dog owner

③ the managers

④ the workers

問3　Summarize the benefits of keeping pets Woodson explains by choosing two
best options to fill in the chart. (The order does not matter.) ⬚26⬚ · ⬚27⬚

① academically

② biologically

③ economically

④ financially

⑤ psychologically

問4　Both writers agree on the advantage pet owners can gain by ☐28☐ .

　　① communicating with their pets non-verbally
　　② interacting with their new acquaintances
　　③ learning about the behaviors of pet animals
　　④ performing daily routines for their pets

問5　Which could be a good way to solve the negative effects of keeping pets that Atwood explains? ☐29☐

　　① go out and take exercise once a week
　　② join a group tour consisting of pet owners
　　③ join a party and talk to people from various backgrounds
　　④ learn about human gestures and facial expressions

Your English teacher has told everyone in your class to find an inspiring story and present it to a discussion group, using notes. You have found a story written by an American journalist.

The Legendary Couple: Herb & Dorothy

Bill Jordan

Herbert Vogel was born in 1922 in Harlem, New York City, the son of a Russian Jewish garment worker. He dropped out of high school, served in the U.S. Army during World War II, and worked as a mail sorter for the U.S. Postal Service until he retired in 1979.

Dorothy Faye Hoffman was born to a Jewish stationery merchant. She earned a bachelor's degree in library science from Syracuse University and a master's degree from the University of Denver, and worked as a librarian at the Brooklyn Public Library until her retirement in 1990.

Herbert and Dorothy met in 1960, fell in love, and got married in 1962. From the beginning of their marriage, the Vogels' life revolved around art. Herbert worked the night shift at the post office while studying at the Institute of Fine Arts during the day. Dorothy followed suit and began taking painting and drawing classes at New York University. They both studied painting and drawing for a while, but realized that they didn't have enough talent to become artists. Soon the couple chose to view and collect art rather than paint on their own.

Their first art purchase was a small sculpture of crushed metal by John Chamberlain. Since they were both on modest salaries, the couple couldn't afford expensive pictures by famous artists. Within their means, the Vogels bought what they liked little by little. Walking hand in hand through SoHo in Manhattan, the Vogels visited numerous galleries and began collecting works of art, mostly minimalist and conceptual art, which were not very popular in the early 1960s.

Their way of acquiring artwork was to make friends with young, promising artists who were still unknown. The Vogels attended nightly gallery events and talked with many such artists as Robert and Sylvia Mangold, Donald Judd, Richard Tuttle, and Sol LeWitt. Not being wealthy, they bought the artists' works in monthly installments, and sometimes fell behind on their payments. However, the artists recognized the Vogels' aesthetic sensibilities and their financial situation, so they never complained when the payment was delayed. Eventually, they became known as "Herb & Dorothy" and gained fame and popularity in the New York art community.

Herb & Dorothy's basic policy for collecting was to live on Dorothy's salary and spend all of Herb's income on purchasing art. They did not own a car, take vacations, or travel abroad, and often spent their evenings at a nearby Chinese deli. They had one more purchase policy: Herb & Dorothy purchased what they could take home by subway or cab. The reason was simple: they lived in a tiny one-bedroom apartment in Harlem.

In the early 1990s, Herb & Dorothy's apartment was overflowing with their collection in every available space from floor to ceiling, kitchen to bathroom, and door to wall. It primarily consisted of drawings, but it also included paintings, sculptures, photographs, and prints by more than 170 artists. Amazingly, their collection had grown to over 4,000 works of art, assembling one of the most significant and comprehensive collections of minimalist and conceptual art in the world.

In 1992, Herb & Dorothy decided to donate their entire collection to the National Gallery of Art in Washington, D.C. To their surprise, it took five trucks to transport them! Then, in 2008, the National Gallery announced their support for "Fifty Works for Fifty States," a plan to donate 50 works from Vogel's collection to galleries in all 50 states.

The collection of contemporary art that a public servant couple had accumulated in their one-bedroom apartment over half a century is now managed by the National Gallery of Art. Even though their collection was worth several million dollars, the Vogels never considered selling any of their artwork. They simply wanted the American people to enjoy their collection for free.

Herbert Vogel passed away in 2012 at the age of 89, but he left behind a remarkable collection of contemporary art that he amassed with his wife over half a century. Their collection and love for art can be seen in the National Gallery of Art and galleries around the country.

Your presentation notes:

Herb & Dorothy's Life

Herbert Vogel and Dorothy Hoffman

· Herbert was [30] .

· Dorothy worked as a librarian.

Married life of Herbert and Dorothy

· Their life revolved around art.

· They chose to [31] rather than to become artists.

Important events in Herb & Dorothy's life

[32] → Their first art purchase → [33] → [34] → [35]

Why did Herb & Dorothy donate their collection to the National Gallery of Art?

Because [36] .

What we can learn from this story

· [37]

· [38]

問1　Choose the best option for [30] .

① a garment worker

② a modern artist

③ a postal worker

④ a school teacher

問2　Choose the best option for ☐31☐ .

　　① appreciate and collect works of art

　　② buy expensive pictures by famous artists

　　③ run an art gallery

　　④ sponsor young, promising artists

問3　Choose four out of the five options (① ~ ⑤) and rearrange them in the order

　　they happened. ☐32☐ → ☐33☐ → ☐34☐ → ☐35☐

　　① Attending nightly gallery events

　　② Buying a small sculpture of crushed metal

　　③ Donating their collection to the National Gallery of Art

　　④ Project of "Fifty Works for Fifty States"

　　⑤ Taking painting and drawing classes

問4　Choose the best option for ⬚36⬚ .

 ① it has branch museums in all the states

 ② it is located in the capital of the U.S.

 ③ it specializes in displaying contemporary art

 ④ it would display their collection for free

問5　Choose the best two options for ⬚37⬚ and ⬚38⬚ . (The order does not matter.)

 ① Herb & Dorothy built a famous art museum that showcases historical art.

 ② Herb & Dorothy had a reputation among artists for their taste in buying art.

 ③ Herb & Dorothy made a fortune in the art business.

 ④ Herb & Dorothy never sold their collection.

 ⑤ Herb & Dorothy often rented trucks and other large vehicles when buying large art objects.

第6問 (配点 24)

A You are in a discussion group in school. You have been asked to summarize the following article. You will speak about it, using only notes.

Research on Expert Performance in Team Sports

In pretty much every area, a sign of expert performance is the ability to see patterns in a collection of things that would seem random or confusing to people with less well-developed mental representations.

In other words, experts see the forest when everyone else sees only trees. This is perhaps most obvious in team sports. Take soccer, for instance. You have eleven players on a side moving around in a way that to the inexperienced seems a furious chaos with no apparent pattern beyond the obvious fact that some players are drawn to the soccer ball whenever it comes near. To those who know and love the game, however, and particularly to those who play the game well, this chaos is no chaos at all. It is all a beautifully nuanced and constantly shifting pattern created as the players move in response to the ball and the movements of the other players. The best players recognize and respond to the patterns almost immediately, taking advantage of weaknesses or openings as soon as they appear.

To study this phenomenon, I and two colleagues, Paul Ward and Mark Williams, investigated how well soccer players can predict what's coming next from what has already happened on the field. To do this we showed them videos of real soccer matches and suddenly stopped the video when a player had just received the ball. Then we asked our subjects to predict what would happen next. Would the player with the ball keep it, attempt a shot at the goal, or pass the ball to a teammate? We found that the more accomplished players were much better at predicting what the player with the ball should do. We also tested the players' memory for where the relevant players were located and in what directions they were moving by asking them to recall as much as they could from the last frame of the video before it was hidden from them. Again, the better players outperformed the weaker ones.

We concluded that the advantages better players had in predicting future events were related to their ability to predict more possible outcomes and quickly analyze through them and come up with the most promising action. In short, the better players had a more highly developed ability to interpret the pattern of action on the field. This ability allowed them to perceive which players' movements and interactions mattered most, which allowed them to make better decisions about where to go on the field, when to pass the ball and to whom, and so on.

Something very similar is true for football, although it is mainly the quarterback who needs to develop mental representations of events on the field. This explains why the most successful quarterbacks are generally the ones who spend the most time in the film room watching and analyzing the plays of their own team and their opponents. The best quarterbacks keep track of what's happening everywhere on the field, and after the game they can generally recall most of the game's plays, providing detailed descriptions of the movements of many players on each team. More importantly, effective mental representations allow a quarterback to make good decisions quickly: whether to pass the ball, whom to pass to, when to pass, and so on. Being able to make the right decision a tenth of a second faster can be the difference between a good play and a disastrous one — between, say, a completed pass and an interception.

For the experts we just described, the key benefit of mental representations lies in how they help us deal with information: understanding and interpreting it, holding it in memory, organizing it, analyzing it, and making decisions with it. The same is true for all experts — and most of us are experts at something, whether we realize it or not.

Your notes:

Expert Performance in Team Sports

Introduction
◆ Experts see the forest while everyone else sees only trees.
◆ Those who play the game of soccer well can ⬚39⬚ .

Investigation
◆ Method: ⬚40⬚
◆ Conclusion: The better soccer players can ⬚41⬚ and they have developed the ability to ⬚42⬚ .

In the case of football
◆ ⬚43⬚

問1　Choose the best option for ⬚39⬚ .

① enjoy the chaos caused by other players during the game

② keep up with even the fastest moves of the opposing players

③ see patterns in a collection of things that would seem random

④ turn the teammates' weaknesses into their strengths

問2　Choose the best option for ⬚40⬚ .

① Ask the players' health conditions before the soccer match

② Investigate each player's advantages by interviewing them

③ Show the subjects videos of real soccer matches

④ Test how quickly the subjects respond to the ball

問3　Choose the best options for ⬚41⬚ and ⬚42⬚ . (The order does not matter.)

① decide what to do after the game

② interpret the pattern of action

③ predict what will happen next

④ realize how to improve relationship among teammates

⑤ respond to the patterns calmly

問4　Choose the best option for ⬚43⬚ .

① Quarterbacks require more physical strength than other positions.

② Successful quarterbacks spend time watching only their teammates.

③ The best quarterbacks have resembling traits to the best soccer players.

④ The most accomplished quarterbacks can coach their teammates into better
   players.

B You are in a student group preparing for an international science presentation contest. You are using the following passage to create your part of the presentation on an interesting creature.

Octopuses are fascinating creatures that you can learn so much from. There are close to 300 species, and they come in many different shapes and sizes. The smallest species would be smaller than 2.5 centimeters long weighing less than a gram, while the largest species are an average of 4 meters weighing 50 kilograms. Octopuses, along with squid and cuttlefish, make up the cephalopod class of marine animals. They have evolved dramatically since the cephalopods originated more than 600 million years ago. These animals have many unique characteristics that set them apart from other invertebrates, or spineless animals.

The word "cephalopod" means "head-foot" in Greek. It refers to the octopus' unique body structure in which its arms branch directly from its head. Directly opposite of its arms, or above its head, there is a highly muscled, balloon-like structure called the mantle. The mantle is filled with most of the animal's organs such as gills, digestive systems, and others, which explains its swollen shape. The mantle's strong muscles protect these vital organs and help with breathing and body shrinkage. The mouth is located on its underside, where the eight arms meet. Its beak is the only hard part of the animal's skeleton-less body. This enables the octopus to squeeze and fit its entire body through any small spaces that its beak can go through. When the food is taken in from the mouth, it is then moved to the muscular crop. The crop holds the food before it is digested in the stomach. The partially digested food then moves into the intestine, where nutrients are absorbed into the bloodstream. By the time it reaches the end of the intestine, or the entrance of the funnel, it is fully converted to stool. The stool is ejected from the funnel, forming into slender ribbon-like substance. There are more functions the funnel is responsible for, which will be discussed later.

Another feature that sets them apart from other animals is their multiple brains, not just two or three, but nine in fact! The central brain is located between their eyes, so when the food is chewed up in the mouth, it goes past it. In general, the central brain contains roughly 180 million neurons out of 500 million in total. The remaining neurons are evenly distributed in the 8 tentacles. If you do the math, you'll find more than half of the neurons are in the tentacles, rather than the central brain! With each tentacle having its own ganglia, or group of neurons, they can act individually from each other and from the central brain. This is advantageous to octopuses as their bodies are fluid and lack any skeleton, resulting in a lack of proprioception, or in other words, the sense of where its body part is located or doing. For instance, we can locate the back of our heads without seeing it, thanks to proprioception. However, octopuses constantly reshape their fluid bodies to adapt to their surroundings, thus they lack proprioception. This is substituted by having smaller brains in each tentacle.

The octopus' movement is another feature worth noting. Generally, octopuses move in the form of crawling. They can crawl vertically or even upside-down with the tentacle's row of suckers. A more interesting method of moving can be seen when the octopus is in danger. In such circumstances, the octopus maneuvers more quickly by using its funnel. The octopus first fills the mantle with water and closes it, like a water balloon. Imagine holding a water balloon and you let go of the opening, as it flies away violently while squirting away water. The octopus uses a similar principle by releasing the water from the mantle and out through the funnel, which jets the octopus in the opposite direction at a maximum of 40 kph. The octopus can alter its course by pointing its funnel in different directions.

There are many more unique features of an octopus, as one scientist mentioned that they are considered the closest living form to an alien on earth. From the octopus' origin and evolutionary process, it can be said that they are the most complex species with the least common factors of humans. As octopuses are the most distant from the human evolutionary process, they yet have a clear consciousness like humans. From this reason, researchers are focusing on octopus brain waves as a possible clue to the mechanisms of human consciousness. This may unlock not just the mysteries of octopus' traits like its brain systems and movement patterns, but the fundamental understanding of how the consciousness of all possible organisms on earth may have been established.

Your presentation slides:

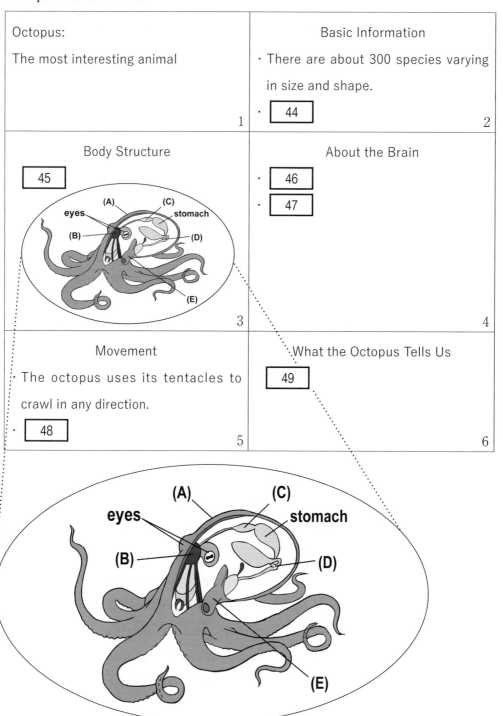

Octopus: The most interesting animal 1	Basic Information · There are about 300 species varying in size and shape. · 44 2
Body Structure 45 (A) (C) eyes stomach (B) (D) (E) 3	About the Brain · 46 · 47 4
Movement · The octopus uses its tentacles to crawl in any direction. · 48 5	What the Octopus Tells Us 49 6

(A) (C)
eyes stomach
(B) (D)
(E)

問 1　Which of the following should you include for ⬚ 44 ⬚ ?

    ① Octopuses are not relatives of ocean animals with shells, as they do not have any.

    ② Octopuses have spines, which sets them apart from other invertebrates.

    ③ Some octopuses have no more than a gram of body weight.

    ④ The average size of all species of octopuses is around 4 meters.

    ⑤ The octopus belongs to "cephalopod", which means "head-foot", as both its arms and head have neurons.

問 2　Complete the missing labels on the illustration of an octopus for the **Body Structure** slide. ⬚ 45 ⬚

	(A)	(B)	(C)	(D)	(E)
①	central brain	mantle	crop	funnel	intestine
②	central brain	mantle	crop	intestine	funnel
③	crop	central brain	funnel	mantle	intestine
④	mantle	central brain	crop	funnel	intestine
⑤	mantle	central brain	crop	intestine	funnel

問 3　For the **About the Brain** slide, select two features of an octopus' brain that are true. (The order does not matter.) ⬚ 46 ⬚ · ⬚ 47 ⬚

    ① Close to 40 million neurons are in each tentacle.

    ② Neurons are in their tentacles so that the octopus' skeletons can be fluid.

    ③ The ganglia in each tentacle allow the octopus to have proprioception.

    ④ The ganglia in each tentacle allow them to act in a different way from each other without the central brain's command.

    ⑤ The number of neurons in the central brain is twice the number of neurons in their tentacles.

問 4   For the **Movement** slide, select a feature of an octopus that is true. [48]

① The octopus fills up its body with air like a balloon and releases it to move its body.
② The octopus jets away by pointing the funnel to control the course.
③ The octopus produces a balloon-like substance and fills it with water.
④ The octopus takes in water from the funnel and fills its body up in preparation to jet away.
⑤ Water comes out directly from the mantle, causing the octopus to jet off in the opposite direction.

問 5   Which is the best statement for the final slide? [49]

① It is best to research octopuses to find out about alien consciousness.
② Octopus brain activities may be the key to unlocking the mystery of the origins of consciousness in living organisms.
③ Studying octopuses may help apply the octopus' unique features to the human body.
④ The human and octopus evolutionary processes are said to be different because they have very different consciousness.

リーディング―――第3回

時間　80分　　　　　　100点　満点

1 ―― 解答にあたっては，実際に試験を受けるつもりで，時間を厳守し真剣に取りくむこと。

2 ―― 巻末にマークシートをつけてあるので，切り離しのうえ練習用として利用すること。

3 ―― 解答終了後には，自己採点により学力チェックを行い，別冊の解答・解説をじっくり
　　　読んで，弱点補強，知識や考え方の整理などに努めること。

　※「リーディング」問題構成について
　　2022 年に大学入試センターにて実施された「2025 年度大学入学共通テスト試作問
　　題モニター調査」では，大問数が第 8 問構成へと変更されています。ただしこの
　　問題構成はモニター調査で必要な情報を収集するために構成したもので，本番に
　　向けて問題構成は今後も引き続き検討をするとの付記があります。
　　この問題集では新しい第 8 問構成の問題（第 5 回）とこれまで通りの第 6 問構成
　　の問題（第 1 ～ 4 回）の両パターンの問題を収録しています。

英　語（リーディング）

各大問の英文や図表を読み，解答番号 ┃ 1 ┃ ～ ┃ 50 ┃ にあてはまるものとして最も適当な選択肢を選びなさい。

第1問 (配点　10)

A　You come back home to find a message from your mother on your desk.

I'm really sorry. I had promised to go shopping with you this evening, but I can't. Grandpa phoned me to say that Grandma fell down the stairs and broke her arm. I have to go to Grandma's home now to prepare for her hospital stay. Depending on her condition, I may stay there for several days. I left some money on the table in the living room, so please make do with that.

By the way, Dad said he would be late coming home today, so you don't have to prepare dinner for him.

Call me if you need anything.

問1　What is your mother most likely to have done after writing this message?

　　　$\boxed{\quad 1 \quad}$

　　① Called an ambulance.

　　② Gone to Grandma's house.

　　③ Phoned Grandpa.

　　④ Prepared dinner for you.

問2　What can you tell from this message?　$\boxed{\quad 2 \quad}$

　　① Your father is going to drop by the hospital before coming back home.

　　② Your grandmother does not live with you.

　　③ Your grandmother was injured because of a traffic accident.

　　④ Your mother does not want to go shopping with you.

B   You are looking at the website of Wakaba University in Japan, and you find an interesting contest announcement. You are thinking about participating in the contest.

Wakaba University Writing Contest for High School Students

This creative writing contest hosted by Wakaba University is open to high school students of all ages. You can submit your work in any of the three categories: poem, short story and essay.

Application Requirements

Please read the following before submitting your work:
- (1)   Applicants must be high school students.
- (2)   All entries must be original works.
- (3)   You may submit entries to more than one category at a time.
- (4)   The word limits below must be strictly adhered to.
    Poem: 2,000 words or less
    Short Story: 8,000 words or less
    Essay: 2,000 words or less
- (5)   Entries that have been previously submitted to other contests are acceptable unless they have already won a prize.
- (6)   All entries must be typed. Include your full name, address, and the title of the work on the first page of the work.
- (7)   All entries must be sent via email to writingcontest@wakaba-u.ac.jp.

Awards

Significant works in each category will be awarded the Grand Prize or the Encouragement Prize.

Grand Prize: A certificate, a trophy and 100,000 yen
Encouragement Prize: A certificate and 30,000 yen

Schedule

Submissions will be accepted August 1 through September 30.

A list of winners will be posted online by November 1.

The award ceremony will be held at Wakaba University on November 23.

問1 If you participate in the Wakaba University Writing Contest, you must submit your work ☐3☐ .

① by November 1
② by the end of November
③ in August and September
④ on August 1

問2 When submitting your work, ☐4☐ .

① the work must be within 2,000 words
② you have to be a student at Wakaba University
③ you have to ensure that it has not yet won a prize in other contests
④ you must type your full name, address, and the title on all the pages

問3 If your work is chosen as the Grand Prize, ☐5☐ .

① you will be awarded a trophy, a certificate, and 100,000 yen
② you will be invited to the award ceremony on November 1
③ you will receive a certificate and 10,000 yen
④ your name will appear online on November 23

第2問 (配点 20)

A You are planning a camping trip for your 18th birthday next month. You are looking at the website of a campground your friend told you about.

⟨ **Stone River Campground** ⟩

Stone River Campground is rich in nature with a river flowing nearby and many kinds of animals. We have more than 30 cottages and well-equipped facilities, which allow even beginners to camp comfortably. Only small dogs and cats are allowed.

Charges:	Adult	Child (Under 15 years old)	Pet
1 Night	$10	$5	$3
2 Nights or more	$9 / night	$4 / night	$3 / night

Cottage

Each of our cottages is equipped with four beds, a refrigerator, and a TV. The cottages themselves don't have Wi-Fi access, but rental Wi-Fi devices are available for $2 per night if you need to access the Internet.

Cooking

The public area, which is located outdoors, has kitchens for several families and you can cook only there. Cooking utensils are available with no additional fee. If you need them, just let us know when you make a reservation. There is a supermarket near the campground, so you don't have to bring large amounts of food from home.

Others

Shower rooms are in the public space and you can use them for up to 20 minutes a day. In the shower room, you can use amenities such as soap and shampoo, which are offered at the reception. As for garbage disposal, please dispose of food scraps in the garbage dump and take home all other garbage with you.

Comments from users

● The campground is easy to access because it is a ten-minute walk from the station. For those who have a lot of baggage for camping, free shuttle buses are in service from the station to the campground. On the other hand, if you want to bring your pet, it is the best to drive there yourself.

● When I went deep into the forest of the campground, I saw various animals such as deer, squirrels, and woodpeckers. Also, many people were camping with their pets, so I felt as if I was in a small zoo!

● I was happy to see my wife and kids enjoying nature. But unfortunately, we couldn't make a campfire because the use of fire is banned in the campground except in the public area, which was so crowded that it would have been impossible for my family to enjoy a campfire alone.

● My first time camping with my dog was very exciting. However, I regret forgetting to bring a pet cage because my dog was so excited that he ran around in the cottage while I was sleeping.

問1 ┃ 6 ┃ are two things that are true about the campground.

    A：All kinds of animals are allowed to be brought to the campground.

    B：Most of the animals there are protected by the staff.

    C：You can rent a Wi-Fi device by paying an additional fee.

    D：You can use the shower rooms as long as you want.

    E：You may not cook in the cottage you are staying in.

    ①   A and B

    ②   A and C

    ③   B and D

    ④   C and E

    ⑤   D and E

問2   If you break your flashlight in the campground and you want to dispose of it, you need to ┃ 7 ┃.

    ①   ask the staff to throw it away

    ②   bring it to the reception

    ③   take it back home with you

    ④   throw it in the campground garbage dump

問3   To use cooking tools belonging to the campground, you have to ┃ 8 ┃.

    ①   apply for them on the day of camping

    ②   pay an additional fee

    ③   reserve them in advance

    ④   show your identification

問4　If you are planning to camp with your 17-year-old friend and your two pet dogs for two nights, the total fee will be 　9　.

① $28

② $32

③ $48

④ $52

問5　One **fact** stated by the users of the campground is that 　10　.

① a pet cage is important to spend time with your pet in the cottage

② camping with animals there is as exciting as touring a zoo

③ you are allowed to have a campfire in a limited area

④ you have to drive there because there isn't much transportation

B You are the editor of "Wanna See Japan," an English website promoting tourism in Japan. You have received an article from David, an American travel journalist, in which he wrote about Japan's international airports and sightseeing spots.

More than half of the tourists visiting Japan use two airports: Narita International Airport (NRT) and Kansai International Airport (KIX). NRT had long been the most important airport in Japan, but in recent years KIX has become increasingly popular, especially among travelers from Asian countries.

Do you know which country or region sends the most visitors to KIX? In 2019, China ranked first, South Korea second, Taiwan third, Hong Kong fourth, and Thailand fifth. So, where do these people visit after arriving at KIX?

An analysis of search data from a navigation app for tourists visiting Japan shows that Osaka Castle is most frequently searched by foreign tourists, followed by Kinkakuji Temple, Nara Park, Tokyo Tower, Fushimi Inari Shrine, Dotonbori, and Universal Studios Japan. Amazingly, three of the top seven spots are in Osaka.

Why is Osaka so popular among foreign visitors to Japan? According to the 2017 survey of 1,236 foreign tourists at KIX, the reasons for choosing Osaka as a destination were as follows: 48% of them said it was an attractive place to visit, 44% said the food was appealing, and 41% said shopping was attractive. 26% of them said they would visit Dotonbori, where almost all of them wanted to enjoy Osaka's unique cuisine such as *takoyaki*, *okonomiyaki*, and *kushikatsu*.

It is hoped that KIX will be crowded with more foreign tourists in the future: the World Exposition will be held in Osaka in 2025. Approximately 28 million people are expected to visit the Expo over the period of six months.

問1　According to David's article, which of the following statements is true about Japan's international airports?　| 11 |

① KIX is an international airport that operates 24 hours a day.

② More than half of the foreign visitors to Japan arrive at KIX.

③ NRT and KIX are the only international airports in Japan.

④ The popularity of KIX is on the rise these days.

問2　Which of the following was ranked fourth in terms of the number of foreign visitors to KIX in 2019?　| 12 |

① Hong Kong

② South Korea

③ Taiwan

④ Thailand

問3　According to the 2017 survey of foreign tourists at KIX, about a quarter of the respondents wanted to visit Dotonbori because　| 13 |　.

① it is a very beautiful place to see

② it is close to Osaka Castle and KIX

③ it is where they can find Osaka's unique cuisine

④ it is where you can buy almost anything

問4 Which is the third most frequently searched place on a navigation app by foreign visitors to Japan? ☐14

① Dotonbori

② Fushimi Inari Shrine

③ Kinkakuji Temple

④ Nara Park

⑤ Tokyo Tower

⑥ Universal Studios Japan

問5 Which is the most suitable title for the article? ☐15

① KIX and Sightseeing Spots in Osaka

② Popular Sightseeing Spots in Japan

③ Positive Impacts of the Expo 2025 Osaka

④ The Battle between NRT and KIX

第3問 （配点 15）

A You are interested in going on a day trip. You are reading a blog post about a nearby tourist attraction by a UK college student in your neighbourhood.

Dave Simpson
Wednesday, 5 July, 6.32 pm

My roommate and I went out to a neighbourhood amusement park. It is a theme park whose main character is a beagle. Many attractions are available there. We rode a roller coaster and were amazed at the speed. I heard that it reaches 60 mph in 2 seconds. The free fall was so terrifying that I felt a little dizzy after the ride, but I hope everyone gives it a try.

We saw three performances in the park. One of them was a musical comedy show. A beagle mascot and other characters were dancing to songs on the stage. The characters were so cute that I really enjoyed the show. Other performances we saw included live music by men dressed in cowboy costumes and a performance by Native Americans using long ribbons. Many people stopped to watch, but we were not interested because we'd seen similar performances in another place.

We also attended valuable and enjoyable workshops. We experienced gold panning, which is an activity to separate gold dust from sand and gravel. We learnt how to use bowls to get the gold out of the muddy water. We also fed the horses. It was interesting to see that carrots were their favourite food, just as expected.

If you ever visit this theme park, please let me know what you think.

問 1　In Dave's blog, you read that he ⬚16⬚ .

　　①　bought a gold ring at the gift shop

　　②　enjoyed a character musical

　　③　learnt how to ride a horse

　　④　saw a beagle's street performance

問 2　Dave was most likely ⬚17⬚ when he was watching cowboys play music.

　　①　amazed

　　②　bored

　　③　pleased

　　④　thrilled

B Your history club will hold a "history experience exhibition" at the school festival. For reference, you are reading an article written by a professor who had his students experience the culture of England in old times.

In order to have my students experience the life of people in 19th century England, I had to consider several things.

First, I decided which social class to focus on. The class society of the time was really complex, but anyway I focused on the life of the common people.

Next, I determined the order of the events that the students would experience. At the beginning, I asked them to wear the clothes of the common people of the time, which I borrowed from a local historian. Then, the students experienced things in the following order: they ate breakfast, experienced the entertainment of the time and did some evening activities.

I purposely left the clothes I had borrowed torn. This is because it was usual for the common people at that time to make repairs, not being able to afford to buy new ones. As an evening activity, I had the students have the experience of sewing clothes with a needle.

Entertainment for the common people at that time included watching street performers and going to the zoo. However, it was not possible for me to prepare these things, so I exhibited panoramic paintings of other countries that were appreciated by the common people, who could not easily travel abroad.

As for food, the English are said to have had two meals a day in the Middle Ages, but after that they began having three meals a day. The most interesting of the three meals is breakfast. The common people's breakfast consisted of a kind of porridge made from oats and very sweet tea. Instead of giving an answer as to why such sweet tea was drunk for breakfast, I asked my students to think about it and write a report after all the events.

My students said they really enjoyed the experience.

問1　Put the following events (①~④) into the order in which the professor's students did them. 18 → 19 → 20 → 21

- ①　They ate porridge and drank sweet tea.
- ②　They changed their clothes.
- ③　They mended the clothes.
- ④　They wrote a report on sweet tea.

問2　According to the professor, in 19th century England, 22 .

- ①　it was rare for the common people to go out for entertainment
- ②　people had just begun to eat three meals a day
- ③　the common people often had difficulty buying new clothes
- ④　travelling abroad was popular among the common people

問3　From this article, you learnt that the professor 23 .

- ①　explained to his students why sweet tea was popular
- ②　gave students an opportunity to consider a question
- ③　hired a street performer to hold a show
- ④　spent a lot of money to remake clothes

第4問 （配点 16）

Your group is holding an event for exchange students in your city. You are reading the messages from two members of the group, Chiaki and Robin, discussing the event plan.

Chiaki   October 9 10:50 p.m.

I found an interesting workshop on the Momiji City Museum's website. In the workshop, we can make pottery on our own. Our city is known for pottery, so I think this is very nice for the event. Also, it will be fun to form clay and make our special pots, cups, or plates. According to the website, after you finish forming the pieces, they are stored in the museum for three days until they dry and then fired in a nearby kiln. The pottery is delivered to our home in about a week.

The workshops are held twice a day on weekends — from 10:00 a.m. and from 2:00 p.m. — and each is two hours. How about seeing the exhibitions in the museum in the morning, and then attending the workshop in the afternoon? The exhibitions are about the history, the industry and the culture of this city, and there we can listen to a thirty-minute English lecture about the pottery industry beginning at noon. It would be good to look around the exhibitions for an hour before attending the lecture.

As for lunch, there is a restaurant in the museum, but it would be nice to walk ten minutes to Momiji Park with lunch boxes. The maple trees in the park will have turned red before the day of the event. Our participants will enjoy the beautiful sight.

What do you think? I would like to hear your opinions.

Thank you, Chiaki! I thought the pottery workshop great. My host family has some flower-patterned ceramic plates. Can we make unique pottery like them? It will surely be fun.

The exhibitions in the museum also seem interesting. However, I suggest we visit Coast Park, instead. Recently I found some social media posts with photos of the palm-lined beach taken in the park and got interested in it. It seems that the park is becoming famous among shutterbugs, who seek spots where they can take nice photographs. We can take a walk on the beach, take photos, and enjoy a picnic with the view of the beautiful horizon and coastline. So, the event participants will learn about the beautiful natural environment of our city.

What do you say to meeting up at Coast Park bus stop at around 11:00 a.m.? Then, let's guide the participants in the park and have lunch, and leave the park at around 1:00 p.m. The Momiji City Museum is 30 minutes from the park by bus, so we can participate in the pottery class after that.

I think this plan lets the participants learn about both the tradition and natural environment of Momiji City. If it rains, however, let's go with Chiaki's plan. As for lunch, it would be better to eat at the restaurant Chiaki mentioned.

What do you guys think? Let's discuss it at the next web meeting!

問1　What is probably the main purpose of the event?　24

① To help exchange students with their studies

② To introduce the city

③ To make and eat lunch together

④ To support the pottery industry

問2　Which of the following is best for Chiaki's event plan?　25

①

Start	End	Activity
10:00 a.m.	12:00 p.m.	Attend the workshop
12:00 p.m.	12:30 p.m.	Listen to the lecture
12:30 p.m.	2:00 p.m.	Go to the park and have lunch
2:00 p.m.	4:00 p.m.	See the exhibitions in the museum

②

Start	End	Activity
10:00 a.m.	12:00 p.m.	Attend the workshop
12:00 p.m.	1:00 p.m.	Visit the kiln
1:00 p.m.	2:00 p.m.	Go to the park and have lunch
2:00 p.m.	4:00 p.m.	See the exhibitions in the museum

③

Start	End	Activity
10:00 a.m.	12:00 p.m.	See the exhibitions in the museum
12:00 p.m.	2:00 p.m.	Go to the park and have lunch
2:00 p.m.	4:00 p.m.	Attend the workshop
4:00 p.m.	5:00 p.m.	Visit the kiln

④

Start	End	Activity
11:00 a.m.	12:00 p.m.	See the exhibitions in the museum
12:00 p.m.	12:30 p.m.	Listen to the lecture
12:30 p.m.	2:00 p.m.	Go to the park and have lunch
2:00 p.m.	4:00 p.m.	Attend the workshop

問3　According to Robin's message, 　26　 .

   ① he has learned about Coast Park online

   ② he has taken photos in Coast Park before

   ③ he thinks the museum's exhibitions are boring

   ④ his host family has made pottery themselves

問4　Robin suggests that if the weather is fine they eat lunch 　27　 and if it rains they eat lunch 　28　 .

   ① at the pottery workshop

   ② at the restaurant in the Momiji City Museum

   ③ in Coast Park

   ④ in Momiji Park

問5　Neither Chiaki nor Robin plans 　29　 .

   ① to contact participants with social media

   ② to go to see autumn leaves in the park

   ③ to learn about the pottery industry in the museum

   ④ to use the bus for transportation

You have been asked by your teacher to present an impressive story in the discussion class. You have found a story written by a student in the US.

Fallen in Love with a Store Clerk

February 23, 2018　Randy Valentine

"Thank you for the heartfelt letter, Randy. I'm so happy such a nice person as you has feelings for me. You say in the letter that our current relationship, a customer and a clerk, may discourage us from becoming friends. But that's not really true."

It all started three months before I gave Karen the letter. I dropped into a newly opened drugstore on my way back from school. As I was picking up some snacks and drinks, I saw a smiling angel at the cash desk. Should I call it "love at first sight"? Definitely!

The next day, I visited the store again and there she was! Though I wasn't feeling sick, I asked her for some headache medicine. She took a bottle from the shelf behind the counter and said, "How about these pills? They should work quite quickly." "Thank you very much. I'll take that," I replied, pretending to be troubled with my pain. "Please take care of yourself," she said with a soft smile — it melted my heart.

On the following day, I wanted to visit Karen again but decided not to, for fear she would notice my feelings if I kept coming back every day. So, I spent the whole week holding back my desire to see her, as I didn't want to give her the impression that I was too eager. The third meeting was far more moving than I had expected. As I was handing her some money for a small item, she said to me, "Is your headache gone?" Oh, at least I was on her radar! "Y-Yes." "Good." I barely remembered our short exchanges at that moment.

The only person who knew this situation of mine was Joe, my older brother.

That evening, I said to him, "I was wondering if I could hand something to the girl personally. Could I give her a piece of paper with my email address on it?" Joe replied, "No. It's too early. What kind of girl wants to make friends with someone she hardly knows? Don't rush it, or you'll just embarrass her, as I once did with another girl. Start your relationship by greeting again and talking to her casually."

Two days later, I went to the store again and saw her as usual. This was the first time our dialogue began with my words. "Good morning. How are you?" "I'm fine, thank you. It's a cold day, isn't it?" she replied with that smile. In our five or six meetings, I succeeded in exchanging a few words with her. She told me that her name was Karen and that she was a college student earning her living expenses as a part-timer at the drugstore. The more I talked to her, the more I liked her.

One day, I said to Joe, "How I wish I could tell Karen that I've fallen for her! But I'm not confident enough. What if she rejects me? I would be messed up!" Joe said, "Come on, Randy. Do you want to spend years regretting not taking any action? I've been rejected by girls five times in my life, but I never regretted telling them my honest feelings. Be a man!" He added, "How about handing her a love letter? It may sound old-fashioned, but since Karen sounds like a very attractive girl, she might be used to receiving emails from boys. A handwritten letter will impress her."

I wrote a letter to Karen that night, telling her I had fallen in love with her and how happy I would be if we could go out. The following day, I gave her the letter, and two days later I was handed a reply from her. The letter began with the sentences mentioned in the beginning. This was followed by, "But I'm sorry, I'm already going out with someone else from the same college. Let's just stay friends." Reading her reply, I sobbed. My heart was completely broken. This happened five years ago, and it still hurts me, but I never regret what I did.

Your presentation notes:

Fallen in Love with a Store Clerk

Characters

Randy · A male student who is in love with Karen

· [30]

Karen · A female university student who works part-time at a drugstore

Joe · Randy's older brother

· [31]

How Randy's story of love progresses

Randy fell in love with Karen

↓

[32]

↓

[33]

↓

[34]

↓

[35]

What can be inferred about Karen's feelings?

[36]

How does Randy look back on this experience?

" [37] "

問1　Choose the best option for ┌─ 30 ─┐ .

① Good at building a relationship with a girl

② Has sometimes fallen in love with someone at first sight

③ Tends to lose control of himself when he's in love

④ Wants to behave carefully and gently towards the lady he likes

問2　Choose the best option for ┌─ 31 ─┐ .

① Advises his brother to refrain from telling Karen his feelings

② Doesn't know his brother's situation in detail

③ Encourages Randy to ask Karen out in an email

④ Gives some clues how Randy should act, based on his own experience

問3　Choose **four** out of the five options (①～⑤) and rearrange them in the order they happened. ┌─ 32 ─┐ → ┌─ 33 ─┐ → ┌─ 34 ─┐ → ┌─ 35 ─┐

① Randy asked Karen to exchange emails

② Randy greeted Karen for the first time

③ Randy handed Karen a letter

④ Randy read the letter from Karen

⑤ Randy was glad to know Karen recognized him

問4　Choose the best option for ┃ 36 ┃.

   ① She believes that one's personality is the most important in deciding who to go out with.

   ② She implies she may change her mind though she is now going out with someone else.

   ③ She thinks that a store clerk shouldn't become her customer's girlfriend.

   ④ She wants to keep the relationship with her boyfriend, but that's not because she doesn't like Randy.

問5　Choose the best option for ┃ 37 ┃.

   ① I never regret giving Karen a love letter several times.

   ② I should have told Karen earlier how much I loved her.

   ③ I still recall it as a bitter memory though I have no regret.

   ④ I wish I'd had a little more courage to take another step.

A You are going to hold a discussion on the history of fashion in a class. You are making a summary of the following article. Using the summary, you will talk about it.

History of Cosmetics

The earliest use of makeup was not necessarily for the purpose of seeking beauty. The ancient Egyptians, both men and women, would paint *kohl*, a mixture of lead, iron, copper, ash and burnt almonds, around their eyes. The circles of kohl were thought to drive away evil spirits and to relieve the effect of the harsh desert sun on their eyes. Today, scientists think that the kohl makeup may also have helped protect the Egyptians from infectious diseases since the lead would kill off bacteria, though they could not have known this at the time. In addition to Egyptians, ancient Greeks, Romans and Chinese are also believed to have worn some kind of makeup on their face.

During the European Middle Ages, pale skin was popular, as it was a sign of wealth. Women painted their faces and necks with a mixture of lead and vinegar to lighten the face, which was actually harmful to the wearer. Elizabeth I of England, with her white face and large forehead, is famous for this look, which was popular for centuries. Around the same time, however, cosmetics became recognized as a health threat.

Towards the end of the 1800s, portrait photography became popular. Putting on some makeup before having one's photo taken became common. Mirrors also became readily available to ordinary people. To be sure, these two factors were important in making makeup common among the general public, but nothing played a greater role than motion pictures. When actors were on the stage, they usually wore very heavy makeup that made them appealing to the audience sitting far from the stage. But faces with such makeup did not look good on the screen. So, in 1914, Max Factor, a Polish businessman who provided wigs to Hollywood studios, developed a new type of paint for foundation that made actors look better through a camera. In the 1920s, he began selling his makeup to the public with the claims that they could look like their favorite movie stars. His products proved very successful.

Around the same time, the US car companies began to use new paints in multiple colors on their vehicles. The main ingredients of the paints were nitrocellulose, a substance which was also used to make gun powder. As this paint dried faster than traditional ones, cosmetics companies wondered if they could use it for nail polish, a cosmetic paint that is applied to the nails. In 1932, the first nail polish using the same material as that used in car paint appeared on the market. Revlon, the manufacturer of this product, successfully promoted it and it soon became popular. Also, in the 1950s, the company ran campaigns for matching nail polishes and lipsticks. One of their advertisements said, "If you are the type of woman who wants to bleach your hair platinum without your husband's consent, then you are the perfect candidate for this new color of lipstick and nail polish." In fact, the ad accelerated the sales of the polish.

The popularity of false nails, or artificial nail products which people put over their natural fingernails, among ordinary people accidentally began in 1954, when a US dentist named Frederick Slack damaged his fingernail while at work. He put an artificial nail over his damaged one, using dental acrylics, material used for mending bad teeth. Since then, false nails have progressed into what is worn by many people today as a beautiful fashion.

Throughout history, humans have tried putting on some sort of artificial materials on themselves. Especially in the modern era, they have added to themselves what they expect to make them more confident and happier, or else to cover up parts of their body they don't like. Can you imagine how people will look 100 years from now? They might be wearing 'fashionable' nose paint, or false ears. Who knows?

Your summary notes:

Cosmetics

History

● Earliest makeup in Egypt

Egyptians painted a circle around their eyes [38] .

↓

● The Middle Ages in Europe

Pale skin was popular.

Cosmetics which were harmful to humans were used.

↓

● Popularization of makeup among the general public

The most important factor: [39]

New Type of Cosmetics

Nail products — nail polish & false nails

Conclusion gained from the article

1. Clues to popularize new products

● [40]

● [41]

2. Author's projections on the future of cosmetics

● [42]

問1　Choose the best option for [38] .

① as the effect of the sun was harsher than anywhere else on earth

② because they wanted to feel more confident and happier

③ for both spiritual and practical purposes

④ in order to avoid suffering from infectious diseases

問2　Choose the best option for 　39　 .

① People had more opportunities to go to see a motion picture than before.

② People were inspired to wear the same makeup as that of their favorite stars.

③ Putting on some makeup before having a portrait photo taken became popular.

④ The price of a mirror became low enough for ordinary people to own one.

問3　Choose the best options for 　40　 and 　41　 . （The order does not matter.）

① Considering application of one technology to another use

② Emphasizing the importance of believing in one's inner beauty

③ Making commercials in which popular movie stars introduce new products

④ Putting in advertisements to urge people to be more interested in the movie industry

⑤ Setting up campaigns to stimulate people's desire to change their own appearance

⑥ Writing articles which introduce effective uses of new products

問4　Choose the best option for 　42　 .

① Nose paint and false ears will be more popular than ever.

② People's wish to be more beautiful will become stronger as time goes by.

③ The technology for cosmetics will make greater progress.

④ There is no telling what will happen in the world of cosmetics.

B You are preparing for a presentation on strange creatures for your science class. You are using the following article for your presentation.

Human fathers may be better than those of other creatures in their active involvement in child-raising. They teach their children how to play a ball game, or how to behave in a decent way. But, in one particular respect, human fathers can never beat the males of certain species, which become pregnant and give birth to their children instead of the females. This trait is peculiar to a strange kind of fish, widely known as "seahorses." Like a kangaroo, a male seahorse has a pocket of skin on its stomach to carry babies in. A female produces eggs and transfers them into her mate's pocket, where they hatch. The pocket can hold as many as 2,000 babies at a time. By keeping the babies inside the pocket, the father offers oxygen and necessary nutrients to the babies as well as protects them from the dangers in the sea.

The reproduction of seahorses begins when a male and a female seahorse start to dance together before dawn, twisting their tails, changing their body color, and swimming side by side. Eventually, they engage in a true dance of courtship, that is, a request for mating. In this phase, the movements of the couple synchronize so that the male can easily receive the eggs when the female is ready to lay them. The male inflates his pocket with water to show that it is empty. The process ends when the male has received the eggs. The pregnancy lasts 10 to 25 days, depending on the species. The eggs hatch in the father's pocket, and then the father swims a long distance to set the newborn babies free.

What evolutionary advantages does male pregnancy give seahorses? Science has not yet revealed the truth. One theory is that it enables a shorter cycle of reproduction by sharing the burden of the process between the father and the mother. While the father is keeping the babies in his pocket, the mother can prepare more eggs to give to the father soon after he has set the babies free. It is said that some seahorses can give birth in the morning and be pregnant again by evening.

Seahorses range from less than one to thirty centimeters in length. They have some unique characteristics in appearance. For example, they have a tube-shaped mouth for sucking in very tiny sea creatures as food, a curling tail for clinging to sea grass to avoid drifting, and hard plates that cover their body for protection. The plates make them less attractive as food to predators. The exception is humans, who have caught them to make some traditional medicines.

Then, what is the current population of seahorses? No such statistical data exists because relatively little research on them has been carried out so far. But fishers have mentioned a decline in the number of seahorses they catch, according to some research on seahorses. It is also pointed out by scientists that seahorses have been threatened by the damage caused by humans to the coastal areas they live in as well as overfishing for the purpose mentioned above.

Scientists have been trying to save seahorses by breeding them in water pools. Breeding seahorses in captivity, however, is not easy, partly because the babies are so tiny that it is hard to keep them alive. They cannot eat most of the tiny plankton that is usually eaten by grownup seahorses. So, special baby food has to be grown for them. New technologies for more efficient breeding are under way now.

Once a seahorse father sets the babies free in the ocean, the parents do not provide their tiny children with any care or protection. Infant seahorses can easily fall victim to predators or be swept away by ocean currents, where they drift away from their feeding areas. Only about five infant seahorses in every 1,000 survive to adulthood. If only seahorse parents would make half the effort that human parents do to protect their children after birth! In this respect, human fathers do surpass seahorses.

Your presentation slides:

<table>
<tr>
<td>

Seahorses:

Cooperative

parenting

</td>
<td>

1. Male Seahorses

· can be pregnant and give birth

· have a pocket on their stomach

· | 43 |

</td>
</tr>
<tr>
<td>

2. How a male seahorse becomes pregnant

A male and a female start dancing in the early morning
↓
The movements of the pair synchronize
The male shows the pocket is available
↓
The male receives the eggs from the female

</td>
<td>

3. Male Pregnancy

Advantages of male pregnancy

→ not yet revealed

One theory: | 44 |

</td>
</tr>
<tr>
<td>

4. Body Parts and Functions

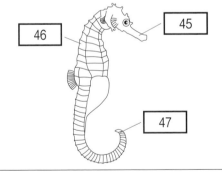

| 45 |

| 46 |

| 47 |

</td>
<td>

5. Population Decrease and Solution

· Fishers have reported that the number of seahorses they catch is declining.

· Possible Reasons: | 48 |, | 49 |

· Solution: New technologies for breeding are being developed.

</td>
</tr>
</table>

問1　For the **Male Seahorses** slide, which of the following fits ⟨ 43 ⟩ ?

    ① feed and protect newborn babies in their pocket

    ② lay eggs like females of other kinds of fish

    ③ take eggs out of the pocket before they hatch

    ④ transfer eggs to the pocket of a female seahorse

問2　Which is the best statement for ⟨ 44 ⟩ in the **Male Pregnancy** slide?

    ① To ensure the safety of the babies

    ② To give birth in the morning

    ③ To raise the frequency of giving birth

    ④ To share the burden of caring for the grown-up children

問3　For the **Body Parts and Functions** slide, which of the following fit ⟨ 45 ⟩, ⟨ 46 ⟩, and ⟨ 47 ⟩, respectively?

    ① absorbs oxygen to breathe

    ② helps them swim smoothly

    ③ keeps their body temperature

    ④ prevents them from being eaten

    ⑤ prevents them from drifting away

    ⑥ takes in necessary nourishment

問4　For the **Population Decrease and Solution** slide, select two possible causes of the decrease in the seahorse population. (The order does not matter.) ⬚48 ・ ⬚49

   ① Baby seahorses cannot tolerate rising ocean temperatures.

   ② Humans have harmed the environment where seahorses live.

   ③ More infant seahorses have fallen victim to predators than before.

   ④ Only about five infant seahorses out of 1,000 can be fed by their parents.

   ⑤ People have caught too many seahorses for medical purposes.

   ⑥ The number of the tiny plankton seahorses eat has decreased due to climate change.

問5　What can be inferred about the author's attitude toward parents' involvement in child-raising? ⬚50

   ① The author criticizes seahorse mothers for not getting involved in taking care of the eggs laid by themselves.

   ② The author feels that male seahorses are better fathers than human ones when it comes to raising their babies.

   ③ The author is sorry that seahorses do not care for their children once they are set free.

   ④ The author thinks that human fathers surpass seahorse fathers during pregnancy.

リーディング————第4回

時間　80分　　　　100点　満点

1 ══ 解答にあたっては，実際に試験を受けるつもりで，時間を厳守し真剣に取りくむこと。

2 ══ 巻末にマークシートをつけてあるので，切り離しのうえ練習用として利用すること。

3 ══ 解答終了後には，自己採点により学力チェックを行い，別冊の解答・解説をじっくり
　　読んで，弱点補強，知識や考え方の整理などに努めること。

　※「リーディング」問題構成について
　　2022年に大学入試センターにて実施された「2025年度大学入学共通テスト試作問
　　題モニター調査」では，大問数が第8問構成へと変更されています。ただしこの
　　問題構成はモニター調査で必要な情報を収集するために構成したもので，本番に
　　向けて問題構成は今後も引き続き検討をするとの付記があります。
　　この問題集では新しい第8問構成の問題（第5回）とこれまで通りの第6問構成
　　の問題（第1〜4回）の両パターンの問題を収録しています。

英　語（リーディング）

各大問の英文や図表を読み，解答番号 $\boxed{1}$ ～ $\boxed{48}$ に当てはまるものとして最も適切な選択肢を選びなさい。

第１問 (配点　10)

A　Your friend Rebecca has sent you a message on social media asking for your help.

Rebecca　　　September 25, 2023, 12:08 p.m.

> I'm in trouble!　I have a presentation in my next class, and I forgot to bring my computer with me to campus today.　I have the file saved in the cloud, so I can access it from there.　I just need a computer to use for the presentation.　Can I borrow yours?

September 25, 2023, 12:14 p.m.

> Sorry, Rebecca.　I didn't bring mine with me either since I only have my art class on Thursdays.　I'm on my way home now though.　Should I go to your house to get your computer for you?

Rebecca　　　September 25, 2023, 12:21 p.m.

> I appreciate it, but no one's there now.　My roommate said that she wouldn't be back until tonight.　Any other ideas?

問 1　What does Rebecca ask you to do?　| 1 |

① Bring her computer from her house to campus.

② Download her presentation file and put it on a USB.

③ Help her to improve her presentation for class.

④ Let her borrow your computer for her next class.

問 2　How will you reply to Rebecca's second message?　| 2 |

① Call your roommate and ask her to unlock the door.

② I'm sure that your presentation will be great!

③ Where should I meet you to give you the computer?

④ You should ask your professor if you can use his.

B You are looking at a website about New York City and you find an announcement about an essay contest for students. You are thinking about entering the contest.

	# Essay Contest
	Introduce Your Favorite Memory from New York City

We want to hear about your experiences in our lovely city! Help us to attract more visitors by sharing your best memory from your time in New York City (NYC). You can write about the places you visited, the food you ate, or even the people you met.

Instructions

- Think about the best part of your trip to NYC.
- Write an essay about that experience in 500 to 1,000 words.
- Submit your essay to the following email address: entry@nycessaycontest.com

Rules

- This contest is open only to students up to 18 years old.
- You must not be a resident of New York City.
- Essays must be received no later than Saturday, April 1st.

Prizes

1st Prize	2nd Prize	3rd Prize
Paid travel for 4 to NYC	Paid travel for 4 to NYC	Paid travel for 4 to NYC
Two free nights at a hotel	One free night at a hotel	One free night at a hotel
All meal expenses paid	All meal expenses paid	Free entry to popular sites
Tickets to a musical	Free entry to popular sites	
Free entry to popular sites		

Schedule

April 29th	The three winners will be selected by our judges and the mayor of New York City!
April 30th	Winners will be listed on this website and contacted by email.
May 7th	Winners must reply by email to accept their prizes by this date. Trips will be scheduled with the winners and their families after that.

問1　You must submit your essay by 3.

①　April 1st

②　April 29th

③　April 30th

④　May 7th

問2　In order to enter this contest, you must 4.

①　be more than 18 years old

②　live outside of New York City

③　tell about a place you've never been to

④　write more than 1,000 words

問3　Which can you get only by winning the 1st prize? 5

①　All meal expenses paid for

②　Free entry to popular sites

③　Paid travel to New York City

④　Two nights' stay at a hotel

第2問 (配点 20)

A You are leaving to go on an exchange programme in the UK next week. You are reading information about the building you will live in while you are there.

Riley Hall
Residence for Porter University's international and exchange programme students

Common Area
This large space on the ground floor has several sofas, chairs, and tables, as well as a television. Students often gather here to do their assignments or to watch some football. Cultural exchange events are also organised and held here a few times each year.

Living Arrangements
Students' rooms are above the ground floor on the first, second, and third floors. Unless a single is requested in advance, new residents are assigned to a double with a roommate. In addition, the second and third floors each have suites, a set of rooms, for three to five students who apply as a group during the previous term.

Facilities
There are bathrooms at both ends of the hallway on the floors with student rooms, and one located across from the common room on the ground floor. Except for the ground floor, all bathrooms are equipped with showers. Residents can wash their clothes using the machines in the basement. Shared kitchens are also available on every floor except for the basement, and include a refrigerator, stove, microwave, and sink.

Comments from Current Residents
● "Getting to know students and cultures from other countries through living in Riley Hall has been a great experience!" —— Marcus
● "The kitchens are crowded until 8 pm on weekdays and until the late afternoon on the weekends, so I usually have to eat at the university cafeteria." —— Arjuna

- "It's easy to study in my room, but it's too hard to focus in the common area since someone is usually watching TV." —— Francisco
- "At first, I didn't like the idea of shared bathrooms, but they are kept so clean that I didn't mind." —— Ben
- "The Spanish Food Party this term was quite fun.   They really don't plan enough events where we can meet the other residents." —— Theo
- "Carrying my clothes from the basement to my room on the third floor is the worst with no elevators." —— Kathrin

問 1　As a new exchange student, you will have to live 　6　 unless you make a request.

　① by yourself

　② with a roommate

　③ with two other students

　④ with four other students

問 2　Riley Hall has bathrooms at 　7　 different locations.

　① 4

　② 6

　③ 7

　④ 8

問 3　You live on the first floor of Riley Hall.   You have to 　8　 to wash your clothes.

　① go down one floor

　② go down two floors

　③ go up one floor

　④ go up two floors

問4　The best day and time to cook a meal for yourself in one of the kitchens would be ☐9☐ .

① Sunday at 10 am

② Monday at 6 pm

③ Thursday at 9 pm

④ Saturday at 1 pm

問5　Which students gave both positive and negative comments?　☐10☐

A: Arjuna

B: Ben

C: Francisco

D: Kathrin

E: Marcus

F: Theo

① A and C

② B and E

③ C and F

④ D and F

B Your friend has been studying at a school in the UK for a few months. He has been discussing some of the differences he has experienced with another friend through email and shows you the conversation.

To: Kang, Yona   2022/12/20 at 12:14 pm

From: Takahashi, Yugo

Subject: My UK Experience

Dear Yona,

I'm sorry that I haven't written to you sooner. I've been busy with my studies and learning how everything works here. Life in the UK is very different, so it took me a while to adjust to some things. The meals were easy to adapt to, but after three months, I still can't understand some British words or the public transport system very well.

But the biggest difference is the style of the classes in school. There are a lot more discussions, and the teachers often ask for our opinions. The first time my teacher suddenly asked what I thought about the book we were reading, I was shocked. I didn't know what to say. When I listened to some of the other students, it seemed like giving their opinions and the reasons why they thought so was so easy and natural for them. Since then, I have been working hard to become more like that. Having to give explanations has made me feel more confident about what I think and know.

Best,

Yugo

To: Takahashi, Yugo

2022/12/21 at 7:05 pm

From: Kang, Yona

Subject: Re: My UK Experience

Dear Yugo,

It's great to hear from you. It sounds like you are having a wonderful time in the UK. Your classes seem really interesting. I'm very shy in groups, so I think that kind of experience is valuable. By discussing things with others, you can learn a lot about yourself, too. As students, remembering facts and information is important. However, the ability to express our beliefs and opinions to others is a more necessary skill in global society.

Thank you for sharing your experiences with me. I hope that I have a similar one next year! Please write again soon!

Regards,

Yona

問1　According to Yugo, it was not difficult to adjust to ┃ 11 ┃.

① British food

② his classes at school

③ public transport in the UK

④ understanding British vocabulary

問2 One **fact** stated in Yugo's email is that in the UK, ⬚12⬚ .

① classes are more difficult for students

② he was asked to give his opinion in classes

③ students have no trouble giving opinions

④ teachers have a less important role

問3 Yugo thinks that his experiences at school have ⬚13⬚ .

① helped him feel sure about his own thoughts

② improved his public speaking ability

③ made other students jealous of him

④ taught him that reading books is more interesting

問4 From Yona's email, you learn that she ⬚14⬚ .

① feels comfortable talking with others

② has never been to another country

③ thinks classes in the UK sound boring

④ will study abroad sometime next year

問5 Which best summarises Yona's opinion? ⬚15⬚

① Discussions are more valuable to adults than to students.

② It is impossible to understand what other people think.

③ Remembering facts is the most important skill for students.

④ The skill of sharing opinions is very valuable in today's world.

第3問 (配点 15)

A You are interested in festivals that are held in the UK. You are reading a young UK blogger's post.

Henry Mills

Saturday, 18 November, 9:00 pm

Diwali, the Festival of Lights, is a religious celebration from India that happens sometime between October and November each year. Last night, I went to the Diwali Festival in the city of Leicester, which is one of the biggest Diwali festivals outside of India. It was the last night of the festival, so the atmosphere was full of excitement. It started with a brilliant firework display that lit up the sky. There was also a large Ferris wheel called the Wheel of Light. It looked lovely all lit up with white lights. I would have ridden it if the line hadn't been so long!

As I walked around more, I got to enjoy a few performances too. First, I saw men and women dressed in colourful costumes doing traditional Indian dances. The music was lively and energetic, and the dancers moved beautifully to the rhythm. I also saw a giant mechanical puppet named Dundu walking through the crowd of people. It looked like a person, but it was glowing so brightly that I could see it coming from far away. When it got closer, I could finally see the man who was making it move. I also realised Dundu was three times taller than me! I laughed while watching it do some funny moves in front of me.

Finally, I visited some of the food stands and tried a few different things. I tried a samosa, but it was a bit too spicy for me. I ate laddoo next, which was sweet and delicious. I liked it so much that I got some more to give to my family.

If you are interested in Indian culture, you should definitely go to the Leicester Diwali Festival! Check out the picture of this year's flyer below.

Diwali Festival 2023

Leicester, UK

Sunday, 12 November – Friday, 17 November

Performances	Activities	Food

Traditional dances

Dundu

Fireworks

Wheel of Light (Ferris wheel)

Samosas (fried snack) (PIXTA)

Laddoo (Indian sweet)

問1　In Henry's blog, you read that he ⬚16⬚ .

① bought something for his family

② enjoyed all of the foods he ate

③ learned a traditional Indian dance

④ rode on the Ferris wheel

問2　Henry was most likely ⬚17⬚ when he got close to the Dundu puppet.

① disappointed

② scared

③ surprised

④ upset

B   You are interested in cycling and have found an interesting article in a cycling magazine.

A Cycling Adventure in Ireland

by John Lawrence

It was a cool, sunny morning in Cork, and I was excited to begin my cycling journey through Ireland. I had planned a route that would take me to Limerick and then on to Waterford before returning to Cork, with plenty of beautiful landscapes to see along the way. The first few hours of my ride

went smoothly, and I made good progress through the countryside without getting lost. But soon, I began having some problems.

In the afternoon, the sky became darker, and a light rain began to fall. I had brought a rain jacket, but it was not enough to keep me completely dry. As the rain became heavier, I got wetter and colder. Despite the difficult conditions, I knew that I had to make it to the city before it got too dark. But as I continued, the ride became even more challenging. The Irish hills that seemed so beautiful earlier felt like mountains as I pushed my way up them. And because the roads were wet, I also had to reduce my speed when going down them. As a result, I arrived three hours later than I had planned.

Right away, I began searching for a place to stay. I must have looked terrible, because a woman carrying an umbrella stopped to ask me if I was okay. I told her what I was looking for, and she guided me to a local hotel and restaurant, where I had a nice, warm meal. After a good night's sleep, I was ready for the next section of my trip.

This time, the weather was clear all the way to Waterford, so I was able to enjoy the scenery more than I had the previous day. However, towards the end of the ride, my left knee began to hurt. It soon became too painful, and I had to stop altogether. It was only 3:30 pm, and I wasn't far from my goal, so I took a long rest until the pain went away and then I rode the last few kilometres. Though I was an hour behind schedule, I still got there in time for dinner.

On the final day, I went to see some sights in Waterford before riding again. My favourite was a sword made of a tree that was over 15 metres long. After taking a few photos of it for my sons, I hopped back on my bike and started the trip back to Cork. This time, I had no trouble and finished the ride quicker than expected. I was finally back where I had started my journey. I had done it. Despite the difficulties, my 3-day cycling tour of Ireland was over, and I felt great!

問1　Put the following events (①〜④) into the order they happened.

| 18 | → | 19 | → | 20 | → | 21 |

① A local woman helped the writer.

② The writer arrived at Limerick.

③ The writer had to stop for a long break.

④ The writer went to an interesting sightseeing spot.

問2　What was one reason the writer reached Limerick later than he had expected?

22

① He got lost while riding through the countryside.

② He had difficulty riding up some mountains.

③ He had to ride slower because of the rain.

④ He stopped to take photos along the way.

問3　From this story, you learnt the writer 23 .

① arrived at each city later than planned

② prepared clothing for bad weather

③ regretted making such a difficult trip

④ will go sightseeing in Cork next

第4問 (配点 16)

You are a university student in the UK and are thinking about studying in France. Your friend asked his adviser for help choosing a programme and shows you the email exchanges.

Dear Professor Mizenko,

I want to study abroad in France next year, but I'm having trouble selecting a programme. The two that I have heard about only offer courses in French. I want to continue taking courses for my science major, but my French is not that good. My understanding is fine, but I'm worried the assignments will take me too long to finish.

I also want to spend some time learning about art since the country is famous for it.

Can you tell me which programme would be best?

Kind regards,
Yutaro Suzuki

Dear Yutaro,

First, it's great you want to keep studying science, but studying abroad is about experiencing things that you can't in your own country. If there is a unique science class at one of the universities, then take it. Otherwise, focus on making the most of being in France. Why not take more French classes? Then, you could try taking easier courses taught in French, such as art.

If that doesn't sound good, then there are two other programmes that our university started offering this year. One is the year in Paris. Courses are offered in both English and French, so you can take anything that interests you. The other is the half-year in Grenoble. Like the Paris programme, you can take courses in English, and the city is known for its scientific research. You are sure to find a science course that you can't take here.

I am sending you the updated programme guide.

Regards,
Michael Mizenko

Dear Professor Mizenko,

Thank you for your reply. It gave me a lot to consider, and I think I know what I am going to do.

I would love to spend a year in France, but the cost is too high. However, after reading your email, I now think three months would not be enough. I want to experience the culture as much as possible.

Your advice to focus on the things that I can't do in the UK convinced me. My main goals will be to improve my French and learn more about art. I enjoy studying science though, so I'd like to be able to take any courses that I think are interesting. Therefore, I'm going to choose a place that also offers courses in English.

Now I need to think about my housing options.

Kind regards,
Yutaro Suzuki

Programme Information:

Grenoble, France		
Grenoble is recognised for being a centre of scientific research.		
Courses offered in:	Length:	Cost:
English, French	6 months	£7,200
Lyon, France		
France's third largest city is famous for art but even more for food.		
Courses offered in:	Length:	Cost:
French	3 months	£3,600
Nice, France		
Nice is a great mix of classical and modern French culture.		
Courses offered in:	Length:	Cost:
French	6 months	£6,700
Paris, France		
The capital of France is known for its modern fashion and world-famous art.		
Courses offered in:	Length:	Cost:
English, French	1 year	£18,000
Housing		
Students can live with a host family or in university housing. The costs listed below are per month: Host family: £800 University housing: £600		

問1　Before receiving Professor Mizenko's reply, Yutaro was thinking about studying in ⬚24⬚ or ⬚25⬚．　(The order does not matter.)

① Grenoble

② Lyon

③ Nice

④ Paris

問2　Yutaro is worried about taking a science course in French because ☐26☐.

① he has trouble understanding when someone speaks quickly

② he knows very little science vocabulary in French

③ the professors will not answer questions he asks in English

④ the work for the class will take him more time to do

問3　Professor Mizenko suggests that ☐27☐.

① it is better to focus on things Yutaro can only do in France

② studying in France for one year would be best for Yutaro

③ there are very few interesting science courses in France

④ Yutaro should not take any science classes while in France

問4　Yutaro thinks that Professor Mizenko's advice is ☐28☐.

① confusing

② helpful

③ lacking

④ troubling

問5　If Yutaro stays with a host family, what will be the total cost of the programme he has chosen?　☐29☐

① £10,800

② £11,500

③ £12,000

④ £27,600

第5問 （配点 15）

In your English class, you are going to give a presentation about an engineer. You found the following article online and prepared notes for your presentation.

In the early 2000s, a young boy from Malawi in Africa became famous for building machines that produced electricity for his village. His name is William Kamkwamba. Born in 1987 in the village of Masitala, William grew up on a corn and tobacco farm where he lived with his parents and six sisters. In 2002, when he was only 14, there was a long shortage of water that led to terrible hunger in his country. William's parents even had to stop paying the $80 yearly fee for his school so that they could buy a bit of food. Hungry and with no access to education, William instead spent his time in the local library, away from his family's farm. He was excited by science and technology, so he read every book and magazine about them that the library had.

One day, William found a textbook called *Using Energy*. It showed how to construct a machine called a windmill that uses the wind to make electricity. Inspired by this idea, he decided to build his own windmill to help the village. Following the English instructions in the textbook as best as he could, he began searching the pile of garbage in his village for spare parts that he could use. But many of the people in his community laughed at him and called him crazy. Back then, only 1% of the people living in the rural areas of Malawi had electricity. They could not imagine a young boy like William being able to build a machine that provided them with electricity.

William never gave up, however. Using some wood, bicycle parts, and other materials he found, he built a small windmill behind his house. He connected the windmill to an old car battery to store the electricity it made, which was enough to power four lights and a radio in his home. As a result, William could stay up reading books at night even after it became dark outside. Soon, he built a bigger windmill that brought electricity to his entire village. The people there were both surprised and delighted. They thought that William must be using some kind of magic.

News of William's larger windmill quickly spread, and he became well known in Malawi and abroad. He was invited to speak at conferences and events around the world, and his story was told in several news articles. Sponsors rushed to give him money, which he used to improve his windmills and make water pumps that ran using the increased electricity. This brought drinking water to his village for the first time and allowed farmers to water their crops when there was no rain.

After becoming famous, William was finally able to go back to school. Then, in 2009, he published a book about his experiences, which became a *New York Times* best seller. He went on to study at Dartmouth College in the United States, from which he graduated in 2014. Five years later, in 2019, William's story was also made into a hit movie for Netflix.

Today, he is a recognized engineer and inventor known for his generous spirit. He continues to work on projects to bring clean energy and other technologies to his community and others who need them. He also fights for access to education and resources for young people in poorer countries. He hopes to inspire younger generations of people to follow their interests and have a positive impact on the world.

Your presentation notes:

William Kamkwamba

- [30] -

Childhood

   - was born in Masitala, Malawi in 1987.

   - [31]

   - [32]

Sequence of Key Events

     [33]

     [34]

     William built his first windmill.

     [35]

     [36]

     William made water pumps for his village.

Character

   - William was [37] .

Achievements and Current Work

   - wrote a best-selling book about his experiences.

   - was invited to speak at global conferences.

   - [38] .

問 1　What is the best subtitle for your presentation?　30

① From Farmer to Successful Author

② The Boy Who Used Wind to Power a Village

③ The Creator of Malawi's First Water Pumps

④ The Self-Taught Inventor Who Never Studied at School

問 2　Choose the best two options for　31　and　32　to complete Childhood.
(The order does not matter.)

① became interested in science and technology

② had a comfortable life thanks to his wealthy parents

③ quit school because he was bored with all of his classes

④ spent a lot of time reading at his local library

⑤ worked in his family's corn and tobacco fields

問3　Choose four out of the five events (①~⑤) in the order they happened to complete Sequence of Key Events.

　33　→　34　→　35　→　36

① News of William's achievements spread around the world.

② William found the textbook called *Using Energy*.

③ William received financial support from sponsors.

④ William searched for parts in the garbage.

⑤ William wrote a science textbook for children.

問4　Choose the best option for ☐37☐ to complete <u>Character</u>.

   ① so determined that he never gave up even when he was laughed at

   ② so generous that he gave money to support children's education

   ③ such a clever boy that he built windmills without any hints

   ④ such a creative person that he built things no one had seen before

問5　Choose the best option for ☐38☐ to complete <u>Achievements and Current Work</u>.

   ① fights with Malawian children to make them stay in school

   ② produced a Netflix movie about his life

   ③ still works to supply his community with clean energy

   ④ tries to convince young people to become inventors like him

第6問 (配点 24)

A You are working on a class project about factors that affect people's personalities and abilities. While researching online, you found the following article. Use the information to complete your poster.

What Makes Southpaws Different?

Are you a "southpaw"? Chances are that you answered "no." That's because southpaws make up only 10% of the world's population compared to about 89% for "righties," or those who prefer to do things with their right hand. Scientists have been interested in southpaws for a long time. Many studies have been conducted on the characteristics and abilities of southpaws, with the goal of understanding whether there are any distinct differences between them and righties. Through these studies, several features have been found to be more common in southpaws.

Research conducted in the 1970s found that southpaws are more likely to avoid social gatherings, preferring a quiet time alone to being with other people. They may also have higher levels of stress, perhaps due to the challenges of living in a world that is designed for righties. After all, many things were not made for southpaws, from scissors to the desks with arm supports used in some schools. However, this may make southpaws better at adapting to new and unexpected situations than righties. Southpaws may also be more creative, with some research showing that southpaws have a natural talent for things like art, music, and design. This may be because the right side of the brain, which controls the left hand, is responsible for creative thinking. This also makes southpaws better at problem-solving tasks that require looking at things in different ways.

In addition, southpaws may be better at doing more than one thing at a time, as they are used to processing information across both sides of their brains to complete tasks. This makes their reaction speed faster too. These two things combined are especially useful in tasks that require speed, including many sports and activities such as typing on a keyboard. In fact, there are several studies that have shown southpaws are more likely to be good at sports like tennis. However, this may not actually be a result of having more skill. Some experts have pointed out that because there are fewer southpaws, most righties rarely get to play matches against them. This gives southpaws an advantage because most of the players they play against are righties, so they know what to expect.

Finally, southpaws tend to be more careful people who think about things in detail. While righties often make decisions and take action quickly, southpaws take longer to get started on a task. They spend more time thinking about all of their options, and the strengths and weaknesses of each one. This means that southpaws may take longer to get a job done than righties.

Are these things true of all southpaws? Definitely not. Researchers have found that these features are just more common in southpaws. There are still other features not mentioned here that are being tested too. In the end, it is important to remember that every individual is unique and cannot be fully understood just by the hand they use the most in their daily lives.

Your poster:

What Makes Southpaws Different?

What is a southpaw?

A southpaw is a person who [39] .

Interesting Details

- Only 10% of all people are southpaws.
- Research has shown that southpaws have some characteristics in common.

Features More Common in Southpaws

Positive	Negative
• can adapt to new things better	• dislike social events
• [40]	• take longer to finish tasks
• are more careful before acting	• [41]

Reasons Why More Research Is Necessary

- In sports, southpaws may be [42] not because they have more skill, but because righties are not as [43] with playing against them.
- Some other characteristics are still being studied, so we cannot say whether those are more common in southpaws or not yet.

問 1 Choose the best option for [39] .

① cannot be found in most places on Earth

② is from the southern part of the world

③ prefers noisy places to quiet ones

④ uses their left hand for most things

問2　Choose the best option for ⬚40⬚ .

  ① are good at focusing on one thing

  ② have faster reactions

  ③ play all sports well

  ④ start tasks right away

問3　Choose the best option for ⬚41⬚ .

  ① are not good at thinking of new ideas

  ② get confused when doing several things at once

  ③ need to deal with many items made for righties

  ④ often make mistakes because they act too quickly

問4　Choose the best options for ⬚42⬚ and ⬚43⬚ .

  ① admired

  ② defeated

  ③ familiar

  ④ pleased

  ⑤ successful

  ⑥ tired

B You are learning about the effects of social media on the mental health and development of young people. Your teacher gives you the following article to read.

Social media has become an important part of modern life for many young people, providing a place for connecting with friends and staying informed about things such as current events and popular trends. However, research has shown that it can have negative effects on young people's mental health and development. One of those potential negative consequences is the impact on confidence. Seeing other people's stories and photos on social media can make young people feel like they are not as attractive or interesting, leading to a decrease in confidence. This effect can be particularly strong in kids between the ages of 10 and 19, who are already likely to worry about others' opinions of them. A study found that young people who spent more time on social media reported having lower confidence and feeling less satisfied with their bodies.

Bullying on the internet, or "cyberbullying" as it is often called, has also turned into a major issue for young people. With the spread of social media, it has become much easier for people to make negative comments and tell lies about others without receiving punishment for their bad behavior. These things are done to hurt the victim's feelings, even though the victim is usually innocent and did nothing to deserve the terrible treatment. Cyberbullying can have serious consequences for young people, including feelings of extreme sadness and anxiety. According to a survey conducted by the Cyberbullying Research Center, approximately 27% of young people between the ages of 13 and 19 have experienced cyberbullying at least once in their lives.

Social media can also affect the quality and amount of sleep that young people get. Studies have shown that too much social media use can ruin sleep patterns, leading to increased tiredness and negative effects on mental health. One study found that young people who spent more than three hours per day on social media were more likely to have sleep problems than those who used it less. Another study showed that 60% of young people check their smartphones before bed, which causes an average of one hour less sleep each night. This can harm other areas of a young person's life, such as their academic performance and relationships with friends, classmates, and family members.

In addition to these mental health issues, using social media can also impact children's communication skills. A lot of the text on social media is not written in proper English, so young people develop problems with grammar. They also like to replace words with numbers, such as "2" for "too," or spell words differently to make their writing seem cooler. However, this can cause children to forget the correct spelling of those words. Likewise, spending too much time on social media reduces the amount of time that young people spend talking with people face to face. As a result, they may have a weaker speaking ability and other social skills.

It's important to remember that not all young people will experience negative effects from social media, and the impacts can vary widely from one child to another. However, it is necessary for young people to be aware of the risks and to use social media in a balanced and healthy way. This might include setting limits on daily usage, taking regular breaks, and doing other activities such as exercise or hobbies.

問 1　You saw the word "cyberbullying" in the article and you want to write down the meaning in your notes. Which of the following is the most appropriate? ｜ 44 ｜

① It is a popular form of communication among young people.

② It is an illness that makes a person feel anxious and sad.

③ It is a way to punish people for their bad behavior on social media.

④ It is writing harmful comments or lies about someone on the internet.

問2　Which of the following is NOT mentioned in the article about the effect of social media on young people's communication skills?　45

① They are not good at speaking to others in person.

② They begin having trouble using correct grammar.

③ They do not remember the proper way to spell words.

④ They face problems in understanding what others say.

問3　According to the article you read, which two of the following are true? (Choose two options.　The order does not matter.)　46 ・ 47

① Children under 10 years old are the ones influenced most by social media.

② Kids often compare themselves to those they see on social media.

③ Most young people have experienced cyberbullying at least once.

④ Sleep problems can occur from using social media for over three hours daily.

⑤ Young people's confidence tends to improve from social media use.

問4　Which of the following is the most appropriate to describe the author's point? 48

① The author claims that young people need to know about the dangers of social media.

② The author insists that there is no safe way for young people to use social media.

③ The author states that limits on social media use do not decrease the risks.

④ The author thinks that social media affects all young people in the same way.

リーディング―――第5回

時間　80分　　　　　100点　満点

1 ―― 解答にあたっては，実際に試験を受けるつもりで，時間を厳守し真剣に取りくむこと。

2 ―― 巻末にマークシートをつけてあるので，切り離しのうえ練習用として利用すること。

3 ―― 解答終了後には，自己採点により学力チェックを行い，別冊の解答・解説をじっくり読んで，弱点補強，知識や考え方の整理などに努めること。

※「リーディング」問題構成について

　2022 年に大学入試センターにて実施された「2025 年度大学入学共通テスト試作問題モニター調査」では，大問数が第 8 問構成へと変更されています。ただしこの問題構成はモニター調査で必要な情報を収集するために構成したもので，本番に向けて問題構成は今後も引き続き検討をするとの付記があります。

　この問題集では新しい第 8 問構成の問題（第 5 回）とこれまで通りの第 6 問構成の問題（第 1～4 回）の両パターンの問題を収録しています。

英　語 (リーディング)

（解答番号　1　～　47　）

第1問 （配点 10）

A You are going on a school trip to a historical city, and your teacher gives you a handout about two guided tours you can choose from.

Historical Tours

◆ **Old Town Walking Tour**	◆ **Riverboat Cruise Tour**
Step back in time and explore the rich history of the city's colonial era	Discover the city's history while enjoying a sightseeing cruise along the river
· Starts at 9:00 a.m. and continues for 2 hours and 30 minutes (short breaks included) · Informed by guides dressed in old-fashioned costumes · Stops at historic buildings and famous sites · No food allowed during the tour	· Cruise begins at 11:30 a.m. and lasts for two hours · Experienced guides tell stories of "the city of rivers" in the old days · A great view of the city's bay area and the mountains behind it · Café on ships offering snacks and drinks

Instructions: Which guided tour would you like to join? Fill in the form below and hand it to your teacher today.

- -

Choose (✓) one: Old Town Walking Tour　☐　　Riverboat Cruise Tour　☐

Name: _____

問 1　What is the purpose of the handout?　1

① To guide students during their school trip.

② To introduce the city's traditional architecture.

③ To present options in taking guided tours.

④ To provide information about historical sites.

問 2　What is true about both tours?　2

① You can eat and drink anytime during the tour.

② You can get historical information from guides.

③ You can get the tours finished in the morning.

④ You can wear historical costumes.

B You are a senior high school student studying in the US, and interested in improving your musical skills during the summer vacation. You come across an advertisement for a music workshop planned by a famous music school.

Melody Music Workshop

Melody Music Workshop (MMW) has been providing music workshops for high school students since 1995. Spend two weeks in a fully musical environment!

Dates: July 15-28, 2024
Location: Harmony Hall, San Francisco, California
Cost: $800 (includes instruction and access to musical instruments; for optional private lessons and instrument rentals, additional fee is required)

Workshops Offered

◆**VOCALS**: Learn vocal techniques, stage presence, and perform popular songs in a group. Your instructors have teaching experience in the music industry and have performed in various concerts and events. Take part in the contest and show your skills on the last day of the workshop.

◆**INSTRUMENTS**: Choose an instrument of your choice (guitar, piano, drums, or violin) and receive specialized instruction. Instructors for each instrument have a strong background in music education and performance. Join a band with fellow participants and compete with other bands for a prize on the final day.

◆**SONGWRITING**: Develop your songwriting skills and collaborate with other participants to create original songs. Your instructors are music teachers as well as professional singer-songwriters, who have written songs for popular artists. Participate in the contest to show your original composition in the musical event on July 28.

▲ **Application**
Step 1: Fill out the online application form **HERE** by June 15, 2024.
Step 2: We'll contact you and schedule a face-to-face interview to know more about you and your musical abilities.
Step 3: You'll be assigned to a workshop based on your musical skills and interests.

問1 All instructors in Melody Music Workshop have 3 .

① performed in music concerts

② won national music competitions

③ worked in music education

④ written songs for popular artists

問2 On the last day of the workshop, all participants will 4 .

① compete to show their improvement

② evaluate each other's performances

③ join a band with other workshop members

④ make your original compositions

問3 What will happen after submitting your workshop application? 5

① You will attend whichever workshop you like.

② You will be invited for a face-to-face interview.

③ You will show your musical abilities at an online interview.

④ Your paper application will be checked by instructors.

第2問 (配点 20)

A You want to buy an e-book reading device as you have too many books in your bookshelf and no more space is left. You are searching on a UK website and find this advertisement.

Cozy Electro presents the new *Brain SP* e-book reader

Brain SP is an e-book reader which improves your reading life.
It is available in three colours.

Special Features

Brain SP e-book reader provides smoother and quicker responses than ever: you can flip the pages without stress. In addition, by using the included touch-pen or the software keyboard, you can underline the text and make notes on the e-books. Your notes can be arranged freely so that you can find your specific note without difficulty. Tap a note on the list, and you can jump to the page on which the note was made. As with other Cozy Electro e-book readers, it has a long-lasting battery and a large amount of storage (32 gigabytes or 64 gigabytes). It is not waterproof, though.

Advantages

Audio Book: You can listen to audio books with headphones or the built-in speaker.

Automatic Light Adjustment: The built-in sensor checks the surrounding brightness and adjusts the intensity of light, which enables you to read comfortably whether you are on a train, on a park bench or in bed.

Recommendation of New Books: Based on your choices, it recommends books that you may like.

Scanned Data Available: Send your own books to our office, and you can get the scanned data as a form of e-book. (*You can't get your books back. **Some books are not accepted due to copyright problems.)

Customers' Comments

- It recommends a variety of books, and I find most of them interesting.

- I download books that have no picture or sound, and it seems that the storage will never be full. I would prefer a less expensive one with smaller storage.

- Easy to use! I have been a booklover since childhood, and now I enjoy reading books as I did with paper books.

- One thing I want to complain about is that it isn't waterproof. I wish I could take it to the beach.

- I find it quite useful that I can make notes and find them easily. I prefer typing to using the included pen when I write down many words.

- I listen to audio books with the built-in speaker while I'm trying to sleep.

- When I read in a dark room, its light tends to be too bright. I have to lower the brightness by myself.

問1 According to the maker's statements, which is NOT an appropriate use of the new e-book reader? ☐ 6 ☐

① Listening to an audio book on the train

② Reading a novel while having a bath

③ Viewing a photo book in the garden

④ Writing notes on an e-book recipe

問2 Which benefit offered by the *Brain SP* e-book reader is most likely to appeal to you? ☐ 7 ☐

① Getting scanned data from paper books

② Having brightness adjusted automatically

③ Making notes on e-books

④ Receiving recommendation of new books

問3　One **opinion** stated by a customer is that 　8　 .

① audio books can be heard without headphones

② reading on the device is totally different from reading paper books

③ the recommended books are enjoyable

④ the storage is too small for a booklover

問4　One customer's comment mentions a problem while reading in a dark room. Which feature is this comment based on? 　9　

① Audio Book

② Automatic Light Adjustment

③ Recommendation of New Books

④ Scanned Data Available

問5　According to one customer's opinion, 　10　 is a good idea.

① additional storage for the reader

② ignoring the maker's recommendation

③ making the light as bright as possible

④ taking notes by typing

B You belong to the math club at high school. The club members have been planning an event to encourage more students to be interested in math. You have found a school article written by a student in the UK.

Ascotfield School Math Competition

Some students dislike studying math at school. You may often see or hear them struggling with math especially during their exam periods. Studying math, however, is interesting, and there are a lot of problems in our daily lives that can be solved with math as well as in textbooks. Last autumn on 7th and 8th October our math club held an online math competition where students in Year 11–13 answered math questions related to real life. Every participant had to submit their answer within two hours on the internet. This competition gathered 120 students: more than half of them were Year 12; about two-fifths were Year 11; the number of the Year 13 participants was only 10. Why did more students in Year 12 participate than students in Year 11 or Year 13? The participants' comments below may help to answer this question.

Participants' Comments

LT: One of my Year 13 friends couldn't take part in this math contest because she was too busy preparing for her university application. This may also be the case with other Year 13 students.

RS: This competition motivated me to study harder. After the competition, I got the highest score ever in a math exam at school.

BJ: I think the math problems were worth solving, but I couldn't upload my answer due to computer trouble. I wish there had been another way to submit it.

TM: I'm a student in Year 11 and really enjoyed this challenge, but it's a pity a lot of my classmates only noticed this event after the entry period.

DC: Thank you for holding a special event like this. I felt it was difficult to understand how to upload my answer. It was complicated and should be changed next time.

問 1　The purpose of Ascotfield School Math Competition was to 　11　.

   ① encourage students to study math at university

   ② help students realise how interesting math is

   ③ improve students' calculation skills efficiently

   ④ show students the difficulty of mathematics

問 2　One **fact** about Ascotfield School Math Competition is that 　12　.

   ① fewer than one tenth of the participants were in Year 13

   ② over half of the competitors were students in Year 11

   ③ participants were allowed to submit their answers on paper

   ④ students had to get a good math score before the competition

問 3　From the participants' comments, Ascotfield School Math Competition enabled a student to 　13　.

   ① do better in a math test at school

   ② make several friends who love math

   ③ pass a college entrance examination

   ④ realise math can change daily life

問 4　Some participants in Ascotfield School Math Competition think that 　14　.

   ① the math competition should be cancelled next year

   ② the math questions were too difficult to answer

   ③ the two-hour testing time should be changed

   ④ the way to submit answers should be reconsidered

問5　The author's question can be answered by comments from ⬚15⬚ .

① BJ　& DC

② BJ　& TM

③ DC & RS

④ DC & TM

⑤ LT & TM

⑥ LT & RS

第3問 （配点　4）

You are studying at a high school in Sydney. To prepare for a cooking class, you are now reading a textbook.

How to Make a Hamburger

First you need to make a burger patty. It is important to prepare ground beef that has some fat. This will make the burger juicier. Put salt and black pepper on the ground beef and mix it until you cannot see any of the salt or pepper. If it is not mixed well enough, the beef patty will fall apart while you are frying it. Then put the ground beef into the pan and gently press it into a 1/2-inch-thick patty. Fry it till it gets brown. To prevent food poisoning, make sure the patty is well-done. The recommended heating time is about ten minutes.

Before serving, spread the bottom half of the toasted hamburger bun with tomato ketchup and mayonnaise, and put vegetables on the bun. The vegetables' order does not matter. The oil in the mayonnaise keeps the bun from absorbing the water contained in the vegetables. Then, place the beef patty on them. Finally put the upper half of the hamburger bun on top and lightly press the hamburger together.

問1 In order to prepare a hamburger that is safe to eat, you have to 16 .

① choose meat which contains a little fat

② heat the beef patty for sufficient time

③ mix the ground beef with salt and black pepper well

④ use salad oil instead of animal fat

問2　If you follow the advice, how should you make a hamburger? 　17

①

hamburger bun
beef patty
ketchup, mayonnaise
lettuce, tomato, onion
hamburger bun

②

hamburger bun
beef patty
lettuce, tomato, onion
ketchup, mayonnaise
hamburger bun

③

hamburger bun
ketchup, mayonnaise
beef patty
lettuce, tomato, onion
hamburger bun

④

hamburger bun
lettuce, tomato, onion
beef patty
ketchup, mayonnaise
hamburger bun

第4問 （配点　8）

In English class you are writing an essay on a topic you are interested in. This is your most recent draft. You are now working on revisions based on comments from your teacher.

The Roles of Museums

Museums play a variety of roles in society though many of us are not fully aware of them. It is said that there are more than 4,000 museums or facilities with a similar purpose in Japan and that a total of around three hundred thousand people visit museums in a year. This essay will discuss three main roles that museums play.

First, museums preserve culturally and historically valuable things in a good condition. There are a lot of heritages in each part of the world, but without proper care, they will soon break and lose their beauty. *(1)*∧ Thus, it can be said that museums are the keepers of our past.

In addition, museums play an educational role by displaying their collections in proper arrangements. Visitors can learn about history through what they see. *(2)*∧ Looking at the pots and tools from ancient Egypt can help you imagine life in those times more vividly than just reading about it.

Finally, museums *(3)*<u>are wonderful places</u>. In fact, many of the world-famous tourist cities, such as Paris, London and New York, have great museums, which are one of the most popular destinations for tourists. It is pointed out that museums not only bring money to the cities but also improve their images as cities of culture and art.

In conclusion, museums are beneficial to society in that they hand down valuable things to the future generations, *(4)*<u>show the collections</u>, and attract tourists from around the world.

(1) You are missing something here. Add more information between the two sentences to connect them.

(2) Insert a connecting expression here.

(3) This topic sentence doesn't really match this paragraph. Rewrite it.

(4) The underlined phrase doesn't summarize your essay content enough. Change it.

Overall comment:

Your essay is getting better. Keep up the good work. (Do you often visit museums? Tell me about your favorite if you have any! ☺)

問 1 Based on comment (1), which is the best sentence to add? 18

　　① Museums admit that they should be to blame for this.

　　② Museums prevent this by providing a proper environment.

　　③ Museums try to make this known to many people.

　　④ Museums use special techniques to make this happen.

問 2 Based on comment (2), which is the best expression to add? 19

　　① as a result

　　② for instance

　　③ in contrast

　　④ moreover

問 3 Based on comment (3), which is the most appropriate way to rewrite the topic sentence? 20

　　① are located in big cities

　　② create a new trend

　　③ improve local employment

　　④ lead to increased tourism

問 4 Based on comment (4), which is the best replacement? 21

　　① bring profits to the local communities

　　② collect the latest information from around the world

　　③ help visitors learn about the past

　　④ provide a standard educational system

第5問 （配点 16）

Your teacher has asked you to read two articles about anger. You will discuss what you learned in your next class.

Feeling Angry

Arnold Stallone

Science Teacher, Rock City High School

Pretty much everyone feels angry sometimes. It doesn't mean you're a bad person. Some feelings of anger come from not being in control. Sometimes it really does feel as if the world is against you, when you try to do your best and things still go wrong or you get into trouble for something that feels unfair.

Anger is an instinctive reaction, a very powerful automatic response which begins in the emotional parts of your brain, particularly a part called the amygdala. The amygdala responds instantly and you feel a surge of anger before the more "thinking" parts of your brain have stepped in to rationalize or control it. We know that the amygdala and other emotional areas are well-developed in teenagers (in fact, from birth) but that the controlling prefrontal cortex is less well-developed.

Emotions are also affected by hormones, some of which go up and down wildly during adolescence in both boys and girls. An increase of testosterone, the mostly male hormone, can cause aggression and the desire to lash out and fight. And swings in levels of oestrogen and progesterone can affect emotions and behavior in girls, sometimes leading to the very distressing condition called PMS. Hormones are powerful and important chemicals that we can't control by will-power, though we can learn to control our reactions. Once you realize that some of your feelings are caused by chemicals in your body and brain, you'll find it easier to predict when you'll feel bad and then you will be better able to control your reactions. Also, just knowing that something has a physical cause can make you less stressed about it.

So, anger is normal. But feeling angry very often or all the time is not a good thing; it will distract you from focusing properly and may harm relationships with friends and family. Not being able to control your anger and perhaps harming someone else or yourself is definitely something you want to avoid.

Continued anger is sometimes a sign of depression. Also, research suggests that boys and men often express depression through anger, perhaps more so than girls and women, whose depression looks more obviously like sadness and feeling low.

The Happiness Hormone

Harrison Willis

Professor, Rock City University

I agree with Mr. Stallone's idea that feeling angry very often or all the time is not a good thing. In order to cooperate with others and maintain a good relationship, we must learn to deal with anger. However, I was surprised at the statement that we cannot control hormones by will-power. There have been various experiments proving that humans have the ability to control hormones, and this is one of the most important things in coping with anger effectively.

How do we control hormones? This can easily be understood by imagining ourselves before an important exam or a tennis match. The more we focus on the event, the more energetic and more confident we feel. This is the effect of adrenaline, a hormone that makes our body active.

Another hormone that we can control is serotonin, which makes us feel happy. It is produced in your brain and plays a key role in regulating mood; therefore the lack of serotonin may cause anxiousness or anger.

Let me introduce two ways to increase the amount of serotonin in your body. The first is choosing food rich in protein. Though taking in serotonin directly from food is impossible, you can take in tryptophan, an amino acid which changes into serotonin in your brain. Tryptophan is found mostly in high protein foods such as tofu and cheese. The second is regular exercise. A good workout tells the body to release tryptophan into your blood. This also causes other amino acids to become less, which creates a good environment for more serotonin to be produced in your brain. One thing you might want to remember is that spending time in the sunshine increases the amount of serotonin. So when you exercise, it is better to do it before dark, ideally in the morning.

All of the above show that we can control the amount of serotonin, the happiness hormone, in our bodies. Therefore your will to change your diet and do exercise can help you handle anger, and can be the first step to leading a cooperative, social life.

問 1　Stallone believes that ☐ 22 ☐ .

① anger can be controlled better if we get enough sleep

② anger is not a normal mental condition

③ we are likely to get angry when we are hungry

④ we may keep being angry when we are depressed

問 2　According to Stallone, emotional parts of a brain such as ☐ 23 ☐ are well-developed in teenagers, while thinking parts such as ☐ 24 ☐ are not.

① amygdala

② oestrogen

③ prefrontal cortex

④ progesterone

⑤ testosterone

⑥ tryptophan

問3　Serotonin is a hormone which ☐25☐.

   ① can be taken directly from food

   ② causes depression as well as anger

   ③ helps us to control negative feelings

   ④ is found basically in females only

問4　Both writers agree that ☐26☐.

   ① anger often leads to a lack of exercise

   ② long-term anger ought to be avoided

   ③ more women suffer from depression than men

   ④ we must not get angry even if the world is against us

問5　A difference of the opinions between the two writers is whether ☐27☐ or not.

   ① boys and girls have the same mechanism about anger

   ② feeling angry all the time is a bad thing

   ③ food with high adrenaline is effective against depression

   ④ we can control hormones by strength of will

第6問 (配点 15)

Your English teacher has told everyone in your class to find an interesting story and present it to a discussion group, using notes. You have found a story written by a high school student in the UK.

Be Honest with Yourself

George Thomas

At dinner on my fifteenth birthday, I made a speech in front of my parents. "I'll work harder on my study this year," I said, "to get a good grade." My father, nodding with satisfaction, said, "Now is an important time in your life, George. Work hard for the exam next year." He went on to point out my poor scores in the recent tests and stress the importance of being honest and diligent, so that by the time we started eating, the food had already gone cold. At the dinner table, my father and mother mostly talked about my test scores and my future career, which I listened to quietly.

I was going to take a national exam the next year, at the age of sixteen. The exam is important for students who want to go on to higher education. My future dream had always been to be a doctor since I was small, and the exam meant a great deal to me. My parents cared about my schoolwork very much, probably more than I did: "Listen to your teachers carefully in class and review each class at home." "Don't leave what you don't understand as it is." "Are you tired? It's important to refresh your body and mind." ... Probably all of them were right, and I could only answer, "OK, I know."

When the summer vacation was around the corner, I asked my parents if I could go for a two-day trip with my friends. My mother frowned and said, "But we've made a study plan for the summer. You have a tutor three times a week. You need time to review by yourself and..." "Just three days," I said. "You always say it's important to refresh my mind. It'll help me feel refreshed and concentrate on my study." My parents finally let me go for a trip on condition that I wouldn't fall behind schedule.

One morning in August, I set out on a trip — alone. I had long been determined to travel by myself at the age of sixteen like Joseph, the main character in *Summer Adventure of Joseph Bronson*, one of my favourite stories. Joseph, a sixteen-year-old boy living in the countryside of England, hitchhiked around the country by himself. He met various people on the way, learning a lot about life, friendship and love. I had been dreaming of making a trip as he did since I first read it when I was nine. I didn't tell my parents that I was going alone because, if I had, they wouldn't have given permission. I felt guilty, but realising my long-held ambition was much more important.

After leaving home, I walked to Aisby, the next town, and held up a sign saying "York" beside the road. In fact, the purpose of my trip was to travel by hitchhiking and I didn't care where I was going. I just thought that York would be a common destination for vehicles running there. After I saw dozens of cars passing by, a blue family car stopped in front of me. In the car were a middle-aged couple, probably a little younger than my parents. A man, who was the driver, said, "We're going to Holden. Is it OK with you?" Holden is a small town on the way to York. I said thank you and got into the car. When they asked me why I was hitchhiking, I answered that I was visiting my grandmother living in York. Talking with the kind man and woman, I was excited that one of my dreams was coming true. After arriving in Holden, I took a walk around, hitchhiked to the suburb of York in a car of another kind driver, and stayed at a small hostel there.

The next morning, a large delivery van stopped to pick me up. To my surprise, the driver was a young woman — probably in her late twenties or early thirties. Ella, the driver, was a friendly and talkative woman. As soon as I got into the van, she struck up a conversation as if we were old friends; she talked about various things — from her difficult customer and her pretty three-month-old nephew to the recent unusually hot weather. I enjoyed listening to her and found myself telling her about myself. When I said that my future dream was to be a doctor, Ella asked, "Why a doctor?" I answered, "I want to help people in need." She asked again, "And?" Not figuring out what she meant, I couldn't answer. Ella said, "I mean, there are a lot of occupations you can take to help people in need. Why do you want to be a doctor among others?" "OK, I see. Well..." At that moment, I realised that I hadn't given much thought to this kind of question. My parents always told me to be a doctor, and I accepted it without any doubt. I was at a loss what to say and became less certain about my determination. As if she were reading my mind, Ella said, "I know little about you, so all I can say is, *be honest with yourself. You* choose your way." "So, why did you choose your way as a driver?" I asked. "I always feel thrilled when I'm driving a large car. That's it. My parents were against my being a truck driver at first, but now they think it can't be helped," she replied with a smile.

After saying goodbye to Ella, two other drivers gave me a ride, and I safely came home. As I expected, my lie became known to my parents right away and they got mad at me. "I always tell you to be *honest.* Why don't you understand?" I had no choice but to apologise for what I had done; I knew that I was totally to blame. They said that I couldn't go out without permission any more during the summer vacation. I spent the rest of the summer studying in the house.

Now I study at high school. Ella's words, "be honest with yourself," have kept occurring to my mind repeatedly since we talked in her van. I have been thinking about what I really want to do — what makes me feel thrilled. I am curious about how machines and robots work, so mechanics or robotics might be a good choice for my career. At the same time, being a doctor is still attractive. I haven't told my parents what I'm thinking about, but someday I will tell them about my true determination.

Be Honest with Yourself

About the author (George Thomas)

· Studying hard to be a doctor in the future.

· Went hitchhiking by himself because | 28 |.

Other important people

· George's parents: Strict with his study and caring about his future very much.

· Ella: A truck driver, who | 29 |.

Events around his memorable trip in summer

| 30 | → | 31 | → | 32 | → | 33 |

What George realised after having a conversation with Ella

· | 34 |

What we can learn from this story

· | 35 |

· | 36 |

問1　Choose the best option for ⬚28⬚ .

 ① he decided to find out what he would do in the future

 ② he hoped to escape from his stressful life

 ③ he planned to go to see his grandmother living in a distant place

 ④ he wanted to have an experience similar to a story character's

問2　Choose the best option for ⬚29⬚ .

 ① advised him to travel alone and meet a lot of people

 ② asked him why he didn't get along with his parents

 ③ gave him an opportunity to think twice about his dream

 ④ made him realise how lazy he was in study

問3　Choose four out of the five options (①～⑤) and rearrange them in the order they happened.

 ⬚30⬚ → ⬚31⬚ → ⬚32⬚ → ⬚33⬚

 ① Apologised to his parents for telling a lie

 ② Asked his parents if he could make a trip

 ③ Hitched a ride in a kind couple's car

 ④ Read a book on how doctors save people

 ⑤ Talked about his dream to a female driver

問4　Choose the best option for ⬚34⬚ .

 ① He hadn't been fully aware of the dangers of travelling alone.

 ② He hadn't been truly honest with his parents about his trip.

 ③ He hadn't thought seriously enough about his future career.

 ④ He hadn't worked so hard as to make his dream come true.

問5　Choose the best two options for 　35　 and 　36　. (The order does not matter.)

① A stranger can have a great effect on our way of thinking.

② Confidence is important in persuading other people.

③ Expressing your goal to others is a good way to achieve it.

④ Sticking to one goal is more likely to lead to success.

⑤ We should follow our own heart in determining our future.

第7問 (配点 12)

In history class, your study group is going to give a presentation on changes in society. You have found an article you want to share with your group. Complete the summary notes for your next meeting.

The Luddite Movement

When we think about technological advancement and how people react to it, there are lessons to be learned from history, one of which is the Luddite movement. It was named after Ned Ludd, an Englishman who is said to have destroyed machines that took away his job. The Luddite movement took place in England in the early 19th century, when workers, especially those who had high skill in the cloth-making industry, took part in the destruction of machines for fear that new technology would threaten their living. They are called the Luddites.

During this time, a great change was taking place in the cloth-making industry. New machines were introduced that could produce fine cloth, which was possible only by skilled workers until then. The machines promised higher efficiency, increased production, and reduced costs. However, the Luddites saw them as a threat to jobs, wages, and also their pride. This was because machines enabled low-skilled workers to perform just as well as, or even better than, high-skilled ones. As a response to the new technology the Luddites formed groups, broke into factories at night, and destroyed machines so that they could no longer be used.

The Luddite movement gained significant attention and support from workers in the cloth-making industry. The Luddites were seen by some as defenders of traditional and skilled labor against the cold, cruel machines of the industrial revolution. However, the government and factory owners saw them as criminals and a threat to society. They responded with force, passing strict laws and sending in the military to stop the movement. The Luddites were caught and severely punished. The movement grew less and less frequent, and factory owners rebuilt their factories and machines. In addition, many workers eventually adapted to the change and found new jobs in the technologically advanced society.

The Luddite movement failed to achieve its goals but played an important role in shaping our modern society. It proved how large the impact of technological advancement could be, and the need to protect workers during times of rapid change. Today, the term "Luddite" is used all over the world to describe people who resist or fear technological advancement. Though the time when people destroyed machines is long gone, the fear for new technologies is as great as ever. The lesson Ned Ludd left us is still alive to this day.

Your summary notes:

The Luddite Movement
Introduction
◆ A social movement in early 19th-century England against the use of machines
◆ The Luddites were \boxed{37} .
Facts
◆ New technologies were introduced in the cloth-making industry.
◆ Machines enabled low-skilled workers to perform as well as highly skilled ones.
◆ \boxed{38}
◆ \boxed{39}
Reasons
The Luddites were concerned that:
◆ they might no longer be needed in their workplace.
◆ they would receive less money for their work.
◆ \boxed{40} .
Lesson to be learned
◆ \boxed{41}

問 1　Choose the best option for ☐ 37 ☐ on your summary notes.

① factory owners
② government officials
③ highly trained laborers
④ unskilled laborers

問 2　Choose the best two options for ☐ 38 ☐ and ☐ 39 ☐ on your summary notes. (The order does not matter.)

① The Luddites attacked factories in order to protect the natural environment.
② The Luddites destroyed new machines that could cause them to lose their jobs.
③ The movement caused low-skilled workers to lose new employment opportunities.
④ The movement took place less and less frequently because of new government rules.
⑤ The movement was named after Ned Ludd, who took away others' jobs.
⑥ The movement was supported by factory owners in the cloth-making industry.

問 3　Choose the best option for ☐ 40 ☐ on your summary notes.

① they could no longer be proud of their jobs
② they would be required to gain a higher skill
③ they would have to replace old machines with newer ones
④ they would have to work for longer hours after dark

問4　Choose the best option for 　41　 on your summary notes.

① Destruction and violence is a great threat to the modern society.

② Governments need to protect factory owners as well as workers.

③ New technologies should be introduced to make our society richer.

④ Society should consider how to protect workers in times of change.

第8問 (配点 15)

You are interested in insects and going to enter a biology presentation contest. You have written the essay below and are making your presentation slides.

When fall comes in Japan, you sometimes hear insects singing beautifully in the grass or on a flower bed. Which insects are good singers? In many cases, as you may guess, crickets are.

Crickets are from 10 mm to 40 mm in length. Their body color is usually black or brown. On the head are two eyes and two antennae. On each side of their body they have three legs, two wings, and a special sense organ called a cercus. Females also have a long tube-shaped organ called an ovipositor, which is used to lay eggs, at the end part of the body. At first sight, crickets may appear to have only one pair of wings, but in fact they have two pairs: a pair in the front and a pair in the back. Since the back wings are folded under the front wings, they may be difficult to find. But having wings doesn't allow them to fly. Rather it is their back legs, which are big and long, that enable them to jump a long distance, as if they were flying. And surprisingly, their ears are located in their front legs — which are very sensitive, allowing them to catch another cricket's song from far away.

As of behavior, crickets love grassy places such as forests and are difficult to find in the daytime because they become active at night. Most of them eat leaves, flowers, other insects, and dead animals, while their natural enemies are spiders, frogs, and birds. Basically they are born in early summer, grow to become adults in one to two months, and die in fall after the females lay eggs. Temperature strongly affects crickets, especially their songs — the cooler it is, the less they sing. For instance, according to an experiment, the average number of times a cricket will sing in 15 seconds is 46 times at 30℃ but drops to 19 times at 15℃ .

By rubbing their wings together crickets sing or make high-pitched sounds. In fact, the sounds are so high that they cannot be caught by telephones; you can't use the telephone to send their songs to someone else. Similar to other animals, it is basically the males that sing. The songs are used to attract females, and we have enjoyed listening to their love songs since ancient times. The early records of their songs can be found in the oldest collection of Japanese poems, *Manyoshu.*

In some regions or countries in the world, crickets have been eaten as daily food. Since they have a mild taste, they are sometimes called "land shrimps." Interestingly, their taste is affected by what they eat — if you give them fruit, they will become fruit-flavored. As a source of nutrition, crickets are rich in minerals and vitamins, and contain as much protein as meat such as beef, pork, or chicken.

You may hesitate to eat crickets, especially if you do not like insects, but in recent years they have been in the spotlight around the world as a sustainable source of food. This is because the world population has been increasing dramatically — some experts expect that the number will reach ten billion in 2050, and that we will suffer from serious food crisis in the future. In 2013, FAO (Food and Agriculture Organization) suggested that we make better use of insects as a food source. Crickets are a strong candidate for the following reasons: they need far less space and water than large animals; they produce much less carbon dioxide (CO_2) than pigs or cows; they are easy to reproduce and nutritious. Cricket protein bars, snacks containing cricket powder, are sold in the UK, and in 2020 cricket crackers gathered so much attention in Japan that they were sold out soon after they went on sale. Though their popularity as a food source is still low, and we must find a way to raise a larger number of crickets economically, human beings need to obtain a new and more ecofriendly food source. If you have a chance to eat them, please give it a try, and help save the Earth.

Your presentation slides:

<table>
<tr>
<td>

Crickets:

Singers that will Save the Earth

</td>
<td>

1. Basic Features

· 10 mm–40 mm in length

· black or brown colored

·

· ⬛ 42

·

</td>
</tr>
<tr>
<td>

2. Body Structure (Female)

⬛ 43

</td>
<td>

3. Songs

· ⬛ 44

· ⬛ 45

</td>
</tr>
<tr>
<td>

4. As Food

· taste like shrimps

· contain a lot of vitamins and protein

· attract attention as sustainable food

· ecofriendly

</td>
<td>

5. Power of Crickets

⬛ 46

</td>
</tr>
</table>

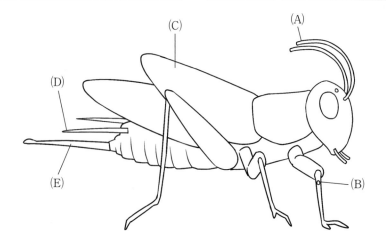

問 1 Which of the following is **not** suitable for | 42 |?

   ① easily affected by temperature

   ② eat plants and animals

   ③ have four legs on their bodies

   ④ have two pairs of wings

   ⑤ not active in the daytime

問 2 Complete the blank labels on the illustration of a cricket for the **Body Structure (Female)** slide. | 43 |

   ① (A) Antenna   (B) Cercus   (C) Back wing
      (D) Ear   (E) Ovipositor

   ② (A) Antenna   (B) Ear   (C) Front wing
      (D) Cercus   (E) Ovipositor

   ③ (A) Antenna   (B) Ear   (C) Back wing
      (D) Ovipositor   (E) Cercus

   ④ (A) Cercus   (B) Ear   (C) Front wing
      (D) Ovipositor   (E) Antenna

   ⑤ (A) Cercus   (B) Ovipositor   (C) Front wing
      (D) Ear   (E) Antenna

問 3 Which are the best two options for | 44 | and | 45 | to complete the **Songs** slide? (The order does not matter.)

   ① As crickets grow older, they begin to sing less often.

   ② Crickets sing more often at 30 ℃ than at 15 ℃ .

   ③ Female crickets make short and high sounds to attract males.

   ④ Some people become nervous or irritated when they hear crickets singing.

   ⑤ There are some classical works in literature which describe crickets' songs.

問 4 Which is the best statement for the last slide? 46

① Although crickets have the potential to save the world, we should pay more attention to the danger of eating insects.

② Crickets as food are expected to save the planet in the future because they have helped us solve a serious food crisis in the world.

③ It is true that some people do not want to eat crickets, but crickets can be a global food source in the future and are worth eating.

④ Recently cricket food has been so popular around the world that animal meat will be completely replaced in the future.

問 5 What can you infer about the life cycle of crickets? 47

① It is impossible for adult crickets to survive winter.

② It takes two to three weeks for crickets to become adults.

③ On average adult crickets live for a few years.

④ The life cycle of crickets is yet to be made clear.

大学入学共通テスト試作問題
［リーディング］
(2022年11月公表)

●大学入試センターによる試作問題（2022年11月公表）は，新課程での共通テスト実施に向け，作問の方向性や具体的なイメージを共有するため，理科以外の6教科それぞれの全科目または一部科目について作成されたものです。本番の試験ではこの試作問題と同じような内容，形式，配点等の問題が必ずしも出題されるものではありません。

○掲載している試作問題
第A問（配点18点）　　　第B問（配点12点）

※本問題集収録にあたっては，A4サイズで公表された問題をB5サイズに縮小しています。また，公表時の問題をベースとして編集部にて一部修正・変更等を行っています。

第A問

You are working on an essay about whether high school students should be allowed to use their smartphones in class. You will follow the steps below.

Step 1: Read and understand various viewpoints about smartphone use.
Step 2: Take a position on high school students' use of their smartphones in class.
Step 3: Create an outline for an essay using additional sources.

[Step 1] Read various sources

Author A (Teacher)

My colleagues often question whether smartphones can help students develop life-long knowledge and skills. I believe that they can, as long as their use is carefully planned. Smartphones support various activities in class that can enhance learning. Some examples include making surveys for projects and sharing one's learning with others. Another advantage is that we do not have to provide students with devices; they can use their phones! Schools should take full advantage of students' powerful computing devices.

Author B (Psychologist)

It is a widespread opinion that smartphones can encourage student learning. Being believed by many, though, does not make an opinion correct. A recent study found that when high school students were allowed to use their smartphones in class, it was impossible for them to concentrate on learning. In fact, even if students were not using their own smartphones, seeing their classmates using smartphones was a distraction. It is clear that schools should make the classroom a place that is free from the interference of smartphones.

Author C (Parent)

I recently bought a smartphone for my son who is a high school student. This is because his school is located far from our town. He usually leaves home early and returns late. Now, he can contact me or access essential information if he has trouble. On the other hand, I sometimes see him walking while looking at his smartphone. If he is not careful, he could have an accident. Generally, I think that high school students are safer with smartphones, but parents still need to be aware of the risks. I also wonder how he is using it in class.

Author D (High school student)

At school, we are allowed to use our phones in class. It makes sense for our school to permit us to use them because most students have smartphones. During class, we make use of foreign language learning apps on our smartphones, which is really helpful to me. I am now more interested in learning than I used to be, and my test scores have improved. The other day, though, my teacher got mad at me when she caught me reading online comics in class. Occasionally these things happen, but overall, smartphones have improved my learning.

Author E (School principal)

Teachers at my school were initially skeptical of smartphones because they thought students would use them to socialize with friends during class. Thus, we banned them. As more educational apps became available, however, we started to think that smartphones could be utilized as learning aids in the classroom. Last year, we decided to allow smartphone use in class. Unfortunately, we did not have the results we wanted. We found that smartphones distracted students unless rules for their use were in place and students followed them. This was easier said than done, though.

問1　Both Authors A and D mention that 1 .

① apps for learning on smartphones can help students perform better on exams

② one reason to use smartphones as an educational tool is that most students possess one

③ smartphones can be used to support activities for learning both at school and at home

④ smartphones make it possible for students to share their ideas with classmates

問2　Author B implies that 2 .

① having time away from digital devices interferes with students' motivation to learn

② sometimes commonly held beliefs can be different from the facts that research reveals

③ students who do not have smartphones are likely to consider themselves better learners

④ the classroom should be a place where students can learn without the interference of teachers

[Step 2] Take a position

問3 Now that you understand the various viewpoints, you have taken a position on high school students' use of their smartphones in class, and have written it out as below. Choose the best options to complete ┌ 3 ┐, ┌ 4 ┐, and ┌ 5 ┐.

Your position: High school students should not be allowed to use their smartphones in class.

● Authors ┌ 3 ┐ and ┌ 4 ┐ support your position.
● The main argument of the two authors: ┌ 5 ┐.

Options for ┌ 3 ┐ and ┌ 4 ┐ (The order does not matter.)
① A
② B
③ C
④ D
⑤ E

Options for ┌ 5 ┐
① Making practical rules for smartphone use in class is difficult for school teachers
② Smartphones may distract learning because the educational apps are difficult to use
③ Smartphones were designed for communication and not for classroom learning
④ Students cannot focus on studying as long as they have access to smartphones in class

[Step 3] Create an outline using Sources A and B

Outline of your essay:

Using smartphones in class is not a good idea

Introduction

　Smartphones have become essential for modern life, but students should be prohibited from using their phones during class.

Body

　Reason 1: [From Step 2]

　Reason 2: [Based on Source A]　·········　| 6 |

　Reason 3: [Based on Source B]　·········　| 7 |

Conclusion

　High schools should not allow students to use their smartphones in class.

Source A

Mobile devices offer advantages for learning. For example, one study showed that university students learned psychology better when using their interactive mobile apps compared with their digital textbooks. Although the information was the same, extra features in the apps, such as 3D images, enhanced students' learning. It is important to note, however, that digital devices are not all equally effective. Another study found that students understand content better using their laptop computers rather than their smartphones because of the larger screen size. Schools must select the type of digital device that will maximize students' learning, and there is a strong argument for schools to provide computers or tablets rather than to have students use their smartphones. If all students are provided with computers or tablets with the same apps installed, there will be fewer technical problems and it will be easier for teachers to conduct class. This also enables students without their own smartphones to participate in all class activities.

Source B

A study conducted in the U.S. found that numerous teenagers are addicted to their smartphones. The study surveyed about 1,000 students between the ages of 13 and 18. The graph below shows the percentages of students who agreed with the statements about their smartphone use.

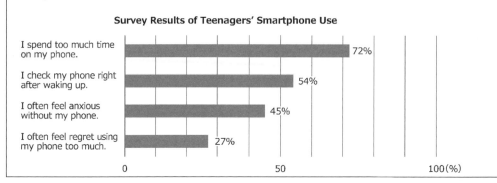

問 4　Based on Source A, which of the following is the most appropriate for Reason 2?　6

① Apps that display 3D images are essential for learning, but not all students have these apps on their smartphones.

② Certain kinds of digital devices can enhance educational effectiveness, but smartphones are not the best.

③ Students should obtain digital skills not only on smartphones but also on other devices to prepare for university.

④ We should stick to textbooks because psychology studies have not shown the positive effects of digital devices on learning.

問 5　For Reason 3, you have decided to write, "Young students are facing the danger of smartphone addiction." Based on Source B, which option best supports this statement?
　7

① Although more than half of teenagers reported using their smartphones too much, less than a quarter actually feel regret about it. This may indicate unawareness of a dependency problem.

② Close to three in four teenagers spend too much time on their phones. In fact, over 50% check their phones immediately after waking. Many teenagers cannot resist using their phones.

③ Over 70% of teenagers think they spend too much time on their phones, and more than half feel anxious without them. This kind of dependence can negatively impact their daily lives.

④ Teenagers are always using smartphones. In fact, more than three-quarters admit to using their phones too much. Their lives are controlled by smartphones from morning to night.

第Ｂ問

In English class you are writing an essay on a social issue you are interested in. This is your most recent draft. You are now working on revisions based on comments from your teacher.

Eco-friendly Action with Fashion	**Comments**
Many people love fashion. Clothes are important for self-expression, but fashion can be harmful to the environment. In Japan, about 480,000 tons of clothes are said to be thrown away every year. This is equal to about 130 large trucks a day. We need to change our "throw-away" behavior. This essay will highlight three ways to be more sustainable.	
First, when shopping, avoid making unplanned purchases. According to a government survey, approximately 64% of shoppers do not think about what is already in their closet. *(1)*⋀So, try to plan your choices carefully when you are shopping.	*(1) You are missing something here. Add more information between the two sentences to connect them.*
In addition, purchase high-quality clothes which usually last longer. Even though the price might be higher, it is good value when an item can be worn for several years. *(2)*⋀Cheaper fabrics can lose their color or start to look old quickly, so they need to be thrown away sooner.	*(2) Insert a connecting expression here.*
Finally, *(3)*<u>think about your clothes</u>. For example, sell them to used clothing stores. That way other people can enjoy wearing them. You could also donate clothes to a charity for people who need them. Another way is to find a new purpose for them. There are many ways to transform outfits into useful items such as quilts or bags.	*(3) This topic sentence doesn't really match this paragraph. Rewrite it.*
In conclusion, it is time for a lifestyle change. From now on, check your closet before you go shopping, *(4)* <u>select better things,</u> and lastly, give your clothes a second life. In this way, we can all become more sustainable with fashion.	*(4) The underlined phrase doesn't summarize your essay content enough. Change it.*

Overall Comment:
Your essay is getting better. Keep up the good work. (Have you checked your own closet? I have checked mine! ☺)

問 1　Based on comment (1), which is the best sentence to add?　1

① As a result, people buy many similar items they do not need.
② Because of this, customers cannot enjoy clothes shopping.
③ Due to this, shop clerks want to know what customers need.
④ In this situation, consumers tend to avoid going shopping.

問 2　Based on comment (2), which is the best expression to add?　2

① for instance
② in contrast
③ nevertheless
④ therefore

問 3　Based on comment (3), which is the most appropriate way to rewrite the topic sentence?　3

① buy fewer new clothes
② dispose of old clothes
③ find ways to reuse clothes
④ give unwanted clothes away

問 4　Based on comment (4), which is the best replacement?　4

① buy items that maintain their condition
② choose inexpensive fashionable clothes
③ pick items that can be transformed
④ purchase clothes that are second-hand

大学入学共通テスト本試験
［リーディング］
（2024 年 1 月 13 日実施）

時間　80分　　　　　100点　満点

1 ══ 解答にあたっては，実際に試験を受けるつもりで，時間を厳守し真剣に取りくむこと。

2 ══ 巻末にマークシートをつけてあるので，切り離しのうえ練習用として利用すること。

3 ══ 解答終了後には，自己採点により学力チェックを行い，別冊の解答・解説をじっくり読んで，弱点補強，知識や考え方の整理などに努めること。

※ 2024 共通テスト本試験問題を編集部にて一部修正して作成しています。

英　　語（リーディング）

各大問の英文や図表を読み，解答番号 | 1 | ～ | 49 | にあてはまるものとして最も適当な選択肢を選びなさい。

第1問　(配点　10)

A　You are studying English at a language school in the US. The school is planning an event. You want to attend, so you are reading the flyer.

The Thorpe English Language School

International Night

Friday, May 24, 5 p.m.-8 p.m.

Entrance Fee: $5

The Thorpe English Language School (TELS) is organizing an international exchange event. TELS students don't need to pay the entrance fee. Please present your student ID at the reception desk in the Student Lobby.

● **Enjoy foods from various parts of the world**
　Have you ever tasted hummus from the Middle East? How about tacos from Mexico? Couscous from North Africa? Try them all!

● **Experience different languages and new ways to communicate**
　Write basic expressions such as "hello" and "thank you" in Arabic, Italian, Japanese, and Spanish. Learn how people from these cultures use facial expressions and their hands to communicate.

● **Watch dance performances**
　From 7 p.m. watch flamenco, hula, and samba dance shows on the stage! After each dance, performers will teach some basic steps. Please join in.

Lots of pictures, flags, maps, textiles, crafts, and games will be displayed in the hall. If you have some pictures or items from your home country which can be displayed at the event, let a school staff member know by May 17!

問 1　To join the event free of charge, you must ☐1☐ .

①　bring pictures from your home country

②　consult a staff member about the display

③　fill out a form in the Student Lobby

④　show proof that you are a TELS student

問 2　At the event, you can ☐2☐ .

①　learn about gestures in various cultures

②　participate in a dance competition

③　read short stories in foreign languages

④　try cooking international dishes

B You are an exchange student in the US and next week your class will go on a day trip. The teacher has provided some information.

Tours of Yentonville

The Yentonville Tourist Office offers three city tours.

The History Tour

The day will begin with a visit to St. Patrick's Church, which was built when the city was established in the mid-1800s. Opposite the church is the early-20th-century Mayor's House. There will be a tour of the house and its beautiful garden.  Finally, cross the city by public bus and visit the Peace Park. Opened soon after World War Ⅱ, it was the site of many demonstrations in the 1960s.

The Arts Tour

 The morning will be spent in the Yentonville Arts District. We will begin in the Art Gallery where there are many paintings from Europe and the US. After lunch, enjoy a concert across the street at the Bruton Concert Hall before walking a short distance to the Artists' Avenue. This part of the district was developed several years ago when new artists' studios and the nearby Sculpture Park were created. Watch artists at work in their studios and afterwards wander around the park, finding sculptures among the trees.

The Sports Tour

First thing in the morning, you can watch the Yentonville Lions football team training at their open-air facility in the suburbs. In the afternoon, travel by subway to the Yentonville Hockey Arena, completed last fall. Spend some time in its exhibition hall to learn about the arena's  unique design. Finally, enjoy a professional hockey game in the arena.

Yentonville Tourist Office, January, 2024

問 1　Yentonville has ☐ 3 ☐ .

① a church built 250 years ago when the city was constructed

② a unique football training facility in the center of the town

③ an art studio where visitors can create original works of art

④ an arts area with both an art gallery and a concert hall

問 2　On all three tours, you will ☐ 4 ☐ .

① learn about historic events in the city

② see people demonstrate their skills

③ spend time both indoors and outdoors

④ use public transportation to get around

問 3　Which is the newest place in Yentonville you can visit on the tours?
☐ 5 ☐

① The Hockey Arena

② The Mayor's House

③ The Peace Park

④ The Sculpture Park

第2問 (配点 20)

A You are an exchange student at a high school in the UK and find this flyer.

Invitation to the Strategy Game Club

Have you ever wanted to learn strategy games like chess, *shogi*, or *go*? They are actually more than just games. You can learn skills such as thinking logically and deeply without distractions. Plus, these games are really fun! This club is open to all students of our school. Regardless of skill level, you are welcome to join.

We play strategy games together and. . .

- learn basic moves from demonstrations by club members
- play online against club friends
- share tips on our club webpage
- learn the history and etiquette of each game
- analyse games using computer software
- participate in local and national tournaments

Regular meetings: Wednesday afternoons in Room 301, Student Centre

----

Member Comments

- My mind is clearer, calmer, and more focused in class.
- It's cool to learn how some games have certain similarities.
- At tournaments, I like discussing strategies with other participants.
- Members share Internet videos that explain practical strategies for chess.
- It's nice to have friends who give good advice about *go*.
- I was a complete beginner when I joined, and I had no problem!

問 1 According to the flyer, which is true about the club? [6]

① Absolute beginners are welcome.

② Members edit computer programs.

③ Professional players give formal demonstrations.

④ Students from other schools can join.

問 2 Which of the following is **not** mentioned as a club activity? [7]

① Having games with non-club members

② Playing matches against computers

③ Sharing game-playing ideas on the Internet

④ Studying the backgrounds of strategy games

問 3 One **opinion** stated by a member is that [8] .

① comparing different games is interesting

② many videos about *go* are useful

③ members learn tips at competitions

④ regular meetings are held off campus

問 4　The club invitation and a member's comment both mention that [　9　].

① new members must demonstrate experience

② online support is necessary to be a good player

③ *shogi* is a logical and stimulating game

④ strategy games help improve one's concentration

問 5　This club is most likely suitable for students who want to [　10　].

① create their own computer strategy games

② improve their skill level of playing strategy games

③ learn proper British etiquette through playing strategy games

④ spend weekends playing strategy games in the club room

B You are a college student going to study in the US and need travel insurance. You find this review of an insurance plan written by a female international student who studied in the US for six months.

There are many things to consider before traveling abroad: pack appropriate clothes, prepare your travel expenses, and don't forget medication (if necessary). Also, you should purchase travel insurance.

When I studied at Fairville University in California, I bought travel insurance from TravSafer International. I signed up online in less than 15 minutes and was immediately covered. They accept any form of payment, usually on a monthly basis. There were three plans. All plans include a one-time health check-up.

The Premium Plan is $100/month. The plan provides 24-hour medical support through a smartphone app and telephone service. Immediate financial support will be authorized if you need to stay in a hospital.

The Standard Plan worked best for me. It had the 24-hour telephone assistance and included a weekly email with tips for staying healthy in a foreign country. It wasn't cheap: $75/month. However, it was nice to get the optional 15% discount because I paid for six months of coverage in advance.

If your budget is limited, you can choose the Economy Plan, which is $25/month. It has the 24-hour telephone support like the other plans but only covers emergency care. Also, they can arrange a taxi to a hospital at a reduced cost if considered necessary by the support center.

I never got sick or hurt, so I thought it was a waste of money to get insurance. Then my friend from Brazil broke his leg while playing soccer and had to spend a few days in a hospital. He had chosen the Premium Plan and it covered everything! I realized how important insurance is—you know that you will be supported when you are in trouble.

問 1　According to the review, which of the following is true?　11

① Day and night medical assistance is available with the most expensive
plan.

② The cheapest plan includes free hospitalization for any reason.

③ The mid-level plan does not include the one-time health check-up.

④ The writer's plan cost her over $100 every month.

問 2　Which is **not** included in the cheapest option?　12

① Email support

② Emergency treatment

③ Telephone help desk

④ Transport assistance

問 3　Which is the best combination that describes TravSafer International?

　　　| 13 |

　　A : They allow monthly payments.

　　B : They design scholarship plans for students.

　　C : They help you remember your medication.

　　D : They offer an Internet-based registration system.

　　E : They require a few days to process the application form.

　　① 　A and D

　　② 　A and E

　　③ 　B and D

　　④ 　B and E

　　⑤ 　C and D

問 4　The writer's **opinion** of her chosen plan is that | 14 | .

　　① 　it prevented her from being health conscious

　　② 　she was not satisfied with the telephone assistance

　　③ 　the option for cost reduction was attractive

　　④ 　the treatment for her broken leg was covered

問 5　Which of the following best describes the writer's attitude? | 15 |

　　① 　She believes the smartphone app is useful.

　　② 　She considers travel preparation to be important.

　　③ 　She feels the US medical system is unique in the world.

　　④ 　She thinks a different hospital would have been better for her friend.

第 3 問 (配点 15)

A Susan, your English ALT's sister, visited your class last month. Now back in the UK, she wrote on her blog about an event she took part in.

Hi!

I participated in a photo rally for foreign tourists with my friends: See the rules on the right. As photo rally beginners, we decided to aim for only five of the checkpoints. In three minutes, we arrived at our first target, the city museum. In quick succession, we made the second, third, and fourth targets. Things were going smoothly! But, on the way to the last target, the statue of a famous samurai from the city, we got lost. Time was running out and my feet were hurting from walking

Sakura City Photo Rally Rules

- Each group can only use the **camera** and **paper map**, both provided by us
- Take as many photos of **25 checkpoints** (designated sightseeing spots) as possible
- **3-hour** time limit
- Photos must include **all 3 team members**
- All members must move **together**
- **No** mobile phones
- **No** transport

for over two hours. We stopped a man with a pet monkey for help, but neither our Japanese nor his English were good enough. After he'd explained the way using gestures, we realised we wouldn't have enough time to get there and would have to give up. We took a photo with him and said goodbye. When we got back to Sakura City Hall, we were surprised to hear that the winning team had completed 19 checkpoints. One of our photos was selected to be on the event website (click here). It reminds me of the man's warmth and kindness: our own "gold medal."

問 1　You click the link in the blog.　Which picture appears?　16

問 2　You are asked to comment on Susan's blog.　Which would be an appropriate comment to her?　17

① I want to see a picture of you wearing the gold medal!

② You did your best.　Come back to Japan and try again!

③ You reached 19 checkpoints in three hours?　Really?　Wow!!

④ Your photo is great!　Did you upgrade your phone?

B You are going to participate in an English Day. As preparation, you are reading an article in the school newspaper written by Yuzu, who took part in it last year.

Virtual Field Trip to a South Sea Island

This year, for our English Day, we participated in a virtual science tour. The winter weather had been terrible, so we were excited to see the tropical scenery of the volcanic island projected on the screen.

First, we "took a road trip" to learn about the geography of the island, using navigation software to view the route. We "got into the car," which our teacher, Mr Leach, sometimes stopped so we could look out of the window and get a better sense of the rainforest. Afterwards, we asked Mr Leach about what we'd seen.

Later, we "dived into the ocean" and learnt about the diversity of marine creatures. We observed a coral reef via a live camera. Mr Leach asked us if we could count the number of creatures, but there were too many! Then he showed us an image of the ocean 10 years ago. The reef we'd seen on camera was dynamic, but in the photo it was even more full of life. It looked so different after only 10 years! Mr Leach told us human activity was affecting the ocean and it could be totally ruined if we didn't act now.

In the evening, we studied astronomy under a "perfect starry sky." We put up tents in the gymnasium and created a temporary planetarium on the ceiling using a projector. We were fascinated by the sky full of constellations, shooting stars, and the Milky Way. Someone pointed out one of the brightest lights and asked Mr Leach if it was Venus, a planet close to Earth. He nodded and explained that humans have created so much artificial light that hardly anything is visible in our city's night sky.

On my way home after school, the weather had improved and the sky was now cloudless. I looked up at the moonless sky and realised what Mr Leach had told us was true.

問 1 Yuzu's article also included student comments (①～④) describing the events in the virtual tour. Put the comments in the order in which the events happened.

①

I was wondering how dangerous the island was. I saw beautiful birds and a huge snake in the jungle.

②

It was really shocking that there had been many more creatures before. We should protect our beautiful oceans!

③

Setting up a camping site in the gymnasium was kind of weird, but great fun! Better than outside, because we weren't bitten by bugs!

④

We were lost for words during the space show and realised we often don't notice things even though they're there.

問 2　From the tour, Yuzu did **not** learn about the ⬚22⬚ of the south sea island.

① marine ecosystem

② night-time sky

③ seasonal weather

④ trees and plants

問 3　On the way home, Yuzu looked up and most likely saw ⬚23⬚ in the night sky.

① a shooting star

② just a few stars

③ the full moon

④ the Milky Way

Your college English club's room has several problems and you want to redesign it. Based on the following article and the results of a questionnaire given to members, you make a handout for a group discussion.

What Makes a Good Classroom?

Diana Bashworth, writer at *Trends in Education*

As many schools work to improve their classrooms, it is important to have some ideas for making design decisions. SIN, which stands for *Stimulation, Individualization*, and *Naturalness*, is a framework that might be helpful to consider when designing classrooms.

The first, Stimulation, has two aspects: color and complexity. This has to do with the ceiling, floor, walls, and interior furnishings. For example, a classroom that lacks colors might be uninteresting. On the other hand, a classroom should not be too colorful. A bright color could be used on one wall, on the floor, window coverings, or furniture. In addition, it can be visually distracting to have too many things displayed on walls. It is suggested that 20 to 30 percent of wall space remain free.

The next item in the framework is Individualization, which includes two considerations: ownership and flexibility. Ownership refers to whether the classroom feels personalized. Examples of this include having chairs and desks that are suitable for student sizes and ages, and providing storage space and areas for displaying student works or projects. Flexibility is about having a classroom that allows for different kinds of activities.

Naturalness relates to the quality and quantity of light, both natural and artificial, and the temperature of the classroom. Too much natural light may make screens and boards difficult to see; students may have difficulty reading or writing if there is a lack of light. In addition, hot summer classrooms do not promote effective study. Schools should install systems allowing for the adjustment of both light and temperature.

While Naturalness is more familiar to us, and therefore often considered the priority, the other components are equally important. Hopefully, these ideas can guide your project to a successful end.

Results of the Questionnaire

Q1: Choose any items that match your use of the English club's room.

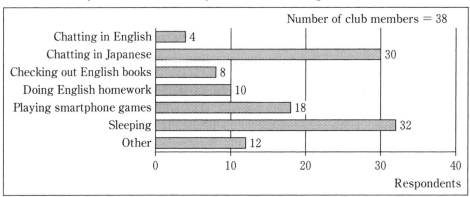

Q2: What do you think about the current English club's room?

Main comments:

Student 1 (S 1): I can't see the projector screen and whiteboard well on a sunny day. Also, there's no way to control the temperature.

S 2: By the windows, the sunlight makes it hard to read. The other side of the room doesn't get enough light. Also, the books are disorganized and the walls are covered with posters. It makes me feel uncomfortable.

S 3: The chairs don't really fit me and the desks are hard to move when we work in small groups. Also, lots of members speak Japanese, even though it's an English club.

S 4: The pictures of foreign countries on the walls make me want to speak English. Everyone likes the sofas — they are so comfortable that we often use the room for sleeping!

S 5: The room is so far away, so I hardly ever go there! Aren't there other rooms available?

S 6: There's so much gray in the room. I don't like it. But it's good that there are plenty of everyday English phrases on the walls!

Your discussion handout:

Room Improvement Project

■ SIN Framework
- What it is: [24]
- SIN = Stimulation, Individualization, Naturalness

■ Design Recommendations Based on SIN and Questionnaire Results
- Stimulation:

  Cover the floor with a colorful rug and [25].

- Individualization:

  Replace room furniture.

  (tables with wheels → easy to move around)

- Naturalness:

  [26]

  A. Install blinds on windows.

  B. Make temperature control possible.

  C. Move projector screen away from windows.

  D. Place sofas near walls.

  E. Put floor lamp in darker corner.

■ Other Issues to Discuss
- The majority of members [27] the room as [28]'s comment mentioned. How can we solve this?
- Based on both the graph and [29]'s comment, should we set a language rule in the room to motivate members to speak English more?
- S 5 doesn't like the location, but we can't change the room, so let's think about how to encourage members to visit more often.

問 1　Choose the best option for ⬚24⬚ .

① A guide to show which colors are appropriate to use in classrooms

② A method to prioritize the needs of students and teachers in classrooms

③ A model to follow when planning classroom environments

④ A system to understand how classrooms influence students' performance

問 2　Choose the best option for ⬚25⬚ .

① move the screen to a better place

② paint each wall a different color

③ put books on shelves

④ reduce displayed items

問 3　You are checking the handout. You notice an error in the recommendations under Naturalness. Which of the following should you **remove**? ⬚26⬚

① A

② B

③ C

④ D

⑤ E

問 4　Choose the best options for ┌ 27 ┐ and ┌ 28 ┐.

┌ 27 ┐

① borrow books from

② can't easily get to

③ don't use Japanese in

④ feel anxious in

⑤ take naps in

┌ 28 ┐

① S 1

② S 2

③ S 3

④ S 4

⑤ S 5

⑥ S 6

問 5　Choose the best option for ┌ 29 ┐.

① S 1

② S 2

③ S 3

④ S 4

⑤ S 5

⑥ S 6

You are in an English discussion group, and it is your turn to introduce a story. You have found a story in an English language magazine in Japan. You are preparing notes for your presentation.

Maki's Kitchen

"*Irasshai-mase*," said Maki as two customers entered her restaurant, Maki's Kitchen. Maki had joined her family business at the age of 19 when her father became ill. After he recovered, Maki decided to continue. Eventually, Maki's parents retired and she became the owner. Maki had many regular customers who came not only for the delicious food, but also to sit at the counter and talk to her. Although her business was doing very well, Maki occasionally daydreamed about doing something different.

"Can we sit at the counter?" she heard. It was her old friends, Takuya and Kasumi. A phone call a few weeks earlier from Kasumi to Takuya had given them the idea to visit Maki and surprise her.

Takuya's phone vibrated, and he saw a familiar name, Kasumi.

"Kasumi!"

"Hi Takuya, I saw you in the newspaper. Congratulations!"

"Thanks. Hey, you weren't at our 20th high school reunion last month."

"No, I couldn't make it. I can't believe it's been 20 years since we graduated. Actually, I was calling to ask if you've seen Maki recently."

Takuya's family had moved to Kawanaka Town shortly before he started high school. He joined the drama club, where he met Maki and Kasumi. The three became inseparable. After graduation, Takuya left Kawanaka to become an actor, while Maki and Kasumi remained. Maki had decided she wanted to study at university and enrolled in a preparatory school. Kasumi, on the other hand, started her career. Takuya tried out for various acting roles but was constantly rejected; eventually, he quit.

Exactly one year after graduation, Takuya returned to Kawanaka with his dreams destroyed. He called Maki, who offered her sympathy. He was surprised to learn that Maki had abandoned her plan to attend university because she had to manage her family's restaurant. Her first day of work had been the day he called. For some reason, Takuya could not resist giving Maki some advice.

"Maki, I've always thought your family's restaurant should change the coffee it serves. I think people in Kawanaka want a bolder flavor. I'd be happy to recommend a different brand," he said.

"Takuya, you really know your coffee. Hey, I was walking by Café Kawanaka and saw a help-wanted sign. You should apply!" Maki replied.

Takuya was hired by Café Kawanaka and became fascinated by the science of coffee making. On the one-year anniversary of his employment, Takuya was talking to Maki at her restaurant.

"Maki," he said, "do you know what my dream is?"

"It must have something to do with coffee."

"That's right! It's to have my own coffee business."

"I can't imagine a better person for it. What are you waiting for?"

Maki's encouragement inspired Takuya. He quit his job, purchased a coffee bean roaster, and began roasting beans. Maki had a sign in her restaurant saying, "We proudly serve Takuya's Coffee," and this publicity helped the coffee gain popularity in Kawanaka. Takuya started making good money selling his beans. Eventually, he opened his own café and became a successful business owner.

Kasumi was reading the newspaper when she saw the headline: *TAKUYA'S CAFÉ ATTRACTING TOURISTS TO KAWANAKA TOWN.* "Who would have thought that Takuya would be so successful?" Kasumi thought to herself as she reflected on her past.

In the high school drama club, Kasumi's duty was to put make-up on the actors. No one could do it better than her. Maki noticed this and saw that a cosmetics company called Beautella was advertising for salespeople. She encouraged Kasumi to apply, and, after graduation, she became an employee of Beautella.

The work was tough; Kasumi went door to door selling cosmetics. On bad days, she would call Maki, who would lift her spirits. One day, Maki had an idea, "Doesn't Beautella do make-up workshops? I think you are more suited for that. You can show people how to use the make-up. They'll love the way they look and buy lots of cosmetics!"

Kasumi's company agreed to let her do workshops, and they were a hit! Kasumi's sales were so good that eight months out of high school, she had been promoted, moving to the big city of Ishijima. Since then, she had steadily climbed her way up the company ladder until she had been named vice-president of Beautella this year.

"I wouldn't be vice-president now without Maki," she thought, "she helped me when I was struggling, but I was too absorbed with my work in Ishijima to give her support when she had to quit her preparatory school." Glancing back to the article, she decided to call Takuya.

"Maki wasn't at the reunion. I haven't seen her in ages," said Takuya.

"Same here. It's a pity. Where would we be without her?" asked Kasumi.

The conversation became silent, as they wordlessly communicated their guilt. Then, Kasumi had an idea.

The three friends were talking and laughing when Maki asked, "By the way, I'm really happy to see you two, but what brings you here?"

"Payback," said Takuya.

"Have I done something wrong?" asked Maki.

"No. The opposite. You understand people incredibly well. You can identify others' strengths and show them how to make use of them. We're proof of this. You made us aware of our gifts," said Takuya.

"The irony is that you couldn't do the same for yourself," added Kasumi.

"I think Ishijima University would be ideal for you. It offers a degree program in counseling that's designed for people with jobs," said Takuya.

"You'd have to go there a few times a month, but you could stay with me. Also, Takuya can help you find staff for your restaurant," said Kasumi.

Maki closed her eyes and imagined Kawanaka having both "Maki's Kitchen" and "Maki's Counseling." She liked that idea.

Your notes:

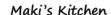

Maki's Kitchen

Story outline

Maki, Takuya, and Kasumi graduate from high school.

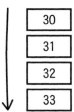
| 30 |
| 31 |
| 32 |
| 33 |

Maki begins to think about a second career.

About Maki

- Age: ☐ 34
- Occupation: restaurant owner
- How she supported her friends:

    Provided Takuya with encouragement and ☐ 35 ☐ .

    〃　　Kasumi　〃　　　　〃　　and ☐ 36 ☐ .

Interpretation of key moments

- Kasumi and Takuya experience an uncomfortable silence on the phone because they ☐ 37 ☐ .
- In the final scene, Kasumi uses the word "irony" with Maki. The irony is that Maki does not ☐ 38 ☐ .

問 1　Choose **four** out of the five events (①~⑤) and rearrange them in the order they happened. 　30　→　31　→　32　→　33

① Kasumi becomes vice-president of her company.

② Kasumi gets in touch with Takuya.

③ Maki gets her university degree.

④ Maki starts working in her family business.

⑤ Takuya is inspired to start his own business.

問 2　Choose the best option for 　34　.

① early 30s

② late 30s

③ early 40s

④ late 40s

問 3　Choose the best options for 　35　 and 　36　.

① made the product known to people

② proposed a successful business idea

③ purchased equipment for the business

④ suggested moving to a bigger city

⑤ taught the necessary skills for success

問 4　Choose the best option for 　37　 .

① 　do not want to discuss their success

② 　have not spoken in a long time

③ 　regret not appreciating their friend more

④ 　think Maki was envious of their achievements

問 5　Choose the best option for 　38　 .

① 　like to try different things

② 　recognize her own talent

③ 　understand the ability she lacks

④ 　want to pursue her dreams

第6問 (配点 24)

A Your English teacher has assigned this article to you. You need to prepare notes to give a short talk.

Perceptions of Time

When you hear the word "time," it is probably hours, minutes, and seconds that immediately come to mind. In the late 19th century, however, philosopher Henri Bergson described how people usually do not experience time as it is measured by clocks (**clock time**). Humans do not have a known biological mechanism to measure clock time, so they use mental processes instead. This is called **psychological time**, which everyone perceives differently.

If you were asked how long it had taken to finish your homework, you probably would not know exactly. You would think back and make an estimate. In a 1975 experiment, participants were shown either simple or complex shapes for a fixed amount of time and asked to memorize them. Afterwards, they were asked how long they had looked at the shapes. To answer, they used a mental process called **retrospective timing**, which is estimating time based on the information retrieved from memory. Participants who were shown the complex shapes felt the time was longer, while the people who saw the simple shapes experienced the opposite.

Another process to measure psychological time is called **prospective timing**. It is used when you are actively keeping track of time while doing something. Instead of using the amount of information recalled, the level of attention given to time while doing the activity is used. In several studies, the participants performed tasks while estimating the time needed to complete them. Time seemed shorter for the people doing more challenging mental activities which required them to place more focus on the task than on time.

Time felt longer for the participants who did simpler tasks and the longest for those who were waiting or doing nothing.

Your emotional state can influence your awareness of time, too. For example, you can be enjoying a concert so much that you forget about time. Afterwards, you are shocked that hours have passed by in what seemed to be the blink of an eye. To explain this, we often say, "Time flies when you're having fun." The opposite occurs when you are bored. Instead of being focused on an activity, you notice the time. It seems to go very slowly as you cannot wait for your boredom to end. Fear also affects our perception of time. In a 2006 study, more than 60 people experienced skydiving for the first time. Participants with high levels of unpleasant emotions perceived the time spent skydiving to be much longer than it was in reality.

Psychological time also seems to move differently during life stages. Children constantly encounter new information and have new experiences, which makes each day memorable and seem longer when recalled. Also, time creeps by for them as they anticipate upcoming events such as birthdays and trips. For most adults, unknown information is rarely encountered and new experiences become less frequent, so less mental focus is required and each day becomes less memorable. However, this is not always the case. Daily routines are shaken up when drastic changes occur, such as changing jobs or relocating to a new city. In such cases, the passage of time for those people is similar to that for children. But generally speaking, time seems to accelerate as we mature.

Knowledge of psychological time can be helpful in our daily lives, as it may help us deal with boredom. Because time passes slowly when we are not mentally focused and thinking about time, changing to a more engaging activity, such as reading a book, will help ease our boredom and speed up the time. The next occasion that you hear "Time flies when you're having fun," you will be reminded of this.

Your notes:

Perceptions of Time

Outline by paragraph

1. [39]

2. Retrospective timing

3. Prospective timing

4. [40]

> ➤ Skydiving

5. Effects of age

> ➤ Time speeds up as we mature, but a [41] .

6. Practical tips

My original examples to help the audience

A. Retrospective timing

Example: [42]

B. Prospective timing

Example: [43]

問 1　Choose the best options for [39] and [40] .

① Biological mechanisms

② Effects of our feelings

③ Kinds of memory

④ Life stages

⑤ Ongoing research

⑥ Types of time

問 2　Choose the best option for ┃ 41 ┃.

   ① major lifestyle change at any age will likely make time slow down

   ② major lifestyle change regardless of age will likely make time speed up

   ③ minor lifestyle change for adults will likely make time slow down

   ④ minor lifestyle change for children will likely make time speed up

問 3　Choose the best option for ┃ 42 ┃.

   ① anticipating a message from a classmate

   ② memorizing your mother's cellphone number

   ③ reflecting on how many hours you worked today

   ④ remembering that you have a meeting tomorrow

問 4　Choose the best option for ┃ 43 ┃.

   ① guessing how long you've been jogging so far

   ② making a schedule for the basketball team summer camp

   ③ running into your tennis coach at the railway station

   ④ thinking about your last family vacation to a hot spring

B You are preparing a presentation for your science club, using the following passage from a science website.

Chili Peppers: The Spice of Life

Tiny pieces of red spice in chili chicken add a nice touch of color, but biting into even a small piece can make a person's mouth burn as if it were on fire. While some people love this, others want to avoid the painful sensation. At the same time, though, they can eat sashimi with wasabi. This might lead one to wonder what spiciness actually is and to ask where the difference between chili and wasabi comes from.

Unlike sweetness, saltiness, and sourness, spiciness is not a taste. In fact, we do not actually taste heat, or spiciness, when we eat spicy foods. The bite we feel from eating chili peppers and wasabi is derived from different types of compounds. Chili peppers get their heat from a heavier, oil-like element called capsaicin. Capsaicin leaves a lingering, fire-like sensation in our mouths because it triggers a receptor called TRPV1. TRPV1 induces stress and tells us when something is burning our mouths. Interestingly, there is a wide range of heat across the different varieties of chili peppers, and the level depends on the amount of capsaicin they contain. This is measured using the Scoville Scale, which is also called Scoville Heat Units (SHU). SHUs range from the sweet and mild *shishito* pepper at 50-200 SHUs to the Carolina Reaper pepper, which can reach up to 2.2 million.

Wasabi is considered a root, not a pepper, and does not contain capsaicin. Thus, wasabi is not ranked on the Scoville Scale. However, people have compared the level of spice in it to chilis with around 1,000 SHUs, which is on the lower end of the scale. The reason some people cannot tolerate chili spice but can eat foods flavored with wasabi is that the spice compounds in it are low in density. The compounds in wasabi vaporize easily, delivering a blast of spiciness to our nose when we eat it.

Consuming chili peppers can have positive effects on our health, and much research has been conducted into the benefits of capsaicin. When capsaicin activates the TRPV1 receptor in a person's body, it is similar to what happens when they experience stress or pain from an injury. Strangely, capsaicin can also make pain go away. Scientists found that TRPV1 ceases to be turned on after long-term exposure to chili peppers, temporarily easing painful sensations. Thus, skin creams containing capsaicin might be useful for people who experience muscle aches.

Another benefit of eating chili peppers is that they accelerate the metabolism. A group of researchers analyzed 90 studies on capsaicin and body weight and found that people had a reduced appetite when they ate spicy foods. This is because spicy foods increase the heart rate, send more energy to the muscles, and convert fat into energy. Recently, scientists at the University of Wyoming have created a weight-loss drug with capsaicin as a main ingredient.

It is also believed that chili peppers are connected with food safety, which might lead to a healthier life. When food is left outside of a refrigerated environment, microorganisms multiply on it, which may cause sickness if eaten. Studies have shown that capsaicin and other chemicals found in chili peppers have antibacterial properties that can slow down or even stop microorganism growth. As a result, food lasts longer and there are fewer food-borne illnesses. This may explain why people in hot climates have a tendency to use more chili peppers, and therefore, be more tolerant of spicier foods due to repeated exposure. Also, in the past, before there were refrigerators, they were less likely to have food poisoning than people in cooler climates.

Chili peppers seem to have health benefits, but can they also be bad for our health? Peppers that are high on the Scoville Scale can cause physical discomfort when eaten in large quantities. People who have eaten several of the world's hottest chilis in a short time have reported experiencing upset stomachs, diarrhea, numb hands, and symptoms similar to a heart attack. Ghost peppers, which contain one million SHUs, can even burn a person's skin if they are touched.

Luckily the discomfort some people feel after eating spicy foods tends to go away soon—usually within a few hours. Despite some negative side effects, spicy foods remain popular around the world and add a flavorful touch to the table. Remember, it is safe to consume spicy foods, but you might want to be careful about the amount of peppers you put in your dishes.

Presentation slides:

Chili Peppers: The Spice of Life	Characteristics

Slide 1: **Chili Peppers:** **The Spice of Life**

Slide 2: **Characteristics**

chili peppers	wasabi
· oil-like elements	· 44
· triggering TRPV1	· changing to vapor
· persistent feeling	· spicy rush

Slide 3: **Positive Effects**

Capsaicin can...   45

   A．reduce pain.

   B．give you more energy.

   C．speed up your metabolism.

   D．make you feel less stress.

   E．decrease food poisoning.

Slide 4: **Negative Effects**

When eating too many strong chili peppers in a short time,

   · 46

   · 47

Slide 5: **Spice Tolerance**

48

Slide 6: **Closing Remark**

49

問 1 What is the first characteristic of wasabi on Slide 2? $\boxed{44}$

① burning taste

② fire-like sensation

③ lasting feeling

④ light compounds

問 2 Which is an **error** you found on Slide 3? $\boxed{45}$

① A

② B

③ C

④ D

⑤ E

問 3 Choose two options for Slide 4. (The order does not matter.)
$\boxed{46}$ · $\boxed{47}$

① you might activate harmful bacteria.

② you might experience stomach pain.

③ you might lose feeling in your hands.

④ your fingers might feel like they are on fire.

⑤ your nose might start hurting.

問 4 What can be inferred about tolerance for spices for Slide 5? [48]

① People with a high tolerance to chili peppers pay attention to the spices used in their food.

② People with a high tolerance to wasabi are scared of chili peppers' negative effects.

③ People with a low tolerance to chili peppers can get used to their heat.

④ People with a low tolerance to wasabi cannot endure high SHU levels.

問 5 Choose the most appropriate remark for Slide 6. [49]

① Don't be afraid. Eating spicy foods will boost your confidence.

② Next time you eat chili chicken, remember its punch only stays for a second.

③ Personality plays a big role in our spice preference, so don't worry.

④ Unfortunately, there are no cures for a low wasabi tolerance.

⑤ When someone offers you some spicy food, remember it has some benefits.

リスニング問題音声配信について

本書に掲載のリスニング問題の音声は，音声専用サイトにて配信しております。
サイトへは下記アドレスよりアクセスしてくだい。ユーザー名とパスワードの入力が必要です。

https://www.yozemi.ac.jp/yozemi/download/book2025shirohoneigo

■ユーザー名：lib7ET8p
■パスワード：8696Xs5K
■利用期間
  2024 年 7 月 10 日〜 2027 年 6 月 30 日（期限内でも配信は予告なく終了する場合がございます）

推奨 OS・ブラウザ (2024 年 6 月現在)

▶パソコン

Microsoft Edge ※／ Google Chrome ※／ Mozilla Firefox ※／ Apple Safari ※
※最新版

▶スマートフォン・タブレット

Android 4.4 以上／ iOS 9 以上

ご利用にあたって

※音声専用サイトの音声のご利用は、『2025 大学入学共通テスト実戦問題集英語』をご利用いただいているお客様に限らせていただきます。それ以外の方の、本サイトの音声のご利用はご遠慮くださいますようお願いいたします。

※音声は無料ですが、音声を聴くこと、ダウンロードには、別途通信料がかかる場合があります（お客様のご負担になります）。

※ファイルは MP3 形式です。音声はダウンロードすることも可能です。ダウンロードした音声の再生には MP3 を再生できる機器をご使用ください。また、ご使用の機器や音声再生ソフト、インターネット環境などに関するご質問につきましては、当社では対応いたしかねます。各製品のメーカーまでお尋ねください。

※本サイトの音声データは著作権法等で保護されています。音声データのご利用は、私的利用の場合に限られます。

※本データの全部もしくは一部を複製、または加工し、第三者に譲渡・販売することは法律で禁止されています。

※本サービスで提供されているコンテンツは、予告なしに変更・追加・中止されることがあります。

※お客様のネット環境および端末により、ご利用いただけない場合がございます。ご理解、ご了承いただきますようお願いいたします。

リスニング──第1回

時間　30分　　　　　100点　満点

1 ══ 解答にあたっては，実際に試験を受けるつもりで，時間を厳守し真剣に取りくむこと。

2 ══ 巻末にマークシートをつけてあるので，切り離しのうえ練習用として利用すること。

3 ══ 解答終了後には，自己採点により学力チェックを行い，別冊の解答・解説をじっくり
　　読んで，弱点補強，知識や考え方の整理などに努めること。

英　語　（リスニング）

(解答番号 | 1 | ～ | 37 |)

第1問　(配点　25)　音声は2回流れます。

第1問は **A** と **B** の二つの部分に分かれています。

A　第1問Aは問1から問4までの4問です。英語を聞き，それぞれの内容と最もよく合っているものを，四つの選択肢（①～④）のうちから一つずつ選びなさい。

問1　| 1 |

① Both Mike and the speaker like to go to the library.

② Mike was surprised to see the speaker in the library.

③ The speaker hadn't expected to meet Mike in the library.

④ The speaker is going to meet Mike in the library.

問2　| 2 |

① The speaker couldn't arrive at the destination on time.

② The speaker gave up walking and got to the destination by bus.

③ The speaker reached the destination on time though he had to walk.

④ The speaker was late because he got caught in a traffic jam.

問3 ☐ 3

① John doesn't really want to go to the gym.
② John has been busy working out at the gym.
③ John has decided to make time to go to the gym.
④ John won't have enough time to go to the gym.

問4 ☐ 4

① Alison's advice enabled the speaker to save 1,000 dollars.
② Owing to Alison's advice, the speaker wasted as much as 100 dollars.
③ Thanks to Alison's advice, the speaker was able to save 100 dollars.
④ The speaker wasted as much as 1,000 dollars despite Alison's advice.

これで第1問Aは終わりです。

B 第1問**B**は問5から問7までの3問です。英語を聞き，それぞれの内容と最もよく合っている絵を，四つの選択肢 (①～④) のうちから一つずつ選びなさい。

問5 　5

①

②

③

④

問6　　6

問7

①

②

③

④

これで第1問Bは終わりです。

第2問 （配点　16）　　音声は２回流れます。

　第２問は問８から問11までの４問です。それぞれの問いについて，対話の場面が日本語で書かれています。対話とそれについての問いを聞き，その答えとして最も適切なものを，四つの選択肢（①〜④）のうちから一つずつ選びなさい。

問８　妹が兄に話しかけています。　8

①

②

③

④

問9 母親と息子が話をしています。 9

①

②

③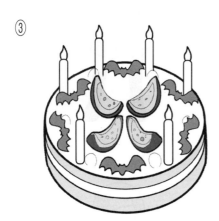

④

問10　父親と娘が話をしています。　10

①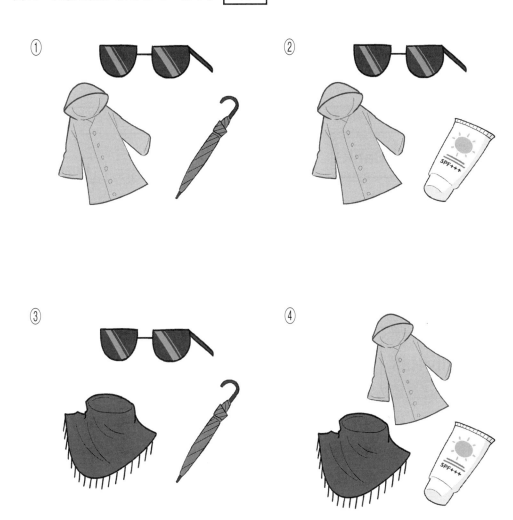

②

③

④

— 231 —

問11　男性のアルバイト先について話しています。　11

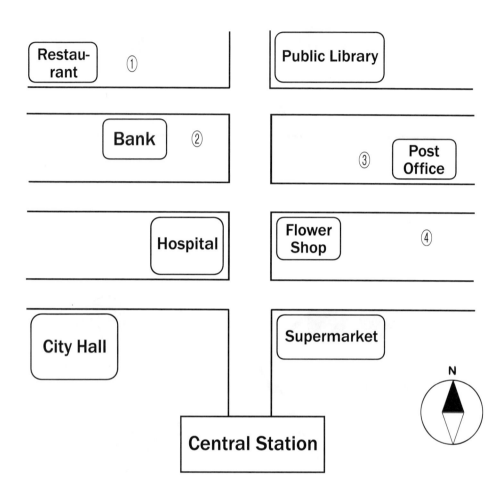

第3問 (配点 18)　　**音声は1回流れます。**

　第3問は問12から問17までの6問です。それぞれの問いについて，対話の場面が日本語で書かれています。対話を聞き，問いの答えとして最も適切なものを，四つの選択肢（①〜④）のうちから一つずつ選びなさい。（問いの英文は書かれています。）

問12　学校で，友人同士が話をしています。

What is the man likely to do right after the conversation?　12

① Borrow the book from the woman
② Give up reading the book
③ Lend the book to the woman
④ Start reading the book again

問13　男性が女性と話をしています。

When will the man and the woman meet?　13

① On Friday　　　　　② On Saturday
③ On Sunday　　　　　④ On Tuesday

問14　大学の教室で，学生同士が話をしています。

What is the woman likely to do?　14

① Attend the lecture on political science
② Go down the stairs to the first floor
③ Go to Room 115
④ Remain in Room 105

問15　空港で，男性が女性係員に話しかけています。

Why is the man upset?　15

① He won't make it to the meeting in London.
② His flight to London was canceled.
③ The starting time of the conference was changed.
④ The woman insisted that he take a later flight.

問16　母親が息子に話しかけています。

Which is true according to the conversation?　16

① The mother is angry that her son isn't studying hard.
② The mother will have the air conditioner fixed.
③ The son has been studying in his father's study.
④ The son thinks it is possible to concentrate in a hot room.

問17　Hiroaki と Cathy が大学での専攻科目について話をしています。

What will Cathy most likely major in at university?　17

① Chemistry
② Geology
③ Medicine
④ Physics

これで第３問は終わりです。

第4問 （配点 12）　**音声は１回流れます。**

第4問は **A** と **B** の二つの部分に分かれています。

A　　第４問**A**は問18から問25までの８問です。話を聞き，それぞれの問いの答えとして最も適切なものを，選択肢のうちから選びなさい。<u>問題文と図表を読む時間が与えられた後，音声が流れます。</u>

問18〜21　男性が，先日の出来事について話しています。話を聞き，その内容を表した四つのイラスト（①〜④）を，出来事が起きた順番に並べなさい。

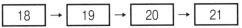

①

②

③

問22〜25　あなたは，友人の家で，スーパーマーケットで購入した食品を冷蔵庫に入れようとしています。友人の話を聞き，次の表の四つの空欄 22 〜 25 に入れるのに最も適切なものを，五つの選択肢 (①〜⑤) のうちから一つずつ選びなさい。選択肢は2回以上使ってもかまいません。

Food Item	Section of the Refrigerator
Grapefruit	22
Grape Juice	23
Lettuce	
Meat Sauce (frozen)	24
Milk	
Tuna (frozen)	25

①　Section 1
②　Section 2
③　Section 3
④　Section 4
⑤　Section 5

これで第4問Aは終わりです。

B　第4問 **B** は問26の1問です。話を聞き，示された条件に最も合うものを，四つの選択肢（①～④）のうちから一つ選びなさい。後の表を参考にしてメモを取ってもかまいません。状況と条件を読む時間が与えられた後，音声が流れます。

状況

　あなたは，学園祭で行われるワークショップの中から，参加するものを一つ決めるために，四人の学生の説明を聞いています。

あなたが考えている条件

　A．参加費が1,000円以下であること

　B．所要時間が1時間以内であること

　C．日本以外の国の文学作品について学べること

	Workshop	Condition A	Condition B	Condition C
①	Workshop No. 1			
②	Workshop No. 2			
③	Workshop No. 3			
④	Workshop No. 4			

問26　| 26 |　is the workshop you are most likely to choose.

①　Workshop No. 1

②　Workshop No. 2

③　Workshop No. 3

④　Workshop No. 4

これで第4問 **B** は終わりです。

第5問 （配点 15） 音声は1回流れます。

第5問は問27から問33までの7問です。

最初に講義を聞き，問27から問32に答えなさい。次に続きを聞き，問33に答えなさ
い。状況，ワークシート，問い及び図表を読む時間が与えられた後，音声が流れます。

状況

あなたはアメリカの大学で，廃棄食品についての講義を，ワークシートにメモ
を取りながら聞いています。

ワークシート

Wasted Food in the World

○**Amount of food production and wasted food**

  ・The Food and Agriculture Organization of the United Nations:

    About 4 billion tons of food are produced every year

      ⇒ About ┃ 27 ┃ is wasted

  ・The Obama administration and the United Nations:

    Promised to cut wasted food in ┃ 28 ┃ by 2030

  ★Wasted food is widespread both in developed and developing countries.

○**Major cause of wasted food**

  ・Developing countries: ┃ 29 ┃
  ・Developed countries: ┃ 30 ┃ ◀━ with the ┃ 31 ┃ emphasized

問27・28 ワークシートの空欄 27 ・ 28 に入れるのに最も適切なものを，四つの選択肢 (①〜④) のうちから一つずつ選びなさい。選択肢は2回以上使ってもかまいません。

① 1/5　　　② 1/4　　　③ 1/3　　　④ 1/2

問29〜31 ワークシートの空欄 29 〜 31 に入れるのに最も適切なものを，五つの選択肢 (①〜⑤) のうちから一つずつ選びなさい。

① consumers' behavior and customs

② freshness of food

③ inadequate facilities to store and distribute food

④ inefficient government intervention

⑤ visual appeal of food

問32 講義の内容と一致するものはどれか。最も適切なものを，四つの選択肢 (①〜④) のうちから一つ選びなさい。 32

① The problem of wasted food is difficult to solve because retail sectors are not interested in it.

② The problem of wasted food is more serious in developing countries than in developed countries.

③ The problem of wasted food occurs for various reasons, so different approaches will be needed.

④ The problem of wasted food will be solved due to the efforts of both grocery stores and supermarkets.

第5問はさらに続きます。

問33 講義の続きを聞き, 次の図から読み取れる情報と講義全体の内容からどのようなことが言えるか, 最も適切なものを, 四つの選択肢 (①〜④) のうちから一つ選びなさい。 33

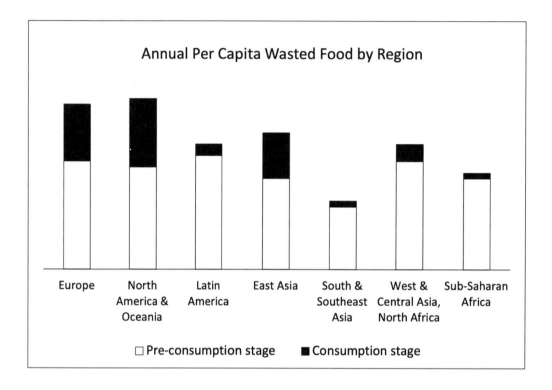

① Consumers in developed countries should raise their awareness of reduction in wasted food.

② Consumers in Latin America don't pay as much attention to wasted food as those in Europe.

③ In developing countries, wasted food at the pre-consumption stage is no longer a serious problem.

④ In sub-Saharan Africa, more than half of wasted food occurs at the consumption stage.

これで第5問は終わりです。

第6問 （配点 14）　音声は１回流れます。

第6問は **A** と **B** の二つの部分に分かれています。

A　　第6問**A**は問34・問35の２問です。二人の対話を聞き，それぞれの問いの答え
として最も適切なものを，四つの選択肢（①～④）のうちから一つずつ選びなさ
い。（問いの英文は書かれています。）状況と問いを読む時間が与えられた後，音
声が流れます。

状況

Tom が Kate と旅行について話をしています。

問34　**What is Tom's main point?**　　34

①　Interacting with local people is the most interesting part of a trip.

②　Online tours are becoming popular among young people.

③　There are many photos of famous tourist spots on the internet.

④　You can't enjoy a trip without using all of the five senses.

問35　**What does Kate think about online tours?**　　35

①　It's possible to have an enjoyable experience even on an online tour.

②　Online tours lack a sense of realism and still need to be improved.

③　Traditional tours will soon be completely replaced by online tours.

④　You should do careful research before participating in an online tour.

これで第6問**A**は終わりです。

B 　第6問 **B** は問36・問37の2問です。会話を聞き，それぞれの問いの答えとして最も適切なものを，選択肢のうちから一つずつ選びなさい。後の表を参考にしてメモを取ってもかまいません。<u>状況と問いを読む時間が与えられた後，音声が流れます。</u>

状況

　四人の学生（Yua, Sammy, Jane, Manabu）が，動物園のあり方について話をしています。

Yua	
Sammy	
Jane	
Manabu	

問36　四人のうち，動物園を<u>廃止すべきだと考えている</u>のは何人ですか。四つの選択肢（①～④）のうちから一つ選びなさい。　36

① 　1人

② 　2人

③ 　3人

④ 　4人

問37 会話を踏まえて，Jane の考えの根拠となる図表を，四つの選択肢（①〜④）の
うちから一つ選びなさい。 37

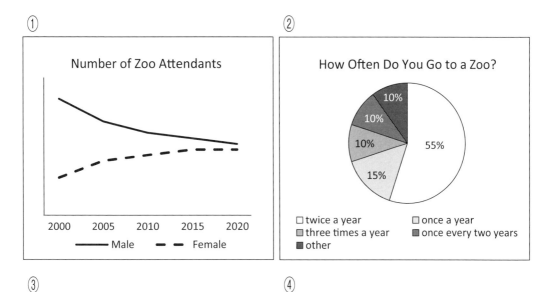

① Number of Zoo Attendants

2000 2005 2010 2015 2020
—— Male - - - Female

② How Often Do You Go to a Zoo?

10%
10%
10%
15%
55%

□ twice a year   □ once a year
□ three times a year   ■ once every two years
■ other

③ What Do you Expect from a Zoo?

1	Variety of animal species
2	Good breeding environment
3	Feeding Experience
4	Low admission fee

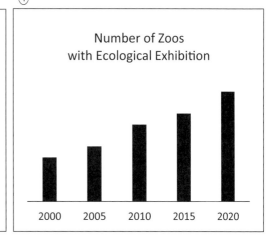

④ Number of Zoos
with Ecological Exhibition

2000 2005 2010 2015 2020

これで第6問Bは終わりです。

リスニング——第2回

時間　30分　　　　　100点　満点

1 ══ 解答にあたっては，実際に試験を受けるつもりで，時間を厳守し真剣に取りくむこと。

2 ══ 巻末にマークシートをつけてあるので，切り離しのうえ練習用として利用すること。

3 ══ 解答終了後には，自己採点により学力チェックを行い，別冊の解答・解説をじっくり
読んで，弱点補強，知識や考え方の整理などに努めること。

英　語　（リスニング）

（ 解答番号 1 ～ 37 ）

第１問　(配点　25)　**音声は２回流れます。**

第１問は **A** と **B** の二つの部分に分かれています。

A　第１問Aは問１から問４までの４問です。英語を聞き，それぞれの内容と最もよく合っているものを，四つの選択肢 (① ～ ④) のうちから一つずつ選びなさい。

問１　1

① The movie will be over at two o'clock.

② The movie will end at five o'clock.

③ The movie will last about three hours.

④ The movie will start at three thirty.

問２　2

① Julie decided to study math hard just before the exam.

② Julie failed the exam and decided to study math hard.

③ Julie studied math hard but she failed the exam.

④ Julie studied math harder before than she does now.

問3　　3

① The speaker behaves appropriately as Tom's boss.

② The speaker doesn't like the way his boss behaves.

③ Tom will be the speaker's boss in the near future.

④ Tom's way of speaking makes the speaker uncomfortable.

問4　　4

① The hotel's service was the worst the speaker had ever received.

② The hotel's service wasn't so good as the speaker had expected.

③ The speaker was greatly satisfied with the hotel's service.

④ The speaker wasn't satisfied with the hotel's service.

これで第1問Aは終わりです。

B 第1問**B**は問5から問7までの3問です。英語を聞き，それぞれの内容と最もよく合っている絵を，四つの選択肢 (①〜④) のうちから一つずつ選びなさい。

問5 [5]

①

②

③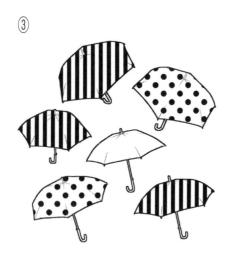

④

問6　　6

①

②

③

④

問7 ☐7☐

①

②

③

④

これで第1問Bは終わりです。

第2問 （配点 16）　音声は2回流れます。

　第2問は問8から問11までの4問です。それぞれの問いについて，対話の場面が日本語で書かれています。対話とそれについての問いを聞き，その答えとして最も適切なものを，四つの選択肢 (①〜④) のうちから一つずつ選びなさい。

問8　教室で友人同士が話をしています。　8

①

②

③

④

問9　家具店で夫婦が話をしています。 9

①

②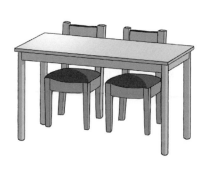

③

④

問10 女性と男性が写真を見ています。 10

①

②

③

④

問11　男性と女性が電話で話をしています。 11

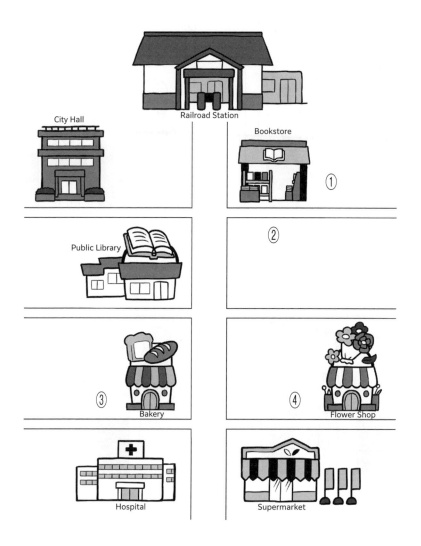

これで第2問は終わりです。

第3問 (配点 18)　音声は1回流れます。

第3問は問12から問17までの6問です。それぞれの問いについて，対話の場面が日本語で書かれています。対話を聞き，問いの答えとして最も適切なものを，四つの選択肢 (①〜④) のうちから一つずつ選びなさい。(問いの英文は書かれています。)

問12　オフィスで男性が女性と話をしています。

Which is true according to the conversation?　　12

① Both the man and the woman have a runny nose.
② Neither the man nor the woman is suffering from hay fever.
③ The man has caught a cold and can't stop coughing.
④ The woman thinks she has caught the flu.

問13　大学で友人同士が話をしています。

Which language has the man learned?　　13

① Danish　　　　　　② Finnish
③ German　　　　　　④ Norwegian

問14　男性と女性が電話で話をしています。

What is the woman likely to do?　　14

① Ask her friend to attend the party
② Attend the party by herself
③ Attend the party with her friend
④ Decide not to attend the party

問15 夫婦が明日の結婚記念日について話をしています。

What do the man and the woman decide to do? 15

① Go to "Miguel River" tomorrow

② Have dinner at the restaurant they often go to

③ Make a reservation at "Round Grill"

④ Stay at home tomorrow

問16 パソコンの前でカップルが話をしています。

Why was the man having a problem? 16

① He got the password mixed up.

② He mistyped his username.

③ He remembered Lucy's birthday incorrectly.

④ He wasn't able to reach the login screen.

問17 父親が娘に話しかけています。

What does the girl think about her new school? 17

① She finds it difficult to make new friends.

② She has no clubs she wants to join.

③ She is fed up with doing homework.

④ She wishes her homeroom teacher were a fun person.

これで第３問は終わりです。

第4問 （配点 12）　音声は１回流れます。

第４問は **A** と **B** の二つの部分に分かれています。

A　第４問**A**は問18から問25までの８問です。話を聞き，それぞれの問いの答えとして最も適切なものを，選択肢のうちから選びなさい。問題文と図表を読む時間が与えられた後，音声が流れます。

問18～21　あなたは，授業で配られたワークシートのグラフを完成させようとしています。説明を聞き，四つの空欄 　18　 ～ 　21　 に入れるのに最も適切なものを，四つの選択肢 （①～④） のうちから一つずつ選びなさい。

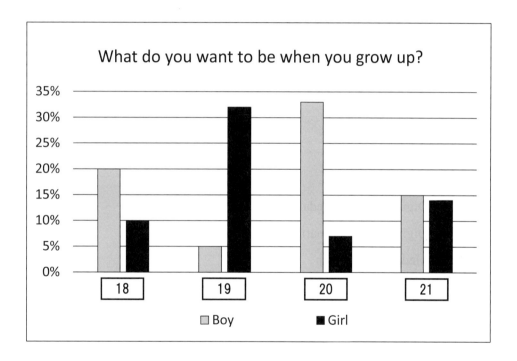

① Athlete

② Doctor

③ Police Officer

④ Teacher

問22〜25　あなたは，ロボットコンテストに参加しています。結果と賞品に関する主催者の話を聞き，次の表の四つの空欄 22 〜 25 に入れるのに最も適切なものを，六つの選択肢（①〜⑥）のうちから一つずつ選びなさい。選択肢は2回以上使ってもかまいません。

International Robot Competition: Summary of the Results

Participant	Score	Prize
Anne Thatcher	152.5	22
Michael Wong	124.7	23
Thomas Trump	89.9	24
Yua Maruyama	205.6	25

① Digital camera

② Medal

③ Smartwatch

④ Digital camera, Medal

⑤ Digital camera, Smartwatch

⑥ Medal, Smartwatch

これで第4問Aは終わりです。

B 第4問 **B** は問26の1問です。話を聞き，示された条件に最も合うものを，四つの選択肢（①〜④）のうちから一つ選びなさい。後の表を参考にしてメモを取ってもかまいません。状況と条件を読む時間が与えられた後，音声が流れます。

状況

あなたは，母親に贈る誕生日プレゼントを決めるために，友人や家族の意見を聞いています。

あなたが考えている条件

A．価格が50ドル以上100ドル以下であること

B．1週間以内に入手できること

C．オンラインで注文できること

Items	Condition A	Condition B	Condition C
① Accessory			
② Bouquet			
③ Hand Cream			
④ Assortment of Sweets			

問26 " **26** " is the item you are most likely to choose.

① Accessory

② Bouquet

③ Hand Cream

④ Assortment of Sweets

これで第4問**B**は終わりです。

第5問 (配点 15) 音声は1回流れます。

第5問は問27から問33までの7問です。

最初に講義を聞き，問27から問32に答えなさい。次に続きを聞き，問33に答えなさい。状況，ワークシート，問い及び図表を読む時間が与えられた後，音声が流れます。

状況

　あなたは大学で，日本のバイオームについての講義を，ワークシートにメモを取りながら聞いています。

ワークシート

Biomes in Japan

○**What is a Biome?**

　· the vegetation of an area

　· primarily depending on average yearly ⬚27⬚ and amounts of rainfall

○**Characteristics of Japan**

　· rainy and humid

　· long from north to south

　· significantly different in altitude

○**Vertical Distribution of Biomes**

Zone	Altitude	Main Tree
low	below 700m	⬚28⬚ & evergreen
mountain	700 - 1,500m	⬚29⬚ & summer-green
subalpine	1,500 - 2,500m	needle-leaved & ⬚30⬚
alpine	above 2,500m	⬚31⬚ & alpine meadow

問27　ワークシートの空欄 27 に入れるのに最も適切なものを，四つの選択肢
（①〜④）のうちから一つ選びなさい。

① carbon dioxide 　　② humidity

③ nutrients 　　④ temperature

問28〜31　ワークシートの空欄 28 〜 31 に入れるのに最も適切なものを，
六つの選択肢（①〜⑥）のうちから一つずつ選びなさい。選択肢は２回以上使っ
てもかまいません。

① broad-leaved 　　② evergreen 　　③ low tree

④ needle-leaved 　　⑤ summer-green 　　⑥ young tree

問32　講義の内容と一致するものはどれか。最も適切なものを，四つの選択肢（①〜④）
のうちから一つ選びなさい。 32

① A biome is the vegetation of an area and doesn't include animal groups.

② In general, the temperature drops by 6 degrees Celsius with each increase of
100 meters in altitude.

③ The "forest limit" means the upper limit of the "subalpine zone."

④ Though Japan is long from north to south, the horizontal distribution of
biomes is rarely found.

第５問はさらに続きます。

問33　グループの発表を聞き，次の図から読み取れる情報と講義全体の内容からどのようなことが言えるか，最も適切なものを，四つの選択肢（①〜④）のうちから一つ選びなさい。　33

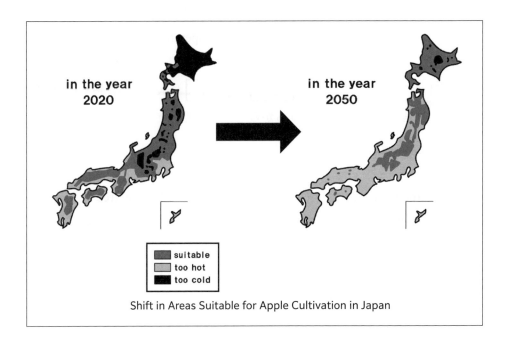

Shift in Areas Suitable for Apple Cultivation in Japan

① By the year 2050, there will be quite a few areas suitable for apple cultivation in Western Japan.

② Climatic differences have a significant impact both on vertical distribution and horizontal distribution of biomes.

③ Forest biomes in Eastern Japan may become more diverse because of global warming.

④ Global warming will lower the "forest limit" and make apple cultivation more difficult.

これで第5問は終わりです。

第6問 （配点 14）　音声は1回流れます。

第6問は **A** と **B** の二つの部分に分かれています。

 　　第6問**A**は問34・問35の2問です。二人の対話を聞き，それぞれの問いの答えとして最も適切なものを，四つの選択肢（①〜④）のうちから一つずつ選びなさい。（問いの英文は書かれています。）状況と問いを読む時間が与えられた後，音声が流れます。

状況

Sophia が Bailey とコーヒーについて話をしています。

問34　**What is Bailey's main point?**　　34

① Buying fairtrade products can help improve the situation of producers.

② Consumers should change their tendency to seek expensive products.

③ Developing countries depend on coffee bean production for much of their income.

④ Fairtrade coffee is becoming popular because of its excellent flavor and aroma.

問35　**What does Sophia think about fairtrade products?**　　35

① Fairtrade products are of poor quality despite their high prices.

② Fairtrade products can lower the living standards in developing countries.

③ Some people avoid buying fairtrade products due to their high prices.

④ The certification process of a fairtrade product is too complex.

これで第6問**A**は終わりです。

B　第6問**B**は問36・問37の2問です。会話を聞き，それぞれの問いの答えとして最も適切なものを，選択肢のうちから一つずつ選びなさい。後の表を参考にしてメモを取ってもかまいません。状況と問いを読む時間が与えられた後，音声が流れます。

状況

　四人の学生（Mike, Nobuko, Boris, Kate）が，昆虫食について話し合っています。

Mike	
Nobuko	
Boris	
Kate	

問36　会話が終わった時点で，昆虫食を肯定している人を，四つの選択肢（①～④）のうちから一つ選びなさい。　[36]

①　Nobuko

②　Kate, Nobuko

③　Mike, Nobuko

④　Boris, Mike, Nobuko

問37 会話を踏まえて，Nobuko の発言の根拠となる図表を，四つの選択肢（①〜④）のうちから一つ選びなさい。 37

①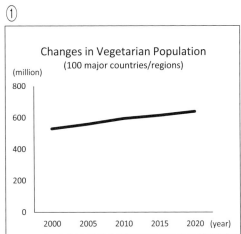

②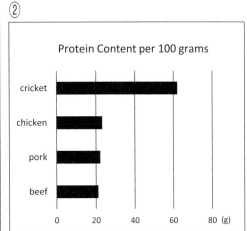

③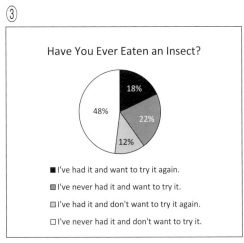

④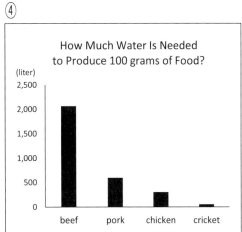

これで第6問Bは終わりです。

リスニング――――第3回

時間　30分　　　　　100点　満点

1 ――解答にあたっては，実際に試験を受けるつもりで，時間を厳守し真剣に取りくむこと。

2 ――巻末にマークシートをつけてあるので，切り離しのうえ練習用として利用すること。

3 ――解答終了後には，自己採点により学力チェックを行い，別冊の解答・解説をじっくり読んで，弱点補強，知識や考え方の整理などに努めること。

英　語　（リスニング）

（解答番号　1　〜　37　）

第１問　(配点　25)　音声は２回流れます。

第１問は **A** と **B** の二つの部分に分かれています。

A　　第１問Aは問１から問４までの４問です。英語を聞き，それぞれの内容と最もよく合っているものを，四つの選択肢(①〜④)のうちから一つずつ選びなさい。

問1　　1

① Mike is shorter than Kevin and the speaker.

② Mike is taller than Kevin and the speaker.

③ The speaker is shorter than Mike and Kevin.

④ The speaker is taller than Mike and Kevin.

問2　　2

① The speaker didn't expect to pass the math exam.

② The speaker didn't make any effort to pass the exams.

③ The speaker succeeded in all the exams except math.

④ The speaker was able to pass the math exam.

問3　3

　　① The speaker forgot to close the window.

　　② The speaker is asking Jennie to open the window.

　　③ The speaker wants to let in cool air.

　　④ The speaker will turn on the air conditioner.

問4　4

　　① Meg has her birthday on October 19th.

　　② Meg's birthday is October 5th.

　　③ The speaker has her birthday on October 12th.

　　④ The speaker's birthday is October 19th.

これで第1問Aは終わりです。

第1問**B**は問5から問7までの3問です。英語を聞き，それぞれの内容と最もよく合っている絵を，四つの選択肢(①〜④)のうちから一つずつ選びなさい。

問5 5

①

②

③

④

問6 　6

①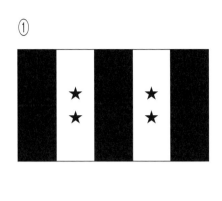

②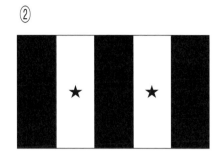

③

④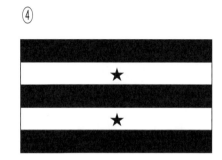

これで第1問Bは終わりです。

第2問 （配点 16） 音声は２回流れます。

　　第２問は問８から問11までの４問です。それぞれの問いについて，対話の場面が日本語で書かれています。対話とそれについての問いを聞き，その答えとして最も適切なものを，四つの選択肢（①〜④）のうちから一つずつ選びなさい。

問8　自動販売機の前で，父親と娘が話をしています。　8

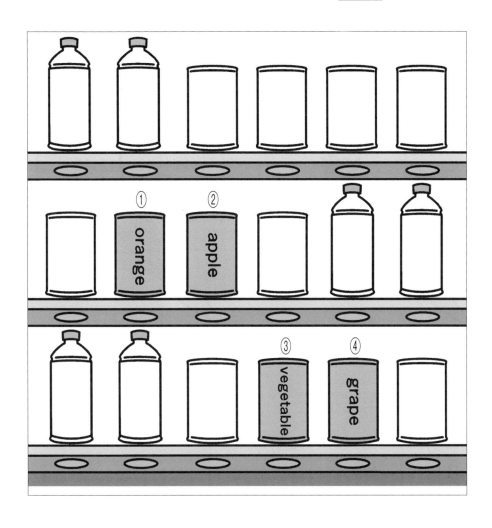

問9 レストランで，女性店員と男性客が話をしています。 9

①

②

③

④

問10　友人同士が話をしています。 10

①

②

③

④

問11　路線図を見ながら，男性と女性が話をしています。　11

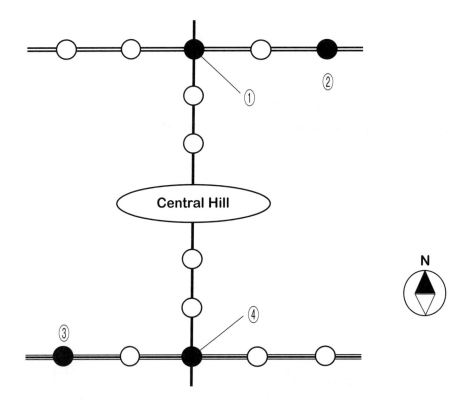

これで第2問は終わりです。

第3問 (配点 18) 音声は1回流れます。

　第3問は問12から問17までの6問です。それぞれの問いについて，対話の場面が日本語で書かれています。対話を聞き，問いの答えとして最も適切なものを，四つの選択肢(①～④)のうちから一つずつ選びなさい。(問いの英文は書かれています。)

問12　同僚同士が，休暇明けに話をしています。

Which is true according to the conversation?　12

① 　The woman doesn't have a younger sister.
② 　The woman has an older brother.
③ 　The woman's father likes to take pictures.
④ 　The woman's mother is away on a business trip.

問13　娘と父親が，夕食について話し合っています。

What will the girl do?　13

① 　Bake an apple pie
② 　Buy some apples
③ 　Grill the meat
④ 　Make a salad

問14　男性と女性が，レストランで話をしています。

What will they do?　14

① 　The man will pay $50 and the woman will pay $5.
② 　The man will pay $30 and the woman will pay $25.
③ 　The man will pay $25 and the woman will pay $30.
④ 　The man will pay $5 and the woman will pay $50.

問15　男性と女性が，待ち合わせ場所で話をしています。

What is true about the man and the woman? | 15 |

① The man took a bus instead of a train.

② The woman had to wait for thirty minutes.

③ They promised to meet in front of the stadium.

④ They will go to the live concert together.

問16　夫婦が，自宅で話をしています。

What will the man do right after the conversation? | 16 |

① Attend the online meeting at home

② Drive the woman to the dentist

③ Make an appointment at the dentist

④ Pass the time in a café with the woman

問17　高校生同士が，昼休みに話をしています。

What is the girl going to do? | 17 |

① Buy some sandwiches

② Eat nothing for lunch

③ Get a banana from the boy

④ Go to the cafeteria

これで第3問は終わりです。

第4問 （配点 12） 音声は1回流れます。

第4問は **A** と **B** の二つの部分に分かれています。

A　第4問**A**は問18から問25までの8問です。話を聞き，それぞれの問いの答えとして最も適切なものを，選択肢のうちから選びなさい。問題文と図表を読む時間が与えられた後，音声が流れます。

問18〜21　あなたは，大学の授業で配られたワークシートのグラフを完成させようとしています。先生の説明を聞き，四つの空欄 　18　 〜 　21　 に入れるのに最も適切なものを，四つの選択肢（①〜④）のうちから一つずつ選びなさい。

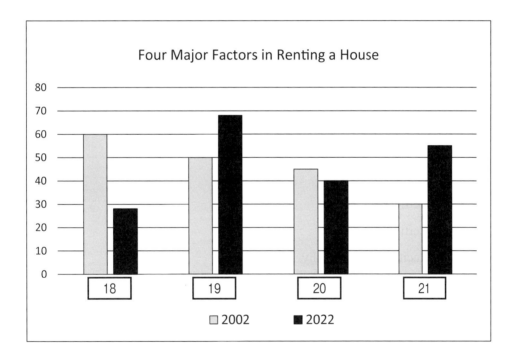

① Distance to railroad station

② Distance to supermarket

③ Floor plan

④ Rent

問22〜25 あなたはピアノのコンクールに参加しています。結果と賞品に関する主催者の話を聞き，次の表の四つの空欄 22 〜 25 に入れるのに最も適切なものを，六つの選択肢(①〜⑥)のうちから一つずつ選びなさい。選択肢は2回以上使ってもかまいません。

Hamaya International Piano Competition: Finalists' Results

Finalist	Expression Score	Technical Score	Final Rank	Prize
Karsten Walter	87	97	3rd	22
Michael Rivas	95	93	1st	23
Nobuko Davis	89	94	4th	24
Yui Narusawa	91	96	2nd	25

① Certificate
② Medal
③ Recital Ticket
④ Certificate, Medal
⑤ Certificate, Trophy
⑥ Recital Ticket, Trophy

これで第4問Aは終わりです。

第4問**B**は問26の1問です。話を聞き，示された条件に最も合うものを，四つの選択肢（①〜④）のうちから一つ選びなさい。後の表を参考にしてメモを取ってもかまいません。<u>状況と条件を読む時間が与えられた後，音声が流れます。</u>

状況

あなたは，夏休みの旅行先を一つ決めるために，四人の友人の説明を聞いています。

あなたが考えている条件

A. 公共交通機関でアクセスしやすいこと

B. 歴史的な遺産が近辺にあること

C. 自然が豊かであること

Destinations	Condition A	Condition B	Condition C
① Coneberry			
② Endoll			
③ Goodland			
④ Rosehill			

問26 | 26 | is the destination you are most likely to choose.

① Coneberry

② Endoll

③ Goodland

④ Rosehill

これで第4問**B**は終わりです。

第5問 （配点 15） 音声は1回流れます。

第5問は問27から問33までの7問です。

最初に講義を聞き，問27から問32に答えなさい。次に続きを聞き，問33に答えなさい。状況，ワークシート，問い及び図表を読む時間が与えられた後，音声が流れます。

状況

あなたはアメリカの大学で，単身世帯の動向に関する講義を，ワークシートにメモを取りながら聞いています。

ワークシート

Trend of One-Person Households

◇ **Global Trend**

· More and more people live alone.

· [27] has the lower rate of one-person households

than other Western countries.

· One-person household rates are also increasing

in China, India and Brazil.

◇ **Background of the Trend**

· [28] is playing a bigger role than [29].

· Living alone is no longer associated with [30].

· We are able to have [31] more freely than ever.

問27　ワークシートの空欄 　27　 に入れるのに最も適切なものを，五つの選択肢
（①〜⑤）のうちから一つ選びなさい。

① France　　　　　　　　　　② Germany

③ Sweden　　　　　　　　　④ The United Kingdom

⑤ The United States

問28〜31　ワークシートの空欄 　28　 〜 　31　 に入れるのに最も適切なものを，
六つの選択肢（①〜⑥）のうちから一つずつ選びなさい。文頭に来る語も小文字で
示してある。

① communication　　② culture　　　　③ economy

④ individualism　　　⑤ isolation　　　⑥ self-reliance

問32　講義の内容と一致するものはどれか。最も適切なものを，四つの選択肢
（①〜④）のうちから一つ選びなさい。 　32　

① As the number of single-person households increases, human nature as a
group-oriented animal is changing.

② Living alone is less lonely than it once was, but it still means less social
contact with other people.

③ Thanks to globalization and technology, it is possible for us to live alone and
have more social contact.

④ The increase in the number of single-person households is a phenomenon
observed mainly in Western countries.

第５問はさらに続きます。

問33　グループの発表を聞き，次の図から読み取れる情報と講義全体の内容からどのようなことが言えるか，最も適切なものを，四つの選択肢（①〜④）のうちから一つ選びなさい。　33

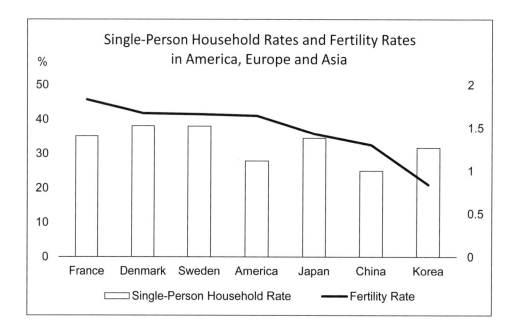

① Countries with a low percentage of single-person households generally do not face declining fertility problems.

② In general, the higher the percentage of single-person households is, the lower the fertility rate is.

③ It seems that there is no correlation between the rate of single-person households and the fertility rate.

④ The increase in the percentage of single-person households is considered to be a consequence of the declining birthrate.

これで第5問は終わりです。

第6問 （配点 14） 音声は１回流れます。

第6問は **A** と **B** の二つの部分に分かれています。

A　第6問Aは問34・問35の２問です。二人の対話を聞き，それぞれの問いの答えとして最も適切なものを，四つの選択肢(①〜④)のうちから一つずつ選びなさい。(問いの英文は書かれています。) <u>状況と問いを読む時間が与えられた後，音声が流れます。</u>

状況

Matthew が Akina とマスクの使用について話をしています。

問34　**What is Matthew's main point?**　| 34 |

① The increase of CO_2 in the air makes it easier for bacteria to grow.

② There are some disadvantages to wearing a mask continuously.

③ We must be careful not to breathe through our mouth.

④ Wearing a mask is effective in preventing headaches.

問35　**Which statement would Akina agree with the most?**　| 35 |

① Aging increases the risk of blood vessel expansion in the brain.

② Headaches are more serious than stiff necks and earaches.

③ The effectiveness of masks in preventing infection can't be ignored.

④ Wearing a mask every day will improve our health in the long run.

これで第6問Aは終わりです。

B 　第6問**B**は問36・問37の2問です。会話を聞き，それぞれの問いの答えとして最も適切なものを，選択肢のうちから一つずつ選びなさい。後の表を参考にしてメモを取ってもかまいません。<u>状況と問いを読む時間が与えられた後，音声が流れます</u>。

状況

　日本に住んでいる四人の学生（Miki, Steve, Irene, Viktor）が話をしています。

Miki	
Steve	
Irene	
Viktor	

問36　出身国の自宅において<u>太陽光発電を導入する可能性が低い人の組み合わせ</u>を，四つの選択肢（①〜④）のうちから一つ選びなさい。　 36

① 　Miki, Irene

② 　Miki, Viktor

③ 　Steve, Irene

④ 　Steve, Viktor

問37　会話を踏まえて，Viktor の考えの根拠となる図表を，四つの選択肢(①〜④)のうちから一つ選びなさい。　37

①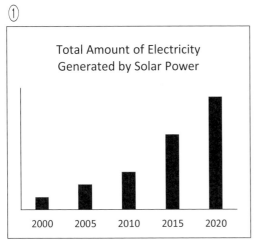

②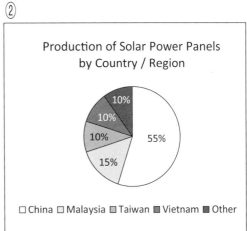

③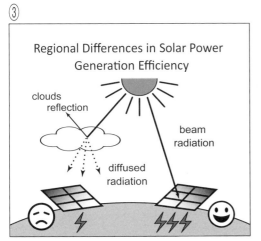

④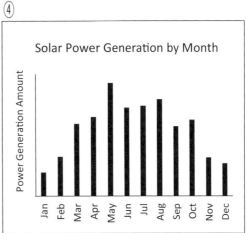

これで第6問Bは終わりです。

リスニング──第4回

時間 30分　　　　　100点 満点

1 ══ 解答にあたっては，実際に試験を受けるつもりで，時間を厳守し真剣に取りくむこと。

2 ══ 巻末にマークシートをつけてあるので，切り離しのうえ練習用として利用すること。

3 ══ 解答終了後には，自己採点により学力チェックを行い，別冊の解答・解説をじっくり
　　読んで，弱点補強，知識や考え方の整理などに努めること。

英　語（リスニング）

（解答番号 [1] ～ [37]）

第1問 （配点 25） <u>音声は2回流れます。</u>

第1問は**A**と**B**の二つの部分に分かれています。

A　　第1問**A**は**問1**から**問4**までの4問です。英語を聞き，それぞれの内容と最もよく合っているものを，四つの選択肢（①～④）のうちから一つずつ選びなさい。

問1 [1]

① The speaker can't decide which dessert to have.

② The speaker is full and will not want dessert.

③ The speaker might have dessert after dinner.

④ The speaker will choose his dessert later.

問2 [2]

① The speaker will be absent from soccer practice on Friday.

② The speaker will go to soccer practice late on Friday.

③ The speaker will have soccer practice on Saturday.

④ The speaker will watch a soccer game on Saturday.

問3 　3

① The speaker came to London before classes began.

② The speaker left London to study abroad last week.

③ The speaker went to London for a holiday last week.

④ The speaker will start classes in London this week.

問4 　4

① Bill and Ted couldn't get on the crowded train.

② Bill and Ted let others be seated on the train.

③ Bill gave his seat on the train to Ted.

④ Ted got a seat on the train, but Bill didn't.

これで第1問Aは終わりです。

B　第1問Bは問5から問7までの3問です。英語を聞き，それぞれの内容と最もよく合っている絵を，四つの選択肢(①〜④)のうちから一つずつ選びなさい。

問5　　5

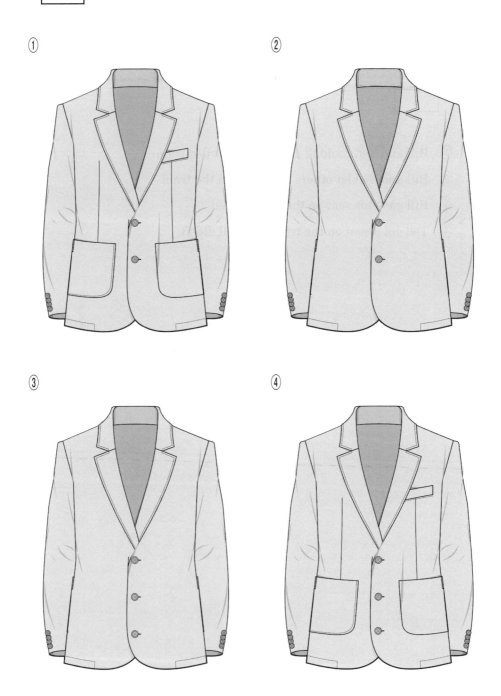

問6 6

①

②

③

④

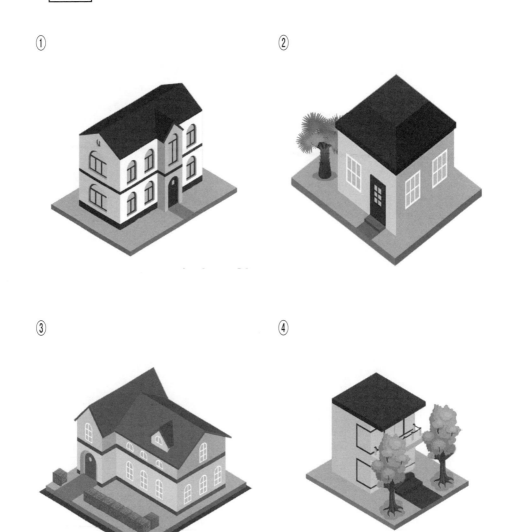

①   ②

③   ④

これで第1問Bは終わりです。

第2問 （配点 16） 音声は2回流れます。

第2問は**問8**から**問11**までの4問です。それぞれの問いについて，対話の場面が日本語で書かれています。対話とそれについての問いを聞き，その答えとして最も適切なものを，四つの選択肢（①～④）のうちから一つずつ選びなさい。

問8 父親が，友人の家に書道の練習をしに行く娘と話をしています。 8

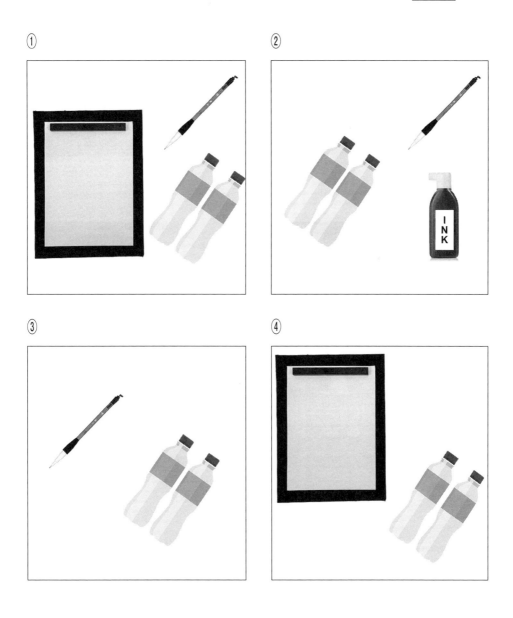

問9　駅で待ち合わせをしている友人と電話で話しています。　9

①

②

③

④

問10　息子が，母親と美術館のホームページを見ています。 ⬚10⬚

①

②

③

④

問11　デパートで買い物をしている女性が，店員に質問をしています。 ⎡11⎤

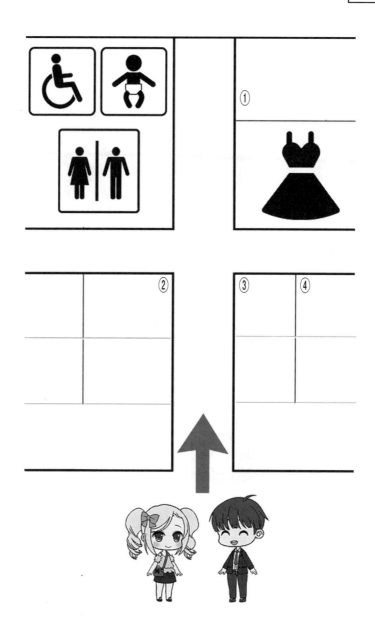

これで第2問は終わりです。

第3問 （配点 18） 音声は1回流れます。

第3問は問12から問17までの6問です。それぞれの問いについて，対話の場面が日本語で書かれています。対話を聞き，問いの答えとして最も適切なものを，四つの選択肢（①～④）のうちから一つずつ選びなさい。（問いの英文は書かれています。）

問12 友人同士が，互いの予定について話しています。

When will the two friends have a meal together? 　12

① Dinner on Friday

② Dinner on Sunday

③ Lunch on Friday

④ Lunch on Sunday

問13 男性が，インターネットでコンサートのチケットを買おうとしています。

What is the man having trouble with? 　13

① He cannot enter his information.

② He cannot use his credit card anymore.

③ The tickets cannot be bought until December.

④ The tickets were all sold out in November.

問14 女性が，友人と今週末の予定について話しています。

What is the woman likely to do? 　14

① She will go on the whole camping trip.

② She will join her friends after the rain stops.

③ She will only go on the first day of the trip.

④ She will stay home and won't join the trip.

問15　学校で，生徒同士が話をしています。

What is the boy's problem?　15

① He didn't sleep the night before the test.

② He expected the math test to be easier.

③ He feels he wasted time by studying so much.

④ He thinks he got a bad score on the test.

問16　兄妹が，両親に贈るプレゼントについて話しています。

What will the brother and sister buy for their parents?　16

① A movie ticket and a new wallet

② A new purse and a new wallet

③ One new wallet for each of them

④ Two tickets to a new movie

問17　男性が，ホテルのマネジャーと話しています。

What did the man dislike about his hotel room?　17

① A smoking place was not provided.

② A working space was not provided.

③ The bathroom was dirty.

④ The bed was uncomfortable.

これで第３問は終わりです。

第4問 （配点 12） 音声は1回流れます。

第4問はAとBの二つの部分に分かれています。

A 第4問Aは問18から問25までの8問です。話を聞き，それぞれの問いの答えとして最も適切なものを，選択肢から選びなさい。**問題文と図表を読む時間が与えられた後，音声が流れます。**

問18～21 友人が，ある日の出来事について話しています。話を聞き，その内容を表した四つのイラスト（①～④）を，出来事が起きた順番に並べなさい。

①

②

③

④

― 301 ―

問22～25　あなたは，留学先の高校で生徒の睡眠時間に関するアンケート結果の発表を聞いています。話を聞き，次の表の四つの空欄 22 ～ 25 に入れるのに最も適切なものを，五つの選択肢(①～⑤)のうちから一つずつ選びなさい。選択肢は2回以上使ってもかまいません。

Sleeping Habits Survey Results

Grade	Gender	Hours of Sleep per Day
Senior 1	Girls	22
Senior 1	Boys	23
Senior 2	Girls	Around 8 hours
Senior 2	Boys	24
Senior 3	Girls	25
Senior 3	Boys	Less than 5 hours

① 5 hours or less

② 6 hours

③ 7 hours

④ 8 hours

⑤ 9 hours or more

これで第4問Aは終わりです。

B 　第4問Bは問26の1問です。話を聞き，示された条件に最も合うものを，四つの選択肢（①～④）のうちから一つ選びなさい。後の表を参考にしてメモを取ってもかまいません。**状況と条件を読む時間が与えられた後，音声が流れます。**

状況

　あなたは，冬休みの間の旅行先を決めるために，四人の友人にお薦めの場所を聞いています。

あなたが考えている条件

　A. 昼間の天気が暖かいこと

　B. おいしい食事を楽しめること

　C. 混雑していない静かな所があること

	Locations	Condition A	Condition B	Condition C
①	Anaheim			
②	Kakslauttanen			
③	Manila			
④	Sydney			

問26　| 26 | is the location you are most likely to choose.

① Anaheim

② Kakslauttanen

③ Manila

④ Sydney

これで第4問Bは終わりです。

第５問 （配点 15） **音声は１回流れます。**

第５問は問27から問33までの７問です。

最初に講義を聞き，問27から問32に答えなさい。次に続きを聞き，問33に答えなさい。**状況，ワークシート，問い及び図表を読む時間が与えられた後，音声が流れます。**

状況

あなたはアメリカの大学で，テレワークについての講義を，ワークシートにメモを取りながら聞いています。

ワークシート

Remote and Hybrid Work Models

○ **Remote Work Models**
   ● Meaning: models where employees work entirely at home

○ **Hybrid Work Models**
   ● Meaning: models where employees [27]

○ **Advantages and Disadvantages**

	Advantages	Disadvantages
Employees	● more flexibility ● [28]	● [29] ● less access to resources
Management	● more productive workers ● [30]	● harder to watch workers ● more difficult to give [31]

問27 ワークシートの空欄 27 に入れるのに最も適切なものを，四つの選択肢(①〜④)のうちから一つ選びなさい。

① do an even amount of work at home and the office

② do more of their work at the office than remotely

③ perform a mixture of remote and in-person work

④ rarely visit the office to do their work face-to-face

問28〜31 ワークシートの空欄 28 〜 31 に入れるのに最も適切なものを，六つの選択肢(①〜⑥)のうちから一つずつ選びなさい。選択肢は2回以上使ってもかまいません。

① better efficiency   ② decreased teamwork   ③ job tasks

④ less stress   ⑤ more burnout   ⑥ recognition

問32 講義の内容と一致するものはどれか。最も適切なものを，四つの選択肢(①〜④)のうちから一つ選びなさい。 32

① Hybrid and remote work models will become more popular than in-person work in every country.

② Over time, more companies will move from hybrid to remote work models.

③ Remote work models usually benefit workers, while hybrid work models benefit companies.

④ The COVID-19 pandemic led to a delay in companies adopting hybrid work models.

第5問はさらに続きます。

問33　講義の続きを聞き，<u>次の図から読み取れる情報と講義全体の内容から</u>どのようなことが言えるか，最も適切なものを，四つの選択肢（①～④）のうちから一つ選びなさい。 33

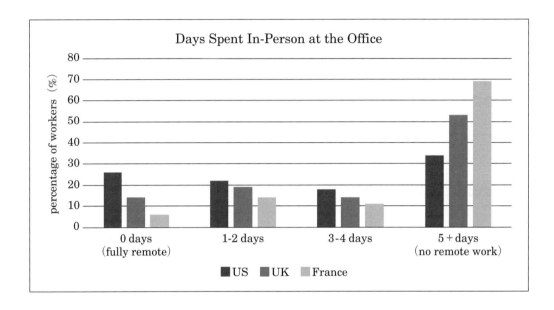

① A majority of workers work remotely at least one day per week in all three countries.

② The percentage of workers who only do remote work is the highest in the UK.

③ There are more US workers who do at least some remote work than those who don't.

④ Workers in all three countries work remotely more than they work in person.

これで第5問は終わりです。

第6問 (配点 14) 音声は1回流れます。

第6問は**A**と**B**の二つの部分に分かれています。

A 　第6問**A**は問34・問35の2問です。二人の対話を聞き，それぞれの問いの答えとして最も適切なものを，四つの選択肢(①〜④)のうちから一つずつ選びなさい。(問いの英文は書かれています。)**状況と問いを読む時間が与えられた後，音声が流れます。**

状況

　Jamie が Taiga と美術館で絵画について話をしています。

問34　**What is Taiga's main point?** 　34

① 　Art should be easy to understand.

② 　Darker paintings are more attractive.

③ 　Skillful artists are very rare.

④ 　The best art is always drawn neatly.

問35　**What does Jamie think about art?** 　35

① 　Artists shouldn't let their feelings affect their art.

② 　Color is the most important aspect of a painting.

③ 　It's fun to think about an artist's message.

④ 　Paintings with a clear meaning are boring.

これで第6問**A**は終わりです。

B 　第6問Bは問36・問37の2問です。会話を聞き，それぞれの問いの答えとして最も適切なものを，選択肢のうちから一つずつ選びなさい。下の表を参考にしてメモを取ってもかまいません。**状況と問いを読む時間が与えられた後，音声が流れます。**

状況

　四人の学生(Yuna, Sarah, Larry, Austin)が，店で電子マネーについて話をしています。

Yuna	
Sarah	
Larry	
Austin	

問36　四人のうち現在電子マネーを<u>利用している</u>のは何人ですか。四つの選択肢
(①～④)のうちから一つ選びなさい。　36

① 　1人

② 　2人

③ 　3人

④ 　4人

問37　会話を踏まえて，Larryの考えの根拠となる図表を，四つの選択肢(①～④)のうちから一つ選びなさい。　37

①

Wallets Stolen（Thousands）

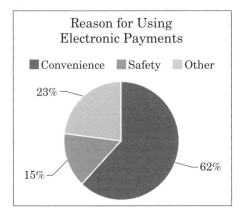

②

Most Popular Electronic Payment Systems	
1	PayBuddy
2	BuyBuy
3	Pineapple Pay

③

Reason for Using Electronic Payments

■Convenience　■Safety　□Other

23%
15%
62%

④

Stores Accepting Electronic Payments（%）

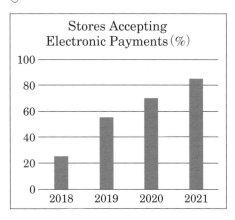

これで第6問Bは終わりです。

リスニング————第5回

時間　30分　　　　　100点　満点

1 —— 解答にあたっては，実際に試験を受けるつもりで，時間を厳守し真剣に取りくむこと。

2 —— 巻末にマークシートをつけてあるので，切り離しのうえ練習用として利用すること。

3 —— 解答終了後には，自己採点により学力チェックを行い，別冊の解答・解説をじっくり
読んで，弱点補強，知識や考え方の整理などに努めること。

英　語　（リスニング）

（ 解答番号 [1] ～ [37] ）

第1問　（配点　25）　**音声は2回流れます。**

第1問は **A** と **B** の二つの部分に分かれています。

A　　第1問Aは問1から問4までの4問です。英語を聞き，それぞれの内容と最もよく合っているものを，四つの選択肢（①～④）のうちから一つずつ選びなさい。

問1　[1]

① The speaker is asking Emily to write a letter.

② The speaker is asking Emily to read a letter in a bright room.

③ The speaker is going to take Emily to a dark room.

④ The speaker is going to turn right to go to the post office.

問2　[2]

① The speaker asked her mother to keep a pet.

② The speaker felt like her dog was a member of her family.

③ The speaker brought the dog up instead of her mother.

④ The speaker looks like her father, and her sister resembles her mother.

問3 　3

① The speaker has been talking with Tom on the phone for many hours.

② The speaker is asking Tom to answer the phone immediately.

③ The speaker has to make a phone call to her husband.

④ The speaker will pick up the phone instead of Tom.

問4 　4

① The speaker is asking someone where she is.

② The speaker is checking the map to see where she is.

③ The speaker is regretting not having a map.

④ The speaker is going back the way she came by herself.

これで第1問Aは終わりです。

B 第1問**B**は問5から問7までの3問です。英語を聞き，それぞれの内容と最もよく合っている絵を，四つの選択肢（①〜④）のうちから一つずつ選びなさい。

問5　5

①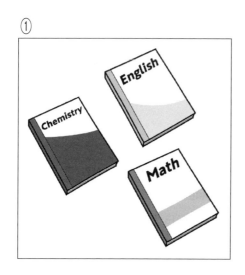

②

③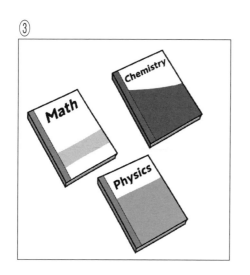

④

①

②

③

④

①

②

③

④

これで第１問**B**は終わりです。

第2問 （配点 16）　**音声は2回流れます。**

　　第2問は問8から問11までの4問です。それぞれの問いについて，対話の場面が日本語で書かれています。対話とそれについての問いを聞き，その答えとして最も適切なものを，四つの選択肢（①〜④）のうちから一つずつ選びなさい。

問8　男女が昼食に何を食べるかを相談しています。　　8

①

②

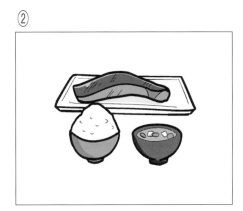

③

④

問9　女性が男性の家について聞いています。　9

①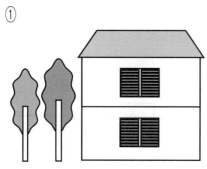

②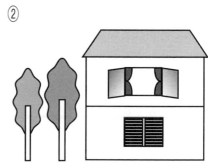

③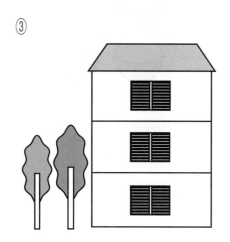

④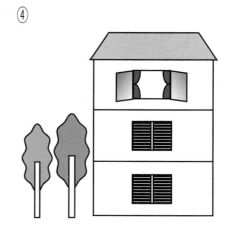

問10　女性が男性のお見舞いをしています。　10

①

②

③

④

問11　男女が地図を見ながら建物の場所を話し合っています。　11

これで第２問は終わりです。

第3問 (配点 18)　音声は1回流れます。

第3問は問12から問17までの6問です。それぞれの問いについて，対話の場面が日本語で書かれています。対話を聞き，問いの答えとして最も適切なものを，四つの選択肢 (①〜④) のうちから一つずつ選びなさい。(問いの英文は書かれています。)

問12　自宅で，母親と息子が話をしています。

What is the boy likely to do?　　12

① Consult a doctor immediately
② Find some good cold medicine by himself
③ Seek advice from other people
④ Try the medicine his mother recommends

問13　職員室で，男性教員と女性教員が話をしています。

Which country is the third most popular this year?　　13

① France
② Germany
③ Italy
④ The United Kingdom

問14　オフィスで，上司と部下が話をしています。

Which is true according to the conversation?　　14

① Ms. Davis was unhappy with being on the late shift.
② Ms. Miller will be on the early shift next month.
③ The man appreciates Ms. Davis taking the late shift.
④ The man doesn't want Ms. Miller to take the early shift.

問15 教室で，生徒が先生に話しかけています。

Which is true about the boy? 15

① The boy has been late before.

② The boy is telling a lie about why he was late.

③ The boy isn't listening to her.

④ The boy won't apologize for being late.

問16 学校で，友人同士が話をしています。

Why is the man upset? 16

① He hasn't yet decided what to wear to the party.

② Miguel found out that a party was going to be held.

③ Preparations for the party are not likely to be finished.

④ The woman promised to meet Miguel in the library.

問17 レストランで，夫婦が話をしています。

What does the woman think about the restaurant? 17

① Her husband should have ordered something else.

② She will never eat at the restaurant again.

③ The chicken tastes better than the steak.

④ The restaurant should be more highly rated.

これで第3問は終わりです。

第4問 （配点 12）　音声は1回流れます。

第4問は **A** と **B** の二つの部分に分かれています。

A　　第4問**A**は問18から問25までの8問です。話を聞き，それぞれの問いの答えとして最も適切なものを，選択肢のうちから選びなさい。<u>問題文と図表を読む時間が与えられた後，音声が流れます。</u>

問18〜21　あなたは，大学の授業で配られたワークシートのグラフを完成させようとしています。先生の説明を聞き，四つの空欄 | 18 | 〜 | 21 | に入れるのに最も適切なものを，四つの選択肢 (①〜④) のうちから一つずつ選びなさい。

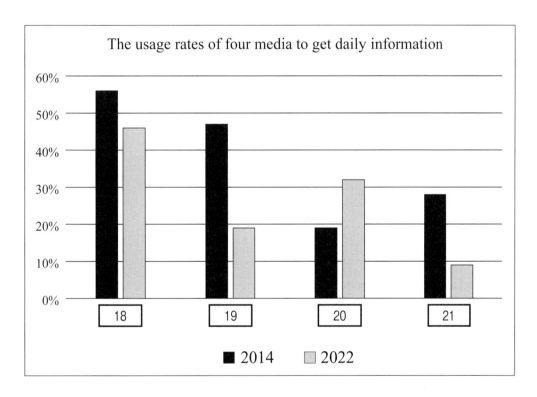

The usage rates of four media to get daily information

■ 2014　　□ 2022

① Newspaper
② Radio
③ SNS
④ TV

問22～25　あなたは，動画配信サイトで，複数のグループアーティストが合同で開催したライブイベントに関する情報を見ています。それぞれのグループへの感想に関するコメンテーターの話を聞き，次の表の四つの空欄 | 22 | ～ | 25 | に入れるのに最も適切なものを，六つの選択肢 (①～⑥) のうちから一つずつ選びなさい。選択肢は2回以上使ってもかまいません。

Super Summer Live Events：Summary of Performers

Teams	Performer's Age	Audience	Good Evaluation
Lemon Knights	18 ～ 19	10,000	22
Cross Gaps	21 ～ 22	5,000	23
Dark Altar	14 ～ 15	20,000	24
Merry Dice	24 ～ 26	35,000	25

① Dance

② Song

③ Stage Direction

④ Dance, Song

⑤ Dance, Stage Direction

⑥ Song, Stage Direction

これで第4問Aは終わりです。

B　第4問 **B**は問26の1問です。話を聞き，示された条件に最も合うものを，四つの選択肢 (①〜④) のうちから一つ選びなさい。後の表を参考にしてメモを取ってもかまいません。<u>状況と条件を読む時間が与えられた後，音声が流れます。</u>

状況

　あなたは，家族で日帰り旅行をする予定で，行き先について四人の友人から話を聞いています。

あなたが考えている条件

　A．電車で1時間以内に行ける場所であること

　B．その土地ならではの食べ物があること

　C．子供でも楽しめる施設があること

Places	Condition A	Condition B	Condition C
① Birchland			
② Gebston			
③ Greenport			
④ Juliapolis			

問26　| 26 |　is the place you are most likely to choose.

① Birchland

② Gebston

③ Greenport

④ Juliapolis

これで第4問 **B**は終わりです。

第5問 (配点 15)　**音声は1回流れます。**

第5問は問27から問33までの7問です。

最初に講義を聞き，問27から問32に答えなさい。次に続きを聞き，問33に答えなさい。状況，ワークシート，問い及び図表を読む時間が与えられた後，音声が流れます。

状況

　あなたは大学で，レジリエンスについての講義を，ワークシートにメモを取りながら聞いています。

ワークシート

Resilience

○What is resilience?　——————→　It is the ability to [27] .

○Ways to strengthen resilience

1. [28]	
2. make healthy lifestyle choices 　　· basic routines 　　　　e.g. [30] , sleep enough, exercise regularly 　　· additional activities 　　　　e.g. keep a diary, practice yoga, [31]	
3. [29]	

問27　ワークシートの空欄　27　に入れるのに最も適切なものを，四つの選択肢 (①〜④) のうちから一つ選びなさい。

① adopt a new approach to solving a problem
② avoid stress in the workplace or at school
③ cope with various stresses and difficulties
④ develop a plan and carry it out effectively

問28・29　ワークシートの空欄　28　・　29　に入れるのに最も適切なものを，四つの選択肢 (①〜④) のうちから一つずつ選びなさい。ただし解答の順序は問わない。

① become accustomed to being alone
② form relationships with others
③ have confidence in yourself
④ look back on your past

問30・31　ワークシートの空欄　30　・　31　に入れるのに最も適切なものを，四つの選択肢 (①〜④) のうちから一つずつ選びなさい。

① eat nutritious food　　② get up early every morning
③ listen to relaxing music　　④ spend time meditating

問32　講義の内容と一致するものはどれか。最も適切なものを，四つの選択肢 (①〜④) のうちから一つ選びなさい。　32

① It is impossible to change the way you respond to stressful events.
② Our body releases endorphins most when we feel anxiety or depression.
③ Resilience can be enhanced, though it takes time and effort.
④ You have to go through a lot of difficulties in order to increase resilience.

第5問はさらに続きます。

問33 講義の続きを聞き，次の図から読み取れる情報と講義全体の内容からどのようなことが言えるか，最も適切なものを，四つの選択肢 (①～④) のうちから一つ選びなさい。 33

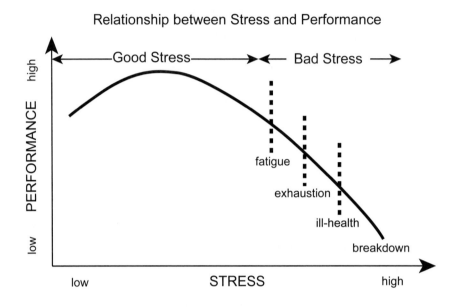

① A certain degree of stress contributes to higher performance.

② Bad stress improves your performance but is not good for your health.

③ It is difficult to distinguish between good stress and bad stress.

④ Too much resilience leads to a decline in good stress.

これで第5問は終わりです。

第6問 （配点 14）　音声は1回流れます。

第6問は **A** と **B** の二つの部分に分かれています。

 　第6問**A**は問34・問35の2問です。二人の対話を聞き，それぞれの問いの答えとして最も適切なものを，四つの選択肢 (①〜④) のうちから一つずつ選びなさい。(問いの英文は書かれています。) 状況と問いを読む時間が与えられた後，音声が流れます。

状況

　Lisa が，Hiro とクラス旅行の行き先について話をしています。

問34　**Why did Hiro choose to go to see the baseball game?** 　34

① He is not interested in the amusement park so much.

② He prefers to watch sports than to do sports himself.

③ He wanted to see a soccer game, but only a baseball game was available.

④ It would be the first time for him to go to see a baseball game.

問35　**Why did Lisa choose to go to the amusement park?** 　35

① She can enjoy rock climbing.

② She likes to exercise.

③ She wants to swim in a big pool.

④ She isn't interested in watching a baseball game.

これで第6問**A**は終わりです。

B 　第6問 **B** は問36・問37の2問です。会話を聞き，それぞれの問いの答えとして最も適切なものを，選択肢のうちから一つずつ選びなさい。後の表を参考にしてメモを取ってもかまいません。<u>状況と問いを読む時間が与えられた後，音声が流れます。</u>

状況

　四人の学生（Yui, Oliver, Jacob, Carol）が，Yui の部屋で話しています。

Yui	
Oliver	
Jacob	
Carol	

問36　宿題の必要性について<u>肯定的な意見を述べている人</u>を，四つの選択肢（①〜④）のうちから一つ選びなさい。　|　36　|

① Carol

② Oliver

③ Carol, Jacob

④ Oliver, Yui

問37　会話を踏まえて，Yui の意見と一致する図表を，四つの選択肢（①～④）のうちから一つ選びなさい。　37

①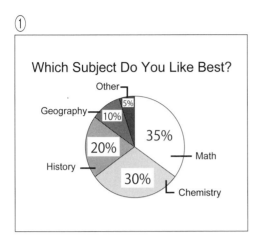

②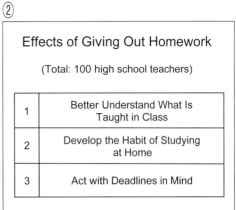

③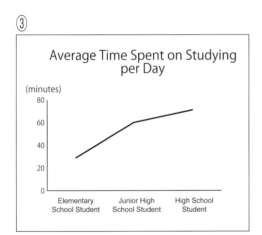

④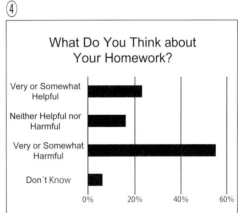

これで第６問 **B** は終わりです。

大学入学共通テスト試作問題
［リスニング］
（2022年11月公表）

●大学入試センターによる試作問題（2022年11月公表）は，新課程での共通テスト実施に向け，作問の方向性や具体的なイメージを共有するため，理科以外の6教科それぞれの全科目または一部科目について作成されたものです。本番の試験ではこの試作問題と同じような内容，形式，配点等の問題が必ずしも出題されるものではありません。

○掲載している試作問題
第C問 （配点15点）

※試作問題の音声配信はありません。

※本問題集収録にあたっては，A4サイズで公表された問題をB5サイズに縮小しています。また，公表時の問題をベースとして編集部にて一部修正・変更等を行っています。

第C問 (配点 15) 音声は1回流れます。

第C問は問27から問33の7問です。

最初に講義を聞き，問27から問31に答えなさい。次に問32と問33の音声を聞き，問いに答えなさい。状況，ワークシート，問い及び図表を読む時間が与えられた後，音声が流れます。

状況

あなたはアメリカの大学で，幸福観についての講義を，ワークシートにメモを取りながら聞いています。

ワークシート

○ **World Happiness Report**

・Purpose: To promote 〔　27　〕 happiness and well-being

・Scandinavian countries: Consistently happiest in the world (since 2012)

　Why? ⇒ **"Hygge"** lifestyle in Denmark

　　　　　↓　spread around the world in 2016

○ **Interpretations of Hygge**

	Popular Image of Hygge	Real Hygge in Denmark
What	28	29
Where	30	31
How	special	ordinary

問27 ワークシートの空欄　27　に入れるのに最も適切なものを，四つの選択肢（①〜④）のうちから一つ選びなさい。

① a sustainable development goal beyond

② a sustainable economy supporting

③ a sustainable natural environment for

④ a sustainable society challenging

問28〜31 ワークシートの空欄　28　〜　31　に入れるのに最も適切なものを，六つの選択肢（①〜⑥）のうちから一つずつ選びなさい。選択肢は2回以上使ってもかまいません。

① goods　　　　　② relationships　　　③ tasks

④ everywhere　　⑤ indoors　　　　　⑥ outdoors

問32 講義後に，あなたは要約を書くために，グループのメンバーA，Bと，講義内容を口頭で確認しています。それぞれの発言が講義の内容と一致するかどうかについて，最も適切なものを四つの選択肢（①〜④）のうちから一つ選びなさい。　32

① Aの発言のみ一致する

② Bの発言のみ一致する

③ どちらの発言も一致する

④ どちらの発言も一致しない

問33 講義の後で，Joe と May が下の図表を見ながらディスカッションをしています。ディスカッションの内容及び講義の内容からどのようなことが言えるか，最も適切なものを，四つの選択肢(①～④)のうちから一つ選びなさい。 33

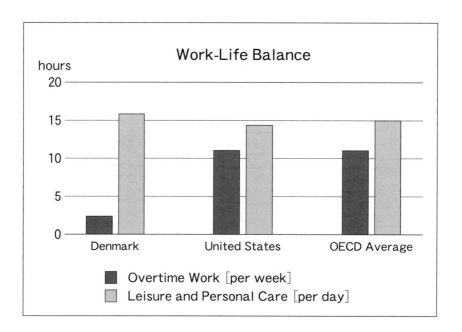

① People in Denmark do less overtime work while maintaining their productivity.

② People in Denmark enjoy working more, even though their income is guaranteed.

③ People in OECD countries are more productive because they work more overtime.

④ People in the US have an expensive lifestyle but the most time for leisure.

大学入学共通テスト本試験
［リスニング］
(2024年1月13日実施)

時間　30分　　　　　　100点　満点

1 ══ 解答にあたっては，実際に試験を受けるつもりで，時間を厳守し真剣に取りくむこと。

2 ══ 巻末にマークシートをつけてあるので，切り離しのうえ練習用として利用すること。

3 ══ 解答終了後には，自己採点により学力チェックを行い，別冊の解答・解説をじっくり読んで，弱点補強，知識や考え方の整理などに努めること。

※ 2024 共通テスト本試験問題を編集部にて一部修正して作成しています。

英　語（リスニング）

$$\left(\text{解答番号}\boxed{1}\sim\boxed{37}\right)$$

第1問　(配点　25)　**音声は2回流れます。**

第1問はAとBの二つの部分に分かれています。

A　　第1問Aは問1から問4までの4問です。英語を聞き，それぞれの内容と最もよく合っているものを，四つの選択肢(①〜④)のうちから一つずつ選びなさい。

問1　　1

①　The speaker brought her pencil.

②　The speaker forgot her notebook.

③　The speaker needs a pencil.

④　The speaker wants a notebook.

問2　　2

①　Ken is offering to buy their lunch.

②　Ken paid for the tickets already.

③　The speaker is offering to buy the tickets.

④　The speaker paid for their lunch yesterday.

問 3　3

① The speaker doesn't know where the old city hall is.

② The speaker has been to the new city hall just one time.

③ The speaker hasn't been to the old city hall before.

④ The speaker wants to know the way to the new city hall.

問 4　4

① The speaker didn't cook enough food.

② The speaker made enough sandwiches.

③ The speaker will serve more pasta.

④ The speaker won't prepare more dishes.

これで第 1 問 A は終わりです。

B 　第1問Bは問5から問7までの3問です。英語を聞き，それぞれの内容と最もよく合っている絵を，四つの選択肢(①〜④)のうちから一つずつ選びなさい。

問5 　　5

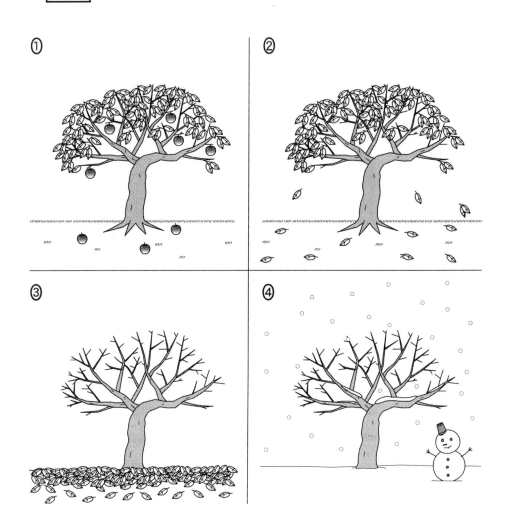

問 6　　6

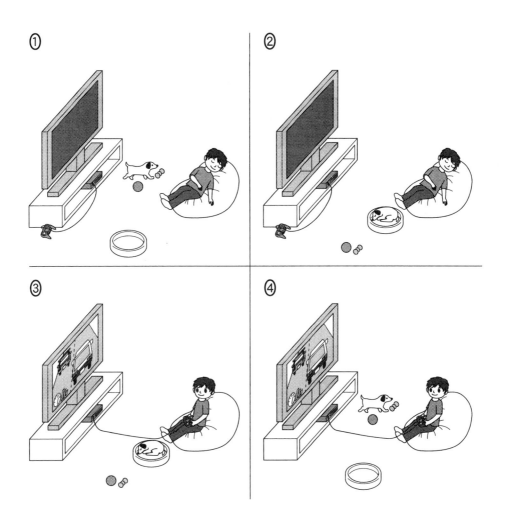

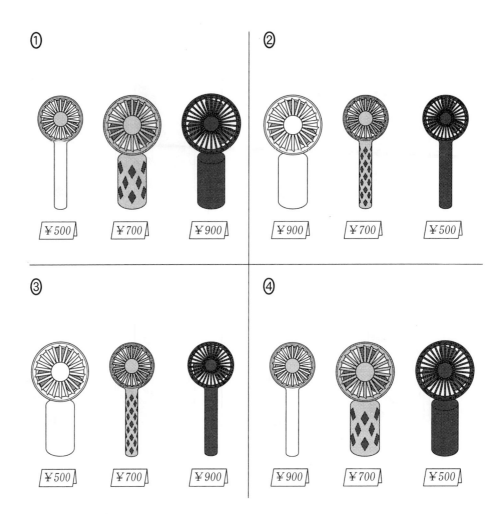

これで第1問Bは終わりです。

第 2 問 （配点 16） 音声は 2 回流れます。

　第 2 問は問 8 から問 11 までの 4 問です。それぞれの問いについて，対話の場面が日本語で書かれています。対話とそれについての問いを聞き，その答えとして最も適切なものを，四つの選択肢（①～④）のうちから一つずつ選びなさい。

問 8　交番で，迷子になった猫の説明をしています。　　8

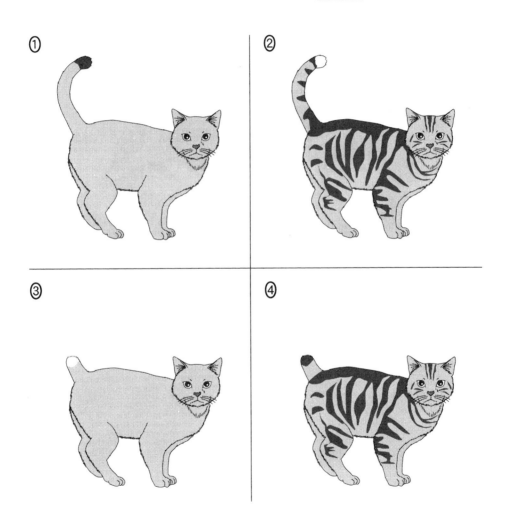

問 9　女性の子ども時代の写真を見ています。　9

問10　母親が，職場から電話をしてきました。　　10

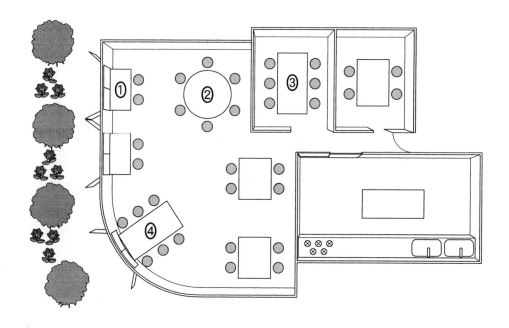

これで第2問は終わりです。

第3問 (配点 18) 音声は1回流れます。

第3問は問12から問17までの6問です。それぞれの問いについて，対話の場面が日本語で書かれています。対話を聞き，問いの答えとして最も適切なものを，四つの選択肢(①～④)のうちから一つずつ選びなさい。(問いの英文は書かれています。)

問12　カフェのカウンターで，店員と客が話をしています。

What will the man do this time? ⬚12

① Ask for a discount
② Pay the full price
③ Purchase a new cup
④ Use his personal cup

問13　男性と女性が，楽器について話をしています。

What is the man going to do? ⬚13

① Begin taking piano lessons
② Buy an electronic keyboard
③ Consider getting another piano
④ Replace the headphones for his keyboard

問14　友人同士が，買い物について話をしています。

What will the woman do? ⬚14

① Buy a jacket at her favorite store
② Go to a used-clothing store today
③ Shop for second-hand clothes next week
④ Take her friend to a bargain sale

問15 荷造りをしている二人が，話をしています。

What is the woman doing now? 15

① Getting things ready in the bedroom

② Helping the man finish in the bedroom

③ Moving everything into the living room

④ Packing all the items in the living room

問16 男性が，友人の女性と明日の予定について話をしています。

What will the man do tomorrow? 16

① Learn to ride a farm horse

② Ride horses with his friend

③ Take pictures of his friend

④ Visit his grandfather's farm

問17 高校生同士が，理科の宿題について話をしています。

What did the boy do? 17

① He finished writing a science report.

② He put off writing a science report.

③ He read two pages from the textbook.

④ He spent a long time reading the textbook.

これで第3問は終わりです。

第4問 （配点 12） 音声は1回流れます。

第4問はAとBの二つの部分に分かれています。

A 第4問Aは問18から問25までの8問です。話を聞き，それぞれの問いの答えとして最も適切なものを，選択肢から選びなさい。**問題文と図表を読む時間が与えられた後，音声が流れます。**

問18～21 友人が，週末に行なったことについて話をしています。話を聞き，その内容を表した四つのイラスト（①～④）を，行なった順番に並べなさい。

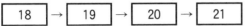

①  ②

③  ④

問22～25　あなたは，留学先の大学で，アドバイザーから夏季講座のスケジュールの説明を聞いています。次のスケジュールの四つの空欄　22　～　25　に入れるのに最も適切なものを，六つの選択肢（①～⑥）のうちから一つずつ選びなさい。選択肢は2回以上使ってもかまいません。

Summer Class Schedule

	Monday	Tuesday	Wednesday	Thursday	Friday
1st	Social Welfare	23	Biology	Social Welfare	World History
2nd	22	Business Studies	Environmental Studies	24	25

① Biology

② Business Studies

③ Environmental Studies

④ Languages

⑤ Math

⑥ World History

これで第4問Aは終わりです。

第4問Bは問26の1問です。話を聞き，次に示された条件に最も合うものを，四つの選択肢(①~④)のうちから一つ選びなさい。後の表を参考にしてメモを取ってもかまいません。**状況と条件を読む時間が与えられた後，音声が流れます。**

状況

あなたは，クラスで行う文化祭の出し物を決めるために，四人のクラスメートからアイデアを聞いています。

あなたが考えている条件

A．参加者が 20 分以内で体験できること

B．一度に 10 人以下で運営できること

C．費用が全くかからないこと

	Ideas	Condition A	Condition B	Condition C
①	Bowling game			
②	Face painting			
③	Fashion show			
④	Tea ceremony			

問26 " $\boxed{26}$ " is what you are most likely to choose.

① Bowling game

② Face painting

③ Fashion show

④ Tea ceremony

これで第4問Bは終わりです。

第 5 問 (配点 15) 音声は 1 回流れます。

第 5 問は問 27 から問 33 までの 7 問です。

最初に講義を聞き，問 27 から問 32 に答えなさい。次に続きを聞き，問 33 に答えなさい。**状況，ワークシート，問い及び図表を読む時間が与えられた後，音声が流れます。**

状況

　あなたは大学で，ガラスに関する講義を，ワークシートにメモを取りながら聞いています。

ワークシート

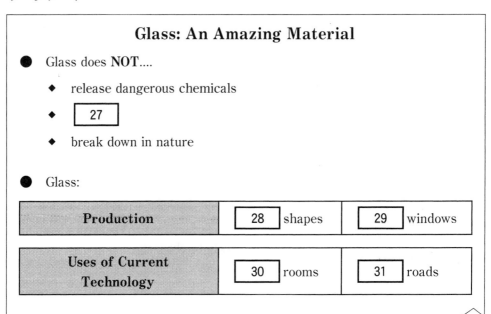

Glass: An Amazing Material

- Glass does **NOT**....
    - ◆ release dangerous chemicals
    - ◆ [27]
    - ◆ break down in nature

- Glass:

Production	28 shapes	29 windows
Uses of Current Technology	30 rooms	31 roads

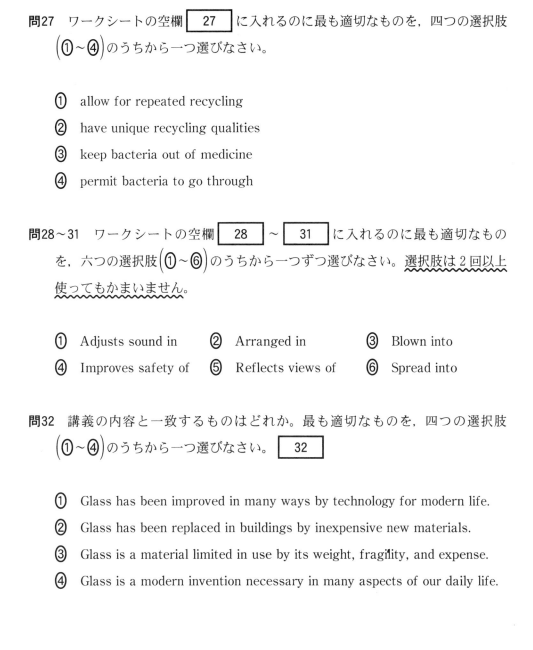

問27 ワークシートの空欄 | 27 | に入れるのに最も適切なものを，四つの選択肢 (①~④)のうちから一つ選びなさい。

① allow for repeated recycling

② have unique recycling qualities

③ keep bacteria out of medicine

④ permit bacteria to go through

問28~31 ワークシートの空欄 | 28 | ~ | 31 | に入れるのに最も適切なもの を，六つの選択肢(①~⑥)のうちから一つずつ選びなさい。選択肢は2回以上 使ってもかまいません。

① Adjusts sound in   ② Arranged in   ③ Blown into

④ Improves safety of   ⑤ Reflects views of   ⑥ Spread into

問32 講義の内容と一致するものはどれか。最も適切なものを，四つの選択肢 (①~④)のうちから一つ選びなさい。 | 32 |

① Glass has been improved in many ways by technology for modern life.

② Glass has been replaced in buildings by inexpensive new materials.

③ Glass is a material limited in use by its weight, fragility, and expense.

④ Glass is a modern invention necessary in many aspects of our daily life.

第5問はさらに続きます。

問33　講義の続きを聞き，**次の図から読み取れる情報と講義全体の内容からどの**ようなことが言えるか，最も適切なものを，四つの選択肢（①～④）のうちから一つ選びなさい。　33

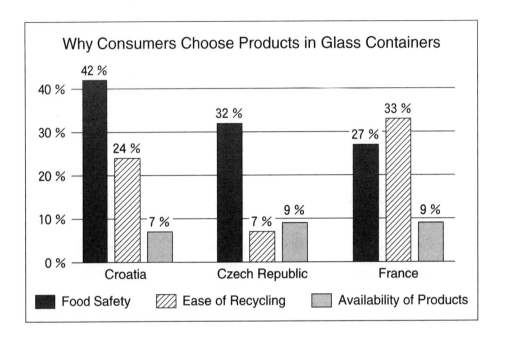

① Glass can be recycled repeatedly, but "ease of recycling" is the least common reason in the Czech Republic and Croatia.

② Glass is harmful to the environment, but "food safety" is the most common reason in the Czech Republic and Croatia.

③ Glass products are preferred by half of Europeans, and "ease of recycling" is the most common reason in France and Croatia.

④ Glass products can be made using ancient techniques, and "availability of products" is the least common reason in France and Croatia.

これで第5問は終わりです。

第6問 (配点 14) <u>音声は1回流れます</u>。

第6問はAとBの二つの部分に分かれています。

A   第6問Aは**問34・問35**の2問です。二人の対話を聞き，それぞれの問いの答えとして最も適切なものを，四つの選択肢(①〜④)のうちから一つずつ選びなさい。(問いの英文は書かれています。)<u>状況と問いを読む時間が与えられた後，音声が流れます</u>。

状況

    Michelle が，いとこの Jack と旅行中の移動の方法について話をしています。

問34 **Which opinion did Michelle express during the conversation?**
    | 34 |

   ①   Booking a hotel room with a view would be reasonable.

   ②   Looking at the scenery from the ferry would be great.

   ③   Smelling the sea air on the ferry would be unpleasant.

   ④   Taking the ferry would be faster than taking the train.

問35 **What did they decide to do by the end of the conversation?**
    | 35 |

   ①   Buy some medicine

   ②   Change their hotel rooms

   ③   Check the ferry schedule

   ④   Take the train to France

これで第6問Aは終わりです。

B 第6問Bは問36・問37の2問です。会話を聞き，それぞれの問いの答えとして最も適切なものを，選択肢のうちから一つずつ選びなさい。後の表を参考にしてメモを取ってもかまいません。**状況と問いを読む時間が与えられた後，音声が流れます。**

状況

　四人の学生(Chris, Amy, Haruki, Linda)が，運動を始めることについて話をしています。

Chris	
Amy	
Haruki	
Linda	

問36　会話が終わった時点で，**ウォーキングをすることに決めた人**を，四つの選択肢(①〜④)のうちから一つ選びなさい。 | 36 |

① Amy
② Haruki
③ Amy, Chris
④ Chris, Linda

— 356 —

問37 会話を踏まえて，Linda の考えの根拠となる図表を，四つの選択肢 (①～④) のうちから一つ選びなさい。 | 37 |

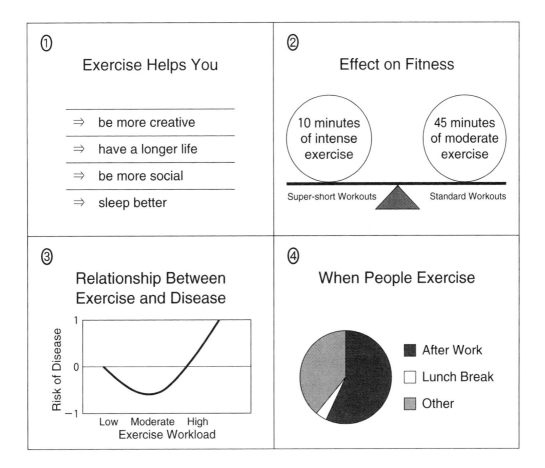

MEMO

MEMO

代々木ゼミナール編

2025大学入学
共通テスト
実戦問題集

英語［リーディング・リスニング］
数学I・A
数学II・B・C
国語
物理
化学
生物
理科基礎［物理/化学/生物/地学］
化学基礎＋生物基礎
生物基礎＋地学基礎
地理総合／歴史総合／公共
歴史総合，日本史探究
歴史総合，世界史探究
地理総合，地理探究
公共，倫理
公共，政治・経済

2025年版／大学入学共通テスト
実戦問題集
英語［リーディング・リスニング］

2024年7月20日　　　初版発行
●
編　者 —— 代々木ゼミナール
発行者 —— 髙宮英郎
発行所 —— 株式会社日本入試センター
　　　　　〒151-0053
　　　　　東京都渋谷区代々木1-27-1
　　　　　代々木ライブラリー
印刷所 —— 三松堂株式会社

●この書籍の編集内容および落丁・乱丁
　についてのお問い合わせは下記までお
　願いいたします
〒151-0053
東京都渋谷区代々木1-38-9
☎03-3370-7409（平日9：00～17：00）
代々木ライブラリー営業部

ISBN978-4-86346-869-6　　Printed in Japan

実戦問題集 英語（リーディング）解答用紙

マーク例

良い例	悪い例
●	· ⊗ ◑ ◐

注意事項

1 訂正は、消しゴムできれいに消し、消しくずを残してはいけません。
2 所定欄以外にはマークしたり、記入したりしてはいけません。
3 汚したり、折り曲げたりしてはいけません。

① 受験番号を記入し、その下のマーク欄にマークしなさい。

受験番号欄

英字	千位	百位	十位	一位
A B C H K M R U X Y Z				

受験番号マーク欄

② 氏名・フリガナ、試験場コードを記入しなさい。

フリガナ	
氏名	
試験場コード	十万位 万位 千位 百位 十位 一位

氏名番号チェック欄

解答欄 (解答番号 1〜25)

解答番号	1	2	3	4	5	6	7	8	9
1	①	②	③	④	⑤	⑥	⑦	⑧	⑨
2	①	②	③	④	⑤	⑥	⑦	⑧	⑨
3	①	②	③	④	⑤	⑥	⑦	⑧	⑨
4	①	②	③	④	⑤	⑥	⑦	⑧	⑨
5	①	②	③	④	⑤	⑥	⑦	⑧	⑨
6	①	②	③	④	⑤	⑥	⑦	⑧	⑨
7	①	②	③	④	⑤	⑥	⑦	⑧	⑨
8	①	②	③	④	⑤	⑥	⑦	⑧	⑨
9	①	②	③	④	⑤	⑥	⑦	⑧	⑨
10	①	②	③	④	⑤	⑥	⑦	⑧	⑨
11	①	②	③	④	⑤	⑥	⑦	⑧	⑨
12	①	②	③	④	⑤	⑥	⑦	⑧	⑨
13	①	②	③	④	⑤	⑥	⑦	⑧	⑨
14	①	②	③	④	⑤	⑥	⑦	⑧	⑨
15	①	②	③	④	⑤	⑥	⑦	⑧	⑨
16	①	②	③	④	⑤	⑥	⑦	⑧	⑨
17	①	②	③	④	⑤	⑥	⑦	⑧	⑨
18	①	②	③	④	⑤	⑥	⑦	⑧	⑨
19	①	②	③	④	⑤	⑥	⑦	⑧	⑨
20	①	②	③	④	⑤	⑥	⑦	⑧	⑨
21	①	②	③	④	⑤	⑥	⑦	⑧	⑨
22	①	②	③	④	⑤	⑥	⑦	⑧	⑨
23	①	②	③	④	⑤	⑥	⑦	⑧	⑨
24	①	②	③	④	⑤	⑥	⑦	⑧	⑨
25	①	②	③	④	⑤	⑥	⑦	⑧	⑨

解答欄 (解答番号 26〜50)

解答番号	1	2	3	4	5	6	7	8	9
26	①	②	③	④	⑤	⑥	⑦	⑧	⑨
27	①	②	③	④	⑤	⑥	⑦	⑧	⑨
28	①	②	③	④	⑤	⑥	⑦	⑧	⑨
29	①	②	③	④	⑤	⑥	⑦	⑧	⑨
30	①	②	③	④	⑤	⑥	⑦	⑧	⑨
31	①	②	③	④	⑤	⑥	⑦	⑧	⑨
32	①	②	③	④	⑤	⑥	⑦	⑧	⑨
33	①	②	③	④	⑤	⑥	⑦	⑧	⑨
34	①	②	③	④	⑤	⑥	⑦	⑧	⑨
35	①	②	③	④	⑤	⑥	⑦	⑧	⑨
36	①	②	③	④	⑤	⑥	⑦	⑧	⑨
37	①	②	③	④	⑤	⑥	⑦	⑧	⑨
38	①	②	③	④	⑤	⑥	⑦	⑧	⑨
39	①	②	③	④	⑤	⑥	⑦	⑧	⑨
40	①	②	③	④	⑤	⑥	⑦	⑧	⑨
41	①	②	③	④	⑤	⑥	⑦	⑧	⑨
42	①	②	③	④	⑤	⑥	⑦	⑧	⑨
43	①	②	③	④	⑤	⑥	⑦	⑧	⑨
44	①	②	③	④	⑤	⑥	⑦	⑧	⑨
45	①	②	③	④	⑤	⑥	⑦	⑧	⑨
46	①	②	③	④	⑤	⑥	⑦	⑧	⑨
47	①	②	③	④	⑤	⑥	⑦	⑧	⑨
48	①	②	③	④	⑤	⑥	⑦	⑧	⑨
49	①	②	③	④	⑤	⑥	⑦	⑧	⑨
50	①	②	③	④	⑤	⑥	⑦	⑧	⑨

解答欄 (解答番号 51〜75)

解答番号	1	2	3	4	5	6	7	8	9
51	①	②	③	④	⑤	⑥	⑦	⑧	⑨
52	①	②	③	④	⑤	⑥	⑦	⑧	⑨
53	①	②	③	④	⑤	⑥	⑦	⑧	⑨
54	①	②	③	④	⑤	⑥	⑦	⑧	⑨
55	①	②	③	④	⑤	⑥	⑦	⑧	⑨
56	①	②	③	④	⑤	⑥	⑦	⑧	⑨
57	①	②	③	④	⑤	⑥	⑦	⑧	⑨
58	①	②	③	④	⑤	⑥	⑦	⑧	⑨
59	①	②	③	④	⑤	⑥	⑦	⑧	⑨
60	①	②	③	④	⑤	⑥	⑦	⑧	⑨
61	①	②	③	④	⑤	⑥	⑦	⑧	⑨
62	①	②	③	④	⑤	⑥	⑦	⑧	⑨
63	①	②	③	④	⑤	⑥	⑦	⑧	⑨
64	①	②	③	④	⑤	⑥	⑦	⑧	⑨
65	①	②	③	④	⑤	⑥	⑦	⑧	⑨
66	①	②	③	④	⑤	⑥	⑦	⑧	⑨
67	①	②	③	④	⑤	⑥	⑦	⑧	⑨
68	①	②	③	④	⑤	⑥	⑦	⑧	⑨
69	①	②	③	④	⑤	⑥	⑦	⑧	⑨
70	①	②	③	④	⑤	⑥	⑦	⑧	⑨
71	①	②	③	④	⑤	⑥	⑦	⑧	⑨
72	①	②	③	④	⑤	⑥	⑦	⑧	⑨
73	①	②	③	④	⑤	⑥	⑦	⑧	⑨
74	①	②	③	④	⑤	⑥	⑦	⑧	⑨
75	①	②	③	④	⑤	⑥	⑦	⑧	⑨

実戦問題集　英語（リーディング）解答用紙

マーク例

良い例	悪い例
●	⊗ ⦸ ◯

注意事項

1 訂正は、消しゴムできれいに消し、消しくずを残してはいけません。

2 所定欄以外にはマークしたり、記入したりしてはいけません。

3 汚したり、折りまげたりしてはいけません。

①

受験番号を記入し、その下のマーク欄にマークしなさい。

受験番号欄

千位	百位	十位	一位	英字

②

氏名・フリガナ、試験場コードを記入しなさい。

フリガナ						
氏 名						
試験場コード	十万位	万位	千位	百位	十位	一位

氏名等チェック欄

解答欄（解答番号 1〜25）

解答番号	解答欄 1 2 3 4 5 6 7 8 9
1	① ② ③ ④ ⑤ ⑥ ⑦ ⑧ ⑨
2	① ② ③ ④ ⑤ ⑥ ⑦ ⑧ ⑨
3	① ② ③ ④ ⑤ ⑥ ⑦ ⑧ ⑨
4	① ② ③ ④ ⑤ ⑥ ⑦ ⑧ ⑨
5	① ② ③ ④ ⑤ ⑥ ⑦ ⑧ ⑨
6	① ② ③ ④ ⑤ ⑥ ⑦ ⑧ ⑨
7	① ② ③ ④ ⑤ ⑥ ⑦ ⑧ ⑨
8	① ② ③ ④ ⑤ ⑥ ⑦ ⑧ ⑨
9	① ② ③ ④ ⑤ ⑥ ⑦ ⑧ ⑨
10	① ② ③ ④ ⑤ ⑥ ⑦ ⑧ ⑨
11	① ② ③ ④ ⑤ ⑥ ⑦ ⑧ ⑨
12	① ② ③ ④ ⑤ ⑥ ⑦ ⑧ ⑨
13	① ② ③ ④ ⑤ ⑥ ⑦ ⑧ ⑨
14	① ② ③ ④ ⑤ ⑥ ⑦ ⑧ ⑨
15	① ② ③ ④ ⑤ ⑥ ⑦ ⑧ ⑨
16	① ② ③ ④ ⑤ ⑥ ⑦ ⑧ ⑨
17	① ② ③ ④ ⑤ ⑥ ⑦ ⑧ ⑨
18	① ② ③ ④ ⑤ ⑥ ⑦ ⑧ ⑨
19	① ② ③ ④ ⑤ ⑥ ⑦ ⑧ ⑨
20	① ② ③ ④ ⑤ ⑥ ⑦ ⑧ ⑨
21	① ② ③ ④ ⑤ ⑥ ⑦ ⑧ ⑨
22	① ② ③ ④ ⑤ ⑥ ⑦ ⑧ ⑨
23	① ② ③ ④ ⑤ ⑥ ⑦ ⑧ ⑨
24	① ② ③ ④ ⑤ ⑥ ⑦ ⑧ ⑨
25	① ② ③ ④ ⑤ ⑥ ⑦ ⑧ ⑨

解答欄（解答番号 26〜50）

解答番号	解答欄 1 2 3 4 5 6 7 8 9
26	① ② ③ ④ ⑤ ⑥ ⑦ ⑧ ⑨
27	① ② ③ ④ ⑤ ⑥ ⑦ ⑧ ⑨
28	① ② ③ ④ ⑤ ⑥ ⑦ ⑧ ⑨
29	① ② ③ ④ ⑤ ⑥ ⑦ ⑧ ⑨
30	① ② ③ ④ ⑤ ⑥ ⑦ ⑧ ⑨
31	① ② ③ ④ ⑤ ⑥ ⑦ ⑧ ⑨
32	① ② ③ ④ ⑤ ⑥ ⑦ ⑧ ⑨
33	① ② ③ ④ ⑤ ⑥ ⑦ ⑧ ⑨
34	① ② ③ ④ ⑤ ⑥ ⑦ ⑧ ⑨
35	① ② ③ ④ ⑤ ⑥ ⑦ ⑧ ⑨
36	① ② ③ ④ ⑤ ⑥ ⑦ ⑧ ⑨
37	① ② ③ ④ ⑤ ⑥ ⑦ ⑧ ⑨
38	① ② ③ ④ ⑤ ⑥ ⑦ ⑧ ⑨
39	① ② ③ ④ ⑤ ⑥ ⑦ ⑧ ⑨
40	① ② ③ ④ ⑤ ⑥ ⑦ ⑧ ⑨
41	① ② ③ ④ ⑤ ⑥ ⑦ ⑧ ⑨
42	① ② ③ ④ ⑤ ⑥ ⑦ ⑧ ⑨
43	① ② ③ ④ ⑤ ⑥ ⑦ ⑧ ⑨
44	① ② ③ ④ ⑤ ⑥ ⑦ ⑧ ⑨
45	① ② ③ ④ ⑤ ⑥ ⑦ ⑧ ⑨
46	① ② ③ ④ ⑤ ⑥ ⑦ ⑧ ⑨
47	① ② ③ ④ ⑤ ⑥ ⑦ ⑧ ⑨
48	① ② ③ ④ ⑤ ⑥ ⑦ ⑧ ⑨
49	① ② ③ ④ ⑤ ⑥ ⑦ ⑧ ⑨
50	① ② ③ ④ ⑤ ⑥ ⑦ ⑧ ⑨

解答欄（解答番号 51〜75）

解答番号	解答欄 1 2 3 4 5 6 7 8 9
51	① ② ③ ④ ⑤ ⑥ ⑦ ⑧ ⑨
52	① ② ③ ④ ⑤ ⑥ ⑦ ⑧ ⑨
53	① ② ③ ④ ⑤ ⑥ ⑦ ⑧ ⑨
54	① ② ③ ④ ⑤ ⑥ ⑦ ⑧ ⑨
55	① ② ③ ④ ⑤ ⑥ ⑦ ⑧ ⑨
56	① ② ③ ④ ⑤ ⑥ ⑦ ⑧ ⑨
57	① ② ③ ④ ⑤ ⑥ ⑦ ⑧ ⑨
58	① ② ③ ④ ⑤ ⑥ ⑦ ⑧ ⑨
59	① ② ③ ④ ⑤ ⑥ ⑦ ⑧ ⑨
60	① ② ③ ④ ⑤ ⑥ ⑦ ⑧ ⑨
61	① ② ③ ④ ⑤ ⑥ ⑦ ⑧ ⑨
62	① ② ③ ④ ⑤ ⑥ ⑦ ⑧ ⑨
63	① ② ③ ④ ⑤ ⑥ ⑦ ⑧ ⑨
64	① ② ③ ④ ⑤ ⑥ ⑦ ⑧ ⑨
65	① ② ③ ④ ⑤ ⑥ ⑦ ⑧ ⑨
66	① ② ③ ④ ⑤ ⑥ ⑦ ⑧ ⑨
67	① ② ③ ④ ⑤ ⑥ ⑦ ⑧ ⑨
68	① ② ③ ④ ⑤ ⑥ ⑦ ⑧ ⑨
69	① ② ③ ④ ⑤ ⑥ ⑦ ⑧ ⑨
70	① ② ③ ④ ⑤ ⑥ ⑦ ⑧ ⑨
71	① ② ③ ④ ⑤ ⑥ ⑦ ⑧ ⑨
72	① ② ③ ④ ⑤ ⑥ ⑦ ⑧ ⑨
73	① ② ③ ④ ⑤ ⑥ ⑦ ⑧ ⑨
74	① ② ③ ④ ⑤ ⑥ ⑦ ⑧ ⑨
75	① ② ③ ④ ⑤ ⑥ ⑦ ⑧ ⑨

（マークセン）

実戦問題集 英語（リーディング） 解答用紙

注意事項

1 訂正は、消しゴムできれいに消し、消しくずを残してはいけません。

2 所定欄以外にはマークしたり、記入したりしてはいけません。

3 汚したり、折りまげたりしてはいけません。

マーク例

良い例	悪い例
●	◌ ⊗ ◐

① 受験番号を記入し、その下のマーク欄にマークしなさい。

② 氏名・フリガナ、試験場コードを記入しなさい。

解答欄（解答番号 1〜25）

各行：解答番号、選択肢 1 2 3 4 5 6 7 8 9

1, 2, 3, 4, 5, 6, 7, 8, 9, 10, 11, 12, 13, 14, 15, 16, 17, 18, 19, 20, 21, 22, 23, 24, 25

解答欄（解答番号 26〜50）

26, 27, 28, 29, 30, 31, 32, 33, 34, 35, 36, 37, 38, 39, 40, 41, 42, 43, 44, 45, 46, 47, 48, 49, 50

解答欄（解答番号 51〜75）

51, 52, 53, 54, 55, 56, 57, 58, 59, 60, 61, 62, 63, 64, 65, 66, 67, 68, 69, 70, 71, 72, 73, 74, 75

受験番号欄：英字 A B C H K M R U X Y Z、千位・百位・十位・一位（0〜9）

受験番号マーク欄

フリガナ 氏名

試験場コード（十万位 万位 千位 百位 十位 一位）

氏名等チェック欄

実戦問題集 英語（リーディング）解答用紙

注意事項

1 訂正は、消しゴムできれいに消し、消しくずを残してはいけません。
2 所定欄以外にはマークしたり、記入したりしてはいけません。
3 汚したり、折りまげたりしてはいけません。

マーク例

良い例	悪い例
●	◐ ⊗ ○

① 受験番号を記入し、その下のマーク欄にマークしなさい。

受験番号マーク正しい例

受験番号欄				
千位	百位	十位	一位	英字

② 氏名・フリガナ、試験場コードを記入しなさい。

フリガナ	
氏 名	
試験場コード	十万位 / 万位 / 千位 / 百位 / 十位 / 一位

氏名等チェック欄

解答欄（解答番号 1〜25、選択肢 1 2 3 4 5 6 7 8 9）

解答欄（解答番号 26〜50、選択肢 1 2 3 4 5 6 7 8 9）

解答欄（解答番号 51〜75、選択肢 1 2 3 4 5 6 7 8 9）

実戦問題集　英語（リーディング）　解答用紙

注意事項

1 訂正は、消しゴムできれいに消し、消しくずを残してはいけません。

2 所定欄以外にはマークしたり、記入したりしてはいけません。

3 汚したり、折りまげたりしてはいけません。

解答番号	解答欄 1 2 3 4 5 6 7 8 9
1	① ② ③ ④ ⑤ ⑥ ⑦ ⑧ ⑨
2	① ② ③ ④ ⑤ ⑥ ⑦ ⑧ ⑨
3	① ② ③ ④ ⑤ ⑥ ⑦ ⑧ ⑨
4	① ② ③ ④ ⑤ ⑥ ⑦ ⑧ ⑨
5	① ② ③ ④ ⑤ ⑥ ⑦ ⑧ ⑨
6	① ② ③ ④ ⑤ ⑥ ⑦ ⑧ ⑨
7	① ② ③ ④ ⑤ ⑥ ⑦ ⑧ ⑨
8	① ② ③ ④ ⑤ ⑥ ⑦ ⑧ ⑨
9	① ② ③ ④ ⑤ ⑥ ⑦ ⑧ ⑨
10	① ② ③ ④ ⑤ ⑥ ⑦ ⑧ ⑨
11	① ② ③ ④ ⑤ ⑥ ⑦ ⑧ ⑨
12	① ② ③ ④ ⑤ ⑥ ⑦ ⑧ ⑨
13	① ② ③ ④ ⑤ ⑥ ⑦ ⑧ ⑨
14	① ② ③ ④ ⑤ ⑥ ⑦ ⑧ ⑨
15	① ② ③ ④ ⑤ ⑥ ⑦ ⑧ ⑨
16	① ② ③ ④ ⑤ ⑥ ⑦ ⑧ ⑨
17	① ② ③ ④ ⑤ ⑥ ⑦ ⑧ ⑨
18	① ② ③ ④ ⑤ ⑥ ⑦ ⑧ ⑨
19	① ② ③ ④ ⑤ ⑥ ⑦ ⑧ ⑨
20	① ② ③ ④ ⑤ ⑥ ⑦ ⑧ ⑨
21	① ② ③ ④ ⑤ ⑥ ⑦ ⑧ ⑨
22	① ② ③ ④ ⑤ ⑥ ⑦ ⑧ ⑨
23	① ② ③ ④ ⑤ ⑥ ⑦ ⑧ ⑨
24	① ② ③ ④ ⑤ ⑥ ⑦ ⑧ ⑨
25	① ② ③ ④ ⑤ ⑥ ⑦ ⑧ ⑨

解答番号	解答欄 1 2 3 4 5 6 7 8 9
26	① ② ③ ④ ⑤ ⑥ ⑦ ⑧ ⑨
27	① ② ③ ④ ⑤ ⑥ ⑦ ⑧ ⑨
28	① ② ③ ④ ⑤ ⑥ ⑦ ⑧ ⑨
29	① ② ③ ④ ⑤ ⑥ ⑦ ⑧ ⑨
30	① ② ③ ④ ⑤ ⑥ ⑦ ⑧ ⑨
31	① ② ③ ④ ⑤ ⑥ ⑦ ⑧ ⑨
32	① ② ③ ④ ⑤ ⑥ ⑦ ⑧ ⑨
33	① ② ③ ④ ⑤ ⑥ ⑦ ⑧ ⑨
34	① ② ③ ④ ⑤ ⑥ ⑦ ⑧ ⑨
35	① ② ③ ④ ⑤ ⑥ ⑦ ⑧ ⑨
36	① ② ③ ④ ⑤ ⑥ ⑦ ⑧ ⑨
37	① ② ③ ④ ⑤ ⑥ ⑦ ⑧ ⑨
38	① ② ③ ④ ⑤ ⑥ ⑦ ⑧ ⑨
39	① ② ③ ④ ⑤ ⑥ ⑦ ⑧ ⑨
40	① ② ③ ④ ⑤ ⑥ ⑦ ⑧ ⑨
41	① ② ③ ④ ⑤ ⑥ ⑦ ⑧ ⑨
42	① ② ③ ④ ⑤ ⑥ ⑦ ⑧ ⑨
43	① ② ③ ④ ⑤ ⑥ ⑦ ⑧ ⑨
44	① ② ③ ④ ⑤ ⑥ ⑦ ⑧ ⑨
45	① ② ③ ④ ⑤ ⑥ ⑦ ⑧ ⑨
46	① ② ③ ④ ⑤ ⑥ ⑦ ⑧ ⑨
47	① ② ③ ④ ⑤ ⑥ ⑦ ⑧ ⑨
48	① ② ③ ④ ⑤ ⑥ ⑦ ⑧ ⑨
49	① ② ③ ④ ⑤ ⑥ ⑦ ⑧ ⑨
50	① ② ③ ④ ⑤ ⑥ ⑦ ⑧ ⑨

解答番号	解答欄 1 2 3 4 5 6 7 8 9
51	① ② ③ ④ ⑤ ⑥ ⑦ ⑧ ⑨
52	① ② ③ ④ ⑤ ⑥ ⑦ ⑧ ⑨
53	① ② ③ ④ ⑤ ⑥ ⑦ ⑧ ⑨
54	① ② ③ ④ ⑤ ⑥ ⑦ ⑧ ⑨
55	① ② ③ ④ ⑤ ⑥ ⑦ ⑧ ⑨
56	① ② ③ ④ ⑤ ⑥ ⑦ ⑧ ⑨
57	① ② ③ ④ ⑤ ⑥ ⑦ ⑧ ⑨
58	① ② ③ ④ ⑤ ⑥ ⑦ ⑧ ⑨
59	① ② ③ ④ ⑤ ⑥ ⑦ ⑧ ⑨
60	① ② ③ ④ ⑤ ⑥ ⑦ ⑧ ⑨
61	① ② ③ ④ ⑤ ⑥ ⑦ ⑧ ⑨
62	① ② ③ ④ ⑤ ⑥ ⑦ ⑧ ⑨
63	① ② ③ ④ ⑤ ⑥ ⑦ ⑧ ⑨
64	① ② ③ ④ ⑤ ⑥ ⑦ ⑧ ⑨
65	① ② ③ ④ ⑤ ⑥ ⑦ ⑧ ⑨
66	① ② ③ ④ ⑤ ⑥ ⑦ ⑧ ⑨
67	① ② ③ ④ ⑤ ⑥ ⑦ ⑧ ⑨
68	① ② ③ ④ ⑤ ⑥ ⑦ ⑧ ⑨
69	① ② ③ ④ ⑤ ⑥ ⑦ ⑧ ⑨
70	① ② ③ ④ ⑤ ⑥ ⑦ ⑧ ⑨
71	① ② ③ ④ ⑤ ⑥ ⑦ ⑧ ⑨
72	① ② ③ ④ ⑤ ⑥ ⑦ ⑧ ⑨
73	① ② ③ ④ ⑤ ⑥ ⑦ ⑧ ⑨
74	① ② ③ ④ ⑤ ⑥ ⑦ ⑧ ⑨
75	① ② ③ ④ ⑤ ⑥ ⑦ ⑧ ⑨

マーク例

良い例	悪い例
●	⊙ ⊗ ◐ ◖

① 受験番号を記入し、その下のマーク欄にマークしなさい。

受験番号欄

英字: Ⓐ Ⓑ Ⓒ Ⓗ Ⓚ Ⓜ Ⓡ Ⓤ Ⓧ Ⓨ Ⓩ

千位	百位	十位	一位	英字
⓪	⓪	⓪	⓪	Ⓐ
①	①	①	①	Ⓑ
②	②	②	②	Ⓒ
③	③	③	③	Ⓗ
④	④	④	④	Ⓚ
⑤	⑤	⑤	⑤	Ⓜ
⑥	⑥	⑥	⑥	Ⓡ
⑦	⑦	⑦	⑦	Ⓤ
⑧	⑧	⑧	⑧	Ⓧ
⑨	⑨	⑨	⑨	Ⓨ
-	-	-	-	Ⓩ

受験番号マークチェック欄

② 氏名・フリガナ、試験場コードを記入しなさい。

フリガナ	
氏　名	
試験場コード	十万位 万位 千位 百位 十位 一位

氏名等チェック欄

実戦問題集 英語（リーディング）解答用紙

マーク例

良い例	悪い例
●	◍ ⊗ ◯

① 受験番号を記入し、その下のマーク欄にマークしなさい。

受験番号欄				
千位	百位	十位	一位	英字

② 氏名・フリガナ、試験場コードを記入しなさい。

フリガナ	
氏名	
試験場コード	

注意事項

1 訂正は、消しゴムできれいに消し、消しくずを残してはいけません。

2 所定欄以外にはマークしたり、記入したりしてはいけません。

3 汚したり、折りまげたりしてはいけません。

解答欄（解答番号 1〜25）

解答番号	解答欄 1 2 3 4 5 6 7 8 9
1	① ② ③ ④ ⑤ ⑥ ⑦ ⑧ ⑨
2	① ② ③ ④ ⑤ ⑥ ⑦ ⑧ ⑨
3	① ② ③ ④ ⑤ ⑥ ⑦ ⑧ ⑨
4	① ② ③ ④ ⑤ ⑥ ⑦ ⑧ ⑨
5	① ② ③ ④ ⑤ ⑥ ⑦ ⑧ ⑨
6	① ② ③ ④ ⑤ ⑥ ⑦ ⑧ ⑨
7	① ② ③ ④ ⑤ ⑥ ⑦ ⑧ ⑨
8	① ② ③ ④ ⑤ ⑥ ⑦ ⑧ ⑨
9	① ② ③ ④ ⑤ ⑥ ⑦ ⑧ ⑨
10	① ② ③ ④ ⑤ ⑥ ⑦ ⑧ ⑨
11	① ② ③ ④ ⑤ ⑥ ⑦ ⑧ ⑨
12	① ② ③ ④ ⑤ ⑥ ⑦ ⑧ ⑨
13	① ② ③ ④ ⑤ ⑥ ⑦ ⑧ ⑨
14	① ② ③ ④ ⑤ ⑥ ⑦ ⑧ ⑨
15	① ② ③ ④ ⑤ ⑥ ⑦ ⑧ ⑨
16	① ② ③ ④ ⑤ ⑥ ⑦ ⑧ ⑨
17	① ② ③ ④ ⑤ ⑥ ⑦ ⑧ ⑨
18	① ② ③ ④ ⑤ ⑥ ⑦ ⑧ ⑨
19	① ② ③ ④ ⑤ ⑥ ⑦ ⑧ ⑨
20	① ② ③ ④ ⑤ ⑥ ⑦ ⑧ ⑨
21	① ② ③ ④ ⑤ ⑥ ⑦ ⑧ ⑨
22	① ② ③ ④ ⑤ ⑥ ⑦ ⑧ ⑨
23	① ② ③ ④ ⑤ ⑥ ⑦ ⑧ ⑨
24	① ② ③ ④ ⑤ ⑥ ⑦ ⑧ ⑨
25	① ② ③ ④ ⑤ ⑥ ⑦ ⑧ ⑨

解答欄（解答番号 26〜50）

解答番号	解答欄 1 2 3 4 5 6 7 8 9
26	① ② ③ ④ ⑤ ⑥ ⑦ ⑧ ⑨
27	① ② ③ ④ ⑤ ⑥ ⑦ ⑧ ⑨
28	① ② ③ ④ ⑤ ⑥ ⑦ ⑧ ⑨
29	① ② ③ ④ ⑤ ⑥ ⑦ ⑧ ⑨
30	① ② ③ ④ ⑤ ⑥ ⑦ ⑧ ⑨
31	① ② ③ ④ ⑤ ⑥ ⑦ ⑧ ⑨
32	① ② ③ ④ ⑤ ⑥ ⑦ ⑧ ⑨
33	① ② ③ ④ ⑤ ⑥ ⑦ ⑧ ⑨
34	① ② ③ ④ ⑤ ⑥ ⑦ ⑧ ⑨
35	① ② ③ ④ ⑤ ⑥ ⑦ ⑧ ⑨
36	① ② ③ ④ ⑤ ⑥ ⑦ ⑧ ⑨
37	① ② ③ ④ ⑤ ⑥ ⑦ ⑧ ⑨
38	① ② ③ ④ ⑤ ⑥ ⑦ ⑧ ⑨
39	① ② ③ ④ ⑤ ⑥ ⑦ ⑧ ⑨
40	① ② ③ ④ ⑤ ⑥ ⑦ ⑧ ⑨
41	① ② ③ ④ ⑤ ⑥ ⑦ ⑧ ⑨
42	① ② ③ ④ ⑤ ⑥ ⑦ ⑧ ⑨
43	① ② ③ ④ ⑤ ⑥ ⑦ ⑧ ⑨
44	① ② ③ ④ ⑤ ⑥ ⑦ ⑧ ⑨
45	① ② ③ ④ ⑤ ⑥ ⑦ ⑧ ⑨
46	① ② ③ ④ ⑤ ⑥ ⑦ ⑧ ⑨
47	① ② ③ ④ ⑤ ⑥ ⑦ ⑧ ⑨
48	① ② ③ ④ ⑤ ⑥ ⑦ ⑧ ⑨
49	① ② ③ ④ ⑤ ⑥ ⑦ ⑧ ⑨
50	① ② ③ ④ ⑤ ⑥ ⑦ ⑧ ⑨

解答欄（解答番号 51〜75）

解答番号	解答欄 1 2 3 4 5 6 7 8 9
51	① ② ③ ④ ⑤ ⑥ ⑦ ⑧ ⑨
52	① ② ③ ④ ⑤ ⑥ ⑦ ⑧ ⑨
53	① ② ③ ④ ⑤ ⑥ ⑦ ⑧ ⑨
54	① ② ③ ④ ⑤ ⑥ ⑦ ⑧ ⑨
55	① ② ③ ④ ⑤ ⑥ ⑦ ⑧ ⑨
56	① ② ③ ④ ⑤ ⑥ ⑦ ⑧ ⑨
57	① ② ③ ④ ⑤ ⑥ ⑦ ⑧ ⑨
58	① ② ③ ④ ⑤ ⑥ ⑦ ⑧ ⑨
59	① ② ③ ④ ⑤ ⑥ ⑦ ⑧ ⑨
60	① ② ③ ④ ⑤ ⑥ ⑦ ⑧ ⑨
61	① ② ③ ④ ⑤ ⑥ ⑦ ⑧ ⑨
62	① ② ③ ④ ⑤ ⑥ ⑦ ⑧ ⑨
63	① ② ③ ④ ⑤ ⑥ ⑦ ⑧ ⑨
64	① ② ③ ④ ⑤ ⑥ ⑦ ⑧ ⑨
65	① ② ③ ④ ⑤ ⑥ ⑦ ⑧ ⑨
66	① ② ③ ④ ⑤ ⑥ ⑦ ⑧ ⑨
67	① ② ③ ④ ⑤ ⑥ ⑦ ⑧ ⑨
68	① ② ③ ④ ⑤ ⑥ ⑦ ⑧ ⑨
69	① ② ③ ④ ⑤ ⑥ ⑦ ⑧ ⑨
70	① ② ③ ④ ⑤ ⑥ ⑦ ⑧ ⑨
71	① ② ③ ④ ⑤ ⑥ ⑦ ⑧ ⑨
72	① ② ③ ④ ⑤ ⑥ ⑦ ⑧ ⑨
73	① ② ③ ④ ⑤ ⑥ ⑦ ⑧ ⑨
74	① ② ③ ④ ⑤ ⑥ ⑦ ⑧ ⑨
75	① ② ③ ④ ⑤ ⑥ ⑦ ⑧ ⑨

注意事項

1　訂正は、消しゴムできれいに消し、消しくずを残してはいけません。

2　所定欄以外にはマークしたり、記入したりしてはいけません。

3　汚したり、折り曲げたりしてはいけません。

解答欄（解答番号 21〜40）

解答番号	1	2	3	4	5	6
21	①	②	③	④	⑤	⑥
22	①	②	③	④	⑤	⑥
23	①	②	③	④	⑤	⑥
24	①	②	③	④	⑤	⑥
25	①	②	③	④	⑤	⑥
26	①	②	③	④	⑤	⑥
27	①	②	③	④	⑤	⑥
28	①	②	③	④	⑤	⑥
29	①	②	③	④	⑤	⑥
30	①	②	③	④	⑤	⑥
31	①	②	③	④	⑤	⑥
32	①	②	③	④	⑤	⑥
33	①	②	③	④	⑤	⑥
34	①	②	③	④	⑤	⑥
35	①	②	③	④	⑤	⑥
36	①	②	③	④	⑤	⑥
37	①	②	③	④	⑤	⑥
38	①	②	③	④	⑤	⑥
39	①	②	③	④	⑤	⑥
40	①	②	③	④	⑤	⑥

解答欄（解答番号 1〜20）

解答番号	1	2	3	4	5	6
1	①	②	③	④	⑤	⑥
2	①	②	③	④	⑤	⑥
3	①	②	③	④	⑤	⑥
4	①	②	③	④	⑤	⑥
5	①	②	③	④	⑤	⑥
6	①	②	③	④	⑤	⑥
7	①	②	③	④	⑤	⑥
8	①	②	③	④	⑤	⑥
9	①	②	③	④	⑤	⑥
10	①	②	③	④	⑤	⑥
11	①	②	③	④	⑤	⑥
12	①	②	③	④	⑤	⑥
13	①	②	③	④	⑤	⑥
14	①	②	③	④	⑤	⑥
15	①	②	③	④	⑤	⑥
16	①	②	③	④	⑤	⑥
17	①	②	③	④	⑤	⑥
18	①	②	③	④	⑤	⑥
19	①	②	③	④	⑤	⑥
20	①	②	③	④	⑤	⑥

マーク例

良い例	悪い例
●	◯ ⊗ ◑ ◓

① 受験番号を記入し、その下のマーク欄にマークしなさい。

受験番号欄

英字	千位	百位	十位	一位
Ⓐ	⓪	⓪	⓪	⓪
Ⓑ	①	①	①	①
Ⓒ	②	②	②	②
Ⓗ	③	③	③	③
Ⓚ	④	④	④	④
Ⓜ	⑤	⑤	⑤	⑤
Ⓡ	⑥	⑥	⑥	⑥
Ⓤ	⑦	⑦	⑦	⑦
Ⓧ	⑧	⑧	⑧	⑧
Ⓨ	⑨	⑨	⑨	⑨
Ⓩ	–	–	–	–

受験番号マークミス欄

② 氏名・フリガナ、試験場コードを記入しなさい。

フリガナ	
氏　名	

試験場コード

十万位	万位	千位	百位	十位	一位

氏名等チェック欄

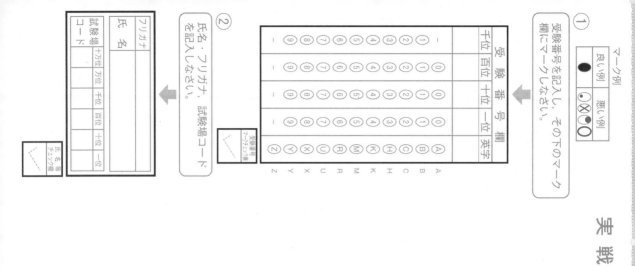

実 戦 問 題 集　英 語 （リスニング） 解 答 用 紙

注意事項

1 訂正欄は、消しゴムできれいに消し、消しくずを残してはいけません。

2 所定欄以外にはマークしたり、記入したりしてはいけません。

3 汚したり、折りまげたりしてはいけません。

実戦問題集　英語（リスニング）解答用紙

注意事項

1　訂正は、消しゴムできれいに消し、消しくずを残してはいけません。

2　所定欄以外にはマークしたり、記入したりしてはいけません。

3　汚したり、折り曲げたりしてはいけません。

解答番号	解答欄 1 2 3 4 5 6
1	① ② ③ ④ ⑤ ⑥
2	① ② ③ ④ ⑤ ⑥
3	① ② ③ ④ ⑤ ⑥
4	① ② ③ ④ ⑤ ⑥
5	① ② ③ ④ ⑤ ⑥
6	① ② ③ ④ ⑤ ⑥
7	① ② ③ ④ ⑤ ⑥
8	① ② ③ ④ ⑤ ⑥
9	① ② ③ ④ ⑤ ⑥
10	① ② ③ ④ ⑤ ⑥
11	① ② ③ ④ ⑤ ⑥
12	① ② ③ ④ ⑤ ⑥
13	① ② ③ ④ ⑤ ⑥
14	① ② ③ ④ ⑤ ⑥
15	① ② ③ ④ ⑤ ⑥
16	① ② ③ ④ ⑤ ⑥
17	① ② ③ ④ ⑤ ⑥
18	① ② ③ ④ ⑤ ⑥
19	① ② ③ ④ ⑤ ⑥
20	① ② ③ ④ ⑤ ⑥

解答番号	解答欄 1 2 3 4 5 6
21	① ② ③ ④ ⑤ ⑥
22	① ② ③ ④ ⑤ ⑥
23	① ② ③ ④ ⑤ ⑥
24	① ② ③ ④ ⑤ ⑥
25	① ② ③ ④ ⑤ ⑥
26	① ② ③ ④ ⑤ ⑥
27	① ② ③ ④ ⑤ ⑥
28	① ② ③ ④ ⑤ ⑥
29	① ② ③ ④ ⑤ ⑥
30	① ② ③ ④ ⑤ ⑥
31	① ② ③ ④ ⑤ ⑥
32	① ② ③ ④ ⑤ ⑥
33	① ② ③ ④ ⑤ ⑥
34	① ② ③ ④ ⑤ ⑥
35	① ② ③ ④ ⑤ ⑥
36	① ② ③ ④ ⑤ ⑥
37	① ② ③ ④ ⑤ ⑥
38	① ② ③ ④ ⑤ ⑥
39	① ② ③ ④ ⑤ ⑥
40	① ② ③ ④ ⑤ ⑥

マーク例
良い例	悪い例
●	◑ ⊗ ◐ ○

① 受験番号を記入し、その下のマーク欄にマークしなさい。

受験番号欄　千位　百位　十位　一位　英字

受験番号マーク欄

② 氏名・フリガナ、試験場コードを記入しなさい。

フリガナ　氏名　試験場コード　十万位　万位　千位　百位　十位　一位

氏名チェック欄

注意事項

1　訂正は、消しゴムできれいに消し、消しくずを残してはいけません。

2　所定欄以外にはマークしたり、記入したりしてはいけません。

3　汚したり、折りまげたりしてはいけません。

マーク例
良い例	悪い例
●	◯ ⊗ ◑

① 受験番号を記入し、その下のマーク欄にマークしなさい。

受験番号欄

千位	百位	十位	一位	英字
－	⓪	⓪	⓪	Ⓐ
①	①	①	①	Ⓑ
②	②	②	②	Ⓒ
③	③	③	③	Ⓗ
④	④	④	④	Ⓚ
⑤	⑤	⑤	⑤	Ⓜ
⑥	⑥	⑥	⑥	Ⓡ
⑦	⑦	⑦	⑦	Ⓤ
⑧	⑧	⑧	⑧	Ⓧ
⑨	⑨	⑨	⑨	Ⓨ
－	－	－	－	Ⓩ

受験番号欄
マークチェック欄

② 氏名・フリガナ、試験場コードを記入しなさい。

フリガナ						
氏名						
試験場コード	十万位	万位	千位	百位	十位	一位

氏名等チェック欄

解答欄

解答番号	解答欄 1	2	3	4	5	6
1	①	②	③	④	⑤	⑥
2	①	②	③	④	⑤	⑥
3	①	②	③	④	⑤	⑥
4	①	②	③	④	⑤	⑥
5	①	②	③	④	⑤	⑥
6	①	②	③	④	⑤	⑥
7	①	②	③	④	⑤	⑥
8	①	②	③	④	⑤	⑥
9	①	②	③	④	⑤	⑥
10	①	②	③	④	⑤	⑥
11	①	②	③	④	⑤	⑥
12	①	②	③	④	⑤	⑥
13	①	②	③	④	⑤	⑥
14	①	②	③	④	⑤	⑥
15	①	②	③	④	⑤	⑥
16	①	②	③	④	⑤	⑥
17	①	②	③	④	⑤	⑥
18	①	②	③	④	⑤	⑥
19	①	②	③	④	⑤	⑥
20	①	②	③	④	⑤	⑥

解答番号	解答欄 1	2	3	4	5	6
21	①	②	③	④	⑤	⑥
22	①	②	③	④	⑤	⑥
23	①	②	③	④	⑤	⑥
24	①	②	③	④	⑤	⑥
25	①	②	③	④	⑤	⑥
26	①	②	③	④	⑤	⑥
27	①	②	③	④	⑤	⑥
28	①	②	③	④	⑤	⑥
29	①	②	③	④	⑤	⑥
30	①	②	③	④	⑤	⑥
31	①	②	③	④	⑤	⑥
32	①	②	③	④	⑤	⑥
33	①	②	③	④	⑤	⑥
34	①	②	③	④	⑤	⑥
35	①	②	③	④	⑤	⑥
36	①	②	③	④	⑤	⑥
37	①	②	③	④	⑤	⑥
38	①	②	③	④	⑤	⑥
39	①	②	③	④	⑤	⑥
40	①	②	③	④	⑤	⑥

実戦問題集　英語（リスニング）解答用紙

（きりとり）

マーク例

良い例	悪い例
●	◐ ⊗ ◖ ○

注意事項

1　訂正は、消しゴムできれいに消し、消しくずを残してはいけません。

2　所定欄以外にはマークしたり、記入したりしてはいけません。

3　汚したり、折り曲げたりしてはいけません。

① 受験番号を記入し、その下のマーク欄にマークしなさい。

受験番号欄

受験番号欄				
千位	百位	十位	一位	英字

受験番号 マークミス欄

② 氏名・フリガナ、試験場コードを記入しなさい。

フリガナ	
氏名	

試験場コード					
十万位	万位	千位	百位	十位	一位

氏名等チェック欄

解答番号 1〜20

解答番号	解答欄 1 2 3 4 5 6
1	① ② ③ ④ ⑤ ⑥
2	① ② ③ ④ ⑤ ⑥
3	① ② ③ ④ ⑤ ⑥
4	① ② ③ ④ ⑤ ⑥
5	① ② ③ ④ ⑤ ⑥
6	① ② ③ ④ ⑤ ⑥
7	① ② ③ ④ ⑤ ⑥
8	① ② ③ ④ ⑤ ⑥
9	① ② ③ ④ ⑤ ⑥
10	① ② ③ ④ ⑤ ⑥
11	① ② ③ ④ ⑤ ⑥
12	① ② ③ ④ ⑤ ⑥
13	① ② ③ ④ ⑤ ⑥
14	① ② ③ ④ ⑤ ⑥
15	① ② ③ ④ ⑤ ⑥
16	① ② ③ ④ ⑤ ⑥
17	① ② ③ ④ ⑤ ⑥
18	① ② ③ ④ ⑤ ⑥
19	① ② ③ ④ ⑤ ⑥
20	① ② ③ ④ ⑤ ⑥

解答番号	解答欄 1 2 3 4 5 6
21	① ② ③ ④ ⑤ ⑥
22	① ② ③ ④ ⑤ ⑥
23	① ② ③ ④ ⑤ ⑥
24	① ② ③ ④ ⑤ ⑥
25	① ② ③ ④ ⑤ ⑥
26	① ② ③ ④ ⑤ ⑥
27	① ② ③ ④ ⑤ ⑥
28	① ② ③ ④ ⑤ ⑥
29	① ② ③ ④ ⑤ ⑥
30	① ② ③ ④ ⑤ ⑥
31	① ② ③ ④ ⑤ ⑥
32	① ② ③ ④ ⑤ ⑥
33	① ② ③ ④ ⑤ ⑥
34	① ② ③ ④ ⑤ ⑥
35	① ② ③ ④ ⑤ ⑥
36	① ② ③ ④ ⑤ ⑥
37	① ② ③ ④ ⑤ ⑥
38	① ② ③ ④ ⑤ ⑥
39	① ② ③ ④ ⑤ ⑥
40	① ② ③ ④ ⑤ ⑥

実戦問題集 英語（リスニング）解答用紙

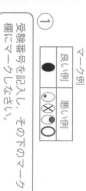

マーク例

良い例	悪い例
●	⊘ ⊗ ◐

① 受験番号を記入し、その下のマーク欄にマークしなさい。

受験番号欄

千位	百位	十位	一位	英字
－	⓪	⓪	⓪	Ⓐ A
①	①	①	①	Ⓑ B
②	②	②	②	Ⓒ C
③	③	③	③	Ⓗ H
④	④	④	④	Ⓚ K
⑤	⑤	⑤	⑤	Ⓜ M
⑥	⑥	⑥	⑥	Ⓡ R
⑦	⑦	⑦	⑦	Ⓤ U
⑧	⑧	⑧	⑧	Ⓨ Y
⑨	⑨	⑨	⑨	Ⓩ Z

受験番号
マークチェック欄

② 氏名・フリガナ、試験場コードを記入しなさい。

フリガナ						
氏名						
試験場コード	十万位	万位	千位	百位	十位	一位

氏名・番号
チェック欄

注意事項

1 訂正は、消しゴムできれいに消し、消しくずを残してはいけません。

2 所定欄以外にはマークしたり、記入したりしてはいけません。

3 汚したり、折り曲げたりしてはいけません。

解答欄

解答番号	1	2	3	4	5	6
1	①	②	③	④	⑤	⑥
2	①	②	③	④	⑤	⑥
3	①	②	③	④	⑤	⑥
4	①	②	③	④	⑤	⑥
5	①	②	③	④	⑤	⑥
6	①	②	③	④	⑤	⑥
7	①	②	③	④	⑤	⑥
8	①	②	③	④	⑤	⑥
9	①	②	③	④	⑤	⑥
10	①	②	③	④	⑤	⑥
11	①	②	③	④	⑤	⑥
12	①	②	③	④	⑤	⑥
13	①	②	③	④	⑤	⑥
14	①	②	③	④	⑤	⑥
15	①	②	③	④	⑤	⑥
16	①	②	③	④	⑤	⑥
17	①	②	③	④	⑤	⑥
18	①	②	③	④	⑤	⑥
19	①	②	③	④	⑤	⑥
20	①	②	③	④	⑤	⑥

解答欄

解答番号	1	2	3	4	5	6
21	①	②	③	④	⑤	⑥
22	①	②	③	④	⑤	⑥
23	①	②	③	④	⑤	⑥
24	①	②	③	④	⑤	⑥
25	①	②	③	④	⑤	⑥
26	①	②	③	④	⑤	⑥
27	①	②	③	④	⑤	⑥
28	①	②	③	④	⑤	⑥
29	①	②	③	④	⑤	⑥
30	①	②	③	④	⑤	⑥
31	①	②	③	④	⑤	⑥
32	①	②	③	④	⑤	⑥
33	①	②	③	④	⑤	⑥
34	①	②	③	④	⑤	⑥
35	①	②	③	④	⑤	⑥
36	①	②	③	④	⑤	⑥
37	①	②	③	④	⑤	⑥
38	①	②	③	④	⑤	⑥
39	①	②	③	④	⑤	⑥
40	①	②	③	④	⑤	⑥

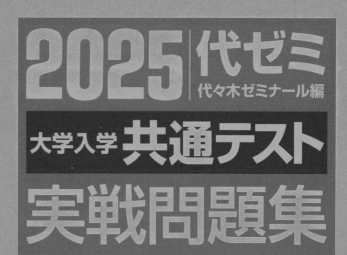

2025 代ゼミ

代々木ゼミナール編

大学入学 共通テスト

実戦問題集

英語

[リーディング・リスニング]

解答・解説

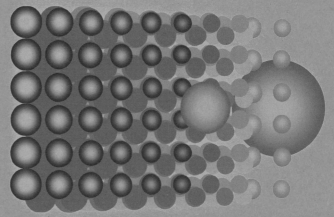

代々木ライブラリー

リーディング・第1回 解 答 と 解 説

問題番号(配点)	設問	解答番号	正解	配点	自己採点
第1問 (10)	A	1	3	2	
	A	2	1	2	
	B	3	4	2	
	B	4	2	2	
	B	5	3	2	
自己採点小計					
第2問 (20)	A	6	5	2	
	A	7	2	2	
	A	8	3	2	
	A	9	1	2	
	A	10	2	2	
	B	11	5	2	
	B	12	2	2	
	B	13	2	2	
	B	14	1	2	
	B	15	2	2	
自己採点小計					
第3問 (15)	A 1	16	1	3	
	A 2	17	4	3	
	B 1	18	2	3*	
		19	1		
		20	3		
		21	4		
	B 2	22	3	3	
	B 3	23	4	3	
自己採点小計					

問題番号(配点)	設問	解答番号	正解	配点	自己採点
第4問 (16)	1	24	1	3	
	2	25	4	2	
	3	26	2	2	
	4	27	1	3	
	5	28	1	3	
	5	29	4	3	
自己採点小計					
第5問 (15)	1	30	1	3*	
		31	3		
		32	4		
		33	5		
		34	2		
	2	35	1	4	
	3	36-37	1-3	4*	
	4	38	4	4	
自己採点小計					
第6問 (24)	A 1	39	3	3	
	A 2	40	4	3	
	A 3	41	1	3	
	A 4	42	3	3	
	B 1	43	3	3	
	B 2	44	4	3	
	B 2	45	3	3	
	B 3	46-47	2-6	3*	
自己採点小計					

自己採点合計

(注)
1 *は全部正解の場合のみ点を与える。
2 −(ハイフン)でつながれた正解は，順序を問わない。

第1問

A

問1 「スケジュールによれば，_____1_____ の両方に応募することはできない」

① アンとエリザ
② アンとオラグ
③ クリストファーとオラグ
④ エリザとオラグ

正解 ⇒ ③

オーディションスケジュールを見ると，日程が同じ5月1日で，時間も似たような午後4時頃となっているのはオラグとクリストファーである。場所もそれぞれ異なる建物にあるため，掛け持ちは厳しいと考えられる。その他の組み合わせは日程が異なっており，掛け持ち可能である。

問2 「もしあなたがどうしてもオラグ役を勝ち取りたかったら，_____2_____」

① 面白い演技を見せて審査員を笑わせる
② 6年間，歌のレッスンを受けてきたことを伝える個人メッセージを送る
③ 審査員にあなたの優雅な踊りを見せる
④ このチャットの人々に，あなたは背が高くてバク転ができることを伝える

正解 ⇒ ①

審査員はオラグに「簡単な演技力」を求めるとともに，「愛嬌があって朗らかな性格の人」であることを期待している。これに応えられるのは①である。②や③はアンやエリザ，④はクリストファーを希望する場合に適する。

【全訳】

クラスメイトのアイリーンが，今度行われるミュージカルのグループチャットにメッセージを送信しました。

皆さん，こんにちは！

秋に行われる文化祭でのミュージカル制作にご参加いただき，ありがとうございます。配役についてですが，人気の高い以下の役はオーディションをすることになりました。日時と場所を確認の上，応募したい方はこのチャットにメッセージを入れて下さい。私に個人メッセージを送っていただいてもかまいません。

アン　　　4月26日午後12時20分　　C302教室にて
エリザ　　4月28日午後12時20分　　C310教室にて
オラグ　　5月1日午後4時　　　　　A棟視聴覚室にて
クリストファー　5月1日午後3時50分　　D棟体育館にて

アンとエリザは歌唱力とダンス，オラグは簡単な演技力，クリストファーは簡単な演技力と身体能力を見たいと思います。オラグ役には，愛嬌があって朗らかな性格の人を募集します。何か特技がある人は，申し込みのメッセージに書き添えて下さい。
たくさんのお申し込みをお待ちしております！

【語句・表現】
・upcoming「今後行われる」
・casting「配役」
・audition「オーディション」
・role「役割」
・private message「個人メッセージ」
・audio-visual room「視聴覚室」
・physical ability「身体能力」
・cheerful「朗らかな，明るい」
・personality「性格」
・application「申し込み」
＜選択肢＞
・backflip「バク転」

B
問1　「8月5日に東京を出発した場合，あなたは8月7日の正午には　3　」

① 東京ターミナルに到着している
② 竿燈祭りを楽しんでいる
③ 弘前市内でお昼を食べている
④ 美しい湖の周辺を散策している

　正解 ⇒ ④

　8月5日に出発した場合，7日は旅程の第3日目に相当する。3日目の昼頃には田沢湖に来ているはずなので，④が正解。

問2　「次のどれが料金に含まれているか」　4

① 田沢湖のお土産屋さんで飲むビール
② 青森に向かうバス車内での弁当
③ 1日目と2日目の朝食
④ ねぶたを見ている時に屋台で食べる焼きそば

　正解 ⇒ ②

　表中の「料金に含まれる食事」の欄を見ると，1日目のバス車内で配布される弁当は料金内であることが分かる。①は表下の注意事項に「料金内の食事ではアルコールの提供はない」と述べられているので，これは当てはまらない。③も1日目の朝食が含まれていないので不適切。④については，1日目の夕食は自由行動のため，含まれない。

問3　「このウェブサイトから分かることとして適切なのは次のどれか」　5

① 竿燈祭りで怪我をした場合，添乗員さんに助けてもらうことができる。
② バスで良い席を取りたかったら，行列に早めに並ぶべきだ。
③ 帰りに，もし群馬SAで夕食をとらないのなら，お土産を選ぶ時間はたっぷりある。
④ 青森に向かう途中で朝食休憩がある。

正解 ⇒ ③

　表下の注意事項を見ていく。①は，注意事項の2番目に「添乗員は夜の祭りには同行しない」とあることから，不適切。②については，最初の注意事項で「席は全席指定」とあることから，並んでも意味がないと分かる。④については，帰りの東京行きのバスでは群馬SAでの休憩が約束されているが，行きについては特に言及されていないので分からない。③は，表中にも「群馬SAで50分間の休憩」とあることから，もし夕食をとるつもりがないのならお土産選びに当てることが可能なので，これが正解。

【全訳】
　あなたは青森のねぶたなどの東北夏祭りを見に行こうかと考え，旅行会社のウェブサイトを見ています。

東京発東北夏祭りツアー
青森ねぶた祭り＋秋田竿燈祭り
2泊3日の旅が49,800円で！！

東北の二大祭りを満喫しましょう。「青森ねぶた祭り」と「秋田竿燈祭り」，さらに美しい東北の観光地巡りを3日間にググッと凝縮！ エネルギーあふれる祭りの魅力をご体感ください！「たつこ姫像」のある田沢湖など，東北の観光名所もふんだんにまわります。

日程	旅程	料金に含まれる食事
1	6:00　東京ターミナルを出発 16:30　青森バスターミナルに到着 　青森ねぶた祭りの夜をお楽しみ下さい 　〜青森駅の近くにあるホテルにご宿泊〜	朝食：× 昼食：○　（バス内でお弁当配布） 夕食：×
2	7:30　青森駅を出発 8:30　弘前城に到着 　弘前市内観光をお楽しみ下さい 13:00　秋田市に向けて出発 16:40　秋田バスターミナルに到着 　秋田竿燈祭りの夜をお楽しみ下さい 　〜秋田市にあるホテルにご宿泊〜	朝食：○ 昼食：○　（弘前市内） 夕食：×
3	8:30　　秋田県田沢湖に向けて出発 　美しい田沢湖観光をお楽しみ下さい 13:00　東京に向けて出発 22:50　東京町ターミナルに到着	朝食：○ 昼食：○　（田沢湖にて） 夕食：×　（群馬SAにて50分間の休憩があります）

✧　当バスは全コース指定席です。当日の先着順に席が決まるわけではありませんので，バス乗り場に早くから並んでいただく必要はありません。ツアー中は常に同じ座席をご利用いただきます。お客さまからの座席についてのご希望はお受けしておりません。

✧　添乗員は弘前城観光と田沢湖観光には同行いたします。1日目と2日目の夜のお祭りには同行いたしません。

✧　1日目と2日目の到着後は市内での自由行動となります。そのため，両日とも夕飯は料金に含まれていません。料金内のお食事には，アルコールのご提供はありません。

✧　3日目の夕飯も料金には含まれていませんが，帰路にて群馬サービスエリアで休憩時間をとります。バス内部座席付近にもトイレは設置されています。

【語句・表現】
・including「〜を含めて」

- travel agency「旅行代理店」
- sightseeing spot「観光名所」
- statue「像，立像」
- attractive「魅力的な」
- castle「城」
- reserved「予約された，指定された」
- line「行列に並ぶ」
- determine「～を決定する」
- on a first-come, first-served basis「先着順」
- accept「受け入れる」
- tour guide「添乗員」
- accompany「～に同行する，ついて行く」
- explore「～を探検する，巡る」
- facility「設備」
- available「利用可能な」
- rear seat「後部座席」

＜選択肢＞
- souvenir「お土産」
- stall「屋台」
- get injured「怪我をする」

第2問

A

問1 「この研究所でできる2つのことは　6　である」

A：図書館で食べ物を持参して食べる
B：1階で入館証をもらう
C：学習エリアでカウンセリングを利用する
D：興味のある分野の研究をする
E：コピー機で本の一部をコピーする

正解 ⇒ ⑤

　Dは学習相談の項目で，学習相談の目的は生徒の興味を明確化することを目的として挙げているので正しい。Eは卒業生のコメントの5つ目に，「面談エリアの隣にあるコピー機は無料で使えますので，本の中の必要なページをコピーすることができます」という記述があるので正しいことが分かる。
　Aは卒業生のコメントの3つ目より誤り。Bは入館証の項目で，メールに添付されている入館証を印刷しなければならないことが分かるので誤り。Cは学習相談の項目で，カウンセリングは学習エリアではなく面談エリアで実施されていることが分かるので誤り。

問2 「今あなたは2階のコンピューターエリアにいて，学習記録の用紙を手に入れたいと思っている。
　　 あなたは　7　ことで入手できる」

① 1階下りる
② 2階上がる
③ 3階上がる
④ 同じ階にとどまる

正解 ⇒ ②

　学習記録の項目の2文目に，「用紙は3階と4階の学習エリアに置いてあります」とあるので，2階から学習記録を入手するためには1階もしくは2階上がらなければいけないことが分かるため，②が正解。イギリス英語では，ground floor が1階，first floor が2階，second floor が3階，third floor が4階を指すことに注意。

問3 「　8　はコピー機のすぐ隣に設けられている」

① コンピューターエリアの一つ
② 学習エリアの一つ
③ 面談エリア
④ Wi-Fi 基地局

正解 ⇒ ③

　卒業生のコメントの5つ目に，「面談エリアの隣にあるコピー機は無料で使えます」という記述があるので，③が正解。

問4 「50分のレッスンを希望し，混雑を避けたい場合は 9 ことができる」

① レッスンを午後3:00までに開始する
② レッスンを午後7:10までに開始する
③ 朝25分間，夜25分間レッスンを受ける
④ 日中30分間，夜20分間レッスンを受ける

正解 ⇒ ①

卒業生のコメントの2つ目に，「レッスンを受けることは朝や日中が楽で，夕方は混み合います」という記載がある。よって①が正解。

問5 「卒業生によって述べられている事実の1つは 10 ということである」

① コンピューターエリアで入館証をカラー印刷することができる
② 研究所では，30,000冊を超えない蔵書がある
③ 長時間の勉強で頭痛に悩む学生を，研究所の落ち着いた音楽が癒す
④ 学習記録用紙は4階の方が取りやすい

正解 ⇒ ②

卒業生のコメントの3つ目に，約20,000冊の蔵書を持つ図書館があると述べられているので，②が正解。
①，③は本文に同様の内容の記述がないため不適。④は卒業生のコメントの2つ目の内容と一致するがこの会員の主観であり，事実とは言えないので誤り。

【全訳】
　あなたは，英国の学習研究所で開催される教育プログラムに参加しています。あなたは，プログラムや研究所の施設に関する情報を読んでいるところです。

学習研究所
月曜日～金曜日：午前9時―午後9時
入館証：研究所にお越しの際は，ウェルカムメールに添付されている入館証をA4カラーで印刷し，お持ちください。

学習相談
グローバルに活躍できる人材になるためのサポートをします。自分の好きなこと，得意なこと，興味のあること，気になることを伸ばし，世界で活躍できる力を最大限に発揮してください。1階の入り口右手の面談エリアで，午前10時から午後8時までカウンセリングを行っています。自分の興味のあるテーマを見つけ，アイデアを形にするための課題に取り組みます。

学習記録
その日に学んだことを記録するために，研究所を訪れるたびに「学習記録」を書くことが義務づけられています。用紙は3階と4階の学習エリアに置いてあります。また，各分野の専門スタッフが1日20～60分程度，あなたのために考えられた授業を実施する時間を設けていますので，記入の際にはご活用ください。

施設情報
研究所を訪問する際には，入館証を提示する必要があります。全フロアでWi-Fiが利用可能です。必要なパスワードは，研究所に到着した際にお渡しします。コンピューターエリアは，2階左側と3階

にあり，終日利用可能です。

> 卒業生のコメント
> ● このプログラムは最高。学校の成績に関係なく，自分の勉強がどのようにして社会貢献につながるかを知ることができます。
> ● レッスンの受講は，朝や日中が楽で，夕方には混雑しています。3階の学習記録用紙のラックが混雑しているので，4階で取ることができます。
> ● 約20,000冊の蔵書を持つ図書館があるので，調べ物には困らないでしょう。食べ物の持ち込みはできませんが，ペットボトル飲料は持ち込めます。
> ● 館内は落ち着いたBGMが流れ，たくさんの植物があり，そこにいるだけで癒されます。コピー機を使うたびに入館証を使わなければならないのは，頭が痛いですが。
> ● 面談エリアの隣にあるコピー機は無料で利用できますので，本の中の必要なページをコピーすることができます。貸出可能な本とそうでない本があります。

【語句・表現】
・institute「研究所，機関」
・attach「〜を貼り付ける，〜を添付する」
・quest「追求，探求」
・competent「能力のある，有能な」
・maximise「〜を最大化する」
・ground floor「（イギリス英語で）1階」；2階がfirst floor，3階がsecond floorとなる。
・insight「理解，見識」
・potential「可能性，潜在能力」
・consultation「相談」
・rack「ラック，棚」
・calm「落ち着いた，穏やかな」
・photocopy「〜を複写機でコピーする」

B

問1 「ビルの記事によると，現在日本の学校給食のメニューにない食品は以下のうちどれか」 □11

> ① カレーライス，揚げパン，ソフト麺，わかめごはん
> ② 鯨の唐揚げ，冷凍みかん，牛乳
> ③ 揚げパン，ソフト麺，脱脂粉乳
> ④ コッペパン，揚げパン，レーズンパン
> ⑤ 脱脂粉乳，鯨の唐揚げ，ソフト麺
> ⑥ ソフト麺，揚げパン，わかめごはん

正解 ⇒ ⑤

　脱脂粉乳については第2段落第2文に，鯨の唐揚げは第5段落第1文に，ソフト麺は第5段落第2〜3文に，それぞれ他のものと置き換えられたか，学校給食から姿を消したという趣旨が書かれている。したがって⑤が正解。

問2 「ビルによると，日本の学校給食の歴史に最も大きな変化をもたらした出来事は以下のうちどれか」 □12

> ① 学校給食にパンと麺の種類が増えた。

② 日本の学校給食にコッペパンが登場した。
③ 米が日本の学校給食の主食になった。
④ 脱脂粉乳が牛乳に変わった。

正解 ⇒ ②

第1段落第1文に「(学校給食が) 最も進歩したのは第二次世界大戦の後になってからだった」と書かれており，その直後で，大戦後に学校給食の主要なメニューになった食品たちが挙げられている。そのうちの一つにコッペパンが含まれているので②が正解となる。①は第2段落第1文，③は第3段落，④は第2段落第2文に記述があるものの，最も大きな変化をもたらした出来事とまでは書かれていないので不適。

問3 「世代別の違いに関する次の記述のうち，正しいものはどれか」 13

① 30代以上の学校での人気メニューはカレーライスである。
② 20代は学校でソフト麺を食べてこなかった。
③ 30代，40代はわかめごはんの給食を食べていた。
④ 30代は鯨肉の給食を食べていた最後の世代である。

正解 ⇒ ②

第5段落第2文にソフト麺に関する記述があり，続く第3文で「ソフト麺は1990年代のある時期から給食で提供されなくなったので，最も若い世代はどういう味がするのか知らない」と述べられているので，②が正解である。

問4 「日本の学校給食に関するビルの記事について正しいのは次のうちどれか」 14

① 日本が豊かになるにつれて，学校給食はより多様なものになった。
② パンもご飯も，学校給食において共に同じくらい重要な食材である。
③ 鯨肉を食べることは，いかなる文化的な理由があっても禁止されるべきではない。
④ ソフト麺は人気があっておいしかったので，復活させるべきだ。

正解 ⇒ ①

第2段落第1文に1960年代に日本社会が豊かになるにつれて，様々な食品が学校給食のメニューに追加されたことが，次いで第3段落でも1980年代に学校給食のメニューがより多様になったことが述べられているので，①が正解である。

問5 「記事に最もふさわしいタイトルはどれか」 15

① 日本人は給食が好き？
② 日本の学校給食はどのように進化してきたのか？
③ 日本の学校給食はどうなっているのか？
④ なぜ日本でパンが人気となったのか？

正解 ⇒ ②

本文全体を通して，日本の学校給食のメニューがどのように移り変わってきたかが述べられているので，②が正解。③は現在にしか焦点が当たっていないので不適。①と④に関しても言及されていないので不適。

【全訳】
　あなたは学校の英字新聞の編集者です。アメリカからの交換留学生であるビルが新聞に記事を書きました。

　　日本の学校給食の歴史は明治時代まで遡るが，最も進歩したのは第二次世界大戦の後になってからだった。1940年代後半に，コッペパン，つまりホットドッグのパン，そして脱脂粉乳が学校給食の主要なメニューとなった。アメリカから輸入された小麦で作られたパンが日本全国で食べられるようになってから日本の食生活は劇的に変化した。

　　1960年代に日本社会が豊かになるにつれ，学校給食のメニューには，揚げパンやレーズンパン，ソフト麺，カレーやミートソースをトッピングした汁なしうどんなどが追加された。同時期，子どもたちに人気のなかった脱脂粉乳は牛乳に取って代わられることとなった。これらの食品が新しく追加されたことで，学校給食の種類は豊富になったのである。

　　結局，1980年代に，パンよりも米が多く出されるようになり，米が学校給食の主食になった。それ以降学校給食のメニューはさらに多様化した。

　　2020年に行われた調査では，20代から50代の人々に「あなたが子どもの頃に食べた学校給食で一番好きな食べ物は何ですか？」と質問した。その回答から抜粋した，4世代で集まった上位4つの食べ物が以下の通りである。
▶ 50s—1. 揚げパン　　　　2. カレーライス　　　3. ソフト麺　　　　4. 鯨の唐揚げ
▶ 40s—1. カレーライス　　2. 揚げパン　　　　　3. ソフト麺　　　　4. 冷凍みかん
▶ 30s—1. カレーライス　　2. 揚げパン　　　　　3. ソフト麺　　　　4. わかめごはん
▶ 20s—1. 揚げパン　　　　2. カレーライス　　　3. 鶏の唐揚げ　　　4. わかめごはん
　　1980年代後半には，営利目的の捕鯨が禁止され，学校給食から鯨の唐揚げが姿を消したが，それ以前は子どもたちのお気に入りの給食メニューの一つだった。同じように，30代から50代の人々の間ではソフト麺が非常に人気だった。しかし，1990年代になって学校給食で提供されなくなったため，最も若い世代はその味を知らないのである。

【語句・表現】
・editor「編集者」
・date back to ~「~に遡る」
・*koppepan*「コッペパン」
・skimmed milk powder「脱脂粉乳」
・diet「食事」
・dramatically「劇的に」
・wheat「小麦」
・import「~を輸入する」
・affluent「豊かな，裕福な」
・fried bread「揚げパン」
・raisin bread「レーズンパン」
・replace「~に取って代わる」
・enrich「~を豊かにする」
・eventually「結局，最終的に」
・staple food「主食」
・diverse「多様な，多種な」
・generation「世代」
・extract「~を抜粋する，~を引き出す」
・commercial「営利目的の，商業上の」
・whaling「捕鯨」
・prohibit「~を禁止する」
・similarly「同じように，同様に」

第3問

A

問1 「マイケルのブログによると，マイケルも友人も [16] 」

> ① ゴーグルで見る建設現場をリアルに感じた
> ② デジタル技術についてのプレゼンは退屈だった
> ③ 今のマンホールは単調だと思った
> ④ 予定通りの数のビスケットを買えた

正解 ⇒ ①

第4段落第2文で，ゴーグルを装着してあたかも現場にいるかのようだったと述べられているので①が適切。

問2 「マイケルと彼の友人は， [17] と思った」

> ① デジタル技術は下水道の補修ではほとんど役に立たない
> ② マンホールはまだ滑りやすいので，改善されなければならない
> ③ 発表者は上手にプレゼンテーションをしていた
> ④ **下水道は環境問題と関係がある**

正解 ⇒ ④

最終段落第1文で，下水道が豪雨といった環境問題と関係している重要なインフラだと二人とも再認識したと述べられているので，④が適切。

【全訳】
　あなたは，下水道システムに興味があります。あなたは，イギリスで工学を学ぶ大学生によるブログ記事を読んでいます。

> マイケル・ウィルソン
> 　私は下水道に関心があります。変な趣味であるのは分かっていますが，興味深いものではあると思います。最近，友人の一人とロンドンで催された下水道展というイベントに参加してきました。
> 　私たちはまず，マンホールを製造している会社のブースを訪れました。私は以前，自転車に乗っていてマンホールで滑ったことがあります。そのため，最近のマンホールは滑らなくなっており，また，ローカルなデザインも含め，様々なデザインがあることに，私たちは感心しました。
> 　次に，私たちは，デジタル技術で効率的に下水管を補修する試みについてのプレゼンを聞きました。私は，この技術が将来AIやロボット技術と組み合わされば，さらに有用になるだろうと思いました。私はこのプレゼンが面白いと思ったのですが，発表をしていた人のしゃべり方がいくぶん単調だったので，友人は興味が持てない様子でした。
> 　最後に，私たちは，下水道の工事現場を見ることのできるバーチャルリアリティーのシステムを体験しました。専用のゴーグルを付けて，私たちは実際に現場にいるように感じました。
> 　私たちは昼食を食べた後，下水管の形をしたユニークなビスケットを購入するためにお土産屋に立ち寄りました。私たちはそれぞれ5個ずつ買って，友人たちにお土産として配ろうと考えていました。しかし，大変な人気商品だったので，一人1個しか買うことができず，そのことに私たちはとてもガッカリしました。
> 　その他にも，展示会ではいろいろな新しい技術が紹介されており，下水道は地球温暖化による豪雨

といった問題と関係しており，重要なインフラであることを再認識させられました。私たちは，展示会を大変楽しみました。

【語句・表現】
〈第1段落〉
・sewage「下水」
〈第2段落〉
・booth「ブース」
・manufacture「〜を製造する」
・manhole「マンホール」
・be impressed to *do*「〜することに感心する」
・various「様々な」
〈第3段落〉
・attempt「試み」
・efficiently「効率的に」
・be combined with 〜「〜と組み合わされる」
・AI「人工知能」：artificial intelligence の略。
・robotics「ロボット技術」
・somewhat「いくぶん」
・monotonous「単調な」
〈第4段落〉
・virtual reality「バーチャルリアリティー，仮想現実」
・construction「建設」
・goggle「ゴーグル」
〈第5段落〉
・souvenir「土産」
・to *one's* disappointment「〜が失望したことに」
〈第6段落〉
・infrastructure「インフラストラクチャー，インフラ」：社会基盤のこと。

B
問1 「次の観光地（①〜④）を，建設された順にならべなさい」

| 18 | → | 19 | → | 20 | → | 21 |

---

① クライスト・チャーチ・カレッジ
② ローマ浴場
③ ロイヤル・クレセント
④ ザ・カヴァーン・クラブ

正解 ⇒ | 18 | ② | | 19 | ① | | 20 | ③ | | 21 | ④ |

②についてはバースの項目の第3文に該当し，現在から約2,000年前に建設されたことがわかる。①については「オックスフォード」の項目の第2文に該当し，1546年に建設されたことがわかる。③については「バース」の項目の第6文に該当し，1767年〜1774年の間に建設されたことがわかる。④については「リバプール」の項目の最終文に該当し，1957年にオープンしたことが分かる。したがって，②→①→③→④の順番である。

問2　「街全体を見渡せる眺めのよい建物はどれか」　22

①　バース修道院
②　クライスト・チャーチ・カレッジ
③　セント・メアリー教会
④　ロイヤル・クレセント

正解 ⇒ ③

「オックスフォード」の項目の最終文に The church's observation deck overlooks this beautiful city.「その教会の展望台からは，この美しい街並みを見渡すことができる」とあるので，③が適当。

問3　「ロンドンからの交通手段に関する次の記述のうち，正しいものはどれか」　23

①　ロンドンからオックスフォードまでは，電車で1時間半かかる。
②　コーチでの移動は，電車を利用するよりも割高になる。
③　リバプールへは電車で1時間30分で行ける。
④　オックスフォード，バース，リバプールへはコーチで行くことができる。

正解 ⇒ ④

　最終段落第5文より，コーチは英国内の著名な都市を結ぶことが分かるので④が適当である。最終段落第2文より，電車でオックスフォードまでは約1時間かかると述べられているので①は不適。最終段落最終文より，コーチならオックスフォードまでは2時間以上かかるが，電車より安いと述べられているので②は不適。最終段落第3文より，リバプールまでは2時間ちょっとかかることが分かるので③は不適。

【全訳】
　この夏，英国を訪れる予定のあなたは，旅行雑誌でロンドンからの日帰り旅行先を紹介する興味深い記事を見つけました。

ロンドンからの最高の日帰り旅行

ダニエル・ジョンソン（著）

　ロンドンは，観光名所の多い大都市として世界中に知られています。しかし，この巨大な都市の周りには，他にも魅力的な都市がたくさんあります。私がお勧めするのは，次の観光地です：オックスフォード，バース，リバプール。
　オックスフォード：この街には，40もの古くからの歴史ある大学があります。特に有名な観光スポットは，1546年に設立された「クライスト・チャーチ・カレッジ」です。その食堂「グレートホール」は，映画『ハリー・ポッター』のロケ地として使用されました。また，オックスフォードには，700万冊以上の蔵書を誇る「ボドリアン図書館」があります。オックスフォード大学の中心にある「セント・メアリー教会」は，美しいステンドグラスの窓で有名です。その展望台からは，この美しい街並みを見渡すことができます。
　バース：その歴史的・建築的価値から街全体が世界遺産に登録されています。最大の観光スポットは「ローマ浴場」です。約2000年前にローマ人によって建てられた古代の公衆浴場です。また，ゴシック様式の教会「バース修道院」も必見です。教会の内部では美しいアーチやステンドグラスを見ることができます。現在，高級ホテルとして利用されている「ロイヤル・クレセント」は，1767年から1774年にかけて建設されました。元々は30軒の建物が曲線状に並んでいたそうです。
　リバプール：ビートルズ発祥の地として知られるイングランド北西部の都市。現在でも，彼らの

ファンが世界中から集まっています。「ビートルズ・ストーリー」はビートルズに特化した博物館
で，歴史上最も重要なロックバンドの写真や貴重な記念品を見ることができます。また，ビートルズ
の歌詞に登場するカフェ「ペニー・レイン」や，1960年代に4人の若者がライブを行ったナイトクラ
ブ「ザ・カヴァーン・クラブ」も見学できます。そのクラブは1957年にオープンしました。
　　この3つの都市は，ロンドンから電車で行くことができます。例えば，オックスフォードまでは電
車で約1時間，バースまでは約1時間20分です。リバプールには電車で2時間強で行くことができま
す。さらに，「コーチ」と呼ばれる交通手段もあります。この長距離バスサービスはこれらのような
英国内の著名な都市を結びます。オックスフォードまではコーチで2時間以上かかりますが，運賃は
かなり安いです。

【語句・表現】
・destination「行先，目的地」
・metropolis「大都市，主要都市」
・gigantic「巨大な，膨大な」
・boast「～を誇る」
・volume「書物，本」
・observation deck「展望台」
・overlook「～を見下ろす」
・World Heritage「世界遺産」
・architectural「建築上の，建築学の」
・arch「アーチ，迫持」
・lay out「～を設計する，～をきちんと並べる」
・birthplace「発祥の地，源」
・dedicated「ある特定の，特化した」
・lyrics「歌詞」
・play live「生演奏をする」
・prominent「著名な，卓越した」
・fare「運賃」

第4問

問1 「ルイスがジムギアでの購入を勧める理由は 24 からである」

> ① あらゆるレベルのジム愛好家のためのアイテムが豊富に揃っている
> ② 大学生に対する割引がある
> ③ お店の評判につながる
> ④ ジムでのエクササイズに必要なアイテムがある

正解 ⇒ ①

　ルイスの投稿の第1段落第7文に「豊富な品揃えで，毎日，初心者から上級者まで多くのジム通いの生徒が集まっています」と書かれているので①が適当である。

問2 「ジェラルドは 25 購入することが適していると考えている」

> ① 1つのショップですべてのアイテムを
> ② 会員割引のある店でアイテムを
> ③ 時間の節約につながるオンラインでアイテムを
> ④ **複数の選択肢から最も安いアイテムを**

正解 ⇒ ④

　ジェラルドの投稿の第2段落第6～7文に，彼が複数の販売先で購入前に価格を比較すれば良かったと後悔していることが書かれているので④が適切。①は，第2段落第5文で一つのショップで全てのアイテムを購入することが苦労の一つであったと述べられているので不適。

問3 「ルイスとジェラルドは共に 26 だと考えている」

> ① ジム用品の購入は特に初心者にとっては重要
> ② **大学を卒業する前にトレーニングを始めるべき**
> ③ ジム用品を買うときは，一番安いものを選ぶことが大切
> ④ 最短時間で筋肉をつけるには，ジム用品の購入が重要

正解 ⇒ ②

　ルイスの投稿の第1段落第3文では，「大学時代は人生の中でそれを行う最も良い時期です」と書かれている。ジェラルドの投稿の第2段落第1～3文を要約すると，社会人生活を始める前に大学生のうちから筋トレを始めるべきだと主張していることが分かる。よって②が適切である。

問4 「ウェイトベルトを購入しようとしているが，重いので自宅まで配送してほしいと思っている。会員にならずに，送料込みで一番安いのは 27 」

> ① **All Hard.com**
> ② Bomb Muscle.com
> ③ Gymgear
> ④ Monster Gear.com

正解 ⇒ ①

　まず，自宅までの配送が条件となるので商品を配送しない③Gymgear は不適であり，ジェラルドが紹介した商品を配送する３つのウェブサイトから最安値を探す必要がある。ジェラルドの投稿の第４段落を参照し，入会せずに送料込みの総額を算出すると以下の通りである。
・All Hard.com の場合，$125 + $20 = $145
・Bomb Muscle.com の場合，$135 + $30 = $165
・Monster Gear.com の場合，$120 + $30 = $150
上記の通り，①が適切。

問５　「会員にならずに，１kgのプロテインパウダーを１回だけ購入する場合，最も安いのは ｜ 28 ｜ である。会費と送料無料を考慮して，１kgのプロテインパウダーを１年間，２ヶ月に１回注文する場合，一番安いのは ｜ 29 ｜ である」

①　**All Hard.com**
②　Bomb Muscle.com
③　Gymgear
④　**Monster Gear.com**

正解 ⇒ ｜ 28 ｜ ①

　1kg のプロテインパウダーを１回注文した時の売り手ごとに総額を算出する必要がある。ジェラルドの投稿の第４段落を参照し，入会せずに送料込みの総額を算出すると以下の通りである。
・All Hard.com の場合，$45+ $20 = $65
・Bomb Muscle.com の場合，$60+ $30 = $90
・Gymgear の場合，$80
・Monster Gear.com の場合，$70 + $30 = $100
上記の通り，①が適切。

正解 ⇒ ｜ 29 ｜ ④

　1kg のプロテインパウダーを１年間，２ヶ月に１回注文した時の売り手ごとに総額を算出する必要がある。会費と送料はジェラルドの投稿の第４段落を参照し，総額を算出すると以下の通りである。
・All Hard.com の場合，（$45+ $20）×6 = $ 390
・Bomb Muscle.com の場合，（$60−$10）×6 + $100 = $400
・Gymgear の場合，$80×6 = $ 480
・Monster Gear.com の場合，（$70−$20）×6 + $80 = $380
上記の通り，④が適切。

【全訳】

　あなたはアメリカのガーバード大学に入学したばかりの学生です。あなたは２人の学生，ルイスとジェラルドのブログを見つけ，役立つ情報を探すために読んでいます。

ガーバード大学での１年目のスタートでお困りですか？

投稿者: ルイス　投稿日時: 2024年９月１日３時００分

　大学１年生になるのを心待ちにしていますか？　新しいクラブに入ったり，インターンシップに応募したり，新しく始められることはたくさんあるけど，何よりも大事なのはジムに通って筋肉をつけることです。大学時代は人生の中でそれを行う最も良い時期です。しかし，ジムへの第一歩を踏み出す前に，ボディビルやフィットネスへの長い旅をうまく始めるために何を買えばいいのか悩むかもしれません。必要な商品がすべて揃っているお店があるので，心配は無用です。そのお店とは「ジムギア」。オンライン販売はしておらず，配送方法もありませんが，豊富な品揃えで，毎日，初心者から上級者まで多くのジム通いの生徒が集まっています。ここでは，特に初心者の方にチェックしていただきたいアイテムをご紹介します。

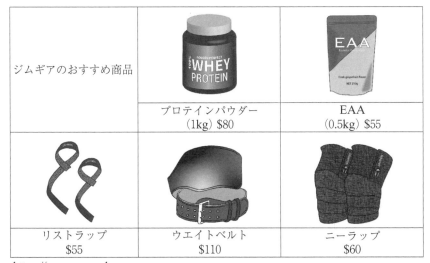

ジムギアのおすすめ商品	プロテインパウダー （1kg）$80	EAA （0.5kg）$55
	リストラップ $55	ウエイトベルト $110

ニーラップ
$60

https://gymgear.web

　上記のジム用品は必須ではありませんが，効率よく筋肉をつけたい，怪我をしたくないという方は是非購入することをおすすめします。後悔しませんよ！

ガーバード大学へようこそ！

投稿者：ジェラルド　投稿日時：2024年９月13日１時００分

　ガーバード大学での大学生活を心待ちにしている新入生へ，ようこそ！　大学ではさまざまな活動がありますが，私の一番のお気に入りはジム通いです。

　せっかく４年間もいるのだから，卒業して社会人になる前にできるだけ筋肉をつけませんか？　社会人になると，毎日時間厳守で早起きしなければならず，毎日ストレスを受けるので，筋肉をつけるのは難しいと聞いています。大学生活の良いところは，ストレスのない環境にいて，毎日の生活を自由に計画できることです。デメリットは，常に予算が限られていることです。私が体を鍛え始めた頃の苦労は，必要なものを１つのショップで買ってしまうことでした。１年後，２年後，もっと安い選択肢が複数あることに気づきました。購入する前に価格を比較すればよかったと思います。

savemoneyforgymtools.com というサイトを見つけたのですが，このサイトはいろいろな e ショップの価格を比較するのにとても役立ちます。このサイトの表を見て，３つのサイトの人気商品の価格を比較してみましょう。

商　品	Monster Gear.com	Bomb Muscle.com	All Hard.com
プロテインパウダー （1kg）	$70	$60	$45
EAA （0.5kg）	$55	$60	$65
リストラップ	$45	$50	$55
ウエイトベルト	$120	$135	$125
ニーラップ	$48	$50	$45

https:// savemoneyforgymtools.com

　　Monster Gear と Bomb Muscle は，オプションで年間会員になることができ，割引があり，送料が無料になります。Monster Gear の会費は年間80ドルで，それぞれの価格から20ドル割引となります。Bomb Muscle の会費は年間100ドルで，それぞれの価格から10ドルの割引があります。１年以内の解約はできません。会員にならない場合，両サイトとも送料は１点につき30ドルです。All Hard. com に関しては，会員制度がなく，送料は１商品につき20ドルです。

【語句・表現】
〈ルイスの投稿〉
・internship「インターンシップ，職業体験」
・journey「旅，道のり」
・bodybuilding「ボディビル」
・fitness「フィットネス，健康」
・gym goer「ジム愛好家，ジム通いする人」
・mandatory「必須の，義務的な」
〈ジェラルドの投稿〉
・why not ～「～すればどうですか」
・enter the workforce「社会人になる，就職する」
・punctual「時間厳守で，時間通りに」
・downside「欠点」
・on a budget「限られた予算で」
・struggle「苦労，苦闘」
・optional「任意の，選択の」
・annual「年間の」
・discount「割引，値引き」
・shipping cost「送料」
〈設問文〉
・take O into consideration「O を考慮する」
・duration「継続，存続期間」

第5問

問1 「あなたのグループのメンバーは，パルマンティエの生涯に関連する重要な出来事を挙げた。その出来事を起きた順番に 30 ～ 34 に入れなさい」

① フランスでジャガイモの栽培が禁止された。
② パルマンティエは自身の提案で賞をもらった。
③ パルマンティエは捕虜としてジャガイモを食べさせられた。
④ パルマンティエがプロイセンからフランスに帰国した。
⑤ パリ大学がジャガイモは食用に適していると宣言した。

正解 ⇒ 30 ①   31 ③   32 ④   33 ⑤   34 ②

　解答根拠となるのは，第2～3段落である。まず第3段落第1文より，フランスでジャガイモの栽培が禁止されたのは1748年であることがわかる。第2段落第2～3文では，パルマンティエが捕虜としてジャガイモを食べたのは七年戦争（1756年～1763年）の期間であったことが述べられているため，①→③となる。第3段落第2文より，パルマンティエがフランスに帰国したのは1763年と述べられていて，七年戦争直後の出来事であると分かるので③→④。第3段落第3文より，パルマンティエがジャガイモを食用にすることを提案して受賞したのは1773年であり，そして第3段落第4文より，パリ大学がジャガイモを食用にすることを認めたのは1772年であると述べられているので，⑤→②となる。

問2 「 35 に入る最も適切なものを1つ選べ」

① ジャガイモは一般に人間の食用に供されていなかった。
② ジャガイモは伝来後すぐに普及した。
③ プロイセン王によってジャガイモの栽培が禁止された。
④ ジャガイモはアイルランドの人々から豚の餌として扱われていた。

正解 ⇒ ①

　まず，問1でみたようにパルマンティエがジャガイモの普及に取り組んだのは18世紀後半なので，それ以前のジャガイモの扱いについての記述を探す。第2段落第4文より，1640年にはジャガイモが全ヨーロッパに伝わったが，アイルランド以外では一般に，家畜の飼料としてのみ使われていたと述べられている。よって①が適切。
　②と④は，この一文と反するため不適。③は，同段落第5文より，「プロイセン王は農民に厳しい罰則のもとに栽培することを義務づけた」という記述があるので，不適。

問3 「 36 ・ 37 に入る最も適切なもの を2つ選べ（順序は問わない）」

① フランス国王と王妃にジャガイモの花を贈った。
② 自分が作った料理にパルマンティエという名前をつけた。
③ 市民にジャガイモを広めるために盗ませた。
④ 一般人を晩餐会に招いてジャガイモを振る舞った。
⑤ 厳しい罰則を設けてジャガイモを栽培するよう人々を脅した。

正解 ⇒ ①・③

　第4段落第2文で，パルマンティエのユニークなジャガイモの普及活動の一つとして，王や王妃にジャ

ガイモの花束を贈ったことが挙げられているので①が適切。同段落第3文より，彼のジャガイモの普及活動の中で最も独特だったのが，ジャガイモの畑を昼間は兵士に護衛させることで貴重な作物を栽培しているように演出し，夜は兵を引き上げさせて，人々に盗ませるという方法だったと述べられている。よって③も適切。

問4 「 38 に入る最も適切なものを1つ選べ」

① 野心的で厳格
② 陽気で友好的
③ 保守的で紳士的
④ 独創的で意志が強い

正解 ⇒ ④

　第4段落でパルマンティエは数多くの独創的なジャガイモの普及活動を行ったことが分かり，また本文全体より彼が様々な困難に直面したにも関わらずジャガイモの普及に成功したことが分かるので，彼は独創的で意志が強い人物だったと言える。

【全訳】

　あなたのグループは，以下の雑誌の記事の情報をもとに，「ジャガイモを広めた男」のポスター発表の準備をしています。

　アントワーネ＝オーギュスタン・パルマンティエは1737年にフランスの北部にあるモンディディエという小さな町で生まれた。彼は薬剤師の職を得たが，農学者，栄養学者としても活躍した。彼にはいくつかの業績があるが，その中でも最も著名なのは，フランスおよびヨーロッパにおいてジャガイモを広めたことである。

　以下は，彼がどうしてジャガイモの推奨者となり，どのようにジャガイモを広めたかのストーリーである。彼は，七年戦争（1756年〜1763年）においてフランス軍に薬剤師として従軍中，プロイセン軍の捕虜となった。プロイセン（現在のドイツ）の獄中で，フランス人には豚の餌としてしか知られていないジャガイモを食べさせられた。ジャガイモは，16世紀頃にスペイン人が南米からヨーロッパに持ち込んだものである。1640年にはヨーロッパの他の地域にも伝わったが，アイルランド以外では一般に，家畜の飼料としてのみ使われていたのである。プロイセン王フリードリヒ2世(1712-1786)は，ジャガイモが寒冷でやせた土地でも生育することに着目し，農民たちに厳しい罰則のもとに栽培することを義務づけた。

　その一方で，フランスでは，ジャガイモは病気の原因になると考えられ，1748年にはジャガイモの栽培が禁止されたほどである。1763年にパリに戻ったパルマンティエは，ジャガイモの栄養学的研究を行った。1769年と1770年の飢饉を受け，1771年に飢饉の際に役立つ食品を獲得するための賞が設けられたコンテストが開催された。パルマンティエはジャガイモの利用を提案し，1773年に賞を獲得したのだった。また，彼の努力のおかげで，パリ大学の医学部は1772年にジャガイモの食用を承認した。しかし，ジャガイモへの抵抗はなおも続き，彼は薬剤師として働いていた病院の試験農場の使用を禁じられたり，病院で希望していたポストへの就任を妨害されたりするなどの苦労も経験した。しかし，彼は決して諦めなかった。

　パルマンティエが，ジャガイモを広めようとした方法はユニークであった。まず，有名人を夕食会に招いてジャガイモ料理を出したり，王や王妃にジャガイモの花束を贈ったりするなどの促進活動を行った。最も面白いのは，ジャガイモの畑を昼間は兵士に護衛させて，貴重な作物を栽培しているのではないかと人々に思わせておき，夜は兵を引き上げさせて，人々に盗ませるという方法であった。1785年は不作の年であったが，フランス北部ではジャガイモによって飢饉を逃れた。このことが，フランスにジャガイモが広まる契機となったのだった。

今日もパルマンティエの名前は，二つの形で我々の間に残っている。一つは，フランスの家庭料理である，牛ひき肉とじゃがいもの重ね焼きアッシ・パルマンティエのように，多くのジャガイモ料理が彼の名前にちなんで名づけられていることである。もう一つは，パリの地下鉄には，彼の功績を記念して，パルマンティエという駅があることである。この駅のホームには，農民にジャガイモを渡す彼の像が立っている。

17世紀末から19世紀まで，ヨーロッパだけでなく全地球上が異常ともいえる低温期にあった。やせた寒い土地でも栽培できるジャガイモは多くの人を飢餓から救うことになった。ジャガイモに対する人々の偏見を取り除くことに成功したパルマンティエの功績は大きいと言えるだろう。

【発表メモの訳】

ジャガイモを広めた男

■重要な出来事

| 30 |
| 31 |
| 32 |
| 33 |
| 34 |

■パルマンティエ以前のヨーロッパにおけるジャガイモ
・16世紀頃にスペイン人が南米から持ち込んだものである。
・ 35

■パルマンティエとジャガイモ
・ 36
・ 37
⇒ヨーロッパ人のジャガイモに対する偏見を払拭することに成功した。

■パルマンティエの人柄
パルマンティエの人柄は，次のように表現できる： 38 。

【語句・構文】

〈第 1 段落〉
・pharmacist「薬剤師」
・profession「職業」
・agronomist「農学者」
・nutritionist「栄養学者」
・be credited with ～「～の功績がある」
・prominent「著名な，卓越した」
〈第 2 段落〉
・advocate「推奨者，擁護者」
・the Seven Years' War「七年戦争」
・feed「餌」
・livestock「家畜」
・King Frederick Ⅱ「フリードリヒ 2 世」
・barren「やせた，不毛な」
・cultivate「～を栽培する，を耕す」

・penalty「罰則」
〈第3段落〉
・on the other hand「一方で」
・famine「飢饉」
・medical faculty「医学部」
・human consumption「食用，人の消費」
・hardship「苦労，困難」
・forbid「〜を禁じる」
〈第4段落〉
・bouquet「花束，ブーケ」
・pull out「撤退する」
〈第5段落〉
・name O C「O を C と名づける」
・minced beef「牛ひき肉」
・metro「地下鉄」
・commemorate「〜を祝う，記念する」
・statue「像」
・hand out 〜「〜を配る，与える」
〈第6段落〉
・starvation「飢餓」
・prejudice「偏見」

第6問

A
問1 「 39 に最も適するものを選びなさい」

① 脳のすぐ後ろの部分
② おでこの前の部分
③ 脳の中で最も前方にある部分
④ 大脳皮質からの信号

正解 ⇒ ③

第4段落第3文に The signal came from a region called the frontopolar cortex, …とあり, この直後で frontopolar cortex について説明されている。「この信号は, 脳の前面, 額のすぐ後ろにある前頭極皮質と呼ばれる領域から発信された」とあるので③が適当である。

問2 「 40 に最も適するものを選びなさい」

① 人間の手の反応は, 脳から送られる信号に基づいている
② 意識と違って脳は数百ミリ秒で判断している
③ 何かをしようと意識したとき, 脳は多くの選択肢を検討した上で1つに絞る
④ あなたが決断することを意識する前にあなたの脳はすでに決断している

正解 ⇒ ④

本文の趣旨は, 第1段落第1文の「あなたの脳は, あなたが気づくより最大10秒前に意思決定をしている」という記述でまとめることができ, 本文に挙がっている実験はその趣旨を検証するためのものである。よって④が適当である。
①については, 実験は被験者の手の反応を調査対象として意志決定における脳内活動を検証しており, 手の反応そのものを調査目的としていないため不適。②と③は本文には述べられていない。

問3 「 41 に最も適するものを選びなさい」

① 脳の反応が特定の意識的な意思決定と結びついていることを確認する
② 使用する手によって脳の反応速度が異なることを示す
③ 人間の精神には意識と無意識があることを保証する
④ 手の動きと意識の働きが分離できることを明らかにする

正解 ⇒ ①

第6段落第1文で, リベットの実験が計測した時間は, 脳の反応が特定の意思決定に関連した活動時間ではなく, 単に運動の一般的な準備時間であったかもしれないという理由で批判を浴びていたことが分かる。第6段落第2～3文で, リベットの実験が受けた批判を踏まえ, ヘインズが被験者に左右の手で意志決定できるように自身の実験を改良した理由は, 左右の手による異なる脳信号で純粋に2つの決定のうちの1つを反映していることを示すことができるからと述べられている。この部分にあてはまる①が適当である。

問4 「 42 に最も適するものを選べ」

① 脳活動
② 創造力
❸ **自由意志**
④ 幻想
⑤ 自己意識

正解 ⇒ ③

最終段落最終文の「神経科学が自由意志の意味を変えてしまう」というトンの主張から， 42 は③が適当である。

【全訳】

あなたの研究グループは，どのように「意思決定をしている」かについて学んでいます。あなたは共有したい記事を見つけました。次のミーティングのための要約ノートを完成させてください。

脳は，あなたが気づかないうちに意思決定している

研究者によると，あなたの脳は，あなたが気づくより最大10秒前に意思決定をしている。研究者らは，意思決定中の脳活動を調べることで，人間が自分で意思決定したことを意識する前に，どのような選択をするかを予測することができた。この研究は，私たちの決断の「意識」に疑問を投げかけるものであり，私たちが特定の時点でどの程度「自由」に選択できるかについての考えさえも覆すかもしれない。

この研究を率いたドイツのマックス・プランク研究所の神経科学者ジョン=ディラン・ヘインズは，「私たちは自分の意思決定が意識的であると思っていますが，これらのデータは意識が氷山の一角であることを示しています」と述べている。ヴァンダービルト大学の神経科学者であるフランク・トンは，「この結果は目を見張るものです」と言う。10秒というのは，脳の活動から見れば「一生分」だと彼は付け加えている。

ヘインズと彼の同僚たちは，14人の被験者の脳を画像化し，意思決定タスクを実行させた。被験者は，衝動を感じたら2つのボタンのうち1つを押すように指示された。それぞれのボタンは別の手で操作された。同時に，スクリーンには0.5秒間隔で文字が表示され，被験者は，ボタンを押す時にどの文字が表示されているかを記憶する必要があった。

研究チームがデータを分析したところ，最も早い信号は，被験者が決断したと報告する7秒前から検出された。画像表示には数秒の遅れがあるため，脳活動は意識的な意思決定の10秒も前に始まっていたことになる。この信号は，脳の前面，額のすぐ後ろにある前頭極皮質と呼ばれる領域から発信された。この領域は，意思決定が開始される脳の領域である可能性が高いと，ヘインズは言う。ヘインズはこの結果を『Nature Neuroscience』誌のオンライン版で報告している。

次のステップは，データ解析の速度を上げて脳が判断している最中に人々の選択を予測できるようにすることである。今回の成果は，1980年代にカリフォルニア大学サンフランシスコ校に在籍していた神経生理学者の故ベンジャミン・リベットが行った，自由意志に関する有名な研究に基づいている。リベットは，ヘインズと同じような実験装置を使ったが，ボタンを1つだけ使って被験者の脳の電気的活動を測定したのである。その結果，意識的な決断が下される数百ミリ秒前に運動を司る領域が反応することを発見した。

しかし，リベットの研究は，その時間の計測方法と，脳の反応が特定の意思決定に関連した活動ではなく単に運動の一般的な準備であったかもしれないという理由で，その後の数十年の間，批判を浴び続けた。ヘインズと彼のチームは，被験者に左と右の2つの選択肢を選んでもらうことでこの方法を改良した。左右の手を動かすと，それぞれ異なる脳信号が発生するので，研究者たちはその活動が

純粋に２つの決定のうちの１つを反映していることを示すことができる。

　しかしこの実験は，人々の選択が実際にどの程度『自由』であるかを制限している可能性がある，とユニバーシティ・カレッジ・ロンドンで意識について研究しているクリス・フリスは言う。被験者は，いつ，どのボタンを押すかを自由に選択できるが，この実験ではこれらの行動だけに制限され，それ以上のことはできない，と彼は言う。「被験者はスキャナーに入ることに同意した時点で，彼らの自由を実験者に譲り渡すことになるのです」と彼は言う。では，自由意志という漠然とした概念にとってこれは何を意味するのだろうか？　もし本当に意識の数秒前に選択が行われているとしたら，「自由意志が働く余地はあまりありません」とヘインズは言う。

　しかし，この結果は自由意志が幻想であることをフリスに納得させるに十分なものではない。「われわれの決断は，無意識に支配されることがあることを，われわれはすでに知っています」と彼は言う。脳活動は意思決定のプロセスではなく，この支配の一部である可能性がある，と彼はつけ加えている。

　問題となる部分は，『自由意志』とは何を意味するのかを定義することである。しかし，今回のような結果はその定義を確定するのに役立つかもしれない。「神経科学によって，私たちが自由意志と呼ぶものの意味が変わってくるかもしれません」とトンは言う。

【要約メモの訳】

脳は，あなたが気づかないうちに意思決定している

語彙：
　意識：あなたが認識していること

　前頭極皮質：　| 39 |

要点：
● 人が意思決定をする際に，意志が本当に自由なのかどうかを知るための研究が必要である。
● ある科学者は，意思決定において，意識は小さな要素に過ぎないと言う。
● ある神経科学者によると，脳にとっての10秒は人間の一生と同じ長さである。
● 一連の実験により，| 40 | であることが明らかになった。
● 人は意識的に意思決定をする前に，無意識の習慣から意思決定をすることがある。

興味深い詳細：
● ヘインズの実験では，| 41 | ためにボランティアに左手と右手のボタンを押させた。
● トンは，神経科学が | 42 | の定義を変えてしまうと考えている。

[出典]　Brain makes decisions before you even know it by Kerri Smith, from Nature, Apr 11, 2008. Reproduced with permission from Springer Nature.
※問題作成の都合上，一部原文を改変しています。

【語句・表現】
〈第１段落〉
・up to「最大〜まで」
・call A into question「A（人・事）に疑問を投げかける」
・be aware of 〜「〜に気づいている」
・consciousness「意識」
・challenge「〜に異議を唱える」
〈第２段落〉
・the tip of the iceberg「氷山の一角」
・neuroscientist「神経科学者」

・the Max Planck Institute「マックス・プランク協会」
・lifetime「一生，生涯」
・in terms of ～「～から見ると，～の点から」
〈第3段落〉
・image「～を画像化する」
・press「～を押す」
・button「ボタン」
・stream「連続，流れ」
・interval「間隔，合間」
〈第4段落〉
・delay「遅れ，遅延」
・the frontopolar cortex「前頭極皮質」
・forehead「額」
・initiate「～を始める」
〈第5段落〉
・experimental「実験の」
・millisecond「ミリ秒（1秒の1000分の1）」
〈第6段落〉
・intervening「間の，間に起こる」
・merely「単に」
・A rather than B「BではなくA，BよりもむしろA」
・alternative「選択肢，代わるもの」
・generate「～を生み出す，～を作り出す」
・distinct「全く異なる，はっきりわかる」
・genuinely「純粋に，本当に」
〈第7段落〉
・limit「～を制限する」
・subject「被験者」
・hand over「～を譲り渡す」
・freedom「自由」
・awareness「気づき，意識」
〈第8段落〉
・convince「～を納得させる」
・illusion「幻想」
・define「～を定義する，～を限定する」
・settle on ～「～に決める，～を選ぶ」
・likely「可能性がある」
・alter「～を変える」

B
問1　「あなたのグループは最初のポスターの見出しの下で，文章で説明されているように必須アミノ酸を紹介したい。 43 に最も適するものを選べ」

①　大豆製品からしか得られないタンパク質の種類であり，それぞれが独自に健康増進に寄与している。
②　20種類のタンパク質からなる分子で，筋肉の増量や回復に欠かせない。
③　人間の体が自分で作ることができず，体外から摂取する必要があるタンパク質の小さな物質である。
④　人間の体が自分で作ることができる11種類のタンパク質分子である。

正解 ⇒ ③

　第1段落第3～7文を要約すると，タンパク質の構成要素であるアミノ酸という物質は，体内に20種類あり，そのうち11種類が体内生成可能な非必須アミノ酸で，残りが体内生成不可能で食品から摂取する必要がある必須アミノ酸となる。よって，③が適当である。

　①は，第1段落第8文より，EAAは大豆製品のみならず，肉類などの動物性タンパク質にも含まれていることが分かるので不適。②は，第1段落第3文より，タンパク質を構成しているのはアミノ酸であり，アミノ酸を構成しているのはタンパク質ではないことが分かるので不適。④は，第1段落第5～6文より，11種類の体内生成可能なものは必須アミノ酸ではなく非必須アミノ酸であることが分かるので不適。

問2　「 44 と 45 に最も適当なものを選べ」

44

```
①　イソロイシン
②　ヒスチジン
③　フェニルアラニン
④　バリン
```

正解 ⇒ ④

　BCAAについては，第2段落で説明されており，第12文でバリンは「皮膚のコラーゲンの結合を強化するタンパク質の一種であるエラスチンの主成分の一つであることから，肌のハリに寄与すると言われている」と述べられている。よって④が適当である。

　②は第3段落第5文で，③は第3段落第8文で，両者ともに肌の健康向上の働きがあるという記述があるものの，BCAAではないため不適。

45

```
①　メラトニンを吸収してセロトニンを作り，心の健康や正しい睡眠・覚醒サイクルに貢献する
②　セロトニンを作り出し，心の健康に貢献すると共に，メラトニンを全身に運び，睡眠・覚醒のサイクルを正す
③　心の健康を保つセロトニンを作ることに貢献し，睡眠・覚醒のサイクルを正すメラトニンに変化する
④　セロトニンとメラトニンを除去し，心の健全化と正しい睡眠・覚醒サイクルを実現する
```

正解 ⇒ ③

　トリプトファンについては第3段落第14～16文で説明されており，「トリプトファンは，脳内でセロトニンという物質を作り出し，心の健康維持に役立つ。夜間は，セロトニンを使ってメラトニンを作り，体の睡眠・覚醒のサイクルを正す働きがある」と述べられている。よって③が適切である。

問3　「あなたは共通の特徴をもつ必須アミノ酸の説明を作っている。記事によると適当な2つは次のうちどれか。（順序は問わない） 46 ・ 47 」

```
①　ヒスチジン，フェニルアラニンは共にウロカニン酸の生成を促進することが証明されている。
②　イソロイシンとロイシンは，共に血糖値の調整の手助けをしてくれる。
③　リジンとメチオニンは，共に体内のエネルギー貯蔵を助ける働きがある。
④　イソロイシン，ロイシンは赤血球を作るのに有効である。
```

⑤ ケラチンとメチオニンを摂取することで，抜け毛を予防することができる。
⑥ うつ病に関しては，フェニルアラニンやトリプトファンを摂取することが有効である。

正解 ⇒ ②・⑥

　②については，まず第2段落第6文より，ロイシンは血糖値をコントロールすることが分かる。また，第
2段落第8文より，イソロイシンもロイシンと同様に血糖値を調整する機能があることが分かる。よって②
は正しいことが分かる。
　⑥については，まず第3段落8文より，フェニルアラニンは身体と心の健康に寄与するドーパミンを作る
材料であることが分かる。また，第3段落第15文より，人間の体はトリプトファンを使い，心の健康を保つ
のに役立つセロトニンという物質を脳内で生成することが分かる。よって⑥も正しいことが分かる。
　①は，ヒスチジンがウロカニン酸の生成を促進する働きがあることは正しいが，フェニルアラニンも同様
の働きをするという記述が本文にないので不適。③は，第3段落最終文より，メチオニンもリジンも，体内
で脂肪をエネルギーに変える働きをするカルニチンの材料として使われるため，脂肪燃焼に役立つという記
述があるものの，エネルギーを貯蔵する機能については本文にはないので不適。④は，第2段落第9文よ
り，イソロイシンはロイシンと似た機能を持つが，ヘモグロビンの生成という機能を持つという違いがある
ことが分かる。ロイシンはヘモグロビンの生成をしないことが分かるので不適。⑤は，ケラチンとメチオニ
ンについては正しいが，第3段落第11～12文より，「人体は硫黄を必要とする分子を作るためにメチオニンを
必要とし，その分子の一例として毛髪の主成分であるケラチンが挙げられる」と要約することができ，ケラ
チンはアミノ酸ではなく，タンパク質であることが分かるので不適。

【全訳】
　あなたは学生グループに所属し，「健康増進のためにすべきこと」をテーマにした科学発表会用のポス
ターを作成しています。あなたは以下の文章を参考にして，ポスターを作成しています。

必須アミノ酸

　タンパク質は，人体に必須な構成要素である。骨，筋肉，目，爪，そして髪に至るまで，あらゆる
ところに含まれている。タンパク質は，アミノ酸と呼ばれる小さな物質に分解することができる。ア
ミノ酸は体の約20％を占め，全部で20種類ある。そのうち11種類は非必須アミノ酸と呼ばれ，残りは
必須アミノ酸（EAA）と呼ばれる。非必須アミノ酸は体内で生成することができるが，EAAはそう
はいかない。EAAを摂取するには，EAAを含む食品を食べるしかない。肉などの動物性タンパク質
や，豆腐や枝豆などの大豆製品は，EAAの主な供給源である。タンパク質を含む食品を摂取する
と，タンパク質はアミノ酸に分解される。

　必須アミノ酸のうち，ロイシン，イソロイシン，バリンと呼ばれる3つのアミノ酸がある。これら
は分子構造が枝分かれしているのが特徴で，分岐鎖アミノ酸（BCAA）と呼ばれている。BCAA
は，筋肉の成長や回復という私たちの体に共通する働きを持つことから，アスリートの間で人気があ
る。しかし，よく調べてみると，私たちの体に与える影響には一定の違いがある。例えば，ロイシン
には，体内でタンパク質を作るのをサポートする働きがある。ロイシンの摂取は，肝機能の改善や血
糖値のバランスを整える効果があるとされている。また，ロイシンのサプリメントは，空腹感をコン
トロールするホルモンであるレプチンを増加させることが示されているため，体重減少を促進する可
能性がある。イソロイシンは，筋肉を強化し，肝機能を向上させ，そして血糖値をコントロールする
というロイシンと同じ働きをする。しかし，イソロイシンはロイシンとは異なり，赤血球中のヘモグ
ロビンを作る働きがあるため，失血回復に重要なアミノ酸となる。ヘモグロビンは，酸素と結合して
体中に運ぶタンパク質分子である。バリンは肝機能をサポートし，血液中の窒素の量をコントロール
する。また，皮膚のコラーゲンの結合を強めるタンパク質の一種であるエラスチンの主成分の一つで
あることから，肌のハリに寄与すると言われている。エラスチンが不足すると，肌のたるみにつなが
る可能性がある。

　BCAAを除く他のEAAも同様に人体に大きく寄与している。ヒスチジンは，体内で生成できる唯

一の必須アミノ酸であることが特徴だ。しかし，それができるのは大人だけで，子どもにはできない。ある研究では，ヒスチジンのサプリメントを摂取すると体脂肪が減少することが示された。また，別の研究では，体内でヒスチジンを使って，ウロカニン酸という，太陽光の紫外線を吸収して皮膚をダメージから守る物質が皮膚に作られることがわかった。スレオニンは，肝臓に脂肪が蓄積されるのを防ぐことが知られている。また，スレオニンは，胃を保護する粘性のある液体を作るのに大きな役割を果たすと言われており，胃の健康に寄与している。フェニルアラニンは，皮膚疾患の回復を促進することが知られており，心身の健康に寄与するドーパミンを作る材料となる。フェニルアラニンには血圧を上昇させる作用があるため，あまり大量に摂取しないようにすべきである。メチオニンの特徴は，硫黄を含む唯一のEAAであることだ。そのため，人体が硫黄を必要とする分子を作るためにメチオニンが必要となる。その一例が、髪の毛の主成分であるケラチンというタンパク質である。メチオニンが不足すると抜け毛が増えるという研究結果がある。トリプトファンは，もともと牛乳から発見されたアミノ酸の一種である。人間の体はトリプトファンを使って，心の健康を保つのに役立つセロトニンという物質を脳内で作り出す。また，夜間ではセロトニンからメラトニンが作られ，睡眠と覚醒のサイクルを調整する働きがある。リジンはトリプトファンと同じく牛乳に含まれ，体内のタンパク質の約２～10％を占めている。リジンを摂取すると，人体のカルシウムの吸収率が高まるという研究結果もある。また，メチオニンもリジンも，体内でカルニチンという脂肪をエネルギーに変えるための物質を作るのに使われるため，脂肪燃焼に役立つとされている。

　以上，紹介した各必須アミノ酸の知識は，アミノ酸不足による不調をより早く回復させるために有効だ。筋肉の増強と維持に関しては，濃縮されたBCAAを摂取することがフィットネス業界では常識となっている。しかし，EAAを摂取することでBCAAをより効率的に体内に吸収できることが研究により明らかになり，EAAをオールインワンで摂取することが徐々に主流になりつつある。アスリートの方もそうでない方も，アミノ酸について学ぶことは心身の健康に大いに役立つことだろう。

【ポスター原稿】

必須アミノ酸

必須アミノ酸とは何か？

43

必須アミノ酸の種類と機能

種類	名称	機能
BCAA以外	スレオニン	肝臓の脂肪貯蔵防止，胃を保護する液体の生成による胃の健康への貢献
BCAA	44	肌の健康維持など
BCAA以外	トリプトファン	45

共通の機能を持つ必須アミノ酸

46　　47

【語句・表現】

＜第1段落＞

・protein「タンパク質」

・essential「不可欠な」

・building block「構成要素」

・break down ～「～を分解する」

・substance「物質」

・amino acid「アミノ酸」

・contain「～を含む」

＜第2段落＞

・leucine「ロイシン」

・isoleucine「イソロイシン」

・valine「バリン」

・molecular「分子の」

・structure「構造」

・branched-chain amino acid「BCAA，分岐鎖アミノ酸」

・examine「～を調査する，～を検査する」

・blood sugar「血糖値」

・red blood cell「赤血球」

・nitrogen「窒素」

・elastin「エラスチン」

・collagen「コラーゲン」

・sagging「たるんだ」

＜第3段落＞

・excluding「～以外の，～を除いた」

・histidine「ヒスチジン」

・urocanic acid「ウロカニン酸」

・threonine「スレオニン」

・buildup「貯蔵」

・phenylalanine「フェニルアラニン」

・facilitate「～を促進する，～を容易にする」

・disorder「（心身機能の）障害，異常」

・dopamine「ドーパミン」

・methionine「メチオニン」

・sulfur「硫黄」

・keratin「ケラチン」

・tryptophan「トリプトファン」

・serotonin「セロトニン」

・melatonin「メラトニン」

・lysine「リジン」

・absorb「～を吸収する」

・calcium「カルシウム」

＜第4段落＞

・concentrated「濃縮された」

・mainstream「主流」

解 答 と 解 説

問題番号 (配点)	設問		解答番号	正解	配点	自己採点
第1問 (10)	A	1	1	2	2	
		2	2	4	2	
	B	1	3	1	2	
		2	4	4	2	
		3	5	3	2	
自己採点小計						
第2問 (20)	A	1	6	3	2	
		2	7	2	2	
		3	8	3	2	
		4	9	4	2	
		5	10	1	2	
	B	1	11	3	2	
		2	12	2	2	
		3	13	3	2	
		4	14	4	2	
		5	15	5	2	
自己採点小計						
第3問 (15)	A	1	16	3	3	
		2	17	4	3	
	B	1	18	3	3*	
			19	2		
			20	4		
			21	1		
		2	22	2	3	
		3	23	1	3	
自己採点小計						

問題番号 (配点)	設問		解答番号	正解	配点	自己採点
第4問 (16)		1	24	2	3	
		2	25	4	3	
		3	26-27	2-5	4*	
		4	28	2	3	
		5	29	3	3	
自己採点小計						
第5問 (15)		1	30	3	3	
		2	31	1	3	
		3	32	5	3*	
			33	1		
			34	3		
			35	4		
		4	36	4	3	
		5	37-38	2-4	3*	
自己採点小計						
第6問 (24)	A	1	39	3	3	
		2	40	3	3	
		3	41-42	2-3	3*	
		4	43	3	3	
	B	1	44	3	2	
		2	45	5	2	
		3	46-47	1-4	3*	
		4	48	2	2	
		5	49	2	3	
自己採点小計						

自己採点合計 ☐

（注）
1　*は全部正解の場合のみ点を与える。
2　–（ハイフン）でつながれた正解は，順序を問わない。

第1問

A

問1 「プリントには遠足について何をするように書かれているか。」 ☐1

> ① 先生に，訪れる場所を慎重に選んでもらう。
> **②** プリントに必要事項を記入し，先生に提出する。
> ③ 次の夏の遠足の場所について調べる。
> ④ あなたが遠足で見た動物の中で一番好きな動物に焦点を当てたレポートを書く。

正解 ⇒ ②

「あなたがすべきこと」の項目の最終文より，Circle the places you have decided to go and submit this printout. とあり，「あなたが行くことに決めた場所に丸をつけ，このプリントを提出してください」と述べられているので，②が適当である。①，③，④は，本文では言及されていないため不適。

問2 「次のうち，どちらの場所にも当てはまるのはどれか。」 ☐2

> ① 施設内での飲食禁止。
> ② 営業時間が同じである。
> ③ チケット代が大人と高齢者で異なる。
> **④** 様々な生き物に出会える。

正解 ⇒ ④

「アクアリウム・オブ・ザ・ブルー」の項目で，様々な海洋生物の不思議が発見できるという記述があり，「アミーゴ・ワイルドライフ・パーク」の項目では，世界中の生き物を体験することができるという記述があることから，④が適当である。①は，「アミーゴ・ワイルドライフ・パーク」はアルコールが禁止されていることが述べられているものの，「アクアリウム・オブ・ザ・ブルー」のように飲食が禁止されているという記述がないため，不適。③は，本文より，両者ともチケット代が異なるのは大人と子供であり，高齢者に関しての言及がないので不適。

【全訳】
　あなたは8月に学校の遠足に行きます。行き先については以下のプリントが生徒に配られます。

名前 ＿＿＿＿＿＿＿＿＿＿＿＿＿＿＿＿＿＿＿＿＿

遠足レポート

アクアリウム・オブ・ザ・ブルー
多種多様な海洋生物の不思議を発見しよう！
▶ 開館時間：午前8時～午後8時
▶ 大人：42.00ドル　子供（3～11歳）：21.00ドル
▶ イルカのエサやり体験
▶ 飲食物の持ち込みはご遠慮ください

アミーゴ・ワイルドライフ・パーク
世界中の生き物を体験しよう
▶ 営業時間：午前10時～午後5時
▶ 大人（13～61歳）：21.95ドル　子供：17.95ドル
▶ アジアゾウの生態を観察する
▶ 動きやすい服装でお越しください
▶ 園内は禁酒・禁煙です

あなたがすべきこと

上記の2つのオプションを慎重に比較してください。遠足レポート課題として，1カ所を選びましょう。（あなたが行くことに決めた場所に丸をつけ，このプリントを先生に提出してください）

【語句・表現】

・field trip「遠足」

・pass out「～を配る」

・feed「～を育てる，～に餌をやる」

・observe「～を観察する，～を注意深く見る」

・wear「～を着る，～を身に付ける」

・above「～の上に」

・submit「～を提出する」

〈選択肢〉

・apply「適用される，当てはまる」

・hours of operation「営業時間」

B

問1　「すべてのESWコースには　3　がある。」

① グループ学習
② 体験型実験
③ 望遠鏡観察
④ 証明書の授与

正解 ⇒ ①

　天体地質学コースの項目ではポスターを他の生徒と一緒に作成するという記述があり，社会科コースの項目では宇宙ステーションについて指定された学習パートナーたちと学ぶという記述があり，文学コースでも研究グループに割り当てられるという記述があることから，①が適当である。

問2　「全てのESWコースの終盤に，参加者は　4　だろう。」

① 卒業式に出席する
② コース登録を完了する
③ お互いのプレゼンテーションを採点する
④ 勉強したことについてレポートを書く

正解 ⇒ ④

　各コースの項目より，全てのコースにプレゼン課題が設けられていることが分かるので，④が適当である。①と③は，本文では言及されていないので不適。②は，プログラム前の登録段階を指すため，不適。

問3 「オンライン申請を提出した後，あなたは何をするだろうか。」 ⬜5

> ① オンライン面接のためにスタッフに連絡する。
> ② 宇宙について事前に知っていることを説明する。
> ③ ワークショップで何を求めているかを説明する。
> ④ 学生証をアップロードします。

正解 ⇒ ③

「2024年夏期募集」の項目の Step 3より，オンライン申請の提出後，生徒は自らコースを決め，何を学びたいかを発表する手順が設けられていることが分かる。よって，③が適当である。

【全訳】
　あなたは夏休みに宇宙の不思議について調査したいと思っている高校生である。あなたは天文台兼研究機関が主催する，星や宇宙についての楽しいサマーキャンプを宣伝しているウェブサイトを見つける。

 エリックのスペース・ワークショップ（ESW）は2001年以来，高校生のための没入型の宇宙探検キャンプを提供している。美しい星空の下，2週間の冒険に没頭しよう！

日程：2024年8月3日～17日
場所：ハンニバル公園内ザウルス山
費用：1,000ドル，食費・宿泊費込み。（ロボット作りや望遠鏡作りなどのオプショナル・アクティビティは追加料金）

提供コース

◆天体地質学：星空観測のほか，本物の隕石を専用の顕微鏡で分析し，分析・分類した結果を他の生徒と共にポスターにまとめ，過去に地球に落下した隕石について調べ，資料を作成し，8月17日に発表する。
◆社会科：星を観測することに加え，地球を周回する宇宙ステーションを観察する。宇宙ステーションの地上からの高さ，地球を一周する時間，宇宙ステーションの役割などを指定された学習パートナーたちと共に調べる。最終日の発表までにレポートを作成する。
◆文学：夜空の星を観測し，星座にまつわる物語や国の行事との繋がりを調べ，文化的な違いを見つける。研究グループに割り当てられるので，負担を感じる必要はない。プログラム最終日の発表までに調査結果をレポートにまとめる。

▲2024年夏期募集： 6月27日～7月28日
ステップ1：オンライン申込フォームに記入して申し込みます。
ステップ2：ESWからオンライン面接の日程について連絡があります。
ステップ3：面接当日では，あなたが参加したいコースと，そのコースに期待することについて質問されます。
ステップ4：ESWからコース申し込み完了のお知らせが届きます。

【語句・表現】

・host「～を主催する」

・observe「～を観察する，～を目撃する，～に気付く」

・authentic「本物の，真正の，実際の，確実な」

・classification「分類，部門」

・assign「～を割り当てる，～を振り分ける，～を配属する，～を任命する」

・associate「～を関係させる，～を関連づける」

・compile「～を編集する，～を一つにまとめる，～を集計する，資料を集める」

・application「応募，申し込み，申込書」

・contact「～に連絡する，～に接触する」

・notify「～に知らせる，～に告知する，～に通知する」

〈選択肢〉

・grade「～を評価する，～を格付けする」

・submit「～を提出する，～を送付する，～を投稿する」

・workshop「作業場，工房，講習会」

第２問

A
問１　「メーカーの説明によると，この新しいダンベルを最もよく表しているのはどれか。」　6

> ① お手頃価格のダンベル
> ② 色とりどりのダンベル
> ❸ 独創的なダンベル
> ④ 昔ながらのダンベル
> ⑤ 防水ダンベル

　正解 ⇒ ③

　本文全体は，モーツァルト・ダンベルがアプリと連携して使える機能やAI搭載されていることを中心に説明しており，それが一般的なダンベルとの大きな違いであることが分かるので，③が適当である。

問２　「ダンベルが提供する利点の中で，あなたが最も魅力を感じそうなものはどれか。」　7

> ① もっと運動しようという気にさせる
> ❷ ダンベルの携帯性を高める
> ③ パフォーマンスを記録し，情報を非公開にする
> ④ 怪我のリスクを減らす

　正解 ⇒ ②

　本文冒頭に，あなたは旅先でのエクササイズのために携帯用ダンベルを買いたいという記述がある。その購入目的に該当するものは②となる。

問３　「顧客から寄せられた意見として，　8　というものがある。」

> ① ダンベルの重さを加減するのが難しい
> ② 自分のパフォーマンスデータを他のアプリメンバーと共有できるのが楽しい
> ❸ ダンベルは他のものより耐久性がある
> ④ アプリを使用せずにダンベルを使うだけで，こんなに早く減量できる

　正解 ⇒ ③

　お客様の声の４点目より，他のダンベルよりダイヤルが壊れにくいことを挙げているので，③が適当である。④は，お客様の声の２点目より，アプリの中のフィットネス・プログラムで減量に成功したことが述べられているものの，ダンベルのみで減量に成功したとは述べられていないため不適である。

問４　「ある顧客のコメントがフィットネス・プログラムについて言及している。このコメントはどの利点に基づくものか。」　9

> ① バランス向上
> ② 携帯性の向上
> ③ 情報セキュリティー
> ❹ 運動の促進

正解 ⇒ ④

　お客様の声の2点目より，フィットネス・プログラムはアプリ内に含まれているものだということが分かる。「様々な利点」の箇所を確認すると，その内容に最も関連しているのが，独自のエクササイズをアプリが提供していることを述べている「運動の促進」という項目であることが分かる。よって，④が適当である。

問5　「ある顧客の意見によると，　10　が推奨されている。」

① アプリに慣れる時間を設けること
② 使用前にダンベルのバッテリーを最大まで充電すること
③ ダンベルのダイヤルを他と比較すること
④ ダンベルを使う前にアプリをダウンロードすること

正解 ⇒ ①

　お客様の声の3点目より，アプリを使いこなすのに何日間かかると述べられているので，①が適当である。③は，お客様の声の4点目より，他のダンベルのダイヤルは早く壊れたことを述べているが，ダンベルの比較を推奨しているとまでは言えないので不適。

【全訳】
　あなたは旅行中のエクササイズ用に携帯用ダンベルを購入したい。イギリスのウェブサイトで検索していたところ，この広告を見つける。

フィットネス・モーツァルトが新しいモーツァルト・ダンベルを発表

　モーツァルト・ダンベルは，家庭での完璧なウェイトリフティング体験を実現するために，世界一流の機械エンジニアが設計した，簡単に調整可能なダンベルだ。

特別な機能

モーツァルト・ダンベルは，3つの方法で重量を切り替えられる重量調整機能を内蔵している：
1. 手動でハンドルのダイヤルを回して，重量を追加または取り外す
2. モーツァルト・ダンベル・アプリに希望の重量を入力すると，ダンベルがそれに応じて反応する
3. モーツァルト・ダンベル・アプリで自動調整モードを選択すると，AIがパフォーマンスに応じて自動的に重量を選択する

このアプリはトレーニングの結果も記録できる。何回ダンベルを持ち上げたか，どれくらいの重さを持ち上げたか，どれくらいの時間パフォーマンスしたか，などなど！さらに，アプリのコミュニティーと即座に共有することもできる。これにより，お互いのフィットネスの進歩を励まし，サポートするグローバル・コミュニティの一員となることができる。また，世界的に有名なフィットネスインストラクターがデザインしたフィットネスプログラムを選択したり，オンラインフィットネスクラスに参加することができる。

モーツァルト・ダンベルは，フィットネス業界とフィットネス体験を革新する。

様々な利点

バランス向上：モーツァルト・ダンベルは，両端が同じ重さになるように精密に作られているため，

　　　　　　使用中に怪我をする危険性が低くなる。

携帯性の向上：ダンベルの重量を簡単に取り外せるので，収納が簡単だ。

運動の促進：このアプリは，ユーザーの体に合わせたユニークなエクササイズを提供する。まるで
　　　　　　ウェイトリフティングのビデオゲームをしているかのような感覚を味わえる。

情報セキュリティー：アプリの記録は公開，非公開，または選択したメンバーにのみ共有することが
　　　　　　　　　　できる。

お客様の声
●ダンベルの重さを物理的にもデジタルでも調整できるのがいいですね！
●とても楽しかったので，アプリのフィットネス・プログラムに従うだけで，10 kg 痩せました！
●このダンベルは素晴らしいですが，アプリに慣れるのに２，３日必要でした。
●このダンベルを使うのに問題はなかった！　他の調節可能なダンベルはダイヤルがすぐ壊れるので
　使いにくかった。
●アプリのコミュニティーで自分のパフォーマンスを共有するのはモチベーションが上がる！　ただ，最近リリースされたばかりなので，メンバーが少ない。

【語句・表現】
・portable「携帯用の，持ち運びできる，運搬できる，ポータブル」
・exercise「運動する，練習する，エクササイズ」
・search「〜を探す，〜を検索する，〜を捜す」
・present「〜を贈呈する，〜を示す」
・easily「簡単に，気楽に，楽に」
・mechanical「機械的な，機械の，機械で動く」
・feature「特徴，要点，主要な点，機能」
・handle「手すり，取っ手」
・mode「方式，方法」
・track「〜をたどる，〜を追跡する」
・share「〜を共有する，〜を配分する，〜を分ける」
・precisely「正確に，確実に，厳密に，きっかり，明確に，几帳面に」
・usage「使用」
・promote「〜を昇進させる，〜を奨励する，〜を促進する」
・motivate「動機を与える，〜を動機づける」
〈選択肢〉
・statement「声明，声明書，陳述書，宣言，公の場での発言」
・affordable「利用できる，入手可能な，手頃な，手に入れる」
・likely「ありそうな，らしく」
・state「〜を述べる，〜を明言する，〜をはっきり言う」
・charge「〜を充電する」

B

問1 「勉強アプリ大会の目的は，　11　だった。」

① 学生同士が学校の時間外でも助け合えるようなオンライン・コミュニティーを作ること
② 生徒に自分のアプリを作る機会を与えること
③ **生徒の勉強意欲を高めること**
④ 学生を自己学習アプリの勉強に動機付けること

正解 ⇒ ③

　第1段落第3文より，勉強アプリ大会を始めた目的は，学生たちがスマートフォンでゲームをする代わりに，その時間を勉強に使ってもらうことだと述べられているので，③が適当である。

問2 「勉強アプリ大会に関する事実の1つは，　12　ということである。」

① 2年生は参加者の50%未満だった
② **冬の間，約4週間開催された**
③ 学生はスマートフォンを使って参加しなければならなかった
④ 参加者の大半は男性であった

正解 ⇒ ②

　第1段落第4文より，生徒たちは1月17日から2月17日までクイズを受けなければならなかったことが述べられているので，②が適切である。③は，参加者NI氏のフィードバックを確認すると，アプリを自宅パソコンで少し使用したという記述があるため，不適。

問3 「フィードバックによると，　13　ことは，学習アプリでできる活動として参加者から報告されている。」

A: 授業に関連する問題に答える
B: 他の学生と交流する
C: オーディオファイルを聴く
D: アプリでメモを取る

① AとB
② AとC
③ **AとD**
④ BとC
⑤ BとD
⑥ CとD

正解 ⇒ ③

　参加者AB氏のフィードバックの第1文より，学習アプリを使うことが授業の理解の手助けとなったという記述があることや，RT氏のフィードバックの第3文より4択の問題に答えるものだと述べられていることからAは正しいことが分かる。また，参加者AB氏のフィードバックの第2文より，アプリでメモを取ることができて，授業中便利であることを述べているので，Dも正しいことが分かる。よって③が適切である。

問4 「勉強アプリ大会についての参加者の意見の１つは，　14　というものだ。」

① アプリ内の音声教材が役に立った
② 賞金が生徒のモチベーションを上げるのに役立った
③ 勉強アプリは歴史の得点向上に特に効果的であった
④ アプリを操作する上で問題はなかった

正解 ⇒ ④

　参加者 VA 氏のフィードバックの第１文より，アプリ自体は使いやすかったという記述があるので，④が適当である。

問5 「筆者の疑問には　15　が答えている。」

① AB
② AJ
③ NI
④ RT
⑤ VA

正解 ⇒ ⑤

　第１段落第８文より，３年生の参加者が少なかったことに筆者が疑問を感じていることが分かる。参加者 VA 氏のフィードバックの最終文の，３年生が勉強アプリ大会に参加しなかったのは大学入試の準備で忙しかったからという記述は，筆者の疑問に答えていると言えるので，⑤が適当である。

【全訳】
　あなたは生徒会のメンバーの１人である。メンバーたちは，勉強意欲を高める生徒プロジェクトについて話し合っている。考えを得るために，あなたは学校の挑戦についてのレポートを読んでいる。それは，日本の他の学校に留学した交換留学生によって書かれている。

画面に釘付け

昨年，本校の生徒の時間の使い方についてアンケートを実施した。その結果，スマートフォンの使用時間が長すぎること，ゲームをしている時間が長いことがわかった。だから，スマートフォンでゲームをする代わりに，勉強に時間を使ってもらうために，私たちはこの勉強アプリ大会を始めた。生徒は，１月17日から２月17日までの期間中，クイズに挑戦しなければならなかった。このクイズで獲得したポイントの合計に応じて賞品がもらえることになっていた。１位は2000円，２位は1000円，３位は500円であった。全校生徒のうち30人が参加し，３分の２以上が２年生で，１年生が７人，残りが３年生だった。なぜ３年生が少なかったか？　以下のフィードバックがその疑問に答えてくれるかもしれない。

参加者からのフィードバック

AB：バスの中ではほとんど勉強アプリを使っていたが，授業の理解が深まった。また，アプリ上でノートを追加できるので，授業中に便利だ。バスに乗っている間にすでに授業の復習をしているので，家に帰ってから復習する必要はないと感じた！
AJ：２年生の友達の中には，この勉強アプリの大会を知らない子もいたと聞いた。彼らが知ったと

きにはすでに大会は終わっていた。2,000円なんてバイト代より安いから，知っていたとしても参加したくはならなかったと思う。

NI：いつもは小さなスマートフォンでアプリを使う。自宅のパソコンでも少し使いましたけど。それに，このアプリには備わってないが，音声で勉強する方が得意なんです。

RT：数学のテストで過去最高点を取りました！　勉強アプリ大会のおかげで勉強がはかどった！各問題に4つの選択肢があり，正しいものを選ぶ。シンプルでいい！

VA：勉強アプリ自体は使いやすかった。3年生は大学受験の準備で忙しいので，勉強アプリ大会に参加できなかったのは意外じゃない。

【語句・表現】
・motivate「～を動機づける」
・glue「～を糊付けする，釘付けになる」
・earn「～を得る，～を稼ぐ，～を獲得する」
・participant「参加者，参加」
〈選択肢〉
・app = application「アプリ，アプリケーション」
・relate「～を関連づける，～を関連させる」

第3問

問1 「グレッグのアドバイスに従うなら，バッグはどのように整理すべきだろうか？」　16

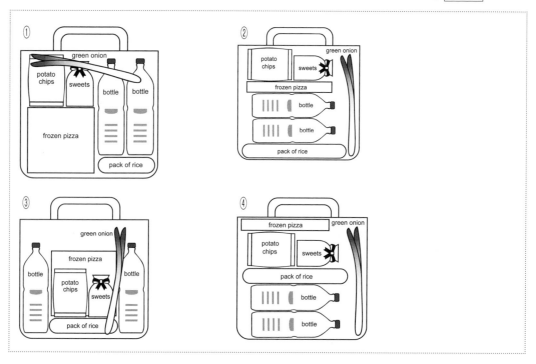

正解 ⇒ ③

　本文全体をまとめると，グレッグが提唱する袋の詰め方としては，まず硬くて長いものを柱にして，次に重いもので床を作り，さらに平たいもので壁を作り，それから中央に重いものから軽い物へと順に置いていく。最後に柔らかくて細長い物があれば，それを隙間に埋めていけばよいと締めくくっている。bottle は硬く長いもの，pack of rice は重いもの，frozen pizza は平たいものにあたる。以上の内容を踏まえると，③ が適当である。

問2 「グレッグによれば，バッグに物を入れる最善の方法は，　17　ことだという。」

① 硬いものや小さいもので隙間を埋める
② コーナーに広いオープンスペースを作る
③ 冷凍食品が一番下になるように商品を置く
④ まるで家を建てるかのように商品を並べる

正解 ⇒ ④

　第2段落第1文より，袋詰めの基本構造は家を建てるときと同じであるとグレッグが語っていることが分かるので，④ が適当である。

【全訳】

あなたはグレッグというブロガーの記事を読んでいる。そこで彼は，買い物をするときに効率よく荷物をまとめる方法を説明している。

買い物袋を整理する最善の方法

こんにちは，グレッグです。スーパーやコンビニで働いたことはありますか？ 僕はコンビニで半年ほど働いていて，商品を上手に素早く袋に入れる方法を学びました。

袋に物を入れるのは，家を建てるのと同じです。まず，背の高いもの，硬いものは袋の隅に入れる。これは家の柱を立てるのと同じではないですか。次に，重いもので床を作るようにバッグの底に置く。そして，平らなものを家の壁のように側面に置く。ここまでで，基本的な構造は完成しました。

さて，真ん中が広く空いていることに気づくでしょう。そこに，重いものから軽いものへと順番に積み上げていく。ポテトチップスや小さなスナック菓子を買うなら，それを一番上に置く。

最後に，新聞紙やネギ，スナックバーなど細長くて柔らかいもので隙間を埋めるように置く。これが最後の仕上げとなります。

いかがですか？ ここで説明した方法を覚えていれば，壊れやすいものを傷つけずに買い物袋を整理することができます。バッグの中の商品は，持ち運ぶときに落ちることはありません。

【語句・表現】

・pack「～を荷造りする，荷造りをする」
・convenience store「コンビニ」
・pole「極，ポール，棒，柱，さお」
・heavy「重い，厚い，重大な」
・flat「平坦な」
・structure「構造，建造物」
・middle「ど真ん中」
・direction「方向，方面，方角，方位，指示」
・fragile「壊れやすい，もろい，破れやすい」

B

問1 「次の出来事（①～④）を起こった順，あるいは起こるであろう順に並べなさい。」

| 18 | → | 19 | → | 20 | → | 21 |

---
① 都市と田舎を結ぶ高速道路の建設
② 「グリーン・ウェーブ」システムの導入
③ 無料の公共自転車共有システムを開始
④ サイクリストからの要望を受け付けるウェブサイトを開設

正解 ⇒ 　18　③　　19　②　　20　④　　21　①

③については第2段落に述べられており，同段落第2文より，CitiBikeは1995年に設立されたことがわかる。②については第3段落に述べられており，同段落第2文より，2007年にGreen Waveが初めて導入されたことがわかる。④については第4段落に述べられており，同段落第1文より，ウェブサイトは2010年に開設されたことが分かる。①については第5段落に述べられており，第3文より，高速道路は現在建設中で2045年に完成する予定であることが分かる。したがって，③→②→④→①の順番である。

問2 「どのように『グリーンウェーブ』は機能するのか。」 ☐22

① 自転車を電車やバスに持ち込むことができる。
② 自転車は赤信号の少ない交差点を通過することができる。
③ サイクリストは事前にウェブサイトで信号が青になるタイミングをリクエストできる。
④ 通勤時間帯に赤信号で自転車を止めなくてよい。

正解 ⇒ ②

　第3段落第1文より，「グリーンウェーブ」は，通勤時間帯の信号のタイミングを管理し，サイクリストが通過する交差点を進みやすくするシステムであることが分かるので，②が適当である。④は，同段落第3文より，「グリーンウェーブ」導入後，自転車は以前より赤信号で止まる必要が少なくなったと述べられており，赤信号の際は止まらないといけないことが分かるので，不適。

問3 「『自転車高速道路』について正しいのはどれか。」 ☐23

① 都市部以外でのサイクリストを増やすことを目的としている。
② 現在建設中で，2025年に完成する予定だ。
③ 当面の間，田舎だけに建設される予定だ。
④ 他の道路に比べ，路面損傷のリスクがない。

正解 ⇒ ①

　第5段落第4文より，政府が「自転車高速道路」を建設している狙いは，地方での自転車利用者を増やすことであることが分かるので，①が適当である。

【全訳】
　この夏，北欧を訪れる予定のあなたは，旅行雑誌でデンマークの首都に関する興味深い記事を見つけました。

コペンハーゲンの魅力とは？

　コペンハーゲンは世界で最も自転車に優しい都市として知られている。コペンハーゲンでは，通学や通勤の交通手段の約50％を自転車が占めている。なぜデンマークの首都ではこれほど多くの人が自転車を利用するのだろうか。

　その答えは，コペンハーゲン市庁が自転車中心のライフスタイルを推進してきたからだ。1995年，コペンハーゲンは市民や観光客に環境に優しい新しい交通手段をつくりだすため，無料の自転車シェアシステム「シティバイク」を導入した。広告で資金を調達し，市が支援する基金が管理した。利用者は払い戻し可能なコインを入れることで，ドッキングステーションから自転車のロックを解除できる。

　さらに，コペンハーゲンの自転車システムには「グリーンウェーブ」と呼ばれるシステムがあり，通勤時間帯の信号のタイミングを管理することで，サイクリストが通過する交差点をよりスムーズに通行できるようにしている。2007年に主要な自転車のルートにこのシステムが導入される以前は，信号機は自動車優先で調整されていた。その後，サイクリストは以前より赤信号で止まる必要が少なくなった。このシステムにより，彼らの通勤はより快適になった。

　2010年，コペンハーゲン市はサイクリストからの要望を受け付けるウェブサイトを開設した。道路損傷に関する情報や，交差点でのサイクリスト専用待機ゾーンの設置など，さまざまな要望の受付を開始した。コペンハーゲン市庁によると，2013年には7,944件の道路損傷に関する修理補修を受け，

そのうち6,396件を修理したという。

　コペンハーゲンは，2025年までに初の CO_2 ニュートラルな首都，グリーンテクノロジーとグリーンイノベーションの欧州のリーダーになることを目指している。市は，都市と地方を結ぶ45ルート（総延長746km）の「自転車高速道路」を建設する。建設は2045年の終了を予定している。一般的な自転車の利用は，現在，大都市で増加しているため，政府は「自転車高速道路」によって地方での自転車利用者が増えることを期待している。高速道路が完成すれば，年間1,500トンの CO_2 排出量を削減できると言われている。

【語句・表現】
・promote「～を昇進させる，～を奨励する，～を促進する」
・introduce「～を紹介する，～を導入する，～を案内する」
・mode「方式，方法」
・manage「～を管理する，～を運営する，～を経営する，～を担当する」
・fund「資金，基金，ファンド」
・insert「～を挿入する，～を差し込む」
・coin「小銭」
・traffic「交通，通行，トラフィック，往来，運輸」
・commute「通勤，通学」
・proceed「前進する，続ける，手続きする，処分する」
・easily「簡単に，気楽に，楽に」
・establish「～を設置する，～を確立する，～を立証する」
・launch「～を発射する，～を始める」
・establishment「施設，創立，創業，設立」
・dedicated「熱心な，打ち込んだ，献身的な，ひたむきな」
・neutral「中立の」
・innovation「革新，刷新，革命的な変化」
・emission「排出，放出，放射，排気ガス」

第４問

問１ 「ウッドソンは，　24　と言う。」

① 犬の飼い主は早起きだから健康だ
② 犬を飼うことは楽しい職場の雰囲気と活発なライフスタイルにつながる
③ ペットを飼うことは飼い主に害を与えるよりも，はるかに多くの良いことをもたらす
④ 人は気づかないうちに特定の種類のペットを好むものだ

正解 ⇒ ②

ウッドソンの投稿の第１段落最終文より，とある研究によるとオフィスに犬を飼うと従業員のストレスレベルを下げる効果が見受けられたことが分かる。また，第３段落第１文より，ペットを飼う方が日常業務が増えることがわかる。よって，②が適当である。

問２ 「ある研究によると，オフィスで犬を飼うと，　25　ストレスレベルが低下した。」

① 犬自身の
② 犬の飼い主の
③ 管理職の
④ 労働者の

正解 ⇒ ④

ウッドソンの投稿の第１段落最終文より，とある研究によるとオフィスに犬を飼うと従業員のストレスレベルを下げる効果が見受けられたことが分かるので，④が適当である。

問３ 「図を埋めるのに最も適切なものを２つ選び，ウッドソンが説明するペットを飼うことの利点をまとめよ。（順序は問わない。）」　26　・　27

① 学術的
② 生物学的
③ 経済的
④ 金銭的
⑤ 心理的

正解 ⇒ ②，⑤

ウッドソンの投稿に挙がっているペットを飼うことの利点をまとめるとすると，表に挙がっている「身体的」，「社会的」以外に「生物学的」と「心理的」が適切である。まず，第１段落第５文より，ストレスホルモンの値を下げる「生物学的」な利点を挙げている。次に，第２段落第１文より，ペットを飼うことが幸福感の向上につながり，同段落第２文より，自尊心を高めるという「心理的」な利点を挙げている。第３段落より生活習慣や運動量によって健康になるというのが「身体的」利点，第４段落よりペットを飼うと交友関係が増えて社会的孤立感がなくなるというのが「社会的」な利点といえる。

問4 「どちらの筆者も，　28　ことで飼い主が得られる利点については同意している。」

① ペットと非言語でコミュニケーションをとる
② 新しい知り合いと交流する
③ ペットの行動を学ぶ
④ ペットのために日課をこなす

正解 ⇒ ②

　ウッドソンの投稿の第4段落最終文より，ペットの飼育は他者との交流につながると述べられており，アトウッドの投稿の第2段落第1文より，ペットを飼うことは他のペットの飼い主と交流する機会を増やすことになると述べられているので，②が適当である。

問5 「アトウッドが説明するペット飼育の弊害を解決する良い方法はどれか。」　29

① 週に一度は外出し，運動をする
② ペットオーナーのグループツアーに参加する
③ パーティーに参加し，様々な背景を持つ人々と話す
④ 人間のしぐさや表情について学ぶ

正解 ⇒ ③

　アトウッドが挙げているペットを飼うことの短所は，第3段落第2～3文より，ペットを飼うことは他の飼い主との交流を促進するかもしれないが，ペットを飼っていない人との交流の妨げになる可能性がある。そして交流する人の種類を制限することは，社会的孤立やコミュニケーション能力の低下につながる恐れがあると述べられている。よって，様々な人との交流を増やすことにつながる③が適当である。

【全訳】
　あなたはペットを飼うことで得られる利点について勉強しています。次の授業では，以下の2つの記事を参照して，学んだことについて話し合います。

ペットを飼うメリット： あなたも飼ってみませんか？
カリム・ウッドソン
モス市立動物診療所 獣医外科医

　人はなぜペットを飼うのか？　多くの人は「理由はない。ただ愛すべき仲間が欲しいだけだ」と答えるかもしれない。しかし，知らず知らずのうちに，ペットはあなたが思っている以上にあなたに利益をもたらしているのである。いくつかの観点から説明しよう。まず，ペットを飼うことでストレスホルモンのレベルが下がり，不安の症状が軽減される。International Journal of Workplace Health Management に掲載された研究では，オフィスで犬を飼うことで，従業員の自覚ストレスのレベルが低下したと報告されている。

　また，ペットとの触れ合いは気分を高め，幸福感を増大させる。そのため，ペットを飼っている人は，そうでない人に比べて自尊心が高く，幸せであることが多い。実際，ある研究では，たった15分犬と一緒に過ごすだけで，社会的なつながりと脳内の快楽に関連するホルモンであるオキシトシンのレベルが上昇することがわかった。

　ペットと一緒に過ごすと，飼い主はペットを飼っていない人よりも多くの日課をこなさなければならない。一緒に遊んだり，餌をやったり，床やケージを掃除したり，散歩をしたりする。これにより，飼い主はより身体を動かすことになる。特に犬は，この点で飼い主に恩恵をもたらす。犬の飼い

主は，そうでない飼い主よりも，１日の身体活動ガイドラインを満たす可能性が高い。さらに，犬の散歩はより健康的な体重を維持し，医者にかかる回数を減らすという報告もある。

　最後に，ペットは飼い主に交友関係をもたらし，社会的孤立感を軽減することができる。ペットを飼うことで孤独感が軽減され，ペットを飼うことで獣医や他の飼い主など，ペットの世話をしているときに出会う人たちとの社会的交流が促進されるからだ。

<h2 style="text-align:center">ペットを飼うことで得られる効果： 良いことだけではない</h2>
セス・アトウッド
バークレン動物専門学校アニマルセラピー講師

　私はアニマル・セラピストを目指す学生を指導しており，私自身も犬を飼っている。ここ数年，私はペットを飼うことが飼い主のコミュニケーション能力に及ぼす影響について研究してきた。いくつかの研究では，これらの効果について調査している。

　まず，ペットを飼うことで，他の飼い主と交流する機会が増え，新たな友情を育むことにつながる。International Journal of Workplace Health Management に掲載された研究によると，ペットを飼っている人はそうでない人に比べて，同僚からの社会的支援のレベルが高いことが報告されている。他者との交流が増えることで，コミュニケーション能力にも良い影響があるかもしれない。さらに，ペットは非言語でコミュニケーションをとるため，ペットの飼い主はボディランゲージや発声を通してペットの感情や意図を理解することに慣れていく。その結果，飼い主は人と接するときに非言語的コミュニケーションを解釈し，利用する能力を向上させることができる。

　しかし，ペットと暮らすことの利点が弊害をもたらすこともある。ペットを飼うことで，他の飼い主との社会的交流は深まるが，ペットを飼っていない人との交流については同じことは言えない。特に飼い主のペットへの依存度が高すぎる場合，交流する人の種類を制限することで，社会的孤立やコミュニケーション能力の低下につながる可能性がある。飼い主が自分とは異なる価値観や嗜好に共感しにくくなる。

　ペットとの生活を楽しく有益なものにしたいのであれば，ペットとの交流と他の人間との交流のバランスを保ちながら，潜在的な弊害を認識しておく必要がある。

【語句・表現】
〈ウッドソンの投稿〉
・surgeon「外科医」
・municipal「市の，都市の，地方自治体の，市営の」
・symptom「兆し，兆候，症状，症候」
・journal「ジャーナル，日誌，雑誌」
・workplace「職場」
・perceive「〜を知覚する，〜を感知する，〜を認識する」
・associate「関連する，交際する，〜を関係させる，〜を関連づける」
・bonding「束縛，結合，繋がり」
・feed「〜を育てる，〜に餌をやる」
・active「活発な，積極的な」
・likely「ありそうな」
・physical「肉体的な，身体の」
・guideline「指針，指標」
・isolation「分離，孤立，隔離，孤独，疎外感」
・loneliness「孤独，寂しさ」
・ownership「所有権」

・promote「～を昇進させる，～を奨励する，～を促進する」
・interaction「相互作用，人とのやり取り」
〈アトゥッドの投稿〉
・therapist「療法士」
・positive「肯定的な，積極的な，楽観的な」
・interpret「～を通訳する，～を解釈する，～を説明する」
・verbal「言葉の，口頭の，口述の」
・excessive「過度の，極端の，度を超した，やり過ぎの」
・sympathetic「同情的な，共感する，思いやりのある」
〈選択肢〉
・specific「具体的な，明確な，特定の，固有の，個別の」
・summarize「～を要約する，～を集約する」
・acquaintance「知り合い，知人，面識」
・exercise「運動，訓練」
・gesture「身振り，手振り」
・facial「顔の」

第5問

問1 「 30 に入る最も適切なものを1つ選べ。」

① 縫製工
② 現代芸術家
③ **郵便局員**
④ 学校の教師

正解 ⇒ ③

　第1段落第2文より，ハーバートは1979年に退職するまでアメリカ郵便公社で郵便仕分け人として働いていたことが分かるので，③が適当である。

問2 「 31 に入る最も適切なものを1つ選べ。」

① **美術品の鑑賞と収集をする**
② 有名画家の高価な絵を買う
③ 画廊を経営する
④ 有望な若手アーティストのスポンサーになる

正解 ⇒ ①

　ヴォーゲル夫妻が芸術との関わり方を決めたことを記した箇所は第3段落である。同段落最終文より，夫婦自身で絵を描くよりも，美術品を鑑賞したり収集したりすることを選んだことが分かるので，①が適当である。

問3 「5つの選択肢（①～⑤）から4つを選び，起こった順に並べ替えなさい。」

　　　 32 → 33 → 34 → 35

① 夜のギャラリーイベントに参加する
② ひしゃげた金属でできた小さな彫刻を買う
③ ナショナル・ギャラリー・オブ・アートにコレクションを寄贈する
④ 「50州のための50作品」プロジェクト
⑤ 絵画・デッサン教室に通う

正解 ⇒ 32 ⑤　　 33 ①　　 34 ③　　 35 ④

　発表ノートを確認すると， 32 と 33 の間に「彼らが初めて美術品を購入」と記載されている。第4段落第1文より，彼らが最初に購入した美術品は，ジョン・チェンバレンの金属を砕いた小さな彫刻だったことが分かる。②は，この内容と重複するため，使用しない選択肢であることが分かる。第3段落第3～4文に，彼らが美術品を収集することを決める前には絵画・デッサン教室に通っていたことが述べられているので，最初の美術品購入より前の出来事であることが分かる。よって 32 は⑤が適当である。また，第5段落第2文より，夫妻は美術品を収集していくために，夜のギャラリーイベントに参加していたことが述べられているので， 33 は①が適当である。第8段落第1文より，1992年にヴォーゲル夫妻が美術品を寄贈したこと，続いて第8段落第3文より，2008年にナショナル・ギャラリー・オブ・アートが「50州のための50作品」プロジェクトを発表したことが述べられているので③→④となる。

問4 「 36 に入る最も適切なものを1つ選べ。」

① 全州に分館がある
② アメリカの首都にある
③ 現代美術の展示に特化している
④ **彼らのコレクションが無料で展示される**

正解 ⇒ ④

　第9段落第2～3文を要約すると、彼らのコレクションが数百万ドルの価値があったにも関わらず、作品を売ろうとしなかった理由は、彼らは大衆に自分たちのコレクションを無料で楽しんでもらいたかったからだと捉えることができる。よって、④が適当である。

問5 「 37 ・ 38 に入る最も適切なものを2つ選べ。（順序は問わない）」

① ハーブとドロシーは、歴史的な美術品を展示する有名な美術館を建てた。
② **ハーブとドロシーは、美術品を買うセンスでアーティストたちの間で評判だった。**
③ ハーブとドロシーはアート業界で財を成した。
④ **ハーブとドロシーがコレクションを売ることはなかった。**
⑤ ハーブとドロシーは、大きな美術品を運ぶためにトラックなどの大型車をよく借りていた。

正解 ⇒ ②，④

　第5段落第4文より、アーティストたちは彼らの美的感覚と家計状況を認めていたので、支払いが遅れても文句を言うことはなかったと述べられているので、②が適当である。第9段落第2文より、彼らは美術品を売ることは考えなかったと述べられているので、④も適当である。

【全訳】
　あなたの英語教師は、クラスの全員に、感動的な物語を見つけ、ノートを使ってディスカッション・グループで発表するように言いました。あなたはアメリカのジャーナリストが書いた物語を見つけました。

伝説のカップル ハーブ＆ドロシー

ビル・ジョーダン

　ハーバート・ヴォーゲルは1922年、ニューヨークのハーレムでロシア系ユダヤ人の縫製工の息子として生まれた。高校を中退し、第二次世界大戦中は米軍に従軍、1979年に退職するまで米郵政公社の郵便仕分け人として働いた。
　ドロシー・フェイ・ホフマンは、ユダヤ系の文房具商の家に生まれた。シラキュース大学で図書館学の学士号、デンバー大学で修士号を取得し、1990年に退職するまでブルックリン公共図書館で司書として働いた。
　ハーバートとドロシーは1960年に出会い、恋に落ち、1962年に結婚した。結婚当初から、ヴォーゲル夫妻の生活は芸術を中心に回っていた。ハーバートは郵便局で夜勤をしながら、昼間はインスティテュート・オブ・ファイン・アーツで学んだ。ドロシーもそれに倣い、ニューヨーク大学で絵画とデッサンの授業を受け始めた。ふたりはしばらくの間、絵画とデッサンを学んだが、芸術家になるには才能が足りないと悟った。やがて夫妻は、自分たちで絵を描くよりも、アートを鑑賞したり収集したりすることを選んだ。
　二人が最初に買った美術品は、ジョン・チェンバレンのひしゃげた金属の小さな彫刻だった。ふたりとも給料はあまり多くなかったので、有名画家の高価な絵を買う余裕はなかった。ヴォーゲル夫妻は身の丈に合った範囲で、気に入ったものを少しずつ買っていった。マンハッタンのソーホー地区を

手をつないで歩きながら，ヴォーゲル夫妻は多くのギャラリーを訪れ，1960年代初頭にはあまり人気がなかったミニマル・アートやコンセプチュアル・アートを中心に作品を集め始めた。

　彼らが作品を手に入れる方法は，まだ無名だった若く有望なアーティストと友達になることだった。ヴォーゲル夫妻は夜のギャラリーのイベントに参加し，ロバート＆シルヴィア・マンゴールド，ドナルド・ジャッド，リチャード・タトル，ソル・ルウィットなど多くのアーティストと語り合った。裕福でなかった彼らは，アーティストたちの作品を月賦で購入し，時には支払いが滞ることもあった。しかし，アーティストたちはヴォーゲル夫妻の美的感覚と彼らの家計状況を理解していたので，支払いが遅れても文句を言うことはなかった。やがて彼らは「ハーブ＆ドロシー」として知られるようになり，ニューヨークのアート・コミュニティで名声と人気を得るようになった。

　ハーブ＆ドロシーの収集の基本方針は，ドロシーの給料だけで生活し，ハーブの収入はすべて美術品の購入にあてるというものだった。車も持たず，休暇も取らず，海外旅行もせず，夜は近くの中華デリで過ごすことが多かった。彼らにはもうひとつ購入ポリシーがあった。つまりハーブ＆ドロシーは，地下鉄やタクシーで持ち帰ることができるものだけ購入したのである。理由は簡単で，彼らはハーレムの小さなワンベッドルームのアパートに住んでいたからだ。

　1990年代初頭，ハーブ＆ドロシーのアパートは，床から天井まで，キッチンからバスルームまで，ドアから壁まで，ありとあらゆるスペースにコレクションが溢れていた。170人以上のアーティストによるコレクションは主に絵画で構成されていたが，絵画，彫刻，写真，版画も含まれていた。驚くことに，彼らのコレクションは4,000点以上に増え，ミニマリズムとコンセプチュアル・アートの世界でも最も重要で包括的なコレクションのひとつとなった。

　1992年，ハーブ＆ドロシーは全てのコレクションをワシントンD.C.のナショナル・ギャラリー・オブ・アートに寄贈することを決めた。驚いたことにそれらの運搬にはトラック5台が必要になった。そして2008年，ナショナル・ギャラリーは，ヴォーゲル氏のコレクションから50点を全米50州のギャラリーに寄贈する計画，「フィフティ・ワークス・フォー・フィフティ・ステイツ」への支援を発表した。

　公務員の夫妻がワンベットルームのアパートで半世紀にかけて収集した現代アートのコレクションは，現在ナショナル・ギャラリー・オブ・アートが管理している。彼らはただ，アメリカの人々に自分たちのコレクションを無料で楽しんでもらいたかったのだ。

　ハーバート・ヴォーゲルは2012年に89歳で他界したが，半世紀以上にわたって妻とともに築き上げた現代アートの驚くべきコレクションを残した。彼らのコレクションと芸術への愛情は，ナショナルギャラリーや各地のギャラリーで見ることができる。

【発表メモの訳】

ハーブ＆ドロシーの生涯

ハーバート・ヴォーゲルとドロシー・ホフマン
・ハーバートは　30　だった。
・ドロシーは図書館司書として働いていた。

ハーバートとドロシーの結婚生活
・彼らの生活は芸術を中心に回っていた。
・彼らはアーティストになるよりも，　31　ことを選んだ。

ハーブ＆ドロシーの人生における重要な出来事
　32　→彼らが初めて美術品を購入→　33　→　34　→　35

ハーブとドロシーはなぜナショナル・ギャラリー・オブ・アートにコレクションを寄贈したのか？

```
  36  から。
```

この話から学べること
・ 37
・ 38

【語句・構文】
・present「〜を贈呈する，〜を示す」
・legendary「伝説の」
〈第1段落〉
・garment「衣類，服」
・army「陸軍」
・postal「郵便の，郵便局の」
〈第2段落〉
・earn「〜を得る，〜を稼ぐ，〜を獲得する」
〈第4段落〉
・crush「〜を押しつぶす，〜を踏み潰す，〜に激しくぶつかる」
・modest「腰が低い，控えめな，謙虚な，自慢しない」
・numerous「たくさんの，数え切れないほど多い」
〈第5段落〉
・promising「前途有望な，見込みのある」
・sensibility「感受性」
〈第6段落〉
・policy「方針，政策」
〈第7段落〉
・overflow「溢れる，満ち溢れる」
・ceiling「天井，上限」
・assemble「〜を集める，〜を組み立てる，〜を招集する」
・comprehensive「包括的な，幅広い，総合的な，徹底的な」
〈第8段落〉
・donate「〜を寄付する，〜を提供する」
・state「国家，州」
〈第9段落〉
・accumulate「〜を蓄積する，〜を積む，〜を集める」
・manage「〜を管理する，〜を運営する，〜を経営する，〜を担当する」
〈第10段落〉
・pass away「亡くなる」

第6問

A

問1 「　39　に最も適するものを選びなさい。」

> ① 試合中に他のプレーヤーによって引き起こされる混乱を楽しむ
> ② 相手選手の速い動きにもついていける
> ③ ランダムに見えるものの集まりにパターンを見つける
> ④ チームメイトの弱点を強みに変える

正解 ⇒ ③

　第2段落第4～最終文を要約すると，サッカーに精通している者は，詳しくない者にとっては不規則に見えるプレーの中のパターンを即座に認識し，弱点や隙が現れたらすぐにそれを利用するとなる。よって③が適当である。

問2 「　40　に最も適するものを選びなさい。」

> ① サッカーの試合前に選手の健康状態を聞く
> ② インタビューを通じて各選手の長所を探る
> ③ 実際のサッカーの試合のビデオを被験者に見せる
> ④ 被験者がどれだけ早くボールに反応するかをテストする

正解 ⇒ ③

　第3段落第2～3文を要約すると，実験の方法として述べられているのは，被験者に実際のサッカーの試合のビデオを見せて，選手がボールを受けたところで突然ビデオを止め，次に何が起こるかを予測させたということである。よって③が適当である。

問3 「　41　と　42　に最も適するものを選びなさい（順番は問わない）。」

> ① 試合後に何をするかを決める
> ② 行動パターンを解釈する
> ③ 次に起こることを予測する
> ④ チームメイトとの関係を改善する方法に気づく
> ⑤ パターンに落ち着いて対応する

正解 ⇒ ②，③

　解答根拠は実験の考察をまとめた第4段落にある。同段落第1～2文より，我々は，優れた選手が未来の出来事を予測する上で有利なのは，より多くの可能性のある結果を予測し，それらを素早く分析し，最も有望な行動を思いつく能力に関係していると結論づけたと述べられている。よって，②，③が適当である。

問4 「　43　に最も適するものを選びなさい。」

> ① クォーターバックは，他のポジションよりも身体の強さが要求される。
> ② 優れたクォーターバックは，チームメイトだけを観察している時間が長い。

③　最高のクォーターバックは，最高のサッカー選手と似た特徴を持っている。

④　最も優れたクォーターバックは，チームメイトをより良い選手に指導することができる。

正解 ⇒ ③

第5段落第1文より，サッカーと似たようなことはフットボールにも当てはまるが，フィールド上の出来事の心的表象を発達させる必要があるのは，主にクォーターバックであると述べられている。よって，③が適当である。②は，第5段落第2文より，クオーターバックは自分のチームと対戦相手を観察し，分析すると述べられているため，不適。

【全訳】

あなたは学校でディスカッション・グループに参加しています。あなたは次の記事を要約するよう求められています。あなたはその記事について，メモだけを使って話すことになります。

チームスポーツにおける専門家のパフォーマンスに関する研究

ほとんどすべての分野において，専門家のパフォーマンスの特徴は，あまり発達していない心的表象を持つ人々にはランダムに見えたり混乱したりするような物事の集まりの中にパターンを見出す能力である。

言い換えれば，専門家は，他の人が木しか見ていないときに森を見ているのだ。これはおそらく，チームスポーツで最も顕著に見られる。例えばサッカーだ。片側に11人の選手がいて，その選手が動き回る。経験の浅い人には，サッカーボールが近づくとそのボールに引き寄せられる選手がいる，という明らかな事実以外には，何のパターンもない，渦巻くカオスのように見える。しかし，サッカーを知っている者，サッカーを愛する者，特にサッカーをうまくプレーする者にとっては，このカオスは決してカオスではない。選手たちがボールや他の選手たちの動きに反応して動くことによって生まれる，美しくニュアンスのある，絶えず変化するパターンなのだ。一流の選手は，そのパターンをほとんど即座に認識し，対応し，弱点や隙が現れたらすぐにそれを利用する。

この現象を研究するために，私はポール・ワードとマーク・ウィリアムズの2人の同僚とともに，サッカー選手がフィールド上ですでに起こったことから次に起こることをどれだけ予測できるかを調査した。実際のサッカーの試合のビデオを見せ，ある選手がボールを受けたところで突然ビデオを止めた。その上で次に何が起こるかを予測させた。ボールを持った選手はボールをキープするのか，ゴールを狙ってシュートを打つのか，それとも味方にボールを渡すのか。その結果，熟練した選手ほど，ボールを持った選手が何をすべきかを予測するのが得意であることがわかった。また，関連する選手がどこにいて，どの方向に動いているのか，映像が隠される前の最後のフレームからできる限り思い出してもらうことで，選手の記憶力もテストした。ここでも，優れた選手は弱い選手よりも優れていた。

我々は，優れた選手が将来の出来事を予測する上で有利なのは，より多くの可能性のある結果を予測し，それらを素早く分析し，最も有望な行動を思いつく能力に関係していると結論づけた。つまり，優れた選手ほど，フィールド上の行動パターンを解釈する能力がより高度に発達していたのである。この能力によって，どの選手の動きや相互作用が最も重要かを察知することができ，フィールドのどこに行くべきか，いつ誰にボールを渡すべきかなど，より良い決断を下すことができたのである。

きわめて似たようなことはフットボールにも当てはまるが，フィールド上の出来事の心的表象を発達させる必要があるのは主にクォーターバックである。このことは，最も成功したクォーターバックが，一般的に，映像室で自チームと対戦相手のプレーを見て分析することに最も多くの時間を費やしている理由を説明している。最高のクォーターバックは，フィールド上のあらゆる場所で何が起こっているかを把握し続け，試合後にはその試合のプレーのほとんどを思い出し，各チームの多くの選手の動きを詳細に説明することができる。さらに重要なことは，効果的な心的表象によって，クォーターバックはボールをパスするかどうか，誰にパスするか，いつパスするかなど，適切な判断を素早く下すことができるということである。コンマ1秒でも早く正しい判断ができるかどうかが，良いプ

レーと悲惨なプレー，つまりパスがつながるかインターセプトされるか，の分かれ目となる。

先ほど説明した専門家にとって，心的表象の主な利点は，情報を理解し，解釈し，記憶に保持し，整理し，分析し，それを使って意思決定を行うなど，情報の取り扱いにどのように役立つかにある。同じことがすべての専門家にも当てはまる。そして私たちのほとんどは，意識しているかどうかに関係なく，何かの専門家である。

【要約メモの訳】

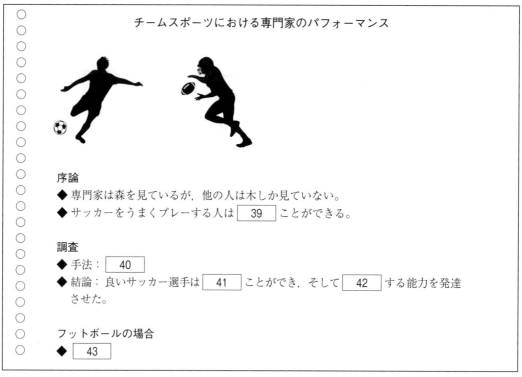

チームスポーツにおける専門家のパフォーマンス

序論
◆ 専門家は森を見ているが，他の人は木しか見ていない。
◆ サッカーをうまくプレーする人は｜ 39 ｜ことができる。

調査
◆ 手法：｜ 40 ｜
◆ 結論：良いサッカー選手は｜ 41 ｜ことができ，そして｜ 42 ｜する能力を発達させた。

フットボールの場合
◆ ｜ 43 ｜

[出典] From Peak by Anders Ericsson and Robert Pool. Copyright (c) 2016 by K. Anders Ericsson and Robert Pool. Used by permission of HarperCollins Publishers.
※問題作成の都合上，一部原文を改変しています。

【語句・表現】
〈第1段落〉
・mental representation「心的表象」
〈第2段落〉
・apparent「明らかな，明白な」
・whenever「～するときはいつでも，～であるときはいつも」
・shift「～を変える，移る」
・immediately「直ちに」
〈第3段落〉
・phenomenon「現象，不思議な現象」
・field「野原，畑，分野」
・accomplish「～をやり遂げる，～を完成する，～を勝ち取る，～を実現する」
・memory「記憶，記憶力，思い出，メモリ」
・direction「方向，方面，方角，方位」

〈第4段落〉
・relate「～を関連づける，～を関連させる」
・outcome「結果，結末，成果」
・promising「前途有望な，見込みのある」
・interpret「～を通訳する，～を解釈する，～を説明する」
・perceive「～を知覚する，～を感知する，～を認識する」
・interaction「相互作用，人とのやり取り」
・matter「重要である，重要になる」
〈第5段落〉
・true「本当の，真実の」
・difference「相違点，不和，差異」
・disastrous「凄惨な，悲惨な，災害的な，破滅的な」
〈選択肢〉
・condition「状態，状況，条件，様態」
・trait「特色，特質，特性」

B
問1 「 44 に入れるべきものはどれか。」

① タコは貝殻を持たないので，貝殻を持つ海洋動物の親戚ではない。
② タコには脊椎があり，他の無脊椎動物とは一線を画している。
③ タコの中には体重が1グラムにも満たないものもいる。
④ 全種類のタコの平均的な大きさは約4メートルである。
⑤ タコは「頭足類」に属するが，「頭足」とは腕と頭の両方にニューロンがあることを意味している。

正解 ⇒ ③

第1段落第2～3文より，「タコは約300種類あり，形も大きさも様々である。最も小さい種は体長2.5センチメートル，重さ1グラム以下，最も大きい種は平均4メートル，重さ50キログラムである」という記述があることから，③が適当である。

①は，本文には述べられていないので，不適。②は，第1段落最終文より，タコは他の無脊椎動物とは一線を画していると述べられているものの，脊椎があると言及されていないので不適。④は，第1段落第3文より，タコの最も大きい種が平均4メートルの大きさであると述べられており，タコ全体の平均的な大きさは言及されていないので不適。⑤は，第2段落第1～2文より，「『頭足類』とはギリシャ語で『頭足』という意味である。頭から直接腕が枝分かれしているタコのユニークな体の構造を指す」という記述があるものの，「頭足」の由来とニューロンは無関係のため不適。

問2 「『体の構造』のスライドで，タコのイラストに欠けているラベルを完成させなさい。」 45

① (A) 中枢脳	(B) 外套膜	(C) 素嚢	(D) 漏斗	(E) 腸
② (A) 中枢脳	(B) 外套膜	(C) 素嚢	(D) 腸	(E) 漏斗
③ (A) 素嚢	(B) 中枢脳	(C) 漏斗	(D) 外套膜	(E) 腸
④ (A) 外套膜	(B) 中枢脳	(C) 素嚢	(D) 漏斗	(E) 腸
⑤ (A) 外套膜	(B) 中枢脳	(C) 素嚢	(D) 腸	(E) 漏斗

正解 ⇒ ⑤

第2段落第3～4文を要約すると，腕の真向かい，つまり頭上には，外套膜と呼ばれる高度に筋肉化した風船のような構造物があり，エラや消化器官などほとんどの器官で満たされているため，膨らんだ形をしているとなる。よって，(A)は mantle になる。次に，第3段落第2文より，中枢脳は目と目の間にあるため，口の中で食べ物を噛み砕くと目の前を通り過ぎると述べられているので，(B)は central brain になる。そして，第2段落第9～10文を要約すると，口から取り込まれた食物は，胃で消化される前の食物を保持する素嚢に移動するとなる。よって，胃の前に位置する(C)は crop であることが分かる。続いて，同段落第11文より，部分的に消化された食物は腸に移動し，そこで栄養素が血流に吸収されると述べられているので，胃の後に位置する(D)は intestine であることが分かる。最後に，同段落第12文より，腸の末端，つまり漏斗の入り口に到達するまでに，完全に便に変わると述べられている。腸の端にある(E)が funnel であることがわかる。以上から，⑤が適当である。

問3　「『脳について』のスライドで，タコの脳の特徴として正しいものを2つ選びなさい（順番は問わない）。」　46　・　47

> ①　それぞれの触手の神経節には4,000万近くのニューロンがある。
> ②　タコの骨格が流動的になれるように，ニューロンは触手にある。
> ③　それぞれの触手にある神経節によって，タコは固有受容感覚を持つことができる。
> ④　それぞれの触手にある神経節は，中枢脳の命令なしに互いに異なる行動をとることを可能にする。
> ⑤　中枢脳のニューロンの数は，触手のニューロンの数の2倍である。

　正解 ⇒ ①，④

　①については，まず第3段落第3～5文の内容から，タコのニューロンは計5億のうち中枢脳の分を除いた3億2,000万が足にあり，それが8本の足に均等に分布していることから，一般的にタコ足一本は4,000万ニューロンを保有していることが分かる。よって，①は正しいことが分かる。
　④については，まず第3段落第6文より，触手にはそれぞれ神経節があるので，互いに，また脳とは独立して作用することができることが分かる。よって④も正しいことが分かる。
　②については，第3段落第7文より，タコは骨格がないと述べられているので，不適。③については，第3段落第9～最終文より，タコは固有受容感覚が備わっておらず，それを補完するために足にニューロンがあると述べられているので，不適。⑤は，同段落第3～5文の内容と反することがわかるので不適。

問4　「『動き方』のスライドで，タコの特徴として正しいものを選びなさい。」　48

> ①　タコは風船のように体に空気を入れ，それを放出して体を動かす。
> ②　タコがジェット噴射で泳ぐコースは，漏斗がどの方向を向いているかによって決まる。
> ③　タコは風船のようなものを作り，その中に水を入れる。
> ④　タコは漏斗から水を取り込み，体をいっぱいにして噴射の準備をする。
> ⑤　外套膜から直接水が出て，タコは逆方向に噴射する。

　正解 ⇒ ②

　第4段落最終文より，タコは漏斗を様々な方向に向けることで進路を変えることができることが述べられているので，②が適当である。⑤は，第4段落第8文より，水は外套膜から噴射されるのではなく，漏斗から噴射されることが分かるので不適。

問5　「最後のスライドに最適な文はどれか。」　49

> ①　エイリアンの意識について知るには，タコを研究するのが一番だ。

　② タコの脳活動が，生物における意識の起源の謎を解く鍵になるかもしれない。
　③ タコを研究することで，タコ特有の特徴を人体に応用できるかもしれない。
　④ 人間とタコは異なる意識を持っているために，両者の進化の過程も異なると言われている。

正解 ⇒ ②

　第5段落最終文より，タコの脳波は，地球上の様々な生物の意識がどのように成立しているのか，その根本的な解明にもつながると述べられているので，②が適当である。①は，本文に言及されていないので不適。③は，第5段落第4文より，研究者たちはタコの脳波が人間の意識のメカニズムを解明する手がかりになる可能性があるとして注目していると述べられており，人体に応用できるかは触れられていないので不適。④は，同段落第3文より，タコは人間の進化の過程から最も遠い存在であるにも関わらず，人間と同じく明確な意識を持っていると述べられているので不適。

【全訳】
　あなたは国際的な科学プレゼンテーション・コンテストの準備をしている学生グループに所属しています。あなたは次の文章を使って，ある興味深い生物に関するプレゼンテーションの一部を作成しています。

　タコは多くのことを学べる魅力的な生き物だ。種は300近くあり，形や大きさも様々である。最小種は体長2.5センチメートル以下，重さ1グラム未満で，最大種は平均4メートル，50キログラムになる。タコはイカやコウイカとともに海洋動物の頭足類を構成している。6億年以上前に頭足類が誕生して以来，彼らは劇的な進化を遂げてきた。この動物は，他の無脊椎動物，つまり脊椎がない動物，とは異なる多くのユニークな特徴を持っている。

　「頭足類」とはギリシャ語で「頭の足」という意味を持つ。これは，頭から直接腕が枝分かれしているタコのユニークな体の構造を指している。腕の反対側，つまり頭の上には，外套膜と呼ばれる非常に筋肉質な風船のような構造がある。外套膜にはエラや消化器官など，動物のほとんどの器官が詰まっており，それがそのふくらんだ形状の理由である。外套膜の強力な筋肉がこれらの重要な器官を保護し，呼吸や体の収縮を助けている。口はその下側，8本の腕が合わさる部分にある。くちばしは，骨格のないこの動物の体の中で唯一の硬い部分である。そのため，タコはくちばしが通る小さな隙間に体全体を押し込んで収めることができる。口から取り込まれた餌は，筋肉質の素嚢に移される。素嚢は胃で消化される前の餌を保持する。その後，部分的に消化された食物は腸に移動し，そこで栄養素が血流に吸収される。腸の末端，つまり漏斗の入り口に到達するまでに，食物は完全に便に変わる。便は漏斗から排出され，細長いリボン状の物質になる。漏斗が担っている機能は他にもあるが，これについては後述する。

　他の動物と違うもうひとつの特徴は，脳が複数あり，しかも2つ，3つではなく9つにもなることだ！中枢脳は目と目の間にあり，食べ物が咀嚼されるときはそこを通過する。一般的に，中枢脳には全5億個のニューロンのうち，およそ1億8,000万個が含まれている。残りのニューロンは8本の触手に均等に分布している。計算すると，ニューロンの半分以上は中枢脳ではなく触手にあることになると分かるだろう！各触手がそれぞれ神経節（ニューロンの塊）を持つことで，触手は互いに，また中枢脳からも独立して動くことができる。これは，タコの体は流動的で骨格がないため，固有受容感覚，つまり体の一部がどこにあるのか，あるいは何をしているのかという感覚が欠如しているので，タコにとって有利に働く。例えば，私たちは固有受容感覚のおかげで，後頭部を見ることなくその位置を把握することができる。しかし，タコは周囲の環境に適応するために常に流動的な体の形を変えているため，固有受容感覚を持たない。その代わりに，各触手に小さな脳がある。

　タコの動きも特筆すべき特徴だ。一般的に，タコは這うように移動する。垂直に這うこともあれば，触手の吸盤の列を使って逆さまに這うこともある。タコが危険にさらされているときは，もっと面白い動き方が見られる。そのような状況では，タコは漏斗を使ってより素早く移動する。タコはまず外套膜から水を取り込み，水風船のように閉じる。水風船を持ったまま口を離すと，水を吹き出しながら激しく飛んでいくのを想像してほしい。タコも同様の原理で外套膜から漏斗を通して水を放出

し，最大時速40キロで逆方向に噴射する。タコは漏斗をさまざまな方向に向けることで進路を変えることができる。

　他にもタコは様々なユニークな特徴を備えており，ある科学者は，タコは地球上で最もエイリアンに近い生物ではないかと述べている。タコの起源と進化の過程から，タコは最も複雑な種であり，人類との共通要素が最も少ない種であると言える。タコは人類の進化過程から最も離れているが，人間のような明確な意識を持っている。このことから，研究者たちはタコの脳波が人間の意識のメカニズムを解明する手がかりになる可能性があるとして注目している。これは，タコの脳の仕組みや運動パターンといった特徴の謎を解き明かすだけでなく，地球上のありとあらゆる生物の意識がどのようにして成立されたのかという根本的な理解につながるかもしれない。

【あなたのプレゼンテーションスライドの訳】

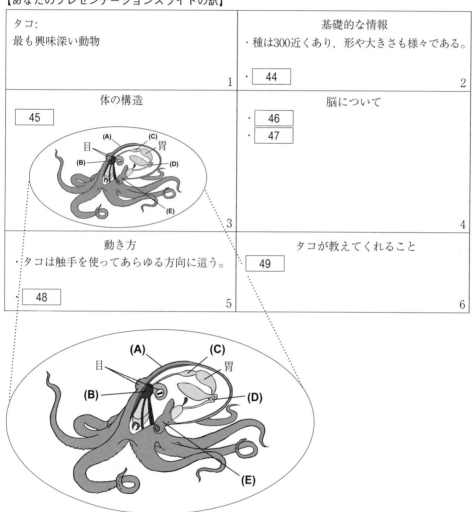

【語句・表現】
〈第1段落〉
・fascinating「魅力的」
・shape「図形，形，形態，輪郭」
・evolve「進化する，発達する」

・drastically「徹底的に，思い切って，抜本的に，根本的に，猛烈に，劇的に」

〈第２段落〉

・structure「構造」

・arm「腕」

・organ「内臓，臓器」

・beak「くちばし，嘴」

・digest「～を消化する」

・partially「部分的に」

・absorb「～を吸収する，～を吸い込む」

・convert「～を転換する，～を変える」

・slender「すらっとした，細い，やせた」

・ribbon「リボン」

・function「機能，作用，役割，働き」

〈第３段落〉

・feature「特徴，特色，特質，要点，機能」

・multiple「多数の，多種多様の，複合的な，多角的な」

・central「中央にある」

・contain「～を含む，～を包括する，～を収容できる」

・roughly「大まかに，荒く，おおよそ，約」

・distribute「～を分配する，～を散布する」

・act「行動する，振る舞う，作用する，作動する，演じる」

・individually「一々，個々に」

・fluid「流動的，液体のような」

・sense「感覚」

〈第４段落〉

・crawl「這う」

・principle「原則，原理，主義，本質，基礎」

・direction「方向，方面，方角，方位」

・course「過程，進路，講座，コース」

〈第５段落〉

・origin「根源，起源，出所，発端，元，原産」

・complex「複雑な，混雑している，込み入った」

・distant「遠い」

・consciousness「意識」

・mechanism「仕組み」

・trait「特色，特質，特性」

・fundamental「基本的な，本質的な，根本的な」

・understanding「理解，合意」

・establish「～を設置する，～を確立する，～を立証する」

〈選択肢〉

・spine「脊椎，背骨」

・label「ラベル，はり紙，はり札，標札」

・illustration「挿絵，イラスト」

・apply A to B「A を B に応用する，適用する」

問題番号(配点)	設	問	解答番号	正解	配点	自己採点
第1問 (10)	A	1	1	2	2	
		2	2	2	2	
	B	1	3	3	2	
		2	4	3	2	
		3	5	1	2	
自己採点小計						
第2問 (20)	A	1	6	4	2	
		2	7	3	2	
		3	8	3	2	
		4	9	3	2	
		5	10	3	2	
	B	1	11	4	2	
		2	12	1	2	
		3	13	3	2	
		4	14	4	2	
		5	15	1	2	
自己採点小計						
第3問 (15)	A	1	16	2	3	
		2	17	2	3	
	B	1	18	2	3*	
			19	1		
			20	3		
			21	4		
		2	22	3	3	
		3	23	2	3	
自己採点小計						

問題番号(配点)	設	問	解答番号	正解	配点	自己採点
第4問 (16)		1	24	2	3	
		2	25	4	3	
		3	26	1	3	
		4	27	3	2	
			28	2	2	
		5	29	1	3	
自己採点小計						
第5問 (15)		1	30	4	3	
		2	31	4	3	
		3	32	5	3*	
			33	2		
			34	3		
			35	4		
		4	36	4	3	
		5	37	3	3	
自己採点小計						
第6問 (24)	A	1	38	3	3	
		2	39	2	3	
		3	40-41	1-5	3*	
		4	42	4	3	
	B	1	43	1	2	
		2	44	3	2	
		3	45	6	3*	
			46	4		
			47	5		
		4	48-49	2-5	3*	
		5	50	3	2	
自己採点小計						

自己採点合計 □

（注）
1　*は，全部正解の場合のみ点を与える。
2　−（ハイフン）でつながれた正解は，順序を問わない。

第1問

A
問1 「このメッセージを書いたあと，あなたの母親は何をした可能性が高いか」 1

① 救急車を呼んだ。
② **おばあちゃんの家に行った。**
③ おじいちゃんに電話をかけた。
④ あなたのために夕食の支度をした。

正解 ⇒ ②

メッセージの中で「これからおばあちゃんの家に行かなくてはならない」とあるため，メッセージを書いた後に実際に行動に移したと考えられる。

【語句・表現】
・ambulance「救急車」

問2 「このメッセージから何が分かるか」 2

① あなたの父親は家に帰る前に病院に立ち寄る予定である。
② **あなたの祖母はあなたと一緒に暮らしていない。**
③ あなたの祖母は交通事故でけがをした。
④ あなたの母親はあなたと一緒に買い物に行きたくないと思っている。

正解 ⇒ ②

家に置いてあったメッセージに「おばあちゃんの家に行かなくてはならない」とあることから，あなたとおばあちゃんは別の家で暮らしていることが分かる。

【語句・表現】
・drop by ～「～に立ち寄る」
・injure「～を傷つける」

【全訳】
あなたが家に帰ると，母親からのメッセージを机の上で見つけます。

> 本当にごめんなさい。夕方に一緒に買い物に行く約束をしていたけど，行けなくなりました。おじいちゃんから電話があって，おばあちゃんが階段から落ちて，腕を骨折したそうです。入院の準備のためにこれからおばあちゃんの家に行かないといけません。おばあちゃんの状態次第では，何日かそこに泊まるかもしれません。リビングのテーブルにお金を置いておいたので，それでどうにかやりくりしてください。
> ところで，お父さんは今日帰りが遅くなると言っていたので，晩ご飯の用意はしなくて大丈夫です。
> 何か用事があったら電話してください。

【語句・表現】
・fall down the stairs「階段で転げ落ちる」
・make do with 〜「〜で間に合わせる」
・be late coming home「帰りが（予定より）遅くなる」

B
問1 「もし若葉大学のライティングコンテストに参加するなら， 3 作品を提出しなくてはならない」

① 11月1日までに
② 11月の終わりまでに
③ 8月と9月の間に
④ 8月1日に

正解 ⇒ ③

コンテストの日程は「スケジュール」の欄に書かれている。ここを見ると「応募作品は8月1日から9月30日まで受け付ける」とあるので，これを言い換えた③が正解である。

問2 「作品を提出する際， 4 」

① その作品は2,000語以内に収まっていなければならない
② あなたは若葉大学の学生でなければならない
③ その作品は他のコンテストで過去に賞を取っていてはならない
④ フルネーム，住所，タイトルを全てのページ上にタイプしなければならない

正解 ⇒ ③

「応募要件」の欄の(5)を見ると，「過去に他のコンテストへ応募したことのあるものでも，未受賞の場合は応募可能です」とある。裏を返せば，他のコンテストで受賞歴のある作品は応募できないということである。この内容に合致する③が正解である。

問3 「作品が大賞に選ばれると， 5 」

① トロフィーと賞状，10万円が授与される
② 11月1日の表彰式に招待される
③ 賞状と1万円が手に入る
④ 名前が11月23日にネット上に掲載される

正解 ⇒ ①

「賞」の欄を見ると，「大賞」の項目の横に「賞状，トロフィー，10万円」との記述がある。

【全訳】

　あなたは日本の若葉大学のウェブサイトを見ていて，面白いコンテストのお知らせを見つけます。あなたはそのコンテストに参加することを考えています。

高校生のための若葉大学ライティングコンテスト

若葉大学主催のこの創造的なライティングコンテストには，全ての年齢の高校生が参加可能です。三つの部門（詩，短編小説，エッセイ）に作品を提出することができます。

応募要件

作品を提出する前に，以下をお読みください：

　(1)　応募は高校生に限ります。

　(2)　応募作品はオリジナルのものでなくてはなりません。

　(3)　一度に一つ以上の部門に応募することもできます。

　(4)　以下の文字数は厳守してください。

　　　詩：2,000語以内

　　　短編小説：8,000語以内

　　　エッセイ：2,000語以内

　(5)　過去に他のコンテストへ応募したことのあるものでも，未受賞の場合は応募可能です。

　(6)　応募作品は全てタイプしてください。氏名，住所，作品タイトルを作品の1ページ目に記載してください。

　(7)　全ての応募作品は電子メールで writingcontest@wakaba-u.ac.jp に送信してください。

賞

各部門における優秀作品には，大賞もしくは奨励賞が与えられます。

大賞：賞状，トロフィー，10万円

奨励賞：賞状，3万円

スケジュール

応募作品は8月1日から9月30日まで受け付けます。

受賞者のリストは9月1日までにネット上に掲載されます。

表彰式は11月23日に若葉大学で行われます。

【語句・表現】

・submit「～を提出する」

・applicant「応募者」

・adhere to ～「(規則など) を固守する」

・entry「参加，出品物」

・type「～をキーボードで打つ」

・via「～を経由して」

・submission「提出，提出物」

第２問

A

問1 「 ⬚6⬚ の二つが，このキャンプ場に関して正しいことである」

A：全ての種類の動物をキャンプ場に連れて行くことができる。
B：そこにいる動物の大半はスタッフによって保護されている。
C：追加料金を払うことで，Wi-Fi 機器を借りることができる。
D：シャワールームは好きなだけ長く利用することができる。
E：泊まっているコテージ内で調理をすることはできない。

  ① 　AとB
  ② 　AとC
  ③ 　BとD
  ④ 　**CとE**
  ⑤ 　DとE

  正解 ⇒ ④

  「コテージ」のセクションを見ると，「コテージ自体には Wi-Fi 接続がないが，レンタル Wi-Fi 機器が１泊あたり２ドルで利用できる」とある。これを言い換えた C が一つ目の正しい記述である。また，「調理」のセクションには「調理はパブリックスペースでのみ可能」との記述があり，この内容と合致する E は正しい。したがって，④が正解である。

問2 「もしこのキャンプ場で懐中電灯を壊してしまって，それを捨てたいと思ったならば， ⬚7⬚ 必要がある」

---

  ① 　スタッフに捨ててもらうようお願いする
  ② 　受付に持っていく
  ③ 　**家に持ち帰る**
  ④ 　キャンプ場のごみ捨て場に捨てる

  正解 ⇒ ③

  ごみの捨て方については「その他」のセクションに書かれている。「生ごみはごみ捨て場に，その他のごみはお持ち帰りください」とあるので，懐中電灯はキャンプ場から持って帰る必要がある。

【語句・表現】
・flashlight「懐中電灯」
・dispose of ～「～を処分する」

問3 「キャンプ場の所有する調理器具を使用するには， ⬚8⬚ 必要がある」

---

  ① 　キャンプをする日にそれを申し込む
  ② 　追加料金を払う
  ③ 　**事前に予約する**
  ④ 　身分証明書を見せる

正解 ⇒ ③

「調理」のセクションに「調理器具は追加料金なしで利用できる」，「必要なら事前に予約のこと」という記述がある。

【語句・表現】
・identification「身分証明書」

問4　「もしあなたが17歳の友人と2匹のペットの犬とともに2泊でキャンプをすることを計画しているなら，合計料金は　9　になる」

① 28ドル
② 32ドル
③ 48ドル
④ 52ドル

正解 ⇒ ③

　2泊のキャンプをする場合は，料金表の「2泊以上」の行が適用される。1泊あたり9ドルの大人が2人，1泊あたり3ドルのペットが2匹で，2泊利用であるので，合計料金は9ドル×2×2＋3ドル×2×2＝48ドルである。

問5　「このキャンプ場の利用者によって述べられている事実の一つは，　10　ということである」

① コテージでペットと過ごすにはペットケージが重要だ
② そこにいる動物とキャンプをするのは動物園の中を見て回るのと同じくらい楽しい
③ **一部の限られた場所ではたき火をすることが許されている**
④ 交通機関が乏しいので，そこまで車を運転しなくてはならない

正解 ⇒ ③

　「利用者のコメント」のセクションを見ると，3番目のコメントで「キャンプ場はパブリックエリア以外では火気の使用が禁止されているので，たき火はできなかった」，「パブリックエリアはとても混んでいたので，家族だけでたき火を楽しむことは不可能だっただろう」と述べられている。つまり，パブリックエリアに限ってはたき火が許可されているということであるので，これを言い換えた③が正解である。①は「利用者のコメント」中の4番目のコメントで述べられている内容と合致するが，事実ではなく意見であるので，解答としては不適切である。

あなたは来月の18歳の誕生日にキャンプ旅行に行こうと計画しています。あなたは，友人に教えてもらったキャンプ場のホームページを見ています。

〈ストーンリバーキャンプ場〉

ストーンリバーキャンプ場は自然豊かで，近くに川が流れ，たくさんの種類の動物がいます。30棟以上のコテージや充実した設備があり，初心者の方でも快適にキャンプをしていただけます。小さい犬と猫のみ同伴可能です。

料金：	大人	子ども (15歳未満)	ペット
1泊	10ドル	5ドル	3ドル
2泊以上	9ドル / 1泊	4ドル / 1泊	3ドル / 1泊

コテージ

各コテージには四つのベッド，冷蔵庫，テレビが備え付けられています。コテージ自体にはWi-Fi接続がありませんが，インターネットにアクセスする必要がある場合は，レンタルWi-Fi機器が1泊あたり2ドルで利用できます。

調理

屋外にあるパブリックエリアには数家族分のキッチンがあり，調理はそこでのみ可能です。調理器具は追加料金なしでご利用いただけます。必要な場合は，予約時にお知らせください。キャンプ場の近くにスーパーマーケットがありますので，自宅から大量の食料を持参する必要はありません。

その他

シャワールームがパブリックスペースにあり，1日20分まで使用可能です。シャワールームでは，受付で提供している石鹸やシャンプーなどのアメニティを使用することができます。ごみの処理については，生ごみはごみ捨て場に捨て，それ以外のごみは各自でお持ち帰りください。

利用者のコメント

● このキャンプ場は駅から徒歩10分なのでアクセスしやすいです。キャンプ用の荷物が多い人には，駅からキャンプ場まで無料のシャトルバスが運行されています。一方で，ペットを連れて行きたい場合は，自分で運転して行くのがベストです。

● キャンプ場の森の奥まで行くと，シカやリス，キツツキなど，さまざまな動物に出会えました。また，多くの人がペットと一緒にキャンプをしていたので，小さな動物園にいるような気分でした！

● 妻や子どもたちが自然を満喫しているのを見て幸せでした。しかし，残念ながらキャンプ場はパブリックエリア以外では火気の使用が禁止されているので，たき火はできませんでした。パブリックエリアはとても混んでいたので，家族だけでたき火を楽しむことは不可能だったことでしょう。

● 愛犬との初めてのキャンプはとても楽しかったです。しかし，愛犬が興奮して私が寝ている間にコテージ内を走り回ってしまったので，ペットケージを持っていくのを忘れたことを後悔しています。

【語句・表現】

・cottage「コテージ」
・well-equipped「設備のよく整った」
・facility「設備，施設」
・be equipped with ~「~を備えている」
・refrigerator「冷蔵庫」
・cooking utensil「調理器具」
・reservation「予約」
・amenity「アメニティ」
・reception「受付，（ホテルの）フロント」
・food scrap「生ごみ，食品廃棄物」
・garbage dump「ごみ捨て場」

B

問1 「デイビッドの記事によると，日本の国際空港に関して正しいものは以下の記述のうちどれか」
　　　11

```
①　KIXは24時間稼働している国際空港である。
②　日本に来る外国人観光客の半数以上がKIXに到着する。
③　NRTとKIXは日本のただ二つの国際空港である。
④　KIXの人気は最近上昇傾向にある。
```

正解 ⇒ ④

　第1パラグラフ最終文を見ると，「近年ではKIXの人気が高まっている」とある。したがって，この内容を言い換えた④が正解である。

問2 「2019年にKIXを訪れた観光客数の点で4位だったのは以下のうちどこか」　12

```
①　香港
②　韓国
③　台湾
④　タイ
```

正解 ⇒ ①

　2019年にKIXを訪れた人がどこから来たかについて述べられているのは，第2パラグラフである。ここを見ると，「香港が4位」とある。

問3 「2017年にKIXで行われた外国人観光客への調査によると，回答者の約4分の1は　13　というのが理由で道頓堀を訪れたいと思っていた」

```
①　そこが非常に美しい観光地である
②　そこが大阪城とKIXに近い
③　そこが大阪ならではの食べ物の見つかる場所である
④　そこがほとんどなんでも買うことのできる場所である
```

正解 ⇒ ③

　「回答者の約4分の1」というのは，第4パラグラフにある26% of them の言い換えである。文の後半に「そのほぼ全ての人が大阪ならではの食べものをそこで堪能したいと思っていた」とあるので，この内容を言い換えた③が正解である。

問4 「日本を訪れた外国人観光客によってナビゲーションアプリ上で3番目によく検索されている場所はどこか」　14

```
①　道頓堀
②　伏見稲荷大社
③　金閣寺
④　奈良公園
⑤　東京タワー
```

⑥　ユニバーサル・スタジオ・ジャパン

　　正解 ⇒ ④

　　第3パラグラフに「大阪城が最も検索されている」,「金閣寺, 奈良公園, 東京タワー, 伏見稲荷大社と続く」とある。したがって, 3番目によく検索されているのは奈良公園であり, ④が正解である。

問5　「この記事のタイトルとして最も適当なものはどれか」　15

① 　KIXと大阪の観光スポット
② 　日本の人気な観光スポット
③ 　2025年大阪万博が与える良い影響
④ 　NRTとKIXの戦い

　　正解 ⇒ ①

　　この記事は冒頭で日本の国際空港について言及した後, その中でも関西国際空港に話題を絞って話を進めている。また, 記事の後半では, 関西国際空港から来た観光客が訪れている大阪の観光地について取り上げている。これらの内容を端的に表現した①が正解である。

【全訳】
　　あなたは「Wanna See Japan」という, 日本の観光産業を推進する英語のウェブサイトの編集者です。あなたは, アメリカ人の旅行記者であるデイビッドから, 日本の国際空港や観光地について書いた記事を受け取りました。

　　　日本を訪れる観光客の半数以上は, 二つの空港を利用している。成田国際空港（NRT）と関西国際空港（KIX）である。NRTは長い間, 日本における最も主要な空港であったが, 近年ではKIXの人気が高まっており, 特にアジア諸国からの訪問客に人気が高い。
　　　どの国や地域から最も多くの旅行者がKIXに来ているか知っているだろうか。2019年は, 中国が1位, 韓国が2位, 台湾が3位, 香港が4位, タイが5位であった。では, その人たちはKIXに到着後, どこを訪れているのだろうか。
　　　訪日観光客向けナビゲーションアプリの検索データを分析したところ, 外国人観光客が最も多く検索しているのは大阪城で, 金閣寺, 奈良公園, 東京タワー, 伏見稲荷大社, 道頓堀, ユニバーサル・スタジオ・ジャパンと続く。驚くことに, トップ7のうち, 3か所のスポットが大阪にあるのだ。
　　　なぜ大阪はそれほどまでに訪日外国人に人気があるのだろうか。2017年にKIXで行われた外国人観光客1,236人への調査によると, 大阪を目的地に選んだ理由は以下のとおりであった。48%は「観光地として魅力的」, 44%は「食べものが魅力的」, 41%は「ショッピングが魅力的」と回答した。彼らのうちの26%は道頓堀を訪れるつもりだと回答したが, そのほぼ全ての人が, たこ焼き, お好み焼き, 串カツといった大阪ならではの食べ物をそこで堪能したいと思っていた。
　　　KIXは将来的により多くの外国人観光客で賑わうと期待されている。というのも, 2025年に大阪で万国博覧会が開催されるからだ。6か月間で約2,800万人の来場が見込まれている。

【語句・表現】
・region「地域」
・ranked「位置する」
・analysis「分析」
・app「アプリケーション, アプリ」

・destination「目的地」
・attractive「魅力的な」
・appealing「魅力的な」
・cuisine「料理」
・the World Exposition「万国博覧会，万博」：Expoと略される。
・approximately「およそ」

第3問

A
問1 「デイヴのブログで，あなたは彼が　16　ことが読める」

① お土産屋で金の指輪を買った
❷ キャラクターのミュージカルを楽しんだ
③ 馬の乗り方を学んだ
④ ビーグルの路上パフォーマンスを見た

正解 ⇒ ②

　第2パラグラフ前半で「キャラクターたちのミュージカル」への言及があり，同パラグラフ第4文後半で「私は本当にそのショーを楽しんだ」とあることから，これに合致する②が正解である。

問2 「カウボーイの演奏を見ていた時，デイヴは　17　可能性が高い」

① 驚いていた
❷ 退屈していた
③ 喜んでいた
④ わくわくしていた

正解 ⇒ ②

　カウボーイの演奏については，第2パラグラフ最終文で Many people stopped to watch, but we were not interested because we'd seen similar performances in another place「多くの人が立ち止まって見ていたが，私たちは同じようなパフォーマンスを別の場所で見たことがあったので，興味を持てなかった」と述べられている。not interestedに対する類似表現である②のboredが正解である。

【全訳】

　あなたは日帰り旅行に関心があります。あなたは，近所に住むイギリスの大学生が書いた，近場の観光地についてのブログの投稿を読んでいます。

デイヴ・シンプソン
7月5日水曜日　午後6時32分

ルームメイトと私は近所の遊園地に行きました。そこはビーグルがメインキャラクターのテーマパークです。そこには多くのアトラクションがあります。私たちはジェットコースターに乗りましたが，そのスピードに驚きました。それは2秒で時速60マイルに達するそうです。フリーフォールは激しすぎて乗った後少しめまいがしましたが，皆さんもぜひ挑戦してみてください。

私たちはその遊園地で三つのパフォーマンスを見ました。そのうちの一つは，ミュージカル・コメディー・ショーでした。ビーグルのマスコットやその他のキャラクターが歌に合わせて舞台上で踊っていました。キャラクターたちがとてもかわいくて，私は本当にそのショーを楽しみました。私たちが見た他のパフォーマンスには，カウボーイに扮した男性たちによる生演奏や，ネイティブ・アメリカンによる長いリボンを使ったパフォーマンスがありました。多くの人が立ち止まって見ていましたが，私たちは同じようなパフォーマンスを別の場所で見たことがあったので，興味を持ちませんでした。

　私たちはまた，貴重で楽しいワークショップにも参加しました。私たちは砂金採りを体験しました。これは，砂や砂利の中から砂金を分離させるというアクティビティです。私たちは泥水の中から金を取り出すためのボウルの使い方を学びました。また，馬の餌やりもしました。思ったとおりニンジンが大好物だったのが面白かったです。

　もしこのテーマパークに行くことがあれば，ぜひ感想を聞かせてください。

【語句・表現】
・attraction「呼び物，魅力」
・roller coaster「ジェットコースター」
・mph「マイル毎時，時速〜マイル」：miles per hour の略。
・dizzy「目まいがする，ふらふらする」
・give 〜 a try「〜を試してみる」
・gravel「砂利」
・muddy「泥の，ぬかるんだ」

B
問1　「次の出来事（①〜④）を，教授の教え子がした順番に並べよ」

18	→	19	→	20	→	21

① おかゆを食べ，甘い紅茶を飲んだ。
② 服を着替えた。
③ 服の補修をした。
④ 甘い紅茶についてのレポートを書いた。

正解 ⇒ 　18 ②　　19 ①　　20 ③　　21 ④

　第3パラグラフ第2文で「始めに，彼らには当時の庶民の服を着てもらった」と述べられているため，最初の 18 に入るのは②である。次に，第3パラグラフ第3文に「その後，生徒は以下の順で物事を体験した。朝食を食べ，当時の娯楽を体験し，夕方のアクティビティをやってもらった」とある。ここで述べられている「朝食」とは，第6パラグラフで述べられているように，おかゆと甘い紅茶のことを指すので，19 には①が入る。また，「夕方のアクティビティ」は，第4パラグラフ第3文に「夕方のアクティビティとして，生徒たちには針で服を縫う体験をさせた」とあることから，服の修理のことを指していると分かる。したがって，20 が③である。そして，第6パラグラフ最終文にて「全てのイベントの後でレポートを書いてもらった」とあるので，21 が④である。

問2　「教授によると，19世紀のイギリスでは， 22 」

① 庶民が娯楽のために出かけることはまれであった
② 人々が一日三食の食事を始めたばかりだった
③ 庶民が新しい服を買うのはしばしば困難だった
④ 庶民の間で海外旅行が盛んであった

正解 ⇒ ③

　第4パラグラフ第2文に「当時の庶民は新しい服を買う余裕がなかった」との記述がある。この内容を言い換えた③が正解である。

問3 「この記事から，教授は　23　ことが分かる」

① なぜ甘い紅茶が人気なのかを学生に説明した
② ある問いについて考察する機会を学生に与えた
③ ショーを開催するために大道芸人を雇った
④ 洋服の作り直しに大金を費やした

正解 ⇒ ②

　第6パラグラフ最終文の記述から，教授は朝食時に甘い紅茶が飲まれていた理由を生徒に考えさせたことが分かる。この内容を言い換えた②が正解である。

【全訳】

　あなたの所属する歴史クラブは，学園祭で「歴史体験展」を開催します。あなたは参考のため，生徒に昔のイングランドの文化を体験させた教授が書いた記事を読んでいます。

　19世紀イングランドの人々の生活を学生に体験させるために，私はいくつかのことを考えなければなりませんでした。

　まず，私はどの社会階級に焦点を当てるかを決めました。当時の階級社会は本当に複雑でしたが，ともかく庶民の暮らしに焦点を当てることにしました。

　次に，生徒たちに体験してもらうイベントの順序を決めました。始めに，彼らには当時の庶民の服を着てもらいました。それは郷土史研究家から私が借りてきたものでした。その後，生徒は以下の順で物事を体験しました。朝食を食べ，当時の娯楽を体験し，夕方のアクティビティをやってもらいました。

　借りた服はわざと破れたままにしておきました。当時の庶民には新しいものを買う余裕がなく，修理をするのが一般的だったからです。夕方のアクティビティとして，生徒たちには針で服を縫う体験をさせました。

　当時の庶民の娯楽は，大道芸人を見たり，動物園に行ったりすることでした。しかし，これらを用意することはできないので，簡単には海外旅行に行けなかった庶民たちが鑑賞していた，他の国を描いたパノラマ画を展示しました。

　食事に関して，イングランド人は中世には1日2食だったと言われていますが，のちに1日3食になりました。3食の中で最も興味深いのは朝食です。庶民の朝食は，オーツ麦から作られるおかゆのようなものと，とても甘い紅茶でした。私は，なぜ朝食にそんなに甘いお茶が飲まれるのかについて，答えを教える代わりに，学生たちにそれについて考えさせ，全てのイベントの後でレポートを書いてもらいました。

　学生たちは，この体験が本当に楽しかったと言っていました。

【語句・表現】
・exhibition「展覧会，展示」
・common people「庶民，一般大衆」
・determine「～を決める」

・local historian「郷土史研究家」
・torn「引き裂けた」: tear「～を引き裂く」の過去分詞形。
・afford to *do*「～する余裕がある」
・exhibit「～を展示する」
・as for ～「～について言えば」
・the Middle Ages「中世」
・porridge「おかゆ」
・oat「オーツ麦」
・as to ～「～について」

第4問

問1 「このイベントの主な目的は何だと思われるか」 24

> ① 留学生の勉強を助けること
> ② **町を紹介すること**
> ③ 昼食を一緒に作って食べること
> ④ 陶磁器産業を支援すること

正解 ⇒ ②

　千秋とロビンのメッセージを見ると，両者とも街の歴史・産業・文化や，街の美しい景色に留学生を触れさせるような計画を立てていることが分かる。したがって，このことを端的に表現した②が正解である。

問2 「千秋のプランとして最も適当なものは次のうちどれか」 25

①

開始	終了	活動
午前10時	午後12時	ワークショップに参加する
午後12時	午後12時30分	講義を聞く
午後12時30分	午後2時	公園に行って昼食をとる
午後2時	午後4時	博物館の展示を見る

②

開始	終了	活動
午前10時	午後12時	ワークショップに参加する
午後12時	午後1時	窯を訪ねる
午後1時	午後2時	公園に行って昼食をとる
午後2時	午後4時	博物館の展示を見る

③

開始	終了	活動
午前10時	午後12時	博物館の展示を見る
午後12時	午後2時	公園に行って昼食をとる
午後2時	午後4時	ワークショップに参加する
午後4時	午後5時	窯を訪ねる

④

開始	終了	活動
午前11時	午後12時	博物館の展示を見る
午後12時	午後12時30分	講義を聞く
午後12時30分	午後2時	公園に行って昼食をとる
午後2時	午後4時	ワークショップに参加する

正解 ⇒ ④

千秋のメッセージを見ると,「午後2時から2時間のワークショップに参加する」,「正午からの30分の講義に参加する前に, 1時間博物館内を見て回る」,「昼食をもみじ公園でとる」というプランであることが分かる。これらの情報と合致するのは④である。

問3 「ロビンのメッセージによると, 26 」

① 彼は海岸公園についてネットを通じて知った
② 彼は以前海岸公園で写真を撮ったことがある
③ 彼は博物館の展示が退屈だと考えている
④ 彼のホストファミリーは陶器を自分たちで作った

正解 ⇒ ①

ロビンは第2パラグラフにて, ソーシャルメディアを通じて海岸公園のことを知ったと述べている。これを言い換えた①が正解である。

問4 「ロビンは, 天気が晴れているなら昼食を 27 食べ, 天気が雨なら昼食を 28 食べることを提案している」

① 陶器のワークショップで
② もみじ市立博物館内のレストランで
③ 海岸公園で
④ もみじ公園で

正解⇒ 27 ③ 28 ②

ロビンは第3パラグラフで「海岸公園で昼食をとろう」と提案している。また, 第4パラグラフで「もし雨ならば千秋のプランで行こう」,「昼食は千秋が言っていたレストランで食べよう」と述べている。このレストランとは, 千秋のメッセージの第3パラグラフ第1文にあるように, もみじ市立博物館内にあるレストランのことである。よって, 27 は③, 28 は②である。

問5 「千秋とロビンのどちらも, 29 することは計画していない」

① 参加者とソーシャルメディアで連絡をとる
② 公園に紅葉を見に行く
③ 博物館で陶磁器産業について学ぶ
④ 移動手段としてバスを使う

正解 ⇒ ①

②と③は千秋が, ④はロビンがそれぞれ計画の中に入れている。したがって, 両者とも計画に入れていないのは①である。

　あなたのグループは，あなたの街で交換留学生のためのイベントを開催します。あなたはイベントの計画について話し合いながら，グループの2人のメンバー，千秋とロビンからのメッセージを読んでいます。

千秋	10月9日　午後10時50分

もみじ市立博物館のホームページで面白いワークショップを見つけました。そのワークショップでは，自分たちで陶器を作ることができます。私たちの街は陶器で有名なので，これはイベントにはとてもいいと思います。また，粘土を成形して，自分の特別な鍋やコップ，お皿を作るのも楽しそうです。ウェブサイトによると，作品の成形が終わった後は，乾燥するまで3日間博物館で保管され，その後近くの窯で焼かれるそうです。陶器は1週間ほどで家に届きます。

ワークショップは週末の午前10時からと午後2時からの1日2回，それぞれ2時間ずつ開催されています。午前中に館内の展示を見て，午後からワークショップに参加するというのはどうでしょうか。展示はこの街の歴史や産業，文化に関するもので，正午から陶磁器産業に関する30分の英語の講義を聞くことができます。その講義に参加する前に，1時間ほど展示を見て回るといいかもしれません。

昼食は，館内にレストランがありますが，弁当を持ってもみじ公園まで10分ほど歩くのがいいかもしれません。公園内のもみじはイベントの日までに紅葉しているだろうと思います。参加者はその美しい光景を楽しめることでしょう。

どう思いますか？　ご意見をお聞かせください。

ロビン	10月10日　午前9時15分

千秋さん，ありがとうございます！　陶芸のワークショップは素晴らしいですね。私のホストファミリーは花柄の陶器のお皿を持っているんです。そのような陶器を作ることができるのでしょうか？きっと楽しいでしょうね。

博物館の展示も面白そうですね。でも，それよりも海岸公園に行くことを提案します。最近，この公園で撮られた，ヤシの木が並んだビーチの写真が載ったソーシャルメディアの投稿を見つけて，興味を持ったんです。この公園は，すてきな写真が撮れる場所を求める写真好きの人たちの間で有名になりつつあるみたいです。美しい水平線や海岸線を眺めながら，ビーチを散歩したり，写真を撮ったり，ピクニックを楽しんだりすることができます。そして，イベントの参加者は，私たちの街の美しい自然環境について知ることができることでしょう。

午前11時頃に海岸公園のバス停に集合するのはどうでしょうか？　その後，参加者に公園を案内し，昼食をとって，午後1時ごろに公園を出ましょう。もみじ市立博物館は公園からバスで30分ほどなので，その後に陶芸教室に参加することができます。

このプランならば，参加者はもみじ市の伝統と自然環境の両方を学ぶことができると思います。でも，雨が降るようなら，千秋さんのプランで行きましょう。昼食は，千秋さんが言っていたレストランで食べた方がいいでしょうね。

皆さんはどう思いますか？　次回のウェブミーティングで話し合いましょう！

【語句・表現】
・exchange student「交換留学生」

- pottery「陶器，陶芸」
- clay「粘土」
- kiln「(陶器などを焼く) 窯」
- ceramic「陶磁器の，セラミックの」
- palm-lined「ヤシの木が並んだ」
- shutterbug「カメラ好き，写真マニア」
- horizon「水平線，地平線」
- coastline「海岸線」
- what do you say to *doing* ～?「～するのはどうですか」

第5問

問1 「　30　にあてはまる最も適当な選択肢を選べ」

> ① 女の子と関係を築くことが得意である
> ② ときどき一目ぼれをしてきた
> ③ 恋に落ちると自制心を失いがちである
> ④ **好きな女性に対して慎重に優しく振る舞いたいと思っている**

　正解 ⇒ ④

　空所は物語の語り手であるランディについてまとめた箇所である。ランディは，カレンに会いたいという気持ちを抑えて店に行くのを控えたり，どうすべきかをジョーに相談したりするなど，カレンに関して慎重に行動しようとしていることがうかがえる。この内容を言い換えた④が正解である。

問2 「　31　にあてはまる最も適当な選択肢を選べ」

> ① カレンに自分の気持ちを伝えるのを控えるよう弟にアドバイスする
> ② 弟の状況を詳細には知らない
> ③ メールでカレンをデートに誘うよう，ランディに勧める
> ④ **自分の経験に基づいて，ランディがどう行動すべきかについての手がかりを与える**

　正解 ⇒ ④

　空所はランディの兄であるジョーについてまとめた箇所である。ジョーは第7パラグラフで，自分の過去の失恋の経験に言及しながら，ラブレターを書くことをランディに提案する。その言葉を聞いたランディは，その後実際にラブレターを書いて渡すという行動をとっている。これら一連の流れを言い換えた④が正解である。

【語句・表現】
・refrain from *doing*「～するのを控える」
・in detail「詳細に」

問3 「五つの出来事（①～⑤）のうちから，起こった順番に四つを選べ」
　　　　　32 → 33 → 34 → 35

> ① ランディがカレンにメールのやり取りをしたいと頼んだ
> ② ランディが初めてカレンにあいさつをした
> ③ ランディがカレンに手紙を手渡した
> ④ ランディがカレンからの手紙を読んだ
> ⑤ カレンがランディを認識していたことにランディが喜んだ

　正解 ⇒ 32 ⑤　　33 ②　　34 ③　　35 ④

　まず，第4パラグラフで，ドラッグストアを訪れたランディのことをカレンが覚えていて，そのことにランディが喜ぶ様子が描かれているので，32 は⑤である。次に，第6パラグラフでは，その2日後にランディが初めてカレンにあいさつをする場面があるので，33 は②である。そして，最終パラグラフを見ると，ランディがカレンに手紙を手渡し，その後カレンからの返事の手紙を読む，という流れになっているので，34 は③，35 は④である。

問4 「 36 」にあてはまる最も適当な選択肢を選べ」

> ① 誰と付き合うか決める上で，その人の性格が一番重要だと思っている。
> ② 今は他の人と付き合っているが，気が変わるかもしれないとほのめかしている。
> ③ 店員が客のガールフレンドになるべきではないと思っている。
> ④ ボーイフレンドとの関係を続けたいと思っているが，それはランディのことが気に入らないからというわけではない。

正解 ⇒ ④

　カレンはランディのラブレターに対する返事として，「付き合っている人がいる」という言葉で断る一方で，「あなたのような素敵な人が私のことを思ってくれているなんてとてもうれしい」と述べている。このことから，現在のボーイフレンドと別れるつもりはないが，ランディのことが気に入らないわけではないということがうかがえる。

問5 「 37 」にあてはまる最も適当な選択肢を選べ」

> ① カレンに数回ラブレターを渡したことを決して後悔していない。
> ② カレンにどれほど好きかをもっと早く伝えるべきだった。
> ③ 後悔はないが，いまだに苦々しい記憶として覚えている。
> ④ もう一歩踏み出す勇気があれば良かったと思っている。

正解 ⇒ ③

　ランディは最後の文で，「いまだに心が痛む」，「決して自分のしたことに後悔はしていない」と語っている。これらの内容を言い換えた③が正解である。

【全訳】
　あなたはディスカッションの授業で，印象的な物語についてプレゼンをするよう先生に言われました。あなたは，あるアメリカの学生が書いた物語を見つけました。

店員と恋に落ちて

2018年2月23日　ランディ・ヴァレンタイン

　「心のこもったお手紙をありがとう，ランディ。あなたのような素敵な人が私のことを思ってくれているなんて，とてもうれしいです。あなたは手紙の中で，私たちの今の関係，客と店員という関係が，友達になることを躊躇させるかもしれないと書いていましたね。でも，そんなことありませんよ」
　事の発端は，カレンに手紙を渡す3カ月前のことだった。僕は学校帰りに新しくオープンしたドラッグストアに立ち寄った。お菓子や飲み物を選んでいると，レジに笑顔の天使を見つけた。これを「一目ぼれ」と呼ぶべきだろうか。そうに違いない！
　翌日，再びその店を訪れると，彼女はそこにいた！　体調が悪いわけでもないのに，僕は彼女に頭痛薬をお願いした。彼女はカウンターの奥の棚からボトルを取り出し，「この錠剤はどうですか？すぐに効くはずですよ」と言った。「ありがとうございます。それにします」と，痛みに悩むふりをして僕は答えた。「お大事に」と柔らかな笑顔で言われ，僕の心はつかまれてしまった。
　次の日，僕はまたカレンに会いに行きたいと思ったが，毎日通い続けると僕の気持ちに彼女が気付いてしまうかもしれないと思い，会いに行かないことにした。だから，まるまる1週間は彼女に会いたいと思う気持ちを抑えて過ごした。というのも，僕が熱を上げすぎているという印象を彼女に与えたくなかったのだ。3度目の出会いは，予想していたよりもはるかに感動的だった。僕が彼女に

ちょっとした品物の代金を渡そうとすると，彼女は「頭痛は治りましたか？」と言ってきた。ああ，少なくとも僕は彼女に認識されていたのだ！　「あ，はい」「それは良かったです」その時の短いやりとりはほとんど覚えていない。

　僕のこの状況を知っているのは，兄のジョーだけだった。その日の夜，僕は彼に言った。「その子に個人的にあるものを渡せないかなと思って。つまり，僕のメールアドレスを書いた紙を彼女に渡せないかな？」ジョーは，「だめだ。まだ早いよ。いったいどんな女の子が，ほとんど知らない人と友達になりたいと思う？　急がない方がいいよ。さもなければ，僕がかつて他の女の子に対してやったように，彼女を困らせるだけだ。さりげなく挨拶をして話をすることから関係を始めるべきだよ」

　2日後，僕は再び店に行き，いつものように彼女に会った。僕の言葉から会話が始まるのは初めてのことだった。「おはようございます。お元気ですか？」「元気です，ありがとうございます。今日は寒いですね」と，彼女はあの笑顔で答えた。5，6回会う中で僕は彼女と言葉を少し交わすことに成功した。彼女は，カレンという名前であることや，ドラッグストアでアルバイトをして生活費を稼いでいる大学生であることを教えてくれた。話せば話すほど，僕は彼女のことが好きになった。

　ある日，僕はジョーに言った。「カレンに彼女のことが好きになったって言えたらなあ！　でも，僕は自信がないんだ。拒絶されたらどうしよう。落ち込んでしまうよ」ジョーは，「いいじゃないか，ランディ。何も行動を起こさなかったことを何年も後悔したいのか？　僕は人生で5回も女の子に振られたけど，自分の正直な気持ちを伝えたことを後悔したことはないんだ。男らしくなれよ！」と言った。彼はさらに，「彼女にラブレターを渡すのはどうだろう？　古臭く思えるかもしれないけど，カレンはとても魅力的な女の子みたいだから，男の子からメールをもらうことには慣れているかもしれない。きっと手書きの手紙は印象的なはずだよ」と付け加えた。

　僕はその夜，カレンに手紙を書き，彼女のことが好きになったこと，付き合えたらどんなに嬉しいかを伝えた。翌日，僕はその手紙を彼女に渡し，2日後には彼女からの返事が手渡された。手紙は冒頭で述べたような文章で始まっていた。その後には，「でも，ごめんなさい，もう同じ大学の人と付き合っているんです。友達でいましょうね」と続いていた。彼女の返事を読んで，僕は号泣した。僕の心は完全に折れてしまった。これは5年前のことであり，今でも心が痛むが，決して自分のしたことに後悔はない。

あなたのプレゼン用メモ：

店員と恋に落ちて

登場人物

ランディ	・カレンに恋をしている男子学生
	・ 30
カレン	・ドラッグストアでアルバイトをする女子大学生
ジョー	・ランディの兄
	・ 31

どのようにランディの恋の物語は進んだのか

ランディがカレンにほれる

↓

32

↓

33

↓

34

↓

35

カレンの気持ちについて分かることは何か
　　36

ランディはこの経験についてどう振り返っているか
「　37　」

【語句・表現】

- impressive「印象的な」
- clerk「店員」
- heartfelt「心からの」
- have feelings for ～「～に（恋愛感情などの）特別な感情を抱く」
- discourage「～を思いとどまらせる」
- drop into ～「～に立ち寄る」
- cash desk「レジ，勘定台」
- love at first sight「一目ぼれ」
- on one's radar「～に存在を認識されている」
- embarrass「～に恥ずかしい思いをさせる」
- casually「気軽に，さりげなく」
- living expenses「生活費」
- messed up「落ち込んで，（精神的に）苦しんで」
- old-fashioned「時代遅れの」
- go out「交際する」
- sob「むせび泣く，泣きじゃくる」

第6問

A
問1 「 38 にあてはまる最も適当な選択肢を選べ」

① 地球上の他のどの場所よりも太陽の影響が過酷なので
② より自信に満ちて幸せになりたいと考えていたため
③ **精神的，実用的な目的のために**
④ 感染症に感染するのを予防するために

正解 ⇒ ③

　第1パラグラフ第3文で「古代エジプトにおける化粧は，悪霊を追い払い，砂漠の厳しい日差しが目に与える影響を和らげると考えられていた」と述べられている。「悪霊を追い払う」という内容を「精神的目的」，「日差しが目に与える影響を和らげる」という内容を「実用的目的」と言い換えた③が正解である。

問2 「 39 にあてはまる最も適当な選択肢を選べ」

① 人々の映画を見に行く機会が以前より増えた。
② **人々がお気に入りのスターと同じメイクをすることに魅力を感じた。**
③ 写真を撮られる前に化粧をすることが人気になった。
④ 鏡の値段が一般の人でも買えるほど安くなった。

正解 ⇒ ②

　空所は，化粧品が大衆にも浸透した最も重要な要因について述べた箇所である。第3パラグラフ第4文には「（化粧品の普及について）映画ほど大きな役割を果たしたものはない」とあり，その後，「映画スターのようになれる」というキャンペーンのおかげで化粧品が普及したことが述べられている。これらを言い換えた②が正解である。

問3 「 40 と 41 にあてはまる最も適当な選択肢を選べ（順序は問わない）」

① **ある技術の別の応用法について考える**
② 人の内なる美を信じることの重要性を強調する
③ 人気の映画スターが新商品を紹介するコマーシャルを作る
④ 人々が映画産業により興味をもつよう仕向けるような広告を出す
⑤ **自身の見た目を変えたいという人々の願望を刺激するキャンペーンを始める**
⑥ 新商品の効果的な使い方を紹介する記事を書く

正解 ⇒ ①，⑤

　空所は，本文の内容を踏まえて，どのようなことが新しい商品の流行のきっかけになったかについてまとめた箇所である。まず，第4パラグラフで車の塗料の話や，第5パラグラフで歯科用アクリルの話があるが，これらはある技術を別の用途に用いて成功を収めた例である。よって，これを言い換えた①が一つ目の正解である。また，第3パラグラフや第4パラグラフで紹介されている，成功を収めた商品の売り出し方は，いずれも「見た目の変化に対する人々の願望」に焦点を当てたものであると言える。これらを端的にまとめた⑤が二つ目の正解である。

問4　「　42　にあてはまる最も適当な選択肢を選べ」

① ノーズペイントや付け耳がかつてないほど人気になるだろう。
② より美しくなりたいという人々の願いは，時代の流れとともに強くなるだろう。
③ コスメのための技術はより進歩を遂げるだろう。
④ **コスメの世界で何が起こるかは分からない。**

正解 ⇒ ④

　筆者は第6パラグラフ第3文で「100年後の人々がどのような見た目であるか想像できるだろうか」と問いかける一方で，同パラグラフを「誰にも分からない」と締めくくっている。したがって，このことを言い換えた④が正解である。

【全訳】
　あなたは，授業でファッションの歴史についてディスカッションをすることになっています。あなたは以下の記事の要約を作成しています。その要約を使って，あなたはそれについて話すことになります。

コスメの歴史

　最古の化粧は，必ずしも美を追求することが目的ではなかった。古代エジプト人は男女を問わず，鉛，鉄，銅，灰，焦がしたアーモンドなどを混ぜた，コールというものを目の周りに塗っていた。コールの円は，悪霊を追い払い，砂漠の厳しい日差しが目に与える影響を和らげると考えられていた。今日，科学者たちは，鉛が細菌を殺すため，コールの化粧がエジプト人を感染症から守るのにも役立ったと考えているが，彼らは当時そんなことについて知らなかったことだろう。エジプト人だけでなく，古代ギリシャ人，ローマ人，中国人も顔に何らかの化粧をしていたと考えられている。

　中世ヨーロッパでは色白の肌が人気になった。というのも，それが富の象徴だったからである。女性は顔を明るく見せるために，鉛や酢を混ぜたものを顔や首に塗っていたが，それは実のところ，使用者に対して有害であった。白い顔と大きな額をしたイングランドのエリザベス1世はその見た目で有名であり，このスタイルは何世紀にもわたって流行した。しかし，同時期に，コスメは健康被害を与えるものとして認識されるようになった。

　1800年代末ごろになると，肖像写真が人気になった。写真撮影の前に化粧をすることが一般的になった。また，鏡が一般庶民の手に入りやすくなった。確かに，化粧が一般大衆に普及したのはこの二つの要因も大きかったが，映画ほど大きな役割を果たしたものはない。俳優が舞台に立つときは，舞台から遠くに座っている観客にも魅力的に映るような，非常に濃い化粧をするのが普通だった。しかし，そのような化粧をした顔は，スクリーンに映ったときに美しくなかった。そこで，1914年，ハリウッドの撮影所にかつらを提供していたポーランドの実業家マックス・ファクターは，カメラを通したときに俳優の顔をより美しく見せるファンデーション用の新しいタイプの塗料を開発した。1920年代には，お気に入りの映画スターのようになれるという売り文句のもと，大衆に向けて化粧品の販売を始めた。彼の製品は十分に成功を収めた。

　ほぼ同じ頃，アメリカの自動車会社はさまざまな色の新塗料を自動車に使い始めた。その塗料の主成分は，銃の火薬を作るのにも使われるニトロセルロースという物質だった。この塗料は従来のものより早く乾いたため，化粧品会社は，爪に塗るメイクであるマニキュアに使えないかと考えた。1932年，車の塗料に用いられるものと同じ素材を使ったマニキュアが初めて市場に出た。製造元であるレブロンはこの製品の宣伝に成功し，すぐにそれは人気商品となった。また，1950年代に同社は，マニキュアと口紅をお揃いにするキャンペーンを実施した。その広告の一つには，「もしあなたが，夫に無断で髪をプラチナ色に染めたいような女性なら，この新しい色の口紅とマニキュアの候補にぴったりです」とあった。実際，この広告はマニキュアの売れ行きを加速させた。

　つけ爪，つまり自然の爪の上につける人工的な爪の製品の一般の人々の間の人気は，1954年に偶然

始まった。それは，フレデリック・スラックという名のアメリカの歯科医が仕事中に爪を傷つけてしまったときである。彼は，悪くなった歯の修復に使われる歯科用アクリルを使って，傷ついた爪の上に人工の爪をかぶせた。それ以来，つけ爪は，美しいファッションとして今日の多くの人が身につけるものへと進化してきた。

　　歴史上，人類は何らかの人工物を身につけることを試みてきた。特に現代では，より自信に満ちて幸せにしたり，あるいは身体の気に入らない部分を隠したりすると思うものを自分自身に着けてきた。今から100年後，人々がどのような見た目であるか想像できるだろうか。「ファッショナブル」なノーズペイントや，付け耳をしているかもしれない。誰にも分からない。

あなたの要約ノート：

コスメ

歴史
　　●エジプトの最古の化粧
　　　　| 38 |エジプト人は目の周りにペイントをしていた
　　　　↓
　　●中世ヨーロッパ
　　　　色白の肌が人気だった
　　　　人にとって有害なコスメが使われていた
　　　　↓
　　●大衆の間での化粧品の普及
　　　　最も重要な要因：| 39 |

新しいタイプのコスメ
　　爪に関する製品 —— マニキュア＆つけ爪

物語から得られる結論
　　1．新しい製品を流行させるための手がかり
　　● | 40 |
　　● | 41 |

　　2．コスメの将来に対する筆者の予想
　　● | 42 |

【語句・表現】
・mixture「混合物，混合」
・lead「鉛」
・copper「銅」
・ash「灰」
・drive away ～「～を追い払う」
・evil「悪い，邪悪な」
・relieve「～を和らげる」
・harsh「過酷な，厳しい」
・desert「砂漠」
・infectious「感染性の，伝染性の」
・pale「（色が）薄い，淡い」
・vinegar「酢」

- forehead「額」
- motion picture「映画」
- wig「かつら，ウィッグ」
- ingredient「成分，材料」
- nitrocellulose「ニトロセルロース」
- nail polish「マニキュア」
- platinum「プラチナ，プラチナ色」
- consent「同意，承諾」
- candidate「候補者」
- false nail「偽の爪，つけ爪」
- acrylics「アクリル塗料」
- mend「～を修復する」

B

問1 「『オスのタツノオトシゴ』のスライドについて，　43　にあてはまるのは次のうちどれか」

① 新しく生まれた赤ちゃんをポケットの中で飼育，保護する
② 他の種類の魚のメスと同様に卵を産む
③ 孵化する前に卵をポケットの外に出す
④ 卵をメスのタツノオトシゴのポケットに運ぶ

正解 ⇒ ①

空所　43　を含むスライドは，タツノオトシゴのオスの特徴についてまとめたものである。第1パラグラフ最終文の内容と合致する①が正解である。

問2 「『オスの妊娠』のスライド中の　44　について，最も適当な記述はどれか」

① 赤ちゃんの安全性を確保するため
② 朝に出産するため
③ 出産の頻度をあげるため
④ 成長した子どもの世話の負担を分け合うため

正解 ⇒ ③

空所にはタツノオトシゴの特徴である，「オスが妊娠する」ことによってもたらされ得る利点が入る。第3パラグラフにおいて一つの説が紹介されており，そこには「生殖のサイクルを短くすることができる」とある。この内容を言い換えた③が正解である。

問3 「『体の部位と機能』のスライドについて，　45　，　46　，　47　それぞれにあてはまるのは次のうちどれか」

① 呼吸のために酸素を吸収する
② スムーズに泳げるようにする
③ 体温を維持する
④ 食べられないようにする
⑤ 流されないようにする
⑥ 必要な栄養素を取り込む

正解 ⇒ 　45　 ⑥　　　46　 ④　　　47　 ⑤

第4パラグラフ第3・4文の「非常に小さな海の生き物を餌として吸い込むための筒状の口」,「流されないように海草にしがみつくための巻き尾」,「捕食者にとって魅力的でないように思わせるための硬い鱗板」という記述から，　45　が⑥，　46　が④，　47　が⑤であると分かる。

問4　「『個体数の減少と解決策』のスライドについて，タツノオトシゴの個体数の減少の考えられる要因を二つ選べ（順序は問わない）」　48　・　49

---

① タツノオトシゴの赤ちゃんが上昇する海水温に耐えられない。
② 人間がタツノオトシゴの住む環境を悪化させている。
③ 以前より多くのタツノオトシゴの子どもが捕食されている。
④ タツノオトシゴの子どもの1,000匹中約5匹ほどしか親から育ててもらえない。
⑤ 人間が医学目的で過度にタツノオトシゴを捕獲してきた。
⑥ 気候変動により，タツノオトシゴが食べる小さいプランクトンの数が減少した。

正解 ⇒ ②，⑤

第5パラグラフ最終文には「前述のような目的での乱獲だけでなく，その生息する沿岸域へ人間が与えたダメージが原因で，タツノオトシゴは脅かされている」とある。「前述のような目的での乱獲」とは，第4パラグラフ最終文で言及されている「伝統的な薬のための捕獲」のことを指す。したがって，これらの内容に合致する②と⑤が正解である。

問5　「親の育児への関わりに対する著者の姿勢について，どのようなことが推測されるか」　50

---

① 筆者は，タツノオトシゴのメスが自分の産んだ卵の世話をしないことを批判している。
② 筆者は，赤ちゃんを育てることに関しては，タツノオトシゴのオスが人間よりも良き父親であると感じている。
③ 筆者は，タツノオトシゴがいったん子どもを放流すると世話をしなくなることに対して気の毒に思っている。
④ 筆者は，妊娠期間中にはタツノオトシゴの父親よりも人間の父親が優れていると思っている。

正解 ⇒ ③

タツノオトシゴの子どもの生存率が低いという話を受けて，最終パラグラフの第4文で筆者は，「タツノオトシゴの親は子どもを守るために努力したら良いのに」と嘆いている。したがって，この筆者の様子を言い換えた③が正解である。

【全訳】

　あなたは，科学の授業に向けて，変わった生き物についてのプレゼンの準備を行っています。プレゼンのために，あなたは以下の記事を使用しています。

　ヒトの父親は，積極的に育児に関わるという点で，他の生物の父親よりも優れているのかもしれない。ヒトの父親は自分の子どもに，球技のやり方や礼儀正しい振る舞い方を教える。しかし，ある一点において，ヒトの父親はとある種のオスに決して勝てない。その生物は，メスの代わりに妊娠して子どもを産むのである。この形質は，「タツノオトシゴ」という名で広く知られる，奇妙な魚の一種に特有のものである。カンガルーのように，タツノオトシゴのオスのおなかには，赤ちゃんを運ぶための皮のポケットがある。メスが卵を産み，それをつがいのポケットに移し，そこで卵が孵化する。ポケットには一度に2,000匹もの赤ちゃんを入れておくことができる。父親はポケットの中に赤ちゃんを入れておくことにより，赤ちゃんを海の危険から守るだけでなく，赤ちゃんに酸素や必要な栄養を供給している。

　タツノオトシゴの繁殖行為は，夜明け前にオスとメスが一緒に踊りだすところから始まり，彼らは尾を巻いたり，体の色を変えたり，並んで泳いだりする。やがて求愛，すなわち交尾の要求のための真のダンスをする。この時，メスが卵を産む準備ができたときにオスがその卵を受け取りやすいように，カップルの動きがシンクロする。オスはポケットが空であることを示すため，水でポケットを膨らませる。オスが卵を受け取るとこのプロセスは終了する。妊娠期間は種によって10日から25日間続く。卵は父親のポケットの中で孵化し，その後，生まれたばかりの赤ちゃんを放流するために，父親は長い距離を泳いでいく。

　オスの妊娠はタツノオトシゴにどんな進化的な利点を与えているのだろうか。科学的にはまだ解明されていない。一つの説は，父親と母親が負担を分け合うことで，生殖のサイクルを短くすることができる，というものだ。父親がポケットに赤ちゃんをとどめている間，母親はより多くの卵を用意して，赤ちゃんを放流したばかりの父親に与えることができるのだ。タツノオトシゴの中には，朝に出産して夕方までに再び妊娠できるものもいると言われている。

　タツノオトシゴは，体長1cm未満から30cmのものまでが存在する。外見にはいくつかの特徴がある。例えば，非常に小さな海の生き物を餌として吸い込むための筒状の口，流されないように海草にしがみつくための巻き尾，体を保護するために覆っている硬い鱗板などだ。この鱗板があることで，捕食者にとっては餌として魅力がないように思わせるのだ。例外は人間で，いくつかの伝統的な薬を作るためにタツノオトシゴが捕獲されてきた。

　では，現在のタツノオトシゴの個体数はどのくらいだろうか。これまでタツノオトシゴに関する調査は比較的少ししか行われていないため，統計的なデータは存在しない。しかし，タツノオトシゴについての一部の研究によると，網にかかるタツノオトシゴの数が減少していることに漁師たちが言及しているそうだ。また，科学者たちは，タツノオトシゴが前述のような目的での乱獲だけでなく，生息する沿岸域へ人間が与えたダメージも原因で脅かされていることを指摘している。

　科学者たちは，タツノオトシゴを水槽で飼育することで救おうとしている。しかし，タツノオトシゴを飼育下で繁殖させるのは容易なことではない。それは一部には，タツノオトシゴの赤ちゃんは小さすぎるがゆえに，死なないようにするのが難しいというのが理由だ。タツノオトシゴの赤ちゃんは，成体のタツノオトシゴが食べるような小さなプランクトンをほとんど食べられない。そのため，特別なベビーフードを栽培しなければならない。現在，より効率的な飼育のための新技術が開発中である。

　いったんタツノオトシゴの父親が赤ちゃんを海に放すと，親はその小さな子どもたちに何の世話や保護も与えない。タツノオトシゴの赤ちゃんは容易に捕食者の犠牲になったり，海流に流され，餌場の遠くまで漂流してしまったりすることがある。1,000匹中約5匹ほどのタツノオトシゴの赤ちゃんしか成体になるまで生き残れないのだ。人間の親が生まれた後の子どもを守るためにする努力の半分を，タツノオトシゴの親がしてくれればいいのだが！　この点では，人間の父親はきっとタツノオトシゴより優れている。

あなたのプレゼン用スライド：

タツノオトシゴ 協力的な子育て	1．オスのタツノオトシゴ ・妊娠・出産することができる ・おなかにポケットがある ・ 43
2．どのようにしてオスのタツノオトシゴが妊娠するか 　オスとメスが早朝にダンスを始める 　　　　　↓ 　ペアの動きがシンクロする 　ポケットが使用可能であることをオスが示す 　　　　　↓ 　オスがメスから卵を受け取る	3．オスの妊娠 オスが妊娠することによる利点 　→未だ解明されていない 一つの説： 44
4．体の部位と機能 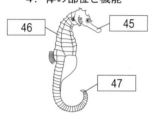	5．個体数の減少と解決策 ・網にかかるタツノオトシゴの数が減少している，と漁師たちが報告している ・考えられる理由： 48 ， 49 ・解決策：飼育のための新技術が開発中である

【語句・表現】
・involvement「参加，関与」
・decent「上品な，礼儀正しい」
・pregnant「妊娠した」
・give birth to ～「～を産む」
・trait「特徴，特性，形質」
・peculiar to ～「～に特有の」
・seahorse「タツノオトシゴ」
・hatch「孵化する」
・nutrient「栄養物，栄養素」
・reproduction「繁殖，生殖」
・dawn「夜明け」
・engage in ～「～に従事する」
・courtship「求愛，求愛行動」
・mating「交配，交尾」
・inflate「～を膨らませる」
・pregnancy「妊娠，妊娠期間」
・burden「負担」
・suck「～を吸う，吸い込む」
・curling「曲がりくねっている，カールしている」
・cling to ～「～にしがみつく」
・drift「漂流する」

・predator「捕食者」
・carry out「〜を実行する」
・overfishing「(魚の) 乱獲」
・breed「〜を育てる」
・captivity「とらわれの身，監禁状態」
・surpass「〜に勝る，〜より優れている」

解 答 と 解 説

問題番号(配点)	設	問	解答番号	正 解	配 点	自己採点
第1問(10)	A	1	1	4	2	
	A	2	2	4	2	
	B	1	3	1	2	
	B	2	4	2	2	
	B	3	5	4	2	
			自己採点小計			
第2問(20)	A	1	6	2	2	
	A	2	7	3	2	
	A	3	8	2	2	
	A	4	9	3	2	
	A	5	10	3	2	
	B	1	11	1	2	
	B	2	12	2	2	
	B	3	13	1	2	
	B	4	14	4	2	
	B	5	15	4	2	
			自己採点小計			
第3問(15)	A	1	16	1	3	
	A	2	17	3	3	
	B	1	18	2	3^{*1}	
			19	1		
			20	3		
			21	4		
	B	2	22	3	3	
	B	3	23	2	3	
			自己採点小計			

問題番号(配点)	設	問	解答番号	正 解	配 点	自己採点
第4問(16)		1	24	$2, 3^{*2}$	2	
			25		2	
		2	26	4	3	
		3	27	1	3	
		4	28	2	3	
		5	29	3	3	
			自己採点小計			
第5問(15)		1	30	2	3	
		2	31	$1, 4^{*2}$	3^{*1}	
			32			
		3	33	2		
			34	4	3^{*1}	
			35	1		
			36	3		
		4	37	1	3	
		5	38	3	3	
			自己採点小計			
第6問(24)	A	1	39	4	3	
	A	2	40	2	3	
	A	3	41	3	3	
	A	4	42	5	3^{*1}	
			43	3		
	B	1	44	4	3	
	B	2	45	4	3	
	B	3	46	$2, 4^{*2}$	3^{*1}	
			47			
	B	4	48	1	3	
			自己採点小計			

(注) ^{*1}は，全部正解の場合のみ点を与える。
　　 ^{*2}は，解答の順序は問わない。

自己採点合計

第1問

A

問1 「レベッカはあなたに何をするように頼んでいるか」 ☐ 1

---
① 彼女の家から大学にコンピューターを持って来る。
② 彼女のプレゼンテーション用ファイルをダウンロードして USB に入れる。
③ 彼女が授業で行うプレゼンテーションを改善するのを手伝う。
④ 次の授業のためにあなたのコンピューターを彼女に貸す。

正解 ⇒ ④

　最初のレベッカからのメッセージに，困っている内容と頼みたいことが書かれている。授業で発表（プレゼンテーション）をする予定であること，そのための資料はクラウドに保存してあるがパソコンを持っていない旨が書かれている。Can I 以降の「あなたのを貸してもらえるかな？」というのが頼みごとなので，正解は④である。

【語句・表現】
・put A on a USB「A を USB に入れる」
・improve「～を改善する」
・let A（人）borrow B「A（人）に B を借りさせる」：「A に B を貸す」という意味。

問2 「あなたはレベッカの二つ目のメッセージにどのように返信するか」 ☐ 2

---
① ルームメイトに電話して，ドアの鍵を開けるように頼んでね。
② プレゼンテーションは絶対うまくいくと思うよ！
③ コンピューターを渡すためにどこで会えばいい？
④ 教授の（パソコン）を貸してもらえるか聞いてみたらどうかな。

正解 ⇒ ④

　レベッカが「ルームメイトは，今日は夜まで戻って来ないと言っていた」と書いているので①は不適切。コンピューターが必要なことは変わりがなく，その問題を解決していない②と，「あなた」は「今帰宅途中」なので③も不適切である。したがって，コンピューターを誰かから借りることを提案している④が正解。

【語句・表現】
・reply「返信する，応える」：名詞も同型で「返信，返事」の意味。
・unlock「～の鍵を開ける」
・be sure that S V「必ず～すると思う」：that 節（名詞節）中は未来のことなので未来時制になる。
・you should *do*「～してみては？」：you had better *do*「～した方がよい」という表現は，言われた側に断る余地がない強い忠告のときに用いるが，should はそれよりも弱い表現。

【全訳】
　あなたの友人のレベッカがあなたに助けを求めるメッセージをソーシャルメディアで送ってきました。

レベッカ　　　　　　　　　　　　　2023/9/25　午後12:08

どうしよう！　次の授業でプレゼンテーションをするんだけど，今日大学にパソコン持って来るの忘

れたの。ファイルはクラウドに保存してあるから，そこからアクセスできるの。プレゼンテーションで使うコンピューターだけ必要なの。あなたのを貸してもらえない？

2023/9/25　午後12：14

ごめん，レベッカ。木曜日は美術の授業しかないから，私も持って来てない。でも，今帰宅途中。だから，あなたの家に行ってパソコン取って来てあげようか？

レベッカ　　　　　　　　　　　　　　　2023/9/25　午後12：21

すごくありがたいんだけど，今は誰も家にいないんだ。ルームメイトは，今日は夜まで戻って来ないって言ってた。どうしたらいいと思う？

【語句・表現】
・be in trouble「困っている」
・forget to *do*「～するのを忘れる」
・have A saved「Aを保存しておく（してある）」：「have / keep A *done*」の構文。
・the cloud「クラウド」：この意味で使うときはふつう the を付ける。
・not ～ either「（否定文で）～もない」
・on *one*'s way home「帰宅途中で」
・though「でも」
・appreciate「～に感謝する」

B

問1　「あなたはエッセーを　3　までに提出しなければならない」

① **4月1日**
② 4月29日
③ 4月30日
④ 5月7日

正解 ⇒ ①

　「規定」の三つ目に「エッセーの提出期限は4月1日土曜日」と記述されているため，①が正解である。それ以外は，「日程」に記載されているエッセーを提出した後の日程なので，全て不適切。

【語句・表現】
・submit「～を提出する」
・by「～までに」：「期限」を表す。

問2　「このコンテストに参加するために，　4　必要がある」

① 18歳より年上である
② **ニューヨーク市外に住んでいる**
③ 訪れたことのない場所について書く
④ 1000語より多く書く

正解 ⇒ ②

　「規定」の二つ目に「ニューヨーク市の居住者ではないこと」と記述されているため，②が正解である。同じく一つ目の項目で「18歳以下の学生」という条件があるため①は誤り。エッセーの内容は，ニューヨーク市で「あなたが経験したことについて」なので③，Instructions の二つ目に「500〜1000語でエッセーを書く」とあるので④も不適切である。

【語句・表現】
・enter「〜に入る・参加する」

問3　「1位に入賞することによってのみ得られるものはどれか」　5

> ①　食費の全額支給
> ②　人気スポットへの無料入場
> ③　ニューヨーク市までの旅行代金
> ④　**2泊分のホテル宿泊**

　正解 ⇒ ④

　「賞品」の項目を見比べると，順位に応じて賞品が減っていることがわかる。1位と2位の賞品を比べると，違いは宿泊の日数とミュージカルのチケットの有無であるため，④が正解。①は1位と2位，②，③は1〜3位全ての賞品になっているため不適切である。

【語句・表現】
・by *doing*「〜することによって」：「手段」を表す。
・win the 1st prize「1位に入賞する・優勝する」
・meal「食事」
・expense「費用」
・entry「入場」
・site「場所」
・paid「支払われた」：主催者側から「支払われた」ということなので，「無料の」を意味する。
・stay「滞在」

【全訳】
　あなたはニューヨーク市に関するウェブサイトを見て，学生のためのエッセーコンテストについてのお知らせを見つけます。そのコンテストに参加することを考えています。

エッセーコンテスト
ニューヨーク市での素敵な思い出を紹介しよう
この素晴らしい街であなたが経験したことについてお聞かせください！　ニューヨーク市（NYC）で過ごした最高の思い出を共有して，より多くの人がこの街に来るお手伝いをしてください。題材は，訪れた場所，食べた物，あるいは出会った人々についてでも構いません。
手順
●ニューヨーク市旅行の一番良かったことについて考えてください。 ●その経験について500〜1000語でエッセーを書いてください。 ●次のメールアドレスにエッセーを送信してください：<u>entry@nycessaycontest.com</u>

規定
●18歳以下の学生のみ参加可能です。
●ニューヨーク市の居住者ではないこと。
●エッセーの提出期限は4月1日土曜日です。

賞品		
1位	2位	3位
ニューヨーク市へ4人分の旅費 ホテル無料宿泊2泊 食費全額支給 ミュージカルのチケット 人気スポットへの無料入場	ニューヨーク市へ4人分の旅費 ホテル無料宿泊1泊 食費全額支給 人気スポットへの無料入場	ニューヨーク市へ4人分の旅費 ホテル無料宿泊1泊 人気スポットへの無料入場

日程	
4月29日	審査員とニューヨーク市長によって入賞者3名が選出されます！
4月30日	入賞者はこのウェブサイトに掲載され，メールでもご連絡いたします。
5月7日	入賞した方は，この日までに賞品を受け取るためにメールで返信してください。その後，ご本人とご家族の旅行日程を調整いたします。

【語句・表現】
・announcement「お知らせ」
・introduce「〜を紹介する」
・favorite「お気に入りの，素敵な」
・attract「〜を引き付ける」
・share「〜を共有する」
・the places you visited「あなたが訪れた場所」：you visited は関係代名詞節。その後に続く，食べ物や人々に関する箇所も同様。目的格の関係代名詞が省略されている。
・instruction「手順」
・following「次（後）に続く」
・up to 〜「〜まで」
・resident「住民」
・no later than 〜「〜より前に」
・entry「入場」
・judge「審査員」
・mayor「市長」
・contact「〜に連絡を取る」

第2問

A

問1 「新規の交換留学生として，あなたは申請をしない限り ☐6☐ 住まなければならない」

① 1人で
② ルームメイトと

③　2人の学生と
④　4人の学生と

正解 ⇒ ②

　「住居の手配」に「事前に1人部屋を申請しない限り，新規居住者はルームメイトとの2人部屋に割り当てられる」とあるため，②が正解である。① by *oneself* は「1人で」という意味。③は two other「他の2人」とあるので合計3人，④は four other「他の4人」とあり，合計5人で住むことになるので，①，③，④はいずれも誤り。

【語句・表現】
・exchange student「(交換) 留学生」
・unless S V「～しない限り」

問2　「ライリーホールには，バスルームが　7　カ所ある」

①　4　　②　6　　③　7　　④　8

正解 ⇒ ③

　「設備」に「バスルームは学生の居室がある階の廊下の両端と，1階の共用ルームの向かいに一つある」とある。学生の居室である2階，3階，4階の両端の計6カ所と1階の1カ所にバスルームがあることになり，全部で7カ所のため，③が正解である。

【語句・表現】
・bathroom「トイレ，バスルーム」
・location「場所」

問3　「あなたはライリーホールの2階に住んでいる。洗濯するために　8　必要がある」

①　1階降りる
②　2階降りる
③　1階上がる
④　2階上がる

正解 ⇒ ②

　「住居の手配」に「学生の居室は1階の上階である2階，3階，4階にある」という記載から，地上階を the ground floor（1階）とし，その上を the first floor（2階に当たる），the second floor（3階に当たる）と数えていることがわかる。これはイギリス特有の表現であるが，この知識がなくても，フロアの数え方が異なることがリーフレットから読み取れるだろう。「あなた」は日本やアメリカで言う「2階」に住んでいることになり，洗濯をするために地下に行くにはフロアを2つ降りなければならない。したがって②が正解。

【語句・表現】
・the first floor「(イギリスの) 1階」：日本やアメリカの2階。

問4　「自分で料理をするために台所を使うのに最も良い曜日と時間は　9　である」

① 日曜日の午前10時
② 月曜日の午後6時
③ 木曜日の午後9時
④ 土曜日の午後1時

正解 ⇒ ③

「平日は午後8時まで，週末は午後遅くまでキッチンが混雑している」とアルジュナがコメントしていることから，平日の午後8時より遅い時間である③が正解。①は週末の午前中のため不適切。②は平日の午後8時より前なので不適切。④は週末だが，午後の遅い時間ではないため不適切である。

【語句・表現】
・for *oneself*「自分で，独力で」

問5 「どの学生が，良い点と悪い点の両方についてコメントしているか」 ⬜10

A: アルジュナ
B: ベン
C: フランシスコ
D: キャサリン
E: マーカス
F: テオ

① AとC
② BとE
③ CとF
④ DとF

正解 ⇒ ③

居住者である学生たちのコメント内容を見ると，フランシスコは「自分の部屋では問題なく勉強できる」が，「共用エリアでは集中できない」と記し，テオは「今学期のスペイン料理パーティーはとても楽しかった」が，そのような「イベントが十分に計画されていない」と記している。この2人だけが良い点と悪い点の両方についてコメントしているので，③が正解である。マーカスとベンは良い点についてだけ，アルジュナとキャサリンは悪い点についてだけコメントしている。

【語句・表現】
・give a comment「コメントする」
・positive「良い，ポジティブな，プラスの」
・negative「悪い，ネガティブな，マイナスの」

【全訳】
あなたは，交換留学プログラムに参加するために，来週イギリスへ出発します。そこにいる間住むことになる建物についての情報を読んでいます。

ライリーホール
ポーター大学の留学生および交換プログラムの学生のための住居

共用エリア
1階のこの広いスペースには，ソファ，椅子，テーブル，テレビが設置されています。よくここに学生が集まって，宿題をしたり，サッカーを見たりします。文化交流イベントも，ここで毎年数回開催されます。

住居の手配
学生の居室は1階の上階である2階，3階，4階にあります。事前に1人部屋を申請しない限り，新規居住者はルームメイトと2人部屋に割り当てられます。また，3階と4階には，前学期中にグループとして申請すれば3～5人の学生で居住できる，複数の部屋がまとまったスイートがあります。

設備
バスルーム（トイレ）は学生の居室がある階の廊下の両端と，1階の共用ルームの向かいに一つあります。1階以外のバスルームにはシャワーが付いています。居住者は地下にある洗濯機を使用できます。地下を除く各フロアに共用キッチンもあり，冷蔵庫，コンロ，電子レンジ，シンクが設置されています。

現在の居住者のコメント
- 「ライリーホールでの生活を通じて他国の学生や文化を知ることができるのは素晴らしい経験です！」──マーカス
- 「平日は午後8時まで，週末は午後遅くまでキッチンが混雑しているので，通常は大学の食堂で食事をしなければなりません」──アルジュナ
- 「自分の部屋では問題なく勉強できますが，共用エリアではたいてい誰かがテレビを見ているので，集中するのはとても難しいです」──フランシスコ
- 「最初は共用バスルームというのが嫌だと思いましたが，とても清潔に保たれているので気になりませんでした」──ベン
- 「今学期のスペイン料理パーティーはとても楽しかったです。他の居住者に出会えるようなイベントが十分に計画されていません」──テオ
- 「エレベーターがないので，地下室から4階の自分の部屋に洗濯物を運ぶのは最悪です」──キャサリン

【語句・表現】
・programme「プログラム」：イギリス式のつづり。アメリカ式では program とつづる。
・residence「家，住宅」
・common「共用の」
・ground floor「1階」
・as well as ～「～も，～同様」
・gather「集まる」
・assignment「課題，宿題」
・cultural exchange「文化交流」
・event「出来事，イベント」
・organise「～を手配する」：イギリス式のつづり。アメリカ式では organize とつづる。
・hold「～を開く」
・each year「毎年」
・arrangement「手配，準備」
・in advance「前もって」
・be assigned to ～「～に割り当てられる」
・in addition「さらに」
・suite「スイートルーム」：数部屋続きの広い部屋のこと。
・apply「申請する，申し込む」

・previous「前の，以前の」
・term「学期」
・facility「設備」
・end「端」
・hallway「廊下」
・(be) located「位置する」
・across from ～「～の向かいに」
・except for ～「～を除いて」
・be equipped with ～「～を備えている」
・resident「居住者」
・basement「地下」
・shared「共用の」
・available「利用できる」
・include「～を含む」
・refrigerator「冷蔵庫」
・stove「ガスコンロ，調理用コンロ」
・microwave「電子レンジ」
・current「現在の」
・get to *do*「～できる，～するようになる」
・crowded「混み合った，満員の」
・cafeteria「カフェテリア，食堂」
・focus「集中する」
・quite「とても」

B

問1 「ユウゴによると，　11　に慣れるのは難しくなかった」

① **イギリスの食事**
② 学校の授業
③ イギリスの公共交通機関
④ イギリス英語の語彙理解

正解 ⇒ ①

　ユウゴのメールの第1段落に「食事には簡単になじめた」が，「イギリス英語特有の単語や公共交通機関」に慣れないとあるので，①が正解，③，④は「まだよくわからない」と書かれているので誤り。②については，学校の授業は「最大の違い」と書かれているだけなので不適切。

【語句・表現】
・according to ～「～によると」
・adjust to ～「～に慣れる・適応する」
・public transport「公共交通機関」
・vocabulary「語彙，単語」

問2 「ユウゴのメールで**事実**として述べられたことは，イギリスでは，　12　ということである」

① 授業が学生にとってより難しい

② 彼は授業で自分の意見を述べることを求められた
③ 学生たちは難なく意見を述べる
④ 教師はあまり重要な役割を持っていない

正解 ⇒ ②

　授業については，ユウゴのメールの第2段落で言及されており，第3文で「どう思うかを突然聞かれた」ことが記述されている。したがって②が正解である。学生たちにとって「意見やその理由を話すのはとても簡単で自然なことみたいだった」と書かれているが，これはユウゴのクラスの学生たちについての感想であるため③は不適切。「授業のスタイル」が違うと書かれているだけで，①と④については記述がないため不適切である。

【語句・表現】
・state「～と述べる」
・give one's opinions「～の意見を言う」
・have no trouble doing「問題なく～する」
・have a role「役割がある」

問3 「ユウゴは，学校での経験で 13 と思っている」

① 自分の考えに確信が持てるようになった
② 公の場で発言する能力が改善した
③ 他の学生をうらやましがらせた
④ 読書をすることはより興味深いと知った

正解 ⇒ ①

　ユウゴのメールの最終文「説明をしなければならないことで，自分の考えや知識に自信が持てるようになった」という記述から，①が正解。②，③，④はメールで言及されておらず，全て不適切。

【語句・表現】
・feel sure「確信する」
・thought「考え」
・improve「～を改善する」
・public speaking「人前で話すこと（の）」
・ability「能力」
・make A B（形容詞）「A を B にする」
・jealous of ～「～がうらやましい」

問4 「ヨナのメールから，彼女は 14 ということがわかる」

① 人と話すのを気楽に感じている
② 他の国に行ったことがない
③ イギリスの授業は退屈だと思っている
④ 来年，留学するつもりである

正解 ⇒ ④

ヨナのメールの最終文「自分も来年同じような体験をしたいなあ」から，④が正解である。「私は大人数だととてもシャイになってしまう」から，①は誤り。②は言及されておらず不明なため不適切。「授業は本当に面白そう」と書かれているため③も誤りである。

【語句・表現】
・feel comfortable「気楽に感じる」
・sound「～のように聞こえる」
・boring「退屈な」
・study abroad「留学する」

問5　「ヨナの意見を最もよくまとめたものはどれか」　15

> ①　議論することは学生よりも大人にとってより価値がある。
> ②　他人が考えていることを理解するのは不可能である。
> ③　学生にとって，事実を覚えることは最も重要なスキルである。
> ④　意見を共有するスキルは現代の世界において大変価値がある。

正解 ⇒ ④

ヨナのメールの第1段落最終文の However から後ろに「自分の信念や意見を伝える能力はグローバル社会においてより必要とされるスキル」と書かれているので，④が正解である。①，②はメールで言及されていないので不適切。「事実や情報をインプットすることは重要。でも，…」と続くので，③も不適切である。

【語句・表現】
・summarise「まとめる」：イギリス式のつづり。アメリカ式では summarize とつづる。
・valuable「価値がある」
・share「～を共有する」

【全訳】
　あなたの友人がイギリスの学校に留学して数カ月たちました。彼が，自分の異文化体験について別の友人と話し合ったメールでのやりとりをあなたに見せています。

宛先：カン　ヨナ　　　　　　　　　　　　　　　2022/12/20 午後12:14
差出人：タカハシ　ユウゴ
件名：イギリスでの体験

ヨナへ
　メールを書くのが遅くなってごめん。勉強もだけど，いろいろなことを学ぶのに忙しくて。イギリスでの生活はすごく違うから，順応するのに時間がかかったことがあってね。食事には簡単になじめたけど，3カ月たった今でも，イギリス英語特有の単語や公共交通機関の使い方がまだよくわからないよ。
　でも，最大の違いは学校の授業のスタイルだ。ものすごくたくさん議論が交わされ，先生たちもよく意見を求めてくる。初めて先生から今読んでいる本についてどう思うか突然聞かれた時は，びっくりした。何を言ったらいいかわからなかった。他の学生が話すのを聞いたけど，彼らにとっては，意見やその理由を話すのはとても簡単で自然なことみたいだった。それ以来，自分ももっとそんなふうになれるように努力している。説明をしなければならないことで，自分の考えや知識に自信が持てるようになったよ。

ではまた。
ユウゴ

宛先：タカハシ　ユウゴ　　　　　　　　　　　　　　　　　　　2022/12/21 午後7：05
差出人：カン　ヨナ
件名：Re: イギリスでの体験

ユウゴへ
　　連絡くれてうれしいよ。イギリスで素晴らしい時間を過ごしているみたいだね。授業は本当に面白そう。私は大人数だととてもシャイになってしまうから，そういう経験は貴重だと思う。他の人と話し合うことで，自分自身についてもたくさんのことがわかるね。学生として，事実や情報をインプットすることは重要。でも，自分の信念や意見を伝える能力はグローバル社会においてより必要とされるスキルだね。
　　経験を共有してくれてありがとう。私も来年同じような体験をしたいなあ！　また連絡ください！

それでは。
ヨナ

【語句・表現】
・another「別の」
・conversation「会話，対話」
〈ユウゴのメール〉
・write to ～「～に手紙・メールを書く」
・be busy with ～「～で忙しい」
・work「作用する」
・it takes A（人）a while to *do*「A（人）が～するのに時間がかかる」
・adapt to ～「～に慣れる・順応する」
・ask for ～「～を求める」
・The first time S V「初めて～する時」
・since then「それ以来」
・work hard「懸命に努力する」
・confident「自信がある」
・Best,「よろしく，それではまた」：文末に使用される決まり文句である Best regards, の簡易表現。
〈ヨナのメール〉
・hear from ～「～から連絡をもらう」
・It sounds like S V「～であるようだ」
・shy「シャイな，恥ずかしがり屋の」
・ability to *do*「～する能力」
・express「～を表現する」
・belief「信念，考え」
・global「グローバルな，国際的な」
・Regards,「よろしく，それではまた」：Best, Best regards, と同意。

第3問

A

問1 「ヘンリーのブログから，彼が ☐16 ことが読み取れた」

---
① 家族に何か買った
② 食べたもの全てを気に入った
③ インドの伝統舞踊を習った
④ 観覧車に乗った

正解 ⇒ ①

Finally から始まる第3段落で，ラドゥーが気に入り「家族への土産に買い足した」とあるので①が正解である。同じ段落で，サモサは「ちょっと辛過ぎた」と書いてあるため②は不適切。インド舞踊は見ただけなので③も不適切。観覧車は「長蛇の列でなかったら乗っていたのに！」と仮定法過去完了で書いてあり，乗らなかったことがわかるので④も不適切。

【語句・表現】
・read that S V「～（ということ）を読んで知る」
・traditional「伝統的な」
・ride on ～「～に乗る」
・Ferris wheel「観覧車」：Ferris と表記するのが一般的だが，全て小文字でも可。

問2 「ダンドゥに近づいた時，ヘンリーはおそらく ☐17 だろう」

---
① がっかりした
② 怖かった
③ 驚いた
④ 気分を害した

正解 ⇒ ③

「ダンドゥは私の身長の3倍も背が高いこともわかった」という記述から，③が正解である。「目の前で面白い動きをしたのを見て笑った」のだから①，②は不適切。④の upset は「動揺する，イライラする」などの「気持ちが落ち着かない感情」全般を意味するので，④も不適切である。

【語句・表現】
・likely「おそらく」
・get close to ～「～に近づく」
・puppet「操り人形」

【全訳】
　あなたはイギリスで開催される祭りに興味を持っています。若いイギリス人のブロガーの投稿を読んでいるところです。

　ヘンリー・ミルズ
　11月18日　土曜日　午後9:00

光の祭典，ディワリは，毎年10月から11月の間のある時期に行われるインドの宗教的な祝典だ。昨夜，インド国外で行われるディワリ祭の中でも最大のものの一つであるレスター市のディワリ祭に行った。祭りの最後の夜だったので，盛り上がっていた。空を照らす華やかな花火から始まった。Wheel of Light（光の輪）と呼ばれる大きな観覧車もあった。白いライトでライトアップされてきれいだった。長蛇の列でなかったら乗っていたのに！

歩き回って，パフォーマンスも楽しんだ。まず，色とりどりの衣装を着た男女が伝統的なインド舞踊をしているのを見た。音楽は活気があり，エネルギッシュで，ダンサーたちはリズムに合わせ優美に動いた。また，ダンドゥという名前の巨大な機械仕掛けの人形が群衆の中を歩いているのも見た。それは一見人間のようだったが，とても明るく光っていたので，遠くからこちらに来るのが見えた。近くに来た時に，ようやくそれを動かしている男性が見えた。そして，ダンドゥは私の３倍も背が高いこともわかった！　目の前で面白い動きをしたのを見て笑った。

最後に，屋台をいくつか訪れ，少しいろいろ食べてみた。サモサを食べたが，僕にはちょっと辛過ぎた。次にラドゥーを食べてみると，甘くておいしかった。とても気に入ったので，家族への土産に買い足した。

インド文化に興味がある方は，ぜひ，レスターのディワリ祭に行ってみてください！　今年のチラシの写真を載せたので，以下をご覧ください。

2023年　ディワリ祭
イギリス　レスター市
11月12日（日）−11月17日（金）

パフォーマンス	アクティビティー	食べ物

花火

 伝統舞踊

 サモサ（揚げ物）（PIXTA）

ダンドゥ
ホイール・オブ・ライト（観覧車）
 ラドゥー（インド菓子）

【語句・表現】
・hold「〜を開催する」
・blogger「ブロガー，ブログを書く人」
・post「投稿」
〈第１段落〉
・religious「宗教的な」

- celebration「祝典」
- atmosphere「雰囲気」
- full of ～「～でいっぱい」
- excitement「興奮」
- start with ～「～から始まる・始める」
- brilliant「素晴らしい」
- firework「花火」
- display「展示」
- light up ～「～を照らす」
- line「列」

〈第2段落〉
- walk around「歩き回る」
- get to do「～する機会を得る」
- be dressed in ～「～を着ている」
- colourful「色とりどりの」：イギリス式のつづり。アメリカ式では colorful とつづる。
- lively「活気のある，陽気な」
- energetic「エネルギッシュな」
- to the rhythm「リズムに合わせて」
- giant「巨大な」
- mechanical「機械式の」
- walk through ～「～の中を歩く，～をかき分けて歩く」
- crowd「集まり」
- glow「光る」
- far away「遠く」
- get close「近づく」
- realise「～だとわかる」：イギリス式のつづり。アメリカ式では realize とつづる。
- ～ times taller than ...「…より～倍背が高い」
- do ～ moves「～な動きをする」

〈第3段落〉
- food stand「屋台，出店」
- a bit「少し」
- spicy「スパイスの効いた」
- delicious「おいしい」

〈第4段落〉
- definitely「絶対に，必ず」
- check out ～「～を確認する・チェックする」
- flyer「チラシ，パンフレット」

B

問1 「次の①～④の出来事を起こった順に並べなさい」

[18] → [19] → [20] → [21]

① 地元の女性が筆者の手助けをした。
② 筆者はリムリックに到着した。
③ 筆者は長時間休憩しなければならなかった。
④ 筆者は興味深い観光地に行った。

正解 ⇒ ②→①→③→④

　第1段落第2文の旅行の計画から，筆者はコーク→リムリック→ウォーターフォード→コークというルートをたどることがわかる。雨の中コークからリムリックに到着し，第3段落で，「傘をさした女性が立ち止まって大丈夫かと尋ねて」きて，宿泊場所を教えてくれたことが記述されている。第4段落では，翌日，ウォーターフォードへと向かう旅行の終盤で左膝が痛くなり始めて「痛みが引くまで長めの休憩を取った」とある。最終段落に，「最終日は，自転車をこぎ出す前にウォーターフォードの観光地を見に行った」とある。したがって，正解は②→①→③→④である。

【語句・表現】
・following「次の，後に続く」
・order「順番」
・local「地域の，地元の」
・break「休憩」
・sightseeing spot「観光地」

問2　「筆者が思ったより遅くリムリックに到着した理由の一つは何だったか」　22

　① 田園地帯を走っている間に道に迷った。
　② 山を登るのに苦労した。
　③ 雨のせいでゆっくりこがなければならなかった。
　④ 道中で写真を撮るために立ち止まった。

正解 ⇒ ③

　第2段落第7文に「道路が濡れていたため，下る時に速度を落とさなければならなかった」とあるので，③が正解である。①の記述はなく，②は同段落に丘が「山のように感じた」とあり，実際に山を登ったわけではないため，どちらも不適切。写真を撮ったのは最終日のウォーターフォードの観光地で，とあるので，④も不適切である。

【語句・表現】
・get lost「道に迷う」
・countryside「田舎，田園地帯」
・along the way「道中，道すがら」

問3　「この話から，筆者が　23　ということがわかった」

　① どの街にも予定より遅れて到着した
　② 悪天候対策の衣類を準備していた
　③ こんなに大変な旅程を立てて後悔した
　④ 次はコークの観光に行くだろう

正解 ⇒ ②

　第2段落第2文に「レインジャケットを持って来ていた」とあるので，②が正解である。最終段落に，予定より早くコークに到着したことが記述されているため①は誤り。記事の最後に I felt great! とあるので，③も不適切。なお，④についての記述はない。

【語句・表現】
・later than planned「予定していたより遅く」
・clothing「衣服，衣類」
・regret *doing*「～したことを後悔する」
・go sightseeing「観光に行く」

【全訳】
　あなたはサイクリングに興味があり，サイクリング雑誌で興味深い記事を見つけました。

アイルランドの自転車旅
ジョン・ローレンス

　コークの涼しく晴れた朝，私はアイルランド国内の自転車旅を開始することに心躍らせていた。道中たくさんの美しい景色を見ながら，リムリックへ行った後ウォーターフォードに行き，コークに戻るというルートを計画していた。最初の数時間は順調で，迷わずに田園地帯を進んだ。しかし，すぐに問題が生じた。

　午後になると空は暗くなり，小雨が降り始めた。レインジャケットを持って来ていたが，雨を完全に防ぐには十分ではなかった。雨が激しくなるにつれて，身体が濡れて寒くなっていった。困難な状況ではあったが，暗くなり過ぎる前に街に到着しなければならないことはわかっていた。しかし，自転車をこぐにつれて，さらに困難になった。さっきまでとても美しく見えたアイルランドの丘は，上るにつれて山のように感じられた。そして，道路が濡れていたため，下る時に速度を落とさなければならなかった。その結果，到着が予定より3時間遅れた。

　すぐに，私は滞在場所を探し始めた。自分はひどいありさまだったに違いない。傘をさした女性が立ち止まって大丈夫かと尋ねてきたからだ。彼女に宿を探していると話すと，おいしくて温かい食事ができるレストランがある地元のホテルに案内してくれた。一晩ぐっすり眠り，次の旅行の行程の準備が整った。

　今回はウォーターフォードまでずっと晴天だったので，前日より景色を楽しむことができた。しかし，旅行の終盤，左膝が痛くなり始めた。すぐに痛みがひどくなり，完全に止まらなければならなかった。まだ午後3時30分で，目標地点まではそれほど離れていなかったため，痛みが引くまで長めの休憩を取ってから，最後の数キロをこいだ。予定より1時間遅れたが，夕食の時間までに到着した。

　最終日は，自転車をこぎ出す前にウォーターフォードの観光地を見に行った。長さ15メートルを超える木製の剣が圧巻だった。息子たちに見せるためにその写真を何枚か撮った後，私は自転車に飛び乗ってコークに戻る旅を始めた。今回はトラブルもなく，思ったより早く旅行を終えた。ついに旅の出発地点に戻った。やり遂げたのだ。困難を乗り越え，アイルランド国内の3日間の自転車の旅を達成した。とても良い気分だった！

【語句・表現】
・article「記事」
〈第1段落〉
・Ireland「アイルランド」
・route「ルート，道のり」
・plenty of ～「たくさんの～」
・landscape「景色，見晴らし」
・smoothly「順調に，スムーズに」
・make（good）progress「はかどる」
〈第2段落〉
・rain jacket「レインジャケット，雨具」
・completely「完全に」
・despite「～にもかかわらず」

・make it（to ～）「（～に）到達する」

・challenging「困難な，やりがいのある」

・feel like ～「～のように感じる」

・pushed *one*'s way up ～「～を（必死で）上る」

・reduce「～を減少させる」

・as a result「結果として」

〈第３段落〉

・right away「すぐに」

・search for ～「～を探す・捜す」

・terrible「ひどい」

・guide A（人）to B「A（人）をBに案内する」

・meal「食事」

・ready for ～「～の準備ができて」

〈第４段落〉

・clear「晴れ渡った」

・all the way to ～「～までずっと」

・scenery「風景，景色」

・previous「前の」

・towards the end of ～「～の終わりの方で」

・knee「膝」

・hurt「痛む」

・painful「痛い」

・altogether「完全に」

・far from ～「～から遠くに」

・take a rest「休息を取る」

・go away「（苦痛などが）とれる」

・behind schedule「予定に遅れて」

・in time for ～「～に間に合って」

〈第５段落〉

・sight「名所」

・favourite「お気に入り人・物」：イギリス式のつづり。アメリカ式では favorite とつづる。

・sword「剣」

・(be) made of ～「～で作られた」

・hop on ～「～に飛び乗る」

・bike「自転車」

第４問

問１ 「ミゼンコ教授からの返信を受け取る前，ユウタロウは　24　か　25　へ留学することを考えていた」（順序は問わない）

> ① グルノーブル　② リヨン　③ ニース　④ パリ

正解 ⇒ ②・③

　ユウタロウの最初のメールに「自分が耳にした二つのコースはフランス語でのみ授業が提供される」と

いう記述がある。ミゼンコ教授の返信の第2段落第1文「本大学が今年提供を始めたプログラムが他に二つある」という記述と，教授が送ったプログラムの情報に合計四つの選択肢が記載されていることから，ユウタロウが考えていたのはリヨンとニースのプログラムということになり，②と③が正解である。

【語句・表現】
・reply「返事」
・order「順序」
・matter「問題である」

問2 「ユウタロウは，| 26 |ので，理系のコースをフランス語で受講することが不安である」

① 速く話されると理解するのが難しい
② フランス語の理系の語彙が乏しい
③ 教授が彼の質問に英語で答えてくれない
④ **授業の課題により時間がかかってしまう**

正解 ⇒ ④

ユウタロウの最初のメールに，フランス語は「理解はできるのですが，課題を終えるのに時間がかかり過ぎるのではないかと心配しています」と書かれているので，④が正解である。聞いて理解することについての不安ではないので，①は不適切。また，②の語彙についてや，③の教授の対応については述べられていない。

【語句・表現】
・have trouble *doing*「〜するのに困難がある」
・vocabulary「語彙」
・take A（人）time to *do*「A（人）が〜するのに時間がかかる」

問3 「ミゼンコ教授は| 27 |と提案している」

① **ユウタロウがフランスでしかできないことに集中した方がいい**
② ユウタロウにとってフランスで1年間留学するのが一番良い
③ フランスには興味深い理系のコースはほとんどない
④ フランスにいる間ユウタロウは理系の授業を一つも取るべきではない

正解 ⇒ ①

ミゼンコ教授のメール第1段落第1文に「留学するというのは，母国では体験できないことを体験するということ」，第3文に「フランスにいることを最大限に活用することに集中してみては」とあることから，正解は①である。②は記述がないので不適切。同メールの第2段落でグルノーブルについても紹介しているが，「本大学では受講できないような理系のコースが必ず見つかる」とあるので，③も不適切。第1段落第2文に「もし，ある大学でそこでしか提供されない理系の授業があるなら，それを受講しましょう」とあるので，④も不適切。

【語句・表現】
・it is better to *do*「〜した方がいい」
・focus on 〜「〜に焦点を当てる・集中する」
・while in 〜「〜にいる間」：while の後に主語と be 動詞が省略されている。

問4 「ユウタロウはミゼンコ教授のアドバイスを [28] と思っている」

① わかりにくい
② 助けになる
③ 物足りない
④ 厄介だ

正解 ⇒ ②

　ユウタロウの2通目のメール第1段落第2文に It gave me a lot to consider と表現されており，同メールの第3段落冒頭に「イギリスでできないことに集中するというアドバイスを頂いたことで決心がつきました」とあることから，正解は②である。

問5 「ユウタロウがホストファミリーの家に滞在した場合，彼が選ぶプログラムの費用は総額いくらになるか」 [29]

① 1万800ポンド
② 1万1500ポンド
③ 1万2000ポンド
④ 2万7600ポンド

正解 ⇒ ③

　ユウタロウの2通目のメールの第2段落にある「1年過ごしたいのですが，費用がかかり過ぎる」「3カ月では十分ではない」という記述から，期間は6カ月，さらに，第3段落第3文「理系の勉強は楽しいので，面白いと思う科目は履修できるようにしたい」という記述から，興味を引かれる理系のコースが見つかるグルノーブルを選択することがわかる。授業料は7200ポンド，ホームステイは1カ月800ポンドなので，7200＋800×6で合計1万2000ポンドになり，正解は③。

【全訳】
　あなたはイギリスの大学生で，フランスに留学しようと考えています。友人が，プログラムの選択について助言を得るためにアドバイザーとやりとりしたメールを，あなたに見せています。

ミゼンコ教授

来年，フランスに留学したいのですが，プログラムの選択に困っています。自分が耳にした二つのコースはフランス語でのみ授業が提供されます。専門である理系のコースを引き続き履修したいのですが，自分はフランス語がそれほど堪能ではありません。理解はできるのですが，課題を終えるのに時間がかかり過ぎるのではないかと心配しています。

また，フランスは芸術で名高いので，芸術についても学びたいと思っています。

どちらのプログラムが最適かご意見頂けますか。

どうぞよろしくお願いいたします。
スズキ　ユウタロウ

ユウタロウ君

まず，理系の学習を続けたいと思うのは素晴らしいことですが，留学するというのは，母国では体験できないことを体験するということです。もし，その大学にしかない理系の授業があるなら，それを受講しましょう。そうでなければ，フランスにいることを最大限に活用することに集中してみては？フランス語の授業をもっと受けてみてはどうでしょうか。そうすれば，フランス語でもより容易に学べる芸術などのコースを受講することも可能でしょう。

これらの案に魅力がなければ，今年うちの大学で始まったプログラムが他に二つあります。一つは，パリでの1年間のプログラムです。英語とフランス語の両言語でコースを提供しているので，何でも興味のあるものを受講できるでしょう。もう一つはグルノーブルでの半年のプログラムです。パリのプログラムと同様に，英語でコースを受講することができ，この都市は科学研究で名高いです。本大学では受講できないような理系のコースが必ず見つかるでしょう。

更新されたプログラム案内を送ります。

それでは。
マイケル・ミゼンコ

ミゼンコ教授

お返事ありがとうございます。教えていただいたことについていろいろと考え，自分がどうしたいかがわかってきたように思います。

フランスで1年過ごしたいのですが，費用がかかり過ぎます。しかし，教授からのメールを読み，今は，3カ月では十分でないと思っています。できるだけ文化を体験したいと思います。

イギリスでできないことに集中するというアドバイスを頂いたことで決心がつきました。自分の主な目標は，フランス語を上達させ，芸術についてもっと学ぶことです。しかし，理系の勉強は楽しいので，やはり面白いと思う科目は履修できるようにしたいと思います。したがって，英語でもコースを提供している所を選択します。

あとは，住む所をどうするかということについて考えなければなりません。

今後ともよろしくお願いいたします。
スズキ　ユウタロウ

プログラム情報：

フランス　グルノーブル
グルノーブルは科学の研究の中心地として有名です。

コースにおける使用言語： 英語，フランス語	期間： 6カ月	費用： 7200ポンド

フランス　リヨン		
フランスで３番目に大きな都市で，芸術で有名ですが，食はさらに有名です。		
コースにおける使用言語： フランス語	期間： ３カ月	費用： 3600ポンド
フランス　ニース		
ニースは，古典と現代のフランス文化が見事に融合した都市です。		
コースにおける使用言語： フランス語	期間： ６カ月	費用： 6700ポンド
フランス　パリ		
フランスの首都で，最新のファッションと世界的に有名な芸術で知られています。		
コースにおける使用言語： 英語，フランス語	期間： １年	費用： １万8000ポンド
住居		
学生はホストファミリーと暮らすか，大学宿舎に住むことができます。以下に示された費用は月額です。 ホストファミリー：800ポンド 大学宿舎：600ポンド		

【語句・表現】
・adviser「アドバイザー」：イギリス式のつづり。アメリカ式では advisor とつづる。
・programme「計画，プログラム」：イギリス式のつづり。アメリカ式では program とつづる。
・exchange「やりとり」
〈ユウタロウの１通目のメール〉
・hear about ～「～について聞く（聞いて知っている）」
・offer「～を提供する」
・continue *doing*「継続して～する」
・major「専攻」
・not that good「それほどうまくない」
・be famous for ～「～で有名である」：＝ be known for ～。
・Kind regards,「（どうぞ）よろしくお願いします」：文末に使用される決まり文句。Best regards, とほぼ同じように用いられる。
〈ミゼンコ教授のメール〉
・study abroad「留学する」
・unique「独特な，唯一の」
・otherwise「そうでなければ」
・focus on ～「～に集中する・焦点を当てる」
・make the most of ～「～を最大限に活用する」
・Why not *do* ?「～してみてはどうですか」
・try *doing*「（試しに）～してみる」
・half-year「半年の」
・scientific「科学の」
・be sure to *do*「必ず～する」
・updated「更新された，アップデートされた」
〈ユウタロウの２通目のメール〉
・consider「～を考える」
・would love to *do*「ぜひ～したい」

・cost「費用」：low / high などと共に用いられることが多い。
・as much as possible「できるだけ多く」
・convince「～を納得させる」
・improve「～を改善する」
・therefore「したがって」
・housing「住居」
・option「選択肢」
〈プログラム情報〉
・recognise「～がわかる，～を認識する」：イギリス式のつづり。アメリカ式では recognize とつづる。
・centre「中心（地）」：イギリス式のつづり。アメリカ式では center とつづる。
・length「長さ，期間」
・capital「首都」
・world-famous「世界的に有名な」
・per month「1 カ月当たりの」

第5問

問1 「あなたの発表の最も適切な副題はどれか」 30

① 農民から成功した作家へ
② **風を使って村に電気をもたらした少年**
③ マラウイで最初にウォーターポンプを作った人
④ 一度も学校で学んでいない独学の発明家

正解 ⇒ ②

　本文の主人公は，独学で電気を生み出す風車を作ったウィリアム・カムクワンバという少年である（第1段落）。図書館で見つけた本を参考にして，手に入る部品を駆使して風車を作ることを試み（第2段落），ついに小さな風車，次に大きな風車を完成させて，村に電力を供給した（第3段落）。これが彼の功績であり，正解は②。彼は本を出版したが，作家ではなくエンジニアなので①は不適切。第4段落にウォーターポンプについて記述があるが，この記事の主なテーマではないので③も不適切。④は第1段落で「学費の支払いをやめなければならなかった」という記述があり，学校に一度も行っていないわけではないので，これも不適切。

【語句・表現】
・subtitle「副題」
・successful「成功した」
・author「作家，筆者」
・power「～に電力を供給する，～を電力で動かす」
・pump「ポンプ」
・self-taught「独学の」
・inventor「発明家」

問2 「 31 と 32 に入る最も適切な選択肢を二つ選び<u>幼少期</u>を完成させなさい」（順序は問わない）

① 科学と技術に興味を持った
② 裕福な両親のおかげで快適な生活を送った

③　全ての授業が退屈だったので学校をやめた
④　**多くの時間を地元の図書館で読書をして過ごした**
⑤　家族が所有するトウモロコシとタバコの畑で働いた

正解 ⇒ ①・④

　第１段落に，学校に行けなかったウィリアムは「家族の農場から離れて地元の図書館で過ごした」「科学技術に心を躍らせた」と記述があるので，正解は①と④である。農場で働いていたという記述はないので⑤は不適切。同じく第１段落で，彼の両親は農業を営んでおり，ウィリアムが学校に行けなかった理由として貧しくて学費が払えなくなったとあるので，②と③も誤り。

【語句・表現】
・option「選択肢」
・complete「～を完成させる」
・childhood「子ども時代，幼少期」
・comfortable「快適な」
・thanks to ～「～のおかげで」
・wealthy「裕福な」
・quit「～をやめる」
・be bored with ～「～に退屈する」
・tobacco「タバコ」
・field「畑」

問３　「起こった順に五つの出来事から四つを選び重要な出来事の時系列を完成させなさい」
　　　33 → 34 → 35 → 36

①　ウィリアムの功績のニュースは世界に知れ渡った。
②　ウィリアムは『エネルギーの利用』という教本を見つけた。
③　ウィリアムはスポンサーから資金の援助を受けた。
④　ウィリアムはゴミの中から部品を探した。
⑤　ウィリアムは子ども向けの科学の教本を書いた。

正解 ⇒ ② → ④ → ① → ③

　第２段落より，ウィリアムは図書館で『エネルギーの利用』という教本を見つけ，村のゴミの中から使用できる部品を探し始めたことがわかる。第４段落から，大きい風車ができたというニュースが世界に知れ渡り，ウィリアムが講演に呼ばれたり，新聞記事に取り上げられたりしてスポンサーが殺到したという記述がある。したがって，②→④→①→③の順が正解となる。

【語句・表現】
・in the order「順番に」
・happen「起こる」
・sequence「時系列，順序」
・key「重要な」
・achievement「功績，業績」
・spread「広がる」
・financial「経済的な」
・search for ～「～を探す」

・garbage「ゴミ」

問4 「 37 に入る最も適切な選択肢を選び性格を完成させなさい」

① とても意志が固く，笑われた時でさえもあきらめなかった
② とても寛大で，子どもたちの教育を支援するためにお金を与えた
③ とても賢い少年で，何のヒントもなく自分で風車を作った
④ とても創造的で，これまで誰も見たことがないものを作った

正解 ⇒ ①

　第2，3段落に，地元の人々がウィリアムを笑い，頭がおかしいと言ったが，彼は決してあきらめなかったという記述があることから，正解は①である。②と④に関しては記述がないため不適切。③は，ウィリアムは本を見て風車を作ったので誤りである。

【語句・表現】
・character「性格」
・determined「意志の固い」
・give up「やめる，あきらめる」
・laugh at ～「～を笑う」
・generous「寛大な」
・clever「利口な，賢い」
・windmill「風車（小屋）」

問5 「 38 に入る最も適切な選択肢を選び功績と現在の取り組みを完成させなさい」

① 学校で学び続けられるようにマラウイの子どもたちと共に闘っている
② 自身の人生について Netflix の映画を製作した
③ 引き続き自分の地域にクリーンエネルギーを供給するために働いている
④ 彼のような発明家になるように若者たちを説得しようとしている

正解 ⇒ ③

　最終段落に，自分のコミュニティーだけでなく，他地域にもクリーンエネルギーを供給するプロジェクトに取り組み続けていると記述があるので，正解は③。①は，「子どもたちと共に」ではなく「子どもたちのために」闘っている，②は，映画はウィリアムが作ったものではない，④は，若い世代が発明家になることを促しているわけではないので，全て誤りである。

【語句・表現】
・current「現在の」
・Netflix「ネットフリックス」
・supply A with B「AにBを供給する」
・community「地域社会，コミュニティー」
・clean energy「クリーンエネルギー（環境に優しいエネルギー）」
・convince A to *do*「Aを～するように説得する」

【全訳】
　あなたは，英語の授業であるエンジニアについての発表を行う予定です。以下の記事をオンラインで見

つけて，発表用のメモを準備しました。

　2000年代初頭，アフリカのマラウイ出身の少年が，村のために電気を生み出す機械を作って有名になった。彼の名前はウィリアム・カムクワンバ。1987年にマシタラの村で生まれたウィリアムは，両親と6人の姉妹と一緒にトウモロコシとタバコの農家で育った。2002年，彼がまだ14歳の時，彼の国でひどい飢餓をもたらした水不足が長く続いた。ウィリアムの両親は，わずかな食べ物を買うために，彼の1年間80ドルの学費の支払いをやめなければならないほどだった。空腹を抱え，教育も受けることができなかったウィリアムは，代わりに家族の農場から離れて地元の図書館で過ごした。彼は科学技術に心を躍らせ，図書館にあるそれらに関する本や雑誌を全て読んだ。

　ある日，ウィリアムは『Using Energy（エネルギーの利用）』という教本を見つけた。本には風を使って電気を作る風車と呼ばれる機械の作り方が示されていた。このアイデアに触発されて，彼は村を助けるために風車を作ることを決意した。教本の英語の指示にできる限り従って，彼は村のゴミの山から，使用できる部品を探し始めた。しかし，地元の人々の多くが彼を笑い，頭がおかしいと言った。当時，マラウイの農村部に住む人々のわずか1％しか電気を利用できなかった。彼らは，ウィリアムのような少年が電気を供給する機械を作ることができるとは想像できなかった。

　しかし，ウィリアムは決してあきらめなかった。見つけた木材や自転車の部品などを使って，家の裏に小さな風車を作った。風車を古い車のバッテリーに接続して電気を蓄え，それは彼の家の四つの照明とラジオをつけるのに十分な電力量であった。その結果，ウィリアムは外が暗くなった後でも夜更かしして本を読むことができた。すぐに，彼は村全体に電気を供給できる，さらに大きい風車を作った。人々は驚き，喜んだ。彼らはウィリアムがある種の魔法を使っているに違いないと思った。

　ウィリアムの大きい風車のニュースはすぐに広まり，彼はマラウイと海外で有名になった。世界中の会議やイベントで講演するよう招待され，彼の話はいくつかの新聞記事にも載った。スポンサーが彼に資金を提供しようと殺到し，彼はその資金を使って風車を改良し，増えた電気で動くウォーターポンプを作るためにその資金を使った。これにより，彼の村に初めて飲料水がもたらされ，雨が降っていないときに農民が作物に水をやることができた。

　有名になった後，ウィリアムはついに学校に戻ることができた。そして，2009年に彼は自身の経験について本を出版し，それは『ニューヨークタイムズ』紙のベストセラーになった。彼はアメリカのダートマス大学へ進学し，2014年に卒業した。5年後の2019年には，ウィリアムの物語がNetflixのヒット映画にもなった。

　今日，彼は寛大な精神で名の知られるエンジニアであり，発明家だ。彼は，クリーンエネルギーやその他の技術を必要としている自分のコミュニティーや他の地域の人々にそれらをもたらすためのプロジェクトに取り組み続けている。彼はまた，貧しい国の若者が教育と資源にアクセスできるように奮闘している。若い世代の人々が自らの興味に従い，世界にプラスの影響を与えることを促したいと思っている。

発表のためのノート：

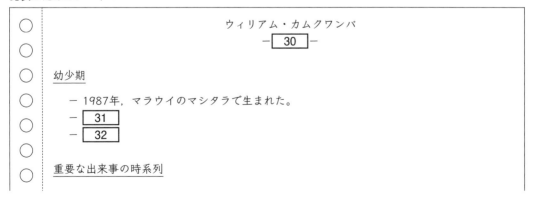

　　　　　　　　　　　　　　ウィリアム・カムクワンバ
　　　　　　　　　　　　　　　　－ 　30 　－

　幼少期

　　－ 1987年，マラウイのマシタラで生まれた。
　　－ 　31
　　－ 　32

　重要な出来事の時系列

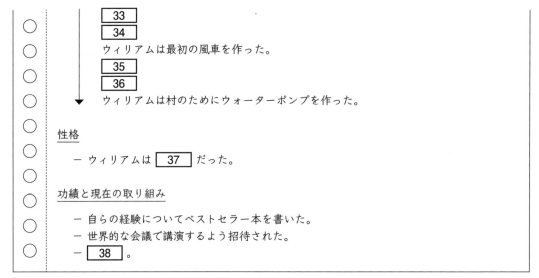

ウィリアムは最初の風車を作った。

| 35 |
| 36 |

↓ ウィリアムは村のためにウォーターポンプを作った。

性格

― ウィリアムは [37] だった。

功績と現在の取り組み

― 自らの経験についてベストセラー本を書いた。
― 世界的な会議で講演するよう招待された。
― [38] 。

【語句・表現】
・engineer「エンジニア，技術者」
・online「オンライン（で）」
〈第1段落〉
・the 2000s「2000年代」
・early「初頭」
・electricity「電気」
・shortage of ～「～の不足」
・lead to ～「～になる」
・terrible「ひどい」
・hunger「飢え，飢餓」
・yearly「年間の」
・fee「料金」
・so that S V「～するために」
・a bit of ～「わずかな～」
・access to ～「～へのアクセス，～を利用する手段・方法」
・instead「代わりに」
・away from ～「～から離れて」
〈第2段落〉
・construct「～を組み立てる・建てる」
・inspire「～を触発する」
・follow「～に従う」
・instruction「指示」
・as ～ as possible「できる限り～」
・pile of ～「～の山」
・spare「余った，予備の」
・back then「その当時」
・rural「田舎の」
・imagine A *doing*「Aが～しているのを想像する」：知覚動詞の用法。
・provide A with B「AにBを供給する」
〈第3段落〉
・material「材料」

・connect A to B「AをBにつなげる」
・battery「バッテリー」
・store「〜を蓄える」
・as a result「その結果」
・stay up *doing*「〜して起きている」
・bring A to B「AをBにもたらす」
・entire「全体の」
・delighted「喜んで」：delight「〜を喜ばせる」という他動詞の過去分詞。
・some kind of 〜「ある種の〜」
〈第4段落〉
・well known「有名な」
・invite「〜を招待する」
・conference「会議」
・rush to *do*「〜しようと殺到する」
・improve「改良する」
・increase「〜を増やす」
・run「動く」
・for the first time「初めて」
・allow A（人）to *do*「A（人）が〜できるようにする」
・water「〜に水をやる」
・crop「作物」
〈第5段落〉
・publish「〜を出版する」
・graduate「卒業する」
〈第6段落〉
・recognized「一般に認められた，名の知れた」
・spirit「精神」
・fight for 〜「〜のために闘う」
・resource「資源」
・generation「世代」
・have a 〜 impact on ...「…に〜な影響を与える」
・positive「プラスの」
〈プレゼン用メモ〉
・best-selling「ベストセラーの」
・global「世界的な」

第6問

A

問1 「 39 に入る最適な選択肢を選びなさい」

① 地球上のほとんどの場所で見つけることができない
② 世界の南の地域出身である
③ 静かな場所よりも騒がしい場所を好む
④ ほとんどのことに左手を使う

正解 ⇒ ④

　第 1 段落第 3 文に righties とは「右手を使うことを好む人」だとあり，compared to about 89% for "righties" と右利きの人と対比されている。よって，southpaw は「左利きの人」のことだとわかる。したがって正解は④である。south は「南」，paw は「人の手，動物の前足」という意味で，語源は諸説あるが，現在は lefty「左利き」の意味として用いられる。

【語句・表現】
・prefer A to B「B よりも A を好む」

問2　「　40　に入る最適な選択肢を選びなさい」

① 一つのことに集中するのが得意
② **反応が速い**
③ 全てのスポーツがうまい
④ タスクをすぐに始める

　正解 ⇒ ②

　第 3 段落に，脳の両側で情報を処理することに慣れていることから，反応速度が速くなる，という主旨の記述があるので，正解は②である。同段落の「一度に複数のことを行うのが得意」という内容から①は誤り。③は「テニスのようなスポーツはうまい」という記述があるが，全てのスポーツではない。④も第 4 段落の内容と異なるため誤り。

【語句・表現】
・be good at 〜「〜が得意である」
・focus on 〜「〜に集中する」
・reaction「反応」
・task「タスク」
・right away「すぐに」

問3　「　41　に入る最適な選択肢を選びなさい」

① 新しいアイデアを考えるのが得意ではない
② 一度に複数のことをすると混乱する
③ **多くの右利き用の物を使わなければならない**
④ 行動が早過ぎるのでよく間違いをする

　正解 ⇒ ③

　第 2 段落に，左利きの人は高いレベルのストレスを抱える理由の一つとして，右利きの人用に作られたはさみや机を使うことが挙げられているので，③が正解。①は同段落に「より創造的である可能性がある」とあること，②は第 3 段落，④は第 4 段落の内容とそれぞれ異なるため，誤りである。

【語句・表現】
・think of 〜「〜のことを考える」
・get confused「混乱する」
・several「いくつかの」

・at once「一度に」
・deal with ～「～を扱う」
・item「アイテム，商品」
・righty「右利きの人」

問4 「　42　と　43　に入る最適な選択肢を選びなさい」

① 賞賛されて
② 負けて
③ **慣れて**
④ 喜んで
⑤ **成功して**
⑥ 疲れて

正解 ⇒ 　42　 ⑤　　43　 ③

　第3段落に，テニスのようなスポーツに長けている理由として，「左利きの人が少ないため，ほとんどの右利きの人が左利きの人と試合をすることはめったにない」と記述されていることから，　42　に⑤ successful，　43　に③ familiar を入れ，「左利きの人は，右利きの人が彼らに慣れていないから，成功する（＝試合に勝つ）のかもしれない」という主旨の文を作る。

【全訳】
　あなたは人々の性格や能力に影響を与える要因についてのクラスプロジェクトに取り組んでいます。インターネットで調べていると，次のような記事を見つけました。この情報を用いてポスターを完成させなさい。

サウスポー（左利きの人）の特異性は何か
　あなたは「サウスポー（左利き）」だろうか。おそらく「いいえ」と答えただろう。なぜなら，左利きの人が世界人口の10%しか占めていないのに対し，「右利き」，つまり右手で物事を行うことを好む人は約89%だからだ。科学者たちは長い間左利きの人に関心を持ってきた。左利きの人の特徴や能力について，右利きの人々と明確な違いがあるかどうかを知ることを目的として，多くの研究が行われてきた。これらの研究を通じて，より一般的な左利きの人の特徴が明らかになってきた。
　1970年代に行われた調査によると，左利きの人は社交的な集まりを避ける傾向が強く，他の人と一緒にいるよりも一人で静かに過ごすことを好むことがわかった。彼らはまた，より高いレベルのストレスを抱えているようで，それはおそらく右利きの人のためにつくられた世界で生きている困難さから生じているのだろう。結局のところ，はさみから一部の学校で使用されている肘掛け付きの机まで，多くの物は左利きの人用に作られていなかった。しかしながら，このことによって，左利きの人は右利きの人よりも予期しない状況に適応する能力を向上させたかもしれない。左利きの人は，また，より創造的である可能性があり，いくつかの研究で，左利きの人が芸術，音楽，デザインなどに生まれながらの才能を持っていることが示された。これは，左手を制御する右脳が創造的思考を担っているからかもしれない。これにより，左利きの人は，物事をさまざまな観点で見ることが要求される問題解決タスクも得意としている。
　さらに，左利きの人は，タスクを完了するために脳の両側で情報を処理することに慣れているため，一度に複数のことを行うのが得意かもしれない。これにより，反応速度も速くなる。これら二つの要素の組み合わせは，多くのスポーツやキーボード入力作業などのスピードが要求される作業では特に有効である。実際，左利きの人がテニスのようなスポーツに長けている可能性が高いことを示した研究もいくつかある。しかし，これは実際には技術が高い結果ではない可能性がある。左利きの人が少ないため，ほとんどの右利きの人が左利きの人と試合をすることはめったにないことが理由だと指摘

している専門家もいる。対戦するプレーヤーのほとんどが右利きであるために，このことが左利きの人を有利にしていて，彼らは何をするべきかわかっているということになる。

最後に，左利きの人は物事を詳細まで考え，より慎重な人である傾向がある。右利きの人はしばしば迅速に決定を下して行動を起こすが，左利きの人はタスクを始めるのにより長い時間がかかる。彼らは全ての選択肢と，それぞれの長所と短所について考えることにより多くの時間をかける。これは，左利きの人が右利きの人よりも仕事を完遂するのに時間がかかる可能性があることを意味する。

これらは全ての左利きの人に当てはまるか。もちろん当てはまらない。研究者たちは，これらの特徴が左利きの人により多く見られることを発見したにすぎない。ここで言及されていない他の特徴についても研究されている。結局のところ，全ての個人は異なり，日常生活で最も使用する利き手だけでは完全に理解できないと覚えておくことが重要なのである。

ポスター:

サウスポーの特異性は何か

サウスポーって何？

サウスポーとは 39 人のこと。

興味深い詳細な情報

● 左利きの人は世界人口のわずか10％である。
● 左利きの人には共通した特性が見られることが研究でわかっている。

左利きの人の一般的な特徴

長所	短所
● 新しい物事によりうまく順応できる ● 40 ● 行動を起こすまで慎重である	● 社交的なイベントが好きではない ● 作業を終えるのにより長い時間がかかる ● 41

さらなる研究が必要な理由

● スポーツにおいて，左利きの人は，より良い技術を持っているからではなく，右利きの人が彼らと対戦するのに 43 いないから 42 しまうのかもしれない。
● 他の特性はまだ研究中であるため，それらが左利きの人の中でより一般的であるかどうかはまだわからない。

【語句・表現】
・work on ～「～に取り組む」
・factor「要因」
・affect「～に影響を与える」
・personality「性格，人格」
・ability「能力」
〈第1段落〉
・southpow「左利きの人」

- (The) chances are (that) S V「～の可能性がある，～の見込みだ」
- make up ～「～を占める・成す」
- compared to ～「～と比べて」
- those who *do*「～する人たち」
- conduct「～を実施する」
- characteristic「特徴」
- with the goal of ～「～を目的に」
- distinct「明確な，際立った」
- feature「特徴」
- common「一般的な」

〈第2段落〉
- the 1970s「1970年代」
- be likely to *do*「～する可能性が高い」
- avoid「～を避ける」
- social gathering「社交的な集まり，親睦会」
- due to ～「～のせいで」
- challenge「困難，難問」
- designed for ～「～のために作られた」
- after all「結局」
- scissors「はさみ」
- arm supports「肘掛け」
- adapt「～に慣れる・適応する」
- unexpected「予期しない」
- natural「生まれながらの」
- talent「才能・適性」
- be responsible for ～「～を担う」
- problem-solving task「問題解決タスク」

〈第3段落〉
- in addition「さらに」
- at a time「一度に」
- be used to *doing*「～に慣れている」
- process information「情報を処理する」
- combine「～を組み合わせる」
- especially「特に」
- eypert「専門家」
- point out ～「～を指摘する」
- rarely「めったに～ない」
- get to *do*「～する機会を得る」
- play (matches) against ～「～と（試合で）戦う」
- advantage「利点」

〈第4段落〉
- tend to *do*「～する傾向がある」
- in detail「詳細に」
- make decisions「決定する」
- take action「動く，動き出す」
- get started「始める」
- strength「長所」
- weakness「短所」

・get a job done「仕事を完了する」
〈第5段落〉
・true of 〜「〜に当てはまる」
・definitely not「まさか，絶対に違う」
・mention「〜について言及する」
・test「〜を試験する・調べる」
・in the end「最後に」
・individual「個人」
・unique「独特の，異なる」
・fully「完全に」
〈ポスター〉
・in common「共通した，共通して」
・dislike「〜が好きではない」

B

問1 「あなたは，記事で『ネットいじめ』という言葉を見て，ノートに意味を書き留めたいと思う。次のうちどれが最も適切か」 44

① 若者の間で人気のあるコミュニケーションの形態。
② 人を不安や悲しい気持ちにさせる病気。
③ ソーシャルメディア上で悪い行いをした人を罰する方法。
④ インターネット上で誰かについて有害なコメントやうそを書くこと。

正解 ⇒ ④

第2段落に「ネットいじめ」についての記述があり，「他人について否定的なコメントをしたり，うそをついたりすること」がいじめの内容であることがわかる。したがって，正解は④である。「ネットいじめ」が①の「人気のあるコミュニケーションの形態」や，②の「病気」であるという記述はないので，いずれも誤り。③は第2段落で言及されているが，これも「ネットいじめ」の定義ではないので誤り。

【語句・表現】
・cyberbullying「ネットいじめ」
・note「メモ」
・appropriate「適切な」
・illness「病気」
・anxious「不安な，心配な」
・punish A for B「AをBを理由に罰する」
・behavior「行い，行動」
・social media「ソーシャルメディア」
・harmful「有害な」
・lie「うそ」

問2 「ソーシャルメディアが若者のコミュニケーションスキルに与える影響に関する記事の中で言及されていないのは次のどれか」 45

① 彼らは他者と面と向かって話すのが得意ではない。
② 彼らは正しい文法を使うのに苦労し始めている。

③　彼らは単語の正しいつづりを覚えない。
④　彼らは他者の言うことが理解できないという問題に直面している。

正解 ⇒ ④

　①～③は全て第4段落に記述がある。第4段落の最終文にある「若者の話す能力が弱くなっている」というのは「他者の言うことが理解できない」ということではないので，述べられていないのは④である。

【語句・表現】
・effect「影響，効果」
・in person「面と向かって，直々に」
・have trouble (in) *doing*「～するのに苦労する」
・correct「正しい」
・grammar「文法」
・proper「正しい，適切な」
・spell「～をつづる」
・face「～に直面する」

問3　「あなたが読んだ記事によると，次のうちどれが正しいか」（二つ選びなさい。順序は問わない）
　　　46　　47

①　10歳未満の子どもが，ソーシャルメディアの影響を最も受けている。
②　**子どもたちは，ソーシャルメディア上で見る子どもたちと自分をしばしば比較する。**
③　ほとんどの若者は少なくとも一度はネットいじめを経験している。
④　**睡眠障害は，ソーシャルメディアを毎日3時間を超えて使用することで生じる可能性がある。**
⑤　若者の自信は，ソーシャルメディアの使用によって向上する傾向がある。

正解 ⇒ ②・④

　自信の低下などの影響を強く受けるのは10歳から19歳までの子どもたちであるため，①は誤り。②については，第1段落に記述があり，子どもたちはソーシャルメディア上の他者と自分を比較するという記述があるので正解。第2段落の最終文に「若者の約27％」が少なくとも一度はネットいじめを経験していると記述があるので③は誤り。第3段落には睡眠障害を起こす可能性についての記述があるので，④は正解である。⑤の内容は言及されておらず，むしろ自信が低下すると書かれているため誤り。

【語句・表現】
・influence「～に影響を及ぼす」
・compare A to B「AとBを比較する」
・experience「～を経験する」
・occur「起こる」
・confidence「自信」
・tend to *do*「～する傾向がある」

問4　「筆者の要点を最もよく説明しているものは次のうちどれか」　48

①　**筆者は，若者はソーシャルメディアの危険性について知る必要があると主張している。**
②　筆者は，若者がソーシャルメディアを使用するための安全な方法はないと主張している。
③　筆者は，ソーシャルメディアの使用制限はリスクを減少させないと述べている。

④　筆者は，ソーシャルメディアは全ての若者に同じように影響を与えると考えている。

正解 ⇒ ①

　第5段落の第2文，However から始まる文章に筆者が特に強調したい内容が書かれている。したがって，正解は①である。②〜④は，全て第5段落の内容と反することから，誤りである。

【語句・表現】
- author「筆者」
- describe「〜について説明する・述べる」
- claim (that) S V「〜と主張する」
- danger of 〜「〜の危険（性）」
- insist (that) S V「〜と主張する」
- state「〜と述べる」
- limit on 〜「〜に対する制限」
- decrease「〜を減少させる」
- affect「影響を及ぼす」

【全訳】
　あなたはソーシャルメディアが若者のメンタルヘルスと発達に及ぼす影響について学んでいます。先生から次の記事を読んでおくように言われています。

　ソーシャルメディアは多くの若者にとって現代の生活で重要性を持ち，友人とつながったり，現在行われている出来事や流行などの情報を入手したりするための場所を提供している。しかし，研究によると，ソーシャルメディアは若者の精神上の健康とその発達に悪影響を与える可能性がある。潜在的な悪影響の一つは，自信への影響である。ソーシャルメディアで他の人の話や写真を見ると，若者は自分が魅力的でも面白くもないと感じ，自信の低下につながる可能性がある。この影響は，自分に対する他者の意見をすでに気にしているであろう10歳から19歳までの子どもに特に強く及ぶ可能性がある。ある研究では，ソーシャルメディアにより多くの時間を費やしている若者は，自信が低く，自分の体型に満足していないと感じていることが示された。

　インターネット上のいじめ，または「ネットいじめ」としばしば呼ばれるものも，若者にとって大きな問題になっている。ソーシャルメディアの普及により，人々は自分の悪い行動を罰せられることなく，他人について否定的なコメントをしたり，うそをついたりすることがはるかに簡単になった。これらのことは，彼らは通常いわれもなく，そのようなひどい扱いを受けるようなことは何もしなかったにもかかわらず，被害者の感情を傷つけるために行われる。ネットいじめは，極度の悲しみや不安など，若者に深刻な影響をもたらす可能性がある。ネットいじめ研究センターが実施した調査によると，13歳から19歳までの若者の約27％が，人生で少なくとも一度はネットいじめを経験している。

　ソーシャルメディアは，若者の睡眠の質と量にも影響を与える可能性がある。研究によると，ソーシャルメディアの使用が多過ぎると，睡眠パターンが乱れ，倦怠感の増加とメンタルヘルスへの悪影響につながる可能性がある。ある研究では，ソーシャルメディアを1日3時間を超えて使用する若者は，使用が少ない若者よりも睡眠障害を起こす可能性が高いことがわかった。別の研究では，若者の60％が就寝前にスマートフォンをチェックし，そのことが毎晩平均1時間の睡眠を減らすことが示された。このことが，学校での成績や，友人，クラスメート，家族との関係など，若者の生活の他の領域に害を及ぼす可能性がある。

　これらのメンタルヘルスの問題に加えて，ソーシャルメディアの使用は子どもたちのコミュニケーションスキルにも影響を与える可能性がある。ソーシャルメディアに書かれる文章の多くは正しい英語で書かれないため，若者は文法に問題を抱えるようになる。彼らはまた，単語の「too」を「2」という数字に置き換えたり，単語のスペルを変えたりするなど，文章をよりクールに見せることも好

む。しかし，このことが，子どもたちにそういった単語の正しいスペルを忘れさせる可能性がある。同様に，ソーシャルメディアに多くの時間を費やすことで，人と対面で話す時間が減る。その結果，若者の話す能力や他の社会的スキルが弱くなっている可能性がある。

　　全ての若者がソーシャルメディアの悪影響を経験するわけではなく，その影響は子どもによって大きく異なる可能性があることを覚えておくことが重要である。しかし，若者は，リスクを認識し，バランスの取れた健全な方法でソーシャルメディアを使用する必要がある。これには，毎日の使用に制限を設定すること，定期的な休憩を取ること，運動や趣味などの他の活動を行うことが含まれるであろう。

【語句・表現】

・mental health「メンタルヘルス，精神上の健康」
・development「発達」

〈第1段落〉
・provide A with B「AにBを供給する・整備する」
・connect with ～「～とつながる」
・stay informed「情報をいつも入手している」
・current「今の」
・trend「トレンド，流行」
・negative「マイナスの」
・potential「潜在的な」
・consequence「影響，結果」
・feel like ～「～のように感じる」
・attractive「魅力的な」
・lead to ～「～に至る，～を引き起こす」
・decrease「減少」
・particularly「特に」
・be likely to do「～しそうである，たぶん～するであろう」
・satisfied「満足して」：satisfy「～を満足させる」という他動詞の過去分詞。

〈第2段落〉
・bullying「いじめ」
・turn into ～「～になる」
・issue「問題」
・with the spread of ～「～の普及にともない」
・tell a lie「うそをつく」
・punishment「罰」
・hurt「～を傷付ける」
・victim「犠牲者」
・innocent「無実の」
・deserve「～に値する」
・terrible「ひどい」
・treatment「扱い」
・serious「重大な，深刻な」
・extreme「極度の」
・sadness「悲しみ」
・anxiety「不安」
・survey「調査」
・conduct「～を行う」
・approximately「およそ」

〈第3段落〉
・affect「～に影響を及ぼす」
・ruin「～をだめにする」
・tiredness「疲労」
・per「～ごとに」
・cause「～を引き起こす」
・average「平均」
・harm「～を傷付ける」
・academic performance「学業成績」
・relationship「関係」
〈第4段落〉
・text「メッセージ，文章」
・proper「適切な」
・replace A with B「A を B に置き換える」
・cool「クールな」
・spelling「つづり，スペル」
・likewise「同様に」
・face to face「顔を合わせて，面と向かって」
〈第5段落〉
・vary from one ～ to another「～によって異なる」
・be aware of ～「～を知る」
・balanced「バランスの取れた」
・set a limit on ～「～に制限を加える」
・usage「使用」
・take a break「休憩する」
・exercise「運動」
・hobby「趣味」

問題番号（配点）	設問		解答番号	正 解	配 点	自己採点
第1問 (10)	A	1	1	3	2	
		2	2	2	2	
	B	1	3	3	2	
		2	4	1	2	
		3	5	2	2	
			自己採点小計			
第2問 (20)	A	1	6	2	2	
		2	7	1	2	
		3	8	3	2	
		4	9	2	2	
		5	10	4	2	
	B	1	11	2	2	
		2	12	1	2	
		3	13	1	2	
		4	14	4	2	
		5	15	5	2	
			自己採点小計			
第3問 (4)		1	16	2	2	
		2	17	2	2	
			自己採点小計			
第4問 (8)		1	18	2	2	
		2	19	2	2	
		3	20	4	2	
		4	21	3	2	
			自己採点小計			

問題番号（配点）	設問	解答番号	正 解	配 点	自己採点
第5問 (16)	1	22	4	3	
	2	23	1	2	
		24	3	2	
	3	25	3	3	
	4	26	2	3	
	5	27	4	3	
		自己採点小計			
第6問 (15)	1	28	4	3	
	2	29	3	3	
	3	30	2	3*1	
		31	3		
		32	5		
		33	1		
	4	34	3	3	
	5	35	1,5*2	3*1	
		36			
		自己採点小計			
第7問 (12)	1	37	3	3	
	2	38	2,4*2	3*1	
		39			
	3	40	1	3	
	4	41	4	3	
		自己採点小計			
第8問 (15)	1	42	3	3	
	2	43	2	3	
	3	44	2,5*2	3*1	
		45			
	4	46	3	3	
	5	47	1	3	
		自己採点小計			
		自己採点合計			

（注）
*1は，全部正解の場合のみ点を与える。
*2は，解答の順序は問わない。

第1問

A

問1 「チラシの目的は何か」 ⬚ 1 ⬚

① 生徒に修学旅行中の案内をすること
② 街の伝統的な建築物を紹介すること
③ ガイドツアーの選択肢を提示すること
④ 史跡に関する情報を提供すること

正解 ⇒ ③

導入文に「あなたは修学旅行で歴史的な街を訪れる予定です。選択可能な二つのガイドツアーについて書かれたプリントを教師から渡されました」とあるので，③が正解。

【語句・表現】
・handout「プリント，ビラ」
・school trip「修学旅行」
・architecture「建築物」
・guided「ガイド付きの，案内のある」
・historical「歴史的な」
・site「遺跡，場所」

問2 「両方のツアーについて正しいものはどれか」 ⬚ 2 ⬚

① ツアー中はいつでも飲食できる。
② ガイドから歴史的な情報を得ることができる。
③ 午前中にツアーを終えることができる。
④ 時代衣装を着ることができる。

正解 ⇒ ②

旧市街ウォーキングツアーには「時代をさかのぼり，植民地時代の街の豊かな歴史を探訪しましょう」「昔ながらの衣装に身を包んだガイドが案内します」，川下りツアーには「経験豊かなガイドが『川の街』の昔話をします」とあることから，正解は②。旧市街ウォーキングツアーの説明の四つ目に「ツアー中の食事は禁止です」とあることから，①は誤り。③については，川下りツアーが「午前11時30分に出発する2時間のクルーズ」とあることから，終了時刻が午後1時30分になることがわかるため誤り。④は旧市街ウォーキングツアーに「昔ながらの衣装に身を包んだガイドが案内します」とあるが，参加者が着用できるわけではない。また，川下りツアーに衣装についての記述はないので誤り。

【語句・表現】
・costume「衣装」

【全訳】
あなたは修学旅行で歴史的な街を訪れる予定です。選択可能な二つのガイドツアーについて書かれたプリントを教師から渡されました。

歴史ツアー	
◆　旧市街ウォーキングツアー 時代をさかのぼり，植民地時代の街の豊かな歴史を探訪しましょう ・　開始は午前9時からで，所要時間は2時間30分（休憩あり）です ・　昔ながらの衣装に身を包んだガイドが案内します ・　歴史的建造物や名所に立ち寄ります ・　ツアー中の食事は禁止です	◆　川下りツアー 川下り観光を楽しみながら，街の歴史を発見しましょう ・　午前11時30分に出発する2時間のクルーズです ・　経験豊かなガイドが「川の街」の昔話をします ・　街の湾岸地域と背後の山々を一望できます ・　船内のカフェで軽食や飲み物が楽しめます
参加方法：どちらのガイドツアーに参加したいですか？ 下記の欄に記入の上，本日中に担任の先生に提出してください。	
1つ（✓）選びなさい：　　旧市街ウォーキングツアー □　　　　川下りツアー □ 名前：_____	

【語句・表現】
〈旧市街ウォーキングツアー〉
・step back「さかのぼる，後ろへ戻る」
・explore「～を探索する」
・colonial「植民地の」
・era「時代」
・continue「続く」
・break「休憩」
・inform「～に知らせる」
・dressed「身にまとった，着用した」
・old-fashioned「昔ながらの」
・historic「歴史上重要な」
・allowed「許された」
〈川下りツアー〉
・cruise「巡航，船旅」
・sightseeing「観光」
・last「続く」
・experienced「経験豊かな」
・bay「湾，入江」
・offer「～を提供する」
・snack「軽食」

B
問1　「メロディー・ミュージック・ワークショップの全ての講師は　3　ことがある」

---
① 音楽コンサートに出演した
② 全国音楽コンクールで優勝した
③ **音楽教育に携わった**
④ 人気アーティストに楽曲を提供した

正解 ⇒ ③

全員の講師に共通する経験は指導・教育なので，③が正解。①について当てはまるのは「歌唱」の講師だけ。②に該当する講師はいない。作詞作曲の講師のみが④の経験をもつ。

【語句・表現】
・instructor「講師，指導員」
・workshop「講習会，研修」
・perform「実演する，歌を歌う」
・competition「コンクール，コンテスト」
・education「教育」

問2　「講習会の最終日，全ての参加者は　4　」

①　上達を披露するために競い合う
②　互いの実演を評価し合う
③　他の講習参加者とバンドを組む
④　オリジナル曲を作る

　正解 ⇒ ①

　全ての講習会で，最終日に指示されているのはコンテストに参加することなので，①が正解。②は記述がない。また③，④はそれぞれ「楽器」と「作詞作曲」の講習会だけで行う活動だ。

【語句・表現】
・participant「参加者」
・compete「競争する，競う」
・improvement「上達，向上」
・evaluate「～を評価する」
・join「～に加わる，参加する」
・composition「作品，曲」

問3　「講習会に申し込んだ後に何があるか」　5

①　どれでも好きな講習会に参加する。
②　対面での面接に招かれる。
③　オンラインの面接で音楽の能力を見せる。
④　講師によって紙の申込書が確認される。

　正解 ⇒ ②

　「申込方法」の手順2から正解は②だ。①は手順3から誤り。③は「オンラインの面接で」能力を見せるという記述がないので誤り。④については手順1から，申し込みは「紙」ではなく「オンライン」だということが分かる。また申込書が講師によって確認されるという記述はないので誤り。

【語句・表現】
・submit「～を提出する」
・application「申し込み」
・attend「～に参加する」
・whichever 名詞 S'V'「～するどの…でも」

・interview「面接」
・online「オンラインの，ネットワークを利用した」

【全訳】

　あなたはアメリカに留学している高校生で，夏休み中に音楽の腕前を上げたいと考えています。ある有名な音楽学校が企画する音楽講習会の広告を目にしました。

メロディー・ミュージック・ワークショップ
メロディー・ミュージック・ワークショップ（MMW）は1995年から，高校生のための音楽講習会を提供しています。音楽漬けの２週間を過ごしましょう！

日程：2024年７月15日～28日
場所：ハーモニーホール（カリフォルニア州サンフランシスコ）
費用：800ドル（指導料と楽器の利用料を含みます。個人レッスンと，その際の楽器レンタルは別途料金が必要）

講習内容

◆**歌唱**：歌唱技術や舞台度胸を学び，流行歌をグループで演奏します。講師は音楽業界での指導経験があり，様々なコンサートやイベントに出演しています。講習会の最終日にはコンテストに参加し，実力を発揮してください。

◆**楽器**：好きな楽器（ギター・ピアノ・ドラム・バイオリン）を選び，専門的な指導を受けることができます。各楽器の講師は，音楽教育や演奏に精通しています。参加者同士でバンドを組み，最終日に賞を狙って他のバンドと競い合ってください。

◆**作詞作曲**：作曲技術を磨き，他の参加者と協力してオリジナル曲を作りましょう。講師は音楽教師でありかつ，人気アーティストの楽曲も手がけるプロのシンガーソングライターです。７月28日の音楽イベントで，あなたたちのオリジナル曲を披露するコンテストに参加しましょう。

▲**申込方法**
手順１：2024年６月15日までに，<u>こちら</u>のオンライン応募フォームに入力してください。
手順２：当方から連絡してあなた自身と音楽の力を詳しく知るための，対面での面接日時を設定します。
手順３：あなたの音楽の力や興味に応じて，いずれかの講習会に割り振られます。

【語句・表現】
〈導入文〉
・improve「～を向上させる」
・skill「腕前，技能」
・come across「～を見つける」
・advertisement「広告」
・plan「～を計画する」
〈チラシ冒頭〉
・fully「たっぷり，まるまる」
・include「～を含む」
・instruction「指導」
・access to ～「～の利用」
・musical instrument「楽器」
・optional「選択制の」

・private「個人的な」
・rental「貸し付け」
・additional fee「追加料金」
・require「～を必要とする」
〈歌唱〉
・vocal「ボーカル，音声の」
・technique「技術」
・stage presence「舞台度胸」
・industry「業界」
・take part in ～「～に参加する」
〈楽器〉
・receive「～を受ける」
・specialized「専門的な」
・background「経歴」
・fellow「仲間」
・prize「賞」
〈作詞作曲〉
・develop「～を発達させる」
・songwriting「作詞作曲」
・collaborate「協力する」
・A as well as B「Bだけでなく A も」
・participate in「～に参加する」

第2問

A

問1 「メーカーが述べている内容によると，新しい電子書籍リーダーの使い方として適切で<u>ない</u>のはどれか」 ┃ 6 ┃

> ① 電車でオーディオブックを聞くこと
> ② **入浴中に小説を読むこと**
> ③ 庭で写真集を見ること
> ④ 電子書籍のレシピにメモを書くこと

　正解 ⇒ ②

　「特色」の末尾に「ただし，防水機能はありません」とあることから，入浴中に使用してはいけないことがわかるので，正解は②。「強み」の欄で，ヘッドフォンを使ってオーディオブックを聞くことができると書かれていることから，①は問題ない。③，④についても，使用上問題となるような記述はない。

【語句・表現】
・maker「製造業者，メーカー」
・statement「陳述，述べること」
・appropriate「適切な」
・e-book reader「電子書籍リーダー」
・audio book「オーディオブック」：書籍の内容の朗読を録音したもの。
・recipe「レシピ」

問2 「ブレイン **SP** 電子書籍リーダーが提供する恩恵のうち，あなたにとって最も魅力的でありそうなのはどれか」 ☐ 7

> ① 紙の書籍からスキャンデータを得られること
> ② 自動で明るさが調節されること
> ③ 電子書籍上にメモをとること
> ④ 新しい書籍のお勧めを受け取ること

正解 ⇒ ①

リード文に「あなたは本棚に本があり過ぎて，スペースがなくなってしまったため，電子書籍リーダーを買いたいと思っています」とあることから，紙の本を電子化してくれるサービスに最も魅力を感じると思われる。正解は①。

【語句・表現】
・benefit「恩恵，利益」
・be likely to *do*「〜しそうである」
・appeal to 〜「〜の心に訴える」
・brightness「明るさ」
・adjust「〜を調節する」
・automatically「自動で」
・recommendation「お勧め」

問3 「利用者が述べているひとつの意見は ☐ 8 というものだ」

> ① オーディオブックはヘッドフォンなしでも聞くことができる
> ② 機器を使っての読書は紙の本を読むこととは全く異なる
> ③ お勧めされる本は面白い
> ④ 読書好きにとってストレージが小さ過ぎる

正解 ⇒ ③

利用者の最初のコメントに「さまざまな書籍を紹介してくれますが，その多くが興味深いです」とあるので，③が正解。①は事実としては正しいが，利用者の「意見」ではない。②は「私は子供のころからの本好きですが，今は紙の本で読んでいた時と同じように読書を楽しんでいます」，④は「もっと小容量でいいのでもっと安いのがあればいいと思います」というコメントとそれぞれ矛盾するため，不正解。

【語句・表現】
・state「〜を述べる」
・customer「顧客」
・device「機器」
・totally「全く，完全に」
・recommend「〜を勧める」
・storage「ストレージ」：パソコンなどの電子機器がデータを記憶する場所。

問4 「ある利用者が暗い部屋で読書をする際の問題点に言及している。このコメントはどの特徴に基づいているか」 ☐ 9

① オーディオブック
② **明るさの自動調節**
③ 新しい本のお勧め
④ スキャンデータの利用

正解 ⇒ ②

　利用者のコメントの中に「暗い部屋で読書をする時にライトが明る過ぎることがあり，自分で明度を下げる必要があります」というものがあり，これが該当のコメントであることがわかる。これに関連するのは，周囲の明るさによって自動で明るさを調整する機能であるので，正解は②。

【語句・表現】
・mention「〜に言及する」
・feature「特徴」
・be based on 〜「〜に基づいている」
・automatic「自動的な」
・adjustment「調節」
・available「利用可能な」

問5　「ある利用者のコメントによると，　10　は良い考えである」

① 書籍リーダーへの追加のストレージ
② メーカーのお勧めを無視すること
③ ライトをできるだけ明るくすること
④ **タイピングでメモをとること**

正解 ⇒ ④

　利用者のコメントに「たくさん書く際は付属のペンを使うよりもタイピングで入力する方が好きです」とあることから，④が正解。他の選択肢については，該当する内容が述べられているコメントがない。

【語句・表現】
・additional「追加の」
・ignore「〜を無視する」
・bright「明るい」

【全訳】
　あなたは本棚に本があり過ぎて，スペースがなくなってしまったため，電子書籍リーダーを買いたいと思っています。あなたはイギリスのウェブサイトを調べており，この広告を見つけました。

コージー電子が新しいブレイン SP 電子書籍リーダーを発表

ブレイン SP はあなたの読書生活をより良くする電子書籍リーダーです。3 色でお求めいただけます。

特色
ブレイン SP 電子書籍リーダーは，これまでにないくらい滑らかで素早い反応をもたらし，ストレスなくページをめくることができます。さらに，付属のタッチペンまたはソフトウェアのキーボードを使って文章に線を引いたり電子書籍上にメモをとったりすることができます。メモは自由に並べ替えること

ができるので，特定のメモを難なく見つけることができます。リスト上のメモをクリックすれば，そのメモを書いたページに飛ぶことができます。他のコージー電子製の電子書籍リーダーと同様に，長時間使用できる電池と大容量のストレージ（32ギガバイトまたは64ギガバイト）を備えています。ただし，防水機能はありません。

強み

オーディオブック：ヘッドフォンまたは内蔵のスピーカーでオーディオブックを聞くことができます。
明るさの自動調整：内蔵センサーが周囲の明るさを感知し，明度を調整します。これにより，電車でも公園のベンチでもベッドの中でも快適に読書をすることができます。
新しい本のお勧め：あなたの選択に基づいて，好みに合いそうな本を紹介します。
スキャンデータの利用：自分の書籍をオフィスにお送りいただければ，電子書籍の形のスキャンデータを得られます。（*お送りいただいた書籍の返却はできません。**一部の書籍は著作権上の問題で受け入れられません）

利用者のコメント
- さまざまな書籍を紹介してくれますが，その多くが興味深いです。
- 私は写真や音のない本をダウンロードしていますが，ストレージがいっぱいになりそうにありません。もっと小容量でいいのでもっと安いのがあればいいと思います。
- 使いやすい！　私は子供のころからの本好きですが，今は紙の本で読んでいた時と同じように読書を楽しんでいます。
- 一つ不満があるとすれば，防水でないことです。ビーチに持っていきたいのですが。
- メモをとって簡単に見つけられるのがとても役立ちます。たくさん書く際は付属のペンを使うよりもタイピングで入力する方が好きです。
- 眠りにつこうとする時に内蔵スピーカーでオーディオブックを聞いています。
- 暗い部屋で読書をする時にライトが明る過ぎることがあり，自分で明度を下げる必要があります。

【語句・表現】
・bookshelf「本棚」
・advertisement「広告」
・present「～を発表する，提示する」
・improve「～を向上させる」
〈特色〉
・provide「～を提供する」
・smooth「滑らかな，スムーズな」
・response「反応，応答」
・flip「～をめくる」
・arrange「～を並べる」
・specific「特定の」
・tap「～を軽くたたく，タップする」
・as with ～「～と同様に」
・long-lasting「長持ちする」
・battery「電池」
・amount「量」
・gigabyte「ギガバイト」：記憶容量の単位。
〈強み〉
・built-in「内蔵の，組み込みの」
・sensor「センサー」

・surrounding「周囲の」

・intensity「強さ」

・enable A to *do*「A が～するのを可能にする」

・comfortably「快適に」

・accept「～を受け入れる」

・due to ～「～のせいで」

・copyright「著作権」

〈利用者のコメント〉

・a variety of ～「さまざまな～」

・prefer「～をより好む」

・childhood「子供の頃」

・complain about ～「～について不満を言う」

・waterproof「防水の」

・quite「かなり」

・lower「～を下げる」

B

問1 「アスコットフィールド校内数学大会の目的は ☐ 11 ☐ ことであった」

> ① 生徒に大学で数学を研究することを奨励する
> ② **生徒に数学がどれほど興味深いのか気づいてもらう手助けをする**
> ③ 生徒の計算力を効率的に向上させる
> ④ 生徒に数学の難しさを示す

正解 ⇒ ②

　イギリス人学生が書いた記事の第3，4文において「しかし，数学を学ぶことは興味深く，教科書は言うまでもなく私たちの日常生活にも数学によって解ける問題が多く存在する。昨秋の10月7日，8日に，私たちの数学研究部は11年生から13年生の生徒が実生活に関わる数学の問題に答えるオンライン数学大会を開催した」とあることから，②が正解。

【語句・表現】

・competition「大会，競争」

・encourage A to *do*「A を～するように励ます」

・realise「～に気がつく」：イギリス式つづり。アメリカ英語では realize とつづる。

・improve「～を向上させる」

・calculation「計算」

・efficiently「効率的に，効果的に」

問2 「アスコットフィールド校内数学大会に関するある事実は ☐ 12 ☐ ことである」

> ① **参加者の10分の1以下は13年生であった**
> ② 参加者の半数以上が11年生の生徒であった
> ③ 参加者は自身の答案を紙面で提出することが許されていた
> ④ 生徒たちは大会前に数学の良い成績をとる必要があった

正解 ⇒ ①

　イギリス人学生が書いた記事の第6文において「この大会は120名の参加者を集めたが，その内の半数以上は12年生であり，約5分の2が11年生，13年生の参加者数はたったの10人であった」という記述より，②は誤りで①が正解。③に関しては，第5文の「各参加者は2時間以内に自身の答えをインターネット上で提出しなければならなかった」という記述より，誤り。④に関しては，該当する記述が本文中に存在しないため，不適。

【語句・表現】
・fewer than ～「～未満」
・participant「参加者」
・Year 13「（イギリスの学制における）13年生」：イギリスでは，Year 11は15歳から16歳，Year 12は16歳から17歳，Year 13は17歳から18歳の学年にあたる。
・competitor「競技参加者」
・allow A to *do*「Aが～するのを許可する」
・submit「～を提出する」

問3　「参加者のコメントによると，アスコットフィールド校内数学大会によってある生徒は　13　ことができた」

---

①　学校の数学のテストでよりうまくいく
②　数学を愛する友達を何人もつくる
③　大学の入学試験に合格する
④　数学は日常生活を変えることができることに気がつく

　正解 ⇒ ①

　記事中の参加者たちのコメントにおける2人目のRSさんの「この大会で私はもっと勉強する気になりました。大会の後，学校の数学のテストで過去最高得点をとりました」という記述から，①が正解。

【語句・表現】
・enable A to *do*「Aが～するのを可能にする」
・several「何人かの」
・entrance examination「入学試験」
・daily life「日常生活」

問4　「アスコットフィールド校内数学大会の参加者の何人かは　14　と考えている」

---

①　来年の数学大会は中止すべきである
②　数学の問題は難しすぎて答えられなかった
③　2時間の試験時間を変更すべきである
④　答案の提出方法を再検討すべきである

　正解 ⇒ ④

　記事中の参加者たちのコメントにおける3人目BJさんの「大会の数学の問題は解く価値があると思いましたが，コンピューターのトラブルで自分の答えをアップロードすることができませんでした。別の提出方法があったらいいなと感じます」という記述，及び5人目DCさんの「私には自分の答えのアップロードの仕方を理解するのが難しく感じました。複雑だったので次回は変更すべきです」という記述より，④が正解。

【語句・表現】

・cancel「～を中止する」：過去形・過去分詞形の cancelled はイギリス式つづり。アメリカ英語では canceled とつづる。

・testing time「試験時間」

・reconsider「～を再検討する」

問5 「　15　のコメントによって筆者の問いに答えることができる」

① BJ & DC
② BJ & TM
③ DC & RS
④ DC & TM
⑤ **LT & TM**
⑥ LT & RS

正解 ⇒ ⑤

　　本文第7文より，筆者の問いは「なぜ12年生の参加者数は11年生や13年生よりも多かったのか」であり，これに対して参加者 LT さんの「13年生の友達のひとりは，大学の出願準備に忙しすぎて，この数学のコンテストに参加できませんでした。他の13年生にも当てはまるかもしれません」というコメント，加えて参加者 TM さんの「私は11年生でこの挑戦を本当に楽しみましたが，参加登録期間後になって初めてこのイベントの存在を知ったクラスメイトが多かったのは残念でした」というコメントが参考になる。よって，⑤の組み合わせが正解。

【語句・表現】

・author「著者」

【全訳】

　　あなたは高校で数学研究部に所属している。部員たちはより多くの生徒に数学に興味を抱いてもらえるようなイベントを計画している。あなたはイギリスの学生が書いた学校の記事を見つけた。

アスコットフィールド校内数学大会

　　学校で数学を学ぶことが嫌いな生徒もいる。特に試験期間中に彼らが数学に悪戦苦闘している声を耳にしたり姿を目にしたりすることも多いかもしれない。しかし，数学を学ぶことは興味深く，教科書は言うまでもなく私たちの日常生活にも数学によって解ける問題が多く存在する。昨秋の10月7日，8日に，私たちの数学研究部は11年生から13年生の生徒が実生活に関わる数学の問題に答えるオンライン数学大会を開催した。各参加者は2時間以内に自身の答えをインターネット上で提出しなければならなかった。この大会は120名の参加者を集めたが，その内の半数以上は12年生であり，約5分の2が11年生，13年生の参加者数はたった10人であった。なぜ12年生の参加者数は11年生や13年生よりも多かったのか。以下の参加者たちのコメントがこの問いに答える手助けになるかもしれない。

参加者のコメント

LT：　13年生の友達のひとりは，大学の出願準備に忙しすぎて，この数学のコンテストに参加できませんでした。他の13年生にも当てはまるかもしれません。

RS：　この大会で私はもっと勉強する気になりました。大会の後，学校の数学のテストで過去最高得点をとりました。

BJ：　大会の数学の問題は解く価値があると思いましたが，コンピューターのトラブルで自分の答えをアップロードすることができませんでした。別の提出方法があったらいいなと感じます。

TM：　私は11年生でこの挑戦を本当に楽しみましたが，参加登録期間後になって初めてこのイベントの存在を知ったクラスメイトが多かったのは残念でした。

DC：　このような特別なイベントを開催してもらいありがとうございます。私には自分の答えのアップロードの仕方を理解するのが難しく感じました。複雑だったので次回は変更すべきです。

【語句・表現】
・dislike「～を嫌う」
・struggle with ～「～に苦戦する」
・especially「特に」
・period「期間」
・A as well as B「B は言うまでもなく A も，B と同様に A も」
・related to ～「～に関連する」
・within「～以内に」
・gather「～を集める」
・more than ～「～以上」
・half「半分」
・participate「参加する」
・below「以下に」
・help to *do*「～するのに役立つ」
・take part in ～「～に参加する」
・be busy *doing*「～するのに忙しい」
・prepare for ～「～の準備をする」
・application「応募，申請」
・be the case with ～「～に当てはまる」
・motivate A to *do*「A を動機づけて～させる」
・ever「今までに」
・worth「～の価値がある」
・upload「～をアップロードする」
・due to ～「～のせいで，～が原因で」
・wish（that）S V「～を願う」：事実に反するあるいは可能性が低い願望を表し，that に続く文では仮定法を用いる。
・it's a pity（that）S V「～は残念なことである」
・notice「～に気がつく」
・entry「参加登録」
・complicated「複雑な」

第3問

問1 「食べるのに安全なハンバーガーを用意するためには，　16　必要がある」

① 少し脂肪分のある肉を選ぶ
② ビーフパティを十分な時間加熱する
③ 牛ひき肉を塩や黒コショウと十分に混ぜる
④ 動物の油ではなくサラダ油を使う

正解 ⇒ ②

　第1段落第8〜9文に「食中毒を防ぐためにパティを確実によく加熱してください。推奨される加熱時間はおよそ10分です」とあることから，②が正解。脂肪分のある肉を選ぶのはハンバーガーをおいしくするためであり，安全性とは関係がないため，①は誤り。牛ひき肉を塩や黒コショウと十分に混ぜるのはパティがバラバラにならないようにするためなので，③も誤り。サラダ油については記述がないため，④も誤り。

【語句・表現】
・prepare「〜を用意する」
・contain「〜を含む」
・heat「〜を加熱する」
・ground beef「牛ひき肉」
・salt「塩」
・pepper「コショウ」
・salad oil「サラダ油」

問2　「アドバイスに従うなら，どのようにハンバーガーを作るべきか」　　17

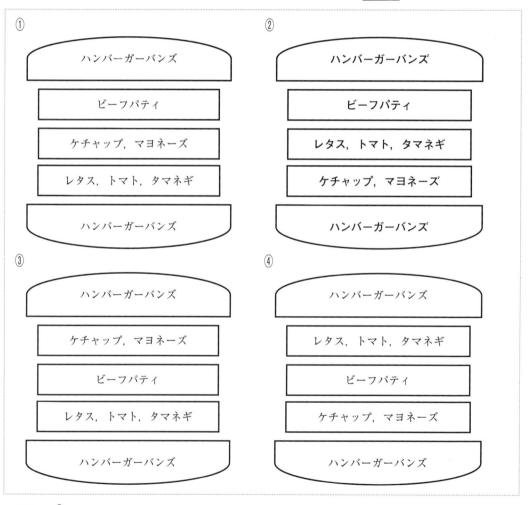

正解 ⇒ ②

　具材の順序については第2段落に書かれている。「トーストしたハンバーガーバンズの下半分にトマトケチャップとマヨネーズを塗り広げて，バンズの上に野菜を乗せます」より，下のバンズの上がケチャップとマヨネーズ，その上が野菜だと分かる。次に「そしてその上にビーフパティを乗せます。最後に一番上にハンバーガーバンズの上半分を乗せ」という記述より，野菜の上がビーフパティだと分かる。したがって，適切なのは②だ。

【語句・表現】
・follow「～に従う」
・hamburger bun「ハンバーガーバンズ」
・patty「パティ」
・ketchup「ケチャップ」
・mayonnaise「マヨネーズ」
・lettuce「レタス」

【全訳】
　あなたはシドニーの高校で学んでいます。調理実習の準備をするために教科書を読んでいるところです。

ハンバーガーの作り方

　まずはバーガーパティを作る必要があります。いくらか脂肪分を含んだ牛ひき肉を用意するのが大切です。これによりハンバーガーがよりジューシーになります。牛ひき肉に塩と黒コショウを加えて，それらが見えなくなるまで混ぜます。もし十分に混ざっていないと，焼いている間にビーフパティがバラバラになってしまいます。そして牛ひき肉をフライパンに入れ，2分の1インチの厚さのパティになるように軽く押し広げます。茶色くなるまで焼きます。食中毒を防ぐためにパティを確実によく加熱してください。推奨される加熱時間はおよそ10分です。

　提供する前に，トーストしたハンバーガーバンズの下半分にトマトケチャップとマヨネーズを塗り広げて，バンズの上に野菜を乗せます。野菜の順序は問いません。マヨネーズに含まれる油分が，バンズが野菜の水分を吸収するのを防ぎます。そしてその上にビーフパティを乗せます。最後に一番上にハンバーガーバンズの上半分を乗せ，ハンバーガーを一緒に軽く押し付けます。

【語句・表現】
・prepare for ～「～に備える」
〈第1段落〉
・juicy「汁気が多くておいしい，ジューシーな」
・fall apart「バラバラになる」
・fry「～を焼く」
・gently「優しく」
・1/2-inch-thick「2分の1インチの厚みの」
・prevent「～を防ぐ」
・food poisoning「食中毒」
・make sure S V「～するのを確実にする」
・well-done「よく焼かれた」
・recommend「～を勧める」
〈第2段落〉
・serve「提供する」
・spread A with B「AにBを塗る」
・order「順番」

・matter「重要である」
・keep A from *doing*「A が〜するのを防ぐ」
・absorb「〜を吸収する」
・place「〜を置く」
・lightly「軽く」

第4問

問1 「コメント(1)に基づくと，どの文を加えるのが最適か」 <u>18</u>

> ① 博物館は自分たちがこのことの責任を負うべきだと認めている。
> **② 博物館は適切な環境を用意することでこれを防いでいる。**
> ③ 博物館はこのことを多くの人に知らせようとしている。
> ④ 博物館はこれを生じさせるために特別な技術を用いている。

正解 ⇒ ②

　空所の前の文は「世界の各地域にはたくさんの遺産が存在しているが，適切に手入れをしなければ，それらはすぐに壊れて美しさを失ってしまうだろう」となっており，これが各選択肢にある this の指す内容だと言える。後ろには「したがって，博物館は私たちの過去を守る存在だと言うことができる」という内容が続いていることから，空所には前文の内容に対して博物館がどのように対処しているかを述べた文を入れるべきである。また，第2段落第1文に「第一に，博物館は文化的，歴史的に価値のあるものを良い状態で保存している」とあることから，博物館は適切な手入れをすることで遺産が「すぐに壊れて美しさを失ってしまう」のを防いでおり，「私たちの過去を守る存在」になっていることがわかる。したがって，正解は②。遺産が失われてしまうことの責任が博物館にあるという記述はないため，①は誤り。③や④を入れても「博物館が私たちの過去を守る存在」という内容にうまくつながらない。

【語句・表現】
・based on 〜「〜に基づいて」
・sentence「文」
・add「〜を加える」
・admit「〜を認める」
・be to blame for 〜「〜に対して責任がある」
・prevent「〜を防ぐ」
・provide「〜を与える，用意する」
・proper「適切な」
・technique「技術」

問2 「コメント(2)に基づくと，どの表現を加えるのが最適か」 <u>19</u>

> ① その結果
> **② 例えば**
> ③ 対照的に
> ④ さらに

正解 ⇒ ②

　これも空所の前後を確認しよう。後ろの文の「古代エジプトのつぼや道具を見ると，当時の生活につい

て，単に書物を読むよりも，生き生きと想像することができる」というのは，前文の「自分が目にしているものを通して歴史について学ぶことができる」という内容の具体例と言うことができる。したがって，正解は②。

【語句・表現】

・expression「表現」

問3　「コメント⑶に基づくと，どれがトピックセンテンスを書き換える最適の方法か」 ☐20

> ① 大都市に位置している
> ② 新しい流行を生み出す
> ③ 地域の雇用を改善する
> **④ 観光業の増加につながる**

　正解 ⇒ ④

　topic sentence「トピックセンテンス」とは，その段落の概要を端的に表した文のことだ。この段落では，観光都市の多くに博物館があり人気の観光地になっていること，文化と芸術の街としてのイメージを向上させることに寄与することが挙げられている。これらの内容を最も適切にまとめたのは，観光業への利点について触れている④だ。本文中では，観光都市の例としてパリやロンドン，ニューヨークといった大都市が挙げられているが，大都市に位置していることが博物館の役割というわけではないので①は誤り。

【語句・表現】

・appropriate「適切な」
・rewrite「～を書き直す」
・be located「位置している」
・create「～を生み出す，創造する」
・trend「流行」
・improve「～を改善する」
・local「地域の」
・employment「雇用」
・lead to ～「～につながる，～をもたらす」
・tourism「観光業」

問4　「コメント⑷に基づくと，どれが最も適切な置き換えか」 ☐21

> ① 地域社会に利益をもたらす
> ② 世界中から最新の情報を集める
> **③ 見物客が過去について学ぶ助けとなる**
> ④ 標準的な教育制度を提供する

　正解 ⇒ ③

　最終段落では全体の結論を述べており，「貴重なものを将来の世代に伝える」というのが第2段落，「世界中から観光客を集める」というのが第4段落の要旨となっており，下線部（4）は第3段落のまとめとなればよいことがわかる。第3段落では，展示物を通して見物客が歴史について学べるという，博物館の教育的な役割について言及している。これを端的に表したのは③だ。

【語句・表現】
・replacement「置き換え」
・profit「利益」
・community「共同体」
・collect「～を集める」
・latest「最新の」
・standard「標準的な」
・educational system「教育制度」

【全訳】
　英語の授業であなたは自分の興味のあるテーマについて作文を書いています。これはあなたが書いた直近の原稿です。あなたは今，先生のコメントに基づいて修正をしているところです。

博物館の役割	
多くの人はしっかりと認識していないものの，博物館は社会においてさまざまな役割を果たしている。日本には4,000以上の博物館あるいは同様の目的を持った施設があり，１年で合計30万人ほどが博物館を訪れていると言われている。この作文は博物館が果たしている３つの主な役割について論じる。	
第一に，博物館は文化的，歴史的に価値のあるものを良い状態で保存している。世界の各地域にはたくさんの遺産が存在しているが，適切に手入れをしなければ，それらはすぐに壊れて美しさを失ってしまうだろう。⁽¹⁾∧ したがって，博物館は私たちの過去を守る存在だと言うことができる。	(1)　ここに足りないものがあります。２文の間をつなぐために情報を加えましょう。
加えて，博物館は収集物を適切な配置で展示することで教育的な役割を果たしている。見学者は自分が目にしているものを通して歴史について学ぶことができる。⁽²⁾∧ 古代エジプトのつぼや道具を見ると，当時の生活について，単に書物を読むよりも，生き生きと想像することができる。	(2)　ここに接続表現を挿入しましょう。
最後に，博物館は₍₃₎<u>素晴らしい場所だ</u>。実際，パリやロンドン，ニューヨークといった世界的に有名な観光都市には著名な博物館があり，最も人気のある観光地の一つとなっている。博物館は都市にお金をもたらすだけでなく，文化と芸術の都市としてイメージを高めている。	(3)　このトピックセンテンスはこの段落にあまりふさわしくありません。書き直しましょう。
結論として，博物館は貴重なものを将来の世代に伝え，₍₄₎<u>収集物を見せ，世界中から観光客を集める</u>という点で社会にとって有益なものである。	(4)　下線部の表現はあなたの作文の内容を十分にまとめていません。変えましょう。
総評： あなたの作文は良くなっていますね。この調子で頑張ってください。（博物館はよく訪れますか。お気に入りがあればぜひ教えてください！☺）	

【語句・表現】
・draft「原稿」
・work on ～「～に取り組む」

・revision「修正，改訂」
〈第 1 段落〉
・a variety of ～「さまざまな～」
・role「役割」
・fully「十分に」
・be aware of ～「～に気づいている」
・facility「施設」
・similar「似た」
・purpose「目的」
〈第 2 段落〉
・preserve「～を保存する」
・valuable「価値のある」
・heritage「遺産」
・keeper「保持者，管理人」
〈第 3 段落〉
・in addition「加えて，さらに」
・display「～を展示する」
・arrangement「配置，配列」
・pot「つぼ，かめ」
・ancient「古代の」
・Egypt「エジプト」
・imagine「～を想像する」
・vividly「生き生きと，鮮明に」
〈第 4 段落〉
・in fact「実際に」
・destination「目的地」
・tourist「観光客」
・point out「～を指摘する」
〈第 5 段落〉
・in conclusion「結論として，要するに」
・beneficial「有益な」
・in that S V「～という点で」
・hand down「～を（後世に）残す，伝える」
・generation「世代」
・attract「～を引きつける」

第 5 問

問 1 「スタローンは　 22 　と考えている」

① 怒りは十分な睡眠を取るとより良くコントロールできる
② 怒りは普通の精神状態ではない
③ 空腹の時に怒りを感じやすい
④ うつ状態の時に怒りを感じ続けることがある

正解 ⇒ ④

　スタローンの意見に関する設問なので，一つ目の記事を参照する。第 5 段落第 1 文に「怒りが続くのは，

時にうつ病の兆候である」とあるため，④が正解。睡眠や空腹時について述べられている箇所はないので，①と③は誤り。第４段落第１文に「怒るのは普通のことだ」とあるので，②も誤り。

【語句・表現】
・mental「精神の，心理的な」
・condition「状態」
・be likely to *do*「～しやすい」
・depressed「うつ状態の」

問２ 「スターローンによると　23　のような脳の感情に関する部分は10代の頃によく発達するが，一方で　24　のような思考に関する部分は違う」

① **扁桃体**
② エストロゲン
③ **前頭前皮質**
④ プロゲステロン
⑤ テストステロン
⑥ トリプトファン

正解 ⇒　23　①　　24　③

　問題文に「スターローンによると」とあるので，一つ目の記事を参照する。問題文にあるような感情と思考の対比については，第２段落に記述がある。第３文に「扁桃体をはじめとする感情的な領域は，10代では（実際，生まれたときから）よく発達しているが，感情を制御する前頭前皮質はあまり発達していないことがわかっている」とあることから，10代で発達しているのは扁桃体，発達していないのは前頭前皮質だとわかる。したがって，正解は　23　が①，　24　が③。

【語句・表現】
・according to ～「～によると」
・well-developed「よく発達した」
・amygdala「扁桃体」
・oestrogen「エストロゲン」
・prefrontal cortex「前頭前皮質」
・progesterone「プロゲステロン」
・testosterone「テストステロン」
・tryptophan「トリプトファン」

問３ 「セロトニンとは　25　ホルモンである」

① 食べ物から直接摂取できる
② 怒りだけでなくうつも引き起こす
③ **我々が悪い感情を制御するのを助けてくれる**
④ 基本的に女性にのみ見られる

正解 ⇒ ③

　セロトニンの話が出てくる二つ目の記事を参照する。第３段落第１～２文で「私たちが制御できるもう一つのホルモンは，幸せを感じさせるセロトニンである。セロトニンは脳内で生成され，気分の調節に重

要な役割を果たしている」と述べられていることから，③が正解。第 4 段落第 3 文に「食べ物から直接セロトニンを摂取することは不可能」とあるため①は誤り。②の怒りやうつを引き起こすホルモンや，④の女性にのみ見られるホルモンについては二つ目の記事には言及がないため，これらも誤り。

【語句・表現】
・hormone「ホルモン」
・directly「直接に」
・cause「～を引き起こす」
・depression「うつ」
・help A to *do*「A が～するのを手助けする」
・basically「基本的に」
・female「女性」

問 4　「筆者は二人とも　26　という点で同意している」

①	怒りはしばしば運動不足につながる
②	**長期にわたる怒りは避けられるべきだ**
③	男性よりも女性の方がうつになりやすい
④	たとえ世界が敵対していても，我々は怒ってはならない

　正解 ⇒ ②

　二つ目の記事の第 1 段落第 1 文に「頻繁に，あるいは常に怒りを感じるのは良いことではないというスタローン氏の考えに私は賛同する」とあるため，②が正解。①，③，④と合致する記述はどちらの記事にもないため，誤り。

【語句・表現】
・lead to ～「～につながる」
・lack「不足」
・long-term「長期の」
・ought to *do*「～すべきである」
・suffer from ～「～に苦しむ」
・even if「たとえ～だとしても」
・be against ～「～に反対している」

問 5　「二人の著者の意見が異なるのは，　27　かどうかだ」

①	少年も少女も怒りについて同じ仕組みを持っている
②	常に怒りを感じるのは悪いことである
③	アドレナリンを多く含む食品はうつに対して効果的である
④	**意志の強さによりホルモンを制御できる**

　正解 ⇒ ④

　二つ目のウィリス教授の記事の第 1 段落第 3 ～ 4 文に「しかし，意志の力でホルモンを制御することはできないという言葉には驚いた。人間にはホルモンを制御する能力があることを証明する様々な実験があり，これは怒りに効果的に対処する上で最も重要なことの一つである」とあり，ウィリスがスタローンと意見が異なる点が述べられているため④が正解。①は，一つ目の記事の第 3 段落第 2 ～ 3 文に「主に男性

ホルモンであるテストステロンが増加すると，攻撃的になり，暴れたり戦ったりしたくなることがある。また，エストロゲンとプロゲステロン値の変動は，少女の感情や行動に影響を与え，時には PMS と呼ばれる非常に苦しい状態につながることもある」とあり，性差について言及されているが，ウィリスがこれに反対している記述はないため誤り。②については，二つ目の記事の第1段落第1文に「頻繁に，あるいは常に怒りを感じるのは良いことではないというスタローン氏の考えに私は賛同する」とあり，両方の著者が同意していることであるため誤り。③は，二つ目の記事の第2段落第4文に，アドレナリンは「私たちの体を活動的にするホルモンである」と説明があり，食品に含まれるという記述はなく，一つ目の記事には関連する内容がないため誤り。

【語句・表現】
・whether「〜かどうか」
・mechanism「仕組み」
・all the time「常に」
・adrenaline「アドレナリン」
・effective「効果的な」
・strength「強さ」

【全訳】
　先生から，怒りに関する記事を2つ読むように言われています。学んだことについて次の授業で話し合います。

怒りを感じること

アーノルド・スタローン

ロック・シティ高校　科学教師

　ほとんど誰でも怒りを感じることはある。それはあなたが悪い人間だという意味ではない。怒りの感情の中には，自分が制御できないことから来るものもある。最善を尽くしてもうまくいかなかったり，不公平に思えることで面倒に巻き込まれたりすると，本当に世界が自分に敵対しているように感じることがある。

　怒りは本能的な反応であり，脳の感情的な部分，特に扁桃体と呼ばれる部分から始まる，非常に強力な自動反応である。扁桃体は即座に反応し，脳のより「思考的」な部分が介入して合理化したり制御したりする前に，怒りの高まりを感じる。扁桃体をはじめとする感情的な領域は，10代では（実際，生まれたときから）よく発達しているが，感情を制御する前頭前皮質はあまり発達していないことがわかっている。

　感情はホルモンの影響も受けるが，ホルモンの一部は思春期の間男女ともに乱高下する。主に男性ホルモンであるテストステロンが増加すると，攻撃的になり，暴れたり戦ったりしたくなることがある。また，エストロゲンとプロゲステロン値の変動は，少女の感情や行動に影響を与え，時には PMS と呼ばれる非常に苦しい状態につながることもある。ホルモンは強力で重要な化学物質だが，意志の力で制御することはできない。自分の反応をコントロールできるようにはなるが。自分の感情の一部が体内や脳内の化学物質によって引き起こされていることを理解すれば，いつ気分が悪くなるかを予測しやすくなり，自分の反応を制御しやすくなる。また，物事には物理的な原因があると知るだけで，それに対するストレスが軽減されることもある。

　だから，怒るのは普通のことだ。しかし，頻繁に，あるいは常に怒りを感じることは良いことではない。集中力が散漫になり，友人や家族との関係にも悪影響を及ぼしかねない。怒りを制御できず，他人や自分を傷つけてしまうといったことは，絶対に避けたいことだ。

　怒りが続くのは，時にうつ病の兆候である。また，調査によると，少年や男性は怒りによってうつ病を示すことがおそらく少女や女性より多い。女性のうつ病の方がよりはっきりと悲しみや落ち込みのように見える。

［出典］ Text © 2014 Nicola Morgan From THE TEENAGE GUIDE TO STRESS Written by Nicola Morgan Reproduced by permission of Walker Books Ltd, London, SE11 5HJ www.walker.co.uk

幸せホルモン
ハリソン・ウィリス
ロック・シティ大学　教授

　頻繁に，あるいは常に怒りを感じるのは良いことではないというスタローン氏の考えに私は賛同する。他人と協力し，良好な関係を維持するためには，怒りとうまく付き合うことを学ばなければならない。しかし，意志の力でホルモンを制御することはできないという言葉には驚いた。人間にはホルモンを制御する能力があることを証明する様々な実験があり，これは怒りに効果的に対処する上で最も重要なことの一つである。

　ホルモンを制御する方法とは？ これは，重要な試験やテニスの試合の前の自分を想像するとわかりやすい。その出来事に集中すればするほど，私たちはよりエネルギッシュで自信に満ちた気分になる。これはアドレナリンの作用であり，私たちの体を活動的にするホルモンである。

　私たちが制御できるもう一つのホルモンは，幸せを感じさせるセロトニンである。セロトニンは脳内で生成され，気分の調節に重要な役割を果たしている。したがって，セロトニンが不足すると，不安や怒りを引き起こすかもしれない。

　体内のセロトニン量を増やす方法を二つ紹介しよう。一つ目は，タンパク質を多く含む食品を選ぶことである。食べ物から直接セロトニンを摂取することは不可能だが，脳内でセロトニンに変化するアミノ酸の一種，トリプトファンを摂取することはできる。トリプトファンは，豆腐やチーズなどの高タンパク食品に多く含まれている。二つ目は，定期的な運動だ。適度な運動は，トリプトファンを血中に放出させるように体に働きかける。これにより，他のアミノ酸も少なくなり，脳内でより多くのセロトニンが生成されやすい環境が整う。一つ覚えておきたいのは，太陽の光を浴びて過ごすとセロトニンの量が増えるということだ。したがって，運動するときは暗くなる前，理想的には午前中がよいだろう。

　以上のことから，体内の幸福ホルモンであるセロトニンの量は，制御できることがわかる。したがって，食生活を変え，運動をするというあなたの意志は，怒りを処理するのに役立ち，協調的で社会的な生活を送るための第一歩となり得るのである。

【語句・表現】
・article「記事」
〈スタローンの記事〉
〈第1段落〉
・pretty much「ほとんど」
・be in control「（感情などを）制御している」
・it feels as if S V「〜のように感じられる」
・go wrong「うまくいかない」
・unfair「不公平な」
〈第2段落〉
・instinctive「本能的な」
・reaction「反応」
・automatic「自動の」
・response「反応」
・particularly「特に」
・respond「反応する」
・instantly「即座に」

・surge「高まり」
・step in「干渉する」
・rationalize「〜を合理化する」
・in fact「実際には」
〈第3段落〉
・affect「〜に影響を与える」
・wildly「激しく」
・adolescence「青年期」
・male「男性の」
・aggression「攻撃」
・desire「欲望」
・lash out「襲いかかる」
・swing「変化」
・behavior「行動」
・distressing「苦しい」
・chemical「化学物質」
・will-power「意志の力」
・realize that S V「〜に気がつく」
・predict「〜を予測する」
・physical「物理的な」
〈第4段落〉
・distract「〜の気をそらす」
・focus「集中する」
・properly「適切に」
・harm「〜を害する」
・relationship「関係」
・definitely「絶対に」
〈第5段落〉
・sign「兆候」
・research「研究」
・suggest that S V「〜を示唆する」
・express「〜を示す」
・obviously「明らかに」
〈ウィリスの記事〉
〈第1段落〉
・cooperate with 〜「〜と協力する」
・maintain「〜を維持する」
・deal with 〜「〜に対処する」
・statement「記述，発言」
・various「様々な」
・experiment「実験」
・prove「〜だと証明する」
・ability「能力」
・cope with 〜「〜に対処する」
・effectively「効果的に」
〈第2段落〉
・match「試合」
・focus on 〜「〜に集中する」

・energetic「活力に満ちた」
・confident「自信に満ちた」
・effect「効果，影響」
・active「活動的な」
〈第3段落〉
・produce「～を作り出す」
・key「重要な」
・role「役割」
・regulate「～を統制する」
・mood「気持ち」
・therefore「したがって」
・anxiousness「不安」
〈第4段落〉
・take in ～「～を摂取する」
・amino acid「アミノ酸」
・regular「定期的な」
・workout「運動」
・release「～を放出する」
・blood「血液」
・create「～を作り出す」
・sunshine「日光」
・ideally「理想としては」
〈第5段落〉
・above「上記のこと」
・diet「食事」
・handle「～に対処する」
・lead a ～ life「～な生活を送る」
・cooperative「協力的な」
・social「社会的な」

第6問

問1 「 28 に入る最も適切な選択肢を選びなさい」

① 彼は将来何をするのか見つけようと決めた
② 彼はストレスのある生活から逃れたかった
③ 彼は遠いところに住む祖母に会いに行く計画をしていた
④ **彼は物語の登場人物と似た経験をしたかった**

正解 ⇒ ④

　ジョージが一人でヒッチハイクの旅に出た理由は第4段落に述べられている。お気に入りの物語『ジョセフ・ブロンソンの夏の冒険』の主人公ジョセフが16歳の時に一人でヒッチハイクの旅をした話に夢中になって，自分も同じような旅をしたかったという内容が書かれている。したがって正解は④。第5段落で，車に乗せてくれた男女が旅の目的を尋ねた際に，ヨークに住む祖母を訪ねるつもりだと答えているが，同段落第2文「実際には，旅の目的はヒッチハイクをすることであり，どこへ行くかは問題でなかった」からもわかるように，これはそれらしい理由としてジョージが作り上げたものだ。

【語句・表現】
・option「選択肢」
・find out「〜を見出す，明らかにする」
・escape from 〜「〜から逃れる」
・stressful「ストレスの多い」
・distant「遠くの」
・experience「経験」
・similar to 〜「〜に似た」
・character「登場人物」

問2 「 29 に入る最も適切な選択肢を選びなさい」

① 彼に一人旅をしてたくさんの人に会うように助言した
② 彼になぜ両親とうまくいっていないのか尋ねた
③ 彼に自分の夢について考え直す機会を与えた
④ 彼に自分が勉強をいかに怠けていたか気づかせた

正解 ⇒ ③

　トラック運転手のエラとの話は第6段落で書かれている。彼女になぜとりわけ医者になりたいのか尋ねられて，ジョージはうまく答えられなかった。さらに第8段落では，その時のエラの「自分に正直であれ」という言葉をその後も繰り返し思い返し，将来本当にしたいことは何なのか考え続けていると述べられている。ジョージはそれまでは両親の言葉をそのまま受け入れていたが，エラとの会話をきっかけに自分自身の気持ちを見つめ直すことになったのだ。これらを踏まえると，③が正解。

【語句・表現】
・advise A to *do*「Aに〜するように助言する」
・get along with 〜「〜と仲良くする，うまく付き合う」
・opportunity「機会」
・think twice「考え直す，よく考える」
・realise「〜に気づく，〜を実感する」：イギリス式のつづり。アメリカ式では realize とつづる。
・lazy「怠けた」

問3 「5つの選択肢（①〜⑤）から4つを選び，起こった順に並びかえなさい」
　 30 → 31 → 32 → 33

① 嘘をついたことを両親に謝った
② 旅行をしてもよいか両親に尋ねた
③ 親切な男女の車に乗せてもらった
④ 医者がどのように人々を救うのかについて本を読んだ
⑤ 女性運転手に自分の夢について話した

正解 ⇒ ② → ③ → ⑤ → ①

　第3段落に，ジョージが友達と旅行に行ってもいいかと両親に尋ね，何とか許可をもらったという記述がある。その後ヒッチハイクの旅に出て，まず男女の車に乗せてもらい（第5段落），翌朝にはトラック運転手であるエラに送ってもらった（第6段落）。帰宅後，両親に嘘がばれて謝った。したがって，②→③→⑤→①という順番が正解。④に該当する内容は本文中に書かれていない。

【語句・表現】
・rearrange「〜を並びかえる」
・order「順序」
・apologise「謝る」：イギリス式のつづり。アメリカ式では apologize とつづる。
・hitch a ride「(ヒッチハイクで) 車に乗せてもらう」
・female「女性の」

問4 「 34 に入る最も適切な選択肢を選びなさい」

① 彼は一人旅をすることの危険性に十分には気づいていなかった
② 彼は旅行のことで両親に対して正直ではなかった
③ 彼は自分の将来の仕事についてあまり真剣に考えていなかった
④ 彼は自分の夢を実現させられるほど懸命に取り組んでいなかった

正解 ⇒ ③

　第6段落で，エラからなぜ医者を目指していたかを問われうまく答えられなかった時に，そのような問いについてこれまであまり考えてこなかったことに気づいたと述べられている。両親に言われる通りに医者を目指していたが，エラとの会話により自分の決心に自信が持てなくなった。このことを端的に表している③が正解。

【語句・表現】
・be aware of 〜「〜に気づいている」
・honest「正直な」
・seriously「真剣に」
・career「仕事，キャリア」
・come true「実現する」

問5 「 35 と 36 に入る最も適切な選択肢を2つ選びなさい (順番は問わない)」

① 見知らぬ人が私たちの考え方に大きな影響を与えることがある。
② 他の人を説得する際には自信が重要である。
③ 他人に自分の目標を表明するのはそれを達成する良い方法だ。
④ 一つの目標にこだわる方が成功につながりやすい。
⑤ 将来を決定する際には自分の気持ちに従うべきだ。

正解 ⇒ ①・⑤

　この物語では，ジョージが一人旅中に出会ったエラとの会話を通して自分の将来についてより深く考えるようになったことが大きな主題となっている。初対面のエラがジョージの考え方に大きな影響を与えたということができるので，一つ目の正解は①だ。また，「自分に正直であれ」という言葉からもわかる通り，エラはジョージに将来の道を自分で決めるべきだというメッセージを送った。この内容を表している⑤が二つ目の正解。「他の人を説得する」「他人に自分の目標を表明する」「一つの目標にこだわる」という内容は，この物語から読み取れることではないので，②・③・④は誤り。

【語句・表現】
・stranger「見知らぬ人」
・effect「影響，効果」

- confidence「自信」
- persuade「〜を説得する」
- express「〜を表す」
- achieve「〜を達成する」
- stick to 〜「〜にこだわる，固執する」
- be likely to *do*「〜しそうだ，〜する可能性が高い」
- determine「〜を決定する」

【全訳】

　あなたの英語の先生は，クラスのみんなに興味深い物語を見つけ，メモを使って討論グループに発表するよう言いました。あなたはイギリスの高校生が書いた物語を見つけました。

自分に正直であれ

ジョージ・トーマス

　15歳の誕生日の夕食時に，僕は両親の前でスピーチをした。「今年は良い成績を取るために勉強をもっと頑張るよ」と僕は言った。父は満足そうにうなずきながら，「今はお前の人生で重要な時だ，ジョージ。来年の試験に向けて頑張りなさい」と言った。続けて父は，最近のテストでの僕のひどい成績を指摘し，正直で勤勉であることの大切さを強調した。その結果，みんなが食べ始める頃には食事はすっかり冷めてしまっていた。夕食の席で，父と母は主に僕のテストの点数と将来の仕事について話し，僕はそれを静かに聞いていた。

　僕は翌年，16歳の年に国家試験を受けることになっていた。その試験は高等教育に進みたい学生にとって重要なものだ。小さい頃からずっと将来の夢は医者になることだったので，その試験は僕にとって非常に大きな意味を持つものだった。両親は僕の学業についてとても，おそらく僕以上に，気にしていた。「授業中は先生の話をしっかり聞いて，家では授業の復習を毎回するんだよ」「わからないところを放っておいてはいけないよ」「疲れているの？　身体と心をリフレッシュすることも大切よ」…たぶんこれらは全部正しくて，僕は「うん，わかっているよ」と答えるしかなかった。

　夏休みがもうすぐそこに来ていた時，僕は両親に友達と2泊3日の旅行に出てもいいか尋ねた。母は眉をひそめて言った。「けど夏の学習計画を立てたじゃない。週に3回家庭教師があるのよ。自分で復習する時間も必要だし…」「3日だけだよ」と僕は言った。「心をリフレッシュするのも大事だっていつも言っているじゃないか。気分転換になって勉強に集中できるようになるはずだよ」　両親は，計画に遅れないという条件で，ついに旅行に行くことを許してくれた。

　8月のある朝，僕は旅行に出発した — 一人で。僕は16歳になったら，お気に入りの物語の1つである『ジョセフ・ブロンソンの夏の冒険』の主人公であるジョセフのように一人旅をするとずっと心に決めていた。イングランドの田舎に住む16歳の少年ジョセフは，一人でヒッチハイクをしながら国中を巡った。途中でさまざまな人に会い，人生や友情，愛についてたくさんのことを学んだ。9歳のときに初めて読んでから，僕は同じように旅をすることを夢見ていた。両親には一人で行くことを告げなかった。もし告げたら許してはくれないだろうから。罪悪感はあったが，長年の野望を実現することの方がずっと大切だったのだ。

　家を出た後，僕は隣町のエイズビーへと歩いて行き，道端で「ヨーク」と書かれた標識を掲げた。実際には，旅の目的はヒッチハイクをすることであり，どこへ行くかは問題でなかった。ヨークはそこを走る車両にとって一般的な目的地だと思っただけだ。何十台もの車が通り過ぎるのを見送った後，青色のファミリーカーが目の前に止まった。車の中には中年の男女がいた。たぶん両親より少し若いくらいだ。運転手の男性が「ホールデンに向かっているんだ。それでいいかな？」と言った。ホールデンはヨークに行く途中にある小さな町だ。僕はお礼を言って車に乗り込んだ。2人になぜヒッチハイクをしているのか尋ねられたとき，僕はヨークに住む祖母を訪ねるのだと答えた。親切な男女と話していると，自分の夢の1つが叶いつつあることに興奮してきた。ホールデンに着くと，辺りを歩き回り，別の親切な運転手の車でヨーク郊外まで送ってもらい，そこで小さなホステルに泊まった。

　翌朝，大きな運送トラックが止まって僕を拾ってくれた。驚いたことに，運転手は若い女性 — おそ

らく20代後半か30代前半 — だった。運転手のエラは気さくで話し好きな女性だった。僕がトラックに乗り込むとすぐに，まるで古くからの友人のように会話を始めた。彼女はいろいろなことについて話した — 気難しい顧客や3か月になるかわいい甥っ子のことから，最近の異常な暑さに至るまで。僕は彼女の話を楽しく聞き，気づくと自分のことについても話していた。将来の夢が医者だと言った時，エラは「なぜ医者なの？」と尋ねた。僕は「困っている人を助けたいんです」と答えた。彼女は再び，「それで？」と尋ねた。彼女が何を言いたいのかわからず，僕は答えられなかった。エラは，「つまり，困っている人を助けるためなら他にもたくさんの職業があるでしょう。その中でも医者になりたいのはどうして？」と言った。「なるほど。えっと…」 その時，僕はこういった種類の問いについてあまり考えたことがなかったことに気づいた。両親はいつも医者になるよう言っていたし，僕は疑いなくそれを受け入れていた。何と言っていいかわからず途方に暮れて，自分の決心に自信が持てなくなってきた。彼女は僕の心を読んでいるかのように，「あなたについてはほとんど知らないから，私が言えるのは自分に正直であれということくらいだわ。あなたが自分の道を選ぶのよ」と言った。僕は「なら，あなたはどうして運転手を自分の道に選んだのですか」と尋ねた。「大きな車を運転しているとぞくぞくするの。それだけよ。両親は最初は私がトラックの運転手になるのに反対したけど，いまは仕方ないと諦めているわ」と，彼女は笑って答えた。

　エラにさよならを言った後，別の2人の運転手が車に乗せてくれて，無事に家に帰ることができた。予想通り，僕の嘘はすぐに両親にばれて，ひどく怒られた。「正直でいなさいといつも言っているでしょう。どうしてわからないの？」 僕は自分がしたことについて謝ることしかできなかった。自分が完全に悪いことはわかっていた。両親から，もう夏休みの間は許可なく外出してはいけないと言われた。僕は残りの夏を家で勉強して過ごした。

　今，僕は高校生だ。エラとトラックで話してから，彼女の「自分に正直であれ」という言葉を繰り返し思い出してきた。自分は本当は何をしたいのか — 僕をぞくぞくさせるのは何なのか — についてずっと考え続けている。機械やロボットがどう動くのかに興味があるから，機械学やロボット工学を仕事にするのも良いかもしれない。同時に，医者になることも依然として魅力的だ。今考えていることについて両親に伝えていないが，いつか僕の本当の決心について伝えるつもりだ。

あなたのメモ：

自分に正直であれ

著者について（ジョージ・トーマス）
・将来医者になるために懸命に勉強している
・ 28 から一人でヒッチハイクに出た

他の重要人物
・ジョージの両親：ジョージの勉強に厳しく，彼の将来をひどく心配している
・エラ：トラックの運転手で， 29

彼の忘れられない夏の旅にまつわる出来事
 30 → 31 → 32 → 33

ジョージがエラとの会話の後で気づいたこと
・ 34

この物語から私たちが学べること
・ 35
・ 36

【語句・表現】

・present「～を発表する」
・note「メモ」

〈第1段落〉
・grade「成績」
・nod「うなずく」
・satisfaction「満足」
・go on to *do*「続けて～する」
・point out「～を指摘する」
・stress「～を強調する」
・diligent「勤勉な」
・by the time S V「～するまでに」

〈第2段落〉
・national「国家の」
・go on to ～「～に進学する，進む」
・higher education「高等教育」
・a great deal「大いに，非常に」
・care about ～「～を気にする」
・schoolwork「学業」
・review「～を復習する」
・leave A as it is「A をそのままにしておく」
・refresh「～をリフレッシュする，～の気分をさっぱりさせる」

〈第3段落〉
・around the corner「間近に，すぐ近くに」
・frown「眉をしかめる，しかめ面をする」
・tutor「家庭教師，個人教師」
・concentrate on ～「～に集中する」
・finally「ついに，ようやく」
・on condition that S V「～するという条件で」
・fall behind schedule「予定より遅れる」

〈第4段落〉
・set out「出発する」
・be determined to *do*「～することを決意している」
・favourite「お気に入りの」：イギリス式のつづり。アメリカ式では favorite とつづる。
・various「さまざまな」
・on the way「途中で」
・dream of ～「～を夢見る」
・permission「許可」
・guilty「罪の意識がある」
・long-held「長年抱いてきた，かねての」
・ambition「野望，野心」

〈第5段落〉
・sign「標識，表示」
・in fact「実際に」
・purpose「目的」
・common「一般的な」
・destination「目的地」
・vehicle「車両」

- dozens of ～「何十もの～」
- pass by「通り過ぎる」
- middle-aged「中年の」
- get into ～「～の中に入る，～に乗り込む」
- suburb「郊外」

〈第6段落〉
- van「（荷物運搬用の）トラック，バン」
- pick ～ up「（車で）～を拾う」
- to *one's* surprise「驚いたことに」
- talkative「話し好きの」
- strike up「～を始める」
- as if S V「あたかも～であるかのように」
- customer「顧客」
- nephew「甥」
- in need「困っている，助けが必要な」
- figure out「～を理解する」
- occupation「職業」
- among others「とりわけ，他でもなく」
- accept「～を受け入れる」
- at a loss「途方に暮れて」
- certain「確信した」
- determination「決意，決心」
- choose「～を選ぶ」
- thrilled「ぞくぞくした，興奮した」
- it can't be helped「仕方がない」
- reply「返事をする」

〈第7段落〉
- right away「すぐに，ただちに」
- mad「怒った，頭にきた」
- have no choice but to *do*「～するしかない，～せざるを得ない」
- be to blame「責任がある，責めを負うべきである」
- totally「完全に，全く」
- rest「残り」

〈第8段落〉
- curious「興味がある，知りたがっている」
- mechanics「機械学」
- robotics「ロボット工学」
- at the same time「同時に」
- attractive「魅力的な」

〈メモ〉
- memorable「記憶に残る，忘れられない」

第7問

問1 「要点メモの　37　を埋めるのに最も適切な選択肢を選びなさい」

① 工場主
② 政府職員
③ **高度に訓練を受けた労働者**
④ 技術の低い労働者

正解 ⇒ ③

　第1段落で「特に織物産業において高い技術を持っていた人たち」によって，この運動が引き起こされたとあるので③が正解。①と②は運動を抑えようとしたことが，第3段落から分かる。

【語句・表現】
・option「選択肢」
・summary note「要点メモ」
・owner「所有者」
・official「職員，役人」
・highly「高度に」
・trained「訓練された」
・laborer「労働者」
・unskilled「技術をもっていない」

問2 「要点メモの 38 と 39 を埋めるのに最も適切な選択肢を2つ選びなさい(順番は問わない)」

① ラッダイトたちは自然環境を守るために工場を襲撃した。
② **ラッダイトたちは自分たちの職を奪うかもしれない新しい機械を破壊した。**
③ この運動は技術の低い労働者の新たな雇用機会を奪った。
④ **政府が新しい法律を定めたため，ラッダイト運動は次第に下火になった。**
⑤ この運動は人々の仕事を奪ったネッド・ラッドにちなんで名づけられた。
⑥ この運動は織物産業の工場主によって支持された。

正解 ⇒ ②・④

　第2段落第4文〜第6文に，ラッダイトたちが新しい機械を失業の脅威とみなしたため，工場に打ちこわしに入ったと述べられているので，②は正解。また，第3段落第3文〜第5文に，政府がラッダイト運動をよしとせず，法律を作って，運動を鎮静化させた，とあるので，④も正解。「自然環境」についての記述はないので，①は誤り。第2段落第5文に，技術の有無にかかわらず，機械によって同様の成果があげられるとある。よって，逆に技術の低い労働者に雇用機会が生まれる可能性もあることから，③は誤り。ネッド・ラッドは自分の仕事を奪った最新の機械を破壊し，それが広がったのがラッダイト運動であるので，⑤は誤り。⑥については，第3段落第1文から誤りだと分かる。運動を支持したのは「織物産業の労働者」だ。

【語句・表現】
・order「順序」
・matter「重要である」
・the Luddites「ラッダイト（ラッダイト運動に参加した人々）」
・attack「〜を攻撃する，襲撃する」
・in order to *do*「〜するために」
・protect「〜を守る」

- cause A to *do*「A が～する原因になる」
- movement「運動」
- low-skilled「技術の低い」
- employment opportunity「雇用機会」
- take place「起こる」
- less and less「ますます～ない」
- frequently「頻繁に」
- name A after B「B にちなんで A に名づける」
- take away ～「～を奪う」
- support「～を支持する」
- cloth-making industry「織物産業」

問3 「要点メモの 40 を埋めるのに最も適切な選択肢を選びなさい」

① **自分たちの仕事に誇りを持てなくなるだろう**
② より高い技術の習得を求められるだろう
③ 古い機械を新しいものに入れ替えなければならないだろう
④ 夜遅くまで働かなければならないだろう

　正解 ⇒ ①

　第2段落第4文に，「ラッダイトたちは，機械が雇用や賃金，さらには自分たちの誇りをも脅かすものだと考えた」とあるので，①が正解。②～④の内容については記述がなく誤り。

【語句・表現】
- no longer「もはや～ない」
- be proud of ～「～を誇りに思っている」
- require「～を求める」
- gain「～を手に入れる」
- replace A with B「A を B と取り換える」
- after dark「夜遅く，日が暮れてから」

問4 「要点メモの 41 を埋めるのに最も適切な選択肢を選びなさい」

① 破壊と暴力は現代社会にとって大きな脅威である。
② 政府は労働者だけでなく工場主も保護するべきである。
③ 社会をより豊かにするために新しい技術を導入すべきである。
④ **社会は変化の時代に労働者をどう守るかを考えるべきである。**

　正解 ⇒ ④

　学ぶべき教訓としては，第4段落第2文後半の「急速に時代が変化する中で労働者を保護する必要性」から④が正解。工場主の保護については述べられていないので②は誤り。①と③は常識的に正しいように思われるが，本文に即していないので誤り。

【語句・表現】
- destruction「破壊」
- violence「暴力」

・threat「脅威」
・A as well as B「Bと同様にAも」
・introduce「～を導入する，取り入れる」
・in times of ～「～の時に」

【全訳】

　歴史の授業で，あなたの研究グループは社会の変化について発表することになっています。グループに共有したい記事を見つけました。次回の会議のため，要点メモを完成させましょう。

ラッダイト運動

　技術の進歩とそれに対する人々の反応について考えるとき，歴史から学ぶべき教訓がある。そのひとつがラッダイト運動である。ラッダイト運動は，イギリス人のネッド・ラッドにちなんで名づけられたが，彼は自分の仕事を奪う機械を破壊したと言われている。ラッダイト運動は19世紀初頭にイギリスで起こったもので，労働者，特に織物産業において高い技術を持っていた人たちが，新しい技術によって自分たちの生活が脅かされることを恐れ，機械の破壊運動に参加した。彼らはラッダイトと呼ばれる。

　この時代，織物産業には大きな変化が起きていた。それまで熟練工によってのみ可能であった上質な布地の生産を可能にする新しい機械が導入されたのだ。機械によって，より高い効率性，生産量の増加，コストの削減が期待された。しかし，ラッダイトたちは，機械が雇用や賃金，さらには自分たちの誇りをも脅かすものだと考えた。なぜなら，機械によって技術の低い労働者でも熟練工と同じように，あるいはそれ以上の仕事ができるようになったからだ。ラッダイトたちは新しい技術に対抗するため，集団で夜な夜な工場に侵入し，二度と使えないように機械を破壊した。

　ラッダイト運動は，織物産業の労働者から大きな注目を集め，支持を得た。ラッダイトたちは，一部の人たちから産業革命の冷たく残酷な機械に対抗する，伝統的な熟練労働の擁護者とみなされた。しかし，政府と工場主は彼らを犯罪者であり，社会に対する脅威とみなした。彼らは力ずくで対応に出た。運動を阻止するために厳しい法律を制定し，軍隊を送り込んだのだ。ラッダイトたちは捕らえられ，厳罰に処された。運動は次第に下火になり，工場主たちは工場と機械を再建した。さらに，多くの労働者が最終的には変化に適応し，技術的に進歩した社会で新しい仕事を見つけた。

　ラッダイト運動は目的を達成することはできなかったが，現代社会の形成に重要な役割を果たした。技術の進歩がどれほど大きな影響を及ぼすか，そして急速に時代が変化する中で労働者を保護する必要性を明らかにしたのである。今日，「ラッダイト」という言葉は，技術の進歩に抵抗したり恐れたりする人々を表す言葉として世界中で使われている。人々が機械を破壊したのは遠い昔のことだが，新しいテクノロジーに対する恐怖心は相変わらず大きい。ネッド・ラッドが私たちに残した教訓は，今日まで生きている。

要点メモ：

ラッダイト運動
前書き
◆　19世紀初頭のイギリスで起こった，機械の使用に反対する社会運動
◆　ラッダイトたちは　37　だった。
事実
◆　織物産業に新しい技術が導入された。
◆　機械によって，技術の低い労働者でも熟練工と同じように働くことができるようになった。
◆　38
◆　39

理由
ラッダイトたちが心配したこと：
◆　職場から必要とされなくなるかもしれない。
◆　労働に対する報酬が減るだろう。
◆　 40 。

学ぶべき教訓
◆　 41

【語句・表現】
〈導入文〉
・presentation「口頭発表」
・article「記事」
・share「〜を共有する」
・complete「〜を仕上げる，完成させる」
〈第1段落〉
・react to 〜「〜に対応する」
・lesson「教訓」
・Englishman「英国人」
・be said to *do*「〜すると言われている」
・century「世紀」
・especially「特に」
・cloth-making industry「織物産業，製布業」
・for fear that S V「〜することを恐れて」
・threaten「〜を脅かす」
・living「生計，生活」
〈第2段落〉
・time「時代，時期」
・produce「〜を生産する」
・promise「〜を約束する」
・efficiency「効率，能率」
・production「生産」
・reduce「〜を減らす」
・see A as B「A を B とみなす」
・wage「賃金」
・enable A to *do*「A に〜することを可能にさせる」
・perform「〜を成し遂げる」
・break into 〜「〜に押し入る，侵入する」
〈第3段落〉
・significant「重大な」
・attention「注目」
・defender「擁護者，守護者」
・traditional「伝統的な」
・cruel「冷酷な，無慈悲な」
・criminal「犯罪者」
・force「力」
・strict「厳しい」
・law「法律」

・military「軍隊，軍人」
・severely「厳しく」
・punish「〜を罰する」
・frequent「頻繁な」
・rebuild「〜を再建する」
・in addition「さらに，加えて」
・eventually「ついには，最終的には」
・adapt to 〜「〜に適応する」
・technologically「技術的に」
・advanced「進歩した」
〈第4段落〉
・fail to *do*「〜することができない」
・achieve「〜を達成する」
・goal「目標，目的」
・play a role in *doing*「〜することの役割を果たす」
・shape「〜を形づくる」
・modern「現代の」
・prove「〜を証明する」
・impact「衝撃」
・advancement「前進，進歩」
・rapid「速い，急速な」
・term「用語」
・describe「〜を記述する」
・resist「〜に抵抗する」
・as 〜 as ever「相変わらず〜で，今までと同じように〜で」
・alive「生きている」

第8問

問1 「次のうち [42] に適さないものはどれか」

> ① 気温の影響を受けやすい
> ② 植物と動物を食べる
> ③ **体には4本の脚がある**
> ④ 2組の翅をもっている
> ⑤ 日中は活動的ではない

正解 ⇒ ③

本文の第2段落でコオロギの体の特徴，第3段落でコオロギの生態の特徴が述べられている。それらの記述内容に合致しないものを選ぶのが問1であるが，第2段落第4文の「体の両側には，3本の脚，2つの翅（はね），そして尾毛と呼ばれる特別な感覚器官がついている」という記述より，③の選択肢が合致せず，本問の正答となる。なお，①に関しては第3段落第4，5文，②は第3段落第2文，④は第2段落第6，7文，⑤については第3段落第1文の記述内容にそれぞれ合致する。

【語句・表現】
・following「次に続くもの」
・suitable for 〜「〜に適する」

- affect「〜に影響を与える」
- temperature「気温」
- active「活動的な, 活発な」
- daytime「日中, 昼間」

問2 「体の仕組み（メス）のスライドを完成させるためにコオロギの説明図の空欄の名称を埋めなさい」
　　 43

	(A)	触角	(B)	尾毛	(C)	後翅	(D)	耳	(E)	産卵管
①	(A)	触角	(B)	尾毛	(C)	後翅	(D)	耳	(E)	産卵管
②	**(A)**	**触角**	**(B)**	**耳**	**(C)**	**前翅**	**(D)**	**尾毛**	**(E)**	**産卵管**
③	(A)	触角	(B)	耳	(C)	後翅	(D)	産卵管	(E)	尾毛
④	(A)	尾毛	(B)	耳	(C)	前翅	(D)	産卵管	(E)	触角
⑤	(A)	尾毛	(B)	産卵管	(C)	前翅	(D)	耳	(E)	触角

正解 ⇒ ②

　問2はメスのコオロギの体の構造を問う問題であるが, コオロギの体の特徴に関しては, 本文の第2段落を中心に語られている。(A) に関しては, 同段落第3文の「頭部には2つの目と2本の触角がついている」という記述より, 触角 (antenna) であることが分かる。(B) は, 第10文に「驚くべきことに, 彼らの耳は前脚についており」とあることから, 耳 (ear) であると考えられる。(C) については, 第6, 7文の「実際には2組の翅があり, 前翅の組と後翅の組である。後翅は前翅に隠れている」という箇所より, 前翅 (front wing) と判断できる。(D) は, 第4文に「体の両側には, 3本の脚, 2つの翅, そして尾毛と呼ばれる特別な感覚器官がついている」とあることから, 尾毛 (cercus) にあたる。また, 続く第5文に「メスには体の末端部に産卵管と呼ばれる長い筒状の器官もあり, これを使って卵を産む」とあるので, (E) には産卵管 (ovipositor) が当てはまる。以上より, ②が正解の組み合わせである。

【語句・表現】
- complete「〜を完成させる」
- blank「空欄の, 空白の」
- label「表示, ラベル」
- illustration「説明図, イラスト」
- cricket「コオロギ」
- structure「構造」
- female「メス」
- antenna「触角」
- cercus「尾毛」
- back wing「後翅（こうし）, 後ろの翅（はね）」
- ovipositor「産卵管」
- front wing「前翅（ぜんし）, 前の翅（はね）」

問3 「鳴き声のスライドを完成させるために 44 と 45 に入る最も適切な2つの選択肢はどれか（順番は問わない）」

① コオロギは老いるにつれて, 鳴く回数が減り始める。
② **コオロギは気温15度より気温30度でより頻繁に鳴く。**
③ メスのコオロギはオスをひきつけるために短く高い音で鳴く。
④ コオロギが鳴いているのを聞くと神経質になったりイライラしたりする人がいる。
⑤ **コオロギの鳴き声を描写する文学の古典作品がいくつか存在する。**

正解 ⇒ ②・⑤

　本文の第3段落第5文の「例えば，ある実験によれば，1匹のコオロギが15秒間に鳴く平均的な回数は気温（摂氏）30度で46回であるが，気温15度においては19回に減少する」という記述，及び第4段落第5文の「彼ら[コオロギ]の鳴き声の初期のいくつかの記録は最古の和歌集である『万葉集』に見ることができる」という記述より，②と⑤が正解。

　なお，第3段落第4，5文より，コオロギの鳴く回数が減少するのは涼しくなるにつれてであるため，①は誤り。また，第4段落第3，4文より，オスのコオロギが求愛のために鳴くとあるので，③も誤り。④に関しては，該当する記述が本文中に存在しないため，不適。

【語句・表現】
・option「選択肢」
・order「順番」
・matter「重要である」
・attract「～をひきつける，～を魅了する」
・nervous「神経質な，不安な」
・irritated「イライラしている」
・classical「古典の」
・literature「文学」
・describe「～を描写する」

問4　「最後のスライドを完成させるための最も適切な文はどれか」　46

> ①　コオロギは世界を救う潜在的な力を持っているが，我々は昆虫食の危険性にもっと注意を払うべきである。
> ②　世界的に深刻な食糧危機を解決するのに役立ったことがあるため，食べ物としてのコオロギは将来的に地球を救うと期待されている。
> ③　**コオロギを食べたくない人たちもいることは事実だが，コオロギは将来的に国際的な食料源になる可能性があり，食べる価値がある。**
> ④　最近，コオロギ食品は世界中で人気があり，動物の肉は将来的に完全に代用されるだろう。

正解 ⇒ ③

　第6段落では食品としてのコオロギの将来的な有益性が語られており，同段落第1文の「特に虫が苦手な場合には，コオロギを食べることをためらうかもしれないが，近年，コオロギは持続可能な食料源として世界中で注目されている」という記述，及び第6，7文の「人間は新しくかつもっと地球にやさしい食料源を獲得する必要がある。もしコオロギを食べる機会があれば，ぜひ食べてみて，どうか地球を救う手助けをして下さい」という記述より，③が正解。

　他の選択肢に関しては，①の「我々は昆虫食の危険性にもっと注意を払うべきである」，②の「世界的に深刻な食糧危機を解決するのに役立ったことがある」，④の「動物の肉は将来的に完全に代用されるだろう」というそれぞれの記述が本文から読み取ることができないため，全て誤りとなる。

【語句・表現】
・statement「文，言明」
・potential「潜在的な力」
・attention「注意」
・expect A to *do*「Aに～するように期待する」
・crisis「危機」

・worth *doing*「～する価値がある」
・completely「完全に」
・replace「～に取って代わる」

問５　「コオロギの一生について何を推論することができるか」　47

---

① 成虫のコオロギが冬を越すのは不可能である。
② コオロギが成虫になるには２，３週間かかる。
③ 平均して成虫のコオロギは２，３年生きる。
④ コオロギの一生は未だ明らかになっていない。

正解 ⇒ ①

本文の第３段落第３文の「基本的には，コオロギは初夏に生まれ，１，２か月で成虫になり，メスが卵を産んだ後，秋に寿命を迎える」という記述より，原則コオロギが越冬することはないことが分かり，①が正解。

【語句・表現】
・infer「～を推論する，～を推察する」
・life cycle「一生，ライフサイクル」
・survive「～を乗り越えて生き残る」
・on average「平均して」
・be yet to *do*「未だ～していない，これから～するはずである」
・make A clear「A を明らかにする」

【全訳】
　あなたは昆虫に興味があり，生物に関する発表コンテストに参加する予定です。あなたは以下の文章を書き，自身の発表用のスライドを作っています。

　日本では秋になると，時おり草むらや花壇で虫たちが美しく鳴くのを耳にする。どの虫が美しく鳴いているのか。ご想像通り，多くの場合，コオロギである。
　コオロギの体長は10ミリから40ミリである。体の色はたいてい黒か茶色である。頭部には２つの目と２本の触角がついている。体の両側には，３本の脚，２つの翅（はね），そして尾毛と呼ばれる特別な感覚器官がついている。メスには体の末端部に産卵管と呼ばれる長い筒状の器官もあり，これを使って卵を産む。一見すると，コオロギには１組の翅しかないように思われるかもしれないが，実際には２組の翅があり，前翅の組と後翅の組である。後翅は前翅に隠れているので，見つけるのが難しいかもしれない。しかし，翅を持っていてもコオロギは飛ぶことができない。むしろ，長く太い後ろ脚によって，まるで飛んでいるように，長い距離を跳ぶことができる。加えて，驚くべきことに，彼らの耳は前脚についており，その耳はとても敏感で遠くから他のコオロギの鳴き声を聞くことができる。
　生態に関しては，森のような草が生い茂った場所を好み，夜行性であるため日中に姿を見ることは難しい。ほとんどのコオロギは葉や花，他の昆虫や動物の死骸を食べるが，一方で彼らの天敵はクモ，カエル，鳥である。基本的には，コオロギは初夏に生まれ，１，２か月で成虫になり，メスが卵を産んだ後，秋に寿命を迎える。気温はコオロギ，特に彼らの鳴き声に影響をかなり与え，涼しくなればなるほど，彼らが鳴く回数は少なくなる。例えば，ある実験によれば，１匹のコオロギが15秒間に鳴く平均的な回数は気温（摂氏）30度で46回であるが，気温15度においては19回に減少する。
　翅を一緒にこすり合わせることによって，コオロギは鳴いて高い音を出す。実際に，その音はとても高く電話で伝えることができない。つまり，彼らの鳴き声を他の誰かに電話越しに伝えることはできな

いのである。他の動物と同様に，基本的に鳴くのはオスである。オスはメスをひきつけるために鳴くのであるが，我々は古代より彼らの求愛の鳴き声を聴くことを楽しんでいる。彼らの鳴き声の初期のいくつかの記録は最古の和歌集である『万葉集』に見ることができる。

　世界の一部の地域や国では，コオロギは日常的な食品として食べられている。まろやかな味がするため，コオロギは「陸のエビ」と呼ばれることがある。興味深いことに，コオロギの味は彼らが食べるものに影響される。例えば，コオロギに果物を与えると，彼らは果物の味がするようになる。栄養源としては，コオロギにはミネラルとビタミンが豊富で，牛肉，豚肉，鶏肉などのような食肉と同じくらい多くのタンパク質を含んでいる。

　特に虫が苦手な場合には，コオロギを食べることをためらうかもしれないが，近年，コオロギは持続可能な食料源として世界中で注目されている。これは，世界の人口が劇的に増加しているからである。世界の人口が2050年には100億人に達し，将来的に深刻な食糧不足に我々は苦しむと予想する専門家もいる。2013年に，FAO（国際連合食糧農業機関）は我々が昆虫を食料として有効活用することを提言した。コオロギは以下の理由において有力な候補である。コオロギは大きな動物と比較して格段に必要な場所と水が少ない。コオロギは豚や牛と比較して CO_2（二酸化炭素）の排出量が極めて少ない。コオロギは繁殖させやすく栄養価が高い。コオロギの粉末を含んだ軽食であるコオロギのプロテインバーはイギリスで販売されており，2020年にはコオロギビスケットが日本で注目を集め販売開始直後に売り切れた。食料としての人気はまだ低く，加えて我々はより大量のコオロギを費用を抑えて育てる方法を見つけなければならないが，人間は新しくかつもっと地球にやさしい食料源を獲得する必要がある。もしコオロギを食べる機会があれば，ぜひ食べてみて，どうか地球を救う手助けをして下さい。

あなたの発表用のスライド：

| コオロギ：
地球を救う歌い手たち | 1. 基本的な特徴
・体長10ミリ〜40ミリ
・黒または茶色
・
・ 42
・ |

2. 体の構造（メス）
43

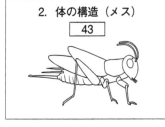

3. 鳴き声
・ 44
・ 45

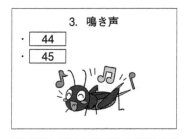

4. 食品として
・エビのような味がする
・ビタミンとタンパク質を豊富に含む
・持続可能な食品として注目を集める
・地球にやさしい

5. コオロギの力

46

【語句・表現】
〈第1段落〉
・grass「芝生，草」

・flower bed「花壇」
・guess「～を推測する，言い当てる」
〈第2段落〉
・sense organ「感覚器官」
・tube-shaped「筒状の」
・lay eggs「卵を産む」
・at first sight「一見すると」
・appear to *do*「～するように見える」
・fold「～をたたむ」
・allow A to *do*「A が～できるようにする，A に～することを許す」
・rather「むしろ，どちらかと言えば」
・enable A to *do*「A が～することを可能にする」
・as if S V「まるで～するように」：as if 以下の文は事実とは異なる場合，仮定法となる。
・be located in ～「～に位置している」
・sensitive「敏感な」
〈第3段落〉
・as of ～「～について，～に関して」
・grassy「草が茂った」
・natural enemy「天敵」
・basically「基本的には」
・strongly「強く」
・for instance「例えば」
・according to ～「～によると」
・experiment「実験」
・second「秒」
・drop to ～「～まで下落する」
〈第4段落〉
・rub「～をこする」
・high-pitched「(音が) 高い」
・similar to ～「～に似ている」
・ancient「古代の」
・record「記録」
〈第5段落〉
・region「地域，地方」
・mild「(味が) まろやかな」
・shrimp「(小さい) エビ」
・interestingly「興味深いことに」
・fruit-flavored「果物の味がする」
・source「源」
・nutrition「栄養」
・mineral「ミネラル」：食品中の栄養素における鉄，カルシウム，亜鉛などの無機物の総称。
・vitamin「ビタミン」
・contain「～を含む」
・protein「タンパク質，プロテイン」
〈第6段落〉
・hesitate to *do*「～することをためらう，～することを躊躇する」
・be in the spotlight「注目されている，注目を集めている」
・sustainable「持続可能な，地球環境にやさしい」

・population「人口」
・dramatically「劇的に」
・expert「専門家」
・reach「～に達する」
・billion「10億」
・suffer from ～「～に苦しむ」
・Food and Agriculture Organization「国際連合食糧農業機関」
・make better use of ～「～を有効活用する，～をより効果的に用いる」
・strong candidate「有力候補」
・reproduce「～を繁殖させる」
・nutritious「栄養価が高い」
・bar「棒状のもの，バー」
・snack「軽食，お菓子」
・cracker「ビスケット，（お菓子の）クラッカー」
・gather「～を集める」
・go on sale「発売される」
・popularity「人気」
・raise「～を育てる」
・economically「経済的に，お金を節約して」
・obtain「～を獲得する」
・give A a try「A をためす」
・help (to) *do*「～する手助けをする，～するのに役立つ」

問　題番　号（配点）	設　問	解　答番　号	正　解	配　点	自　己採　点
第A問 (18)	1	1	2	3	
	2	2	2	3	
	3	3－4	2－5	3	
		5	4	3	
	4	6	2	3	
	5	7	2	3	
自己採点小計					
第B問 (12)	1	1	1	3	
	2	2	2	3	
	3	3	3	3	
	4	4	1	3	
自己採点小計					

自己採点合計

（注）
－(ハイフン)でつながれた正解は，順序を問わない。

第A問

問1　「筆者AとDはどちらも　1　ということに言及している」

> ①　スマートフォンの学習用アプリは，生徒が試験でより良い点数を取るのに役立つ
> ②　スマートフォンを教育ツールとして活用する理由の一つは，ほとんどの生徒がそれを所有しているからである
> ③　スマートフォンは，学校と家庭の両方で学習活動をサポートするのに活用できる
> ④　スマートフォンは，生徒らが自分たちの考えをクラスメートと共有することを可能にする

正解 ⇒ ②

　選択肢②は，筆者Aは第5文「生徒にデバイスを提供する必要がなく，生徒が自分の携帯電話を使える」，筆者Dは第2文「…ほとんどの生徒がスマートフォンを持っている」で言及しているので，これが正解。①は，筆者Dの第3・4文と一致するが，筆者Aは言及していない。③は，筆者A・Dのどちらも「家庭」には言及していない。④は筆者Aが第4文で述べているが，筆者Dは触れていない。

問2　「筆者Bは　2　と示唆している」

> ①　デジタル機器から離れる時間をとることは，生徒の学習意欲を妨げる
> ②　時に，一般的に信じられていることが，調査によって明らかになった事実と異なることがある
> ③　スマートフォンを持っていない生徒たちは，自分たちの方が勉強ができると考えそうだ
> ④　教室は，生徒が教師の干渉を受けずに学べる場であるべきだ

正解 ⇒ ②

　筆者Bは，第1文で「スマートフォンは生徒の学習を促すというのが一般的な意見である」と述べているが，第3文では，最近の研究でスマートフォンを許可されると生徒らは学習に集中できないことがわかったと説明している。よって，これに当てはまる②が正解。①は第3文に矛盾し，③は本文の内容とは無関係のため不適。④は，最終文で「教室をスマートフォンに邪魔されない場所にすべき」と述べられているため，「教師の干渉」が誤り。

【全訳例】
　あなたは高校生が授業中にスマートフォンを使うことを許可すべきかどうかについてのエッセイに取り組んでいます。あなたは以下のステップに従います。

　ステップ1：スマートフォンの使用に関する様々な見解を読み，理解する。
　ステップ2：高校生が授業中にスマートフォンを使用することについて立場をとる。
　ステップ3：追加の情報源を用いつつ，エッセイの概要を作成する。

［ステップ1］様々な情報元を読む

> **筆者A（教師）**
> 私の同僚は，スマートフォンが生徒の生涯にわたって役立つ知識やスキルを身につけるのに役に立ち得るのかどうか，とよく疑問を投げかけます。私はよく考えて使用する限りにおいては，スマートフォンは役に立つと考えています。スマートフォンは，学習効果を高めることができる様々な授業での活動をサポートします。例えば，プロジェクトのためにアンケートを作成したり，自分の学びを他の生徒と共有したりすることが挙げられます。別の利点は，私たちが生徒にデバイスを提供する必要

がないことです。生徒が自分のスマートフォンを使えるのです！ 学校は，生徒の高性能なコンピュータ・デバイスを最大限に活用すべきです。

筆者B（心理学者）

スマートフォンは生徒の学習を促すというのが広く浸透された意見である。しかし，多くの人がそう思うからといって，その意見が正しいとは限らない。最近の研究では，高校生が授業中にスマートフォンを使用することを許可された場合，彼らは学習に集中できないことがわかった。実際，生徒が自分のスマートフォンを使っていなくても，クラスメートがスマートフォンを使っているのを見ることが集中の妨げとなった。学校は教室をスマートフォンに邪魔されない場所にすべきであることは明らかである。

筆者C（保護者）

最近，高校生の息子にスマートフォンを買ってやりました。というのも，学校が私たちの街から遠いのです。息子はいつも早く家を出て，遅くに帰って来ます。今は，彼は私に連絡したり，困ったことがあれば必要な情報にアクセスしたりできます。その一方で，彼がスマートフォンを見ながら歩いているのを時々見かけます。気をつけないと，彼は事故に遭いかねません。一般に，高校生はスマートフォンを持つほうが安全だと思いますが，それでも保護者はその危険性を認識しておく必要があります。また，彼が授業中にどう使っているのかも知りたいと思います。

筆者D（高校生）

学校では，授業中にスマートフォンを使うことが許可されています。ほとんどの生徒がスマートフォンを持っているので，学校が私たちにその使用を許可することは理にかなっています。授業中，私たちはスマートフォンの外国語学習アプリを活用しており，私にはそれがとても役立っています。今は以前よりも勉強が面白いですし，テストの点数も上がりました。しかしこの前，授業中にオンラインコミックを読んでいるところを先生に見つかり，怒られました。たまにこういうことは起こりますが，全般的に言えば，スマートフォンは私の学習を向上させました。

筆者E（校長）

私の学校の教師たちは，生徒たちが授業中に友達とやり取りするためにスマートフォンを使うのではないかと考え，始めはスマートフォン（の使用）に懐疑的でした。そのため，スマートフォンを禁止していました。しかし，利用できる教育用アプリが増えるにつれ，私たちはスマートフォンを教室での学習補助教材として活用できるのではないかと考えるようになりました。昨年，私たちは授業中のスマートフォンの使用を許可することにしました。残念ながら，私たちが望んでいたような結果は得られませんでした。スマートフォンの使用上のルールが機能しており，生徒がそれに従わない限り，スマートフォンは生徒の気を散らすことがわかったのです。もっとも，これは口で言うほど簡単ではありません。

【語句・表現】

・work on ～「～に取り組む」
・allow O to *do*「O が～することを許可する」
・viewpoint「観点，見地，立場」
・take a position「立場をとる」
・outline「概略，骨子，アウトライン」
・additional「追加の」
・source「情報源」
〈筆者A〉
・colleague「同僚」

・life-long「生涯続く」
・as long as ...「…である限りは」
・enhance「～を向上させる，高める」
・include「～を含む」
・provide A with B「A に B を提供する」
・device「装置，デバイス」
・take advantage of ～「（機会など）を利用する」
〈筆者 B〉
・widespread「広く行きわたった，普及した」
・concentrate on ～「～に集中する」
・distraction「気を散らすもの，注意散漫」
・free from ～「～のない」
・interference「じゃま，妨害，干渉」
〈筆者 C〉
・far from ～「～から遠い」
・essential「必要不可欠な」
・on the other hand「一方で」
・generally「一般に，概して，大体，一般的に言って」
・be aware of ～「～に気が付いている，知っている」
・wonder ...「…だろうかと思う，…か知りたいと思う」
〈筆者 D〉
・make sense「道理にかなう」
・permit「～を許可する」
・make use of ～「～を利用する」
・get mad at ～「～に怒る」
・occasionally「時々」
・overall「全体としては，全般的に言えば，概して」
〈筆者 E〉
・initially「初めは」
・skeptical「懐疑的な」
・ban「～を禁止する」
・socialize with ～「～と打ち解けておしゃべりする，（勤務中などに）べらべらしゃべる」
・available「利用できる」
・utilize「～を利用する」
・aid「助け，支援」
・unfortunately「残念ながら」
・distract「～の気を散らす」
・in place「（法律・政策などが）機能している」
・easier said than done「言うは易く行うは難し」
〈設問・選択肢〉
・mention「～に言及する」
・possess「～を所有する，持っている」
・imply「～を暗に意味する，ほのめかす」
・interfere with ～「～を妨げる，邪魔する」
・reveal「～を明らかにする」

[ステップ２] ある立場をとる

問３　さまざまな見地を理解したあなたは，高校生が授業中にスマートフォンを使用することについて次のような立場をとり，それを下記のように書き出しました。　 3 ，　 4 ，　 5 　を完成させるのに最も適切な選択肢を選びなさい。

> あなたの立場：高校生が授業中にスマートフォンを使用することは許されるべきではない。
> ● 筆者　 3 　と　 4 　はあなたの立場を支持している。
> ● 二人の筆者の主な主張：　 5 　。

　 3 　と　 4 　の選択肢（順序は問わない）

> ① A　　　② B　　　③ C　　　④ D　　　⑤ E

　正解 ⇒　 3 　②　　 4 　⑤

　「あなたの立場」は授業中のスマートフォンの使用に反対の立場である。これを支持しているのは，スマートフォンが生徒の学習の妨げとなることを指摘した②の筆者Bと，生徒の気が散ることなくスマートフォンを授業で活用することの困難さを述べた⑤の筆者Eである。筆者Aと筆者Dは，授業中のスマートフォンの使用に賛成の立場なので誤り。筆者Cは，明確に反対の立場をとっているとは言えない。

　 5 　の選択肢

> ①　学校の先生が授業中のスマートフォン使用に関する実用的なルールを作るのは難しい
> ②　教育アプリは使うのが難しいため，スマートフォンは学習の妨げになる可能性がある
> ③　スマートフォンはコミュニケーションを目的として設計されたものであり，授業中の学習向けではない
> ④　生徒は，授業中にスマートフォンを使える状態にしている間は勉強に集中できない

　正解 ⇒ ④

　 3 　と　 4 　より，筆者Bと筆者Eは二人とも「授業中にスマートフォンを使用できる状態だと，生徒が学習に集中できない」という意見なので，④が正解。①は筆者Eのみの主張に当てはまり，②と③のようなことはどちらの筆者も述べていない。

【語句・表現】
・order「順序」
・practical「実用的な」
・focus on ～「～に集中する」

［ステップ3］情報元AとBを用いて概要を作成する

問4 「情報元Aによると，理由2として最も適切なものはどれか」　6

> ① 3D画像を表示するアプリは学習に欠かせないが，すべての生徒がスマートフォンにそのような
> アプリを入れているわけではない。
> ② ある種のデジタル機器は教育効果を高めるが，スマートフォンが最適なわけではない。
> ③ 生徒は，スマートフォンだけでなく他のデバイスも使えるデジタルスキルを身につけ，大学進学
> に備えるべきである。
> ④ 心理学の研究では，デジタル機器が学習に良い影響を与えるという研究結果が出ていないため，
> 私たちは教科書を使い続けるべきである。

正解 ⇒ ②

　情報元Aの第3文まではモバイルデバイスは学習に役立つことが述べられており，第4文以降では，デ
ジタル機器すべてが効果的というわけではなく，スマートフォンよりもノートパソコンやタブレット端末
のほうが授業に適していると主張されていることが説明されている。以上をまとめた②が正解。

問5 「理由3について，あなたは『若い学生はスマホ中毒の危険に直面している』と書くことにした。
　　 情報元Bによると，この記述を最もよく裏付けている選択肢はどれか」　7

> ① ティーンエイジャーの半数以上がスマートフォンを使いすぎていると回答しているが，実際にそ
> のことを後悔しているのは4分の1未満である。これは，スマートフォン依存問題に無自覚である
> ことを示しているのかもしれない。
> ② ティーンエイジャーの若者のおよそ4人に3人がスマートフォンを使いすぎている。実に50％以
> 上が起床後すぐにスマートフォンをチェックする。多くのティーンエイジャーは，スマートフォン
> を使うことを我慢できない。
> ③ 70％を超えるティーンエイジャーが自分はスマホを使いすぎていると考えており，半数以上はス
> マートフォンがないと不安だと感じている。このような依存は，彼らの日常生活に悪影響を及ぼし
> かねない。
> ④ ティーンエイジャーは常にスマートフォンを使っている。実際，4分の3以上がスマートフォン
> の使いすぎを認めている。彼らの生活は朝から晩までスマートフォンに支配されている。

正解 ⇒ ②

　情報元Bに基づいて，「若い学生がスマートフォン中毒の危険に直面している」という記述を最も支持
するのは選択肢②である。上から1～2番目のグラフによると，およそ4人に3人（72％）がスマート
フォンの使用が長すぎると感じており，半数以上（54％）が起床後すぐにスマートフォンを確認している
ことがわかる。
　①は，一番下のグラフにスマートフォンの使い過ぎを後悔している人は27％とあり，4分の1を超える
ので誤り。③は，3番目のグラフによるとスマートフォンがないと不安だと感じる人は45％と半数に届い
ていない。④は，該当する一番上のグラフ（72％）は4分の3未満のため不適。

【全訳例】
あなたのエッセイの概要：

授業中にスマートフォンを使用することは好ましくない

序論
　　スマートフォンは現代人の生活に欠かせないものとなったが，生徒が授業中にスマートフォンを使用することは禁止すべきである。

本文
　　理由1：［ステップ2より］
　　理由2：［情報元Aをもとに］ …………………………… ⬚ 6 ⬚
　　理由3：［情報元Bをもとに］ …………………………… ⬚ 7 ⬚

結論
　　高校は生徒が授業中にスマートフォンを使うことを許可すべきではない。

情報元A
モバイルデバイスは学習に有益である。例えば，ある研究では，大学生が対話型のモバイルアプリを使用した場合，デジタル教科書と比較して，心理学をよりよく学んだことが示された。情報は同じでも，3D画像などのアプリが持つ追加機能が学生の学習効果を高めたのだ。しかし，デジタル機器がすべて等しく効果的というわけではないことを念頭に置くことが重要である。別の研究では，スマートフォンよりもノートパソコンを使った方が，画面サイズが大きいため生徒が内容を理解しやすいということがわかった。学校は，生徒の学習効果を最大化するデジタル機器の種類を選ぶべきであり，生徒に自分のスマートフォンを使わせるよりも，学校がパソコンやタブレット端末を支給するべきだという強い主張がある。すべての生徒に同じアプリがインストールされたパソコンやタブレット端末が支給されれば，技術的な問題が減り，教師も授業を行いやすくなる。また，これなら自分のスマートフォンを持っていない生徒もすべての授業活動に参加することができる。

情報元B
アメリカで行われたある研究では，多くのティーンエイジャーがスマートフォンに依存していることがわかった。この調査は，13歳から18歳までの生徒約1000人を対象に行われた。下のグラフは，スマートフォンの使用についての記述にそう思うと答えた生徒の割合を示している。

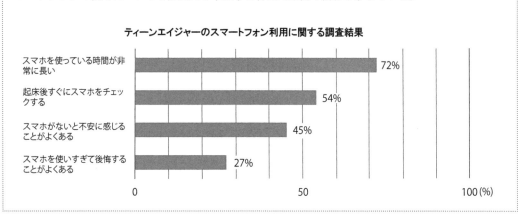

ティーンエイジャーのスマートフォン利用に関する調査結果

記述	割合
スマホを使っている時間が非常に長い	72%
起床後すぐにスマホをチェックする	54%
スマホがないと不安に感じることがよくある	45%
スマホを使いすぎて後悔することがよくある	27%

【語句・表現】
・prohibit「～を禁止する」
〈Source A〉
・psychology「心理学」
・interactive「対話方式の，相互作用を活用した」
・feature「特徴」
・effective「効果的な」
・maximize「～を最大化する」
・conduct「～を行う，運営する」
〈Source B〉
・numerous「たくさんの，数多くの」
・be addicted to ～「～の中毒になる，～におぼれる」
・statement「陳述，発言，意見」
〈設問・選択肢〉
・obtain「～を（努力・計画して）得る」
・positive effect「良い効果」
・addiction「依存症」
・regret「後悔」
・indicate「～を指し示す」
・unawareness「気づいていないこと」
・dependency「依存」
・immediately「すぐに」
・resist「～に抵抗する，（誘惑など）に負けない，～に影響されない」
・anxious「不安な」
・dependence「依存」
・admit to ～「～を（事実であると）認める」

第 B 問

問 1 「コメント(1)に基づくと，付け加えるのに最適な文はどれか」 ［ 1 ］

① その結果，人々は必要のない似たようなものをたくさん買ってしまう。
② このため，客は服を買うことを楽しめない。
③ このため，店員は客が何を必要としているかを知りたがる。
④ このような状況では，消費者は買い物に行くのを避ける傾向がある。

正解 ⇒ ①

(1)の直前は「約64％の買い物客が，すでにクローゼットの中にあるものについて考えていない」である。このような状態で買い物をしてしまうと，すでに持っている服と同じようなものを買ってしまう恐れがあると考えられるため，①が正解。そうすると，(1)の直後の文「そのため，買い物をする時には慎重に服を選ぶ計画を立てるようにしよう」にも上手くつながる。その他の選択肢は，どれも文脈に合わないため不適。

問 2 「コメント(2)に基づくと，付け加えるのに最適な表現はどれか」 ［ 2 ］

① たとえば
② 反対に
③ それにもかかわらず
④ それゆえ

正解 ⇒ ②

(2)の直前は「(高品質のものは) 値段が比較的高かったとしても，何年か着られるものであれば十分にその価値はある」，直後は「安い生地はすぐに色が落ちたり，古く見え始めたりするので，早めに捨てなくてはならない」である。この二文は対比の関係にあるので，②「反対に」が正解。

問 3 「コメント(3)に基づくと，主題文を書き換えるのに最も適切な方法はどれか」 ［ 3 ］

① 新しい服の購入数を減らす
② 古い服を捨てる
③ 服を再利用する方法を探す
④ 不要な服を人に譲る

正解 ⇒ ③

下線部(3)はこの段落の主題文にあたる。後続の文では，その例として「古着屋に売る」「必要とする人に寄付をする」「他の用途を探す」といったことが挙げられている。これらはいずれもいらなくなった服を再利用する方法なので，③が正解。最終段落第2文で give your clothes a second life「自分の服に第二の人生を与えよう」と言い換えられていることもヒントになる。①と②は前述の例に当てはまらない。④は服の再利用の具体例であり，主題文としてはふさわしくない。

問 4 「コメント(4)に基づくと，最適な代替案はどれか」 ［ 4 ］

① 状態を保てるものを買う
② 安価でおしゃれな服を選ぶ

③　作り変えることができるアイテムを選ぶ
④　中古の服を買う

　　正解 ⇒ ①

　最終段落第2文では，第2～4段落で述べられた「持続可能であるための3つの方法」をそれぞれ短く言い変えて再掲されている。下線部は，第3段落の「服を買う際には長持ちする高品質なものを買うべき」という主張の言い換えとなればよいので，①が正解。②は，第3段落の安い生地は早めに捨てなければならないため好ましくないという説明と矛盾するため不適切。③や④のようなことは本文で述べられていない。

【全訳例】

　英語の授業で，あなたは関心のある社会問題についてエッセイを書いています。これはあなたの最新版の原稿です。あなたは今，先生からのコメントに基づいて修正作業を行っています。

ファッションで環境に優しい行動をとる	コメント
多くの人はファッションが大好きである。洋服は自己表現のために大切なものだが，ファッションは環境に有害となる恐れがある。日本では毎年約48万トンの服が捨てられていると言われている。これは1日あたり大型トラック約130台分に相当する。私たちは「捨てる」行動を変える必要がある。このエッセイでは，より持続可能であるための3つの方法を強調する。	
第一に，買い物をする際，計画になかった購入を避けることである。政府の調査によると，約64%の買い物客が，すでにクローゼットの中にあるものについて考えていないという。(1)∧そのため，買い物をする時には慎重に服を選ぶ計画を立てるようにしよう。	(1)ここに何かが欠けています。この二文がつながるようにこの間に情報を追加しましょう。
加えて，通常長持ちする高品質の服を購入すること。値段が比較的高かったとしても，何年か着られるものであれば十分にその価値はある。(2)∧安めの生地はすぐに色が落ちたり古びて見え始めたりするので，早めに捨てなくてはならない。	(2)ここに接続表現を入れましょう。
最後に，(3)自分の服について考えてみよう。例えば，それらを古着屋に売る。そうすれば他の人がそれらを着て楽しむことができる。また，服を必要としている人のために慈善団体に寄付してもよいだろう。もうひとつの方法は，それらの新しい用途を見つけることである。キルトやバッグなど，服を便利なアイテムに作り変える方法はたくさんある。	(3)このトピックセンテンスはこのパラグラフにあまり適していません。書き直しましょう。
結論として，今こそライフスタイルを変える時である。これからは，買い物に行く前に自分のクローゼットを確認し，(4)より良い物を選び，そして最後に，自分の服に第二の人生を与えよう。そうすることで，私たちはみなファッションでより持続可能な存在になれるのである。	(4)下線部の表現はあなたのエッセイの内容の要約として不十分です。変更しましょう。

全体的なコメント：
あなたのエッセイは良くなってきています。この調子で頑張ってください。(自分のクローゼットはチェックしましたか？　私はチェックしましたよ！☺)

【語句・表現】

・social issue「社会問題」
・revision「修正，改訂」

〈第1段落〉
・self-expression「自己表現」
・harmful to ～「～に有害な」
・throw ～ away「～を捨てる」
・highlight「～を強調する」
・sustainable「持続可能な」

〈第2段落〉
・avoid *doing*「～することを避ける」
・purchase「購入，買物」
・approximately「およそ」

〈第3段落〉
・high-quality「質の良い，高品質の」
・last long「長持ちする」
・fabric「布地」

〈第4段落〉
・donate「～を寄付する」
・charity「慈善団体」
・transform A into B「A を B に変形［変質］させる」
・outfit「服装一式」
・quilt「キルト風に仕上げたもの，キルト布団，ベッドカバー」

〈第5段落〉
・from now on「今後は」
・select「～を（多くのものから）選び出す」

〈コメント〉
・miss「～を欠く，抜かす」
・add「～を追加する」
・insert「～を挿入する」
・connecting expression「接続表現」
・topic sentence「主題文，トピックセンテンス」
・match「～と調和する」
・rewrite「～を書き直す」
・summarize「～を要約する，手短に述べる」
・content「内容，中身」
・keep up「～を続ける，実践し続ける」

〈設問・選択肢〉
・due to ～「（原因）～のため」
・shop clerk「店員」
・consumer「消費者」
・tend to *do*「～する傾向がある，～しがちである」
・dispose of ～「～を処分する，捨てる」
・reuse「～を再利用する」
・give away「～をただでやる，寄付する」
・replacement「置き換え」
・pick「～を選ぶ」
・second-hand「中古の」

問題番号 （配点）	設	問	解答番号	正 解	配 点	自己採点
第1問 (10)	A	1	1	4	2	
		2	2	1	2	
	B	1	3	4	2	
		2	4	3	2	
		3	5	1	2	
			自己採点小計			
第2問 (20)	A	1	6	1	2	
		2	7	2	2	
		3	8	1	2	
		4	9	4	2	
		5	10	2	2	
	B	1	11	1	2	
		2	12	1	2	
		3	13	1	2	
		4	14	3	2	
		5	15	2	2	
			自己採点小計			
第3問 (15)	A	1	16	2	3	
		2	17	2	3	
	B	1	18	1	3*	
			19	2		
			20	3		
			21	4		
		2	22	3	3	
		3	23	2	3	
			自己採点小計			

問題番号 （配点）	設	問	解答番号	正 解	配 点	自己採点
第4問 (16)		1	24	3	3	
		2	25	4	3	
		3	26	4	3	
	4		27	5	2	
			28	4	2	
		5	29	3	3	
			自己採点小計			
第5問 (15)		1	30	4	3*	
			31	5		
			32	1		
			33	2		
		2	34	2	3	
		3	35	1	3*	
			36	2		
		4	37	3	3	
		5	38	2	3	
			自己採点小計			
第6問 (24)	A	1	39	6	3*	
			40	2		
		2	41	1	3	
		3	42	3	3	
		4	43	1	3	
	B	1	44	4	2	
		2	45	4	2	
		3	46 – 47	2 - 3	3*	
		4	48	3	3	
		5	49	5	2	
			自己採点小計			

自己採点合計 [　　]

（注）
1 ＊は全部正解の場合のみ点を与える。
2 −(ハイフン)でつながれた正解は，順序を問わない。

第1問

A
問1 「無料イベントに参加するには，[1]」

---
① 自国から写真を持参する
② 展示についてスタッフに相談する
③ 学生ロビーで申込用紙に必要事項を記入する
④ **TELS の学生であることを証明できるものを提示する**

正解 ⇒ ④

第2～3文に「TELS の学生は入場料を支払う必要はありません。学生ロビーの受付デスクで学生証を提示してください」と説明があるため，④が適切。①と②はホール内の展示物に関することであり，無料で参加する方法とは無関係なので誤り。③については本文で述べられていない。

【語句・表現】
・consult「～に相談する」
・fill out ～「～に記入する」
・proof「証明，証拠」

問2 「イベントでは，あなたは[2]ことができる」

---
① 様々な文化のジェスチャーを学ぶ
② ダンス大会に参加する
③ 外国語の短編小説を読む
④ 世界の料理を作ってみる

正解 ⇒ ①

催し物の2つ目の項目の最後「これらの文化圏の人々がどのように表情や手を使ってコミュニケーションをとっているのかを学んでください」より，正解は①である。②は，項目の3つ目で「パフォーマーが基本的なステップを教えます」とは述べられているが，ダンス大会に関する記述ではないので誤り。③のような記述は本文にない。④は，項目の1つ目から分かるように，世界の料理を作るのではなく食べる場なので，これも誤り。

【語句・表現】
・participate in ～「～に参加する」
・competition「コンテスト，競争」

【全訳例】
あなたはアメリカの語学学校で英語を勉強しています。その学校はイベントを企画しています。あなたは参加したいと思い，チラシを読んでいます。

ソープ英語語学学校
インターナショナル・ナイト
5月24日（金）午後5時～午後8時
入場料：5ドル

ソープ英語語学学校（TELS）は国際交流イベントを企画しています。TELS の生徒は入場料を支払う必要はありません。学生ロビー受付にて学生証をご提示ください。

- **・世界各地の料理を楽しもう**
  中東のフムスを食べたことがありますか？ メキシコのタコスは？ 北アフリカのクスクスは？ ぜひ全部試してみてください！
- **・異なる言語や新しいコミュニケーション方法を体験しよう**
  アラビア語，イタリア語，日本語，スペイン語で「こんにちは」「ありがとう」などの基本的な表現を書いてみましょう。これらの文化の人々が表情や手を使ってどのようにコミュニケーションをとるのか学びましょう。
- **・ダンスを鑑賞しよう**
  午後7時からは，ステージで行われるフラメンコ，フラ，サンバのダンスショーを鑑賞しましょう！ 各ダンス終了後，出演者が基本的なステップを教えます。ぜひご参加ください。

ホール内には，たくさんの写真，国旗，地図，織物，工芸品，ゲームなどが展示されます。イベントで展示できるような自国の写真や品物をお持ちの方は，5月17日までに学校スタッフまでお知らせください！

【語句・表現】
〈リード文〉
・attend「出席する」
・flyer「チラシ」
〈本文〉
・entrance fee「入場料」
・organize「〜を計画［準備］する」
・present「〜を提示する」
・reception「受付」
・various「さまざまな」
・facial expression「表情」
・textile「織物」
・craft「工芸品」

B
問1 「イェントンビルには □3□ がある」

- ① 街が建設される250年前に建てられた教会
- ② 町の中心にあるユニークなサッカー練習施設
- ③ 来場者がオリジナルの芸術作品を制作できるアートスタジオ
- ④ アートギャラリーとコンサートホールが併設されたアートエリア

正解 ⇒ ④

①については，「歴史ツアー」の第1文に，教会は1800年代半ばに設立されたとある。これは今から約175年前であることから，計算が合わないため不適切。②は，「スポーツツアー」の第1文より，練習施設は町の中心部ではなく「郊外」にあるので，誤り。③は，「芸術ツアー」の最終文より，アートスタジオは見学するところであって，作品作りはできないため，誤り。④は，「芸術ツアー」の説明の前半より，芸術地区にはアートギャラリーと，その向かいにコンサートホールがあることがわかるので，これが正解。

【語句・表現】
・construct「～を建設する」
・facility「施設」
・works「作品」

問2 「3つの全てのツアーで，あなたは ☐4☐ 」

> ① 市内の歴史的な出来事について学ぶ
> ② 人々が技を披露するのを見る
> ❸ 屋内と屋外の両方で過ごす
> ④ 公共交通機関を利用して移動する

　正解 ⇒ ③

　3つのツアーに共通する点は，屋内と屋外の両方の訪問箇所があることなので，③が正解。①は「歴史ツアー」のみに当てはまる。②は「芸術ツアー」のスタジオ見学と「スポーツツアー」のプロによる試合の2つのみに当てはまる。④については，「歴史ツアー」ではバス，「スポーツツアー」では地下鉄を利用するが，「芸術ツアー」では交通機関に言及されていない。

【語句・表現】
・get around「移動する」

問3 「このツアーで訪れることのできるイェントンビルの中で最も新しい場所はどこか」 ☐5☐

> ① ホッケーアリーナ
> ② 市長邸
> ③ 平和公園
> ④ 彫刻公園

　　正解 ⇒ ①

　①のホッケーアリーナはcompleted last fall「昨年の秋に完成」，②の市長邸は early-20th-century「20世紀初頭」，③の平和公園は Opened soon after World War II「第二次世界大戦後すぐにオープン」，④の彫刻公園は several years ago「何年か前」にできたと述べられている。以上より，この中で最も新しいのは①のホッケーアリーナであるとわかる。

【全訳例】
　あなたはアメリカにいる交換留学生で，来週あなたのクラスは日帰り旅行に出かけます。先生がいくつかの情報を提供してくれました。

イェントンビルのツアー
イェントンビル観光局では，3つの市内ツアーを提供しています。
歴史ツアー
この日はまず，1800年代半ばに市が設立されたときに建てられた聖パトリック教会を訪れます。教会の向かいには，20世紀初頭に建築された市長邸があります。邸宅とその美しい庭を見学するツアーを行います。最後に，公共バスで市内を横断し，平和公園を訪れます。この公園は第二次世界大戦後すぐに開園し，1960年代には多くのデモが行われた場所でした。

芸術ツアー
午前中はイェントンビル芸術地区を訪れます。初めに，ヨーロッパやアメリカの絵画が多数展示されているアートギャラリーを訪れます。昼食後，通り向かいのブルトン・コンサートホールでコンサートを楽しんだ後，アーティスト通りまで少し歩きます。芸術地区のこの部分は，数年前に新しいアーティストのスタジオと近くの彫刻公園が造られたときに開発されました。アーティストたちがスタジオで作業をしているのを見学した後は，公園内を散策し，木々の間にある彫刻を見つけてみましょう。

スポーツツアー
朝一番に，郊外の野外施設でイェントンビル・ライオンズというフットボールチームの練習を見ることができます。午後は，地下鉄で昨年秋に完成したイェントンビル・ホッケーアリーナへ行きます。その展示ホールでしばらく過ごし，アリーナのユニークなデザインについて学びます。最後に，アリーナでプロ・ホッケーの試合を楽しみましょう。

イェントンビル観光局，2024年1月

【語句・表現】
〈歴史ツアー〉
・establish「～を設立，創立する」
・opposite「反対側の」
・cross「～を渡る，横断する」
・demonstration「デモ」
〈アートツアー〉
・district「地区，管区」
・distance「距離，道のり」
・several「いくつかの」
・sculpture「彫刻，彫像」
・afterward(s)「あとで，その後」
・wander「歩き回る，ぶらつく」
〈スポーツツアー〉
・open-air「野外」
・suburb「郊外」
・subway「地下鉄」
・complete「～を仕上げる，完成させる」
・fall「秋」
・spend「（時間）を過ごす」
・exhibition「展覧会，展示会，（スポーツの）エキシビション」
・professional「プロの，本格的な」

第2問

A
問1 「チラシによると，クラブについて正しいのはどれか」 ⬚6

① 全くの初心者も歓迎する。
② 部員がコンピュータープログラムを編集する。
③ プロのプレイヤーが正式に実演をする。
④ 他校の生徒も参加できる。

正解 ⇒ ①

第6文に「スキルのレベルに関係なく，あなたの参加を歓迎します」とあるので，①が正解。②のようなことは本文で述べられていない。③は，箇条書きの1つ目より，実演を行うのはプロのプレイヤーではなく，部員なので誤り。④は，第5文に「クラブは本校の全ての生徒が参加できます」とあるが，他校の生徒についての言及がないので不適切。

【語句・表現】
・absolute「まったくの，純然たる」
・demonstration「実演，実物教授，デモンストレーション」

問2　「クラブ活動として言及されていないのは次のうちどれか」　7

① 部員以外と試合すること
② コンピューターと対戦すること
③ インターネット上で試合に関するアイデアを共有すること
④ 戦略ゲームの背景を研究すること

正解 ⇒ ②

クラブ活動の内容は箇条書きで述べられている。①は，6つ目の「地方や全国の試合に参加する」に当てはまる。②は，5つ目に「コンピューターソフトウェアを使ってゲームを分析する」とはあるが，コンピューターとの対戦には言及がないので，これが正解。③は，3つ目の「クラブのウェブページでヒントを共有する」に一致する。④は，4つ目の「各ゲームの歴史と礼儀作法を学ぶ」のことである。

【語句・表現】
・match「試合，ゲーム」
・background「背景」
・strategy「戦略」

問3　「部員が述べた意見のひとつは，　8　ということである」

① いろいろなゲームを比較するのは面白い
② 囲碁についての動画がたくさんあって役に立つ
③ 部員は大会でヒントを学ぶ
④ 定例会が学外で行われる

正解 ⇒ ①

部員の意見が含まれる「部員のコメント」を参照する。①は，2つ目のコメントの「いくつかのゲームの共通点を学べるのがいい」という意見に該当するので，これが正解。②は4つ目のコメントより，動画は囲碁ではなくチェスについてなので不適切。③はヒントを学べるのはウェブページからであり，④も定例会が行われるのは「学生センターの301教室」なので，いずれも本文と一致せず，かつどちらも意見ではないので誤り。

【語句・表現】
・compare「～を比較する」

問4　「クラブの招待文と部員のコメントの両方に，　9　という言及がある」

> ① 新メンバーは経験を示さなければならない
> ② 良いプレイヤーになるためにはオンラインサポートが必要である
> ③ 将棋は論理的で刺激的なゲームである
> **④ 戦略ゲームは集中力の向上に役立つ**

　正解 ⇒ ④

　正解は④である。これについては，第3文「気を散らすことなく，論理的に深く考えるスキルを学ぶことができます」と，部員のコメントの1つ目「授業でもより頭がクリアになり，落ち着き，集中できています」の両方で言及されている。①と②の内容は，本文で述べられていない。③の「論理的」は将棋に言及した部員のコメントがないので，不適。

【語句・表現】
・necessary「必要な」
・logical「論理的な」
・stimulating「（よい）刺激となる」
・concentration「集中（状態）」

問5　「このクラブは　10　生徒に最も向いている可能性がある」

> ① 自分でコンピューター戦略ゲームを作りたい
> **② 戦略ゲームをプレイするスキルを向上させたい**
> ③ 戦略ゲームを通して，イギリスの正式な礼儀作法を学びたい
> ④ 部室で戦略ゲームをして週末を過ごしたい

　正解 ⇒ ②

　本文全体から，このクラブでは部員とオンラインでヒントを共有したり，試合の分析をしたりと，戦略ゲームのスキルを向上させるための様々な取り組みがされていることが読み取れる。よって，②が正解。①と④はクラブの活動内容や条件にあてはまらない。③は，活動内容の4つ目に「各ゲームの礼儀作法」を学ぶとあるが，イギリスの礼儀作法を学べるわけではない。

【語句・表現】
〈設問〉
・suitable for ～「～に適した，ふさわしい」
〈選択肢〉
・proper「適切な，正式の」
・etiquette「礼儀作法，エチケット」

【全訳例】
　あなたはイギリスの高校に留学中で，次のチラシを見つけました。

戦略ゲームクラブへの招待

チェスや将棋，囲碁などの戦略ゲームを学びたいと思ったことはありませんか？　実はこれらは単なるゲームではありません。気を散らすことなく，論理的に深く考えるスキルを習得することができま

す。しかも，これらのゲームは本当に楽しいです！ このクラブは本校の生徒なら誰でも参加できます。腕前に関係なく，大歓迎です。

一緒に戦略ゲームをしながら…

- ● 部員による実演から基本的な手を学びます。
- ● 部員とオンラインで対戦します。
- ● クラブのウェブページでヒントを共有します。
- ● 各ゲームの歴史と礼儀作法を学びます。
- ● コンピューターソフトウェアを使ってゲームを分析します。
- ● 地方や全国のトーナメントに参加します。

定例会：毎週水曜日の午後，学生センター301教室にて

部員のコメント

- － 授業でもより頭がクリアになり，落ち着き，集中できています。
- － いくつかのゲームの共通点を学べるのがいい。
- － 大会で，他の参加者たちと戦略を話し合うのが好きです。
- － 部員同士で，チェスの実践的な戦略を説明するインターネットの動画を共有しています。
- － 囲碁について良いアドバイスをしてくれる友人がいてよかったです。
- － 入部したときは全くの初心者でしたが，何の問題もありませんでした！

【語句・表現】
- ・invitation to ～「～への招待」
- ・chess「チェス」
- ・deeply「深く」
- ・plus「そしてその上，しかも」
- ・regardless of ～「～にかかわらず」
- ・tip「ヒント，助言」
- ・analyse「～を分析する」：イギリス英語のつづり。アメリ英語では analyze とつづる。
- ・participate in ～「～に参加する」
- ・local「その土地の，地元の，現地の」
- ・national「国内の，全国的な」
- ・mind「精神，心」
- ・focused「集中した」
- ・similarity「類似（点）」
- ・discuss「～を議論する」
- ・participant「参加者」
- ・practical「実際的な，実用的な，効果的な」
- ・complete「まったくの，完全な」

B
問1 「レビューによると，次のうち正しいものはどれか」　11

① 最も高額なプランでは，昼夜を問わず医療サポートが受けられる。
② 最も安いプランでは，いかなる理由でも入院費が無料である。
③ 中級のプランには1回限りの健康診断が含まれていない。
④ 筆者が契約したプランは毎月100ドル以上かかった。

正解 ⇒ ①

　最も高いプレミアムプランについて書かれた第3段落第2文に「このプランでは…24時間医療サポートを提供しています」とあるので，正解は①である。②は，第5段落に記載された最も安いプランの説明にない内容である。③は，第2段落の最終文「すべてのプランに1回きりの健康診断が含まれる」に矛盾するため，誤り。④は，第4段落第3文より，筆者が契約したプランは通常で月75ドルだとわかるので不適。

【語句・表現】
・day and night「昼も夜も」
・include「～を含む」
・hospitalization「入院」
・check-up「健康診断」

問2　「最も安いプランに含まれないものは次のうちどれか」　　12

> ①　メールによるサポート
> ②　救急治療
> ③　電話相談窓口
> ④　輸送の援助

　正解 ⇒ ①

　最も安いエコノミープランについては第5段落に説明がある。このプランに含まれるのは，②と③にあたる救急治療を扱う電話相談と，④にあたる病院に行くためのタクシーの手配である。メールサポートはここには含まれていないので，正解は①である。

【語句・表現】
・emergency「緊急事態」
・transport「輸送（の）」

問3　「TravSafer International を説明するのに最も適した組み合わせはどれか」　　13

> A：月払いが可能である。
> B：学生のための奨学金制度がある。
> C：薬を忘れないようにサポートしてくれる。
> D：インターネット上での登録システムを提供している。
> E：申し込みフォームの処理に数日かかる。
>
> ①　AとD　　　　②　AとE　　　　③　BとD
> ④　BとE　　　　⑤　CとD

　正解 ⇒ ①

　第2段落第2・3文に「オンラインで15分もかからずに契約でき，すぐに保険が適用されました。どんな支払い方法も受けつけており，通常は月払いです」とあるので，①のAとDが正解。BとCのようなことは本文で述べられていない。Eは，「15分で登録できる」という内容に矛盾する。

【語句・表現】
〈設問〉
・combination「組み合わせ」
・describe「～を説明する，（言葉で）描写する，～の特徴を述べる」
〈選択肢〉
・allow「～を許す」
・payment「支払い」
・scholarship「奨学金」
・medication「薬剤，薬物（治療）」
・registration「登録」
・application form「申し込み書，申し込みフォーム」

問4 「筆者が選んだプランに対する彼女自身の意見は，[14]というものである」

① そのプランは彼女の健康志向を妨げるものであった
② 彼女は電話サポートに満足しなかった
③ **費用割引のオプションは魅力的だった**
④ 彼女の足の骨折の治療費が保障された

正解 ⇒ ③

第4段落最終文に「15％値引を受けられたのは良かった」とあることから，正解は③である。①と②のようなことは本文で述べられていない。④は，最終段落によると足を骨折したのは筆者の友達であり，さらに意見ではなく事実にあたる内容であるため，誤り。

【語句・表現】
・prevent O from *doing*「O が～するのを妨げる，阻止する」
・health conscious「健康志向の」
・be satisfied with ～「～に満足している」
・reduction「削減，割引」
・attractive「魅力的な」
・cover「～を扱う，～に適用される」

問5 「次のうち筆者の態度を最もよく表しているものはどれか」[15]

① 彼女はスマートフォンのアプリは便利だと考えている。
② **彼女は旅行の準備は大切だと考えている。**
③ 彼女は米国の医療制度は世界でも独特だと感じている。
④ 友人には別の病院の方が良かっただろうと彼女は思っている。

正解 ⇒ ②

筆者は第1段落で，海外旅行の前には準備に関して多くのことを考えなければならないと述べている。さらに第6段落では，彼女の友人が旅先で骨折をしたものの，全額保険で治療費を賄えたという話を受けて，最終文で「保険がどれだけ大切であるかに気づきました」と述べている。以上より，旅行前の準備は大切だと考えていると読み取れるため，正解は②である。その他の選択肢は，本文では述べられていない内容である。

〈設問〉
・attitude「態度，意見」
〈選択肢〉
・consider O (to be) C「O を C だとみなす［考える］」
・preparation「準備」

【全訳例】
　あなたはアメリカへ留学する予定の大学生で，旅行保険を必要としています。あなたは，6か月間アメリカに留学した女子留学生による保険プランのレビューを見つけました。

海外旅行に行く前に考えなければならないことはたくさんあります。適切な服を用意すること，旅費を準備すること，（必要であれば）薬を忘れないこと。また，旅行保険にも加入すべきです。

私はカリフォルニアのフェアビル大学に留学したとき，TravSafer International の旅行保険に加入しました。オンラインで15分もかからずに契約でき，すぐに保険が適用されました。どんな支払い方法も受けつけており，通常は月払いです。プランは3つありました。すべてのプランに1回限りの健康診断が含まれています。

プレミアムプランは月額100ドルです。このプランは，スマートフォンのアプリと電話サービスを通じて24時間医療サポートを提供しています。入院が必要になった場合は，即座に金銭的なサポートが認められます。

スタンダードプランが私には一番合っていました。24時間の電話サポートがあり，外国で健康を維持するための助言が書かれたメールが毎週送られてきます。月75ドルと安くはありませんでした。しかし，6か月分の保険料を前払いすることでオプションの15％割引を受けられたのは良かったです。

予算が限られている場合は，月25ドルのエコノミープランを選んでもよいでしょう。他のプランと同様に24時間の電話サポートがありますが，救急時のみ利用可能です。また，サポートセンターが必要と判断すれば，病院までのタクシーを割引料金で手配してくれます。

私は病気や怪我をしたことがなかったので，保険に入るのはお金の無駄だと思っていました。そんなとき，ブラジルから来た友人がサッカー中に足を骨折し，数日間入院しなければなりませんでした。彼はプレミアムプランを選んでいたので，すべて保障されたのです！私は保険がどれだけ大切であるかに気づきました。自分が困ったときにサポートしてくれることが分かっているのですから。

【語句・表現】
〈リード文〉
・insurance「保険」
〈第1段落〉
・appropriate「適切な，ふさわしい」
・expense「費用，出費，必要経費」
・if necessary「必要であれば」
・purchase「～を購入する」
〈第2段落〉
・signed up「登録する，契約する」
・immediately「ただちに，すぐに」

・accept「～を受諾する，～に応じる」
・on a ～ basis「～基準で」
・one-time「１回限りの」
〈第３段落〉
・immediate「即時の，じかの」
・financial「財政上の，会計上の」
・authorize「（支払いなど）を承認する，認可する」
〈第４段落〉
・optional「選択の，オプションの，任意の」
・discount「割引」
・coverage「保障範囲」
・in advance「前もって，あらかじめ」
〈第５段落〉
・budget「予算」
・arrange「～を手配する」
〈第６段落〉
・waste「浪費，むだ使い」

第３問

A
問１ 「あなたはブログのリンクをクリックする。どの写真が表れるか」 16

正解 ⇒ ②

第８～10文より，侍像に向かう途中に出会った，猿を連れた男性と写真を撮ったことがわかる。よって，正解は②である。男性と猿が写っていない①と④は不適。③は，第10～11文より，ゴールにたどり着いたのは猿を連れた男性と別れた後なので，誤り。

問２ 「あなたはスーザンのブログにコメントを求められている。彼女への適切なコメントはどれか」
17

> ① あなたが金メダルを身に着けている写真が見たいです！
> ② あなたはベストを尽くしました。日本に戻ってきて，また挑戦してください！
> ③ ３時間で19のチェックポイントを通過したんですか？ 本当に？ すごいですね!!
> ④ あなたの写真は素敵ですね！ 携帯をアップグレードしたのですか？

正解 ⇒ ②

本文はスーザンがイギリスに帰国した後に日本でフォトラリーに参加した時のことを書いたブログであること，スーザンたちは予定していたチェックポイント全てをめぐることはできなかったことを踏まえると，最も適切なコメントは②である。19のチェックポイントを通過して優勝したのはスーザンたちのチームではないので，①と③は誤り。ルール項目の１つ目で，撮影には支給されたカメラのみを使用することが定められており，さらに６つ目に「携帯電話の使用禁止」とあることから，④は２文目が不適。

【全訳例】

　あなたの英語 ALT の姉であるスーザンが，先月あなたのクラスを訪れました。今はイギリスに戻った彼女が，参加したイベントについてブログに書いていました。

こんにちは！
外国人観光客向けのフォトラリーに友達と参加しました。右のルールをご覧ください。フォトラリー初心者の私たちは，チェックポイントのうち5つだけを目指すことにしました。
3分で，最初の目標である市立美術館に到着しました。その後，2つ目，3つ目，4つ目と立て続けにクリアしました。順調に進んでいました！　しかし，最後の目標である，市の有名な侍像に向かう途中で道に迷ってしまいました。制限時間が迫っており，2時間以上歩いたので足が痛くなっていました。ペットの猿を連れた男性を呼び止め助けを求めましたが，私たちの日本語も彼の英語も十分ではありませんでした。彼が身振り手振りを交えて道を説明してくれた後，私たちはそこにたどり着くには時間が足りず，あきらめるしかないと分かりました。私たちは彼と写真を撮って別れました。さくら市役所に戻ると，優勝チームが19のチェックポイントをクリアしたと聞いて驚きました。私たちの写真の1枚が選ばれて，イベントのウェブサイトに掲載されました（ここをクリック）。この写真はあの男性の温かさと親切さを思い出させてくれます。私たちにとっての「金メダル」なのです。

> **さくら市フォトラリールール**
> - 各チームは支給されたカメラと紙の地図のみ使用可能
> - 25か所のチェックポイント（指定された観光スポット）のうち，出来るだけ多くの写真を撮ってください
> - 制限時間は**3時間**
> - 写真には**チームメンバー3人全員**が写っている必要があります
> - チームメンバーは**一緒に移動**しなければなりません
> - 携帯電話の**使用禁止**
> - 交通機関の**使用禁止**

【語句・表現】

・aim for ～「～をねらう，目指す」
・in quick succession「矢つぎ早に」
・smoothly「円滑に」
・on the way to ～「～に行く道中に」
・statue「像」
・run out「（時間が）なくなる」
・neither A nor B「A も B も～ない」
・give up「あきらめる」
・remind O of ～「O に～を思い出させる」
・warmth「思いやり，温情，優しさ」
・kindness「親切心，優しさ，親切な行為」

B

問1　「ユズの記事には，バーチャルツアーでの出来事を説明した学生のコメント（①～④）も掲載されていた。コメントを出来事が起こった順に並べなさい」

　　　| 18 | → | 19 | → | 20 | → | 21 |

---

① 私はこの島がどれほど危険な場所なのか気になりました。ジャングルでは美しい鳥と大きなヘビを見ました。
② 以前はもっとたくさんの生き物がいたなんて，本当に衝撃的でした。私たちは美しい海を守らなければなりません！

③　体育館にキャンプ場を設営するのはなんだか変な感じがしたけど，とても楽しかったです！ 虫に刺されることもなかったので，外よりも良かったです！

④　宇宙ショーの間言葉を失い，私たちはそこにあるのに気づかないことがよくあるということがわかりました。

正解 ⇒　| 18 | ① | | 19 | ② | | 20 | ③ | | 21 | ④ |

　第2段落は，島の地学について学ぶ「ロードトリップ」についての記述なので，最初は①である。第3段落では海の生物について学んでいるので，②が2番目。第4段落は，夜に行った天文学の勉強についての記述である。まず体育館にテントを張り，その天井に映し出された星を観察したとあることから，③→④の順となる。以上より，①→②→③→④が正解。

【語句・表現】
・wonder ...「…だろうかと思う」
・creature「生物」
・protect「～を保護する，守る」
・ocean「海洋，海，大洋」
・set up ～「～を建てる，設置する」
・gymnasium「体育館，ジム」
・weird「不思議な，奇妙な」
・bite「～をかむ，（虫などが）～を刺す」
・bug「昆虫，（刺す）虫」
・even though ...「…であるけれども」

問2　「このツアーで，ユズは南洋の島の　| 22 |　について学ばなかった」

①　海の生態系
②　夜空
③　季節の天候
④　樹木や植物

正解 ⇒ ③

　本文には季節の天候については記述がないので，③が正解。①は第3段落，②は第4段落，④は第2段で学んだ内容である。

【語句・表現】
・marine「海の，海に住む」
・ecosystem「生態系」
・seasonal「季節の，季節ごとの」

問3　「帰り道，ユズは夜空を見上げ，おそらく　| 23 |　を見ただろう」

①　流れ星
②　たった数個の星
③　満月
④　天の川

正解 ⇒ ②

　本文の最終文に「月のない空を見上げると，リーチ先生が私たちに言ったことは本当なのだとわかった」とある。リーチ先生の発言とは，第4段落の最終文にある「人間は人工的な明りを作り過ぎてしまったために，私たちの街の夜空にはほとんど何も見えない」という内容である。したがって，空を見上げても星はほとんど見えなかったということだと考えられるので，②が正解。

【語句・表現】
・shooting star「流れ星」
・just a few「たった数個の」
・full moon「満月」
・the Milky Way「天の川」

【全訳例】

　あなたはイングリッシュ・デイに参加します。準備のために，あなたは昨年参加したユズが書いた学校新聞の記事を読んでいます。

南洋の島へのバーチャル校外学習

今年のイングリッシュ・デイに，私たちはバーチャル・サイエンス・ツアーに参加しました。荒天の冬の日だったので，スクリーンに映し出される火山島の南国の風景を見てわくわくしました。

まず，島の地理を学ぶために，ナビゲーション・ソフトを使ってルートを見ながら「ドライブ旅行」をしました。私たちは「車に乗り込み」，リーチ先生が時々止めてくれることで，窓から熱帯雨林を眺め，熱帯雨林をより感じることができました。その後，私たちは見たものについてリーチ先生に質問しました。

その後，私たちは「海に潜り」，海洋生物の多様性について学びました。私たちはライブカメラでサンゴ礁を観察しました。リーチ先生は，生き物の数を数えられますかと私たちに尋ねましたが，多過ぎました！　それから先生は，10年前の海の画像を見せてくれました。カメラで見たサンゴ礁も迫力がありましたが，写真で見た海は，さらに生命力に溢れていました。たった10年後のものが，大きく違って見えたのです！　リーチ先生は，人間の活動が海に影響を及ぼしており，私たちが今すぐ行動を起こさなければ，海は完全にダメになってしまうかもしれないと，私たちに言いました。

夜は，「完璧な星空」の下で天文学を学びました。体育館にテントを張り，プロジェクターを使って天井に仮設のプラネタリウムを作りました。満天の星座，流れ星，天の川に魅了されました。誰かが最も明るい光のひとつを指さして，あれが地球に近い惑星である金星ですか，とリーチ先生に尋ねました。先生はうなずき，人間が人工的な光をたくさん作り出したため，この街の夜空にはほとんど何も見えないのだと説明しました。

放課後の帰り道，天気は回復し，雲ひとつない空になりました。私は月のない空を見上げて，リーチ先生が話してくれたことが本当だと気づきました。

【語句・表現】
〈第1段落〉
・virtual「仮想の」
・terrible「ひどく悪い」

- be excited「興奮した，うきうきした」
- tropical「熱帯（地方）の，熱帯性の」
- scenery「風景，景色」
- volcanic「火山の（ある），火山の多い」
- project「〜を映写する，投影する」

〈第2段落〉
- geography「地理，地勢，土地の様子」
- route「道，ルート」
- sense「感覚，理解，観念」
- rainforest「熱帯雨林」

〈第3段落〉
- dive into 〜「〜に飛び込む，潜る，没頭する」
- diversity「多様性」
- observe「〜を観察する」
- coral reef「サンゴ礁」
- via 〜「〜経由で，〜を通って」
- dynamic「動的な，活動的な，精力的な」
- affect「〜に影響する，（不利）に作用する」
- ruin「〜をだめにする，荒廃させる，破滅させる」

〈第4段落〉
- astronomy「天文学」
- starry「星の多い，星明りの」
- put up 〜「〜を建てる，掲げる」
- temporary「一時の，一時的な，仮の，臨時の」
- ceiling「天井」
- be fascinated by 〜「〜にうっとりする，ひきつけられる」
- constellation「星座」
- pointed (out) 〜「〜を指し示す，〜に注目させる」
- bright「輝いている，鮮明な（色の)」
- Venus「金星」
- nod「うなずく」
- artificial「人工の，人工的な，人造の」
- visible「目に見える」

〈第5段落〉
- cloudless「雲のない，晴れわたった」
- looked up at 〜「〜を見上げる」
- moonless「月のない」

第4問

問1 「　24　にあてはまる最も適切な選択肢を選べ」

> ① 教室でどの色を使うのが適切かを示す指標
> ② 教室における生徒と教師のニーズに優先順位をつける方法
> **③ 教室の環境を検討する際の見本**
> ④ 教室が生徒の成績にどのような影響を与えるかを理解するための仕組み

正解 ⇒ ③

SIN フレームワークとは何かを答える問題である。第１段落最終文に「SIN とは，（中略）教室をデザインする際に参考になるフレームワーク」とあることから，③が正解。①は S（Stimulation）にあてはまるが，SIN 全体の説明ではないので不適。②や④については，記事の中で言及されていない。

【語句・表現】
・appropriate「適切な」
・prioritize「～の優先順位を決める，～を優先する」
・influence「～に影響を及ぼす」
・performance「成績，（テストなどの）出来ばえ」

問２ 「 25 にあてはまる最も適切な選択肢を選べ」

① スクリーンをより良い場所に移動する
② それぞれの壁を違う色に塗る
③ 本を棚に並べる
④ 展示物を減らす

正解 ⇒ ④

第２段落に Stimulation とは色と複雑さに関する物であり，例えば壁の展示物が多くて気が散ることであると説明されている。またアンケートでは，S ２のコメントの第３・４文に，壁がポスターで埋め尽くされていて居心地が悪いとある。よって， 25 には④が入る。①は，Naturalness に関する記述なので不適。②は，第４文「教室はカラフル過ぎてもいけない」に反するので誤り。③については本文で述べられていない。

【語句・表現】
・shelves：shelf「棚」の複数形。

問３ 「あなたは配布資料をチェックしている。あなたは『自然さ』の推奨事項に誤りがあることに気づいた。次のうち取り除くべきものはどれか」 26

① A（窓にブラインドを取り付ける）
② B（温度調節ができるようにする）
③ C（プロジェクターのスクリーンを窓から離す）
④ D（ソファを壁際に置く）
⑤ E（フロアランプを暗い隅に置く）

正解 ⇒ ④

Naturalness「自然さ」は，第４段落第１文にあるように「自然光と人工光の質と量，教室の温度に関するもの」である。よって選択肢の中で取り除くべきは，光と室温の調整に関係のない④である。

【語句・表現】
・handout「配布資料」

問4 「 27 と 28 にあてはまる最も適切な選択肢を選べ」

27

① ～から本を借りる   ② ～になかなか行けない

③ ～で日本語を使わない   ④ ～で不安を感じる

⑤ ～で昼寝をする

28

① S 1   ② S 2   ③ S 3   **④ S 4**   ⑤ S 5   ⑥ S 6

正解 ⇒ 27 ⑤   28 ④

27 の直前に「多数の部員は」とあるのでグラフを見てみると，「寝る」が最も多く，それに言及しているのは，「ソファはみんなお気に入り。とても気持ちがいいので，部室は寝るときによく使ってる！」と述べているS4である。よって，27 は⑤，28 は④が正解。

問5 「 29 にあてはまる最も適切な選択肢を選べ」

---

① S 1   ② S 2   **③ S 3**   ④ S 4   ⑤ S 5   ⑥ S 6

正解 ⇒ ③

29 を含む一文で挙げられている問題は，「もっと英語を話すようにするために，教室での言語に関するルールを設けたらどうか」である。アンケートのコメントの中でこの点に言及しているのは，「英語サークルなのに，日本語を話す人が多い」と述べているS3である。

【全訳例】

あなたの大学の英語クラブの部室にはいくつかの問題があり，あなたはその部室を設計し直したいと考えています。以下の記事と部員に行ったアンケートの結果に基づき，あなたはグループディスカッション用の資料を作成します。

良い教室とは？
ダイアナ・バシュワース（Trends in Education ライター）

多くの学校が教室の改善に取り組む中，デザインを決めるためにいくつかのアイデアを持つことは重要である。SIN とは，Stimulation（刺激），Individualization（個別化），Naturalness（自然さ）の頭文字をとったもので，教室をデザインする際に参考になるフレームワークである。

最初の「刺激」には，色と複雑さという2つの側面がある。これは，天井，床，壁，室内の備品に関係する。例えば，色のない教室は面白味がないかもしれない。一方で，教室はカラフル過ぎてもいけない。明るい色は壁の一面，床，カーテン類，または家具に使えるだろう。また，壁にあまりに多くのものが飾られていると，視覚的に気が散ってしまう。壁面スペースの20～30％は空けておくことが推奨されている。

フレームワークの次の項目は「個別化」で，所有権と柔軟性の2つを含むものである。所有権とは，教室が自分向けであると感じられるかどうかということである。例えば，生徒の体格や年齢に合った椅子や机を用意すること，収納スペースや，生徒の作品やプロジェクトを展示する場所を提供することなどが挙げられる。柔軟性とは，さまざまな活動を行える教室を作ることである。

「自然さ」とは，自然光と人工光の質と量，そして教室の温度に関するものである。自然光が強す

ぎると，スクリーンや黒板が見づらくなるかもしれない。光が足りなければ，読み書きがしづらくなるかもしれない。また，夏の暑い教室では，効果的な勉強を促せない。学校は，光と温度の両方を調整できるシステムを導入すべきである。

「自然さ」は私たちにとってより身近なものであるため，優先順位が高いと思われがちだが，その他の要素も同様に重要である。これらのアイデアが，プロジェクトを成功に導くことを願っている。

アンケート結果

Q1：英語クラブの部室のあなたの利用状況について，当てはまるものを選んでください。

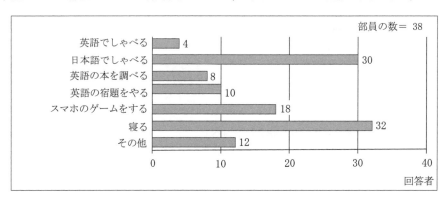

Q2：現在の英語クラブの部室についてどう思いますか？

主なコメント：

生徒1（S1）：晴れた日はプロジェクターのスクリーンやホワイトボードがよく見えない。それと，温度調節ができない。

S2：窓際は日差しが強くて文字が読みにくい。教室の反対側は十分な光が入らない。それに，本が散らかっているし，壁はポスターで埋め尽くされている。そのせいで居心地が悪い。

S3：椅子が自分に合わないし，小人数のグループで活動をするときに机を移動しにくい。また，英語クラブなのに，日本語を話す人が多い。

S4：壁に貼ってある外国の写真を見ると，英語を話したくなる。ソファはみんなお気に入り。とても気持ちがいいので，部室は寝るときによく使ってる！

S5：部室は遠いからほとんど行ってない！他に使える部屋はないの？

S6：部室は灰色だらけ。私は好きじゃない。でも，壁に日常的な英語のフレーズがたくさん書いてあるのは良い！

あなたのディスカッション配布資料：

部屋改善プロジェクト

■ **SIN** フレームワーク
- SIN とは何か： [24]
- SIN ＝刺激，個性化，自然さ

■ **SIN** とアンケート結果に基づくデザインの提案
- 刺激：
 床をカラフルなラグで覆い， [25] 。

- 個性化：

  教室の備品を入れ替える。

    （キャスター付きテーブル → 移動しやすい）

- 自然さ：

  | 26 |

    A．窓にブラインドを取り付ける。
    B．温度調節ができるようにする。
    C．プロジェクターのスクリーンを窓から離す。
    D．ソファを壁際に置く。
    E．フロアランプを暗い隅に置く。

■ その他の話し合うべき問題

- | 28 | のコメントで言及されたように，過半数のメンバーが部屋 | 27 |。これをどう解決するか。
- グラフと | 29 | のコメントの両方から，もっと英語を話すようにするために，教室での言語に関するルールを設けたらどうか。
- S 5は場所が気に入っていないが，部屋を変えるわけにはいかないので，部員にもっと頻繁に来てもらう方法を考えよう。

【語句・表現】
〈第1段落〉
・stand for ～「～を表す，～の略である」
・stimulation「刺激」
・individualization「個別化，個性化」
・naturalness「自然らしさ」
・framework「枠組み，骨子，構造」
〈第2段落〉
・complexity「複雑さ」
・have to do with ～「～と関係がある」
・visually「視覚的に」
・distracting「気を散らす」
・display「～を展示する，飾る」
・It is suggested that S (should) *do*「S が～すべきだと提案されている」
〈第3段落〉
・consideration「考慮（すべきこと）」
・ownership「所有者であること，所有，所有権」
・flexibility「柔軟性」
・refer to ～「～に関係する，あてはまる」
・storage「保管」
〈第4段落〉
・relate to ～「～に関係がある」
・quality「質」
・quantity「量」
・temperature「温度」
・promote「～を促進する」
・install「～を据え付ける」

〈第5段落〉
・familiar to ～「～によく知られた」
・therefore「それゆえ，したがって」
・priority「重要であること，優先事項」
・component「構成要素」
・equally「等しく，同様に，均一に」
・hopefully「できれば，うまくいけば」
〈アンケートとコメント〉
・questionnaire「質問事項，アンケート用紙」
・disorganize「～の秩序を乱す，～を混乱させる」
・cover「～を覆う」
・uncomfortable「不快な」
・fit「～にぴったりの，ふさわしい，適当な」
・hardly ever「ほとんど～ない」
・available「利用可能な」
・plenty of ～「十分な～」
〈ディスカッション用の資料〉
・recommendation「推薦（すること）」
・based on ～「～に基づいて」
・replace「～を取り替える」
・majority「大多数，大部分」
・motivate「～に動機［刺激］を与える」
・location「場所，位置」
・encourage O to *do*「O に～するよう促す，励ます」

第5問

問1 「5つの出来事（①～⑤）のうち**4つ**を選び，起こった順に並べ替えよ」

$$\boxed{30} \rightarrow \boxed{31} \rightarrow \boxed{32} \rightarrow \boxed{33}$$

---

① カスミが会社の副社長になる。
② カスミがタクヤに連絡する。
③ マキが大学の学位を取得する。
④ マキが家業で働き始める。
⑤ タクヤが起業するよう触発される。

正解 ⇒ ┃ 30 ┃ ④ ┃ 31 ┃ ⑤ ┃ 32 ┃ ① ┃ 33 ┃ ②

（解説の都合上，◆◆◆◆◆を区切りとした本文の各場面を【シーン1】～【シーン6】とする）

シーン1で，マキが19歳で家業を手伝うようになった（④）と述べられている。シーン3では，タクヤが高校卒業から1年後に川中に戻り，マキが家業のために大学進学を諦めたことを知り驚く場面がある。さらに1年後，タクヤは自分のコーヒー店を持ちたいとマキに打ち明ける。シーン3の最終段落第1文に「マキの励ましがタクヤを奮い立たせた」とあるように，この場面はマキの励ましによりタクヤが起業しようと思う瞬間（⑤）として描写されている。ここまでで，④→⑤となる。

シーン4後半では，「今年」会社の副社長になったカスミ（①）が，手元の新聞にタクヤの店の記事が載っているのを見て，タクヤに連絡している（②）ので，①→②とつながる。シーン2より，カスミとタクヤがマキの店に訪れた「現在」は，高校卒業から20年後であり，④→⑤から20年弱経過して①→②の出

来事が起きたとわかる。

　以上より，④→⑤→①→②の順が正解。なお本文は，タクヤとカスミが，マキに一度諦めた大学進学を再び目指してみるよう勧めたところで終わっているので，③はこのストーリーに含まれない。

【語句・表現】
・vice-president「副社長」
・get in touch with ～「～と連絡をとる」
・degree「学位」
・inspire「～を触発する」

問2　「　34　にあてはまる最も適切な選択肢を選べ」

① 30代前半
② 30代後半
③ 40代前半
④ 40代後半

　正解 ⇒ ②

　シーン2の「卒業してから20年も経ったなんて信じられない」というカスミのセリフから，マキの年齢は高校卒業から20年後なので30代後半だと考えられる。より正確には，マキが19歳で家業を手伝い始めた日のちょうど1年前が高校卒業の年だったことが，シーン3のタクヤがマキに連絡をとる場面からわかるので，現在マキは38歳ということになる。よって，②が正解。

問3　「　35　と　36　にあてはまる最も適切な選択肢を選べ」

① 製品を人々に広めた
② 成功するビジネスアイデアを提案した
③ ビジネスのための設備を購入した
④ より大きな都市への転居を提案した
⑤ 成功のために必要なスキルを教えた

　正解 ⇒ 　35　① 　　36　②

　シーン3の最後の段落に，「マキは『当店はタクヤのコーヒーを自信を持って提供しています』という掲示を店内に掲げ，このおかげでタクヤのコーヒーは川中町で評判になった」とあることから，　35　はこれに一致する①が正解。また，シーン4の第3段落より，マキがカスミにメイクのワークショップを開くようアドバイスしたことがきっかけで，カスミが成功したことがわかる。よって，　36　には②が入る。

【語句・表現】
・equipment「備品，機器」

問4　「　37　にあてはまる最も適切な選択肢を選べ」

① 自分たちの成功について話したくない
② 長い間話をしていない
③ 友人の良さをもっと理解すべきだったと後悔している

④　マキは彼らの成功をうらやましがっていたと思っている

正解 ⇒ ③

　シーン４の最後でカスミは，「彼女は私が悩んでいたときに助けてくれたのに，私ったら石島での仕事に夢中で，彼女が予備校を辞めなければならなくなったときに支えてあげられなかった」と悔やんでいる様子が述べられており，またシーン５で「無言のうちに二人は罪悪感を覚えていることが互いに伝わってきた」とある。これらの描写を踏まえると，もっとも適切なのは③である。

【語句・表現】
・appreciate「〜の良さを認める，〜をありがたく思う」
・envious of 〜「〜をうらやんで，ねたんで」
・achievement「成功，業績，功績」

問5　「　38　にあてはまる最も適切な選択肢を選べ」

①　様々なことに挑戦するのが好きで
②　彼女の才能に気づいて
③　彼女に足りない能力を理解して
④　彼女の夢を追いかけたく

正解 ⇒ ②

　最後のシーンで，カスミは「皮肉なことに，あなたは自分のためには同じようにできなかった」とマキに言っている。「同じように」が指す内容は，直前のタクヤの発言より，マキがカスミとタクヤの才能を見抜き，成功に導くことができたということである。他の人の才能を活かす力に長けているにもかかわらず，その能力をマキ自身のために使えていないのが皮肉だということである。よって，正解は②である。③は，「彼女に足りない」が誤り。①や④のようなことは本文で述べられていないので不適。

【語句・表現】
・talent「能力」
・pursue「〜を追い求める」

【全訳例】
　あなたは英語のディスカッショングループに所属していて，物語を紹介する順番が来ました。あなたは日本の英字雑誌である物語を見つけました。あなたは発表のためのメモを準備しています。

マキズ・キッチン

【シーン１】
　「いらっしゃいませ」二人の客が彼女のレストラン，マキズ・キッチンに入るとマキは言った。マキは19歳の時に父親が病気になり，家の仕事の手伝いを始めた。父親が回復した後も，マキは仕事を続けることを決めた。やがて両親は引退し，彼女がオーナーとなった。マキのところには常連客が多く，彼らはおいしい料理を食べるだけでなく，カウンターに座ってマキと話をするのを楽しみに来店した。経営はうまくいっていたが，マキは時折，何か違うことをしたいと夢見ることもあった。
　「カウンターに座っていい？」という声が聞こえた。それは旧友のタクヤとカスミだった。数週間前，カスミがタクヤにかけた電話がきっかけで，二人はマキを訪ねて驚かせようと考えたのだった。

【シーン2】
　タクヤの電話が振動し，カスミというよく見知った名前が目に入った。
「カスミ！」
「タクヤ，新聞で見たよ。おめでとう！」
「ありがとう。そういえば，先月の20回目の同窓会に来なかったよね？」
「そう，行けなかったの。卒業してから20年も経ったなんて信じられない。実は，最近マキに会ったかどうか聞きたくて電話したんだ」

【シーン3】
　タクヤの家族が川中町に引っ越してきたのは，高校に入学する少し前のことだった。彼は演劇部に入り，そこでマキとカスミに出会った。3人は切っても切れない関係になった。卒業後，タクヤは役者になるために川中を離れ，マキとカスミは地元に残った。マキは大学進学を志し，予備校に通った。一方，カスミは働き始めた。タクヤはさまざまな役柄に挑戦したが，断られ続け，結局あきらめた。
　卒業からちょうど1年後，タクヤは夢破れて川中に戻ってきた。タクヤはマキに電話をかけ，マキはタクヤに同情した。マキが実家のレストランを経営するため，大学進学を断念したと聞いて，タクヤは驚いた。マキが仕事についた初日は，タクヤが電話をした日だった。タクヤはなぜか，マキにアドバイスをせずにはいられなかった。
　「マキ，君の家のレストランはコーヒーを変えたほうがいいとずっと思っていたんだ。川中の人たちはもっと際立った味を求めていると思う。僕がよろこんで別の銘柄をお勧めするよ」と彼は言った。「タクヤ，あなたは本当にコーヒーに詳しいね。ねえ，カフェ・カワナカの前を通りかかったら，従業員募集の張り紙があったよ。応募してみなよ！」とマキは答えた。
　タクヤはカフェ・カワナカに採用され，コーヒー作りの科学に魅了された。働き始めてちょうど1年目となる日，タクヤはマキの店で彼女と話した。
　「マキ，僕の夢が何だかわかる？」と彼は言った。
　「コーヒーに関係あることでしょうね」
　「そう！自分のコーヒー店を持つことなんだ」
　「タクヤ以上の適任者はいないって。ためらうことないよ」
　マキの励ましがタクヤを奮い立たせた。彼は仕事を辞め，コーヒー豆の焙煎機を購入し，豆の焙煎を始めた。マキは「当店はタクヤのコーヒーを自信を持って提供しています」という掲示を店内に掲げ，このおかげでタクヤのコーヒーは川中町で評判になった。タクヤはコーヒー豆の販売で利益を上げるようになった。やがて，彼は自分のカフェを開き，経営者として成功した。

【シーン4】
　「タクヤズ・カフェ，川中町に観光客呼び込む」カスミが新聞を読んでいると，その見出しが目に入った。「タクヤがこんなに成功するなんて，誰が想像できただろう？」カスミは自分の過去を振り返りながらそう思った。
　高校の演劇部では，カスミの仕事は演者にメイクをすることだった。彼女ほど上手な人はいなかった。そのことに気づいたマキは，ビューテラという化粧品会社が販売員を募集しているのを見つけた。マキはカスミに応募するように勧め，卒業後，カスミはビューテラの社員になった。
　そこの仕事は厳しかった。カスミは一軒一軒化粧品を売り歩いた。上手くいかなかった日にはマキに電話し，励ましてもらった。ある日，マキは思いついた。「ビューテラはメイクのワークショップをやってないの？カスミはその仕事のほうが向いてるよ。あなたなら人々にメイクの仕方を教えられる。みんな化粧の仕上がりが気に入って，化粧品をたくさん買ってくれるよ！」
　カスミの会社は彼女にワークショップをさせることに同意し，それは大当たりだった！カスミの売り上げはとても好調で，高校を卒業して8か月後には昇進し，大都市である石島に移ることになった。それ以来，彼女は着実に出世階段を上り，今年にはビューテラの副社長に任命された。
　「マキがいなかったら，今ごろ副社長になっていなかった」と彼女は思った。「彼女は私が悩んでいたときに助けてくれたのに，私ったら石島での仕事に夢中で，彼女が予備校を辞めなければならなく

なったときに支えてあげられなかった」もう一度記事に目をやると，カスミはタクヤに電話すること
を決めた。

【シーン5】
　「同窓会にマキは来てなかったよね。彼女には長い間会ってないな」とタクヤが言った。
「私もそう。残念ね。彼女がいなかったら，私たちはどうなっていたんだろう？」とカスミが疑問を
投げかけた。
　会話はぷつりととぎれ，無言のうちに二人は罪悪感を覚えていることがお互いに伝わってきた。そ
して，カスミはある考えを思いついた。

【シーン6】
　友人3人が談笑していると，マキが尋ねた。「ところで，二人に会えて嬉しいんだけど，二人はど
うして来たの？」
　「お返しさ」とタクヤが言った。
　「何か悪いことをしちゃったかな？」とマキは尋ねた。
　「いや，逆だよ。マキは信じられないほど人のことをよく分かってる。人の長所を見つけて，それ
を活かす方法を教えることができる。僕らがその証拠だよ。君が僕たちの才能に気づかせてくれたん
だ」とタクヤは言った。
　「皮肉なことに，あなたは自分のためには同じようにできなかった」とカスミが付け加えた。
　「石島大学はマキにとって理想的だと思う。そこには働いている人向けのカウンセリングの学位取
得課程があるんだ」とタクヤは言った。
　「月に何回か通うことになるけど，私の家に泊まることもできる。それに，タクヤがあなたのお店
のスタッフ探しを手伝ってくれるよ」とカスミが言った。
　マキは目を閉じて，川中に「マキズ・キッチン」と「マキズ・カウンセリング」の2店を持つこと
を想像した。マキはそのアイデアが気に入った。

あなたのメモ：

マキズ・キッチン

ストーリーの概要
マキ，タクヤ，カスミが高校を卒業する。

| 30 |
| 31 |
| 32 |
| 33 |

マキはセカンドキャリアについて考え始める。

マキについて
● 年齢： 　34
● 職業：レストランオーナー
● どのように友人を支えたか：
　　　　タクヤを励まし，　35　。
　　　　カスミ　〃　〃　　36　。

重要な場面の解釈
● カスミとタクヤは電話で居心地の悪い沈黙を経験する。なぜなら彼らは　37　からだ。
● 最後のシーンで，カスミはマキのことで「皮肉」という言葉を使う。皮肉なのは，マキが　38

なかったことである。

【語句・表現】
〈シーン1〉
・ill「病気の」
・recover「回復する」
・eventually「最終的に」
・retire「退職する」
・not only ~ but also ...「~だけでなく…も」
・occasionally「時々」
・daydream「空想する」
〈シーン2〉
・vibrate「振動する」
・reunion「同窓会，再会の集い」
〈シーン3〉
・inseparable「切り離せない」
・enroll in ~「~に入学する」
・preparatory「（大学）進学予備の」
・try out for ~「~の試験に挑む」
・constantly「絶えず」
・reject「~を拒絶する」
・quit「辞める」
・exactly「正確に」
・return「戻る」
・destroy「~を破壊する」
・abandon「~を放棄する」
・for some reason「何らかの理由で」
・resist「~に抵抗する」
・bold「はっきりした，大胆な」
・flavor「風味」
・hire「~を雇う」
・be fascinated by ~「~に魅了される」
・anniversary「記念日」
・employment「雇用」
・encouragement「激励，励ますこと」
〈シーン4〉
・reflect on ~「~を回想する」
・duty「義務」
・make-up「化粧」
・cosmetics「化粧品」
・advertise for ~「~を求めて広告を出す」
・salespeople「販売員」
・apply「申し込む，志願する」
・employee「従業員」
・tough「厳しい」
・lift one's spirit「気持ちを高める」
・be suited for ~「~に適している」

・hit「ヒットする」
・promote「〜を昇進させる」
・ladder「(成功，出世への) 階段，はしご」
・struggle「奮闘する」
・be absorbed with 〜「〜に夢中になる」
・glance「ちらっと見る」
〈シーン5〉
・pity「残念な事，惜しい事」
・silent「沈黙の」
・wordlessly「言葉を交わさずに」
・guilt「罪悪感」
〈シーン6〉
・by the way「ところで」
・payback「お返し」
・incredibly「信じられないほど」
・make use of 〜「〜を利用する」
・proof「証拠」
・be aware of 〜「〜を知っている，〜に気づいている」
〈メモ〉
・occupation「職業」
・interpretation「理解，解釈」

第6問

A
問1 「 | 39 | と | 40 | にあてはまる最も適切な選択肢を選べ」

> ① 生物学的仕組み
> ② **私たちの感情の影響**
> ③ 記憶の種類
> ④ ライフステージ
> ⑤ 現在進行中の研究
> ⑥ **時間の類型**

正解 ⇒ | 39 | ⑥ | 40 | ②

　本文の段落ごとの概要として適切な見出しを選択させる設問である。まず第1段落では，私たち人間にとって「時間」とは何か，またその代表例として「時計時間」と「心理的時間」を紹介している。したがって，⑥「時間の類型」が最適である。次に，第4段落では私たちの感情も時間に対する意識に影響を及ぼすと述べている。「楽しいとあっという間に時が過ぎる」「退屈だと時間が経つのが遅い」という趣旨の段落なので，②が最もふさわしい。

【語句・表現】
・ongoing「進行中の，継続している」

問2 「 41 にあてはまる最も適切な選択肢を選べ」

① どの年代でも，生活様式の大きな変化があると，時の経つのが遅く感じる
② 年代に関わらず，生活様式の大きな変化があると，時の経つのが速く感じる
③ 大人の場合，生活様式のちょっとした変化があると，時の経つのが遅く感じる
④ 子供の場合，生活様式のちょっとした変化があると，時の経つのが速く感じる

正解 ⇒ ①

第5段落の「年代の影響」では，「歳をとるほど時が経つのは速く感じられるが，転職や転居など生活の大きな変化がある時には大人でも子供のように遅く感じる」といった内容が述べられている。したがって①が最適である。

問3 「 42 にあてはまる最も適切な選択肢を選べ」

① クラスメートからメッセージが来ることを予期する
② あなたの母親の携帯電話番号を記憶する
③ 今日何時間働いたかを振り返って考える
④ 明日ミーティングがあることを思い出す

正解 ⇒ ③

retrospective timing の例を選ぶ設問である。第2段落第5文にあるように，retrospective timing「追想的時間評価」とは，記憶から取り出された情報に基づいて時間を推定するプロセスである。したがって，③のように過去の出来事の時間を振り返っている行動例を選べば良い。

【語句・表現】
・anticipate「～を予期する，予測する」

問4 「 43 にあてはまる最も適切な選択肢を選べ」

① 今の時点まででどのくらいの間ジョギングをしたかを推測する
② バスケットボールチームが行う夏期キャンプのスケジュールを立てる
③ 鉄道の駅でテニスのコーチと偶然出くわす
④ あなたが家族と最近行った温泉旅行のことを考える

正解 ⇒ ①

prospective timing の例を選ぶ設問である。prospective timing「予期的時間評価」とは，第3段落第2文にある通り，何かをすることと並行して時間を把握しようとするプロセスであるため，①が正解。残りの選択肢はいずれもこのプロセスとは関係のない行動例である。

【語句・表現】
・run into ～「～に偶然出会う」
・railway「鉄道」
・hot spring「温泉」

【全訳例】

英語の先生からこの記事を課題として与えられました。あなたは短いスピーチをするためにメモを準備する必要があります。

時間に対する認識

「時間」と聞いてすぐに思い浮かぶのは，おそらく時，分，秒だろう。しかし19世紀後半，哲学者のアンリ・ベルクソンは，人が通常経験するのは，時計によって計測される時間（時計時間）ではないと説明した。人間には，時計時間を計測する既知の生物学的なメカニズムはないため，代わりに精神的なプロセスを用いるのだ。これは心理的時間と呼ばれ，人によって感じ方が異なる。

宿題を終えるのにかかった時間を聞かれたとしても，おそらく正確にはわからないだろう。尋ねられた人は，思い返して推測することになる。1975年の実験では，被験者に単純な図形または複雑な図形を一定時間見せ，それを記憶させた。その後，どのくらいの時間，その図形を見ていたかを尋ねられた。回答するため，記憶から取り出された情報に基づいて時間を推定する，**追想的時間評価**と呼ばれる精神的プロセスを彼らは用いた。複雑な図形を見せられた参加者は時間を長く感じ，単純な図形を見せられた人はその逆だった。

心理的時間を測定するもう一つのプロセスは，**予期的時間評価**と呼ばれる。これは，何かをすることと並行して積極的に時間を把握しようとしているときに使われる。思い出した情報を用いる代わりに，活動中の時間に対する注意の度合いが使われる。いくつかの研究では，参加者は完了するのに必要な時間を見積もりながらタスクを行った。時間よりもタスクの方に集中しなければならないような，より困難な精神的活動を行った被験者は，時間がより短く感じられた。より単純な作業をした被験者では時間が長く感じられ，待機，つまり何もしなかった被験者は最も長く感じられた。

感情の状態も，時間に対する意識に影響を与える。例えば，コンサートを楽しむあまりに時間を忘れてしまうかもしれない。終わってから，一瞬のように思われる出来事の間に何時間も過ぎてしまったことに愕然とする。これを説明するために，私たちはよく「楽しい時間が過ぎるのは早い」と言う。退屈な時間にはその逆のことが起きる。活動に集中するのではなく，時間に意識が向く。退屈なひとときが終わるのが待ち遠しくなり，時間がとても遅く感じられるのだ。恐怖も時間の認識に影響を与える。2006年の研究では，60人以上が初めてスカイダイビングを体験した。不快な感情の度合いが高かった参加者は，スカイダイビングに費やした時間が実際よりもずっと長く感じられた。

心理的時間の過ぎ方は，ライフステージによっても異なるようだ。子どもたちは常に新しい情報に出会い，新しい経験をする。これにより一日一日が思い出に残り，思い起こしてみると長かったように感じる。また，誕生日や旅行など，これから起こる出来事を楽しみに待つときは，時間はゆっくりと過ぎていく。ほとんどの大人にとって，未知の情報に出会うことは滅多になく，新しい経験をする頻度も少なくなるため，精神的な集中力がさほど必要とされなくなり，一日一日が記憶に残りにくくなる。しかし，常にそうとは限らない。転職や転居など，劇的な変化が起きると，日常は大きく揺れ動く。そのような場合，その人たちの時間の流れは子供のそれと近いものになる。しかし，一般的には，大人になるにつれて時間は加速していくようだ。

心理的時間についての知識は，日常生活で役立つかもしれない。というのも，退屈に対処しやすくなるからだ。精神的に集中しておらず時間について考えているときは，時間はゆっくりと過ぎていくので，本を読むなど，より魅力的な活動に変えることで，退屈を和らげ，時間を速めることができるだろう。次に「楽しい時間が過ぎるのは早い」という言葉を耳にしたとき，あなたはこのことを思い出すだろう。

あなたのメモ：

時間の認識

段落ごとの概要

　1. ☐ 39

2．追想的時間評価
3．予期的時間評価
4． 40
   ➢ スカイダイビング
5．年代による影響
   ➢ 年を取ると時の経つのが早くなるが， 41 。
6．実用的なヒント

聞き手に役立つ私のオリジナル例
A．追想的時間評価
   例： 42
B．予期的時間評価
   例： 43

【語句・表現】
〈第1段落〉
・second「秒，ほんのちょっとの間」
・philosopher「哲学者」
・measure「～を測定する，計る」
・biological「生物学的な，生物学の」
・perceive「～を知覚する」
〈第2段落〉
・exactly「正確に，ちょうど」
・estimate「～を見積もる，推定する」
・complex「複雑な」
・fixed「決められた，変動しない」
・amount「量」
・retrospective「回顧の，回顧的な」
・retrieve「～を引き出す，取り戻す，回収する」
・opposite「反対の事，逆」
〈第3段落〉
・prospective「予期された，見込みのある」
・keep track of ～「～の経過を追う」
〈第4段落〉
・awareness「意識，自覚」
・the blink of an eye「一瞬」
・be bored「飽き飽きしている，退屈している」
・notice「～に気づく」
・boredom「退屈」
・unpleasant「不快な」
＜第5段落〉
・encounter「～に偶然出くわす」
・creep by ～「（時が）ゆっくりと過ぎていく」
・frequent「頻繁に起こる」
・routine「お決まりの仕事，日課」
・drastic「思い切った，抜本的な」
・relocate「転居する」

・generally speaking「一般的に言って，概して」
・accelerate「速度を増す，加速する」
・mature「成熟する，大人になる」
〈第6段落〉
・engaging「人を引き付ける，魅力的な」
・occasion「機会」

B
問1　「スライド2の，ワサビの第1の特徴は何か」　44

① 焼けるような味　　　　　　　② 火のような感覚
③ ずっと残る感覚　　　　　　　**④ 軽い化合物である**

正解 ⇒ ④

　ワサビの特徴については第3段落で詳述されている。第4文に，ワサビのスパイス化合物の濃度が低いため，唐辛子に耐えられなくてもワサビは大丈夫という人もいると述べられていることから，正解は④である。

【語句・表現】
・sensation「感覚」
・lasting「長続きする」
・compound「混合物，化合物」

問2　「スライド3にある間違いはどれか」　45

① A（痛みを軽減する）　　　　② B（より多くのエネルギーを与える）
③ C（新陳代謝を促進する）　　**④ D（ストレスを感じにくくする）**
⑤ E（食中毒を減らす）

正解 ⇒ ④

　A〜Eのうち，本文に書かれていない項目はDの「ストレスを感じにくくする」である。第4段落第3文で筋肉痛などの痛みを和らげるといった効果が述べられているが，ストレスについての言及はない。ほかはそれぞれ，Aが第4段落，BとCが第5段落，Eが第6段落にて言及されている。

問3　「スライド4にあてはまる選択肢を2つ選べ（順序は問わない）」　46 ・ 47

① 有害な細菌を活性化するかもしれない
② 胃痛を経験するかもしれない
③ 手の感覚がなくなるかもしれない
④ 指が燃えているような感じがするかもしれない
⑤ 鼻が痛くなり始めるかもしれない

正解 ⇒ ②，③

　唐辛子を食べた時の弊害については，第7段落第3文に詳述されている。これによれば，短時間であま

りに多量の唐辛子を食べてしまうと，「胃の不調」，「下痢」，「手のしびれ」，「心臓発作に似た症状」が起こるとされている。これに合致するのは②と③である。④は，同段落最終文で言及されているゴースト・ペッパーに触った場合に起こることなので，このスライドには適さない。

【語句・表現】
・activate「〜を活性化する」
・bacteria「細菌」

問4 「スライド5の香辛料への耐性に関して推測できることは何か」 48

① 唐辛子に強い耐性を持つ人は，自分の食べ物に使われている香辛料に注意を払う。
② ワサビに対して強い耐性を持つ人は，唐辛子の弊害を恐れている。
❸ 唐辛子に対して耐性があまりない人は，その辛さに慣れる可能性がある。
④ ワサビに対して耐性があまりない人は，高い SHU レベルに耐えられない。

正解 ⇒ ③

第4段落第4文に，「唐辛子に長期間接すると TRPV1 がオンにならなくなり，一時的に痛みが和らぐ」と書かれていること，また第6段落第5文にも「暑い地域の人々は唐辛子を多く使う傾向があり，何度も唐辛子にさらされることで，より辛い食べ物に対する耐性が強くなる」とあることから考えて，③が最適である。

【語句・表現】
・tolerance「耐性」

問5 「スライド6に最もふさわしい意見を選べ」 49

① 怖がらないで。辛い食べ物を食べれば，自信がいっそう湧いてきます。
② 次にチリチキンを食べる時には，その衝撃はほんの一瞬しか残らないということを思い出して下さい。
③ 香辛料の好みにはその人の性格が大きく影響します。だから，心配しないで。
④ 残念ながら，ワサビに耐性がほとんどない人には改善方法がありません。
❺ 辛い食べ物を出されたら，その食べ物には利点があることを覚えておいて下さい。

正解 ⇒ ⑤

本文を踏まえると，唐辛子には健康面や食料の保存において複数の利点があるとされているため，正解は⑤である。①は「自信が湧いてくる」が間違い。そのようなことは本文中にない。②も，「衝撃が一瞬で消えていく」というところが不適切。第2段落にも書かれている通り，唐辛子の辛さは lingering「いつまでも余韻が残る」ものである。③や④のような内容は本文中に述べられていない。

【語句・表現】
・boost「〜を増大させる，高める」
・confidence「自信」
・play a 〜 role「〜な役割を果たす」

【全訳例】

あなたは次の科学系ウェブサイトの記事を用いて，科学部のプレゼンテーションの準備をしています。

唐辛子：暮らしのスパイス

　チリチキンに含まれる小さな赤いスパイスのかけらは，彩りに良いアクセントを加えるが，たとえ小さなかけらでも，噛むと口の中が燃えるように熱くなることがある。これが好きな人もいれば，この痛みの感覚を避けたい人もいる。けれど同時に，そんな人々でも刺身にワサビを付けて食べることはできたりする。こうなると，辛さとは何だろうとか，唐辛子とワサビの違いはどこから来るのだろうか，などと考える人が出てくるかもしれない。

　甘味，塩味，酸味とは異なり，辛さは味ではない。実は，私たちは辛いものを食べても，実際に熱さや辛さを味わっているわけではない。私たちが唐辛子やワサビを食べて感じる刺激は，様々な化合物に由来する。唐辛子の辛さはカプサイシンと呼ばれる，油に似た比重の大きい成分に由来する。カプサイシンは，TRPV1と呼ばれる受容体を刺激するため，口の中に燃えるような感覚を残す。TRPV1はストレスを誘発し，何かが口の中を焼いているぞ，と伝達してくる。興味深いことに，唐辛子の種類によって辛さの幅があり，そのレベルは含まれるカプサイシンの量に左右される。これは，スコヴィル・ヒート・ユニット（SHU）とも呼ばれるスコヴィル・スケールを用いて測定される。SHUは，甘くてマイルドなシシトウガラシの50〜200SHUから，最大220万SHUに達するキャロライナ・リーパーまで幅広い。

　ワサビは唐辛子ではなく根であり，カプサイシンを含まない。したがって，ワサビはスコヴィル・スケールではランク付けされない。しかし，ワサビの辛さは約1,000SHUの唐辛子と同程度とみなされており，スコヴィル・スケールでは低い方である。唐辛子のスパイスには耐えられないが，ワサビ味の食品なら食べられるという人がいるのは，ワサビに含まれるスパイス化合物の濃度が低いからである。ワサビに含まれる化合物は気化しやすく，食べたときに鼻に抜けるような辛さをもたらす。

　唐辛子を摂取することは健康に良い影響を与える可能性があり，カプサイシンの効能について多くの研究がなされている。カプサイシンが人の体内のTRPV1受容体を活性化するとき，それはストレスや怪我による痛みを経験したときに起こることと似ている。不思議なことに，カプサイシンは痛みを消すこともできる。科学者たちは，唐辛子に長期間接するとTRPV1がオンにならなくなり，一時的に痛みの感覚が和らぐことを発見した。したがって，カプサイシンを含む皮膚クリームは，筋肉痛の人々に有用かもしれない。

　唐辛子を食べることのもう一つの利点は，新陳代謝を促進することである。ある研究グループがカプサイシンと体重に関する90の研究を分析したところ，辛いものを食べると食欲が減退することがわかった。これは，辛い食べ物が心拍数を上げ，筋肉により多くのエネルギーを送り，脂肪をエネルギーに変えるからである。最近，ワイオミング大学の科学者たちは，カプサイシンを主成分とする減量薬を作った。

　また，唐辛子は食品の安全性とも関係があり，より健康的な生活につながるかもしれないと考えられている。食品を冷蔵環境外に放置すると微生物が繁殖し，それを食べると具合が悪くなる可能性がある。唐辛子に含まれるカプサイシンやその他の化学物質には抗菌作用があり，微生物の繁殖を遅らせたり，止めたりさえもできるという研究結果がある。その結果，食べ物が長持ちし，食中毒が少なくなる。このことは，暑い地域の人々が唐辛子を多く使う傾向があり，そのために何度も唐辛子にさらされることで，より辛い食べ物に対する耐性が強いことの理由になるかもしれない。また，冷蔵庫ができる以前は，彼らは涼しい気候の地域の人々よりも食中毒にかかりにくかった。

　唐辛子は健康に良さそうだが，健康に悪いこともあるのだろうか？　スコヴィル・スケールの高い唐辛子は，大量に食べると身体に不調をきたすことがある。世界一辛い唐辛子を短時間に何本も食べた人は，胃の不調，下痢，手のしびれ，心臓発作に似た症状を経験したと報告している。100万SHUを含むゴースト・ペッパーは，触ると皮膚が火傷することさえある。

　幸いなことに，辛いものを食べた後に感じる不快感はすぐに消え去る傾向にあり，かかっても通常は数時間以内だ。副作用があるにもかかわらず，辛い食べ物は世界中で人気があり，食卓に風味を添

えてくれる。辛いものを食べても安全だが，料理に入れる唐辛子の量には注意した方がいいということを覚えておこう。

発表用スライド：

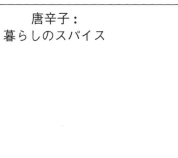

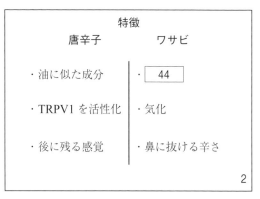

【語句・表現】
〈第1段落〉
・tiny「とても小さい」
・bite into ～「～にかじりつく」
・avoid「～を避ける」
・painful「痛い，痛みを伴う」
・actually「実際に」
〈第2段落〉
・saltiness「塩味」

・sourness「酸味」
・bite「辛さ」
・be derived from ～「～から派生する，～に由来する」
・element「要素，成分」
・capsaicin「カプサイシン（唐辛子の辛味成分）」
・lingering「長引く，（影響などが）なかなか消えない」
・trigger「～を引き起こす，～を誘引する」
・receptor「受容体，レセプター」
・induce「～を誘発する，引き起こす」
・contain「～を含む」
〈第3段落〉
・root「根」
・tolerate「許容する，耐える，我慢する」
・density「濃度」
・vaporize「蒸発する，気化する」
・blast「突風，一吹き」
〈第4段落〉
・consume「～を消費する」
・conduct「～を行う」
・strangely「不思議なことに」
・exposure「さらされること，暴露」
・muscle ache「筋肉痛」
〈第5段落〉
・metabolism「新陳代謝」
・reduce「～を減らす」
・appetite「食欲」
・heart rate「心拍数」
・convert A into B「A を B へと変える」
・ingredient「成分，原材料」
〈第6段落〉
・refrigerated「（冷蔵庫で）冷蔵された」
・microorganism「微生物」
・multiply「どんどん増える，繁殖する」
・antibacterial「抗菌性の」
・property「特性，性質」
・food-borne illness「食物由来の疾患，食中毒」
・tendency「傾向」
・food poisoning「食中毒」
〈第7段落〉
・discomfort「不快，苦痛」
・upset stomach「胃の不調」
・diarrhea「下痢」
・numb hand「手のしびれ」
・symptom「症状」
〈第8段落〉
・side effect「副作用」
・flavorful「風味に富む，味のよい」

リスニング問題音声配信について

本書に掲載のリスニング問題の音声は，音声専用サイトにて配信しております。

サイトへは下記アドレスよりアクセスしてくだい。ユーザー名とパスワードの入力が必要です。

https://www.yozemi.ac.jp/yozemi/download/book2025shirohoneigo

■ユーザー名：lib7ET8p

■パスワード：8696Xs5K

■利用期間

2024 年 7 月 10 日〜2027 年 6 月 30 日（期限内でも配信は予告なく終了する場合がございます）

推奨 OS・ブラウザ (2024 年 6 月現在)

▶パソコン

Microsoft Edge ※／ Google Chrome ※／ Mozilla Firefox ※／ Apple Safari ※

※最新版

▶スマートフォン・タブレット

Android 4.4 以上／ iOS 9 以上

ご利用にあたって

※音声専用サイトの音声のご利用は、『2025 大学入学共通テスト実戦問題集英語』をご利用いただいているお客様に限らせていただきます。それ以外の方の、本サイトの音声のご利用はご遠慮くださいますようお願いいたします。

※音声は無料ですが、音声を聴くこと、ダウンロードには、別途通信料がかかる場合があります（お客様のご負担になります）。

※ファイルは MP3 形式です。音声はダウンロードすることも可能です。ダウンロードした音声の再生には MP3 を再生できる機器をご使用ください。また、ご使用の機器や音声再生ソフト、インターネット環境などに関するご質問につきましては、当社では対応いたしかねます。各製品のメーカーまでお尋ねください。

※本サイトの音声データは著作権法等で保護されています。音声データのご利用は、私的利用の場合に限られます。

※本データの全部もしくは一部を複製、または加工し、第三者に譲渡・販売することは法律で禁止されています。

※本サービスで提供されているコンテンツは、予告なしに変更・追加・中止されることがあります。

※お客様のネット環境および端末により、ご利用いただけない場合がございます。ご理解、ご了承いただきますようお願いいたします。

解 答 と 解 説

問題番号 （配点）	設	問	解答番号	正 解	配 点	自採 己点
第1問 （25）	A	1	1	3	4	
		2	2	3	4	
		3	3	3	4	
		4	4	1	4	
	B	5	5	1	3	
		6	6	4	3	
		7	7	3	3	
自己採点小計						
第2問 （16）		8	8	4	4	
		9	9	4	4	
		10	10	2	4	
		11	11	1	4	
自己採点小計						
第3問 （18）		12	12	4	3	
		13	13	4	3	
		14	14	3	3	
		15	15	1	3	
		16	16	2	3	
		17	17	3	3	
自己採点小計						

問題番号 （配点）	設	問	解答番号	正 解	配 点	自採 己点
第4問 （12）	A	18	18	3	4*	
		19	19	1		
		20	20	2		
		21	21	4		
		22	22	1	1	
		23	23	4	1	
		24	24	5	1	
		25	25	3	1	
	B	26	26	1	4	
自己採点小計						
第5問 （15）		27	27	3	3*	
		28	28	4		
		29	29	3	4*	
		30	30	1		
		31	31	5		
		32	32	3	4	
		33	33	1	4	
自己採点小計						
第6問 （14）	A	34	34	4	3	
		35	35	1	3	
	B	36	36	1	4	
		37	37	4	4	
自己採点小計						

（注）

*は，全部正解の場合のみ点を与える。

自己採点合計 [　　　]

第1問

A
問1 ⬚1⬚
【放送内容と選択肢】

> I saw Mike in the library by chance. It was surprising for me because he rarely goes there.
>
> ① マイクと話者は二人とも図書館に行くのが好きである。
> ② マイクは図書館で話者に会って驚いた。
> ③ 話者は図書館でマイクに会うことを予想していなかった。
> ④ 話者はマイクと図書館で会うつもりである。

正解 ⇒ ③

放送された英文は，「私は図書館でマイクに偶然会った。彼はめったにそこに来ないので私は驚いた」という意味である。話者は「マイクに偶然会った」のであるから，「マイクに会うことを予想していなかった」はずである。よって，③が正解となる。

【語句・表現】
・by chance「偶然に」

問2 ⬚2⬚
【放送内容と選択肢】

> Due to the traffic jam, I had to get off the bus and walk, but managed to get there on time.
>
> ① 話者は時間通りに目的地に到着することができなかった。
> ② 話者は歩くのをやめて，バスで目的地に到着した。
> ③ 話者は歩かなければならなかったが，時間通りに目的地に到着した。
> ④ 話者は交通渋滞に巻き込まれたので遅刻した。

正解 ⇒ ③

放送された英文は，「交通渋滞のせいでバスを降りて歩かなければならなかったが，どうにか時間通りに目的地に到着することができた」という意味である。この内容に一致するのは③である。

【語句・表現】
・due to ～「～が原因で」
・traffic jam「交通渋滞」
・manage to *do*「どうにか～する」
〈選択肢〉
・destination「目的地，行き先」

問3 ☐3
【放送内容と選択肢】

> John has been too busy to go to the gym, but he has made up his mind to change his situation.
>
> ① ジョンはジムに行きたいとあまり思っていない。
> ② ジョンはジムで運動するのに忙しい。
> ❸ ジョンはジムに行く時間を作り出すことに決めた。
> ④ ジョンはジムに行くのに十分な時間がないだろう。

正解 ⇒ ③

　放送された英文は,「ジョンは忙しすぎてジムに行くことができていないが,状況を変えようと決心した」という意味である。「忙しくてジムに行けない状況を変える」ということは「ジムに行く時間を作り出す」ということであるから,③が正解となる。

【語句・表現】
・make up one's mind to *do*「～する決心をする」
〈選択肢〉
・work out「体を鍛える,運動する」

問4 ☐4
【放送内容と選択肢】

> But for Alison's advice, I would have wasted as much as 1,000 dollars.
>
> ❶ アリソンのアドバイスによって,話者は1,000ドルを節約することができた。
> ② アリソンのアドバイスのために,話者は100ドルもの大金を無駄にした。
> ③ アリソンのアドバイスのおかげで,話者は100ドルを節約することができた。
> ④ アリソンのアドバイスにもかかわらず,話者は1,000ドルもの大金を無駄にした。

正解 ⇒ ①

　放送された英文は,「アリソンのアドバイスがなかったら,私は1,000ドルもの大金を無駄にしていただろう」という意味である。仮定法過去完了が用いられている。実際には「アリソンのアドバイスによって1,000ドルを無駄にしないで済んだ」わけであるから,①が正解となる。

【語句・表現】
・but for ～「～がなければ」
・as much as ～「～ほども多く」:量の多さを強調する表現。
〈選択肢〉
・enable O to *do*「O が～することを可能にする」
・owing to ～「～のために,～が原因で」
・despite「～にもかかわらず」

B
問5　5
【放送内容と選択肢】

A swan has just taken off from the lake and there are now two swans on the lake.

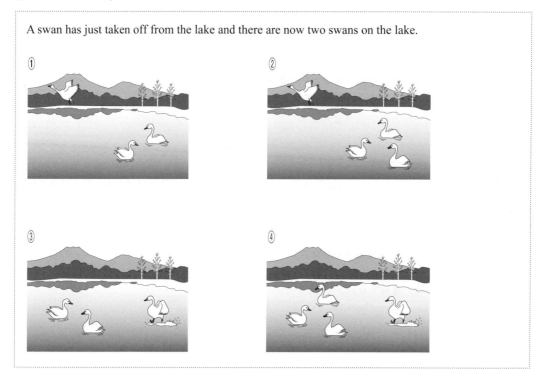

正解 ⇒ ①

　放送された英文は，「1羽の白鳥が飛び立ち，湖には今2羽の白鳥がいる」という意味である。この内容に一致するのは①である。

【語句・表現】
・swan「白鳥」
・take off「飛び立つ」

問6 　6

【放送内容と選択肢】

My grandfather doesn't wear glasses and is slightly shorter than my grandmother.

正解 ⇒ ④

　放送された英文は,「私の祖父はめがねをかけておらず，祖母より少し身長が低い」という意味である。この内容に一致するのは④である。

【語句・表現】
・glasses「めがね」
・slightly「わずかに，かすかに」

【放送内容と選択肢】

A white cat is sleeping curled up on a bookshelf, and a black one is lying stretched out on the floor.

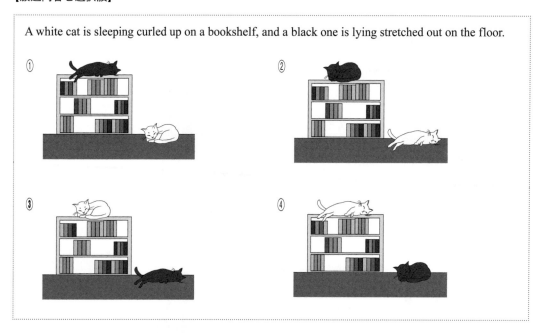

正解 ⇒ ③

　放送された英文は，「白いネコは本棚の上で体を丸めて寝ており，黒いネコは床の上で体を伸ばして寝ている」という意味である。この内容に一致するのは③である。

【語句・表現】
・be curled up「体を丸める，丸まって寝る」
・stretch out ～「～を伸ばす」

第2問

問8　　8
【放送内容と選択肢】

W: I'm going out on a date with Manabu tomorrow. Does this outfit look good on me?
M: Well, tomorrow will be much colder than today. I don't think you should wear that short-sleeved blouse.
W: OK ... I'll wear a long-sleeved blouse instead. I wonder if I should wear my long boots.
M: It'll be too hot if you wear them, I think.
Question:
How will the girl be dressed when she goes out?

W：明日，マナブとデートに行く予定なの。この服装，似合ってる？
M：うーん，明日は今日よりもずっと寒くなりそうだよ。その半袖のブラウスは着ていかない方がいいと思うな。
W：わかった…長袖のブラウスにする。ロングブーツを履いた方がいいかな。
M：ロングブーツを履くのは暑すぎるんじゃないかと思うけど。

問い：

女の子は出かける時，どのような服装をする予定か。

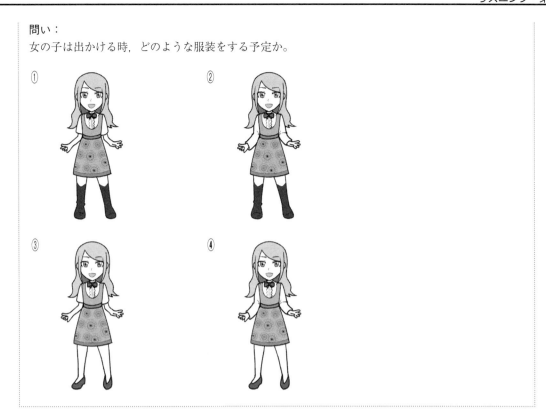

① ② ③ ④

正解 ⇒ ④

　女の子（＝妹）が男の子（＝兄）に，翌日のデートの服装について話している。「その半袖のブラウスは着ていかない方がいい」と言われた女の子は，「長袖のブラウスにする」と述べているので，正解は②か④に絞られる。さらに，ロングブーツを履いていくべきか迷っている様子だが，男の子が「ロングブーツを履くのは暑すぎる」と言っていることから，履いていかない可能性が高い。よって，正解は④となる。

【語句・表現】
・outfit「服装」
・look good on ～「～［人］に似合う」
・short-sleeved「半袖の」
・long-sleeved「長袖の」

問9 　9
【放送内容と選択肢】

W: How would you like your birthday cake decorated?
M: My birthday month is October, so I want it to look like Halloween. I'd like six pieces of chocolate shaped like bats.
W: What else would you like to put on top?
M: I would like four slices of pumpkin and the same number of candles.
Question:
What will the cake look like?

W：あなたのバースデーケーキ，どんな風に飾りつけしてほしい？

M：僕の誕生月は10月だから，ハロウィーン風にしたいな。コウモリの形をしたチョコレートを6個のせたい。

W：他には何をのせたい？

M：カボチャを4切れと，同じ数のキャンドルをのせたいな。

問い：

ケーキはどのようなものになるか。

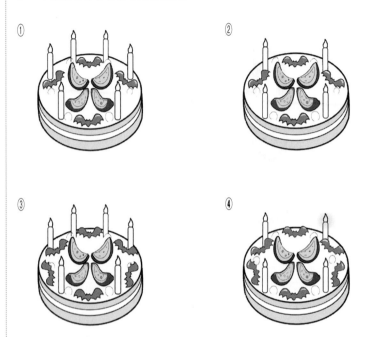

正解 ⇒ ④

　バースデーケーキをどのように飾りつけしてほしいかと尋ねる母親に対して，息子は「ハロウィーン風にしたい」と答えている。具体的には，「コウモリの形をしたチョコレートを6個のせたい」「カボチャを4切れと，同じ数（＝4本）のキャンドルをのせたい」という希望を述べている。したがって，正解は④となる。

【語句・表現】

・decorate「～を飾る，～を装飾する」

・bat「コウモリ」

・on top「上に，表面に」

・pumpkin「カボチャ」

問10　　10
【放送内容と選択肢】

M: Tomorrow you're going hiking. You should bring a raincoat, not an umbrella, in case it rains. You'll also need a scarf.

W: Dad, I understand. But I don't need a scarf.

M: You don't? You might get a lot of sun.

W: I'll bring my sunglasses and sunscreen.

Question:

What will the daughter bring with her tomorrow?

M：明日はハイキングに行くんだよね。雨に備えて，傘ではなくレインコートを持っていくといいよ。スカーフも必要だね。
W：わかったよ，お父さん。でもスカーフは要らないな。
M：そうかい？　日差しが強いかもしれないよ。
W：サングラスと日焼け止めクリームを持っていくから。
問い：
娘は明日何を持っていくか。

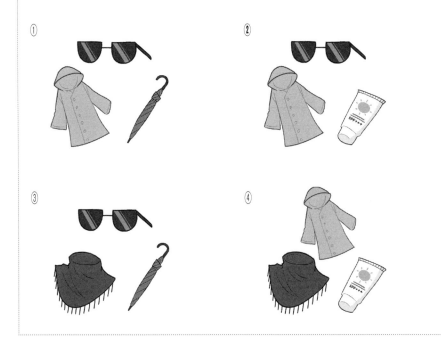

① ② ③ ④

正解 ⇒ ②

　ハイキングの持ち物として，父親は「レインコートを持っていくといい」「スカーフも必要だ」とアドバイスしている。しかし，娘は「スカーフは要らない」と言い，「サングラスと日焼け止めクリームを持っていく」と伝えている。したがって，「レインコート」「サングラス」「日焼け止めクリーム」を持っていくことになるので，正解は②である。

【語句・表現】
・in case ...「…する場合に備えて」
・scarf「スカーフ」
・sunscreen「日焼け止めクリーム」

問11　　11
【放送内容と選択肢】

W: I hear you work part-time at a café. Where is it located?
M: From the Central Station, first go three blocks north, then turn left, and it'll be on your right.
W: There's a post office around there, right?
M: Well, there's a bank, not a post office. The café is across the street from it.

Question:
Where is the café the man works at?

W：カフェでアルバイトをしているって聞いたよ。どこにあるの？
M：セントラル駅からだと，まず3ブロック北に進んで，それから左折すると右側にあるよ。
W：あの辺りには郵便局があるよね？
M：えぇと，郵便局じゃなくて銀行があるよ。カフェは銀行から通りを隔てた向かい側にあるんだ。
問い：
男性の働いているカフェはどこにあるか。

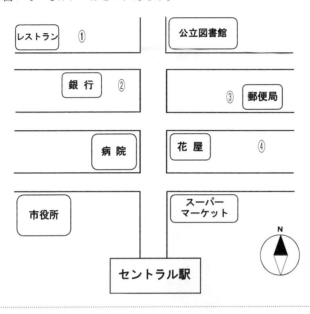

正解 ⇒ ①

　カフェの場所について，男性は1回目の発言で「セントラル駅からだと，まず3ブロック北に進んで，それから左折すると右側にある」と説明している。また，2回目の発言では「カフェは銀行から通りを隔てた向かい側にある」と述べている。したがって，正解は①である。

【語句・表現】
・work part-time「パートタイムで働く，アルバイトをする」
・be located「ある，位置する」

第3問

問12 ⎡12⎤
【放送内容と選択肢】

W: What are you reading, Matthew?
M: Oh, hi, Lucy. It's a detective story. I'm confused because there are so many characters ...
W: May I borrow it when you're done?
M: Of course, but it'll take some time to finish reading it ... Well, let me get back to reading.

W：マシュー，何を読んでいるの？

M：やぁ，ルーシー。探偵小説だよ。登場人物がすごく多いから，頭が混乱しているんだ…。
W：あなたが読み終わったら借りてもいい？
M：いいよ，でも読み終えるのに少し時間がかかりそうなんだ…さて，読書に戻らせて。

男性は会話の直後に何をする可能性が高いか。

① その本を女性から借りる
② その本を読むのをやめる
③ その本を女性に貸す
④ その本をもう一度読み始める

正解 ⇒ ④

「あなたが読み終わったら借りてもいい？」と尋ねる女性に対し，男性は「いいよ」と応じており，女性に本を貸す気はあることがわかる。しかし，続けて「読み終えるのに少し時間がかかりそう」「読書に戻らせて」と言っていることから，会話が終わった直後にはその本をもう一度読み始める可能性が高い。よって，正解は④である。

【語句・表現】
・detective story「探偵小説，推理小説」
・character「登場人物」

問13 ⎡13⎤
【放送内容と選択肢】

M: How about going to the new shopping mall this Friday?
W: Sorry, but I have to work to get ready for an important presentation on Monday.
M: Then, do you have time for dinner on Sunday evening?
W: Well, I may not be finished then. But I'm free on the day after the presentation.
M: OK. Let's meet then.

M：今度の金曜日に，新しいショッピングモールに行くのはどう？
W：悪いけど，仕事をしなければならないの。月曜日の大事なプレゼンの準備があるから。
M：じゃあ，日曜日の夜に食事をする時間はある？
W：うーん，その時はまだ終わっていないかも。でも，プレゼンの翌日は空いているよ。
M：わかった。その日に会おう。

男性と女性はいつ会う予定か。

① 金曜日 ② 土曜日 ③ 日曜日 ④ 火曜日

正解 ⇒ ④

「仕事をしなければならない」「月曜日の大事なプレゼンの準備がある」と言う女性に対し，男性は日曜日の夜に時間があるか尋ねている。女性は「その時（＝日曜日の夜）はまだ終わっていないかも」と答えているため，③は不可である。続けて，女性は「プレゼン（＝月曜日）の翌日は空いている」と言い，男性が「その日に会おう」と応じていることから，④の「火曜日」が正解となる。

問14 　14
【放送内容と選択肢】

W: Excuse me. Is this the right place for the English literature lecture?
M: No, this is Room 105, and the political science lecture is held here. I think the room has been changed. There should be a notice on the door.
W: I see ... Yeah, it says English literature is in Room 115.
M: I think it's just down the hall, past the stairs.
W: Thank you.

W：すみません。英文学の講義はこの教室で合っていますか。
M：いいえ，ここは105教室で政治学の講義です。教室変更があったんだと思います。ドアに掲示があるはずですよ。
W：わかりました…ええ，英文学は115教室と書いてあります。
M：廊下の先の，階段を通り過ぎたところにある教室だと思います。
W：ありがとうございます。

女性は何をする可能性が高いか。

① 政治学の講義に出席する
② 階段を下りて1階へ行く
③ 115教室に行く
④ 105教室にとどまる

正解 ⇒ ③

　女性は英文学の講義に出席したいようだが，男性に尋ねたところ，今いる教室で行われるのは政治学の講義であることがわかる。また，ドアに貼られた掲示を確認すると，英文学の講義は「115教室」に変更されたことが判明する。男性にその教室の場所を教えてもらい，礼を述べていることから，女性は115教室に向かうと考えられる。よって，③が正解である。

【語句・表現】
・literature「文学」
・lecture「講義，講演」
・political science「政治学」
・notice「掲示，貼り紙」
・hall「廊下」
・stair「階段」

問15 　15
【放送内容と選択肢】

M: Excuse me! I have to take the 11 a.m. flight to London.
W: I'm afraid that check-in has already been closed, so you can't take that flight.
M: Oh, no! I need to be in London tomorrow for a conference. What should I do?
W: There is a later flight to London, but you'll arrive the day after tomorrow. I'm sorry, but there's nothing else that we can do.

M：すみません！　午前11時のロンドン行きの便に乗らないといけないのですが。
W：恐れ入りますが，チェックインはすでに終了しておりまして，その便にはご搭乗いただくことができません。
M：ええ，そんな！　会議があるので明日ロンドンに到着しなければならないんです。どうしたらいいですか。
W：ロンドン行きのもっと遅い便がありますが，到着は明後日になります。申し訳ありませんが，私どもは他にどうすることもできません。

男性はなぜうろたえているのか。

① ロンドンで行われる会議に間に合わなさそうである。
② ロンドン行きの便が欠航になった。
③ 会議の開始時刻が変更された。
④ 女性が男性にもっと遅い便に乗るように要求した。

正解 ⇒ ①

　チェックインが終了しており，搭乗する予定だったフライトを利用できないと言われた男性は，「ええ，そんな！」と動揺した様子である。続けて，「会議があるので明日ロンドンに到着しなければならない」と言っていることから，男性がうろたえている理由は，ロンドンで行われる会議に間に合わなさそうだからだとわかる。よって，正解は①となる。

【語句・表現】
・flight「航空便，フライト」
・check-in「チェックイン」：空港で搭乗の手続きを済ませること。
・conference「会議，打ち合わせ」
〈選択肢〉
・make it to ～「～に間に合う，～に参加できる」
・cancel「～［列車など］を運休にする」
・insist that S (should) do「Sが～するように要求する」：insist などの動詞に続く that 節の中では，should が省略されて仮定法現在が用いられることが多い。

問16　　16
【放送内容と選択肢】

W: Oh, Tom! Why are you studying in such a hot room?
M: The air conditioner seems to be out of order, Mom.
W: Then I'll call an electrician right away.
M: Thanks, I can't concentrate at all in this heat.
W: Until then, work in your father's study.
M: OK.

W：あら，トム！　どうしてこんな暑い部屋で勉強しているの？
M：お母さん，エアコンが故障しているみたいなんだよ。
W：それならすぐに電気屋さんを呼ぶわ。
M：ありがとう，この暑さじゃ全然集中できなくて。
W：それまではお父さんの書斎で勉強しなさい。
M：そうするよ。

会話によると正しいものはどれか。

① 母親は息子が一生懸命に勉強していないので腹を立てている。
② **母親はエアコンを修理してもらうつもりである。**
③ 息子はずっと父親の書斎で勉強している。
④ 息子は暑い部屋でも集中することはできると思っている。

正解 ⇒ ②

　暑い部屋で勉強している理由を母親に尋ねられた息子は,「エアコンが故障しているみたいなんだ」と答えている。母親は「それならすぐに電気屋さんを呼ぶ」と言っているので,エアコンの修理を依頼するつもりであると推測できる。よって,②が正解となる。

【語句・表現】
・out of order「故障して」
・electrician「電気工事人,電気技師」
・right away「すぐに,直ちに」
・study「書斎」
〈選択肢〉
・fix「〜を修理する」

問17　　17

【放送内容と選択肢】

M: I've decided to major in geology at university. How about you, Cathy? You're interested in science subjects, aren't you?
W: That's right, Hiroaki. I've been interested in chemistry and physics, but my interest has changed a little.
M: How has it changed?
W: Now I'm most interested in how our body functions. I'd like to improve people's health.

M：僕は大学で地質学を専攻することに決めたんだ。キャシーは？　理系の科目に興味があるんだよね。
W：そうだよ,ヒロアキ。今までは化学や物理学に興味があったんだけど,ちょっと興味が変わってきたんだ。
M：どんな風に変わってきたの？
W：今は私たちの体がどのように機能するのかに一番興味があるよ。人々の健康状態を改善したいんだ。

キャシーが大学で専攻する可能性が最も高いものは何か。

① 化学　　　② 地質学　　　③ **医学**　　　④ 物理学

正解 ⇒ ③

　ヒロアキに「理系の科目に興味があるんだよね」と尋ねられたキャシーは,「今までは化学や物理学に興味があったんだけど,ちょっと興味が変わってきた」と答えている。具体的には,「私たちの体がどのように機能するのかに一番興味がある」「人々の健康状態を改善したい」と述べている。選択肢のうち,

このような内容を研究する学問分野として適切なのは，③の「医学」である。

【語句・表現】
・major in ～「～を専攻する」
・geology「地質学」
・chemistry「化学」
・physics「物理学」

第4問

A
問18〜21　| 18 | | 19 | | 20 | | 21 |
【放送内容と選択肢】

　Last Sunday, one of my friends suggested to me that we should go to a hamburger shop. It was rumored to offer really delicious hamburgers. Of course, I agreed, and we went to the shop together, where we enjoyed delicious hamburgers. Just before leaving the shop, we met the shop owner by chance, who was unexpectedly a foreigner. To our surprise, he kindly showed us how to cook the hamburger we had just eaten! After leaving the shop, I went to a local supermarket, and bought the necessary ingredients. The next day at home, I cooked as instructed and enjoyed the hamburger again!

　先週の日曜日，友人の1人がハンバーガーショップに行かないかと誘ってきました。そのお店はとてもおいしいハンバーガーを提供しているという噂でした。もちろん私は同意し，一緒にお店に行っておいしいハンバーガーを味わいました。お店を出る直前に，私たちは偶然店主に会いました。意外なことに店主は外国人でした。驚いたことに彼は，私たちが食べたハンバーガーの作り方を教えてくれたのです！　お店を出た後，私は地元のスーパーマーケットに行き，必要な材料を買いました。次の日に自宅で指示通りに料理をして，もう一度ハンバーガーを楽しみました！

正解 ⇒　| 18 | ③　| 19 | ①　| 20 | ②　| 21 | ④

まず，第3文で「（友人と）一緒にお店に行っておいしいハンバーガーを味わいました」と述べられているので， 18 には③が入る。

次に，第5文で「驚いたことに彼（＝ハンバーガーショップの店主）は，私たちが食べたハンバーガーの作り方を教えてくれたのです」と述べられていることから， 19 には①が入る。

さらに，第6文に「お店を出た後，私は地元のスーパーマーケットに行き，必要な材料を買いました」とあることから， 20 には②が入る。

そして，最終文に「次の日に自宅で指示通りに料理をして，もう一度ハンバーガーを楽しみました」とあるので， 21 には④を入れるのが適切である。

【語句・表現】
・be rumored to *do*「～すると噂される」
・unexpectedly「意外にも」
・ingredient「（料理などの）材料」
・as instructed「指示通りに，指示に従って」

問22～25   22   23   24   25

【放送内容と選択肢】

Thanks for helping me do the shopping. Please put the food items we bought in the refrigerator in the following way. First, put the fruits and vegetables in Section 1. Meat should go in Section 2 and fish in Section 3. Please put beverages of any kind in Section 4. All frozen foods, regardless of the type, should be kept in Section 5. Oh, I want to defrost the frozen tuna, so please keep it in the fish section.

買い物をするのを手伝ってくれてありがとう。買った食料品は次のように冷蔵庫に入れてください。まず，果物と野菜は「セクション1」に入れてください。肉は「セクション2」，魚は「セクション3」にお願いします。飲み物はすべて「セクション4」に入れてください。冷凍食品は種類に関係なく「セクション5」にお願いします。あ，冷凍マグロは解凍したいので，魚のセクションに入れておいてください。

食料品	冷蔵庫の入れる場所
グレープフルーツ	22
グレープジュース	23
レタス	
ミートソース（冷凍）	24
牛乳	
マグロ（冷凍）	25

① セクション1　　② セクション2　　③ セクション3
④ セクション4　　⑤ セクション5

正解 ⇒   22 ①   23 ④   24 ⑤   25 ③

まず，第3文に「果物と野菜は『セクション1』に入れてください」とあることから， 22 には①が入る。

次に，第5文で「飲み物はすべて『セクション4』に入れてください」と述べられているので，

23 に入るのは④である。

また，第6文に「冷凍食品は種類に関係なく『セクション5』にお願いします」とあることから，24 には⑤が入る。

最後に，第7文で「冷凍マグロは解凍したいので，魚のセクションに入れておいてください」と述べられている。魚のセクションは第4文より「セクション3」だとわかるので，25 は③が正解となる。

【語句・表現】
・refrigerator「冷蔵庫」
・beverage「飲料，飲み物」
・frozen「凍った，冷凍した」
・regardless of 〜「〜にかかわらず，〜に関係なく」
・defrost「〜を解凍する」
・tuna「マグロ」

B
問26 26
【放送内容】

1. Workshop No. 1 allows you to learn about the literature of Latin American countries. For example, you can read a summary of *One Hundred Years of Solitude* by Gabriel García Márquez. This workshop will be held from 10:00 to 11:00 of the festival day and the participation fee is 500 yen.

2. By participating in Workshop No. 2, you can learn about Dutch paintings. This workshop will be enjoyable especially for those interested in the works by 17th-century painters such as Rembrandt and Vermeer. The required time is an hour and a half, and it costs 1,000 yen.

3. Workshop No. 3 enables you to discuss famous Japanese literary works with students from English-speaking countries. They can speak Japanese fluently, so you need not worry about your English proficiency. You can enjoy talking up to half an hour and there is no charge to participate.

4. Through participating in Workshop No. 4, you can learn about contemporary British novels. This workshop covers a variety of genres so that those unfamiliar with modern British literature can enjoy themselves. The duration is about 90 minutes, and it costs 1,500 yen.

1. ワークショップ1では，ラテンアメリカ諸国の文学について学ぶことができます。例えば，ガブリエル・ガルシア＝マルケスの『百年の孤独』の要約を読むことができます。このワークショップは，学園祭当日の10時から11時まで行われます。参加費は500円です。

2. ワークショップ2に参加すると，オランダの絵画について学ぶことができます。このワークショップは，レンブラントやフェルメールなど17世紀の画家による作品に興味のある方にとって，特に楽しめるものになるでしょう。所要時間は1時間半で，料金は1,000円です。

3. ワークショップ3では，英語圏の国から来た学生たちと，日本の有名な文学作品について議論することができます。彼らは日本語を流暢に話せますので，ご自身の英語力について心配する必要はありません。最長で30分まで話すことができます。料金はかかりません。

4. ワークショップ4に参加すると，イギリスの現代小説について学ぶことができます。このワーク

ショップでは，現代のイギリス文学になじみのない人でも楽しめるように，様々なジャンルを取り扱います。所要時間は90分で，料金は1,500円です。

　正解 ⇒ ①

　3つの条件をすべて満たすのは，①の「ワークショップ1」である。
　②は，第1文で「オランダの絵画について学ぶことができます」，第3文で「所要時間は1時間半」と述べられており，条件B・Cに合わない。
　③は，第1文で「日本の有名な文学作品について議論することができます」と述べられていることから，条件Cを満たさない。
　④は，第3文に「所要時間は90分で，料金は1,500円です」とあり，条件A・Bに合わない。

ワークショップ	条件 A	条件 B	条件 C
① ワークショップ1	○	○	○
② ワークショップ2	○	×	×
③ ワークショップ3	○	○	×
④ ワークショップ4	×	×	○

【語句・表現】
〈ワークショップ1〉
・summary「要約，概要」
・participation「参加」
・fee「料金，会費」
〈ワークショップ2〉
・participate in ～「～に参加する」
・Dutch「オランダ（人）の」
・work「作品」
〈ワークショップ3〉
・literary「文学の」
・fluently「流暢に」
・proficiency「技量」
・up to ～「（最大で）～まで」
・charge「料金」
〈ワークショップ4〉
・contemporary「現代の」
・cover「～を扱う」
・genre「ジャンル」
・be unfamiliar with ～「～に親しんでいない」
・duration「継続時間」

第5問

【放送内容】

Wasted food is a global issue for environmental, humanitarian, cultural, economic and public health reasons. During the 2015 Climate Change Conference in Paris, the Obama administration and the United Nations promised to cut wasted food in half by 2030. According to the Food and Agriculture Organization of the United Nations, around 4 billion tons of food are produced for human consumption around the world annually and approximately one third of that is wasted. Waste happens everywhere along the production chain and, interestingly, it is equally widespread among developed and developing countries.

In developing countries, wasted food can be mostly attributed to poorly developed infrastructure preventing the adequate storage of food or delaying its arrival to the market place. An unnecessarily large amount of food, sometimes up to 40 percent of food which does not keep long, doesn't make it to the market and ends up rotting in the fields, trucks or warehouses. In contrast, wasted food in industrialized economies and rich communities around the world is mostly explained by consumer behavior and practices in both the retail sector and the food industry.

Although one of the biggest sources of waste in industrialized economies is household waste, not all wasted food is food that gets thrown away. Some of the food gets wasted before it even reaches the household. The fact that consumer preferences vary drastically with external factors like the weather also explains why much of fresh produce goes bad in the supermarket's shelves. However, whether food looks beautiful or not plays an even larger part. In other words, grocery stores and supermarkets know their customers won't purchase produce that doesn't have the "right" shape, color or size.

　　廃棄食品は，環境，人道，文化，経済，公衆衛生上の理由から世界的な問題となっています。2015年にパリで行われた気候変動会議において，オバマ政権と国際連合は，2030年までに廃棄食品を半減させることを約束しました。国連食糧農業機関によると，世界中で年間約40億トンの食料が人間の消費用に生産されていますが，その約3分の1が廃棄されています。廃棄食品は生産チェーンのあらゆるところで発生しており，また興味深いことに，先進国でも発展途上国でも同じように広まっているのです。

　　発展途上国では，インフラの整備が不十分なために，食品の適切な保存が妨げられたり，市場への到着が遅れたりすることが，廃棄食品の主な原因と考えられます。不必要に大量の食品，時には日持ちのしない食品の最大40％が市場に出回らず，畑やトラック，倉庫で腐敗する結果になっています。一方で，世界中の先進国や豊かな社会における廃棄食品は，その大半が，小売部門および食品産業の両方における消費者の行動と慣習によって説明されます。

　　先進国における最大の廃棄食品発生源の1つは家庭ごみですが，廃棄食品のすべてが捨てられる食品というわけではありません。家庭に届く前に無駄になる食品もあります。消費者の好みが天候などの外的要因で大きく変わることも，生鮮食品の多くがスーパーの棚で腐ってしまう原因になります。しかし，それ以上に大きな原因となっているのは，食品の見た目が美しいかどうかです。つまり，食料品店やスーパーマーケットは，形，色，大きさが「適切」でない製品を客が購入しないことを知っているのです。

世界における廃棄食品

○食料の生産量と廃棄食品の量
・国連食糧農業機関：
　　毎年約40億トンの食料が生産されている ⇒ 約 | 27 | が廃棄されている
・オバマ政権と国連：
　　2030年までに廃棄食品を | 28 | 削減することを約束した
★廃棄食品は先進国と発展途上国の両方で広まっている。

○廃棄食品が生じる主な原因
・発展途上国： | 29 |
・先進国： | 30 | ← | 31 | が重視される

講義の続き

　Now look at the following graph. This graph shows wasted food in various regions of the world, divided into the pre-consumption stage and the consumption stage. The pre-consumption stage means the production-to-retail stage. What should we do to reduce wasted food?

　さて，次のグラフをご覧ください。これは，世界のさまざまな地域における廃棄食品について，消費前の段階と消費段階とに分けたグラフです。消費前の段階とは生産から小売の段階を意味します。廃棄食品を減らすために，私たちは何をすべきでしょうか。

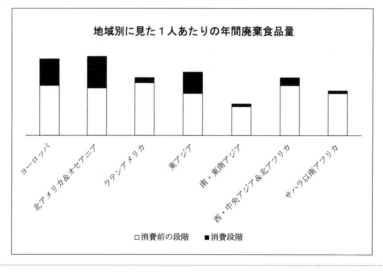

地域別に見た１人あたりの年間廃棄食品量

ヨーロッパ　北アメリカ＆オセアニア　ラテンアメリカ　東アジア　南・東南アジア　西・中央アジア＆北アフリカ　サハラ以南アフリカ

□消費前の段階　■消費段階

［出典］COLUMN: Solve the problem of food waste: eat the ugly by Laura Villegas Ortiz from TECHNICIAN, Aug 15, 2016. Reproduced with permission of Technician.
　※問題作成の都合上，一部原文を改変しています。

問27・28 | 27 | 28 |

| ① 5分の1 | ② 4分の1 | ③ 3分の1 | ④ 2分の1 |

正解 ⇒ | 27 | ③ | 28 | ④

27

　第1段落第3文では，「国連食糧農業機関によると，世界中で年間約40億トンの食料が人間の消費用に生産されていますが，その約3分の1が廃棄されています」と述べられている。したがって，正解は③である。

28

　第1段落第2文では，「2015年にパリで行われた気候変動会議において，オバマ政権と国際連合は，2030年までに廃棄食品を半減させることを約束しました」と述べられている。よって，正解は④である。

問29～31　　29　　30　　31

①	消費者の行動と慣習
②	食品の新鮮さ
③	食品を保存し供給する設備の不十分さ
④	非効率な政府の介入
⑤	食品の見た目の良さ

　正解 ⇒　29　③　　30　①　　31　⑤

29

　第2段落第1文では，「発展途上国では，インフラの整備が不十分なために，食品の適切な保存が妨げられたり，市場への到着が遅れたりすることが，廃棄食品の主な原因と考えられます」と述べられている。よって，③が適切である。

30

　第2段落第3文では，「世界中の先進国や豊かな社会における廃棄食品は，その大半が，小売部門および食品産業の両方における消費者の行動と慣習によって説明されます」と述べられている。したがって，①を入れるのが適切である。

31

　「消費者の行動や慣習」の具体例については，第3段落で言及されている。第4文に「それ（＝消費者の好みが外的要因で大きく変わること）以上に大きな原因となっているのは，食品の見た目が美しいかどうかです」とあるので，⑤が正解となる。

問32　　32

①	廃棄食品の問題は小売部門が関心を持っていないため，解決するのが困難である。
②	廃棄食品の問題は，先進国より発展途上国の方が深刻である。
③	廃棄食品の問題はいろいろな理由で生じるため，さまざまな取り組みが必要になるだろう。
④	廃棄食品の問題は，食料品店とスーパーマーケットの尽力により解決するだろう。

　正解 ⇒ ③

　第2段落では，廃棄食品の発生する原因が先進国と発展途上国で異なることが説明されている。また，第3段落では，先進国の中でも種々の原因が存在することが述べられている。したがって，廃棄食品の問題を解決するためには，さまざまな取り組みが必要であると考えられる。よって，③が正解となる。

問33　　33

①	先進国の消費者は，廃棄食品の削減に対する意識を高めるべきである。
②	ラテンアメリカの消費者は，ヨーロッパの消費者ほど多くの注意を廃棄食品に払っていない。

③ 発展途上国では，消費前の段階で発生する廃棄食品はもはや深刻な問題ではない。
④ サハラ以南のアフリカでは，廃棄食品の半分以上が消費段階で発生している。

正解 ⇒ ①

　グラフを見ると，ヨーロッパや北アメリカ，オセアニア，東アジアといった先進国の比較的多い地域では，「消費段階」で発生する廃棄食品の割合が高いことが読み取れる。また，前半の講義の第3段落では，先進国において「消費前の段階」で廃棄食品が発生する原因として，「消費者の好みが外的要因で大きく変わること」「消費者が食品の見た目を気にすること」が挙げられている。つまり，先進国において廃棄食品を削減するためには，消費者の意識を変える必要があることがわかる。よって，正解は①となる。

【語句・表現】
〈第1段落〉
・humanitarian「人道主義的な」
・conference「会議」
・administration「政権，政府」
・agriculture「農業」
・consumption「消費，飲食」
・annually「毎年」
・approximately「おおよそ」
・widespread「広く行き渡っている」
〈第2段落〉
・attribute A to B「A を B に帰する」
・infrastructure「インフラ」
・adequate「十分な，適当な」
・storage「保管」
・delay「〜を遅らせる」
・make it to 〜「〜にたどり着く」
・end up *doing*「最後には〜することになる」
・rot「腐る」
・warehouse「倉庫」
・in contrast「対照的に」
・industrialized「工業化した，産業化した」
・retail「小売」
・sector「部門，分野」
〈第3段落〉
・household「家族，家庭」
・preference「好み」
・drastically「大幅に，大々的に」
・external「外部の，外的な」
・grocery store「食料品店」
・purchase「〜を買う，〜を購入する」
〈講義の続き〉
・divide A into B「A を分割して B にする」
〈ワークシート〉
・emphasize「〜を強調する，〜を重要視する」
〈選択肢〉
・inadequate「十分でない，不適当な」

・facility「設備，施設」
・store「〜を保管する，〜を貯蔵する」
・distribute「〜を供給する，〜を配送する」
・inefficient「効率の悪い」
・intervention「干渉，介入」
・visual「視覚の，目に見える」
・appeal「魅力」
・approach「取り組み，手法」
・per capita「1 人あたりの」
・awareness「知識，意識」
・reduction「減少，削減」

第6問

A
【放送内容】

Tom: Hi, Kate. I've been stressed lately because I haven't been able to go traveling since the pandemic began.

Kate: Hi, Tom. Hmm ... as for me, looking at pictures of different places on the internet is enough.

Tom: Oh, come on. I want to see many places with my own eyes. I can't be satisfied with just looking at photos and videos.

Kate: Travel agencies are offering online tours these days. I've actually been on one, and it was so realistic. It was like being on a real trip.

Tom: But you can't experience the local atmosphere with all five senses, can you? I mean, you use only sight and hearing on an online tour.

Kate: That's true, but each place may be more memorable because you are focused on the screen. Plus, online tours allow you to do research while participating in them, so you can learn a lot.

Tom: Hmm ... Personally, I prefer to travel in real life. You can't interact with local people online.

Kate: You might change your opinion once you take an online tour.

Tom: OK, I'll try.

トム：やあ，ケイト。パンデミックが始まってからずっと旅行に行けないから，最近ストレスがたまっているよ。

ケイト：あら，トム。うーん…私の場合は，インターネットでいろいろな場所の写真を見れば十分だわ。

トム：おいおい，冗談だろ。僕はたくさんの場所を自分の目で見てみたい。写真や動画を見るだけじゃ満足できないね。

ケイト：最近は旅行会社がオンラインツアーを提供しているよ。私は実際に参加したことがあるけど，すごく臨場感があった。本当に旅行をしているみたいだったよ。

トム：でも，五感のすべてを使って現地の雰囲気を体験することはできないよね。つまり，オンラインツアーでは視覚と聴覚しか使わないっていうことだよ。

ケイト：確かにそうだけど，スクリーンに意識を集中するから，それぞれの場所が記憶に残りやすいかもしれない。それに，オンラインツアーは参加している最中に調べ物をすることができるから，たくさんのことを学べるよ。

トム：うーん…。個人的には，旅行は実際に行く方がいいな。オンラインだと現地の人々と交流ができないし。

ケイト：あなたも一度オンラインツアーに参加してみれば，意見が変わるかもしれないわ。

トム：わかった，試してみるよ。

問34 　34

トムの発言の要点は何か。

① 現地の人々との交流は旅行の最もおもしろい部分である。
② オンラインツアーは若者の間で人気が高まっている。
③ インターネットには有名な観光地の写真が多数存在する。
④ 五感のすべてを使わなければ旅行を楽しむことはできない。

正解 ⇒ ④

ケイトは2回目の発言で，自分が参加したオンラインツアーについて，「すごく臨場感があった」「本当に旅行をしているみたいだった」と肯定的な評価をしている。これに対してトムは，「（オンラインツアーでは）五感のすべてを使って現地の雰囲気を体験することはできない」「オンラインツアーでは視覚と聴覚しか使わない」と言っている。ここから，トムは「旅行を楽しむためには，五感のすべてを使う必要がある」と考えていることがうかがえる。よって，正解は④となる。

問35 　35

ケイトはオンラインツアーについてどのように考えているか。

① オンラインツアーであっても楽しい経験をすることは可能である。
② オンラインツアーは臨場感に欠けるので依然として改良の余地がある。
③ 従来のツアーはまもなくオンラインツアーに完全に取って代わられるだろう。
④ オンラインツアーに参加する前に入念な下調べをするべきである。

正解 ⇒ ①

ケイトがオンラインツアーについて肯定的な評価をしていることは，問34で述べたとおりである。具体的には，2回目の発言で「すごく臨場感があった」「本当に旅行をしているみたいだった」，3回目の発言で「スクリーンに意識を集中するから，それぞれの場所が記憶に残りやすい」「参加している最中に調べ物をすることができるから，たくさんのことを学べる」と言っている。つまり，オンラインツアーであっても楽しむことは可能であると考えているわけであるから，①が正解となる。

【語句・表現】
・stressed「ストレスがたまって」
・pandemic「世界的な流行病」
・as for ～「～については」
・be satisfied with ～「～に満足している」
・travel agency「旅行会社」
・atmosphere「雰囲気」
・sense「感覚」：five senses は sight（視覚）・hearing（聴覚）・smell（嗅覚）・taste（味覚）・touch（触覚）を指す。
・sight「視力，視覚」
・memorable「記憶に残る」
・plus「その上，さらに」
・participate in ～「～に参加する」

- interact with ～「～と交流する」
- once「いったん…すると」
〈選択肢〉
- tourist spot「観光地，観光名所」
- realism「現実感，リアルさ」
- completely「完全に」

B
【放送内容】

Yua: Hi, Sammy. I went to a zoo with my cousins who are elementary school students. We had a great time with many different kinds of animals.

Sammy: Glad to hear you had a good time, Yua. But zoos have been criticized for several reasons. It's unfortunate that animals who are supposed to live in nature spend their whole lives in cages. Don't you think so, Jane?

Jane: I see your point, Sammy. But I think zoos play an important role, for example, in helping children learn about animals. What do you think, Manabu?

Manabu: Well, zoos are necessary now that so many animals are endangered. A large number of zoos are preserving and breeding animals that are at high risk of extinction. What about the zoo you went to, Yua?

Yua: Now that you mention it, the zoo had a breeding program for an animal called okapi. I hope zoos will continue to exist.

Sammy: I know that zoos do conservation work, but it should only be done in the wild. I think zoos should be abolished.

Jane: I don't think so, Sammy. More and more zoos are trying to keep their animals in near-natural conditions.

Manabu: I agree with you, Jane. We should be concerned about animal welfare, but there's a lot to be learned from zoos. Oh, I feel like going to a zoo for the first time in many years!

ユア：ねえ，サミー。私，小学生のいとこたちと一緒に動物園に行ったの。いろんな種類の動物を見られて楽しかった。

サミー：楽しい時間を過ごせたみたいでよかったね，ユア。だけど，動物園はいくつかの理由で批判されているんだ。本来であれば自然の中で生きるはずの動物たちが，一生おりの中で過ごすなんてかわいそうだよ。ジェーン，そう思わない？

ジェーン：サミー，あなたの言いたいことはわかる。でも動物園は，例えば子どもたちが動物について学ぶ上で，重要な役割を果たしていると思うの。マナブ，あなたはどう思う？

マナブ：そうだね，これだけ多くの動物が絶滅の危機にある以上，動物園は必要だよ。絶滅の危険性が高い動物を保護して繁殖させている動物園はたくさんあるんだ。ユア，君が行った動物園はどうだった？

ユア：そう言われてみれば，あの動物園には，オカピっていう動物の繁殖計画があったよ。これからも動物園はなくならないでほしいな。

サミー：動物園で保護活動が行われていることは知っているけど，それは自然の中でだけ行うべきだよ。動物園は廃止すべきだと思うね。

ジェーン：サミー，私はそう思わないな。自然に近い状態で動物を飼育するように努めている動物園は，ますます増えているんだよ。

マナブ：ジェーン，僕も同じ考えだよ。動物福祉には配慮するべきだけど，動物園から学べることはたくさんある。あぁ，久しぶりに動物園に行きたくなってきた！

①　1人　　②　2人　　③　3人　　④　4人

正解 ⇒ ①

　　サミーは,「本来であれば自然の中で生きるはずの動物たちが,一生おりの中で過ごすなんてかわいそうだ」「それ（＝保護活動）は自然の中でだけ行うべきだ」と述べ,最終的に「動物園は廃止すべきだ」と言っている。

　　これに対して,ユアは「これからも動物園はなくならないでほしい」と言っており,動物園の廃止に消極的な立場であることがうかがえる。また,ジェーンは,「動物園は廃止すべきだ」というサミーの意見に「私はそう思わない」と明確に反対している。さらに,マナブも「僕も同じ考えだ」と言い,ジェーンの意見に賛同している。

　　以上より「動物園を廃止すべきだと考えている」のはサミーだけであるから,正解は①となる。

問37　　37

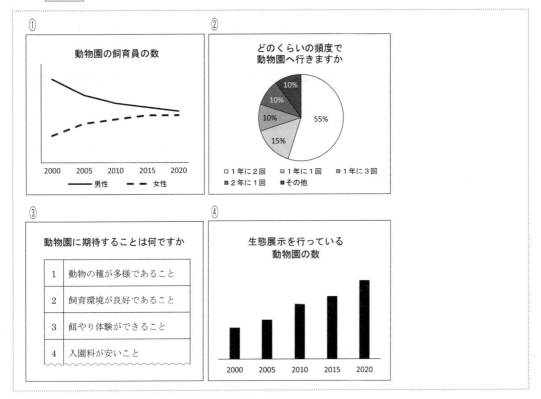

正解 ⇒ ④

　　ジェーンは2回目の発言で,「自然に近い状態で動物を飼育するように努めている動物園は,ますます増えている」と述べている。④のグラフからは,生態展示を実施している動物園の数が増加していることが読み取れる。よって,これが正解である。

【語句・表現】
・cousin「いとこ」
・elementary school「小学校」

・criticize「〜を批判する」
・be supposed to *do*「〜することになっている」
・cage「かご，おり」
・endangered「絶滅の危機に瀕した」
・preserve「〜を保護する」
・breed「〜を育てる，〜を繁殖させる」
・be at high risk of 〜「〜の危険性が高い」
・extinction「絶滅」
・Now that you mention it「言われてみれば」
・conservation「保護」
・wild「自然のままの環境，野生の状態」
・abolish「〜を廃止する」
・animal welfare「動物福祉」
・feel like *doing*「〜したい気がする」
・for the first time in many years「久しぶりに」
〈選択肢〉
・zoo attendant「動物園の飼育員」
・species「（生物の）種」
・feed「〜に食べ物を与える」
・admission fee「入場料，入園料」
・ecological exhibition「生態展示」：動物の本来の生息環境をできる限り再現し，動物と環境全体を観察できる展示のこと。

問題番号（配点）	設問		解答番号	正　解	配　点	自己採点
第1問（25）	A	1	1	4	4	
		2	2	2	4	
		3	3	4	4	
		4	4	3	4	
	B	5	5	1	3	
		6	6	4	3	
		7	7	1	3	
自己採点小計						
第2問（16）		8	8	3	4	
		9	9	3	4	
		10	10	1	4	
		11	11	2	4	
自己採点小計						
第3問（18）		12	12	1	3	
		13	13	3	3	
		14	14	4	3	
		15	15	4	3	
		16	16	1	3	
		17	17	3	3	
自己採点小計						

問題番号（配点）	設問		解答番号	正　解	配　点	自己採点
第4問（12）	A	18	18	1	4*	
		19	19	4		
		20	20	3		
		21	21	2		
		22	22	4	1	
		23	23	4	1	
		24	24	2	1	
		25	25	6	1	
	B	26	26	3	4	
自己採点小計						
第5問（15）		27	27	4	3	
		28	28	1	4*	
		29	29	1		
		30	30	2		
		31	31	3		
		32	32	3	4	
		33	33	2	4	
自己採点小計						
第6問（14）	A	34	34	1	3	
		35	35	3	3	
	B	36	36	4	4	
		37	37	4	4	
自己採点小計						

（注）
*は，全部正解の場合のみ点を与える。

自己採点合計 □

第1問

A
問1 [1]
【放送内容と選択肢】

> It'll be half past five by the time this movie is over. The running time is just two hours.
>
> ① その映画は2時に終わるだろう。
> ② その映画は5時に終わるだろう。
> ③ その映画は約3時間続くだろう。
> ④ その映画は3時半に始まるだろう。

　正解 ⇒ ④

　放送された英文は，「この映画が終わった時には5時半になっているだろう。上映時間はちょうど2時間だから」という意味である。上映時間が「2時間」で終了時刻が「5時半」であるから，開始時刻は「3時半」だとわかる。よって，④が正解となる。

【語句・表現】
・by the time ...「…するまでには」
・running time「（映画などの）上映時間」
〈選択肢〉
・last「続く，継続する」

問2 [2]
【放送内容と選択肢】

> It was not until she failed the exam that Julie decided to study math hard.
>
> ① ジュリーは試験の直前に，数学を熱心に勉強する決心をした。
> ② ジュリーは試験に不合格になり，数学を熱心に勉強する決心をした。
> ③ ジュリーは数学を熱心に勉強したが，試験に合格しなかった。
> ④ ジュリーは現在よりも以前の方が，数学を熱心に勉強していた。

　正解 ⇒ ②

　放送された英文は，「ジュリーは試験に不合格になってようやく，数学を熱心に勉強する決心をした」という意味である。It is not until ～ that ...「～して初めて…する」の表現がポイントである。よって，②が正解となる。

【語句・表現】
・fail「～［試験など］に落ちる」：この意味では他動詞用法が一般的。

問3 [3]
【放送内容と選択肢】

> I don't like the way Tom behaves. He speaks to me as if he were my boss.

① 話者はトムの上司として適切にふるまっている。
② 話者は上司のふるまい方が好きではない。
③ トムは近い将来，話者の上司になるだろう。
④ トムの話し方は話者を不快にさせる。

　正解 ⇒ ④

　放送された英文は，「私はトムのふるまい方が好きではない。彼はまるで私の上司であるかのような話し方をする」という意味である。as if ... 「まるで…であるかのように」の表現がポイントである。「話者はトムの話し方に不快感を抱いている」ということであるから，④が正解となる。

【語句・表現】
・behave「ふるまう，行動する」
・boss「上司」
〈選択肢〉
・appropriately「ふさわしく，適切に」
・uncomfortable「不快な」

問4　　4
【放送内容と選択肢】

The service at the hotel couldn't have been better.

① そのホテルのサービスは，話者が受けた最悪のサービスだった。
② そのホテルのサービスは，話者が期待していたほど良くはなかった。
③ 話者はそのホテルのサービスに大いに満足した。
④ 話者はそのホテルのサービスに満足できなかった。

　正解 ⇒ ③

　放送された英文は，「そのホテルのサービスは最高だった」という意味である。couldn't have been better は直訳すると「それ以上良いものになり得なかっただろう」となり，「最高だった」という意味を表す。つまり，話者は「そのホテルのサービスに大いに満足した」ということであるから，③が正解となる。

【語句・表現】
〈選択肢〉
・be satisfied with ～「～に満足している」

B
問5 ☐ 5
【放送内容と選択肢】

Some umbrellas are plain, others are striped and one of them is white with polka dots.

① ② ③ ④

正解 ⇒ ①

放送された英文は,「何本かの傘は無地,別の何本かはストライプ,1本は白地に水玉模様である」という意味である。この内容に一致するのは①である。

【語句・表現】
・plain「模様のない,無地の」
・striped「しま模様の,ストライプの」
・polka dot「水玉模様」

問6 ☐ 6
【放送内容と選択肢】

There's no room for the two of us to sit side by side. Let's sit separately.

① ② ③ ④

正解 ⇒ ④

　　放送された英文は,「私たち2人が並んで座れるスペースはないね。別々に座ろう」という意味である。この内容に一致するのは④である。

【語句・表現】
・room「空間, 余地」
・side by side「(横に) 並んで」
・separately「別々に, 離れて」

問7　　7
【放送内容と選択肢】

Can you see the woman over there?　She is sitting surrounded by children.

①

②

③

④

正解 ⇒ ①

　　放送された英文は,「あそこにいる女性が見えますか。彼女は子どもたちに囲まれて座っています」という意味である。この内容に一致するのは①である。

【語句・表現】
・be surrounded by ～「～に囲まれている」

第2問

問8 ⬚8⬚

【放送内容と選択肢】

M: Cathy, don't you know where my notebook is?
W: Do you mean your math notebook, James?
M: Yes.　The cover has the subject on the upper left and my name on the bottom right.
W: If I find it, I'll let you know.
Question:
What does the boy's notebook look like?

M：キャシー，僕のノートがどこにあるか知らない？
W：数学のノートのこと，ジェームズ？
M：うん。表紙の左上に科目，右下に僕の名前が書いてあるんだ。
W：もし見つけたら教えるね。
問い：
男の子のノートはどのようなものか。

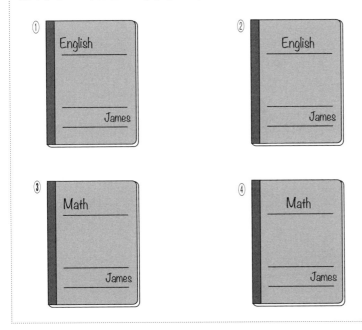

正解 ⇒ ③

　男の子（＝ジェームズ）がノートを探している。女の子（＝キャシー）が「数学」のノートのことかと尋ねると，男の子は「うん」と答え，「表紙の左上に科目，右下に僕の名前が書いてある」と説明している。科目は「数学」，名前は「ジェームズ」であるから，③が正解となる。

【語句・表現】
・cover「表紙」
・subject「科目，教科」
・upper「上部の」
・bottom「下部の」

問9　　9

【放送内容と選択肢】

W: Amy has asked me to buy her a study desk. But I also want to replace the dining table and the chairs.

M: All of that would be way beyond our budget. Oh, look there. I'd love that leather sofa for my room ...

W: You're kidding, right? We don't have money to buy things like that.

M: Yeah, yeah, I know. This time let's give up what we want, OK?

Question:

What will the man and the woman buy?

W：エイミーに学習机を買ってほしいと言われているの。でも，ダイニングテーブルとイスも買い替えたいな。

M：それを全部買ったら，予算を大幅に超えてしまうよ。あ，見て。僕は自分の部屋にあの革張りのソファを置きたいな…。

W：冗談でしょう！　そんな物を買うお金はないわ。

M：はいはい，わかってるよ。今回は僕たちが欲しい物はあきらめよう，いいね？

問い：

男性と女性は何を買うか。

正解 ⇒ ③

　女性の１回目の発言より，夫婦の娘と思われるエイミーは「学習机」を欲しがっていることがわかる。女性は「ダイニングテーブルとイス」，男性は「革張りのソファ」を買いたいと言っているが，「それ（＝学習机，ダイニングテーブル，イス）を全部買ったら，予算を大幅に超えてしまう」「そんな物（＝革張りのソファ）を買うお金はない」とのことで，結局「僕たちが欲しい物はあきらめよう」という結論に至っている。よって，エイミーの学習机のみを購入することになるので，正解は③となる。

【語句・表現】
・way「はるかに」：副詞・前置詞等を強める副詞。
・budget「予算」
・leather「革」
・kid「冗談を言う，からかう」
・give up ～「～をあきらめる」

問10 ☐ 10
【放送内容と選択肢】

W: Here's a picture of my family. I'm now taller than my mother.
M: Wow, and is this your brother?
W: Yes. He is taller than my father, but I'm not taller than my father yet.
M : You are next to your father, and you really look like him.
Question:
What does the picture look like?

W：これはうちの家族の写真だよ。私は母より背が高くなったんだ。
M：そうなんだ。この人は君のお兄さん？
W：うん。彼は父より背が高いけれど，私はまだ父より背が低いの。
M：君はお父さんの隣にいるけど，よく似ているね。
問い：
写真はどのようなものか。

①  ②

③  ④

正解 ⇒ ①

　女性が1回目の発言で「私は母より背が高くなった」と言っていることから，身長は「女性＞母」であるとわかる。また，2回目の発言では「彼（＝女性の兄）は父より背が高いけれど，私はまだ父より背が低い」と述べており，「兄＞父＞女性」の順であることがわかる。以上より，「兄＞父＞女性＞母」となるので，①が正解である。

問11 ☐11☐
【放送内容と選択肢】

> M: I've just arrived at the station. I'll be waiting for you in front of the convenience store.
> W: Which one? The one next to the bakery?
> M: No, the one across from the bookstore.
> W: OK, I'll be with you soon.
> **Question:**
> Where will the man and the woman meet?
>
> M：駅に到着したよ。コンビニの前で待っているね。
> W：どのコンビニ？　パン屋さんの隣にあるコンビニのこと？
> M：ううん，本屋さんの向かい側にあるコンビニだよ。
> W：わかった，すぐに行くね。
> 問い：
> 男性と女性はどこで会うか。

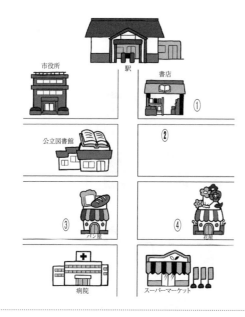

正解 ⇒ ②

　男性が「コンビニの前で待っている」と電話で女性に伝えている。女性が「パン屋さんの隣にあるコンビニ」のことかと尋ねると，男性は「本屋さんの向かい側にあるコンビニ」だと答えている。続けて女性が「わかった，すぐに行くね」と言っていることから，二人が会う場所は②であるとわかる。

【語句・表現】
・in front of ～「～の前に」
・bakery「パン屋，ベーカリー」
・across from ～「～の反対側に，～の向かい側に」

第3問

問12 ☐12☐

【放送内容と選択肢】

W: Achoo!

M: Bless you!

W: Thanks.

M: Are you all right? You don't look very well.

W: It's hay fever. My nose is runny and I can't stop sneezing.

M: Same here. But in my case it's a cold. Or I may have caught the flu.

W: Oh, really? Take care.

W：ハクション！

M：お大事に！

W：ありがとう。

M：大丈夫？　体調があまり良くなさそうだけど。

W：花粉症なの。鼻水が出るし，くしゃみも止まらなくて。

M：僕もだよ。でも，僕の場合は風邪だけど。あるいは，インフルエンザにかかったのかもしれない。

W：あら，本当に？　お大事にね。

会話によると正しいものはどれか。

① 男性も女性も鼻水が出ている。

② 男性も女性も花粉症にかかっていない。

③ 男性は風邪をひいており，せきが止まらない。

④ 女性はインフルエンザにかかったと思っている。

正解 ⇒ ①

　「花粉症なの。鼻水が出るし，くしゃみも止まらなくて」と話す女性に対し，男性は「僕もだよ。でも，僕の場合は風邪だけど。あるいは，インフルエンザにかかったのかもしれない」と言っている。ここから，男性も女性も鼻水が出ていることがわかるので，①が正解となる。

【語句・表現】

・Bless you!「お大事に」：くしゃみをした人に言う決まり文句。

・hay fever「花粉症」

・runny「鼻水の出る」

・sneeze「くしゃみをする」

・flu「インフルエンザ」：influenza の短縮形。

〈選択肢〉

・suffer from ～「～を患う」

・cough「せきをする」

問13 ☐13☐
【放送内容と選択肢】

> W: From what I hear, German, Russian and Finnish are among the hardest languages to learn.
> M: I've learnt German and Russian but I don't know anything about Finnish.
> W: I wonder if it's similar to other Nordic languages such as Norwegian, Swedish and Danish.
> M: Let me see ... According to Wikipedia, the language system is totally different from that of other Nordic languages.
>
> W：ドイツ語，ロシア語，フィンランド語は，習得するのが最も難しい言語だって聞いたけど。
> M：僕はドイツ語とロシア語を学んだことがあるけど，フィンランド語については何も知らないや。
> W：ノルウェー語やスウェーデン語，デンマーク語のような他の北欧の言語と似ているのかしら。
> M：ええと…ウィキペディアによると，フィンランド語の言語体系は，他の北欧の言語と全く違うんだって。

> 男性が学んだことのある言語はどれか。
>
> ① デンマーク語
> ② フィンランド語
> ③ **ドイツ語**
> ④ ノルウェー語

正解 ⇒ ③

　男性は「ドイツ語とロシア語を学んだことがある」と話しているので，正解は③である。フィンランド語については「何も知らない」と言っているので，学習した経験があるとは考えにくい。デンマーク語やノルウェー語に関しても，学んだ経験があることをうかがわせる発言はないので不可である。

【語句・表現】
・from what I hear「私の聞いたところでは」
・learnt：learn の過去分詞。主にイギリス英語で用いられる。
・Nordic「北欧の」
・totally「完全に，まったく」

問14 ☐14☐
【放送内容と選択肢】

> M: I'm having a party at my house on Sunday. Would you like to join us?
> W: I'd love to. Is it all right if I bring a friend with me?
> M: Of course. The party starts at noon. Can you come in time for that?
> W: Oh, no! I thought it would be held in the evening. Both of us have a job during the day. What a pity!
>
> M：日曜日に僕の家でパーティーをするんだ。君も参加しない？
> W：喜んで。友達を連れて行ってもいい？
> M：もちろんだよ。パーティーは正午に始まるんだ。間に合うように来られる？
> W：あら！ 夕方に開催されるのかと思っていたよ。私たち，日中は仕事があるの。残念だなぁ！

女性は何をする可能性が高いか。

① パーティーに参加するように友人に頼む
② 一人でパーティーに参加する
③ 友人と一緒にパーティーに参加する
④ パーティーに参加しないことに決める

正解 ⇒ ④

　パーティーに誘われた女性は,「喜んで。友達を連れて行ってもいい？」と返答しており,参加する気満々である。しかし,パーティーが正午に始まると聞くと,「夕方に開催されるのかと思っていた」「日中は仕事がある」と言っており,女性もその友人も参加は難しい状況だとわかる。最後の「残念だなぁ！」という発言からも参加をあきらめていることがうかがえるので,正解は④となる。

【語句・表現】
・noon「正午」
・What a pity!「それは残念！」
〈選択肢〉
・by oneself「一人で」

問15　　15
【放送内容と選択肢】

W: Why don't we eat dinner at "Miguel River" tomorrow?
M: That restaurant is popular, so it'll be difficult to make a reservation now. How about "Round Grill"?
W: Don't you know? It closed last month.
M: Oh, I didn't know that. Then what about the restaurant we often go to?
W: That wouldn't feel like an anniversary. Let's not go out tomorrow, and instead go to "Miguel River" next weekend.
M: OK. I'll make a reservation.

W：明日は「ミゲル・リバー」で食事をしようよ。
M：あのレストランは人気があるから,今から予約をするのは難しいんじゃないかな。「ラウンド・グリル」はどう？
W：知らないの？　あそこは先月閉店したのよ。
M：えー,それは知らなかった。じゃあ,僕たちがよく行くあのレストランは？
W：それだと記念日っていう感じがしないな。明日は外出を控えて,その代わりに来週末に「ミゲル・リバー」に行こうよ。
M：そうだね。僕が予約しておくよ。

男性と女性は何をすることに決めたか。

① 明日「ミゲル・リバー」に行く
② よく行くレストランで食事をする
③ 「ラウンド・グリル」に予約を入れる
④ 明日は自宅で過ごす

正解 ⇒ ④

　対話を追っていくと，「ミゲル・リバー」は翌日に予約をとるのが難しいこと，「ラウンド・グリル」は閉店したことがわかる。そこで，男性が「よく行くレストラン」を提案するものの，女性は「それだと記念日っていう感じがしない」と言っており，乗り気ではない。最終的に，女性が「明日は外出を控えて，その代わりに来週末に『ミゲル・リバー』に行こう」と提案し，男性も同意しているので，正解は④である。

【語句・表現】
・reservation「予約」

問16 ☐16☐
【放送内容と選択肢】

M: That's strange. I can't log in, Lucy.
W: Did you mistype the username?
M: Ah ... no. The password is also correct.
W: Maybe you've got the wrong password.
M: I don't think so. My password is a combination of your birthday and mine. Oh, wait. Perhaps it
　　was her birthday ... Oh, yes, it worked.
W: Hmm ... Whose birthday, Alex?

M：おかしいな。ログインできないよ，ルーシー。
W：ユーザー名を間違えて入力したんじゃない？
M：えぇと…いや。パスワードも正しいし。
W：パスワードを間違えて覚えているのかもしれないよ。
M：それはないと思う。僕のパスワードは，君の誕生日と僕の誕生日を組み合わせたものだから。ん，
　　待てよ。ひょっとすると彼女の誕生日かも…あ，ログインできた。
W：ふーん…誰の誕生日なの，アレックス？

男性はなぜ問題を抱えていたのか。

① パスワードを勘違いしていた。
② ユーザー名を間違えて入力した。
③ ルーシーの誕生日を間違えて覚えていた。
④ ログイン画面にたどり着けなかった。

正解 ⇒ ①

　ユーザー名もパスワードも正しく入力したと主張する男性（＝アレックス）に，女性（＝ルーシー）は「パスワードを間違えて覚えているのかもしれない」と言っている。男性は「それはないと思う」と答えるが，直後に何かを思い出した様子で「ひょっとすると彼女の誕生日かも」と言っている。結果として無事にログインできたことから，男性はパスワードを勘違いして覚えていたのだとわかる。よって，①が正解となる。

【語句・表現】
・mistype「～を間違ってタイプする」
・combination「組み合わせ」

〈選択肢〉
・get ～ mixed up「～を勘違いする」
・incorrectly「不正確に，間違って」

問17　　17

【放送内容と選択肢】

M: How are you getting along at your new school?
W: I'm doing fine. All my friends are kind.
M: What do you think about your homeroom teacher?
W: She's a fun person. I don't like all the homework she gives us every day, though.
M: Ha-ha! Are you planning to take part in any club activity?
W: I'm trying to decide whether to join the dance club or the music club.

M：新しい学校ではうまくやっているのかい？
W：順調だよ。友達はみんな親切だし。
M：担任の先生についてはどう思っているの？
W：楽しい先生だよ。毎日宿題を出すところは嫌だけど。
M：はは！　部活は何か入るつもりなの？
W：ダンス部に入るか音楽部に入るか，決めかねているの。

女の子は新しい学校についてどう思っているか。

① 新しい友達をつくるのは難しいと感じている。
② 入りたいと思うクラブがない。
③ 宿題をやることにうんざりしている。
④ 担任の先生が楽しい人であればいいのにと思っている。

正解 ⇒ ③

　担任の先生について聞かれた女の子は，「楽しい先生だよ。毎日宿題を出すところは嫌だけど」と答えている。ここから，女の子は宿題を出されることに不満をもっていることがわかるので，③が正解となる。担任の先生に対する印象については，上述のとおり「楽しい先生」と言っているので，④は不適切である。

【語句・表現】
・homeroom teacher「担任の先生」
・take part in ～「～に参加する」
〈選択肢〉
・be fed up with ～「～にうんざりしている」

第4問

【放送内容と選択肢】

We conducted a survey of elementary school children asking them what they wanted to be in the future. It was conducted separately for boys and girls. The graph shows four occupations: "athlete," "doctor," "police officer," and "teacher." The popular choice among boys was "police officer," chosen by about one-third of them. The percentage of girls who chose "teacher" was almost the same as that of boys who chose "police officer." The percentage of boys who chose "athlete" was exactly double that of girls. As for "doctor," there was little difference by gender.

小学生を対象に，将来就きたい職業を聞く調査を実施しました。この調査は男子と女子に分けて行われました。以下のグラフでは，「スポーツ選手」「医師」「警察官」「教師」の4つの職業を示しています。男子の間で人気が高かったのは「警察官」で，約3分の1の人が選びました。「教師」を選んだ女子の割合は，「警察官」を選んだ男子の割合とほぼ同じでした。「スポーツ選手」を選んだ男子の割合は，女子のちょうど2倍でした。「医師」に関しては，性別による違いがほとんどありませんでした。

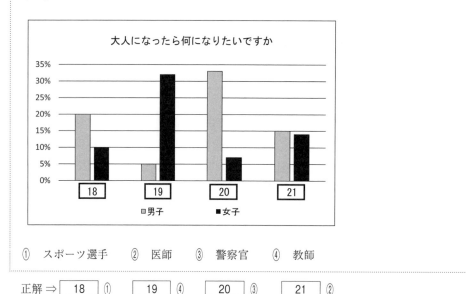

大人になったら何になりたいですか

□男子　■女子

① スポーツ選手　② 医師　③ 警察官　④ 教師

正解 ⇒ | 18 | ① | 19 | ④ | 20 | ③ | 21 | ② |

まず，第4文で「男子の間で人気が高かったのは『警察官』で，約3分の1（＝約33%）の人が選びました」と述べられているので，| 20 |には③が入る。

続く第5文では「『教師』を選んだ女子の割合は，『警察官』を選んだ男子の割合とほぼ同じでした」と述べられており，| 19 |には④が入ることがわかる。

第6文では「『スポーツ選手』を選んだ男子の割合は，女子のちょうど2倍でした」と述べられているので，| 18 |に入るのは①である。

そして，最終文に「『医師』に関しては，性別による違いがほとんどありませんでした」とあるので，| 21 |には②を入れるのが適切である。

【語句・表現】
・conduct「［調査など］を行う」

・survey「調査」
・elementary school「小学校」
・separately「別々に，分けて」
・occupation「職業」
・exactly「正確に，ちょうど」
・gender「（社会的・文化的）性」

問22～25 │ 22 │ │ 23 │ │ 24 │ │ 25 │

【放送内容と選択肢】

Now we will announce the prizes. First, all the participants will receive a commemorative medal. In addition to that, prizes will be awarded according to the scores. Congratulations to those who scored over 200 points! You'll be presented with the latest model smartwatch. The participants whose scores are between 100 and 200 points will receive a digital camera. The prizes will be sent to everyone next month.

それでは賞品を発表いたします。まず，参加者全員に記念のメダルを贈呈します。さらに，得点に応じて賞品が贈られます。200点を超えた方々，おめでとうございます！　最新モデルのスマートウォッチを贈呈します。100点以上200点以下の方々にはデジタルカメラを差し上げます。賞品は来月，みなさんにお送りする予定です。

国際ロボットコンテスト：結果概要

参加者	得　点	賞　品
アン・サッチャー	152.5	22
マイケル・ウォン	124.7	23
トーマス・トランプ	89.9	24
ユア・マルヤマ	205.6	25

① デジタルカメラ　　　　　　　　② メダル
③ スマートウォッチ　　　　　　　④ デジタルカメラ，メダル
⑤ デジタルカメラ，スマートウォッチ　　⑥ メダル，スマートウォッチ

正解 ⇒ │ 22 │ ④　　│ 23 │ ④　　│ 24 │ ②　　│ 25 │ ⑥

　まず，第２文に「参加者全員に記念のメダルを贈呈します」とあることから，①・③・⑤は除外される。
　第４文・第５文で「200点を超えた方々，おめでとうございます！　最新モデルのスマートウォッチを贈呈します」と述べられているので，│ 25 │ に入るのは⑥である。
　また，第６文に「100点以上200点以下の方々にはデジタルカメラを差し上げます」とあることから，│ 22 │ と │ 23 │ には④が入る。
　得点が100点未満の参加者はメダルのみとなるので，│ 24 │ に入るのは②である。

【語句・表現】
・announce「～を知らせる，～を発表する」
・participant「参加者」
・commemorative「記念の」
・award O_1 O_2「O_1 に O_2 を授与する」

· according to ～「～に応じて」
· present A with B「A に B を贈呈する」
· latest「最近の，最新の」：late の最上級の 1 つ。

B
問26　<u>26</u>
【放送内容】

1．I think it's a good idea to give your mother an accessory. The online shop I sometimes use will make an original accessory within one week of ordering. It's a little bit expensive; it costs more than 120 dollars, but I'm sure she will be pleased with it!

2．Don't you think a bouquet will please your mother? The flower shop near the station makes a special bouquet according to your request for 50 dollars. It takes at least one week to have it delivered to your house, so you should visit the shop right away!

3．Mom is always complaining her hands are rough, so hand cream will be a good present for her. A friend of mine, who also suffers from rough hands, recommended some good cream. We can buy the cream for 50 dollars online. If we order it today, it will arrive within a few days!

4．How about giving Mom an assortment of sweets? She has a sweet tooth, so she will definitely enjoy that. I know a good confectionery store. Wait a minute ... This is the store's website. We can order online. I think this 50-dollar gift set is great! It will take around ten days to arrive.

1．お母さんにアクセサリーをあげるのがいいと思うな。私が時々利用するオンラインショップは，注文してから 1 週間以内にオリジナルアクセサリーを作ってくれるの。ちょっと高いけどね，120 ドル以上かかるから。でも，お母さんはきっと喜んでくれるよ！

2．お母さんに花束をあげたら喜ぶと思わない？　駅の近くのお花屋さんは50ドルで，要望に応じて特別な花束を作ってくれるよ。家に配達してもらうまでに少なくとも 1 週間かかるから，すぐにお店に行った方がいいよ！

3．ママはいつも手が荒れていることに不満を言っているから，ハンドクリームはいいプレゼントになると思う。私の友達にも手荒れに悩んでいる子がいて，その子がいいハンドクリームを勧めてくれたんだ。オンラインで50ドルで買えるの。今日注文すれば数日で届くよ！

4．ママにスイーツの詰め合わせを贈るのはどうかな？　ママは甘い物が好きだから絶対に喜ぶよ。私，いいお菓子屋さんを知っているんだ。ちょっと待ってね…これがそのお店のウェブサイトだよ。オンラインで注文できるの。この50ドルのギフトセットがいいんじゃないかな！　届くまでに10日くらいかかるって。

正解 ⇒ ③

　3 つの条件をすべて満たすのは，③の「ハンドクリーム」である。①は，第 3 文で「120ドル以上かかる」と述べられており，条件Aに合わない。②は，第 3 文に「家に配達してもらうまでに少なくとも 1 週間かかる」「すぐにお店に行った方がいい」とあり，条件B・Cを満たすか定かではない。④は，第 8 文に「届くまでに10日くらいかかる」とあり，条件Bに合わない。

品　物	条件 A	条件 B	条件 C
① アクセサリー	×	○	○
② 花束	○	?	?
③ ハンドクリーム	○	○	○
④ スイーツの詰め合わせ	○	×	○

【語句・表現】

〈アクセサリー〉

・a little bit「ちょっと，少し」

・be pleased with ～「～を喜んでいる」

〈花束〉

・bouquet「花束」

・according to ～「～に応じて」

・deliver「～を配達する」

・right away「直ちに，すぐに」

〈ハンドクリーム〉

・rough「（手が）荒れた」

〈スイーツの詰め合わせ〉

・have a sweet tooth「甘い物に目がない」

・definitely「確かに，間違いなく」

・confectionery「菓子類」

第 5 問

【放送内容】

A biome is the vegetation of an area and the group of all living organisms, including animals, that inhabit it. The type and distribution of biomes mainly correspond to average annual temperature and amounts of rainfall.

Since the Japanese Archipelago is almost entirely rainy and humid, forests are formed. For this reason, Japan has a wide variety of forest biomes, apart from some areas such as high mountains like Mt. Fuji or desert areas like the Tottori Sand Dunes. Which type of forests will be formed depends on the temperature. The Japanese Archipelago is unique in two respects: it is long from north to south and its altitude varies remarkably. Therefore, both horizontal and vertical distribution of biomes are found in Japan. Now, we will look at the vertical biome formed by altitude.

Temperatures generally decrease as altitude increases. For every 100 meters of elevation, they decrease by about 0.6 degrees Celsius. On the main island of Japan, you can see the vertical distribution of biomes from low to high elevation.

In the "low zone" at an altitude below 700 meters, evergreen broad-leaved forests are seen. Typical trees found in this type of forest are oak trees. Summer-green forests are formed in the "mountain zone" at elevations from 700 to 1,500 meters. They are dominated by broad-leaved trees that lose their leaves in winter. Maples are representatives of these trees. In the "subalpine zone" at elevations between 1,500 and 2,500 meters, you can see needle-leaved forests. They are made up of evergreen needle-leaved trees. The upper limit of this zone is called the "forest limit," and no tall tree can be seen above there. You can understand it by imagining the area near the top of Mt. Fuji. The area above the forest limit is the "alpine zone," where low trees and alpine meadows can be found.

Now, let's move on to the group presentation. First, Group A will give its report to the class.

バイオームとはある地域の植生のことで，動物を含め，そこに生息するあらゆる生物の集まりを意味します。バイオームの種類と分布は，主に年間平均気温と降水量に対応しています。

日本列島はほぼ全域にわたって雨が多く多湿なため，森林が形成されます。このため日本では，富士山のような高山や鳥取砂丘のような砂漠地帯など一部の地域を除き，多種多様な森林のバイオームが見られます。どのタイプの森林になるかは気温によって決まります。日本列島は2つの点で特徴的です。すなわち，南北に長く，標高に著しい差があるという点です。このため，日本ではバイオームの水平分布と垂直分布が見られます。では，標高によって形成される垂直方向のバイオームについて見ていきましょう。

一般に，標高が高くなるほど気温は低下します。標高が100メートル高くなるごとに，気温は摂氏約0.6度低くなります。日本の本州では低地から高地にかけて，バイオームの垂直分布が見られます。

標高700メートル未満の「低地帯」では，常緑広葉樹林が見られます。このタイプの森林でよく見られる樹木はオークの木です。標高700〜1500メートルの「山地帯」には，夏緑樹林が形成されています。この森林は冬に葉を落とす広葉樹が優占しています。カエデはこのタイプの樹木の代表的なものです。標高1500〜2500メートルの「亜高山帯」では，針葉樹林が見られます。この森林は常緑針葉樹によって形成されています。亜高山帯の上限は「森林限界」と呼ばれ，これより標高の高い場所では高木が見られません。富士山の頂上付近を想像してもらうと理解できるでしょう。森林限界よりも高い場所は「高山帯」で，低木や高山草原が見られます。

ここからはグループ発表に移りましょう。まず，Aグループに調査の内容を発表してもらいます。

【ワークシート】

日本のバイオーム

○バイオームとは何か
  ・ある地域の植生
  ・主に年間の平均 [27] と降水量に依存する

○日本の特徴
  ・雨が多く多湿である
  ・南北に長い
  ・標高に著しい差がある

○バイオームの垂直分布

場所	標高	主な樹木
低地帯	700メートル未満	[28] &常緑
山地帯	700〜1,500メートル	[29] &夏緑
亜高山帯	1,500〜2,500メートル	針葉& [30]
高山帯	2,500メートル超	[31] &高山草原

グループの発表

Due to global warming, the horizontal biome in Japan has been changing. The figure shows the projected movement of areas suitable for apple cultivation. We can see that the areas will have moved considerably northward from their current locations by 2050. If global warming continues at this rate, the areas where apples can be harvested will become very limited.

地球温暖化によって，日本の水平方向のバイオームは変化しています。図は，リンゴの栽培に適し

た地域の移動を予測したものです。2050年には，現在に比べてかなり北上していることがわかります。地球温暖化がこのまま進めば，リンゴを収穫できる地域は非常に限定的になってしまうでしょう。

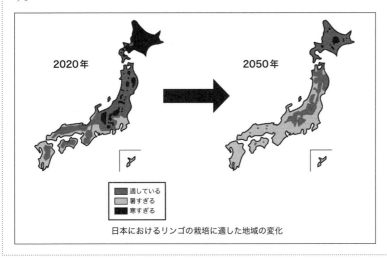

日本におけるリンゴの栽培に適した地域の変化

問27 ☐ 27 ☐

① 二酸化炭素　　② 湿度　　③ 栄養素　　④ 気温

正解 ⇒ ④

　バイオーム一般に関する説明は，第1段落で述べられている。第2文に，「バイオームの種類と分布は，主に年間平均気温と降水量に対応しています」とあるので，正解は④である。

問28〜31 ☐ 28 ☐ 29 ☐ 30 ☐ 31 ☐

① 広葉の　　② 常緑の　　③ 低木
④ 針葉の　　⑤ 夏緑の　　⑥ 若木

正解 ⇒ ☐ 28 ☐ ① ☐ 29 ☐ ① ☐ 30 ☐ ② ☐ 31 ☐ ③

☐ 28 ☐
　「低地帯」については第4段落第1文・第2文に言及がある。第1文で「標高700メートル未満の『低地帯』では，常緑広葉樹林（evergreen broad-leaved forests）が見られます」と述べられているので，①を入れるのが適切である。

☐ 29 ☐
　「山地帯」については第4段落第3文〜第5文で説明されている。第4文に「この森林（＝夏緑樹林）は冬に葉を落とす広葉樹が優占しています」とあるので，①が適切である。

☐ 30 ☐
　「亜高山帯」については第4段落第6文・第7文に言及がある。第7文で「この森林は常緑針葉樹によって形成されています」と述べられているので，②を入れるのが適切である。

☐ 31 ☐
　「高山帯」については第4段落第8文〜第10文で説明されている。第10文に「森林限界よりも高い場所は『高山帯』で，低木や高山草原が見られます」とあるので，③が適切である。

問32　　32

> ① バイオームはある地域の植生のことで，動物の集団は含まれない。
> ② 一般に，標高が100メートル高くなると気温は摂氏6度低くなる。
> ③ 「森林限界」は「亜高山帯」の上限を意味する。
> ④ 日本は南北に長いが，バイオームの水平分布はめったに見られない。

　正解 ⇒ ③

　第4段落第6文および第8文では，「標高1500～2500メートルの『亜高山帯』では，針葉樹林が見られます」「この場所（＝亜高山帯）の上限は『森林限界』と呼ばれ…」と述べられている。③はこの内容と一致するので，これが正解となる。

問33　　33

> ① 2050年までに，西日本ではリンゴの栽培に適した地域がかなり多くなるだろう。
> ② 気候の違いは，バイオームの垂直分布と水平分布の両方に大きな影響を与える。
> ③ 東日本の森林バイオームは，地球温暖化によって多様性を増すかもしれない。
> ④ 地球温暖化によって「森林限界」は低くなり，リンゴの栽培はより困難になるだろう。

　正解 ⇒ ②

　前半の講義の第2段落第4文・第5文では，「日本列島は2つの点で特徴的です。すなわち，南北に長く，標高に著しい差があるという点です。このため，日本ではバイオームの水平分布と垂直分布が見られます」と述べられている。そして，第3段落以降では，日本におけるバイオームの「垂直分布」について説明されている。そこで述べられているのは，標高の差によって気温は変わり，それにともなって形成される森林も異なるという内容である。
　一方，グループの発表では，第1文に「地球温暖化によって，日本の水平方向のバイオームは変化しています」とあることからわかるように，バイオームの「水平分布」に話が移っている。図を見ると，地球温暖化による気温の上昇によって，水平分布が大きく変化する可能性のあることが読み取れる。以上の内容を総合すると，②が適切であると言える。

【語句・表現】
〈第1段落〉
・biome「バイオーム，生物群系」
・vegetation「植物，植生」
・organism「生物」
・inhabit「～に住む，～に生息する」
・distribution「分布」
・correspond to ～「～に対応する」
・annual「1年間の」
・rainfall「降雨，降水量」
〈第2段落〉
・archipelago「列島，諸島」
・entirely「完全に」
・humid「湿気の多い」
・apart from ～「～は別として」
・desert「砂漠」

- sand dune「砂丘」
- altitude「高度，標高」
- remarkably「著しく，非常に」
- horizontal「水平の」
- vertical「垂直の」
〈第3段落〉
- ～ degrees Celsius「摂氏～度」
- elevation「標高，高度」
〈第4段落〉
- oak「オーク」
- dominate「～で優位を占める」
- maple「カエデ」
- representative「代表的なもの」
- subalpine zone「亜高山帯」
- upper limit「上限」
- alpine meadow「高山草原」
〈ワークシート〉
- primarily「主として」
- characteristic「特徴，特色」
〈グループの発表〉
- project「～を見積もる，～を予測する」
- cultivation「栽培」
- considerably「かなり，相当に」
- northward「北へ」
- current「現在の」
- harvest「～を収穫する」
〈選択肢〉
- quite a few ～「かなり多数の～」
- climatic「気候の」
- significant「重大な」
- impact「影響，効果」
- diverse「多様な，さまざまな」
- lower「～を下げる，～を低くする」

第6問

A
【放送内容】

Sophia: Your coffee smells good, Bailey! Where did you get it?

Bailey: Actually, I brewed it at home. I like the rich flavour and aroma. Plus, it's made by a fairtrade brand.

Sophia What's that?

Bailey: Fairtrade products are made by firms that treat the producers fairly.

Sophia: Ah ... Are you saying some firms don't treat producers well?

Bailey: As you know, most coffee beans are produced in developing countries. But importers in developed countries often buy them at unfairly low prices.

Sophia: Is that because they want to sell them at lower prices?

Bailey: Yeah. Consumers prefer low-priced products. But if this situation continues, producers in developing countries won't be able to escape poverty.

Sophia: So, we should pay fair prices to them so that they can improve their livelihoods, right? But wouldn't that lead to an increase in the price of the coffee we buy?

Bailey: Right. Fairtrade products are certainly more expensive. But it's the appropriate price we should pay.

Sophia: Hmm ... I see your point, but I might still choose inexpensive coffee.

ソフィア：ベイリー，あなたのコーヒー，いい香りがするね！　どこで買ったの？

ベイリー：実は自分で家でいれたんだ。この豊かな風味と芳醇な香りが好きでね。それに，フェアトレード・ブランドの製品だし。

ソフィア：何それ？

ベイリー：フェアトレード製品は，生産者を公正に扱う会社によって作られたものなんだ。

ソフィア：えぇと…つまり，生産者を正当に扱わない会社もあるということ？

ベイリー：君も知っていると思うけど，コーヒー豆の大半は発展途上国で生産されているんだ。でも先進国の輸入者は，コーヒー豆を不当に安い価格で購入することがよくあるんだよ。

ソフィア：安い値段で売りたいからそういうことをするのかな？

ベイリー：うん。消費者は安価な製品を好むからね。でも，この状況が続くと，発展途上国の生産者は貧困を免れることができなくなってしまう。

ソフィア：だから，彼らの暮らしが良くなるように，私たちは彼らに適正な価格を支払うべきだというわけね？　だけど，そうすると，私たちが買うコーヒーの値段が高くなるんじゃないかしら？

ベイリー：そうだね。フェアトレード製品は確かに値段が高い。でも，それが僕たちが支払うべき適正な価格なんだよ。

ソフィア：うーん…あなたの言うことはわかるけど，私はやっぱり安いコーヒーを買ってしまうかもしれないよ。

問34　34

ベイリーの発言の要点は何か。

① フェアトレード製品の購入は，生産者の置かれている状況を改善するのに役立つ可能性がある。
② 消費者は，高価な製品を求める傾向を改めるべきである。
③ 発展途上国は，収入の多くの部分をコーヒー豆の生産に依存している。
④ フェアトレード・コーヒーは，味と香りが非常に良いので人気が高まっている。

正解 ⇒①

　ベイリーは３回目・４回目の発言で，「先進国の輸入者は，コーヒー豆を不当に安い価格で購入することがよくある」「この状況が続くと，発展途上国の生産者は貧困を免れることができなくなってしまう」と述べている。その直後にソフィアは，「だから，彼らの暮らしが良くなるように，私たちは彼らに適正な価格を支払うべきだというわけね？」とベイリーの主張内容を確認している。以上の内容を踏まえると，①が正解となる。

問35　35

ソフィアはフェアトレード製品についてどのように考えているか。

① フェアトレード製品は値段が高いにもかかわらず，品質が良くない。
② フェアトレード製品は，発展途上国の生活水準を低下させる可能性がある。

④ 値段が高いため，フェアトレード製品の購入を避ける人もいる。
④ フェアトレード製品の認証手続きは，あまりにも複雑すぎる。

正解 ⇒ ③

　ベイリーが5回目の発言で「フェアトレード製品は確かに値段が高い。でも，それが僕たちが支払うべき適正な価格なんだよ」と述べると，ソフィアは「あなたの言うことはわかるけど，私はやっぱり安いコーヒーを買ってしまうかもしれない」と言っている。ここからソフィアは，価格の高さゆえにフェアトレード製品を敬遠する人がいると考えていることがうかがえる。よって，正解は③となる。

【語句・表現】
・brew「～［コーヒーなど］をいれる」
・flavour「風味，味」：主にイギリス英語で用いられる綴り。アメリカ英語では flavor と綴ることが多い。
・aroma「芳香，香り」
・plus「そのうえ，さらに」
・firm「会社」
・fairly「公正に，公平に」
・bean「豆，豆に似た実」
・consumer「消費者」
・poverty「貧困」
・so that ...「…するために」：「目的」を表す副詞節を導く。
・livelihood「生計，暮らし」
・appropriate「適切な，ふさわしい」
・inexpensive「安価な」
〈選択肢〉
・tendency「傾向」
・seek「～を求める」
・depend on A for B「B を A に依存する」
・income「収入」
・despite「～にもかかわらず」
・living standards「生活水準」
・certification「証明，認定」
・process「過程，手順」
・complex「複雑な」

B
【放送内容】

Mike:　　 What are you eating, Nobuko?

Nobuko:　It's a snack with insect powder, Mike. It's crunchy and delicious. Eating insects is more environmentally friendly than eating beef or pork. Boris, why don't you try some?

Boris:　　I can't imagine eating insects. If beef and pork are not good for the environment, I prefer to eat meat alternatives such as those made from soybeans. What about you, Kate?

Kate:　　 It's absolutely impossible for me to eat insects! And we still don't understand the health risks of eating them.

Mike:　　 Well, humans have a long history of eating insects. Even today, many people around the world eat them. They are rich in nutrients such as protein, fiber and iron. I think it's OK to eat them. Nobuko, give me some of your snack.

Nobuko: Go ahead, Mike. The earth's population is growing, so we can't continue with our current diet. The amount of water needed to raise insects is much less than that needed to raise other livestock.

Kate: If beef and pork are bad for the environment, why don't we just eat vegetables?

Nobuko: You might have a different impression if you actually try them. Boris, try some of this.

Boris: Ah ... OK. Hmm, it's not bad! I'm still a little uncomfortable with the way it looks, but I can eat it. Kate, you should try some too.

Kate: I definitely will not!

マイク：ノブコ，何を食べているの？

ノブコ：昆虫のパウダー入りのスナックだよ，マイク。サクサクしていておいしいの。昆虫食は牛肉や豚肉を食べるより環境に優しいし。ボリス，あなたも食べてみない？

ボリス：昆虫を食べるなんて考えられないよ。牛肉や豚肉が環境に良くないのなら，大豆から作られたものなどの代替肉を食べる方がいいね。ケイト，君はどう？

ケイト：私は昆虫を食べるなんて絶対に無理！　昆虫を食べることによる健康上のリスクはまだわからないし。

マイク：実は，人類には昆虫食の長い歴史があるんだ。今でも昆虫を食べる人々は世界中にたくさんいる。昆虫にはタンパク質や食物繊維，鉄分などの栄養素が豊富に含まれている。僕は食べてもいいと思っているよ。ノブコ，そのスナック，ちょっとちょうだい。

ノブコ：どうぞ，マイク。地球の人口は増え続けているから，私たちが今の食生活を続けることは不可能だよね。昆虫を育てるのに必要な水の量は，他の家畜を飼育するのに必要な水の量と比べて，はるかに少なくて済むのよ。

ケイト：牛肉や豚肉が環境に良くないのなら，野菜を食べればいいんじゃない？

ノブコ：実際に昆虫を食べてみたら印象が変わるかもよ。ボリス，ちょっと食べてみて。

ボリス：あぁ…わかったよ。うーん，悪くないね！　見た目にはまだ少し抵抗があるけど，僕は食べられるよ。ケイト，君も食べてみて。

ケイト：私は絶対に食べたくない！

問36　36

① ノブコ　　　　　② ケイト，ノブコ
③ マイク，ノブコ　④ ボリス，マイク，ノブコ

正解 ⇒ ④

　ノブコは昆虫のパウダー入りスナックを食べながら，「サクサクしていておいしい」「昆虫食は牛肉や豚肉を食べるより環境に優しい」「昆虫を育てるのに必要な水の量は，他の家畜を飼育するのに必要な水の量と比べて，はるかに少なくて済む」と述べており，肯定的な立場であるのは明らかである。

　マイクも「人類には昆虫食の長い歴史がある」「今でも昆虫を食べる人々は世界中にたくさんいる」「昆虫にはタンパク質や食物繊維，鉄分などの栄養素が豊富に含まれている」と述べた後，ノブコからスナックをもらって食べており，肯定的な立場である。

　ボリスは1回目の発言では，「昆虫を食べるなんて考えられない」と否定的な立場をとっているが，ノブコに勧められてスナックを食べた後は，「悪くない」「見た目にはまだ少し抵抗があるけど，僕は食べられる」と肯定的な意見を述べている。

　これに対して，ケイトは「私は昆虫を食べるなんて絶対に無理！」「私は絶対に食べたくない！」と言っており，最後まで昆虫食に抵抗を示している。

　以上より，正解は④となる。

問37　　37

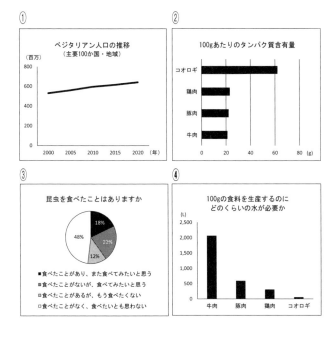

正解 ⇒ ④

　ノブコは２回目の発言で，「昆虫を育てるのに必要な水の量は，他の家畜を飼育するのに必要な水の量と比べて，はるかに少なくて済む」と述べている。④のグラフはこの発言内容に合致するので，これが正解となる。

【語句・表現】
・insect「昆虫」
・crunchy「(食べ物が) サクサクと音がする」
・environmentally friendly「環境に優しい」
・beef「牛肉」
・pork「豚肉」
・meat alternative「代替肉」：植物由来の原料を使い，味と食感を肉に似せて作った食品。
・soybean「大豆」
・absolutely「まったく，絶対に」
・nutrient「栄養素」
・protein「タンパク質」
・fiber「食物繊維」
・iron「鉄，鉄分」
・population「人口」
・current「現在の，今の」
・diet「食事」
・raise「〜 [家畜] を飼育する」
・livestock「家畜」
・impression「印象」
・be uncomfortable with 〜「〜に対して心地よく感じない」
・definitely「絶対に」

問題番号 (配点)	設問		解答番号	正解	配点	自己採点
第1問 (25)	A	1	1	1	4	
		2	2	4	4	
		3	3	3	4	
		4	4	4	4	
	B	5	5	2	3	
		6	6	3	3	
		7	7	1	3	
			自己採点小計			
第2問 (16)		8	8	1	4	
		9	9	2	4	
		10	10	1	4	
		11	11	4	4	
			自己採点小計			
第3問 (18)		12	12	1	3	
		13	13	2	3	
		14	14	3	3	
		15	15	2	3	
		16	16	2	3	
		17	17	2	3	
			自己採点小計			

問題番号 (配点)	設問		解答番号	正解	配点	自己採点
第4問 (12)	A	18	18	1		
		19	19	4	4*	
		20	20	3		
		21	21	2		
		22	22	2	1	
		23	23	5	1	
		24	24	3	1	
		25	25	4	1	
	B	26	26	1	4	
			自己採点小計			
第5問 (15)		27	27	5	3	
		28	28	3	2*	
		29	29	2		
		30	30	5	2*	
		31	31	1		
		32	32	3	4	
		33	33	3	4	
			自己採点小計			
第6問 (14)	A	34	34	2	3	
		35	35	3	3	
	B	36	36	4	4	
		37	37	3	4	
			自己採点小計			

自己採点合計　□

(注)
*は，全部正解の場合のみ点を与える。

第1問

A
問1 | 1 |
【放送内容と選択肢】

Mike is not so tall as me, but I'm shorter than Kevin.

① マイクはケビンや話者より身長が低い。
② マイクはケビンや話者より身長が高い。
③ 話者はマイクやケビンより身長が低い。
④ 話者はマイクやケビンより身長が高い。

正解 ⇒ ①

　放送された英文は,「マイクは私ほど身長が高くないが, 私はケビンより身長が低い」という意味である。前半部分より「マイク<話者」, 後半部分より「話者<ケビン」となるから,「マイク<話者<ケビン」となる。よって, ①が正解である。

問2 | 2 |
【放送内容と選択肢】

Despite my effort, I failed to pass all the exams except math.

① 話者は数学の試験に合格すると思っていなかった。
② 話者は試験に合格するための努力を何もしなかった。
③ 話者は数学以外のすべての試験に合格した。
④ 話者は数学の試験に合格することができた。

正解 ⇒ ④

　放送された英文は,「努力したにもかかわらず, 私は数学以外のすべての試験に合格できなかった」という意味である。fail to *do*「～しそこなう, ～できない」, except「～を除いて, ～以外は」の表現がポイントである。よって, ④が正解となる。

【語句・表現】
・despite「～にもかかわらず」

問3 | 3 |
【放送内容と選択肢】

Jennie, do you mind if I open the window? This room is very hot.

① 話者は窓を閉めるのを忘れた。
② 話者はジェニーに窓を開けてくれるように頼んでいる。
③ 話者は冷たい空気を取り入れたいと思っている。
④ 話者はエアコンをつけるつもりである。

正解 ⇒ ③

　放送された英文は，「ジェニー，窓を開けてもいい？　この部屋はすごく暑いよ」という意味である。Do you mind if I ...? は「（私が）…してもいいですか」と相手に許可を求める表現である。話者は，自分で窓を開けて部屋の中を涼しくしたいと考えているわけであるから，③が正解となる。

【語句・表現】
〈選択肢〉
・let in ～「～を中に入れる」
・turn on ～「～［エアコンなど］をつける」

問4　　4
【放送内容と選択肢】

Today is October 12th, Meg's birthday.　And my birthday is exactly a week away.

① メグは10月19日が誕生日である。
② メグの誕生日は10月5日である。
③ 話者は10月12日が誕生日である。
④ 話者の誕生日は10月19日である。

正解 ⇒ ④

　放送された英文は，「今日は10月12日，メグの誕生日だ。そして，私の誕生日はちょうど1週間後だ」という意味である。ここでの away は「（時間的に）～先で，～後で」の意味を表す。話者の誕生日は「10月19日」であるとわかるから，④が正解となる。

B
問5　　5
【放送内容と選択肢】

This blouse has a loose thread on the shoulder.　Oh, it's missing a button on the right sleeve.

① 　②

③ 　④

正解 ⇒ ②

　放送された英文は,「このブラウスは肩のところの糸がほつれているね。あら,右袖のボタンがなくなっているよ」という意味である。この内容に一致するのは②である。

【語句・表現】
・loose「ほどけた,ゆるんだ」
・thread「糸」
・shoulder「肩」
・miss「〜［あるはずのもの］がない」：通例,進行形で用いられる。
・sleeve「袖」

問6　　6
【放送内容と選択肢】

The flag has five horizontal stripes of black and white alternately, and two stars are drawn on each white one.

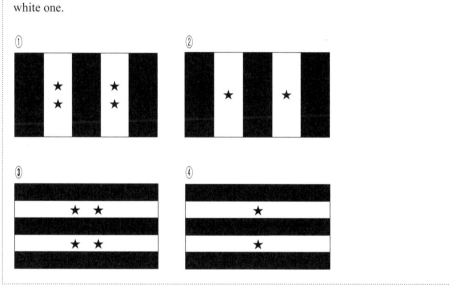

正解 ⇒ ③

　放送された英文は,「その旗は,黒と白が交互に並ぶ5本の横じまで構成されており,白いしまのそれぞれに2つの星が描かれている」という意味である。この内容に一致するのは③である。

【語句・表現】
・horizontal「水平の,横の」
・alternately「交互に」

【放送内容と選択肢】

If he had gone to bed earlier last night, he wouldn't have fallen asleep during the exam.

正解 ⇒ ①

　放送された英文は，「昨晩もっと早く寝ていれば，彼は試験時間中に寝てしまわなかっただろうに」という意味である。仮定法過去完了が用いられている。実際には「昨晩早く寝なかったので，彼は試験時間中に寝てしまった」ということであるから，①が正解である。

【語句・表現】
・fall asleep「眠り込む，寝入る」

第2問

問8　　8
【放送内容と選択肢】

M: Have you decided which drink to buy? I'll take orange juice.
W: Not yet. Which do you think is better, apple juice or grape juice, Dad?
M: How about this juice?
W: I don't like vegetable juice! OK, I've decided. Buy me this, next to the vegetable juice.
Question:
What will the man buy for himself?

M：どの飲み物を買うか決めた？　パパはオレンジジュースにするよ。
W：まだ決めてない。パパはりんごジュースとぶどうジュース，どっちがいいと思う？
M：このジュースはどう？
W：野菜ジュースは好きじゃないよ！　よし，決めた。野菜ジュースの隣のこれを買って。
問い：
男性が自分用に買うものは何か。

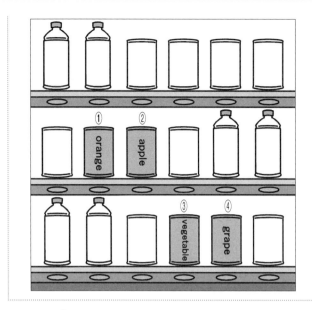

正解 ⇒ ①

　父親は「オレンジジュース」を買うつもりであることが，1回目の発言からわかる。娘は「りんごジュース」と「ぶどうジュース」のどちらにするか迷っていたものの，最終的には「野菜ジュースの隣」の飲み物に決めている。問われているのは「男性（＝父親）が自分用に買うもの」であるから，①のオレンジジュースが正解となる。

【語句・表現】
・next to ～「～の隣に」

問9　　9

【放送内容と選択肢】

W: Are you ready to order, sir?
M: May I ask you something? What ingredients are used in this soup?
W: It includes potatoes and bacon as well as carrots and onions.
M: Then it seems all right. I'm allergic to eggs, and my wife doesn't like tomatoes.
Question:
What ingredients are included in the soup?

W：ご注文はお決まりですか。
M：ちょっとお聞きしてもいいですか。このスープに使われている材料は何ですか。
W：ジャガイモとベーコンです。ニンジンとタマネギも入っています。
M：あぁ，それなら大丈夫そうだ。私は卵アレルギーで，妻はトマトが苦手なので。
問い：
スープに使われている材料は何か。

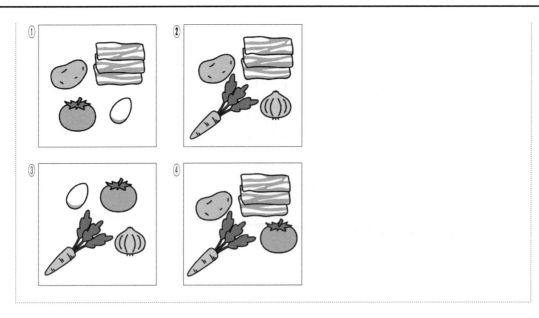

正解 ⇒ ②

　スープに使われている材料を尋ねられた女性店員は,「ジャガイモとベーコンです。ニンジンとタマネギも入っています」と答えている。男性客が最後に「私は卵アレルギーで, 妻はトマトが苦手なので」と言っていることから, 卵とトマトが含まれる選択肢は除外される。以上を踏まえると, 正解は②となる。

【語句・表現】
・order「注文する」
・ingredient「(料理の) 材料」
・A as well as B「Bだけでなく Aも」
・be allergic to ～「～にアレルギーがある」

問10　　10
【放送内容と選択肢】

W: Have you seen the news about the discovery of a new species of fish?
M: Yeah. They have a cut on their back fin, don't they?
W: No, they have one on their tail fin. I want to see them with my own eyes!
M: They seem to live in the deep sea, so it would be difficult for us to see them.
Question:
Which fish are they talking about?

W：新種の魚が発見されたっていうニュース, 見た？
M：見たよ。背びれに切れ目がある魚だっけ？
W：ううん, 尾びれに切れ目があるの。私も自分の目で見てみたいな！
M：深海に住んでいる魚みたいだから, 僕たちが見るのは難しいだろうね。
問い：
彼らはどの魚について話しているか。

正解 ⇒ ①

　新種の魚が発見されたというニュースについて，女性と男性が話している。「背びれに切れ目がある魚だっけ？」と尋ねる男性に対し，女性は「ううん，尾びれに切れ目があるの」と答えているので，正解は①か②に絞られる。男性が最後の発言で「深海に住んでいる魚みたいだから…」と述べていることから，①が正解となる。

【語句・表現】
・discovery「発見」
・species「（生物の）種」
・back fin「背びれ」
・tail fin「尾びれ」

問11 ［ 11 ］
【放送内容と選択肢】

M: Here we are at Central Hill Station. How can we get to City Museum?
W: First, we take the Red Line three stops south to City Park Station.
M: OK.
W: Then we take the Green Line two stops west. City Museum is right in front of the station.
Question:
At which station will they change trains?

M：さあ，セントラル・ヒル駅に着いたよ。市立博物館にはどうやって行けばいいの？
W：最初にレッド・ラインに乗って，南に３駅行くとシティ・パーク駅に着く。
M：うん。
W：その後グリーン・ラインに乗って，西に２駅行く。市立博物館は駅の目の前にあるよ。
問い：
彼らはどの駅で電車を乗り換えるか。

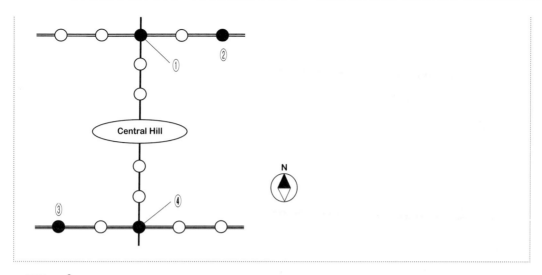

正解 ⇒ ④

「目的地の最寄り駅」ではなく「電車を乗り換える駅」が問われていることに注意する。女性は「最初にレッド・ラインに乗って，南に3駅行くとシティ・パーク駅に着く」「その後グリーン・ラインに乗って…」と説明しているので，乗り換えをする駅は，「セントラル・ヒル駅から南に3駅行った駅」であるとわかる。したがって，正解は④である。

【語句・表現】
・right in front of ～「～のすぐ前に，～の目の前に」：right は「まさに」の意味を表す副詞。

第3問

問12 ⟨12⟩
【放送内容と選択肢】

M: You visited your hometown during the vacation, didn't you?
W: Yes, I was happy to see my family. My father was away on an overseas business trip, though. Look at these pictures of my family.
M: Wow, there are so many! Did you take these?
W: No, most of them were taken by my mother. She likes to take pictures.
M: Who are the people on your left?
W: My older sister and my younger brother. We are a family of five.

M：休暇中に帰省したんだよね？
W：うん，家族に会えてうれしかったな。父は海外出張で不在だったけどね。これ，うちの家族の写真だよ。
M：わぁ，ずいぶんたくさんあるね！　君が撮ったの？
W：ううん，ほとんどは母が撮ったの。母は写真を撮るのが好きだから。
M：君の左側にいる人たちは誰？
W：私の姉と弟だよ。うちは5人家族なの。

会話によると正しいものはどれか。

① 女性には妹がいない。
② 女性には兄がいる。
③ 女性の父親は写真を撮るのが好きである。
④ 女性の母親は出張で不在である。

正解 ⇒ ①

　女性は1回目の発言で「父は海外出張で不在だった」と言っているが，母親が出張中であるとは言っていないから，④は不可。また，2回目の発言で「母は写真を撮るのが好き」と述べているから，③も不適切。最後に「私の姉と弟だよ。うちは5人家族なの」と説明しているので，女性の家族は父親・母親・姉・女性・弟という構成であるとわかり，②は不可，①が正解となる。

【語句・表現】
・hometown「故郷」
・overseas「海外の」
・business trip「出張」

問13　13
【放送内容と選択肢】

W: What shall we eat for dinner, Dad?
M: We have some steaks in the fridge. Let's grill them.
W: Sounds good. Please make a salad too. What about dessert? I want a freshly baked apple pie.
M: I can't bake an apple pie! Can't we just eat apples for dessert instead? I'll go to the supermarket to get some.
W: Dad, I'll go and buy them. You grill the meat, OK?

W：パパ，夕食は何を食べようか？
M：冷蔵庫にステーキ用のお肉があるから，それを焼こう。
W：いいね。サラダも作ってね。デザートはどうする？　焼きたてのアップルパイが食べたいな。
M：僕はアップルパイは焼けないよ！　かわりに，デザートにリンゴを食べるのはだめかな？　スーパーでいくつか買ってくるよ。
W：パパ，私が買いに行く。パパはお肉を焼いてくれる？

女の子は何をするつもりか。

① アップルパイを焼く
② リンゴを買う
③ 肉を焼く
④ サラダを作る

正解 ⇒ ②

　娘は「焼きたてのアップルパイが食べたい」と言うが，父親はアップルパイを作れる自信がない様子である。かわりに「リンゴを食べること」を提案し，スーパーで買ってくると言っている。それに対して，娘は「私が（リンゴを）買いに行く」と言っているので，正解は②となる。

【語句・表現】
・steak「ステーキ」
・fridge「冷蔵庫」
・grill「～をグリルする，～を網焼きにする」：主にイギリス英語で用いられる。
・dessert「デザート」
・freshly-baked「焼きたての」

問14 　14

【放送内容と選択肢】

M: The paella was delicious!
W: Yeah, I'm full.
M: How much is the bill?
W: Well, it's $50. But it's on me this time.
M: No, no. You treated me the other day, so I'll pay today.
W: OK, then let's split it. But let me pay the $5 tip.
M: Thank you.

M：パエリアおいしかったね！
W：うん，お腹いっぱいだよ。
M：お会計はいくら？
W：ええと，50ドルだね。でも今回は私がおごるから。
M：だめだよ。先日ごちそうになったから，今日は僕が支払うよ。
W：わかった，じゃあ割り勘にしよう。でも5ドルのチップは私に支払わせて。
M：ありがとう。

彼らは何をするつもりか。

① 男性が50ドル支払い，女性が5ドル支払う。
② 男性が30ドル支払い，女性が25ドル支払う。
③ **男性が25ドル支払い，女性が30ドル支払う。**
④ 男性が5ドル支払い，女性が50ドル支払う。

正解 ⇒ ③

　女性の2回目の発言より，食事代は「50ドル」であるとわかる。2人はお互いに自分が支払うと主張するが，最終的には女性が「割り勘にしよう。でも5ドルのチップは私に支払わせて」と言い，男性が「ありがとう」とお礼を述べている。以上より，男性は「50ドル÷2＝25ドル」，女性は「50ドル÷2＋5ドル＝30ドル」を支払うことになるので，③が正解である。

【語句・表現】
・paella「パエリア」
・full「満腹の」
・bill「（レストランなどでの）勘定」：主にイギリス英語で用いられる。
・on ～「～のおごりで」
・treat「～におごる」
・split「～を折半する」

問15　15

【放送内容と選択肢】

> M: I'm sorry, Cindy!
> W: Hi, David. I've been waiting for half an hour ...
> M: I couldn't get on the train I wanted to take. The Green Line was so crowded.
> W: I wonder why there were so many people.
> M: Maybe it's because a large live concert will be held at the Central Stadium.
> W: Ah, yeah. It is located along the Green Line.
>
> M：シンディー，ごめん！
> W：やぁ，デイビッド。30分も待ったよ…。
> M：乗りたかった電車に乗れなかったんだ。グリーンラインはすごく混んでいて。
> W：どうしてそんなにたくさんの人がいたのかなぁ。
> M：セントラル・スタジアムで大きなライブが行われるからじゃないかな。
> W：あぁ，そうね。あのスタジアムはグリーンラインの沿線にあるものね。

> 男性と女性について正しいものはどれか。
>
> ①　男性は電車ではなくバスに乗った。
> ②　女性は30分間待たなければならなかった。
> ③　彼らはスタジアムの前で会う約束をした。
> ④　彼らは一緒にライブに行くつもりである。

正解 ⇒ ②

　待ち合わせに遅れてやって来た男性（＝デイビッド）に，女性（＝シンディー）は1回目の発言で「30分も待ったよ」と言っている。ここから，正解は②であるとわかる。男性は「乗りたかった電車に乗れなかった」と説明しているが，「バスに乗った」とは言っていないので，①は不可。③・④のような内容は述べられていない。

【語句・表現】
・hold「～を開く，～を催す」
・be located「ある，位置する」
〈選択肢〉
・instead of ～「～のかわりに，～ではなくて」

問16　16

【放送内容と選択肢】

> W: I have a dentist appointment at four o'clock. Can you drive me there?
> M: I have an online meeting that starts at four.
> W: Then can't you take me right now?
> M: I can, but it's only half past two. Isn't it too early? You'll be there in fifteen minutes.
> W: No problem. I can kill time in a café near the dental clinic.
> M: OK.
>
> W：4時に歯医者の予約があるの。車で送ってくれる？

M：4時からオンライン会議があるんだ。
W：じゃあ，今連れて行ってくれない？
M：いいけど，まだ2時半だよ。早すぎない？　15分で着いちゃうよ。
W：大丈夫。歯医者の近くにあるカフェで時間をつぶすから。
M：わかった。

男性は会話の直後に何をするつもりか。

① 自宅でオンライン会議に参加する
② 女性を車で歯医者まで送っていく
③ 歯医者の予約をする
④ 女性と一緒にカフェで時間をつぶす

正解 ⇒ ②

　妻に「車で（歯医者まで）送ってくれる？」と尋ねられた夫は，「4時からオンライン会議がある」と言って渋っている。すると，妻は「今連れて行ってくれない？」と頼んでいる。夫は到着が早すぎるのではないかと心配するが，妻が「大丈夫」と言うので「わかった」と了承している。よって，②が正解となる。「会話の直後」の行動を問われているので，①は不可である。

【語句・表現】
・dentist「歯医者」
・appointment「（病院などの）予約」
・kill time「時間をつぶす」
・dental clinic「歯科医院」

問17　　17
【放送内容と選択肢】

M: I'm going to the cafeteria to buy some sandwiches. Won't you go with me?
W: I'm on a diet, so I'm skipping lunch these days.
M: That's bad for your health. I have a banana. You can have it.
W: I appreciate your thought, but I want to stick to my diet for a while longer.

M：カフェテリアにサンドイッチを買いに行くんだけど，一緒に行かない？
W：私，ダイエット中で，最近お昼を抜いているの。
M：それは健康に良くないって。バナナがあるから君にあげるよ。
W：気持ちはありがたいけど，もうしばらくの間ダイエットを頑張りたいから。

女の子は何をするつもりか。

① サンドイッチを買う
② 昼食に何も食べない
③ 男の子からバナナをもらう
④ カフェテリアへ行く

正解 ⇒ ②

昼食を買いに行かないかと誘われた女の子は,「ダイエット中で, 最近お昼を抜いている」と答えている。男の子は「それは健康に良くない」「バナナがあるから君にあげる」と言って昼食をとるように勧めるが, 女の子は「もうしばらくの間ダイエットを頑張りたい」と答えており, 何も食べないつもりであることがうかがえる。よって, ②が正解となる。

【語句・表現】
・skip「～を飛ばす, ～を省く」
・appreciate「～に感謝する」
・stick to ～「～［約束など］を守る, ～を実行する」

第4問

A
問18～21 | 18 | 19 | 20 | 21 |
【放送内容と選択肢】

Every year we ask our students why they decided to live in their current apartment. Shown in the graph are the results for 2002 and 2022. We extracted four major factors: "rent," "floor plan," "distance to railroad station," and "distance to supermarket." Factors that increased are "rent" and "distance to supermarket." The former was the most chosen answer in 2022. The latter was the least selected in 2002, but became the second most chosen answer in twenty years. On the other hand, "distance to railroad station" declined significantly to less than half of its 2002 level. "Floor plan" also decreased, but only slightly.

　私たちは本学の学生を対象に, 現在のアパートに住むことに決めた理由を調査しています。グラフに示したのは2002年と2022年の調査結果です。4つの主な要因, すなわち「家賃」「間取り」「駅までの距離」「スーパーマーケットまでの距離」を抽出しました。増加した要因は「家賃」と「スーパーマーケットまでの距離」です。前者は2022年に最も多く選ばれた回答でした。後者は2002年には選んだ人が最も少なかったのですが, 20年後には2番目に多い回答になりました。一方で,「駅までの距離」は大幅に減少し, 2002年の半分に満たない割合でした。「間取り」も減少しましたが微減でした。

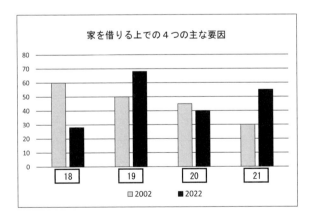

① 駅までの距離　　　② スーパーマーケットまでの距離
③ 間取り　　　　　　④ 家賃

正解 ⇒ | 18 | ① | 19 | ④ | 20 | ③ | 21 | ② |

第4文・第5文に,「増加した要因は『家賃』と『スーパーマーケットまでの距離』です。前者(=家賃)は2022年に最も多く選ばれた回答でした」とあるので,空欄19には④が入る。続く第6文では,「後者(=スーパーマーケットまでの距離)は2002年には選んだ人が最も少なかったのですが,20年後には2番目に多い回答になりました」と述べられているので,空欄21に入るのは②である。

さらに,第7文に「『駅までの距離』は大幅に減少し,2002年の半分に満たない割合でした」とあることから,空欄18に入るのは①である。そして,最終文で「『間取り』も減少しましたが微減でした」と述べられているので,空欄20は③を入れるのが適切である。

【語句・表現】
・current「現在の,今の」
・extract「〜を抽出する,〜を抜粋する」
・factor「要因,要素」
・the former「(2つのうちの)前者」
・the latter「(2つのうちの)後者」
・on the other hand「一方で」
・decline「減少する,低下する」
・significantly「著しく,大きく」
・slightly「わずかに」

問22〜25 | 22 | 23 | 24 | 25 |
【放送内容と選択肢】

Now we will announce the results of the finalists' performance. First, those whose expression score is 90 points or higher will receive a certificate. Next, medals will be awarded to those who got 95 or higher technical score. Lastly, the finalist who got the highest final rank will be presented with a trophy. Those who don't fall into any of the above will receive a ticket to the piano recital that will be hosted by us.

それでは,最終選考通過者の演奏の結果を発表いたします。まず,表現点が90点以上の方には賞状が授与されます。次に,技術点が95点以上の方にはメダルが贈られます。最後に,優勝した方にはトロフィーが贈呈されます。以上のいずれにも該当しない方々には,私どもが主催いたしますピアノリサイタルのチケットをお贈りします。

ハマヤ国際ピアノコンクール:最終選考通過者の結果

最終選考通過者	表現点	技術点	最終順位	賞
カルステン・ヴァルター	87	97	第3位	22
マイケル・リーバス	95	93	第1位	23
ノブコ・デイビス	89	94	第4位	24
ユイ・ナルサワ	91	96	第2位	25

① 賞状　　　　　　　　　　② メダル
③ リサイタルのチケット　　④ 賞状,メダル
⑤ 賞状,トロフィー　　　　⑥ リサイタルのチケット,トロフィー

正解 ⇒ | 22 | ② | 23 | ⑤ | 24 | ③ | 25 | ④ |

第2文に「表現点が90点以上の方には賞状が授与されます」とあり，マイケル・リーバスとユイ・ナルサワがこれに該当する。第3文では「技術点が95点以上の方にはメダルが贈られます」と述べられており，カルステン・ヴァルターとユイ・ナルサワがこれに当てはまる。続いて，第4文で「優勝した方にはトロフィーが贈呈されます」と述べられており，「最終順位」が第1位のマイケル・リーバスがこれに該当する。

以上より，カルステン・ヴァルターは「メダル」，マイケル・リーバスは「賞状，トロフィー」，ユイ・ナルサワは「賞状，メダル」を受け取ることになる。

そして，最終文で「以上のいずれにも該当しない方々には…ピアノリサイタルのチケットをお贈りします」と述べられているので，ノブコ・デイビスが受け取る賞品は「リサイタルのチケット」であるとわかる。

【語句・表現】
・announce「～を知らせる，～を発表する」
・finalist「最終選考通過者」
・expression「表現」
・certificate「証明書」
・award O1 O2「O1 に O2 を授与する」
・technical「技術上の」
・present A with B「A に B を贈呈する」
・fall into ～「～に該当する，～に分類される」
・recital「リサイタル，独奏会」
・host「～を主催する」
〈表〉
・competition「コンクール，コンテスト」

B
問26 26
【放送内容】

1．You should visit the town *Coneberry*. It's a long way from big cities, but that's the very reason why it has many wild plants and animals. If you're interested in history, visit the site of Coneberry Castle. Last year, a new train station was built in this town, which has made it accessible.

2．I'm sure you'll like the city *Endoll*. The city boasts a famous theme park, which is popular among young people. Furthermore, there is a large shopping mall, so you can enjoy shopping too. The public transport system is well-developed and makes it easy to look round the city.

3．The town *Goodland* is an ideal place to spend your vacation. The town has many remains of an ancient civilization. It is also famous for its beautiful river. Fishing or boating in the river is a lot of fun. The number of trains per day is limited, so we recommend you go to the town by car.

4．How about the city *Rosehill*? The award-winning movie, "Metal Quest," was filmed in the city. Every weekend, many fans of the movie enjoy visiting the places where it was set. If you have a car, you can also go to a memorial park in the suburbs which is blessed with nature.

1．「コーンベリー」の町を訪れるといいでしょう。大都市から離れていますが，だからこそ多くの野生動物が見られます。歴史に興味があるなら，コーンベリー城の跡地を訪れてください。昨年，この町に新しい鉄道の駅が開業したので，アクセスしやすくなりました。

2. 「エンドール」の街を気に入ると思います。この街には,若者の間で人気の高い有名なテーマパークがあります。また,大型のショッピングモールがありますので,買い物を楽しむこともできます。公共交通機関が非常に発達しているので,市内を見て回るのが楽です。

3. 「グッドランド」の町は休暇を過ごすのに理想的な場所です。この町には古代文明の遺跡がたくさんあります。美しい川があることでも有名です。川で魚釣りをしたり,ボートに乗ったりするのはとても楽しいです。1日あたりの電車の本数が限られているため,車で行くことをお勧めします。

4. 「ローズヒル」の街はいかがですか。受賞映画「メタル・クエスト」はこの街で撮影されました。毎週末,この映画のファンが大勢,映画の舞台となった場所を巡るのを楽しんでいます。車があれば,郊外にある自然豊かな記念公園へ行くこともできます。

正解 ⇒ ①

　3つの条件をすべて満たすのは,①の「コーンベリー」である。②は,条件B・Cを満たすか判然としない。③は,第5文で「1日あたりの電車の本数が限られているため,車で行くことをお勧めします」と述べられていることから,条件Aを満たさない。④は,条件A・Bを満たすかどうかが不明である。

目的地	条件A	条件B	条件C
① コーンベリー	○	○	○
② エンドール	○	?	?
③ グッドランド	×	○	○
④ ローズヒル	?	?	○

【語句・表現】
〈コーンベリー〉
・a long way from ～「～から遠い」
・site「場所,跡地」
・accessible「(場所などが) 行ける,到達できる」
〈エンドール〉
・boast「(場所などが) ～を持っている,～を誇っている」
・furthermore「さらに,その上」
・transport「交通機関,交通手段」:主にイギリス英語で用いられる。
・look round ～「～ [場所など] を見て回る」:主にイギリス英語で用いられる。
〈グッドランド〉
・ideal「理想的な,申し分ない」
・remain「(通例複数形で) 遺跡」
・ancient「古代の」
・civilization「文明」
〈ローズヒル〉
・award-winning「受賞した」
・film「～ [映画など] を撮影する」
・be set「(映画・小説などの舞台が) 設定される」
・memorial「記念の」
・suburb「郊外」
・be blessed with ～「～に恵まれている」

第5問

【放送内容】

More people live alone now than at any other time in history. In prosperous American cities like Atlanta, Seattle, and San Francisco, 40 percent or more of all households contain a single occupant. In Manhattan and in Washington, nearly half of all households are occupied by a single person. By international standards, these numbers are in fact surprisingly low. In Paris, more than half of all households contain single people, and in Stockholm, the rate tops 60 percent.

The decision to live alone is more of an economic decision than a cultural one. Although Americans pride themselves on their self-reliance and culture of individualism, Germany, France, Britain and Sweden have a greater proportion of one-person households than America, as does Japan. Three of the nations with the fastest-growing populations of single people — China, India and Brazil — are also among those with the fastest growing economies.

In the past, the thought of living alone sparked anxiety, dread and visions of loneliness. But those images are old-fashioned. Now living alone is seen as promoting freedom, personal control and self-realization, which are all prized aspects of contemporary life. Living alone is less frightening than ever simply because it no longer means an isolated or less-social life. After interviewing more than 300 people who live alone, I've concluded that living alone seems to encourage more, not less, social interaction.

Humans have been defined as group-oriented animals, and this basic characteristic hasn't changed because of globalization. On the contrary, global societies have become more interdependent. Dynamic markets, flourishing cities and open communications systems make modern autonomy more appealing. They give us the capacity to live alone but to engage with others when we want to and on our own terms.

Now, let's move on to the group presentation. First, Group A will give its report to the class.

　現在，歴史上最も多くの人々が一人暮らしをしています。アトランタ，シアトル，サンフランシスコといったアメリカの豊かな都市では，全世帯の40％以上が単身世帯です。マンハッタンやワシントンでは，全世帯の半数近くが単身世帯です。国際的に見ると，これらの数値は実のところ驚くほど低いものです。パリでは全世帯の半数以上が単身世帯であり，ストックホルムでは単身世帯の割合が60％を超えます。

　一人暮らしをするのは，文化的な判断というよりはむしろ経済的な判断です。アメリカ人は自立と個人主義の文化を誇りにしていますが，ドイツ，フランス，イギリス，スウェーデンはアメリカより単身世帯の割合が高く，日本も同様です。また，単身者の人口が最も急速に増えている中国，インド，ブラジルの3か国は，経済が最も急速に発展している国々です。

　かつては一人暮らしというと，不安や恐怖，孤独というイメージがありました。しかし，そのようなイメージは古いものです。一人暮らしは自由や自己管理，自己実現など，現代の生活で重要視されるあらゆる要素を促進すると考えられています。一人暮らしはもはや孤立した生活，人付き合いの少ない生活を意味しないので，以前より怖いものではなくなりました。私は300人以上の一人暮らしをしている人たちにインタビューした結果，一人暮らしをすると社会的な交流が少なくなるどころか，むしろ増えるようであるという結論に達しました。

　人間は集団志向の動物であると定義されてきましたが，この基本的な特性はグローバル化によって変わっていません。それどころか，グローバル社会は相互依存を強めています。ダイナミックな市場，繁栄する都市，オープンな通信システムによって，現代の自立性はより魅力的なものになっています。私たちは一人でも生きていけますが，自分の好きな時に，好きなように，他人と関わることができるのです。

　ここからはグループ発表に移りましょう。まず，Aグループに調査の内容を発表してもらいます。

【ワークシート】

単身世帯の動向

◇世界的な動向
- ・一人暮らしをする人たちが増えている。
- ・ 27 は他の西洋諸国より単身世帯率が低い。
- ・単身世帯率は中国，インド，ブラジルでも増加している。

◇このような動向の背景
- ・ 28 が 29 より大きな役割を演じている。
- ・一人暮らしはもはや 30 と結びついていない。
- ・私たちはかつてないほど自由に 31 をすることができる。

グループの発表

Our group examined fertility rates and single-person household rates for the United States, Europe, and Asia. Look at the following graph. A high percentage of single-person households does not necessarily mean a low birthrate. One factor may be the recognition of diverse ways of life, such as marriage without living together, as in Sweden, for example.

　私たちのグループは，アメリカ，ヨーロッパ，アジア諸国の出生率と単身世帯率を調べました。次のグラフをご覧ください。単身世帯の割合が高くても，必ずしも出生率が低くなるとは限りません。例えばスウェーデンのように，結婚していても同居はしないなど，多様な生活様式が認められていることも要因の1つかもしれません。

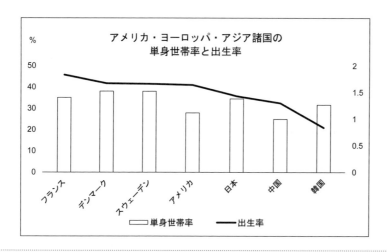

[出典] One's a Crowd by Eric Klinenberg © The New York Times Company
※問題作成の都合上，一部原文を改変しています。

問27 ☐ 27

---
① フランス　　② ドイツ　　③ スウェーデン　　④ イギリス　　⑤ アメリカ

正解 ⇒ ⑤

　第2段落第2文では,「ドイツ, フランス, イギリス, スウェーデンはアメリカより単身世帯の割合が高く…」と述べられている。つまり, アメリカは他の西洋諸国より単身世帯率が低いということであるから, 正解は⑤である。

問28〜31 ☐ 28 ☐ 29 ☐ 30 ☐ 31

---
① 意思疎通　　② 文化　　③ 経済
④ 個人主義　　⑤ 孤立　　⑥ 自立

正解 ⇒ ☐ 28 ③　☐ 29 ②　☐ 30 ⑤　☐ 31 ①

☐ 28 ☐ 29

　第2段落第1文では,「一人暮らしをするのは, 文化的な判断というよりはむしろ経済的な判断です」と述べられている。つまり, 一人暮らしをするかどうかの判断においては「経済が文化より大きな役割を演じている」ということであるから, ☐ 28 には③, ☐ 29 には②を入れるのが適切である。

☐ 30

　第3段落第1文・第2文では,「かつては一人暮らしというと, 不安や恐怖, 孤独というイメージがありました。しかし, そのようなイメージは古いものです」と述べられている。また, 第4文にも「一人暮らしはもはや孤立した生活, 人付き合いの少ない生活を意味しない」とある。したがって, ⑤が正解となる。

☐ 31

　第4段落最終文では,「私たちは…自分の好きな時に, 好きなように, 他人と関わることができるのです」と述べられている。つまり,「かつてないほど自由に意思疎通をすることができる」ということであるから, ①が正解となる。

問32 ☐ 32

---
① 単身世帯数が増加するにつれて, 集団志向の動物であるという人間の性質が変化している。
② 一人暮らしは以前と比べると孤独なものではなくなったが, 他人との社会的な交流は依然として少ない。
③ グローバル化とテクノロジーのおかげで, 私たちは一人暮らしをしながら社会的な交流を増やすことができる。
④ 単身世帯数の増加は主に西洋諸国で見られる現象である。

正解 ⇒ ③

　第3段落最終文では,「私は…一人暮らしをすると社会的な交流が少なくなるどころか, むしろ増えるようであるという結論に達しました」と述べられている。また, 第4段落第2文・第3文には,「グローバル社会は相互依存を強めています。ダイナミックな市場, 繁栄する都市, オープンな通信システムによって, 現代の自立性はより魅力的なものになっています」とあり, 一人暮らしの人々の社会的な交流を可能にしているのは, グローバル化とテクノロジーであることがうかがえる。よって, ③が正解となる。

問33　　33

> ①　単身世帯の割合が低い国は，一般に出生率低下の問題に直面していない。
> ②　一般に，単身世帯の割合が増加すればするほど，出生率は低下する。
> ③　**単身世帯の割合と出生率の間に，相関関係はないようである。**
> ④　単身世帯の割合の増加は，出生率低下の結果であると考えられている。

　正解 ⇒ ③

　「グループの発表」の第3文では，「単身世帯の割合が高くても，必ずしも出生率が低くなるとは限りません」と述べられている。また，グラフを見ると，単身世帯率と出生率には相関関係があるとは言えないことがわかる。よって，正解は③となる。

【語句・表現】
〈第1段落〉
・prosperous「繁栄している」
・household「世帯，所帯」
・occupant「居住者」
・occupy「～を占める」
・top「～を上回る，～を超える」
〈第2段落〉
・more of A than B「B というよりはむしろ A」
・pride oneself on ～「～を誇りにする」
・self-reliance「自立」
・individualism「個人主義」
・proportion「割合，比率」
〈第3段落〉
・spark「～［感情など］を引き起こす」
・anxiety「心配，不安」
・dread「恐怖，不安」
・loneliness「寂しさ，孤独」
・old-fashioned「時代遅れの」
・self-realization「自己実現」
・prize「～を高く評価する，～を重んじる」
・aspect「側面，局面」
・contemporary「現代の」
・frightening「恐ろしい」
・isolated「孤立した，孤独な」
・social「社交の，人付き合いの」
・interaction「交流」
〈第4段落〉
・define A as B「A を B と定義する」
・-oriented「～志向の，～重視の」
・characteristic「特徴，特質」
・on the contrary「それどころか」
・interdependent「相互依存の」
・dynamic「活発な，活動的な」
・flourish「繁栄する，栄える」

- autonomy「自立性」
- appealing「魅力的な」
- capacity「能力，適性」
- engage with ～「～に関わる」
- on one's own terms「～の好きなように」
〈グループの発表〉
- not necessarily ～「必ずしも～でない」
- birthrate「出生率」
- recognition「承認，認識」
- diverse「多様な」
- marriage「結婚」
〈選択肢〉
- phenomenon「現象」
- observe「～を観察する」
- decline「低下する，減少する」
- fertility「出生率」
- correlation「相関関係，相関性」
- consequence「結果，影響」

第6問

A
【放送内容】

Matthew: You seem kind of down, Akina.
Akina: Hi, Matthew. I have a slight headache.
Matthew: I often get headaches too. Especially since I started wearing a mask every day.
Akina: You too? Actually, I never had headaches like this before I started wearing one.
Matthew: If we are wearing a mask for many hours, there's too much carbon dioxide inside it. That can cause expansion of blood vessels in our brain, resulting in headaches.
Akina: How did you learn that?
Matthew: I read it in a newspaper. Our headaches may be caused by excessive CO_2.
Akina: Besides, these masks make my ears hurt and my neck stiff.
Matthew: When we wear a mask, we tend to breathe through our mouth, not through our nose.
Akina: It makes our mouths dry, and makes it easier for bacteria to grow.
Matthew: Right. I don't think it's a good idea to wear a mask every day.
Akina: But if we don't wear one, we'll be at high risk of infection. Hmm ... it's hard to decide which way to go!

マシュー：アキナ，なんだか元気がないね。
アキナ：あら，マシュー。ちょっと頭痛がしてね。
マシュー：僕もよく頭痛がするよ。毎日マスクを着用するようになってからは特に。
アキナ：あなたも？　実はマスクをするようになる前は，こんな頭痛はなかったのよ。
マシュー：長時間マスクを着用していると，マスクの内側に二酸化炭素が過剰にたまるよね。それによって脳の血管が拡張して，頭痛が起きる可能性があるんだ。
アキナ：どうやって知ったの？
マシュー：新聞で読んだんだ。僕たちの頭痛は二酸化炭素過剰が原因かもしれない。
アキナ：それに，こういうマスクって耳が痛くなるし，首が凝るし。

マシュー：マスクをしていると，鼻呼吸ではなく口呼吸になりがちだし。
アキナ：口呼吸だと口が乾いて，細菌が繁殖しやすくなるね。
マシュー：そうそう。毎日マスクを着用するのは良くないと思うな。
アキナ：でも，マスクをしないと感染症にかかるリスクが高くなるし。うーん…どちらがいいのか決めるのは難しいなぁ！

問34　34

マシューの発言の要点は何か。

① 大気中の二酸化炭素の増加によって細菌が繁殖しやすくなる。
② **継続的にマスクを着用することにはいくつかのデメリットがある。**
③ 私たちは口呼吸をしないように注意しなければならない。
④ マスクの着用は頭痛を予防するのに効果的である。

正解 ⇒ ②

　マシューは，「それ（＝マスクの内側に二酸化炭素が過剰にたまること）によって脳の血管が拡張して，頭痛が起きる可能性がある」「マスクをしていると，鼻呼吸ではなく口呼吸になりがち」などと述べ，マスクを着用することによるデメリットを挙げている。そして，6回目の発言で「毎日マスクを着用するのは良くないと思う」と結論を述べている。よって，②が正解である。

問35　35

アキナが最も同意すると思われる発言はどれか。

① 加齢によって脳内の血管が拡張する危険性が高まる。
② 頭痛は首の凝りや耳の痛みよりも深刻である。
③ **感染予防におけるマスクの有効性は無視できない。**
④ 長い目で見れば毎日マスクを着用することで健康が改善するだろう。

正解 ⇒ ③

　アキナは「マスクをするようになる前は，こんな頭痛はなかった」「耳が痛くなるし，首が凝る」「口呼吸だと口が乾いて，細菌が繁殖しやすくなる」などと述べ，マシューと同様，マスクのデメリットを挙げている。しかし，最後の発言では「マスクをしないと感染症にかかるリスクが高くなる」「（マスクを着用するのとしないのと）どちらがいいのか決めるのは難しい」と言っており，感染予防におけるマスクの重要性を軽視できないと考えていることがうかがえる。よって，正解は③となる。

【語句・表現】
・kind of「やや，ちょっと」：断定を避け，表現を和らげるために用いられる。
・slight「わずかな，少しの」
・headache「頭痛」
・carbon dioxide (CO_2)「二酸化炭素」
・expansion「膨張，拡張」
・blood vessel「血管」
・excessive「過度の」
・neck「首」
・stiff「硬直した，凝った」

- breathe「息をする，呼吸する」
- bacteria「バクテリア，細菌」
- infection「感染」

〈選択肢〉
- prevent「〜を予防する，〜を防止する」
- continuously「絶え間なく，連続して」
- earache「耳の痛み」
- in the long run「長い目で見れば，長期的には」

B
【放送内容】

Miki: We're rebuilding our house, and we're putting solar power panels on the roof.

Steve: Really, Miki? My house in the U.S. doesn't have a solar power system installed yet, but some of our neighbors' houses do.

Irene: You know, Steve, the United States ranks second in solar power installation in the world. And my home country China has the world's largest market.

Steve: Oh, so your house in China has one installed, Irene?

Irene: Of course. No one in my neighborhood is without solar power.

Miki: Japan often suffers from natural disasters. If you can generate electricity at home, it'll be useful in case of a blackout.

Irene: Right. Besides, you can sell surplus power. And it doesn't emit any CO_2.

Viktor: Great. In my country, Sweden, solar power generation is not common at all.

Miki: Unfortunately, some areas are not suitable for it, Viktor.

Viktor: I'm sure our area is not a suitable one. If only there was more sunshine there!

Steve: Moreover, the initial investment may be very expensive. Installing large panels on a roof can cost a lot of money. My family can't afford to do that!

ミキ：うちは今，家を建て替えているんだけど，屋根に太陽光発電のパネルを設置するつもりなんだ。

スティーブ：そうなの，ミキ？ 僕のアメリカの家はまだ太陽光発電システムを導入していないけど，近所の家では導入しているところもあるよ。

アイリーン：あのね，スティーブ，アメリカは太陽光発電の導入量が世界第2位なんだよ。そして，私の母国の中国は世界最大の市場を持っているの。

スティーブ：じゃあ，君の家も太陽光発電システムを導入しているの？

アイリーン：もちろん。うちの近所で太陽光を利用していないところはないよ。

ミキ：日本は自然災害に見舞われることが多いの。自宅で発電することができれば，停電した場合に役立つね。

アイリーン：そうだね。それに，余剰電力を売ることもできるし。二酸化炭素を放出することもないしね。

ビクトル：すばらしいね。僕の母国のスウェーデンでは，太陽光発電は全然一般的ではないんだ。

ミキ：残念だけど，太陽光発電には適していない地域もあるのよ，ビクトル。

ビクトル：僕の地域が適していないのは間違いないよ。スウェーデンがもっと日の当たる国であればなぁ！

スティーブ：それに，初期投資が高額になる可能性があるよ。屋根に大きなパネルを設置するには，多額の費用がかかるんじゃないかな。うちの家族にはそんな余裕ないよ！

問36　　36

① ミキ，アイリーン　　　② ミキ，ビクトル
③ スティーブ，アイリーン　　④ **スティーブ，ビクトル**

正解 ⇒ ④

　ミキは「うちは今，家を建て替えているんだけど，屋根に太陽光発電のパネルを設置するつもり」と述べており，自宅で太陽光発電を導入する予定であることがわかる。また，アイリーンは，「君の家も太陽光発電システムを導入しているの？」と聞かれた際に「もちろん」と答えており，中国の自宅では太陽光発電を導入済みであることがわかる。

　これに対して，ビクトルは「僕の地域が（太陽光発電に）適していないのは間違いないよ。スウェーデンがもっと日の当たる国であればなぁ」と言っており，スウェーデンの自宅で太陽光発電を利用する可能性は低い。また，スティーブも「初期投資が高額になる可能性があるよ。…うちの家族にはそんな余裕ないよ」と述べており，アメリカの自宅で太陽光発電を利用する可能性は低そうである。

　以上より，「出身国の自宅において太陽光発電を導入する可能性が低い人」はビクトルとスティーブの2人なので，正解は④となる。

問37　　37

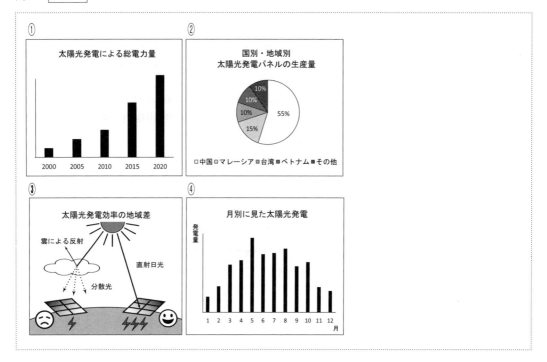

正解 ⇒ ③

　ビクトルは2回目の発言で，「僕の地域が（太陽光発電に）適していないのは間違いないよ。スウェーデンがもっと日の当たる国であればなぁ」と述べている。③の図は，太陽光発電効率が地域によって異なることを示しており，ビクトルの発話内容を裏付けるものとなっている。よって，これが正解である。

【語句・表現】
・rebuild「～を建て直す」
・solar「太陽の，太陽光線を利用した」
・roof「屋根」
・install「～を設置する」
・disaster「災害」
・generate「～を生み出す，～を作り出す」
・electricity「電気，電力」
・blackout「停電」
・surplus「余分な，余剰の」
・emit「～を発する，～を出す」
・suitable「適した，適切な」
・latitude「緯度」
・initial「最初の」
・investment「投資，出資」
・afford to *do*「～できる余裕がある」
・financial「財務の，金銭的な」

リスニング・第4回 解 答 と 解 説

問題番号(配点)	設 問		解答番号	正 解	配 点	自己採点
第1問(25)	A	1	1	2	4	
		2	2	3	4	
		3	3	1	4	
		4	4	2	4	
	B	5	5	2	3	
		6	6	1	3	
		7	7	4	3	
自己採点小計						
第2問(16)		8	8	3	4	
		9	9	1	4	
		10	10	2	4	
		11	11	1	4	
自己採点小計						
第3問(18)		12	12	1	3	
		13	13	2	3	
		14	14	1	3	
		15	15	1	3	
		16	16	4	3	
		17	17	2	3	
自己採点小計						

(注)*は，全部正解の場合のみ点を与える。

問題番号(配点)	設 問		解答番号	正 解	配 点	自己採点
第4問(12)	A	18	18	4	4*	
		19	19	1		
		20	20	3		
		21	21	2		
		22	22	5	1	
		23	23	3	1	
		24	24	2	1	
		25	25	3	1	
	B	26	26	1	4	
自己採点小計						
第5問(15)		27	27	3	3	
		28	28	4	2*	
		29	29	2		
		30	30	1	2*	
		31	31	6		
		32	32	1	4	
		33	33	3	4	
自己採点小計						
第6問(14)	A	34	34	1	3	
		35	35	3	3	
	B	36	36	2	4	
		37	37	4	4	
自己採点小計						

自己採点合計 [　　]

第１問

A

問１　　1

【放送内容と選択肢】

> **I had a lot for dinner, so I can't possibly eat dessert.**
>
> ① 話者はどのデザートを食べるべきか決められない。
> ② **話者はお腹がいっぱいなのでデザートは欲しくならない。**
> ③ 話者は夕食の後にデザートを食べるかもしれない。
> ④ 話者はデザートを後で選ぶだろう。

正解 ⇒ ②

　放送された英文は，「夕食をたくさん食べたので，とてもデザートは食べられない」という意味である。つまり，デザートを食べないので，正解は②。他の選択肢はデザートを食べることを示唆するため不適である。

【語句・表現】
・cannot possibly *do*「とても～できない」
・full「満腹の」

問２　　2

【放送内容と選択肢】

> **Soccer practice is usually on Friday, but it's a day later this week.**
>
> ① 話者は金曜日のサッカーの練習を休むだろう。
> ② 話者は金曜日のサッカーの練習に遅れて行くだろう。
> ③ **話者は土曜日にサッカーの練習があるだろう。**
> ④ 話者は土曜日にサッカーの試合を見るだろう。

正解 ⇒ ③

　放送された英文は，「サッカーの練習は通常金曜日だが，今週は１日後の日になる」という意味。つまり，今週の練習日は，金曜日の次の日である土曜日になるため，正解は③。

【語句・表現】
〈選択肢〉
・be absent from ～「～を欠席する」

問３　　3

【放送内容と選択肢】

I arrived in London last week to adjust to living here before classes started.

① 話者は授業が始まる前にロンドンに来た。
② 話者は先週，留学するためにロンドンを発った。
③ 話者は先週，休暇でロンドンに行った。
④ 話者は今週，ロンドンで授業を始める。

正解 ⇒ ①

　放送された英文は，「私は，（学校の）授業が始まる前にここでの暮らしに慣れるために，先週ロンドンに着いた」という意味である。複数形の classes は学校の「授業（全般）」を指し，その前にロンドンに来たので，正解は①。授業が始まる時期は不明なため，④は不適。

【語句・表現】
・adjust to ～「～に慣れる・適応する」

問4 ☐ 4 ☐
【放送内容と選択肢】

The train was crowded, so Bill and Ted gave their seats to an elderly couple.

① ビルとテッドは混雑した電車に乗れなかった。
② ビルとテッドは電車で他の人を座らせた。
③ ビルは電車で席をテッドに譲った。
④ テッドは電車で座れたが，ビルは座れなかった。

正解 ⇒ ②

　放送された英文は，「電車が混んでいたので，ビルとテッドは座席を老夫婦に譲った」という意味である。これは，「他の人を座らせた」と言い換えられるので，正解は②。

【語句・表現】
・crowded「混んだ」
・give one's seat to ～「～に席を譲る」
・elderly「高齢の」
・let A do「A に～させる」

B

問5 ☐ 5 ☐
【放送内容と選択肢】

I'll take this one.　I like the 2-button design with no pockets.

正解 ⇒ ②

放送された英文は,「これを買います。ボタンが二つでポケットのないデザインが気に入りました」という意味であり,正解は②。リスニングでは,数を表す表現(ここでは two と no)に注意して聞くようにしよう。

【語句・表現】
・2-button design「ボタンが二つのデザイン」: 2-button は形容詞として使われているため,button は複数形にならない。

問6 [6]
【放送内容と選択肢】

Three kids are playing around the tree, another is running, and two others are jumping rope.

①

②

③

④

正解 ⇒ ①

　放送された英文は，「三人の子どもたちが木の周りで遊び，別の一人は走っていて，他の二人は縄跳び
をしている」という意味である。木の周りに三人の子どもたちがいるのは①と②。さらに，走っている子
と二人の縄跳びをしている子どもたちの三人を加えて，全部で六人いる①が正解である。

【語句・表現】
・another「別の（もう）一人」
・jump rope「縄跳びをする」

問7　　7
【放送内容と選択肢】

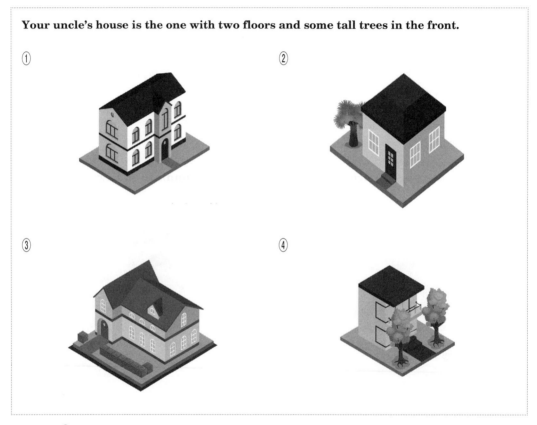

Your uncle's house is the one with two floors and some tall trees in the front.

① ② ③ ④

正解 ⇒ ④

　放送された英文は，「２階建てで家の前に数本背の高い木があるのが，あなたの叔父さんの家です」と
いう意味である。２階建ての家は①③④，家の前に複数の木があるのは④なので，正解は④。①と③の家
の前に高い木はない。

【語句・表現】
・with two floors「２階建てで」
・in the front「正面に」

第2問

問8 [8]
【放送内容と選択肢】

M: Are you going to take paper with you to Yuka's house?
W: No, but I'm taking this.
M: Of course.   That's your favorite one to write with.
W: And we might get thirsty, so I'll take these too.

Question:
What will the daughter take to Yuka's house?

M: 紙はユカの家に持って行くの？
W: いいえ，でも，これは持って行く。
M: もちろんそうだろうね。一番気に入っている筆記用具だね。
W: それと，喉も渇くかもしれないから，これも持って行くわ。

問い：
娘はユカの家に何を持って行くのか。

① ②

③ ④

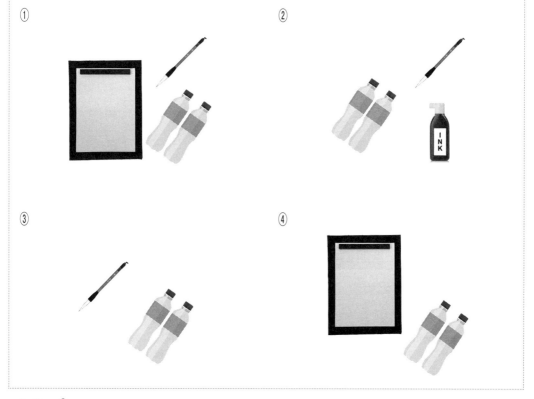

正解 ⇒ ③

　娘の発言の this が指すもの（単数）は，その後の父親の発言 one to write with「書くためのもの（＝筆記用具）」から，筆だとわかる。また，娘の最後の発言にある these は2本のボトルに入った飲み物

（複数）を指す。このことから，娘は，お気に入りの筆と複数の飲み物を持って行くつもりであるとわかるので，正解は③。

【語句・表現】
・write with ～「～で書く」
・get thirsty「喉が渇く」

問9　　9
【放送内容と選択肢】

W: The station is crowded.　I can't find you, Chris.
M: I'm wearing a long winter coat.
W: Okay.　And are you wearing a hat too?
M: No, but I have my sunglasses on.

Question:
Which picture is Chris?

W: 駅が混んでいて，あなたを見つけられないわ，クリス。
M: 丈の長い冬用のコートを着ているよ。
W: わかった。あと，帽子もかぶっている？
M: 帽子はかぶっていないけど，サングラスをかけているよ。

問い：
どの絵がクリスか。

正解 ⇒ ①

　クリスは，long winter coat「丈の長い冬用のコート」を着ていると言い，次に帽子についての質問には No と答え，サングラスをかけていると返答している。したがって，正解は①である。

【語句・表現】
・have A on「Aを身に着けている」

問10 ☐10
【放送内容と選択肢】

M: Can we take Max with us to the art museum?
W: The website says dogs are allowed inside.
M: Great!　I want to take photos of him with some paintings.
W: Unfortunately, it says you can't photograph the art.

Question:
Which picture shows what they are looking at?

M: マックスを美術館に連れて行ける？
W: ウェブサイトには犬も入れるって書いてあるね。
M: やった！　マックスの写真を絵と一緒に撮りたいんだ。
W: 残念だけど，作品の写真を撮ってはいけないと書かれているわ。

問い：
どの絵が，彼らが見ているものを示しているか。

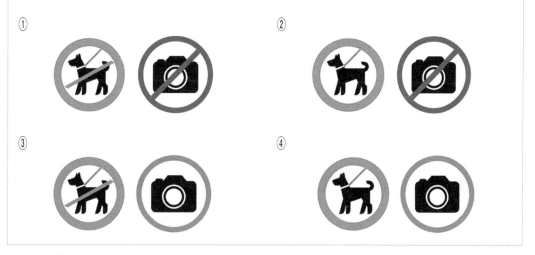

①　②　③　④

正解 ⇒ ②

　母親の最初の発言から，犬を連れて入ることが可能だとわかる。母親は次の発言で「美術品（作品）の写真を撮ることはできないと書いてある」と答えていることから，彼らが見ているのは②の絵である。

【語句・表現】
・say (that) S V「～と書いてある」
・unfortunately「残念ながら」
・photograph「～の写真を撮る」

問11 ☐11
【放送内容と選択肢】

W: Excuse me.　Can you tell me where the shoe section is?
M: Straight ahead on the right, across from the bathrooms.

W: Just at the corner?
M: No, it's at the end, after the dress section.

Question:
Where is the shoe section?

W: すみません，靴売り場はどこか教えてもらえますか。
M: 真っすぐ行って右手，化粧室の向かいにあります。
W: そこの角ですか。
M: いいえ，ドレス売り場の先の，突き当たりです。

問い：
靴売り場はどこか。

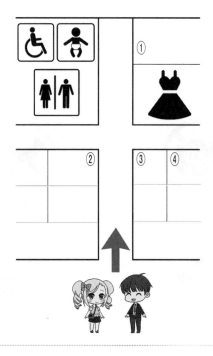

正解 ⇒ ①

　靴売り場がどこか尋ねる女性に，男性（店員）が Straight ahead on the right と言っているので，真っすぐ進んだ右手にあることがわかる。across from the bathroom と言われた女性は，手前の角か，その向こうの突き当たりの右手かを確認し，男性が「突き当たり」で「ドレス売り場の先」と言っていることから，正解は①。

【語句・表現】
・straight ahead「真っすぐ先に（で）」
・on the right「右手に」
・across from ～「～の向かいに」
・bathroom「化粧室，トイレ」
・at the end「突き当たりに」

第3問

問12 ☐ 12
【放送内容と選択肢】

M: When did you want to have lunch together?
W: I'm off this Friday.　How about then?
M: That's no good for me.　I work until five.
W: Well, I'm free again on Sunday.
M: I have plans all day.　Maybe dinner another day is better.
W: Let's do it on Friday after you finish work.

M: いつ昼食を一緒に食べたいって言っていたかな？
W: 今週は金曜日休みなの。その日はどうかな？
M: その日はダメだ。5時まで仕事がある。
W: それじゃあ，私は日曜日も空いているよ。
M: その日は一日中予定があるんだ。別の日の夕食の方がいいかも。
W: 金曜日，あなたの仕事が終わった後にしよう。

二人はいつ一緒に食事をするだろうか。

① 金曜日の夕食
② 日曜日の夕食
③ 金曜日の昼食
④ 日曜日の昼食

正解 ⇒ ①

　男性が，以前話題にしていたと思われる昼食の予定について尋ね，女性が自分の空いている日を伝えている。女性が金曜日（の昼食）を提案したのに対して，男性はダメだと答え，次に提案された日曜日も予定があるため，日曜日以外の夕食の方がいいかもしれない，と発言している。女性がそれに同意して金曜日にしようと答えていることから，正解は①。

【語句・表現】
・off「休みで」
・no good「だめな」：いわゆる「NG」のこと。
・all day「一日中」

問13 ☐ 13
【放送内容と選択肢】

W: Were you able to buy tickets to the concert?
M: Not yet.　It keeps giving me an error.
W: Have you checked that your information is correct?
M: Yes, but it still isn't working.
W: Look!　Your credit card was only good through November.　Today is December 1st!

W: コンサートのチケット，購入できた？

M: まだだよ。エラーが出続けている。

W: 自分の情報が正しいか確認した？

M: うん，でもまだダメだ。

W: 見て！　あなたのクレジットカード，11月末が有効期限だったのよ。今日は12月1日よ！

男性は，どのようなことに困っているのか。

① 自分の情報を入力できない。

② **クレジットカードがもう使用できない。**

③ チケットは12月まで購入できない。

④ チケットは11月で完売してしまった。

正解 ⇒ ②

　男性がコンサートチケットを購入しようとしているが，エラーが出続けて次のステップに進めない状況になっている。女性が最後の発言で Your credit card was only good through November とクレジットカードの有効期限が切れていたと言っているので正解は②。

【語句・表現】

・ticket to 〜「〜の券」

・keep *doing*「〜し続ける」

・give A an error「Aにエラーメッセージを出す」

・work「（機械などが）動く」

・good「有効な」：叙述的用法の形容詞として用いられる。

・through「〜の終わりまで」

〈問い〉

・have trouble with 〜「〜に苦労する」

〈選択肢〉

・be sold out「売り切れている」

問14　14
【放送内容と選択肢】

M: Would you like to go camping this weekend?

W: That sounds great, but what will the weather be like?

M: It's supposed to be cloudy on both Saturday and Sunday.

W: Well, I'll go as long as it doesn't rain.

M: According to the weather report, there's no chance of rain.

M: 今週末キャンプに行かないかい？

W: いいわね，でも天気はどんな感じかな？

M: 土日とも曇りみたいだよ。

W: そうね，雨が降らないなら行くわ。

M: 天気予報によると，雨が降る可能性はないって。

女性はどうすると考えられるか。

① **彼女は両日のキャンプ旅行に行く。**

② 彼女は雨がやんだら友達と合流する。
③ 彼女は旅行の最初の日だけ行く。
④ 彼女は旅行には参加せずに家にいる。

正解 ⇒ ①

　男性から，週末にキャンプに行くかどうかを尋ねられて，女性が天気について質問している。男性の応答から，土日のキャンプ旅行だという情報が得られ，女性が I'll go as long as it doesn't rain. と答えていることから，女性は雨さえ降らなければキャンプに行くつもりであることがわかる。男性の最後の発言から，雨は降りそうにないので，正解は①である。

【語句・表現】
・go camping「キャンプに行く」
・sound「～に聞こえる，～と思われる」
・What be S like?「S はどのようなものか」
・be supposed to be ～「～になるはずだ」
・cloudy「曇った」
・as long as S V「～な限り」：≒ if S V。
・there's no chance of ～「～の見込みはない」
〈問い〉
・be likely to *do*「～しそうである」
〈選択肢〉
・go on a trip「旅行に行く」
・join「～に参加する」
・the first day of ～「～の初日」

問15 　15
【放送内容と選択肢】

W: You don't seem to be in a good mood.
M: I just finished my big math exam.
W: Was it really that bad?
M: No, I think I did fine.　I just stayed up all night studying.
W: That would put anyone in a bad mood.

W: 機嫌が良くなさそうだね。
M: 数学の大事なテストが終わったところでね。
W: そんなにできなかったの？
M: いや，結構できたと思う。ただ徹夜して勉強したんだ。
W: そりゃあ誰でも機嫌が悪くなるね。

男子生徒が抱えている問題は何か。

① **彼はテストの前夜，眠らなかった。**
② 彼は数学のテストはもっと簡単だと思っていた。
③ 彼は勉強し過ぎたことで時間を無駄にしたと感じている。
④ 彼は数学のテストで悪い点数を取ったと思っている。

正解 ⇒ ①

女子生徒の「数学のテストができなかったのか」という質問に対して，男子生徒が応答の中で I just stayed up all night と発言している。これが彼の bad mood の原因なので，正解は①である。

【語句・表現】
・be in a good mood「機嫌が良い」
・math「数学」：＝ mathematics。
・exam「試験」：＝ examination。
・do fine「うまくやる」
・stay up all night「徹夜する」
・put A in B「A を B（の状態）にする」
〈選択肢〉
・expect A to be ～「A が～だと思う」
・waste「～を無駄にする」
・by *doing*「～することによって」
・get a ～ score「～な点数を取る」
・on the test「テストで」

問16　16
【放送内容と選択肢】

> M: What should we get Mom and Dad for their anniversary?
> W: How about a new purse and a new wallet?
> M: Mom has enough purses, though.
> W: Then let's get them something they can enjoy together.
> M: That's a much better idea.
> W: Well, they both love watching movies.
> M: True.　They might like that new comedy.
>
> M: お父さんとお母さんの（結婚）記念日に何を買おうか。
> W: 新しい小銭入れと新しい財布はどうかな？
> M: お母さんはもうたくさん小銭入れを持っているけどなあ。
> W: じゃあ，何か二人で楽しめるものをあげよう。
> M: そっちの方がずっと良い案だね。
> W: そうね，二人とも映画を見るのが好きだよね。
> M: そうだね。あの新作のコメディー，気に入るだろうね。

> 兄妹は両親のプレゼントに何を買うだろうか。
>
> ①　映画の券1枚と新しい財布
> ②　新しい小銭入れと新しい財布
> ③　二人それぞれに新しい財布
> ④　**新作映画の券2枚**

正解 ⇒ ④

両親の結婚記念日に贈るものとして，妹が，それぞれに新しい小銭入れと財布を買うことを提案するが，

母が小銭入れをたくさん持っているため，その案は却下される。妹が something they can enjoy together と別の提案をして，それに兄が同意した後の発言から正解が導き出せる。妹の movies や兄の new comedy などから二人が両親に映画の券を贈ること考えられるので正解は④。

【語句・表現】
・anniversary「記念日」：ここでは両親の記念日なので，「結婚記念日」のこと。
・How about 〜?「〜はどうですか」
・purse「小銭入れ，（がま口付きの）財布」
・though「でも，けれど」：ここでは副詞として使用されている。
・get A B「A に B を買ってあげる」

問17　[17]
【放送内容と選択肢】

W: Thank you for staying with us, sir.　How was your room?
M: The bed was bigger than I expected, and comfortable too.
W: I'm happy to hear that.
M: The bathroom was very clean too, but ...
W: Something wrong, sir?
M: I wish there had been a place for me to do my work.

W: ご宿泊いただき，ありがとうございました。お部屋はいかがでしたか。
M: ベッドは思っていたより大きくて，寝心地も良かったです。
W: それはよかったです。
M: バスルームもとてもきれいでした。でも…
W: 何かお気に召さなかったでしょうか。
M: 仕事をする場所があったらよかったですね。

男性が，ホテルの部屋について気に入らなかったことは何か。

① 喫煙する場所がなかった。
② 仕事をする場所がなかった。
③ バスルームが汚れていた。
④ ベッドの寝心地が悪かった。

正解 ⇒ ②

　ホテルのマネジャーに滞在の感想を聞かれ，男性は，まずベッドについて，次に浴室について満足した旨を伝えている。男性の発言の but ... 以降がホテルに対する不満であり，最後の文の I wish 〜「〜だったらよかった」から，正解は②。

【語句・表現】
・stay with 〜（人）「〜（のところ）に滞在する」
・Something wrong?「何か問題でも？」：Is（または Was）(there) something wrong? の口語表現。
・I wish（that）＋仮定法過去完了表現「〜だったらよかったのに」：過去に起こってしまったことや過去の事実に対して，その逆のことを願う表現。
〈選択肢〉
・space「場所」：不可算名詞なので単数扱い。

· uncomfortable「心地よくない」

第４問

A

問18～21　| 18 |　| 19 |　| 20 |　| 21 |
【放送内容と選択肢】

　　I had a terrible day last week.　One thing after another kept going wrong.　At breakfast, I spilled coffee on my shirt, so I had to put on a new one.　Because of that, I missed my usual train.　While waiting for the next one, I tried to buy a drink, but I didn't have my wallet.　It had fallen out of my bag on the way to the station.　After I finally got to school, the gate was closed and no one else was there.　I checked my phone, and it was Sunday.　I never want to have a day like that again!

　　先週ひどい一日を過ごしました。次々と悪いことが起こったのです。朝食時にシャツにコーヒーをこぼしてしまったので，新しいシャツに着替えなければなりませんでした。そのせいで，いつもの電車に乗り遅れてしまいました。次の電車を待っている間に飲み物を買おうとしたら，財布がありませんでした。駅に向かう途中でバッグから落ちてしまったのです。ようやく学校に着くと，門が閉まっていて誰もいませんでした。携帯電話を確認すると，その日は日曜日でした。あの日のような体験は二度としたくありません！

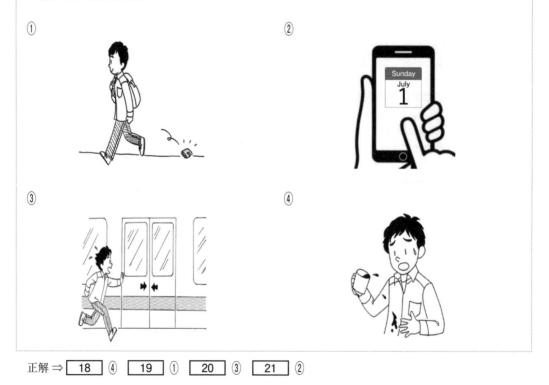

① 　　　　　　　　　　　　　②

③ 　　　　　　　　　　　　　④

正解 ⇒　| 18 | ④　| 19 | ①　| 20 | ③　| 21 | ②

　　出来事を描いたイラストを時系列に沿って並べ替える問題。「私」が，問題が立て続けに起こった日の体験について語っている。財布を落とした（had fallen out：大過去）のは，電車に乗り損ねたり，飲み

物を買おうとしたりする（missed ... / tried to buy ...：過去）ことよりも前だったことに注意。出来事の順番は，④朝食時にコーヒーをこぼす→①駅に向かう途中で財布を落とす→③いつもの電車に乗り遅れる→②日にちを確認するとなる。

【語句・表現】
・terrible「ひどい」
・one thing after another「次々と」
・go wrong「失敗する，うまくいかない」
・spill A on B「BにAをこぼす」
・put on ～「～を着る」
・miss「～に乗り遅れる」
・fall out of ～「～から落ちる」
・on the way to ～「～に行く途中に」
・get to ～「～に到着する」

問22～25 ☐22 ☐23 ☐24 ☐25
【放送内容と選択肢】

　These are the results of last month's survey.　Boys in Senior 1 get 7 hours of sleep, which is the same as Senior 3 girls.　On the other hand, Senior 1 girls get at least 9 hours of sleep on average.　A majority of girls in Senior 2 sleep for around 8 hours, while most of the boys in the same grade sleep for only 6.　Senior 3 boys get the least amount of sleep, with an average of less than 5 hours per night.

　これは先月の調査結果です。高1男子の睡眠時間は7時間で，これは高3女子と同じです。一方，高1女子は少なくとも平均9時間は睡眠を取っています。高2女子の大多数は約8時間寝ていますが，同じ学年のほとんどの男子は6時間しか寝ていません。高3男子は睡眠量が最も少なく，平均5時間未満です。

睡眠習慣の調査結果

学年	性別	1日の睡眠時間
高1	女子	22
高1	男子	23
高2	女子	約8時間
高2	男子	24
高3	女子	25
高3	男子	5時間未満

① 5時間以下
② 6時間
③ 7時間
④ 8時間
⑤ 9時間以上

正解 ⇒ | 22 | ⑤ | 23 | ③ | 24 | ② | 25 | ③ |

　放送された英文では，まず，高1男子の睡眠時間と，同じ睡眠時間である高3女子について言及し，その後，高1女子，高2男女，高3男子の順に説明されている。高1女子の睡眠に関しては，at least 9 hours of sleep「少なくとも9時間は眠っている」から⑤「9時間以上」，最初に言及された高1男子は7 hours of sleep から③「7時間」である。高2男子は A majority of girls in Senior 2 ... から始まる文の while 以降に，②「6時間」とある。高3女子は高1男子と同じ睡眠時間なので，③「7時間」が正解である。

【語句・表現】
・survey「調査」
・senior「高校生」
・on the other hand「一方」
・on average「平均で」
・a majority of ~「~の大多数」
・while S V「~であるが」：対比，または譲歩を表す表現。
・per「~につき」：per night「一晩につき」（= a night）。
〈表〉
・habit「（個人の）習慣」
・gender「（社会的）性差，性別」

B

問26　| 26 |
【放送内容と選択肢】

①　I really enjoyed Anaheim when I went there.　There was a lot of international food, and it was all delicious.　The weather was also warm from late morning to early evening.　Most places were crowded, such as the theme parks, but Yorba Regional Park was a great place where I could enjoy a quiet walk out in nature.

②　Kakslauttanen is my recommendation.　The snowy landscape was beautiful.　You can enjoy quiet nights in a private room.　The room has a glass ceiling and walls so that you can watch the aurora from your bed!　The Finnish food was also wonderful, with some great meat dishes and pies.

③　Manila was my favorite place in winter.　It was hot like summer, so I wore T-shirts every day. If you go to the Camayan Beach Resort, you can enjoy group activities like hiking or you can just sit alone along the beach.　I thought the food was pretty average, but I still had a great time.

④　I think you should try Sydney.　It will be summertime there, so you don't need to pack a coat.　The popular places, like the Sydney Opera House and the Taronga Zoo, were crowded.

However, the shrimp and lamb that I ate there were the best I have ever had!

① アナハイムに行って，本当に楽しかったです。世界の料理がたくさんあって，どれもおいしかったです。天気も，朝遅くから夕方頃まで暖かかったです。テーマパークなどほとんどの場所が混雑していましたが，ヨーバ・リージョナル・パークは自然の中を静かに散歩を楽しめる素晴らしい場所でした。

② カクシラウッタネンが私のお薦めです。雪景色がきれいでした。個室で静かな夜を過ごせます。天井と壁はガラス張りなので，ベッドからオーロラを眺められます！　フィンランド料理も素晴らしく，とてもおいしい肉料理やパイもありました。

③ マニラが私の冬のお気に入りの場所でした。夏のように暑く，毎日Tシャツを着ていました。カマヤン・ビーチリゾートに行くと，ハイキングのようなグループアクティビティーを楽しむことができますし，一人で海岸沿いにただ座ることもできます。食べ物はかなり平均的だと思いましたが，それでも素晴らしい時間を過ごしました。

④ シドニーを試してみるべきだと思います。現地は夏だと思うので，コートを持って行く必要はありません。シドニー・オペラハウスやタロンガ動物園のような人気のある場所は混んでいました。でも，そこで食べたエビとラム肉は今まで食べた中で一番おいしかったです！

正解 ⇒ ①

　最もふさわしいのは①のアナハイムである。②のカクシラウッタネンは雪景色やオーロラについての言及から，気温が低いと考えられるため条件Aに合わず，③のマニラは食べ物が平均的なことから条件Bに，④のシドニーは観光地で他の場所は混んでいたとあるので条件Cにそれぞれ合わない。

場所	条件A （日中暖かい）	条件B （食事がおいしい）	条件C （一人でリラックス）
① アナハイム	○	○	○
② カクシラウッタネン	×	○	○
③ マニラ	○	△	○
④ シドニー	○	○	×

【語句・表現】
・Anaheim「アナハイム」：アメリカ・カリフォルニア州にある都市。
・regional「地域の」
・crowded「混み合った，混雑した」
・such as ～「～のような」
・(out) in nature「自然の中で」：out は室内ではなく「外」を示している。省略可能。
・Kakslauttanen「カクシラウッタネン」：フィンランドのラップランド地方にある宿泊施設。
・recommendation「推薦（するもの）」
・snowy「雪に覆われた」
・landscape「景色」
・ceiling「天井」
・so that S V「～するように」：目的を表す表現。V の前に助動詞（can, will など）が入ることが多い。ここでも目的の意味で使われているが，「オーロラを眺められる」ということに対して「！」が付いているので，英語の語順のまま訳出した。

・aurora「オーロラ」
・Finnish「フィンランドの」
・Manila「マニラ」：フィリピンの首都。
・alone「一人で」
・pretty「かなり」：≒ quite, rather。
・average「平均」
・still「それでも」
・have a great time「素敵な時間を過ごす」
・Sydney「シドニー」：オーストラリア南東部の都市。
・summertime「夏季」
・pack「～を荷造りする」
・shrimp「エビ」
・lamb「ラム肉」

第5問

【放送内容】

Today we'll be talking about the increase in remote and hybrid work models at companies. Are you familiar with these types of models?   Remote work models are ones in which employees do all their work at home.   Hybrid work models, on the other hand, are ones in which employees spend some of their working hours carrying out their tasks remotely while the rest is spent in person at the office.

Both types of models became more popular due to the COVID-19 pandemic.   Since then, a lot of research has been done on the benefits of these models for both workers and their managers. For example, we know that both types of models offer workers greater flexibility in their work and cause less stress and burnout.   Meanwhile, companies have reported higher productivity among workers and a more efficient use of their time.

These models do have some negative aspects, of course.   For one thing, workers have less access to company resources and equipment.   They also cannot work together as easily and may feel disconnected from their company's culture.   Managers also have less ability to monitor their workers and offer help when necessary.   It is also more difficult for them to identify workers who deserve recognition, such as promotions or salary increases.

Despite some of the disadvantages, a majority of US companies have already adopted either a fully remote or hybrid work model, or plan to use one in the near future.   This means that our ideas about work and work-life balance are sure to change in the coming years.   While some countries may be slower than others to move to these work models, in the future, fully in-person jobs will be rarer than other work models everywhere.

今日は，企業におけるリモートワークモデルとハイブリッドワークモデルの増加についてお話しします。これらのモデルについてご存じでしょうか。リモートワークモデルは，従業員が全ての仕事を自宅で行うという就業形態です。一方，ハイブリッドワークモデルは，従業員が勤務時間の一部をリモートで仕事をするのに使い，残りの時間はオフィスで対面式勤務をするという就業形態です。
　どちらのタイプのモデルも，新型コロナウイルス感染症の流行により広まりました。それ以来，従

業員・マネジャーの両者にとってのこれらのモデルの利点について多くの研究が行われてきました。たとえば，どちらのタイプのモデルも，従業員の仕事の自由度を高め，ストレスや極度の疲労を減らすことがわかっています。一方，企業側は，従業員の生産性が向上し，彼らが時間をより効率的に活用していると報告しています。

　もちろん，これらのモデルにはいくつかのマイナス面があります。一つは，従業員の会社のリソースや設備へのアクセスが少なくなることです。また，以前ほど容易に一緒に働くことができず，自分が働く会社の文化へのつながりを感じないかもしれません。マネジャーたちは，従業員をチェックし，必要に応じて支援を提供することもあまりできなくなります。昇進や昇給などの評価に値する従業員を確認することもより困難になります。

　これらの欠点にもかかわらず，アメリカ企業の大多数はすでに完全なリモートワークモデルかハイブリッドワークモデルを採用している，もしくは近い将来にどちらかを利用する予定です。これは，仕事やワークライフバランスに関する私たちの考えが，今後数年間で確実に変化することを意味します。これらのワークモデルへの移行が他の国よりも遅れている国もありますが，将来的には，世界中で完全な対面式勤務は他のワークモデルよりもまれになるでしょう。

【ワークシート】

リモートワークモデルとハイブリッドワークモデル

○ リモートワークモデル
　● 定義：従業員が完全に自宅で仕事をするモデル

○ ハイブリッドワークモデル
　● 定義：従業員が 27 するモデル

○ 利点と欠点

	利点	欠点
従業員	● 自由度の向上 ● 28	● 29 ● リソースへのアクセスの減少
管理職	● より生産的な従業員 ● 30	● 従業員の監督が難しい ● 31 を与えるのが難しい

講義の続き（問33）

　Here is a graph based on data from surveys of several US and European companies that were done after the COVID-19 pandemic.　It shows the number of days per week that employees spend at the office among those who work at least five days per week.　What trend can we see happening with remote and hybrid work models?

　これは，新型コロナウイルス感染症の流行後に行われた，アメリカおよびヨーロッパのいくつかの企業の調査データに基づくグラフです。少なくとも週5日働いている従業員のオフィスで過ごす週当たりの日数を示しています。リモートワークモデルやハイブリッドワークモデルではどのような傾向が見られますか。

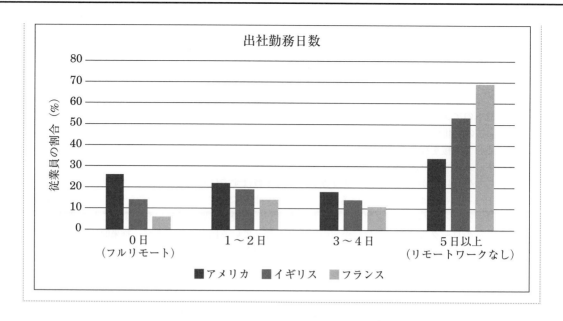

出社勤務日数

従業員の割合 (%)

■アメリカ ■イギリス □フランス

問27 ⌐27⌐

① 自宅とオフィスで同じ量の仕事をする
② リモートよりもオフィスで多くの仕事をする
③ **リモートと対面式勤務を組み合わせて行う**
④ 対面式勤務をするためにオフィスを訪れることはめったにない

正解 ⇒ ③

　放送文の第1段落で，リモートワークモデルとハイブリッドワークモデルについての説明がされている。第4文の in which 以降 employees spend ... at the office「従業員が勤務時間の一部をリモートで仕事をするのに使い，残りの時間はオフィスで対面式勤務をする」がハイブリッドワークの説明となり，リモートワークと対面式勤務の両方を，割合に関係なく組み合わせる就業形態を指す。したがって③が正解となる。

問28〜31 ⌐28⌐ ⌐29⌐ ⌐30⌐ ⌐31⌐

① 効率の向上　　② チームワークの減少　　③ 仕事タスク
④ ストレスの減少　⑤ 極度の疲労の増加　　⑥ 評価

正解 ⇒ ⌐28⌐ ④ ⌐29⌐ ② ⌐30⌐ ① ⌐31⌐ ⑥

　放送文の第2段落，For example 以降で利点が，第3段落全体で欠点が言及されており，For one thing 以降で欠点の具体例が挙げられている。従業員側の利点は greater flexibility in their work「仕事の自由度の向上」と less stress and burnout「ストレスや極度の疲労の減少」なので，⌐28⌐には④「ストレスの減少」が入る。一方，欠点は less access to company resources and equipment「会社のリソースや設備へのアクセスが少ない」と cannot work together as easily and may feel disconnected ...「以前ほど容易に一緒に働くことができず，自分が…つながりを感じないかもしれない」なので，⌐29⌐には②「チームワークの減少」が入る。管理職（企業）側の利点は higher productivity among workers「従業員の生産性の向上」と more efficient use of their time「より効率的な時間の活用」なので，⌐30⌐

には①「効率の向上」が入る。一方，欠点は less ability to monitor their workers と more difficult for them to identify workers who deserve recognition「評価に値する従業員を確認することがより困難である」なので，　31　には⑥「評価」が入る。

問32　32

> ①　全ての国で，ハイブリッドおよびリモートワークモデルは，対面式勤務よりも広まるだろう。
> ②　今後，より多くの企業がハイブリッドワークモデルからリモートワークモデルに移行していくだろう。
> ③　リモートワークモデルは通常，従業員に利益をもたらすが，ハイブリッドワークモデルは企業に利益をもたらす。
> ④　新型コロナウイルス感染症の流行により，企業においてハイブリッドワークモデルの採用が遅れた。

正解 ⇒ ①

　放送文の最終文 in the future 以降で将来の展望が述べられている。その後に続く fully in-person jobs will be rarer than other work models everywhere「世界中で，完全な対面式勤務は他のワークモデルよりもまれになるだろう」ということから，正解は①である。放送文中では，ハイブリッドワークモデルからリモートワークモデルへの移行については言及されていないので②は不適。リモートワークモデル，ハイブリッドワークモデルのそれぞれに，従業員と企業の両者にもたらす利益・不利益があるため③も不適。第2段落の冒頭で Both types of models became more popular due to the COVID-19 pandemic「どちらのタイプのモデル（リモートワークとハイブリッドワークモデル）も，新型コロナウイルス感染症の流行により広まった」と述べられているため，④も不適。

問33　33

> ①　3カ国全てで，従業員の大多数は少なくとも週に1日リモートワークをしている。
> ②　リモートワークのみを行う従業員の割合は，イギリスが最も高い。
> ③　アメリカでは少しでもリモートワークをする従業員は，そうでない人よりも多い。
> ④　3カ国全ての従業員は，対面で働くよりもリモートで働くことが多い。

正解 ⇒ ③

　講義の続きを聞き，図表と併せて考える問題である。放送文でも説明されている通り，グラフはアメリカ，イギリス，フランスにおける「従業員がオフィスで過ごす週当たりの日数」を示している。フランスでは「リモートワークなし」の従業員の割合が最も多く，70%近くに上るため，①は不適。オフィスワークが0日の従業員（リモートワークでのみ働く従業員）の割合は，アメリカが最も多いため②も不適となる。グラフを見ると，アメリカ以外は「リモートワークなし」の従業員の割合が最も多いため④も不適となり，正解は③。アメリカでは少しでもリモートワークをする従業員の割合は，「0日」「1〜2日」「3〜4日」の全てを足して，およそ65%となり，「リモートワークなし」の割合の35%弱より多い。

【語句・表現】
〈第1段落〉
・remote「遠隔の」
・hybrid「混種の，混合の」
・be familiar with 〜「〜について知っている」
・employee「従業員」

・on the other hand「一方」
・working hour「就業時間」
・carry out ～「～を実行する・遂行する」
・the rest「残り」
・in person「対面で」
〈第2段落〉
・the COVID-19「新型コロナウイルス感染症」
・pandemic「(病気などの) 大流行」
・on「～について」：research on ～「～についての研究」。
・benefit「利益」
・manager「管理職，経営者」
・flexibility「自由度，柔軟性」
・cause「～を引き起こす」
・burnout「バーンアウト，燃え尽き症候群」
・meanwhile「一方」
・productivity「生産性」
・efficient「効率的な，有能な」
〈第3段落〉
・negative「マイナスの」
・aspect「点，側面」
・for one thing「一つには」
・resource「リソース，資源」
・equipment「設備」
・as easily「(～と同じくらい) 容易に」：後ろに続く as before「以前と」が省略された表現。
・feel disconnected from ～「～から切り離されている感じがする」
・monitor「～を観察する」
・when necessary「必要なときに」：when の後の代名詞主語と be 動詞 [本文では it (= help) is] が省略されている。
・identify「～を識別する・特定する」
・deserve「～に値する」
・recognition「評価，表彰」
・promotion「昇進」
〈第4段落〉
・despite「～にもかかわらず」
・disadvantage「欠点」：= negative aspect。
・adopt「～を採用する」
・fully remote「フルリモートの」
・in the near future「近い将来に」
・work-life balance「ワークライフバランス」：「仕事と生活の調和」を意味する。
・be sure to *do*「必ず～する」
・coming「これから来る，今後の」
・rare「まれな，珍しい」
〈講義の続き〉
・based on ～「～に基づいて」
・per「～につき」
・trend「傾向」
〈ワークシート〉
・entirely「まったく」

・management「経営力」
・flexible「柔軟な」
〈選択肢〉
・even「同等の」
・perform「～を行う」
・mixture「組み合わせ」
・rarely「ほとんど～ない」
・face-to-face「対面で」
・efficiency「効率」
・decreased「減少した」
・over time「時がたつにつれて」
・benefit「～に利益を与える」：この文では動詞で用いられている。
・lead to ～「～になる・至る」
・delay「遅れ」

第6問

A

【放送内容】

Jamie: What do you think of this painting, Taiga?　I really like the colors.
Taiga: I don't really get it, Jamie.
Jamie: What do you mean?
Taiga: I just don't understand what the artist is trying to say.　What's the message?
Jamie: Isn't that part of what makes art great?　You have to think about what the artist wanted to say.
Taiga: Maybe, but this looks like the artist just put random spots of paint on the paper.　I prefer this kind of painting over here.
Jamie: What do you like better about this one?　I don't really like the dark mood.
Taiga: Well, I can tell what kind of feeling and message the artist wanted to give by looking at the expressions of the people in the painting.
Jamie: I see.　You're more attracted to art that has a clear meaning and focus.
Taiga: I guess you're right.　When I understand what's happening or what the painting is about, I appreciate the artist's skill more.
Jamie: If a painting has a nice use of color and technique, then I can enjoy it.
Taiga: Even that first painting?
Jamie: Sure!　I think the artist used a unique technique to express her feelings.

ジェイミー：タイガ，この絵，どう思う？　私はこの色がすごく好きだな。
タイガ　　：ジェイミー，僕にはよくわからないや。
ジェイミー：どういう意味？
タイガ　　：この画家が何を言おうとしているのかわからないっていうこと。伝えたいことは何だろう。
ジェイミー：それが芸術の素晴らしいところじゃない？　画家が何を伝えたかったか，自分で考えなければいけない。
タイガ　　：たぶんね。だけど，これはただ単に紙の上に絵の具をでたらめに飛び散らせたように見

えるけど。僕はこっちにあるこういう絵の方が好きだな。

ジェイミー：この絵のどういうところが好きなの？　私は暗い感じがあまり好きじゃないな。

タイガ　　：ええと，絵の中の人たちの表情を見れば，画家がどのような気持ちやメッセージを伝えたかったのかわかるところ。

ジェイミー：なるほど。あなたは明確な意味と焦点のある作品により引かれるということね。

タイガ　　：たぶんそうだと思う。何が起こっているかとか，何が描かれているのかがわかれば，画家のスキルの高さをもっと楽しめるよ。

ジェイミー：私は，色やテクニックがうまく使われていれば，絵を楽しむことができるわ。

タイガ　　：最初に見た絵でも？

ジェイミー：もちろん！　あの画家は自分の気持ちを表現するための独特なテクニックを使ったんだと思うわ。

問34　34

タイガの意見の要点は何か。

① 芸術はわかりやすい方が良い。
② 暗い絵の方が魅力的である。
③ 熟練した画家は大変まれである。
④ 最高の芸術品はいつもきちんと描かれている。

正解 ⇒ ①

ジェイミーとタイガが展示された絵画を見て対話をしている。2種類の異なる技法で描かれた絵画をめぐる対話から，それぞれの芸術に対する好みや意見を聞き取る問題である。ジェイミーが最初に示した絵画に対して，タイガは，「画家が伝えたいことがわからない」と言い，ジェイミーは，「それを自分で考えるのが芸術の素晴らしいところ」と発言している。次にタイガが「こっちにあるこういう絵の方が好きだ」と違う絵をジェイミーに示し，「画家がどのような気持ちやメッセージを伝えたかったのかわかるところが好き」と答えている。したがって，①が正解となる。

問35　35

ジェイミーは芸術についてどう考えているか。

① 画家は，自分の感情を作品に反映させるべきではない。
② 色は絵の最も重要なものである。
③ 画家が伝えたいことについて考えるのは楽しい。
④ 明確な意味を持っている絵はつまらない。

正解 ⇒ ③

ジェイミーの三つ目の発言に「それ（画家が伝えたいことがわからないこと）が芸術の素晴らしいところじゃない？　画家が何を伝えたかったか，自分で考えなければいけない」とあることから，正解は③である。

【語句・表現】
・painting「絵」

・get「〜を理解する」
・random「でたらめの」
・spot「点」
・over here「こっちに」
・mood「雰囲気，ムード」
・expression「表情」
・attract A to B「A を B に引き付ける」
・focus「焦点，中心点」
・guess「〜と思う・推測する」：I guess ... は，自分の考えを述べるときに使う口語表現。
・appreciate「〜を高く評価する，〜の良さがわかる」
・skill「技術」
・have a nice use of 〜「〜をうまく使う」
・unique「独特の，唯一無二の」
〈選択肢〉
・attractive「魅力的な」
・skillful「熟練した」
・draw「〜を描く」
・neatly「素晴らしく，きちんと」
・affect「〜に影響を及ぼす」
・aspect「面，側面」
・boring「つまらない」

B

【放送内容】

Yuna:　Hey, Sarah.　I saw that you paid for your food with your smartphone just now.

Sarah:　That's right, Yuna.　Electronic payments make things so much easier.

Yuna:　I see.　But are they safe?　Aren't you worried that your information could be stolen?

Sarah:　Not as much as I worry about losing my wallet or having that stolen.　What do you think, Larry?

Larry:　I agree.　Even if my smartphone is stolen, they can't use the payment system without my password.

Yuna:　Isn't it easy to spend too much money, though?　With cash, I can't use more than what I have in my wallet.

Larry:　That's true, Yuna, but it's the same as credit cards.　You have to be careful.

Austin:　My parents use electronic payments for most things, but I haven't tried them yet.　There are too many different kinds!

Sarah:　Don't worry, Austin.　Most stores accept several types, so you can just pick one.

Yuna:　But what happens when a store only accepts cash?

Larry:　That's a bit of an inconvenience, but more stores are accepting electronic payments, and using electronic payments is becoming more and more popular.

Austin:　That's a good point, Larry.　Lately, I see more stores that accept them than stores that don't.

Sarah:　Exactly.　I never have to think about how much money I need to take before I go out.

Larry:　Or try to search for an ATM when I'm low on cash.

Austin:　Hmm ...　Maybe I'll try setting one up when I get home.

Yuna:　You too, Austin?　I guess I just don't trust technology.

ユナ	：ねえ，サラ。今，食事代をスマホで支払ったでしょ。
サラ	：そうよ，ユナ。電子決済って本当にいろいろ便利よ。
ユナ	：そうなんだ。でも安全なの？　個人情報が盗まれるのではと心配じゃない？
サラ	：財布をなくしたり，盗まれたりすることほど心配じゃないよ。どう思う，ラリー？
ラリー	：僕も同感だ。たとえスマホが盗まれても，本人のパスワードがないと決済できないからね。
ユナ	：でも，お金を使いやすくなり過ぎない？　現金なら，財布に入っている以上のお金は使えないよ。
ラリー	：本当にそうだね，ユナ，でもクレジットカードと同じだよ。気を付けなくちゃいけないってこと。
オースティン	：うちの両親はほとんどのことに電子決済を使っているけど，僕はまだ試したことないな。種類が多過ぎて！
サラ	：心配ないよ，オースティン。ほとんどの店で数種類取り扱っているから，どれか一つを選べばいいのよ。
ユナ	：でも，現金しか受け付けない店だとどうなるの？
ラリー	：それがちょっと不便だけど，電子決済が可能な店は日々増えているし，電子決済はますます一般的になってきているよ。
オースティン	：確かにそうだね，ラリー。最近は電子決済できない店よりもできる店の方が多いよ。
サラ	：その通りだね。外出する前に，お金をいくら持っていく必要があるか考える必要がない。
ラリー	：それに，現金をあまり持っていないときにATMを探す必要もない。
オースティン	：うーん…家に帰ったら設定してみようかな。
ユナ	：オースティン，あなたも？　私は，テクノロジーを信用していないだけかな。

問36 　36

① 1人
② **2人**
③ 3人
④ 4人

正解 ⇒ ②

　電子マネーによる決済について，四人が会話をしている。それぞれの意見が聞き取れたかどうかを確認する問題である。ユナが，サラがelectronic paymentsを使うのを見たことで，電子決済についての会話が始まる。まず，情報が盗まれないかなどの安全性についてユナが質問していることから，ユナは電子決済を使っていないことがうかがえる。サラが自分の意見を述べた後にラリーに意見を求める。ラリーは最初の発言でサラに同意を示し，「スマホが盗まれても，本人のパスワードがないと決済できない」と答えていることから，ラリーも電子マネーを使っていることがわかる。オースティンが「両親はほとんどのことに電子決済を使っているけど，自分はまだ試したことない」と発言していることから彼が使っていないことが明らかとなる。その後は，電子決済を導入する店が増えている，という内容で会話が進み，これまで電子決済の不安について質問してきたユナが，最後に「私は，テクノロジーを信用していない」と発言している。したがって，電子マネーを使っていないのはユナとオースティン，使っているのはサラとラリーの二人となり，正解は②。

問37 　37

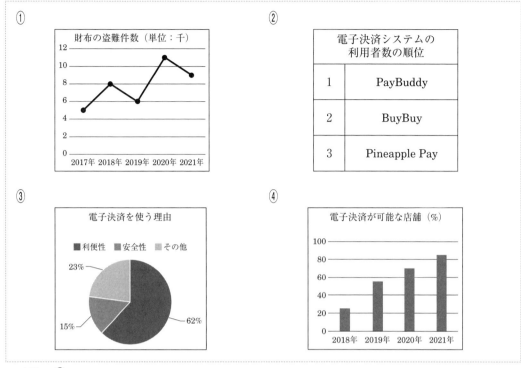

①
財布の盗難件数（単位：千）

②
電子決済システムの
利用者数の順位

1	PayBuddy
2	BuyBuy
3	Pineapple Pay

③
電子決済を使う理由

■利便性　■安全性　□その他

23%　15%　62%

④
電子決済が可能な店舗（%）

正解 ⇒ ④

　それぞれの意見を聞き取った上で，ラリーの考えの根拠まで把握できたかを確かめる問題である。具体的な盗難件数には触れていないが，財布の盗難に言及したのはサラであるため①は不適。電子決済の種類が多過ぎることについて言及したのはオースティンとサラであるため②も不適である。サラ，ラリーの二人が電子決済は便利であると思っていることがうかがえるが，人々が電子決済を使う理由について話されたわけではないので③も不適。④は毎年電子決済のできる店が増加していることを示しており，ラリーの「電子決済が可能な店は日々増えている」という発言の根拠となるので正解である。

【語句・表現】
・pay for A with B「Bを使ってAの代金を支払う」
・smartphone「スマートフォン，スマホ」
・electronic payment「電子決済」：現金を使わず電子的に支払うこと。
・things「物事」
・(A) not as much as B「(Aは) Bほどではない」
・even if S V「たとえ～でも」
・a bit of ～「少しの～」
・inconvenience「不便」：↔ convenience「利便性」。
・That's a good point.「確かにそうだね」：直訳は「それは良い指摘だ」という意味で，相手が的を射ていることを言ったときなどに使う。
・lately「最近」
・exactly「まさに，そのとおり」
・low on cash「現金不足で，現金の持ち合わせが少ない」
・get home「帰宅する」

リスニング・第5回 解答と解説

問題番号 （配点）	設問		解答番号	正解	配点	自己採点
第1問 (25)	A	1	1	2	4	
		2	2	2	4	
		3	3	2	4	
		4	4	3	4	
	B	5	5	1	3	
		6	6	2	3	
		7	7	4	3	
自己採点小計						
第2問 (16)		8	8	3	4	
		9	9	4	4	
		10	10	4	4	
		11	11	4	4	
自己採点小計						
第3問 (18)		12	12	1	3	
		13	13	4	3	
		14	14	2	3	
		15	15	1	3	
		16	16	2	3	
		17	17	2	3	
自己採点小計						

問題番号 （配点）	設問		解答番号	正解	配点	自己採点
第4問 (12)	A	18	18	4	4*	
		19	19	1		
		20	20	3		
		21	21	2		
		22	22	6	1	
		23	23	3	1	
		24	24	6	1	
		25	25	1	1	
	B	26	26	4	4	
自己採点小計						
第5問 (15)		27	27	3	2	
		28	28	2-3	4*	
		29	29			
		30	30	1	2	
		31	31	4	2	
		32	32	3	2	
		33	33	1	3	
自己採点小計						
第6問 (14)	A	34	34	4	3	
		35	35	2	3	
	B	36	36	2	4	
		37	37	4	4	
自己採点小計						

自己採点合計 □

(注)
　1 *は，全部正解の場合のみ点を与える。
　2 −(ハイフン)でつながれた正解は順序を問
　　わない。

第1問

A
問1 　1　
【放送内容と選択肢】

Emily, are you reading a letter? It's dark, so turn on the light in your room.

① 話者はエミリーに手紙を書くよう頼んでいる。
❷ 話者はエミリーに明るい部屋で手紙を読むよう頼んでいる。
③ 話者はエミリーを暗い部屋へ案内しようとしている。
④ 話者は右に曲がって郵便局へ行こうとしている。

正解 ⇒ ②

　放送された英文は,「エミリー,手紙を読んでいるの？　暗いから部屋の明かりを点けなさい」という意味である。手紙を読むには部屋が暗すぎるので,明かりを点けて部屋を明るくしてから読むようにとエミリーを促しているため,正解は②である。

問2 　2　
【放送内容と選択肢】

In my childhood, my mother bought a puppy for me, which was like a younger sister.

① 話者はペットを飼うように母親に頼んだ。
❷ 話者は自分の犬を家族の一員のように感じていた。
③ 話者は母親の代わりにその犬を育てた。
④ 話者は父親に似ていて,話者の妹は母親に似ている。

正解 ⇒ ②

　放送された英文は,「子供の頃に,私の母が子犬を買ってくれて,それを妹のように思っていた」という意味である。話者が飼っている犬を妹,つまり家族の一員のように思っていたことから,正解は②である。

問3 　3　
【放送内容と選択肢】

The phone is ringing, Tom. Hurry up. My hands are full right now.

① 話者は電話でトムと長時間話している。
❷ 話者はトムに今すぐ電話に応対させようとしている。
③ 話者は夫に電話しなければならない。
④ 話者はトムの代わりに電話に出るつもりである。

正解 ⇒ ②

放送された英文は「電話が鳴っているよ,トム。急いで。私は今手が離せないの」という意味である。

つまり，話者はトムに電話に出るよう促しているのであるから，②が正解となる。

【語句・表現】
〈選択肢〉
・instead of ~「~の代わりに」

問4　　4
【放送内容と選択肢】

I got completely lost while sightseeing. I wish I had a map to know where I am.

① 話者は誰かに現在地を尋ねている。
② 話者はどこにいるかを知るために地図を確認している。
③ 話者は地図を持っていないことを後悔している。
④ 話者は自分で来た道を戻っている。

　正解 ⇒ ③

　放送された英文は「観光中に完全に道に迷ってしまった。今どこにいるか知るために地図を持っていればなあ」という意味である。I wish ＋仮定法過去で，実現しがたい現在の願望を表すので，地図を持っていない現状を憂いていることがわかる。したがって，③が正解となる。

【語句・表現】
・get lost「道に迷った，当惑した」

B
問5　　5
【放送内容と選択肢】

I have two other textbooks besides English.

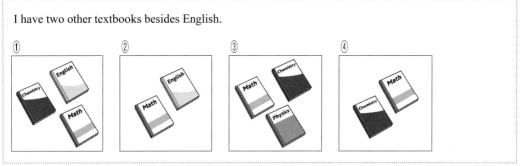

　正解 ⇒ ①

　放送された英文は，「私は英語の他に教科書を2冊持っている」という意味である。「besides」は「~の他に」という表現であり，これを表すイラストは①となる。

問6　　6

【放送内容と選択肢】

The man is walking along the street, and so is the woman.

① ② ③ ④

正解 ⇒ ②

　　放送された英文は,「男性が通りに沿って歩いていて, 女性もまた通りに沿って歩いている」という意味である。「so+(助)動詞+主語」は「～もまた…だ」という意味を表す。よって, 男女2人が同じ行動をしている②と③のうち, 通りに沿って歩いている②が正解である。

【語句・表現】

・so+(助)動詞+主語「～もまた…だ」

問7　　7

【放送内容と選択肢】

Look at the thick book with big letters.

① ② ③ ④

正解 ⇒ ④

　　放送された英文は,「大きな文字が書かれた厚い本を見てください」という意味である。この内容に一致するのは④である。

【語句・表現】

・thick「厚い」

・letter「文字」

第２問

問8 ☐8☐
【放送内容と選択肢】

W：Would you like to go to the Italian restaurant?
M：Sounds nice, but I had pizza yesterday.
W：How about Chinese food? There is a restaurant over there.
M：Good! Let's go.
Question:
Which are they most likely to eat?

W：イタリアンレストランに行かない？
M：それは素敵だね，でも僕は昨日ピザを食べてしまったんだ。
W：中華料理は？　あそこにレストランがあるのよ。
M：いいね！行こう。

問い：
彼らが食べる可能性が最も高いのはどれか。

① 　② 　③ 　④

正解 ⇒ ③

　女性は２回目の発言で中華料理を提案しており，男性も２回目の発言で賛成している。よって，彼らが最も食べる可能性があるものは③である。

【語句・表現】
・over there「あそこに」
・be likely to *do* ～「～しそうである，～する可能性が高い」

問9 ☐9☐
【放送内容と選択肢】

W：Which is your house?
M：Can you see that three-storied one?
W：I found it! Did you leave a window open?
M：Oh, no! I forgot to close it this morning.
Question:
Which is the man's house?

W：あなたの家はどれ？

M：あの3階建ての家が見える？
W：見つけた！　窓を開けっぱなしにしたの？
M：うわー！　今朝閉め忘れたんだ。

問い：
男性の家はどれか。

① 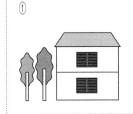　② 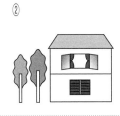　③ 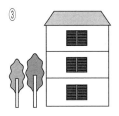　④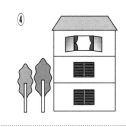

正解 ⇒ ④

　男性の1回目の発言から，男性の家は3階建てであることがわかる。また，男性と女性のそれぞれ2回目の発言から，窓が開いていることが分かる。したがって，正解は④である。

【語句・表現】
・three-storied「3階建ての」

問10　　10
【放送内容と選択肢】

W：Are you feeling better?
M：I have a headache.
W：Really? I assumed you had a sore throat.
M：Ah, this is just for cold prevention.
Question:
What does the man look like?

W：気分は良くなった？
M：頭が痛いんだ。
W：本当？　のどが痛いのかと思ったよ。
M：ああ，これはただ風邪予防のためなんだ。

問い：
男性はどのように見えるか。

① 　② 　③ 　④

正解 ⇒ ④

女性の2回目の発言から，男性はのどの痛みがあると誤解されるような見た目をしていることがわかる。また，男性は2回目の発言で「風邪予防のため」と言っていることからマスク姿の④が正解。

【語句・表現】
・sore throat「のどの痛み」
・cold prevention「風邪予防」

問11 ☐11☐
【放送内容と選択肢】

W：The post office is next to the hospital.
M：Where is the bank?
W：It's across from the hospital.
M：I see, it's next to the drugstore.
Question:
Where is the drugstore?

W：郵便局は病院のとなりにあるね。
M：銀行はどこかな？
W：病院の向かいだよ。
M：なるほど，薬局のとなりだね。

問い：
薬局はどこか。

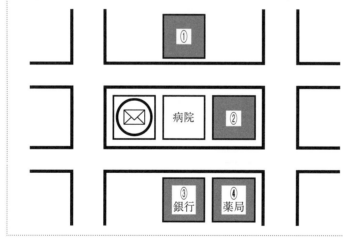

正解 ⇒ ④

女性の1回目の発言から，病院は郵便局のとなりにあると分かる。男性の1回目の発言と女性の2回目の発言から，銀行は①もしくは③の位置にあると分かる。男性の2回目の発言によると，銀行と薬局は横並びにあるため，銀行が③の位置にあると分かり，薬局は④が正解となる。

第3問

問12　12
【放送内容と選択肢】

W：You seem to have a bad cold. Go to see a doctor at once.
M：I don't want to. Don't you have some good cold medicine?
W：Wait a minute ... I bought this last time I had a cold.
M：What on earth is that? Looks like the root of some plant.
W：It looks a bit grotesque, but it really works. You should try it!
M：Never ever! I'll follow your first suggestion.

W：ひどい風邪をひいているみたいね。すぐに病院に行きなさい。
M：行きたくない。何かいい風邪薬を持ってない？
W：ちょっと待ってね…前回私が風邪をひいた時はこれを買ったの。
M：それはいったい何？　何かの植物の根っこみたいだけど。
W：見た目はちょっとグロテスクだけど，よく効くのよ。飲んでみて！
M：絶対にいやだ！　最初のアドバイスに従うことにするよ。

男の子は何をする可能性が高いか。

① すぐに医者の診断を受ける
② よい風邪薬を自分で見つける
③ 他の人たちにアドバイスを求める
④ 母親が勧める薬を飲む

正解 ⇒ ①

　「すぐに病院に行きなさい」と言われた息子は最初「行きたくない」と言い，よい風邪薬を持っていないか母親に尋ねている。しかし，母親が勧めてきた薬は植物の根っこのようなもので，「飲んでみて」と言われた息子は「絶対にいやだ」と拒絶している。そして，「（母親の）最初のアドバイスに従うことにする」と言っているので，息子はすぐに病院に行くことにしたのだとわかる。よって，正解は①である。

【語句・表現】
・at once「すぐに，直ちに」
・疑問詞 + on earth「いったい」
・root「根」
・grotesque「奇怪な，グロテスクな」
〈選択肢〉
・consult「～に相談する，（医師の診断）を受ける」
・immediately「すぐに，直ちに」
・recommend「～を勧める」

問13 ☐13☐

【放送内容と選択肢】

> M: Out of the five countries, which is the most popular destination among the students?
> W: Well, the questionnaire shows that France beats all the others, followed by Germany.
> M: How about Italy? Last year it was by far the top choice, wasn't it?
> W: Yes, but this year Italy is in the fourth place, behind the United Kingdom.
> M: That's surprising.
>
> M：5か国の中で，生徒たちに一番人気のある行き先はどこですか。
> W：えぇと，アンケートの結果によると，フランスが一番人気があって，ドイツが次に続いています。
> M：イタリアはどうですか。昨年は断トツの第1位でしたよね。
> W：えぇ，でも今年はイタリアは第4位で，イギリスよりも順位が下です。
> M：それは意外ですね。

> 今年，3番目に人気のある国はどこか。
>
> ① フランス
> ② ドイツ
> ③ イタリア
> ④ **イギリス**

正解 ⇒ ④

　女性は1回目の発言で「フランスが一番人気があって，ドイツが次に続いています」と述べているので，第1位はフランス，第2位はドイツであるとわかる。また，女性の2回目の発言では「イタリアは第4位で，イギリスよりも順位が下です」と言っているので，第3位がイギリス，第4位がイタリアとなる。よって，「3番目に人気のある国」はイギリスであるから，正解は④となる。

【語句・表現】
・destination「目的地，行き先」
・questionnaire「アンケート」
・beat「～にまさる，～をしのぐ」
・by far「はるかに，断然」：比較級や最上級を強調する表現。

問14 ☐14☐

【放送内容と選択肢】

> M：Here's your work schedule for next month, Ms. Miller.
> W：Oh, you've put me on the early shift. I didn't expect that.
> M：Well, Ms. Davis complained about being on the early shift for so long.
> W：All right. It might not be a bad idea to work earlier in the day.
> M：I appreciate you saying so.
>
> M：ミラーさん，あなたの来月の勤務スケジュールです。
> W：あら，私は早番になったのですね。それは予想していませんでした。
> M：えぇ，デービスさんが，ずっと早番に入っていることに不満を言っていたんです。
> W：わかりました。早い時間帯に仕事をするのも悪くないかもしれません。

M：そう言ってもらえると助かります。

会話によると正しいものはどれか。

① デービスさんは遅番に入っていることが不満だった。
② ミラーさんは来月早番に入る予定である。
③ 男性はデービスさんが遅番に入ってくれることに感謝している。
④ 男性はミラーさんに早番に入ってほしくないと思っている。

正解 ⇒ ②

　　上司の男性が部下の女性（＝ミラーさん）に来月の勤務スケジュールを渡している。女性は早番に入っていることを知って少々驚くが，男性が事情を説明すると「わかりました」と応じている。そして，「早い時間帯に仕事をするのも悪くないかもしれません」と述べていることから，早番に入る来月のシフトに納得した様子がうかがえる。よって，②が正解となる。

【語句・表現】
・shift「シフト，（交替制の）勤務時間」
・complain about ～「～のことで不満を言う」
・appreciate O *doing*「O が～することをありがたく思う」

問15　　15
【放送内容と選択肢】

M：Ah, good morning, Ms. Jones. I'm sorry I'm late.
W：What's the excuse this time? Did your alarm not go off again?
M：Well, I just overslept and missed the bus.
W：All right. But let this be the last time, OK?
M：Yes, I understand. I'm really sorry.

M：あの，ジョーンズ先生，おはようございます。遅刻してすみません。
W：今回はどんな理由？　また目覚まし時計が鳴らなかったの？
M：えぇと，寝坊してバスに間に合わなかっただけです。
W：わかりました。でも，今後は二度とこういうことがないように。
M：はい，わかりました。本当にすみません。

その男の子について正しいのはどれか。

① 男の子はこれまでにも遅刻したことがある。
② 男の子は遅刻した理由について嘘を言っている。
③ 男の子が女性の話を聞いていない。
④ 男の子は遅刻したことについて謝ろうとしない。

正解 ⇒ ①

　　「遅刻してすみません」と謝る生徒に対して，先生は「今回はどんな理由？　また目覚まし時計が鳴らなかったの？」と尋ねている。「今回は」「また」と言っていることから，この生徒が遅刻をしたのは，この日が初めてではないことがうかがえる。よって，正解は①となる。

【語句・表現】
・excuse「理由，弁解」
・alarm「目覚まし時計」
・go off「(目覚まし時計などが)鳴る」
・oversleep「寝過ごす，寝坊する」
〈選択肢〉
・tell a lie「嘘をつく」
・apologize for ～「～のことで謝罪する」

問16 　16

【放送内容と選択肢】

W：How are the birthday party preparations coming along?
M：They are going well. It'll be so much fun!
W：That's good to hear. Miguel is really excited.
M：What? You told Miguel?
W：Yeah ... I saw him in the library and asked him what he was going to wear to the party.
M：Oh, gosh! It was supposed to be a surprise for him!

W：誕生日パーティーの準備は進んでる？
M：順調に進んでいるよ。すごく楽しくなりそうだ！
W：それならよかった。ミゲルもすごく楽しみにしているよ。
M：何だって？　ミゲルに話したの？
W：うん…図書館で彼に会って，パーティーに何を着ていく予定なのか聞いたの。
M：あぁ，何てこった！　ミゲルへのサプライズのつもりだったのに！

男性はなぜうろたえているのか。

① 　彼はまだパーティーに何を着ていくか決めていない。
② 　パーティーが開催されることをミゲルが知ってしまった。
③ 　パーティーの準備が終わりそうにない。
④ 　女性がミゲルと図書館で会う約束をした。

正解 ⇒ ②

　女性が「ミゲルもすごく楽しみにしているよ」と話すのを聞いて，男性は「何だって？　ミゲルに話したの？」と動揺し，最後に「ミゲルへのサプライズパーティーのつもりだったのに！」と言っている。男性は，ミゲルには知らせずにパーティーを開いて驚かせるつもりだったのだが，女性が教えてしまったのでうろたえている。よって，②が正解となる。

【語句・表現】
・come along「(事が) 進む，進展する」
・be supposed to do「～することになっている」

問17 　17　
【放送内容と選択肢】

W：How's your steak, Manabu?
M：Hmm ... I should have ordered something else. What's your chicken like, Alison?
W：It doesn't taste as good as it looks.
M：This is the first and last time we come here.
W：Yeah. This restaurant was highly rated in online reviews, though.

W：マナブ，あなたのステーキはどう？
M：うーん…他のものを注文するべきだったな。アリソン，君のチキンはどう？
W：見た目ほどおいしくはないよ。
M：僕たちがここに来るのは，今回が最初で最後だね。
W：ええ。このレストランはネットのレビューでは評価が高かったんだけど。

女性はそのレストランについてどう思っているか。

① 　夫は他のものを注文するべきだった。
② 　彼女は二度とそのレストランで食事をしないだろう。
③ 　チキンはステーキよりおいしい。
④ 　そのレストランはもっと高く評価されるべきである。

正解 ⇒ ②

　男女はそれぞれステーキとチキンを注文したが，男性は「他のものを注文するべきだった」，女性は「見た目ほどおいしくはない」と言っており，料理に不満を感じている様子である。続けて，男性が「僕たちがここに来るのは，今回が最初で最後だね」と言うと，女性も「ええ」と同意している。以上を踏まえると，女性は二度とこのレストランに来るつもりがないことがうかがえるので，正解は②となる。

【語句・表現】
・steak「ステーキ」
・should have *done*「～すべきだったのに」：実際にはしなかったことが含意される。
・highly「高く，好意的に」
・rate「～を評価する」

第4問

A
問18～21 　18　 　19　 　20　 　21　
【放送内容と選択肢】

　We researched what media people often use to get daily information. As for the four media, "TV", "Newspaper", "SNS" and "Radio", we compared the usage rates for 2014 and 2022. According to the graph, "SNS" was the only medium which increased during this period. "Newspaper" was the second most used in 2014 but moved down to the third place in 2022. Even though "TV" decreased a little, it was still the top. Finally, "Radio" was used less than 10 percent in 2022.

　私たちは日々の情報を入手するために人々がどんなメディアをよく使うのかを調べました。4つの

メディア，「テレビ」，「新聞」，「SNS」，「ラジオ」に関して，2014年と2022年における使用率を比較しました。グラフによれば，「SNS」だけが唯一その期間に使用率が上昇しているメディアです。「新聞」は2014年においては二番目に多く使用されていますが，2022年には3位に順位を下げました。「テレビ」の割合は多少減少していますが，依然として使用率はトップです。最後に「ラジオ」は2022年の時点で使用率が10パーセント以下です。

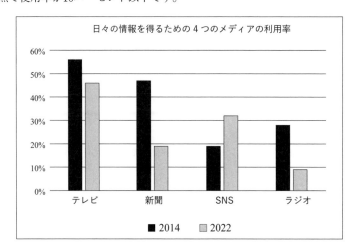

① 新聞
② ラジオ
③ SNS
④ テレビ

正解 ⇒ | 18 | ④ | 19 | ① | 20 | ③ | 21 | ② |

まず第3文で，「SNSだけが唯一使用率が上昇しているメディアである」と述べられているので，
  20 には③が入る。次に第4文で「新聞は2014年では二番目に使用率が高く，2022年には3位にまで順位が下がっている」と述べられているので， 19 には①が入る。さらに第5文では「テレビの使用率は減少しているが，トップである」と述べられているので， 18 には④が入る。そして最終文では「ラジオは2022年の時点で使用率が10パーセント以下である」と述べられているので， 21 には②が入る。

【語句・表現】
・as for ～「～に関して」
・compare「～を比較する」
・move down「下がる」

問22～25 | 22 | 23 | 24 | 25 |
【放送内容と選択肢】

All the performers this time were excellent! It's very difficult to rank them. Okay, then, I would like to mention the good points of their performances. First, in terms of singing, the youngest and the second youngest team were exciting. As for the dancing, the team that drew the largest audience was the most innovative. I have never seen such dances. However, the stage direction of this team was not so good, while all the other teams were good.

今回の出演者はどれも素晴らしかった。彼らに順位をつけるのはとても難しいね。それじゃあ，彼らのパフォーマンスの良かったところを述べていこうと思う。まず，歌に関して言うと一番若いチー

ムと二番目に若いチームは刺激的だったよ。ダンスに関しては，最も多くの観客を集めたチームが最も革新的だった。あんなダンスは見たことがない。ただ，このチームは舞台演出があまり良くなくて，他のチームはどれも良かったよ。

スーパーサマーライブイベント：出演者一覧

チーム	出演者の年齢	観客	好評価
Lemon Knights	18 ～ 19	10,000	22
Cross Gaps	21 ～ 22	5,000	23
Dark Altar	14 ～ 15	20,000	24
Merry Dice	24 ～ 26	35,000	25

① ダンス
② 歌
③ 舞台演出
④ ダンス，歌
⑤ ダンス，舞台演出
⑥ 歌，舞台演出

正解 ⇒ 　22　 ⑥ 　　23　 ③ 　　24　 ⑥ 　　25　 ①

　まず，第4文で「歌に関しては一番年齢が若いグループと，二番目に若いグループが良かった」と述べられているので，これに該当するのは Dark Altar と Lemon Knights である。第5文では「ダンスに関しては観客を最も動員したチームが革新的だった」と述べられているので，Merry Dice が該当する。第7文では「このチーム（＝ Merry Dice）以外の舞台演出は良かった」と述べられているので，Lemon Knights，Cross Gaps，Dark Altar が舞台演出に関して評価を得ていることが分かる。よって，　22　 には⑥，　23　 には③，　24　 には⑥，　25　 には①が入る。

【語句・表現】
・rank「～に順位をつける」
・in terms of ～「～に関して」
・draw「～を引き寄せる，動員する」
・innovative「革新的な」
・stage direction「舞台演出」

B
問26　 26
【放送内容】

① I recommend Birchland as a travel destination. It is a very large city and the cityscape is beautiful. There are many stores and restaurants where you can enjoy shopping and eating. It takes about 30 minutes by train from here to Birchland.

② Gebston is a great place to travel. It's famous for the Gebston Zoo. The monkey show is popular with children. As agriculture is flourishing, a stew using local products is a specialty. However, you need to drive there because there are no stations nearby.

③   Greenport is the best choice. It is a sightseeing spot with many buildings designated as World Heritage Sites. The stained-glass windows of the cathedral are especially worth seeing. Greenport is a city near the sea, with delicious seafood dishes.

④   How about Juliapolis? It's less than an hour away by train. A popular tourist attraction is the Juliapolis Flower Garden. Parents and children can enjoy a walk together, looking at seasonal flowers. If you get hungry, you should try some traditional sweets of the region.

①   旅行先としてバーチランドをお勧めします。とても大きな街で，街並みも綺麗です。お店やレストランがたくさんあり買い物や食事を楽しむことができます。ここからバーチランドまでは電車で約30分です。

②   ゲブストンは旅行に最適な場所です。ゲブストン動物園で有名です。サルのショーが子供たちに人気です。農業が盛んなので，地元の食材を使ったシチューが名物です。ただし，近くに駅がないので，車で行く必要があります。

③   グリーンポートが最善の選択です。世界遺産に指定されている建物が多くあり，観光スポットになっています。特に大聖堂のステンドグラスの窓は一見の価値あります。グリーンポートは海に近い街で，魚介料理がおいしいです。

④   ジュリアポリスはどうでしょう。ここから電車で1時間以内の距離です。人気の観光スポットはジュリアポリスフラワーガーデンです。季節の花々を眺めながら親子で散歩を楽しむことができます。お腹が空いたらその地方の伝統的なお菓子を食べてみるのもよいでしょう。

正解 ⇒ ④

　4つの候補のうち，「電車で1時間以内に行ける」「その土地ならではの食べ物がある」「子供でも楽しめる施設がある」の条件をすべて満たすのは④である。①は，「お店やレストランがたくさんあり買い物や食事を楽しむことができます」とあるが，レストランで提供されるものがその土地ならではの食べ物であるとは限らず，また子供が買い物を楽しめるかは不明なため，BとCの条件を満たさない。②は，電車で行くことができないため，Aの条件を満たさない。③は，行くための手段や所要時間について触れられておらず，大聖堂などの観光スポットも子供が楽しめるとは述べられていないため，AとCの条件を満たさない。

※表の書き込みイメージ

Places	Condition A	Condition B	Condition C
① Birchland	○	×	×
② Gebston	×	○	○
③ Greenport	×	○	×
④ Juliapolis	○	○	○

【語句・表現】
〈バーチランド〉
・destination「目的地，行き先」
・cityscape「都市の景観」
〈ゲブストン〉
・specialty「名物」

― 340 ―

〈グリーンポート〉
・World Heritage Site「世界遺産」
・cathedral「大聖堂」
〈ジュリアポリス〉
・tourist attraction「観光地」

第5問

【放送内容】

What is resilience? Psychologists say that resilience is the skill to handle stress well. Please note that it doesn't mean you can avoid hard times or stress. Stress can come from problems in the family, health, work, school, money, or everyday challenges. Resilience enables you to recover quickly from difficult events. Here are some ways to strengthen your resilience.

First of all, connecting with others reminds you that you don't have to face your problems alone. Talk to kind people who understand you. Sometimes, people want to be alone after bad experiences. But remember, you are not alone. It is okay to get help and support from people who care about you.

Secondly, making healthy lifestyle choices, such as getting proper nutrition, getting enough sleep, and exercising regularly helps a lot in managing stress. Such basic routines can strengthen your ability to cope with stress and reduce the feeling of worry or sadness. When you exercise, your body makes endorphins. These are the chemicals that reduce stress and make you feel happy. Also, as additional activities, keeping a diary, doing yoga, or meditating to calm down can be effective.

Lastly, your attitude plays an important role in how well you can handle tough situations. If you feel the problem is too big, remind yourself that you are not helpless. Past mistakes do not determine your future. You may not be able to change the stressful event itself, but you can change your reaction to it. Even in difficult times, stay confident.

Building resilience takes time and effort, just like building stronger muscles. However, becoming more resilient is not a special matter. It is a common skill and anyone can learn it. So let's become more resilient!

レジリエンスとは何か？ 心理学者によれば，レジリエンスとはストレスにうまく対処する技術のことである。これは，つらい時やストレスを避けることができるということではないということに注意してほしい。ストレスは，家族，健康，仕事，学校，お金の問題，あるいは日常的な課題から生じることがある。レジリエンスがあれば，つらい出来事からすぐに立ち直ることができる。レジリエンスを強化する方法をいくつか紹介しよう。

第一に，人とつながることで，自分一人で問題に立ち向かわなくてよいということを気づかせてくれる。あなたを理解してくれる親切な人たちと話しなさい。嫌な経験をすると，人は一人になりたくなることがある。しかし，あなたは一人ではないことを忘れてはならない。あなたを心配してくれる人たちから助けやサポートを得ても構わないのである。

次に，適切な栄養を取り，十分な睡眠を取り，定期的に運動するなど，健康的なライフスタイルを選択することはストレス管理に大いに役立つ。このような基本的習慣は，ストレスに対処する能力を強化し，心配や悲しみの感情を軽減する。運動すると，体内でエンドルフィンが作られる。これはスト

レスを軽減し，幸せな気分にさせる化学物質である。また，付加的な活動として，日記をつけたり，ヨガをしたり，瞑想をしたりして気持ちを落ち着かせるのも効果的である。

最後に，厳しい状況にどれだけ上手く対処できるかは，あなたの態度が重要な役割を果たす。問題が大きすぎると感じたら，自分は無力ではないということを思い出しなさい。過去の失敗があなたの未来を決めるわけではない。ストレスになる出来事そのものは変えられないかもしれないが，それに対する反応は変えることができる。困難な時でも，自信を持ち続けなさい。

レジリエンスを高めるには，筋肉を強くするのと同じように時間と努力が必要である。しかし，レジリエンスを高めることは特別なことではない。一般的なスキルであり，誰でも身につけることができる。さあ，もっとレジリエンスを高めよう！

問33

Actually, there is good stress and bad stress. Look at the graph showing the relationship between stress and performance. Good stress is exciting and challenging, and improves performance and the quality of life. On the other hand, bad stress is damaging to performance and health, and can even lead to breakdown.

実のところ，ストレスには良いストレスと悪いストレスが存在する。ストレスとパフォーマンスの関係を示したグラフを見てほしい。良いストレスは刺激的でやりがいを感じさせるものであり，パフォーマンスや生活の質を向上させる。その一方で，悪いストレスはパフォーマンスや健康を損なうものであり，心身を衰弱させる可能性さえある。

【ワークシート】

レジリエンス

○レジリエンスとは何か ──────▶ それは 27 能力である。
○レジリエンスを高める方法

1.	28	
2.	日常生活において健康的なライフスタイル選択をする	
	・基本的な習慣	
	例） 30 ，十分な睡眠をとる，定期的に運動をする	
	・付加的な活動	
	例）日記をつける，ヨガをする， 31	
3.	29	

問27 27

① 問題解決のための新しい手法を採用する
② 職場や学校におけるストレスを回避する
③ さまざまなストレスや困難に対処する
④ 計画を立てそれを効率よく実行する

正解 ⇒ ③

　「レジリエンス」の内容については第1段落で言及されている。第2文で「ストレスにうまく対処する技術」，第5文で「レジリエンスがあれば，つらい出来事からすぐ立ち直ることができる」と述べられているので，正解は③である。②は，第1段落第3文に「つらい時やストレスを避けることができるというわけではない」とあるので不適。

【語句・表現】
〈選択肢〉
・adopt「～を採用する」
・approach「取り組み方，手法」
・carry ～ out「～（計画など）を実行する」
・effectively「効果的に，効率的に」

問28・29 　28　 　29

① 孤独な状態に慣れる
② 他者と関係を築く
③ 自分に自信をもつ
④ 過去を振り返る

　正解 ⇒ ②，③（順不同）

　「レジリエンスを高める方法」については，第2段落～第4段落で説明されている。まず第2段落では，「他人とつながりを持つこと」の大切さについて言及されている。次に第3段落では，「健康的なライフスタイルを選択すること」による効果が述べられている。これは，ワークシートの「レジリエンスを高める方法」の2番目の項目に該当する内容である。続いて第4段落では，「自分に自信をもつこと」の重要性が述べられている。よって，　28　 及び 　29　 には②と③を入れるのが適切である。

【語句・表現】
〈選択肢〉
・become accustomed to ～「～に慣れる」
・confidence「自信」
・look back on ～「～を振り返る，～を回想する」

問30・31 　30　 　31

① 栄養のある食品を食べる
② 毎朝早起きをする
③ リラックスできる音楽を聴く
④ 瞑想をして時間を過ごす

　正解 ⇒ 　30　 ①　 　31　 ④

　30

　第3段落で述べられている「健康的なライフスタイルの選択」のうち「日常における基本的習慣」に関するものが問われている。第1文に「きちんと栄養のあるものをとる，睡眠を十分にとる，定期的に運動をするなど，健康的なライフスタイルを選択すれば…」とあるので，①が正解となる。

[31]

　「健康的なライフスタイルの選択」のうち「付加的な活動」に関するものが問われている。第5文に「日記をつけたり，ヨガをしたり，瞑想したりすることも…」とあるので，④が正解となる。

【語句・表現】
〈選択肢〉
・nutritious「栄養のある」
・meditate「瞑想する」

問32　[32]

> ① ストレスの多い出来事に対する反応の仕方を変えることは，不可能である。
> ② 私たちの体は，不安や憂鬱を感じる時に最もエンドルフィンを放出する。
> ③ 時間と労力を必要とするが，レジリエンスは高めることが可能である。
> ④ レジリエンスを高めるためには，数多くの困難を経験する必要がある。

　正解 ⇒ ③

　第5段落第1文・第2文では，「レジリエンスを高めるには，筋肉を強くするのと同様に時間と労力を要するが，一般的なスキルであり，誰でも身につけることができる」と述べられている。③はこの内容と一致するので，これが正解となる。

【語句・表現】
〈選択肢〉
・respond to ～「～に反応する」
・release「～を放出する」
・anxiety「心配，不安」
・depression「憂鬱，意気消沈」
・resilience「（苦境などからの）回復力」
・enhance「～を高める」
・go through ～「～を経験する」

問33 　33

【グラフ】

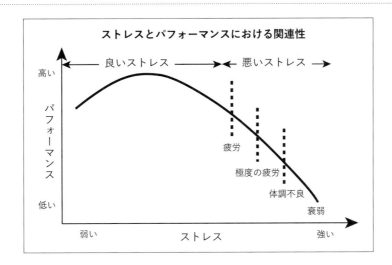

ストレスとパフォーマンスにおける関連性

① ある程度のストレスはより優れたパフォーマンスを発揮するのに役に立つ。
② 悪いストレスはパフォーマンスを向上させるが，健康には良くない。
③ 良いストレスと悪いストレスを区別するのは難しい。
④ レジリエンスが高すぎると良いストレスが減少する。

正解 ⇒ ①

　「講義の続き」では「良いストレス」と「悪いストレス」について言及しており，第3文では「良いストレスは刺激的でやりがいを感じさせるものであり，パフォーマンスや生活の質を向上させる」と述べられている。また，「ストレスとパフォーマンスの関係」を示したグラフを見ると，fatigue「疲労」に至るまでの段階においては，ストレスが増加するにつれてパフォーマンスが向上する部分があることが読み取れる。以上を踏まえると，①が正解であるとわかる。

【語句・表現】
〈選択肢〉
・contribute to ～「～に貢献する，～に寄与する」
・distinguish between A and B「A と B を区別する」
・decline「減少，低下」
〈図〉
・fatigue「疲労，過労」
・exhaustion「極度の疲労」

【語句・表現】
問27～問32
〈第1段落〉
・psychologist「心理学者」
・avoid「～を避ける」
・handle「～を処理する」
・challenge「課題，難題」
・enable O to do「O が～するのを可能にする」

· strengthen「～を強化する」
〈第2段落〉
· face「～に直面する」
〈第3段落〉
· proper「適切な」
· nutrition「栄養」
· endorphin「(通例複数形で) エンドルフィン」
· chemical「(通例複数形で) 化学物質」
· effective「効果的な」
〈第4段落〉
· tough「厳しい」
· determine「～を決める」
問33
· challenging「やりがいのある」
· breakdown「(心身の) 衰弱，(健康状態の) 破綻」

第6問

A
【放送内容】

Lisa: Hiro, you voted for the amusement park, right?

Hiro: Oh, no, Lisa. I chose the baseball game.

Lisa: Really? I thought you were a soccer fan.

Hiro: I like both. I have been to soccer games at a stadium many times, but haven't gone to see a baseball game. So I thought it would be a good opportunity.

Lisa: I understand. I like watching sport games too, but I like playing sports better.

Hiro: So you want to go to the amusement park to enjoy working out. I hear it has a big pool with a thrilling slide!

Lisa: Well, I like physical activity, so I chose the amusement park, but I'm not good at swimming, actually.

Hiro: Then are you going to try rock climbing?

Lisa: That sounds fun. I want to try it. But I'm happy if I can just enjoy the park with friends.

Hiro: There are rides and attractions that you can enjoy in a group. I especially recommend the Dragon Swing!

Lisa: You must have done a lot of research.

Hiro: I want to be as prepared as possible to make better choices.

リサ：ヒロ，あなたはアミューズメントパークに投票したんでしょう？

ヒロ：いや，リサ。僕は野球の試合を選んだよ。

リサ：そうなの？　あなたはサッカーファンだと思ってたのに。

ヒロ：どっちも好きだよ。サッカーの試合はスタジアムで何度も見たことあるけど，野球の試合は見に行ったことがないんだ。それで良い機会だと思ってね。

リサ：なるほどね。私もスポーツを見るのは好きだけど，スポーツをする方が好きかな。

ヒロ：じゃあアミューズメントパークに行って体を動かしたいってことかな。スリリングな滑り台付きの大きなプールがあるって聞いたよ。

リサ：ええと，私は体を動かすことが好きだから，アミューズメントパークを選んだけど，実は泳ぐのは得意じゃないの。

ヒロ：じゃあロッククライミングをやってみるとか。
リサ：それは面白そう。やってみたいな。でも友達と一緒にパークを楽しめればそれで満足。
ヒロ：みんなで楽しめる乗り物やアトラクションがあるよ。ドラゴン・スイングは特におすすめだね！
リサ：ずいぶんよく調べたのね。
ヒロ：良い選択のためにはできるだけ準備しないとね。

問34 ⬚34⬚
「なぜヒロは野球の試合を見に行くことを選んだか」

① アミューズメントパークにはあまり興味がないから。
② 自分でスポーツをするよりスポーツを見る方が好きだから。
③ サッカーの試合が見たかったが野球の試合しか選べなかったから。
④ 野球の試合を見に行くのは初めてだから。

正解 ⇒ ④

ヒロは2回目の発言で，野球の試合を選んだ理由として，野球の試合を見に行ったことはないので良い機会だと思った，と説明している。

問35 ⬚35⬚
「なぜリサはアミューズメントパークに行くことを選んだか」

① ロッククライミングを楽しめるから。
② 体を動かすのが好きだから。
③ 大きなプールで泳ぎたいから。
④ 野球の試合を見るのに興味が無いから。

正解 ⇒ ②

リサの4回目の発言で，体を動かすことが好きだから，アミューズメントパークを選んだとあるので②が正解。①のロッククライミングは，ヒロに聞くまで知らなかったのでアミューズメントパークを選んだ理由ではないと考えられる。③のプールについては泳ぐのが苦手と答えており，④については言及されていない。

【語句・表現】
・opportunity「機会」
・work out「体を動かす」

B
【放送内容】

Yui: Phew! I finally finished it.
Oliver: Oh, are you done already, Yui? I still need some time ... How about you, Jacob?
Jacob: Not likely to finish for a while, Oliver. Our math teacher gives us too much homework!
Yui: Yeah. I don't think homework is necessary. It merely imposes a large amount of meaningless work on students. Do you think so too, Oliver?
Oliver: Well ... I don't like homework, of course, but I can understand its importance. If I didn't have

any homework, I wouldn't study at home at all, and my grades would be disastrous. I haven't developed the habit of studying of my own will.

Jacob:　I know what you mean, Oliver, but I agree with Yui. Most of us do our homework just because we don't want to be scolded by our teachers. I don't think it will help us retain what we have learned.

Yui:　Carol, you are a bright student. So, homework is not a big deal for you, is it?

Carol:　Hmm ... I don't think I'm bright. But anyway, I'm skeptical about the need for homework.

Oliver:　Really? It's surprising you say that!

Carol:　Well, studying is not something we are forced to do. It's something we should do voluntarily. It's not right to let someone other than yourself decide what you study and how much you study. Don't you think so?

Yui:　Phew! You're on a different level, Carol! Amazing!

ユイ　　　：やれやれ！　ようやく終わった。

オリバー：あれ，もう終わったの，ユイ？　僕はまだ時間がかかりそうだ…ジェイコブは？

ジェイコブ：しばらく終わりそうにないよ，オリバー。数学の先生は宿題を出しすぎだ！

ユイ　　　：そうだよね。私，宿題は必要ないと思うんだ。生徒に意味のない課題をたくさん押しつけるだけだもの。オリバーもそう思うでしょう？

オリバー：うーん…宿題はもちろん好きじゃないけど，大切だってことは理解できるんだ。もし宿題がなかったら，僕は家でまったく勉強しないだろうし，成績は悲惨なことになると思う。自主的に勉強する習慣がついていないからさ。

ジェイコブ：オリバー，君の言いたいことはわかる。でも，僕はユイの意見に賛成だな。僕たちのほとんどは，先生に叱られたくないから宿題をやるだけだよね。学んだ内容を覚えておくのに，それが役に立つとは思えないな。

ユイ　　　：キャロル，あなたは優秀だから，宿題なんて大したことじゃないでしょう？

キャロル：うーん…私は自分が優秀だとは思っていないけど。それはともかく，宿題が必要かどうかは疑わしいと思っているよ。

オリバー：本当に？　君がそんなことを言うなんて意外だ！

キャロル：だって，勉強は強制されてやるものではなくて，自発的に取り組むべきものでしょう。何を勉強するか，どのくらい勉強するかを，自分以外の人に決めてもらうのはいやだよ。そう思わない？

ユイ　　　：やれやれ！　キャロルはレベルが違うね！　さすがだよ！

問36　　[36]

① キャロル
② オリバー
③ キャロル，ジェイコブ
④ オリバー，ユイ

正解 ⇒ ②

　ユイは２回目の発言で「宿題は必要ないと思う」と述べている。また，ジェイコブは２回目の発言で「僕はユイの意見に賛成だ」と言っている。さらに，キャロルは１回目の発言で「宿題が必要かどうかは疑わしいと思っている」と述べている。よって，ユイ，ジェイコブ，キャロルは宿題の必要性について否定的な立場である。

　これに対して，オリバーは２回目の発言で「宿題はもちろん好きじゃないけど，大切だってことは理解

できる」と言い，続けてそのように考える理由を説明している。

　以上より，宿題の必要性について肯定的な意見を述べているのはオリバーのみであるから，正解は②となる。

問37　　37
【グラフ】

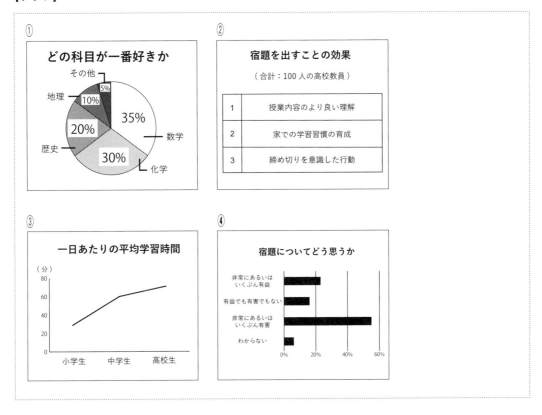

正解 ⇒ ④

　ユイは2回目の発言で，「（宿題は）生徒に意味のない課題をたくさん押しつけるだけだ」と述べている。④のグラフは，宿題について「非常にあるいはいくぶん有害である」と考えている人が多いことを示しており，ユイの発言内容に一致すると言える。よって，これが正解となる。

【語句・表現】
・be done「終わっている」
・for a while「しばらくの間」
・merely「単に」
・impose A on B「A を B に課す」
・meaningless「無意味な」
・disastrous「悲惨な，ひどい」
・of one's own will「自分の意志で」
・scold「～を叱る，～を怒る」
・retain「～を保持する，～を覚えておく」
・bright「頭の良い」
・big deal「大したこと」

・force O to *do*「O に～することを強いる」
・voluntarily「自発的に，自ら進んで」
・other than ～「～以外」
〈選択肢〉
・deadline「締切」
・somewhat「やや，いくぶん」
・harmful「有害な」

問 題番 号（配点）	設 問	解 答番 号	正 解	配 点	自 己採 点
第C問（15）	27	27	2	3	
	28	28	1	2*	
	29	29	2		
	30	30	5	2*	
	31	31	4		
	32	32	3	4	
	33	33	1	4	
自己採点小計					

自己採点合計

（注）
*は全部正解の場合のみ点を与える。

第 C 問

What is happiness? Can we be happy and promote sustainable development? Since 2012, the *World Happiness Report* has been issued by a United Nations organization to develop new approaches to economic sustainability for the sake of happiness and well-being. The reports show that Scandinavian countries are consistently ranked as the happiest societies on earth. But what makes them so happy? In Denmark, for example, leisure time is often spent with others. That kind of environment makes Danish people happy thanks to a tradition called "hygge," spelled H-Y-G-G-E. Hygge means coziness or comfort and describes the feeling of being loved.

This word became well-known worldwide in 2016 as an interpretation of mindfulness or wellness. Now, hygge is at risk of being commercialized. But hygge is not about the material things we see in popular images like candlelit rooms and cozy bedrooms with hand-knit blankets. Real hygge happens anywhere — in public or in private, indoors or outdoors, with or without candles. The main point of hygge is to live a life connected with loved ones while making ordinary essential tasks meaningful and joyful.

Perhaps Danish people are better at appreciating the small, "hygge" things in life because they have no worries about basic necessities. Danish people willingly pay from 30 to 50 percent of their income in tax. These high taxes pay for a good welfare system that provides free healthcare and education. Once basic needs are met, more money doesn't guarantee more happiness. While money and material goods seem to be highly valued in some countries like the US, people in Denmark place more value on socializing. Nevertheless, Denmark has above-average productivity according to the OECD.

幸せとは何でしょうか。私達は幸せになり，持続可能な発展を進めていくことができるのでしょうか。2012年から国連機関が「世界幸福度報告書」を発行し，幸福と健康のため，経済の持続可能性に向けた新たな取り組みを展開しています。報告書によると，北欧諸国は常に地球上で最も幸福な社会として評価されています。しかし，なぜ彼らはそれほどまでに幸せなのでしょうか。例えばデンマークでは，余暇を他人と一緒に過ごすことが多いです。このような環境があるためにデンマーク人は幸せを感じられるのですが，それは H-Y-G-G-E と綴られる「ヒュッゲ」と呼ばれる伝統のおかげです。ヒュッゲは，居心地の良さや快適さを意味し，愛されているという感覚を表します。

この言葉は2016年にマインドフルネス（自分の意識に注意深くなること）やウェルネス（健康）の解釈として世界的に知られるようになりました。現在，ヒュッゲは商業化の危険にさらされています。しかしヒュッゲとは，キャンドルの灯る部屋や，手編みのブランケットを敷いた居心地の良いベッドルームのような一般的なイメージに見られる物質的なものではありません。本当のヒュッゲは，公共の場でもプライベートでも，室内でも屋外でも，キャンドルの有無に関わらず，どこでも起こります。ヒュッゲの要点は，愛する人たちとのつながりにおいて，普段の生活に必要な仕事を有意義で楽しいものにしていくことです。

デンマーク人は，生活必需品についての心配がないため，生活の中のささやかな「ヒュッゲ」な物事を察する力が優れているのかもしれません。デンマーク人は，所得の30％から50％の税金を快く支払っています。これらの高い税金は，無償の医療と教育を提供する充実した福祉制度のために使われています。ひとたび基本的ニーズが満たされてしまえば，より多くのお金を持つことはより大きな幸せの保証にはなりません。アメリカのようないくつかの国々では，お金や物に大きな価値があるとみなされているようですが，デンマークの人々は社交性により重きを置いています。それにもかかわら

ず，OECDによればデンマークは平均以上の生産性を誇っているのです。

問32
Student A：Danish people accept high taxes which provide basic needs.
Student B：Danish people value spending time with friends more than pursuing money.

生徒A：デンマークの人々は基本的ニーズを得るための高い税金を受け入れている。
生徒B：デンマーク人はお金を追い求めるよりも，友達と過ごす時間に重きを置いている。

問33
　Joe： Look at this graph, May. People in Denmark value private life over work. How can they be so productive?
　May： Well, based on my research, studies show that working too much overtime leads to lower productivity.
　Joe： So, working too long isn't efficient. That's interesting.

　Joe： このグラフを見て，メイ。デンマークの人々は仕事よりもプライベートを大切にしているね。どうしてこんなに生産性が高いんだろう？
　May： そうね，私の調査によると，残業のしすぎは生産性の低下につながるらしいよ。
　Joe： つまり，長く働きすぎるのは効率的ではないということか。興味深いね。

【ワークシート】

○世界幸福度報告書
・目的：幸福と健康〔　27　〕を推進すること
・北欧諸国：一貫して世界で最も幸せな国々とされている（2012年以来）
なぜか　⇒　「ヒュッゲ」デンマークの生活様式
　　　　　　⇓ 2016年に世界へ広まった
○ヒュッゲの解釈

	ヒュッゲの一般的なイメージ	デンマークの本来のヒュッゲ
何を	28	29
どこで	30	31
どのように	特別な	普段の

問27　　27

①　〜を超えた持続可能な発展目標
②　**〜を支える持続可能な経済**
③　〜のための持続可能な自然環境
④　〜に挑む持続可能な社会

正解 ⇒ ②

「世界幸福度報告書」の目的は，第1段落第2文に「幸福と健康のため，経済の持続可能性に向けた新たな取り組みを展開していく」ことであると述べられている。よって，②が正解。

問28～31 | 28 |～| 31 |

①	物	②	関係性	③	課題
④	どこでも	⑤	室内で	⑥	屋外で

正解 ⇒ | 28 | ① | 29 | ② | 30 | ⑤ | 31 | ④

　表の「一般的なヒュッゲのイメージ」については，第2段落第3文に「ヒュッゲとは，キャンドルの灯る部屋や，手編みのブランケットを敷いた居心地の良いベッドルームのような一般的なイメージに見られる物質的なものではありません」とある。室内を快適にする物質的なものといったイメージを抱きがちということなので，| 28 |は①，| 30 |は⑤である。これに対しデンマークにおける本来のヒュッゲは，第4・5文に「どこでも起こります」「ヒュッゲの要点は，愛する人たちとのつながりにおいて，普段の生活に必要な仕事を有意義で楽しいものにしていくことです」とあることから，| 29 |は②の「関係性」，| 31 |は④の「どこでも」となる。

問32 | 32 |

①	Aの発言のみ一致する
②	Bの発言のみ一致する
③	どちらの発言も一致する
④	どちらの発言も一致しない

正解 ⇒ ③

　Aの「デンマークの人々は基本的ニーズを得るための高い税金を受け入れている」という発言は，第3段落2文目の「デンマーク人が，所得の30％から50％の税金を快く支払っています」という記述に当てはまる。Bの「デンマーク人はお金を追い求めるよりも，友達と過ごす時間に重きを置いている」という発言は，最後から2文目「アメリカのようないくつかの国々では，お金や物に大きな価値があるとみなされているようですが，デンマークの人々は社交性により重きを置いています」に当てはまる。よって，どちらの発言も講義内容に一致するので，正解は③である。

問33 | 33 |

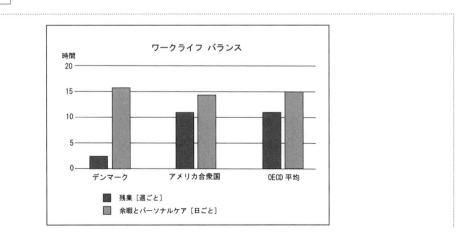

①　デンマークの人々は生産性を維持しつつも，あまり残業をしていない。
②　デンマークの人々は収入が保証されていてもなお，さらに働くことを楽しんでいる。
③　OECD 諸国の人々は比較的残業が多いので，より生産性が高い。
④　アメリカの人々はお金のかかる生活を送っているが，余暇の時間は最も多い。

正解 ⇒ ①

　本文とグラフに一致しているのは①である。グラフの中で，デンマークは「残業」の時間が最も少ない。また本文の最終文で「OECD によると平均以上の生産性を誇っている」と述べられている。②や③のようなことは述べられていない。④は，アメリカ人の「余暇とパーソナルケア」に当てる時間がデンマークや OECD 平均よりも少ないことから，不適切である。

【語句・表現】
問27〜31
〈第1段落〉
・promote「〜を促進する」
・sustainable「持続可能な」
・issue「発行する，発刊する」
・United Nations organization「国際連合機関」
・for the sake of 〜「〜のために」
・well-being「安寧，幸福，健康」
・Scandinavian「スカンジナビアの，北欧の」
・consistently「一貫して」
・leisure「余暇」
・environment「環境」
・coziness（＞ cozy）「快適さ，居心地の良さ」
・comfort「快適さ，心地よさ」
〈第2段落〉
・well-known「よく知られた」
・worldwide「世界中に」
・interpretation「解釈」
・mindfulness「注意深さ」：ここでは，「マインドフルネス」として知られている，今この瞬間の体験に
　意識を向ける心理的な過程のこと。
・wellness「健康」
・commercialize「〜を商品化する」
・candlelit「ろうそくに照らされた」
・hand-knit「手編みの」
・blanket「毛布，ブランケット」
・ordinary「普通の，通常の」
・essential「必要不可欠な」
・meaningful「意味のある，有意義な」
・joyful「楽しい」
〈第3段落〉
・appreciate「〜の良さを正しく理解する」
・necessity「必要性，必要なこと」
・willingly「いとわず，快く」
・income「収入」
・tax「税金」

・welfare「福祉」

・guarantee「～を保証する」

・socialize「打ち解けて交際する，社会活動に参加する」

・nevertheless「それにもかかわらず」

・productivity「生産性」

・OECD「経済協力開発機構」：Organization for Economic Cooperation and Development の略。

問32

・pursue「～を追い求める」

問33

・productive「生産的な」

・be based on ～「～に基づいている」

・efficient「効率が良い」

・overtime work「残業」

解 答 と 解 説

問題番号 （配点）	設	問	解答番号	正 解	配 点	自己採点
第1問 (25)	A	1	1	3	4	
		2	2	3	4	
		3	3	4	4	
		4	4	1	4	
	B	5	5	2	3	
		6	6	3	3	
		7	7	4	3	
自己採点小計						
第2問 (16)		8	8	2	4	
		9	9	4	4	
		10	10	1	4	
		11	11	4	4	
自己採点小計						
第3問 (18)		12	12	2	3	
		13	13	2	3	
		14	14	2	3	
		15	15	4	3	
		16	16	3	3	
		17	17	1	3	
自己採点小計						

問題番号 （配点）	設	問	解答番号	正 解	配 点	自己採点
第4問 (12)	A	18	18	2	4*	
		19	19	1		
		20	20	4		
		21	21	3		
		22	22	5	1	
		23	23	6	1	
		24	24	4	1	
		25	25	2	1	
	B	26	26	1	4	
自己採点小計						
第5問 (15)		27	27	4	3	
		28	28	3	2*	
		29	29	6		
		30	30	1	2*	
		31	31	4		
		32	32	1	4	
		33	33	4	4	
自己採点小計						
第6問 (14)	A	34	34	2	3	
		35	35	4	3	
	B	36	36	1	4	
		37	37	2	4	
自己採点小計						

（注）

*は，全部正解の場合のみ点を与える。

自己採点合計 □

リスニング・共通テスト本試験

第1問

A
問1 　1
【放送内容と選択肢】

> **I have my notebook, but I forgot my pencil. Can I borrow yours?**
>
> ① 話者は鉛筆を持ってきた。
> ② 話者はノートを忘れた。
> ❸ 話者は鉛筆が必要である。
> ④ 話者はノートが欲しい。

　　正解 ⇒ ③

　　放送された英文は,「ノートは持ってるけど, 鉛筆を忘れちゃった。あなたのを貸してくれる？」という意味。話者はノートを持っていて鉛筆を持っていないという状況なので, ③が正解。

問2 　2
【放送内容と選択肢】

> **You bought me lunch yesterday, Ken. So, shall I buy our movie tickets tonight?**
>
> ① ケンは彼らの昼食をおごると言っている。
> ② ケンはすでにチケット代を支払った。
> ❸ 話者はチケットを買うと申し出ている。
> ④ 話者は昨日彼らの昼食代を支払った。

　　正解 ⇒ ③

　　放送された英文は,「昨日お昼をおごってくれたよね, ケン。だから, 今夜の映画のチケットは私が買おうか？」という意味である。この英文に当てはまるのは③である。

【語句・表現】
・Shall I 〜？「私が〜しましょうか」
〈選択肢〉
・offer to *do*「〜してもよいと申し出る」

問3 　3
【放送内容と選択肢】

> **Do you know how to get to the new city hall? I've only been to the old one.**
>
> ① 話者は旧市役所がどこにあるか知らない。
> ② 話者は新市役所に一度だけ行ったことがある。
> ③ 話者は旧市役所に行ったことがない。
> ❹ 話者は新市役所に行く道を知りたがっている。

正解 ⇒ ④

　放送された英文は,「新市役所への行き方を知ってる？ 私は旧市役所にしか行ったことがないの」という意味である。話者は新市役所に行く道を尋ねているので,正解は④である。他の選択肢は第2文に矛盾するため,誤り。

【語句・表現】
・how to *do*「～のやり方」
・get to ～「～に行く,着く」
・city hall「市役所,市庁舎」
・have been to ～「～に行ったことがある」

問4　　4
【放送内容と選択肢】

> **This pasta I made isn't enough for five people. So, I'll make sandwiches and salad, too.**
>
> ①　話者は十分な量の料理を作らなかった。
> ②　話者は十分な量のサンドイッチを作った。
> ③　話者はもっとパスタを出すつもりである。
> ④　話者は追加の料理を作るつもりはない。

正解 ⇒ ①

　放送された英文は,「私が作ったパスタは5人分には足りない。だから,サンドイッチとサラダも作るよ」という意味。この内容に一致するのは①である。第2文から,サンドイッチはこの発言の後に追加で作られることがわかるので,②～④は不適切である。

【語句・表現】
・enough「十分な」
〈選択肢〉
・prepare「～を用意する,調理する」

B
問5　　5
【放送内容】

> **The season's changing. See, the leaves are falling.**

正解 ⇒ ②

　放送された英文は,「季節の変わり目だね。ほら,木の葉が散っているよ」という意味である。leaves are falling と現在進行形であるため,木の葉が落ちている最中である様子を表した②が正解。葉が全て散った状態の③は不適切である。

【語句・表現】
・leaves：leaf「葉」の複数形
・fall「落ちる」

問6　6

【放送内容】

> **Our dog always sleeps by my brother while he plays video games. It's so cute.**

正解 ⇒ ③

　放送された英文は，「うちの犬は弟がビデオゲームをしている間，いつもそばで寝ているんだ。とてもかわいいんだよ」という意味である。選択肢の中でこの発言に合うのは③のイラストである。

【語句・表現】
・while「～の間」

問7　7

【放送内容】

> **The white fan is the slimmest, but the black one is the cheapest. Hmm.... Which to choose?**

正解 ⇒ ④

　放送された英文は，「白い扇風機が一番スリムだけど，黒い扇風機が一番安いね。うーん，どっちにしよう？」という意味である。この特徴に当てはまるのは，白い扇風機の持ち手が細く，黒い扇風機が最安値の④である。

【語句・表現】
・fan「扇風機，ファン」
・slimmest：slim「ほっそりとした，スリムな」の最上級。
・which to *do*「どちら［どれ］を～すべきか」

第2問

問8　8

【放送内容】

> W: So, what does your cat look like?
> M: He's gray with black stripes.
> W: Could you describe him in more detail?
> M: He has a long tail. Oh, and its tip is white.
> **Question:**
> Which is the man's cat?
>
> W：それで，あなたの猫はどんな見た目ですか。
> M：彼はグレーで黒い縞模様があります。
> W：もう少し詳しく彼のことを教えてくれますか。
> M：尻尾が長いんです。あ，それと尻尾の先は白いです。
> 問い：

男性の猫はどれか。

正解 ⇒ ②

　男性の発言より，猫はグレーで黒の縞模様があり，尻尾は長く先が白いことがわかる。これに当てはまる②が正解。

【語句・表現】
・stripe「縞，ストライプ」
・describe「～を描写する，説明する」
・in detail「詳細に」
・tip「先，先端」

問9 　9

【放送内容】

M: The girl holding the book looks like you.
W: Actually, that's my best friend. I'm in the front.
M: Ah, you're the one with the hat!
W: That's right!
Question:
Which girl in the photo is the woman?

M：本を持っている女の子はあなたに似ているね。
W：実は，それは私の親友なんだ。私は前にいるよ。
M：ああ，あなたは帽子をかぶってる人だね！
W：その通り！
問い：
写真の中の少女のうち，女性はどれか。

正解 ⇒ ④

　男女の1回目の発話より，女性は後ろで本を持っている少女ではなく，前の列にいることがわかる。さらに会話の後半で，女性は帽子をかぶっていることがわかるので，④の少女が正解。

【語句・表現】
・hold「～を持っている」
・front「前部，前方」

問10 　10

【放送内容】

W: Can you look on my desk for a white envelope?
M: Is it the large one?
W: No, it's smaller. Can you check under the computer?
M: Yes, here it is.
Question:
Which envelope does the woman want?

W：机の上に白い封筒がないか探してくれる？
M：それは大きいやつ？
W：ううん，小さいほうだよ。パソコンの下を確認してくれる？
M：うん，ここにあるよ。
問い：
女性が必要としている封筒はどれか。

正解 ⇒ ①

　女性の1回目の発言より，女性は白い封筒が必要であること，2回目の発言より，それは小さいサイズのものでパソコンの下にあることがわかる。よって，①が正解。

【語句・表現】
・envelope「封筒」

問11 　11
【放送内容】

W: Can I reserve a private room for six people tonight?
M: Sorry, it's already booked.　But we do have two tables available in the main dining room.
W: Do you have a window table?
M: We sure do.
Question:
Which table will the woman probably reserve?

W：今夜，6人用の個室を予約できますか。
M：申し訳ありませんが，もう予約が入っています。でも，メインダイニングに2卓空きがありますよ。
W：窓際のテーブルはありますか。
M：ございます。
問い：
女性はどのテーブルを予約する可能性が高いか。

正解 ⇒ ④

　男性の1回目の発言より，6人用の個室は予約済みのため③は候補から外れ，またメインダイニングに2卓空きがあるというので，②か④に絞られる。会話の後半から，窓際のテーブルが利用できるということなので，④が正解。

【語句・表現】
・reserve「～を予約する」
・book「～を予約する」
・private room「個室」
・available「利用可能な」

第3問

問12 ☐12
【放送内容と選択肢】

M: I'll have a large cup of hot tea.
W: Certainly. That'll be ¥400, but you can get a ¥30 discount if you have your own cup.
M: Really? I didn't know that! I don't have one today, but I'll bring one next time.
W: OK, great. Anything else?
M: No, thank you.

M：ホットティーのラージを一つください。
W：かしこまりました。400円になりますが，マイカップをお持ちでしたら30円引きになりますよ。
M：そうなんですか？ それは知りませんでした！ 今日は持ってないけど，次回は持ってきます。
W：わかりました，それがいいですね。他にご注文はありますか。
M：いえ，結構です。

男性は今回どうするか。

① 値引きを求める
② 全額を支払う
③ 新しいカップを買う
④ 自分のカップを使う

正解 ⇒ ②

女性の1回目の発言によると，男性がマイカップを持参していれば30円引きになる。しかし男性の2回目の発言により，男性はマイカップを持参してないことがわかる。さらに会話の最後「他にご注文はありますか」「いえ，結構です」より，男性はホットティーのみを定価で購入したということである。よって，②が正解。

【語句・表現】
・discount「割引，値引き」

問13 ☐13
【放送内容と選択肢】

M: I'm thinking about buying a piano. I've really been enjoying my piano lessons.
W: That's great!
M: But I don't want to disturb my neighbors when I practice at home.
W: How about getting an electronic keyboard? You can control the volume of the music or even use headphones.
M: That's a good idea! I'll get that instead!

M：ピアノを買おうと思っているんだ。ピアノのレッスンがとても楽しいからね。
W：それはいいね！
M：でも，家で練習するときに近所迷惑にならないようにしたいんだ。
W：電子キーボードを買うのはどう？ 演奏の音量を調節できるし，ヘッドフォンも使えるよ。

M：それはいい考えだね！代わりにそれを買うよ！

男性はどうするか。

① ピアノを習い始める
② 電子キーボードを買う
③ ピアノをもう1台買うことを検討する
④ キーボード用にヘッドフォンを取り替える

正解 ⇒ ②

　ピアノを買いたいが近所迷惑になりたくないという男性に対して，女性は2回目の発言で代わりに電子キーボードを買うことを提案し，男性もそれに賛同している。よって，正解は②である。

【語句・表現】
・disturb「～に迷惑をかける，～を困らせる」
・neighbor「近所の人，隣人」
・electronic「電気の，電動の」
・even「～だって，～さえ」
・instead「代わりに」

問14　[14]
【放送内容と選択肢】

W: I'd like to buy a jacket this afternoon.
M: Have you ever been to a second-hand shop?
W: No ...
M: I went to one last week. You have to look around, but you can find some good bargains.
W: That sounds like an adventure! Can you take me now?
M: Sure, let's go!

W：今日の午後にジャケットを買いたいな。
M：古着屋に行ったことはある？
W：ない…
M：僕は先週行ったよ。見て回らないといけないけど，良い掘り出し物が見つかるよ。
W：それは冒険みたいだね！今から連れて行ってくれる？
M：うん，行こう！

女性はどうするか。

① 彼女のお気に入りの店でジャケットを買う
② 今日，古着屋に行く
③ 来週，古着を買いに行く
④ 友人をバーゲンセールに連れて行く

正解 ⇒ ②

　ジャケットを買いたいという女性に，男性は古着屋に行くことを勧めている。女性は，3回目の発言で

「今から連れて行ってくれる？」と言っており，男性もそれに賛成していることから，このあと古着屋に行くと考えられる。よって，②が正解。

【語句・表現】
・second-hand「中古の」
・bargain「掘り出し物，値引き品」
〈選択肢〉
・favorite「最も好きな，最も気に入りの」
・used-clothing「古着の」

問15 ［ 15 ］
【放送内容と選択肢】

W: The moving company is coming soon.
M: I thought that was later this afternoon.
W: No, they'll be here in an hour. I'm putting everything here in the living room into boxes. Can you help me?
M: OK, I'll just finish packing up the bedroom first.
W: All right, I'll keep working in here then.

W：引越し屋さんがもうすぐ来るよ。
M：今日の午後に来るのかと思ってた。
W：いや，1時間後には来るよ。今リビングにあるものを全部箱に詰めているの。手伝ってくれる？
M：いいよ，先に寝室の荷造りを済ませるね。
W：わかった，じゃあ私はここで作業を続けているね。

女性は今何をしているか。

① 寝室で準備をしている
② 男性が寝室での作業を終えるのを手伝っている
③ すべての物をリビングルームに運んでいる
④ リビングルームにある物をすべて梱包している

正解 ⇒ ④

女性の2回目の発言「今リビングにあるものを全部箱に詰めているの」と，最後の発言「じゃあ私はここで作業を続けているね」から，女性はリビングルームで梱包作業をしていることがわかる。よって，④が正解。

【語句・表現】
・moving company「引っ越し業者」
・pack O up「～を荷造りする，梱包する」

問16 ［ 16 ］
【放送内容と選択肢】

M: What will you do tomorrow?
W: I'll visit my grandfather's horse farm. I'll go riding and then take a hike. Would you like to come?

M: Sure, but I'll just take photos of you riding. I'm afraid of horses.
W: Well, OK. After that, we can go hiking together.
M: That sounds nice!

M：明日は何をするの？
W：祖父の馬牧場に行くの。乗馬して，ハイキングもするよ。あなたも来る？
M：うん，でも君が乗馬しているところを写真に撮るだけにするよ。馬が怖いんだ。
W：そう，わかった。その後，一緒にハイキングに行けるよ。
M：それはいいね！

男性は明日何をするか。

① 牧場の馬に乗れるようにする
② 友達と馬に乗る
③ **友達の写真を撮る**
④ 彼の祖父の農場を訪れる

正解 ⇒ ③

　男性は，女性と馬牧場に行くことにしたが，2回目の発言で「君が乗馬しているところを写真に撮るだけにするよ。馬が怖いんだ」と述べている。よって，正解は③である。男性は馬に乗る予定はないので，①と②は不適。女性の1回目の発言より，女性の祖父の馬牧場に行くという話なので，④も誤り。

【語句・表現】
・farm「農場」
・take a hike「ハイキングをする」
・be afraid of ～「～が怖い」

問17　　17
【放送内容と選択肢】

W: Did you finish your homework?
M: Yes. It took so long.
W: Why? We just had to read two pages from the textbook.
M: What? I thought the assignment was to write a report on our experiments.
W: No, we were only told to read those pages for homework.
M: Oh, I didn't do that.

W：宿題は終わった？
M：うん。すごく時間がかかったよ。
W：どうして？ 教科書を2ページ読めばいいだけなのに。
M：えっ？ 課題は実験のレポートを書くことだと思ってた。
W：いや，宿題として該当のページを読むように言われただけだよ。
M：あ，それはやってない。

男性が行ったことは何か。

① 彼は科学のレポートを書き終えた。

② 彼は科学のレポートを書くのを先延ばしにした。
③ 彼は教科書を2ページ読んだ。
④ 彼は長時間かけて教科書を読んだ。

正解 ⇒ ①

　男性は宿題として実験のレポートを書いたと述べているが，女性の指摘により，実は宿題は教科書を2ページ読むことであり，男性は勘違いしていたことがわかる。また会話の最後で，男性は教科書の該当ページを読む宿題は「やっていない」と述べている。よって，正解は①である。

【語句・表現】
・assignment「課題」
・experiment「実験」
〈選択肢〉
・put off ～「～を延期する，先延ばしにする」
・spent O（時間）*doing*「（時間）を～するのに使う」

第4問

A
問18〜21　| 18 | | 19 | | 20 | | 21 |
【放送内容と選択肢】

　　We went to Midori Mountain Amusement Park yesterday. To start off, we purchased some limited-edition souvenirs and put them into lockers. Then we dashed to the recently reopened roller coaster, but the line was too long so we decided to eat lunch instead. After lunch, we saw a parade marching by, and we enjoyed watching that. Finally, we rode the roller coaster before we left the park.

　　昨日，私たちは緑山遊園地に行きました。はじめに，限定版のお土産を買ってロッカーに入れました。その後，私たちは最近再開したジェットコースターへと急行しましたが，列があまりに長かったので，代わりに昼食を食べることにしました。昼食後，パレードが行進しているのが見えたので，私たちはそれを見て楽しみました。最後に，ジェットコースターに乗ってから遊園地を後にしました。

正解 ⇒　| 18 | ② |　| 19 | ① |　| 20 | ④ |　| 21 | ③ |

　第2文「はじめに，限定版のお土産を買ってロッカーに入れた」より，②が最初である。第3文より，ジェットコースターに乗る代わりに昼食にしたとあるので，次は①である。第4文に昼食後はパレードを楽しんだとあるので，④が3番目。最終文より，最後にジェットコースターに乗ったとあるので，最後が③となる。

【語句・表現】
・amusement park「遊園地」
・purchase「～を購入する」
・limited-edition「限定版の，限定販売品の」
・souvenir「お土産」
・dash「急行する，突進する」
・reopen「～を再開する」
・roller coaster「ジェットコースター」

· line「列」
· saw O *doing*「O が〜しているのを見る」

問22〜25　| 22 |　| 23 |　| 24 |　| 25 |

【放送内容】

Here's your schedule for this year's summer classes. Monday and Thursday will begin with Social Welfare classes. Immediately after the Monday Social Welfare class, you'll have Math class. On Tuesday and Friday, you'll hear lectures about ancient Egypt and the Roman Empire during first period. These lectures will be followed by Business Studies on both days. On Wednesday, you'll have Biology first period, and second period will be Environmental Studies. Finally, after Social Welfare on Thursday, you'll have your French or Spanish class.

　これがあなたの今年の夏季講座のスケジュールです。月曜日と木曜日は社会福祉の授業から始まります。月曜日の社会福祉の授業のすぐ後に，数学の授業があります。火曜日と金曜日は，1限目に古代エジプトとローマ帝国についての講義を聞きます。これらの講義の後，両日とも経営学があります。水曜日は，1限目は生物学，2限目は環境学です。最後に，木曜日は社会福祉の後，フランス語またはスペイン語の授業があります。

【表】　　　　　　　　　　　　　夏季講座のスケジュール

	月曜日	火曜日	水曜日	木曜日	金曜日
1限目	社会福祉	23	生物学	社会福祉	世界史
2限目	22	経営学	環境学	24	25

① 生物学	② 経営学	③ 環境学
④ 語学	⑤ 数学	⑥ 世界史

正解 ⇒　| 22 | ⑤　| 23 | ⑥　| 24 | ④　| 25 | ②

　第3文に，「月曜日の社会福祉の授業の直後に，数学の授業があります」とあるので，| 22 | には⑤が入る。第4文「火曜日と金曜日は，1限目に古代エジプトとローマ帝国についての講義を聞きます」より，| 23 | は金曜日の1限目と同じ⑥の世界史である。「これらの講義の後，両日とも経営学があります」と説明が続くので，| 25 | は②の経営学が入る。最終文に「木曜日は社会福祉の後，フランス語またはスペイン語の授業があります」とあるので，| 24 | には「フランス語またはスペイン語の授業」を言い換えた④の語学が当てはまる。

【語句・表現】
· immediately「直ちに，早速，すぐに」
· ancient「古代の」
· empire「帝国」
· period「期間，（学校の）時限」
· follow「〜の次にくる」

B
問26 ☐ 26
【放送内容】

① It would be fun to have a bowling game as our group's activity. Everybody loves bowling, and we can prepare the game using free recycled materials! We'll only need 8 people working at one time, and games can finish within 15 minutes!

② How about doing a face painting activity this year? I think we can finish painting each person's face in about 30 minutes, and the theater club already has face paint we can use. It will take all 20 of us to run the whole event.

③ Let's have a fashion show for our activity! We can do it for free by using our own clothes to create matching looks for couples. Visitors can be the models and 12 of us will work during the show. The show will be less than 20 minutes.

④ I think having visitors experience a tea ceremony would be fun. Each ceremony will take about 10 to 15 minutes and we only need 7 people to work each shift. We will just need to buy the tea and Japanese sweets.

① 私たちのグループの出し物として，ボウリングゲームを開催したら楽しいと思う。みんなボウリングが大好きだし，無料のリサイクル資材を使ってゲームを準備できる！ 一回につき働く人は8人しか必要ないし，15分以内にゲームを終わらせられるよ！

② 今年はフェイスペイントの出し物をするのはどう？ 1人30分くらいで顔にペイントできると思うし，演劇部にはすでに私たちが使えるフェイスペイントがある。この出し物全体を運営するには20人全員が必要になるよ。

③ 私たちの出し物はファッションショーにしよう！ 自分たちが持っている服を使って，カップルでおそろいの衣装を作れば無料でできるよ。お客さんにモデルになってもらえて，私たち12人がショーの間に働く。ショーの時間は20分未満だろうね。

④ お客さんに茶会を体験してもらうと楽しいと思う。茶会1回あたり10分から15分くらいで，各シフトで働くのはたった7人で済む。お茶と和菓子だけ買う必要があるよ。

正解 ⇒ ①

3つの条件を満たすのは①のボウリングゲームである。「無料のリサイクル資材を使ってゲームを準備できる」より，条件Cを満たしている。さらに，「8人しか必要ないし，15分以内にゲームを終わらせられる」より，条件AとBも満たしている。

②のフェイスペイントは，「1人30分くらい」「20人全員が必要」という発言より，AとBの条件に合わない。③のファッションショーは，必要人数が12人なので条件Bを満たしていない。④の茶会は，「お茶と和菓子だけ買う必要がある」ということなので，Cを満たしていない。

アイデア	条件 A	条件 B	条件 C
① ボウリングゲーム	○	○	○
② フェイスペイント	×	×	○
③ ファッションショー	○	×	○
④ 茶会	○	○	×

【語句・表現】
・material「材料，素材，道具」
・couple「カップル，（男女の）1組」
・experience「経験，体験」
・tea ceremony「茶会，茶の湯」

第5問

【放送内容】

This afternoon, we're going to talk about the unique characteristics of glass and recent innovations in glass technology. Glass does not release any dangerous chemicals and bacteria cannot pass through it, which makes it suitable for storing food, drinks, and medicine. Glass can also be cleaned easily, reused many times, and recycled repeatedly, making it friendly to the environment. A surprising characteristic of glass is that it doesn't break down in nature. This is why we can still see many examples of ancient glass work at museums.

Glass-making began in Mesopotamia roughly 4,500 years ago. Beads and bottles were some of the first glass items made by hand. As glass-making became more common, different ways of shaping glass developed. One ancient technique uses a long metal tube to blow air into hot glass. This technique allows the glassblower to form round shapes which are used for drinking glasses or flower vases. Spreading hot glass onto a sheet of metal is the technique used to produce large flat pieces of window glass.

Today, new technology allows glass to be used in exciting ways. 3D printers that can make lenses for eyeglasses have been developed. Smart glass can be used to adjust the amount of light that passes through airplane windows. Other types of glasses can help control sound levels in recording studios or homes. Moreover, tiny pieces of glass in road paint reflect light, making it easier to see the road at night.

Due to these characteristics, glass can be found everywhere we go. Our first group investigated the use of glasses in some European countries. Group 1, go ahead.

　　今日の午後は，ガラスのユニークな特性と，ガラス技術における最近のイノベーションについてお話しします。ガラスは危険な化学物質を放出せず，細菌も通過しないため，食品，飲料，医薬品の保存に適しています。また，ガラスは簡単に洗浄でき，何度も再利用でき，繰り返しリサイクルできるので，環境にも優しいです。ガラスの意外な特徴は，自然界では分解されないことです。そのため，今でも博物館などで古代のガラス工芸品を数多く見ることができるのです。

　　ガラス製造はおよそ4500年前にメソポタミアで始まりました。ビーズや瓶は，手作業で作られた最初のガラス製品です。ガラス作りが一般的になるにつれ，ガラスを成形するさまざまな方法が開発されました。古代の技法のひとつに，長い金属管を使って高温のガラスに空気を吹き込むというものがあります。この技法によって，吹きガラス職人は，飲料用グラスや花瓶に使われる丸い形を作ること

ができるのです。熱したガラスを金属板の上に広げる技法は，大きく平らな窓ガラスを作るのに使われます。

今日，新しい技術によってガラスはわくわくするような使い方ができるようになりました。眼鏡のレンズを作ることができる３Ｄプリンターが開発されました。スマートガラスは，飛行機の窓を通過する光の量を調整するために使用できます。別の種類のガラスは，レコーディング・スタジオや家庭の音の大きさを調整するのに役立ちます。さらに，道路用塗料に含まれる小さなガラス片が光を反射することで，夜間の道路が見やすくなります。

このような特徴から，ガラスはどこに行っても見つけることができるのです。最初のグループは，ヨーロッパのいくつかの国でのガラスの用途を調査しました。グループ１，どうぞ。

ワークシート

ガラス：驚くべき物質

● ガラスに当てはまらないのは…
- ◆ 危険な化学物質を放出する
- ◆ 　27
- ◆ 自然に還る

● ガラス：

製品	28 形	29 窓

現在の技術の利用	30 部屋	31 道路

講義の続き

Given a choice of buying a product in a glass container or a different kind of container, approximately 40% of Europeans choose glass. Our group researched why: reasons include food safety, ease of recycling, and availability of products. We focused on the following three countries: Croatia, the Czech Republic, and France. Let's look at the information in detail.

ガラス容器に入った商品を買うか，別の種類の容器に入った商品を買うかを選択する場合，ヨーロッパ人の約40％がガラス容器を選びます。私たちのグループはその理由を調査しました。理由としては，食品の安全性，リサイクルのしやすさ，製品の入手しやすさなどが挙げられます。私たちは次の３カ国に焦点を当てました。クロアチア，チェコ共和国，フランスです。その情報を詳しく見てみましょう。

問27　27

① 繰り返しのリサイクルを想定する
② 特有のリサイクル特性を持つ
③ 細菌が薬に混入しない
④ 細菌を通過させる

正解 ⇒ ④

ワークシートの１つ目の項目である，ガラスに当てはまらないものを選ぶ問題。第１段落の第２文に「細

菌も通過しない」とあるので，これに当てはまる④が正解。①と②は，第3文の後半で「繰り返しリサイクルできる」と述べられており，ガラスに当てはまるので，誤り。③は第2文の「（ガラスは）最近も通過しない」に反する内容のため不適。

問28〜31　| 28 | 29 | 30 | 31 |

| ① | 〜の音を調整する | ② | 〜に配置される | ③ | 吹いて〜にされる |
| ④ | 〜の安全性を高める | ⑤ | 〜の視野を反射する | ⑥ | 広げて〜にされる |

正解 ⇒ | 28 | ③ | | 29 | ⑥ | | 30 | ① | | 31 | ④ |

　ワークシートの2つ目の項目である，ガラスについての表の穴埋め問題である。表の上段は「製造」に関することであるとわかり，これに関しては第2段落で説明されている。ここではガラスの2つの成形方法が紹介されており，1つ目は第4文にある blow air into hot glass「熱したガラスに息を吹き込む」という方法で，| 28 | には③が入る。2つ目は同段落最終文に Spreading hot glass ... is the technique used to produce large flat pieces of window glass「熱したガラスを…広げる技法は，大きく平らな窓ガラスを作るのに使われます」とあるので，| 29 | は⑥である。
　表の下段は，「新しいテクノロジーの利用」に関する内容であり，第3段落がこれに該当する。| 30 | は，第4文で「レコーディング・スタジオや家庭の音の大きさを調整するのに役立つ」と述べられているので，①が当てはまるとわかる。| 31 | は，同段落の最終文に「道路用塗料に含まれる小さなガラス片が光を反射することで，夜間の道路が見やすくなる」とあることから，④が当てはまる。

問32　| 32 |

①	ガラスは現代生活のためにテクノロジーによってさまざまに改良されてきた。
②	ガラスは建築物において，安価な新素材に置き換えられた。
③	ガラスは，その重さ，壊れやすさ，費用によって用途が限定される素材である。
④	ガラスは日常生活の多くの場面で必要とされる近代的な発明品である。

正解 ⇒ ①

　第3段落で，今日の新しいテクノロジーにより，スマートガラス，室内の音の調整，道路の反射など，様々な用途のガラスが登場したことがわかり，これに一致する①が正解。②や③のようなことは本文で述べられていない。④は，英文の後半は正しいが，第2段落冒頭にあるようにガラスは古来から作られていたものなので modern invention「近代的な発明」が誤り。

問33　| 33 |

①	ガラスは繰り返しリサイクルできるが，チェコ共和国とクロアチアでは「リサイクルのしやすさ」という理由が最も少ない。
②	ガラスは環境に有害だが，チェコ共和国とクロアチアでは「食品の安全性」という理由が最も多い。
③	ガラス製品はヨーロッパ人の半数が好むが，フランスとクロアチアでは「リサイクルのしやすさ」という理由が最も多い。
④	ガラス製品は古くからの技術で作ることができ，フランスとクロアチアでは「製品の入手のしやすさ」という理由が最も少ない。

正解 ⇒ ④

　グラフは「消費者がガラス容器に入った商品を買う理由」を表しており，クロアチア・チェコ共和国・フランスの，「食品の安全」「リサイクルのしやすさ」「製品の入手のしやすさ」の項目をパーセントで表している。これを参照しながら選択肢を検討していくと，①はクロアチアの「リサイクルのしやすさ」は2番目に少ないので，誤り。②は，後半は正しいが，「ガラスは環境に害がある」ということは述べられていないので，誤り。③は，講義の続きでガラス製品を好むヨーロッパ人は「約40％」と述べられておりhalf「半分」に満たないし，クロアチアで最も多い理由は「リサイクルのしやすさ」ではなく「食の安全性」なので，これも誤り。④は，第2段落第で古代のガラス製造の技法に言及されており，グラフに関してもフランスとクロアチアの「製品の入手のしやすさ」の値が最も低い。よって，前半・後半とも正しいので④が正解。

【語句・表現】
〈第1パラグラフ〉
・characteristic「特徴」
・release「〜を放出する」
・chemical「化学薬品」
・pass through「〜を通る，通り過ぎる」
・suitable for 〜「〜にふさわしい」
・store「〜を蓄える」
・reuse「〜を再利用する」
・break down 〜「〜を分解する」
・This is why ...「こういう訳で…」
〈第2パラグラフ〉
・Mesopotamia「メソポタミア」
・roughly「おおよそ，概略で」
・shape「〜を形作る；形」
・metal「金属の」
・blow「〜を吹く，吹き動かす」
・allow O to do「Oに〜させてやる」
・vase「花瓶」
・flat「平らな」
・a piece of+〈不可算名詞〉「（独立したものの）1つ」
〈第3パラグラフ〉
・adjust「〜を調整する，適合させる」
・amount「量」
・tiny「ごく小さい，ちっちゃな」
・reflect「（光・熱）を反射する」
〈第4パラグラフ〉
・due to 〜「（理由）のために，〜が原因で」
・investigate「〜を調べる，調査する，研究する」
・go ahead「（何かを始めるよう促して）どうぞ」
〈問33〉
・container「容器」
・approximately「おおよそ，約」
・focus on 〜「〜を重点的に取り扱う」
・in detail「詳細に」
〈選択肢〉
・allow for 〜「〜を考慮に入れる，見越す」
・keep A out of B「AをBに寄せ付けない，加わらせない」

・go through「通り抜ける，通過する」
・improve「～を改善する，向上させる」
・be replaced by ～「～に取って代わられる，～に取り替えられる」
・inexpensive「安価な，費用のかからない」
・limit「～を制限する，限定する」
・fragility「壊れやすさ」
・expense「費用」
・invention「発明，発明品」
・aspect「側面，局面，状況」
・repeatedly「繰り返して」
・common「一般的な」
・Czech Republic「チェコ共和国」：中央ヨーロッパの国。首都はプラハ。
・Croatia「クロアチア」：南ヨーロッパのバルカン半島にある国。首都はザグレブ。
・harmful「有害な」
・prefer「～をより好む」
・availability「利用できること，有用性」

第6問

A
【放送内容】

Michelle: Jack, did you know that there's a ferry from England to France? I've always wanted to see the English coast from the ferry. I imagine it would be so beautiful.

Jack: Hmm, but I thought we should go by train. It'd be much easier.

Michelle: Come on. We can also smell the sea air and feel the wind.

Jack: That's true. But actually, I get seasick whenever I travel by boat.

Michelle: Oh, I didn't know that. Have you tried taking medicine for it?

Jack: Yeah, I've tried, but it never works for me. I know you want to take the ferry, but ...

Michelle: It's OK. I understand. Well, I suppose it is faster to take the train, isn't it?

Jack: Yes. And it's much more convenient because the train takes us directly to the center of the city. Also, the station is close to the hotel we've booked.

Michelle: I see. It does sound like the better option.

Jack: Great. Let's check the schedule.

ミシェル：ジャック，イギリスからフランスにフェリーが出てるの知ってる？　私はいつもフェリーからイギリスの海岸を見てみたいと思っていたの。すごくきれいなんだろうな。
ジャック：うーん，でも列車で行くべきだと思ったんだ。その方がずっと楽だよ。
ミシェル：いいじゃない。海の匂いや風も感じられるし。
ジャック：そうだね。でも実は，船で旅行するときはいつも船酔いするんだ。
ミシェル：あら，知らなかった。薬を飲んでみたことはある？
ジャック：うん，試したけど，僕には全く効かなかったよ。君がフェリーに乗りたいのはわかるけど…。
ミシェル：いいよ。わかった。ねえ，電車に乗ったほうが早いんじゃない？
ジャック：そうだね。それに，電車は街の中心まで直接連れて行ってくれるから，ずっと便利だよ。それに，駅は予約したホテルの近くだし。
ミシェル：なるほど。確かにそのほうがよさそうだね。
ジャック：よかった。スケジュールを確認しようか。

問34 　34

> ミシェルが会話の中で述べた意見はどれか。
>
> ① 眺めのいいホテルの部屋を予約するのが妥当だろう。
> ② フェリーから景色を眺めるのは最高だろう。
> ③ フェリーで嗅ぐ海辺の空気は不快だろう。
> ④ フェリーに乗る方が電車に乗るより早いだろう。

正解 ⇒ ②

　ミシェルは1回目の発言で「私はいつもフェリーからイギリスの海岸を見てみたいと思っていたの。すごくきれいなんだろうな」と述べているので，これに一致する②が正解。③は，ミシェルの2回目の発言から，むしろ海辺の空気を感じたいと思っていると考えられるので不適切。④も，彼女の4回目の発言で「電車に乗ったほうが早いんじゃない？」と言っているので誤り。

問35 　35

> 会話が終わるまでに，彼らは何をすることに決めたか。
>
> ① 薬を買う
> ② ホテルの部屋を変更する
> ③ フェリーのスケジュールを確認する
> ④ フランス行きの列車に乗る

正解 ⇒ ④

　ミシェルがイギリスからフランスにフェリーで行かないかとジャックを誘うが，ジャックが船酔いすることや電車の方が便利だということで，最終的には電車で行くことで合意している。よって，④が正解。①は，ジャックが3回目の発言で，船酔いの薬を試したけど効かなかったと述べているので，不適切。②のようなことは述べられていない。③は，二人は電車で行くことにしたので「フェリー」が誤り。

【語句・表現】
・ferry「フェリー（ボート）」
・coast「沿岸，海岸，沿岸地方」
・imagine S V「…と想像する」
・get seasick「船酔いする」
・whenever S V「…する時はいつでも」
・work「うまくいく，効く」
・I suppose S V「…だと思う，…であると想像する」
・convenient「便利な，都合のよい，使いやすい」
・directly「（寄り道せず）まっすぐに，直行して，直接に」
〈設問・選択肢〉
・express「〜を表現する」
・reasonable「通りにかなった，もっともな」
・scenery「風景，景色」
・sea air「海辺の空気」
・unpleasant「不愉快な，不快にさせる，いやな」

B
【放送内容】

Chris: For my new year's resolution, I've decided to start doing something healthy. Do you have any good suggestions, Amy?

Amy: Good for you, Chris! It's important to find something that you won't give up easily. I also want to do something, like walking, for instance. Chris, why don't we walk in the morning together?

Chris: That sounds good. Haruki, do you want to join us?

Haruki: Sorry. I started running last year. It's tough, but refreshing. Linda, you exercise a lot, don't you?

Linda: Yeah, recently I've been trying "super-short workouts." One workout takes only 10 minutes.

Haruki: Ten minutes? Linda, is that enough? I need at least an hour to feel satisfied.

Linda: Yes. Super-short workouts are really efficient. You just need to push yourself extremely hard for a short time. Why don't you try them too, Chris?

Chris: Yeah, now that I think about it, walking takes too long. But I could easily spare 10 minutes for a workout. That way, I'm definitely not going to quit. Amy, would you like to try the super-short workouts, too?

Amy: It sounds interesting, but I prefer more moderate exercise. So, I'm going to start walking to the station every day. It's only about 30 minutes, which is fine for me.

Chris: OK. So Linda, can we work out together?

Linda: Sure. How about this Saturday? It'll be fun!

クリス：僕の新年の抱負として，何か健康的なことを始めようと決めたんだ。何かいい提案はあるかい，エイミー？

エイミー：いいね，クリス！ 簡単にあきらめないことを見つけるのは大事よ。私も何かやりたいな，例えばウォーキングとか。クリス，朝一緒に歩かない？

クリス：それはいいね。ハルキも一緒にどう？

ハルキ：ごめん。去年からランニングを始めたんだ。きついけど，リフレッシュできる。リンダはよく運動しているよね？

リンダ：ええ，最近は「超短時間ワークアウト」に挑戦しているんだ。1回のワークアウトにかかる時間はたったの10分だよ。

ハルキ：10分？ リンダ，それで十分なの？ 僕は満足感を得るのに最低1時間は必要なんだけど。

リンダ：うん。超短時間のワークアウトは本当に効率的なの。短時間で自分を追い込むだけだから。あなたもやってみたらどう，クリス？

クリス：ああ，今考えると，ウォーキングは時間がかかりすぎる。でも，10分のワークアウトなら時間をとりやすいね。このやり方なら絶対に辞めない。エイミー，君も超短時間ワークアウトをやってみるかい？

エイミー：面白そうだけど，私はもっと適度な運動が好きなんだ。だから，毎日駅まで歩くようにするよ。30分くらいだから，私にはちょうどいい。

クリス：わかった。じゃあリンダ，一緒に運動しない？

リンダ：もちろん。今度の土曜日はどう？ きっと楽しいよ！

問36 [36]

① エイミー 　　　　　② ハルキ
③ エイミー，クリス 　　④ クリス，リンダ

　正解 ⇒ ①

　クリスは，一旦はエイミーのウォーキングに加わることにしたが，リンダが「超短時間ワークアウト」を勧めたことで，時間のかかるウォーキングから，超短時間ワークアウトに変更している。よって，クリスが含まれる③と④は候補から外れる。エイミーは，1回目の発言で「私も何かやりたいな，例えばウォーキングとか」，2回目の発言で「毎日駅まで歩くことにする」と述べているので，ウォーキングをすることに決めている。残るハルキは，1回目の発言で「去年からランニングを始めたんだ」と述べ，クリスからのウォーキングの誘いを断わっている。よって，①のエイミーが正解。

問37 [37]

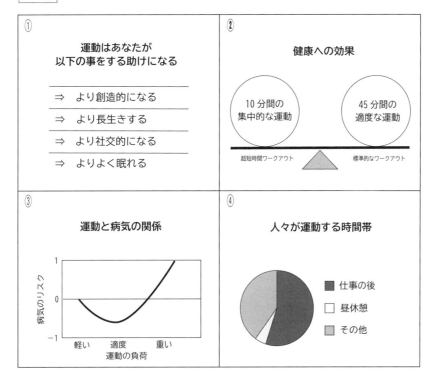

　正解 ⇒ ②

　リンダは「超短時間ワークアウト」について説明している。まず，1回目の発言で「1回のワークアウトにかかる時間はたったの10分」と述べており，さらに2回目の発言で，ハルキが10分だけで十分なのかという問いに「うん。超短時間ワークアウトは本当に効率的なの。短時間で自分を追い込むだけだから」と返答している。以上より，「超短時間ワークアウト」は10分間の集中的な運動でも効果が得られることを示した②の図が正解である。

【語句・表現】
・resolution「決心，決意」：New Year's resolution で「新年の決意，今年の目標」の意味。
・tough「骨の折れる，難しい」

・refreshing「元気づける，心身をさわやかにする，すがすがしい」
・push *oneself*「（必死に）努力する，無理をする，頑張る」
・extremely「極度に，極端に」
・definitely「確かに，間違いなく，絶対に」
・quit「やめる」
・moderate「適度の，並みの，節度のある」
〈選択肢〉
・intense「激しい，強烈な」
・disease「病気，疾病」

受験は
くるしむだけが正解、
とは限らない。

心を、敵にしないで。

SAPIX YOZEMI GROUP 模試 2024/2025 <高3・高卒生対象>

7/13（土）・14（日）	第1回東大入試プレ
7/21（日）	第1回京大入試プレ
8/ 4（日）	九大入試プレ
8/11（日・祝）	第1回大学入学共通テスト入試プレ
8/18（日）	東北大入試プレ
8/18（日）	阪大入試プレ
10/20（日）	早大入試プレ〈代ゼミ・駿台共催〉
11/ 4（月・振）	慶大入試プレ〈代ゼミ・駿台共催〉
11/10（日）	第2回京大入試プレ
11/10（日）	北大入試プレ
11/16（土）・17（日）	第2回東大入試プレ
11/24（日）	第2回大学入学共通テスト入試プレ

実施日は地区により異なる場合があります。詳細は、代々木ゼミナール各校へお問い合わせください。

代々木ゼミナール
代ゼミサテライン予備校

本部校／札幌校／新潟校／名古屋校／
大阪南校／福岡校／仙台教育センター
／代ゼミオンラインコース

詳細はこちら
X @yozemi_official
LINE @yozemi
www.yozemi.ac.jp
代ゼミ 検索

あなたの街で代ゼミの授業を

最寄りの代ゼミサテライン予備校を
検索できます。www.yozemi-sateline.ac